T0234627

Lecture Notes in Computer Science   10157

Commenced Publication in 1973
Founding and Former Series Editors:
Gerhard Goos, Juris Hartmanis, and Jan van Leeuwen

More information about this series at http://www.springer.com/series/7410

Seokhie Hong · Jong Hwan Park (Eds.)

Information Security and Cryptology – ICISC 2016

19th International Conference
Seoul, South Korea, November 30 – December 2, 2016
Revised Selected Papers

 Springer

Editors
Seokhie Hong
CIST, Korea University
Seoul
Korea (Republic of)

Jong Hwan Park
Sangmyung University
Seoul
Korea (Republic of)

ISSN 0302-9743   ISSN 1611-3349   (electronic)
Lecture Notes in Computer Science
ISBN 978-3-319-53176-2   ISBN 978-3-319-53177-9   (eBook)
DOI 10.1007/978-3-319-53177-9

Library of Congress Control Number: 2017930645

LNCS Sublibrary: SL4 – Security and Cryptology

Printed on acid-free paper

This Springer imprint is published by Springer Nature
The registered company is Springer International Publishing AG
The registered company address is: Gewerbestrasse 11, 6330 Cham, Switzerland

Preface

ICISC 2016, the 19th International Conference on Information Security and Cryptology, was held in Seoul, Korea, from November 30 to December 2, 2016. This year the conference was hosted by the KIISC (Korea Institute of Information Security and Cryptology) jointly with the NSR (National Security Research Institute).

The aim of this conference is to provide an international forum for the latest results of research, development, and applications in the field of information security and cryptology. This year we received 69 submissions, and were able to accept 18 papers from 10 countries, with an acceptance rate of 26%. The review and selection processes were carried out by the Program Committee (PC) members, 44 prominent international experts, via the EasyChair review system. First, each paper was blind reviewed, by at least three PC members for most cases. Second, for resolving conflicts on the reviewers' decisions, the individual review reports were open to all PC members, and detailed interactive discussions on each paper followed.

The conference featured two invited talks: "Multivariate Public Key Cryptography" by Jintai Ding; "On Practical Functional Encryption" by Michel Abdalla. We thank those invited speakers for their kind acceptance and interesting presentations. We would like to thank all authors who submitted their papers to ICISC 2016 and all 44 PC members. It was a truly nice experience to work with such talented and hard-working researchers. We also appreciate the external reviewers for assisting the PC members in their particular areas of expertise.

We would like to thank all attendees for their active participation and the Organizing Committee members who managed this conference. Finally, we thank the sponsors NSR (National Security Research Institute) and KONAI.

December 2016

Seokhie Hong
Jong Hwan Park

Organization

ICISC 2016 was organized by the Korea Institute of Information Security and Cryptology (KIISC) and NSR (National Security Research Institute)

Executive Committee

General Chair

Im-Yeong Lee   Soonchunhyang University, Korea

Program Chairs

Seokhie Hong   CIST, Korea University, Korea
Jong Hwan Park   Sangmyung University, Korea

Organizing Chair

Okyeon Yi   Kookmin University, Korea

Program Committee

Olivier Blazy	XLim, Université de Limoges, France
Andrey Bogdanov	Technical University of Denmark, Denmark
Zhenfu Cao	East China Normal University, China
Donghoon Chang	IIIT-Delhi, India
Paolo D'Arco	University of Salerno, Italy
Keita Emura	NICT, Japan
Dong-Guk Han	Kookmin University, South Korea
Swee-Huay Heng	Multimedia University
Deukjo Hong	Chonbuk National University
Xinyi Huang	Fujian Normal University, China
David Jao	University of Waterloo, Canada
Dong Seong Kim	University of Canterbury, New Zealand
Dong-Chan Kim	Kookmin University, South Korea
Howon Kim	Pusan National University, South Korea
Huy Kang Kim	Korea University, South Korea
Alptekin Küpçü	Koc University, Turkey
Taekyoung Kwon	Yonsei University, South Korea
Hyung Tae Lee	Nanyang Technological University, Singapore
Kwangsu Lee	Sejong University, South Korea

Moon Sung Lee	Seoul National University, South Korea
Mun-Kyu Lee	Inha University, South Korea
Pil Joong Lee	POSTECH, South Korea
Joseph K. Liu	Monash University, Australia
Zhe Liu	Nanjing University of Aeronautics and Astronautics, Singapore
Jiqiang Lu	Institute for Infocomm Research, Singapore
Sjouke Mauw	University of Luxembourg, Luxembourg
Florian Mendel	Graz University of Technology, Austria
Atsuko Miyaji	JAIST, Japan
Tarik Moataz	Brown University, USA
Raphael C.-W. Phan	Multimedia University
Josef Pieprzyk	Queensland University of Technology, Australia
Christian Rechberger	DTU, Denmark and Graz University of Technology, Austria
Kouichi Sakurai	Kyushu University, Japan
Jae Hong Seo	Myongji University, South Korea
Rainer Steinwandt	Florida Atlantic University, USA
Marion Videau	Quarkslab and Loria, France
Wenling Wu	Institute of Software, Chinese Academy of Sciences, China
Shouhuai Xu	University of Texas at San Antonio, USA
Toshihiro Yamauchi	Okayama University, Japan
Masaya Yasuda	Kyushu University, Japan
Wei-Chuen Yau	Xiamen University, Malaysia
Dae Hyun Yum	Myongji University, South Korea
Aaram Yun	UNIST

Additional Reviewers

Hiroaki Anada
Selcuk Baktir
Sanaz Taheri Boshrooyeh
Ji-Jian Chin
Emmanuel Conchon
Deepak Dalai
Christoph Dobraunig
Mohammad Etemad
Olga Gadyatskaya
Yiwen Gao
Junqing Gong
Feng Hao
Yahya Hassanzadeh-Nazarabadi
Shoichi Hirose
Zhi Hu
Devriş İşler
Ravi Jhawar

Saqib A. Kakvi
İpek Kızl
Stefan Koelbl
Thomas Korak
Mario Larangeira
Zhen Liu
Willi Meier
Kirill Morozov
Johannes Mueller
Koji Nuida
Cristina Onete
Jiaxin Pan
Geovandro Pereira
Somindu C. Ramanna
Arnab Roy
Sushmita Ruj
Yumi Sakemi

Pinaki Sarkar
Sumanta Sarkar
Masaya Sato
Peter Scholl
Hwajeong Seo
Jun Shao
Koutarou Suzuki

Syh-Yuan Tan
Tyge Tiessen
Jorge Toro-Pozo
Rolando Trujillo
Berkant Ustaoglu
Licheng Wang

Abstracts of Invited Talks

Multivariate Public Key Cryptography

Jintai Ding

University of Cincinnati, Cincinnati, US
jintai.ding@uc.edu

Abstract. Multivariate public key cryptosystems (MPKC) are one of the four main families of post-quantum public key cryptosystems. In a MPKC, the public key is given by a set of quadratic polynomials and its security is based on the hardness of solving a set of multivariate polynomials. In this tutorial, we will give a general introduction to the multivariate public key cryptosystems including the main designs, the main attack tools and the mathematical theory behind. We will also present state of the art research in the area.

Can Functional Encryption Be Practical?

Michel Abdalla

ENS and PSL Research University, Paris, France
michel.abdalla@ens.fr

Abstract. Functional encryption is a paradigm that allows users to finely control the amount of information that is revealed by a ciphertext to a given receiver. In this talk, we will discuss some of the main results in the area for both general and specific functionalities. While constructions for general functionalities tend to be quite inefficient, we will see how one can significantly improve the efficiency of such schemes by focusing on specific functionalities, such as inner products. Though less general, such functionalities still seem expressive enough for use in practical settings.

Contents

Signatures (and Protocol)

Analysis

Protocols

A Secure Group-Based AKA Protocol for Machine-Type Communications

Rosario Giustolisi[✉], Christian Gehrmann, Markus Ahlström,
and Simon Holmberg

Swedish Institute of Computer Science, Stockholm, Sweden
`rosario.giustolisi@sics.se`

Abstract. The fifth generation wireless system (5G) is expected to handle with an unpredictable number of heterogeneous connected devices while guaranteeing a high level of security. This paper advances a group-based Authentication and Key Agreement (AKA) protocol that contributes to reduce latency and bandwidth consumption, and scales up to a very large number of devices. A central feature of the proposed protocol is that it provides a way to dynamically customize the trade-off between security and efficiency. The protocol is lightweight as it resorts on symmetric key encryption only, hence it supports low-end devices and can be already adopted in current standards with little effort. Using ProVerif, we prove that the protocol meets mutual authentication, key confidentiality, and device privacy also in presence of corrupted devices, a threat model not being addressed in the state-of-the-art group-based AKA proposals. We evaluate the protocol performances in terms of latency and bandwidth consumption, and obtain promising results.

1 Introduction

The evolution of mobile networks has made a key achievement in each of its generations: 1G established the foundation of mobile networks; 2G increased the voice connectivity capacity to support more users per radio channel; 3G introduced high-speed internet access; 4G provided more data capacity. One of the key achievement for 5G is to be the reference network for the Internet of Things (IoT) connectivity. Analysts forecast more than 25 billion of devices to be interconnected in 2020 [16]. Providing connectivity to such a large number of device s, which may require simultaneous network access, will lead to a potential signaling overload. Signaling data is growing 50% faster than data traffic in mobile networks [22] and is expected to surpass the global IP traffic growth within three years [23]. An increased level of signaling would affect speed and data capacity of 5G. Thus, to fully support IoT connectivity, the contemporary architecture of the mobile network should be revisited, including the aspects related to security.

The Authentication and Key Agreement protocol (AKA) has a central role in the security of mobile networks as it bootstraps the parameters needed to form a security context that is agreed by the parties. The protocol provides mutual

© Springer International Publishing AG 2017
S. Hong and J.H. Park (Eds.): ICISC 2016, LNCS 10157, pp. 3–27, 2017.
DOI: 10.1007/978-3-319-53177-9_1

authentication between device and serving network, and establishes session keys. The state-of-the-art protocol used in 4G (EPS-AKA) [3] is almost identical to its predecessor used in 3G, which was introduced in the late 90s. A limitation of EPS-AKA is that, for each device that requires network access, the protocol requires signaling among the device, the local serving network and the device's remote home network. In particular, the signaling between serving network and home network may introduce a major delay when they are distant, which is the case when users are roaming. This represents a bottleneck for the development of 5G as a low delay and reliable network for IoT devices.

From this situation emerged the need of a *group-based* AKA, which allows the serving network to authenticate a group of devices reducing the signaling and communication latency with the home network. Groups may consist of devices sharing similar features such as functions, locations, or ownership. In the scenario of IoT, devices often operate in groups and some use cases have been recently advanced [11,13,21]. While the functional goals of group-based AKA are clear, new security aspects arise. The group approach introduces additional threats, which mainly originate from colluding corrupted members [18]. This results to a more powerful intruder than one historically considered in the current AKA protocol. Thus, it seems to be an open challenge to design a group-based AKA secure against the extended threats. This paper addresses this very challenge. In particular, the contributions of this paper includes:

- A novel mechanism based on the inverted hash tree that allows the network operator to balance dynamically the requirements of security and efficiency of the designed protocol.
- The formal security analysis of the protocol in ProVerif.
- A prototype implementation of the protocol in the OpenAirInterface platform.
- A performance analysis of the protocol in terms of latency and bandwidth consumption.

Outline. The paper is organized as follows. Section 2 presents a primer on AKA. Section 3 details the group-based AKA protocol. Section 4 describes the formal analysis of the protocol in ProVerif. Section 5 details the implementation of the protocol in OpenAirInterface and discusses its performances. Section 6 analyses some related work. Finally, Sect. 7 draws some conclusions.

2   Background

The three main roles that concern the AKA protocol are the *User Equipment* (UE) or device, the *Mobility Management Entity* (MME) or serving network, and the *Home Subscriber Server* (HSS) or authentication server. The UE role concerns the tasks of the terminal device and USIM. A subscriber identity (IMSI) is permanently stored on the USIM so the network can identify the UE. The USIM also stores a long-term secret key Kthat is shared with the HSS. With the introduction of *machine-type communication* (MTC), the 3GPP consortium released a dedicated specification for MTC devices to enhance the LTE suitability for the IoT market [5]. Thus, we refer to the UE also using the term MTC.

The MME role concerns the tasks of covering the mobility of the MTC. The MME serves a number of MTCs according to its geographical area. Each MTCis connected to a *base station* (eNodeB), which in turn is directly connected to an MME. In the context of AKA, the MME authenticates the MTCand agree on a session master key K_{ASME} from which they can derive further keys to protect the signaling data.

The HSS role concerns the tasks of assisting the MME for the mutual authentication. The signaling between HSS and MME is secured with Diameter [4]. The HSS shares with the MTCIMSI, K, and a *sequence number* (SQN) to support authentication.

2.1   EPS-AKA

The state-of-the-art AKA protocol is EPS-AKA, which is the standard for LTE. The protocol is described in Fig. 1 and consists of five main messages:

– The **Attach request** message bootstraps the protocol. It normally includes the IMSIof the MTC, when the device visits the MME for the first time. Future

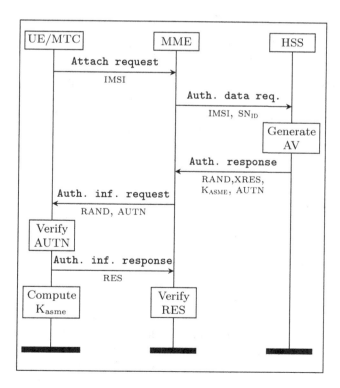

Fig. 1. EPS-AKA message sequence chart

attach requests will include the Globally Unique Temporary Identity (GUTI), which is generated by the MME and assigned to the MTC. In doing so, the MME can translate the GUTI to the corresponding IMSI, preserving the privacy of the MTC.

- The `Authentication data request` message, sent by MME with identity SN_{ID}, requires the HSS to generate an authentication vector consisting of:
  - a random value RAND that provides freshness to the session;
  - the expected response XRES, based on RAND and K, that allows the MME to authenticate the MTC;
  - the session master key K_{ASME}, to encrypt the signaling between MTC and serving network;
  - the authentication token AUTN, based on RAND, K, and SQN, that allows the MTC to authenticate the serving network.
- The `Authentication response` message contains the authentication vector and is transmitted to the MME.
- The `Authentication information request` message consists of RAND and AUTN, which the MME forwards to the MTC. The MTC checks that the SQN matches a valid one and if so, it successfully authenticates the serving network. The MTC computes the session master key K_{ASME} and the response RES, which is based on K and on the received RAND.
- The `Authentication information response` message, which the MTC sends to the MME, contains RES. The MME successfully authenticates the MTC if RES = XRES. The MME computes K_{ASME} so the signaling between serving network and MTC can be protected with session keys derived from K_{ASME}.

The cryptographic functions for the generation of the different terms outlined above are included in *MILENAGE* [2], which is a set of algorithms currently supported by EPS-AKA. The limitation of EPS-AKA is that `Authentication response` and `Authentication data request` are required for *each* device that requires network access. The next section introduces a group-based AKA that addresses this very limitation.

3   Group-Based AKA

The design of the group-based AKA is pivoted on the *inverted hash tree*. Thus, we briefly discuss the notion of inverted hash trees prior to providing a detailed description of the protocol.

Inverted Hash Trees. An inverted hash tree (see Fig. 2) is a data structure in which a node is linked to at most two successors (children), and the value of each node is computed using a family of hash functions h_*. The value of the root is given, while the value associated with any other node is derived from the hash value of its parent. In particular, we consider two hash functions h_0 and h_1 and recursively assign the value of each node n_{ij} located at i^{th} position and j^{th} level as follows.

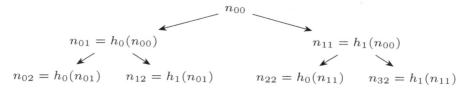

Fig. 2. An inverted hash tree of height 2

$$n_{ij} = \begin{cases} h_0(n_{k(j-1)}) \text{ if } i = 2k & \text{(left children)} \\ h_1(n_{k(j-1)}) \text{ if } i = 2k+1 & \text{(right children)} \\ \text{given value if } i = j = 0 & \text{(root)} \end{cases}$$

The underlying idea of the proposed group-based AKA is to associate each MTC to a value of the leaf node, and to reveal a sub-root node to the MME so that it can authenticate the (sub)group of all MTC descendants. This allows the HSS to control the trade-off between security and efficiency dynamically. In fact, the HSS can reveal sub-roots at different levels. Revealing a sub-root at a higher level supports security at the cost of efficiency because the MME can authenticate a smaller group of MTC without involving the home network. Conversely, revealing a sub-root at lower level supports efficiency at the cost of security because the MME can authenticate a large group of MTC without involving the home network. The proposed group-based AKA protocol supports MILENAGE. It does not introduce new primitives (e.g., secret sharing or public key encryption) to favour backward compatibility with existing mobile telephony systems and uses most of the functions already available in MILENAGE (i.e., kdf, $f2$, $f3$, $f4$, and $f5$).

3.1 Protocol Description

The protocol assumes two inverted hash trees of height $\mathcal{H}$, both generated by the home network. The structures of the two inverted hash trees are identical, and each MTC$_i$ is associated with the leaf nodes with PATH $= (i, \mathcal{H})$ in both trees. The *GK tree* serves as group key tree, and the value of its root can be seen as a *master group key*. Each leaf node of the tree (GK$_{i\mathcal{H}}$) serves as master individual key and is associated to each MTC$_i$. Several session individual keys HGK$_{(i\mathcal{H}, N)} = hash(\text{GK}_{ij, N})$, which are keyed with a sequence number N, can be derived from the master individual key. The generation of several session individual keys enables for several secure AKA runs using the same GK$_{i\mathcal{H}}$. The *CH tree* serves as challenge key tree. Also in this case, each leaf value of the tree (CH$_{i\mathcal{H}}$) is associated to an MTC$_i$ and acts as individual challenge key. Several session challenge keys HCH$_{(i\mathcal{H}, N)} = hash(\text{CH}_{ij, N})$ can be generated from CH$_{i\mathcal{H}}$.

As we shall see later, the MME will send HCH$_{(i\mathcal{H}, N)}$ to the MTC so that the device can compute HGK$_{(i\mathcal{H}, N)}$. In fact, each MTC$_i$ knows no keys initially, but is given an obfuscated value O$_{(i\mathcal{H}, N)} = hash(\text{K}, \text{HCH}_{(i\mathcal{H}, N)}) \oplus$ HGK$_{(i\mathcal{H}, N)}$.

As soon as the MTC receives HcH and N, it can use them with o and K to retrieve HGK. The obfuscation binds both session keys to K. This choice prevents that two corrupted MTCs, say MTC_1 and MTC_2, swap their keys to break authentication.

Table 1. Description of the terms introduced in the group-based AKA

Term	Description
GID	Group identifier
NONCE	Random number
GK_{ij}	The key associated with the value of the node at the ith position and j^{th} level of the inverted hash tree GK
CH_{ij}	The challenge key associated to the value of the node at the ith position and j^{th} level of the inverted hash tree CH
$HGK_{(ij, N)}$	The result of hashing GK_{ij} and N
$HCH_{(ij, N)}$	The result of hashing CH_{ij} and N
$O_{(ij, N)}$	The obfuscated value that hides the hashed keys GK_{ij} and CH_{ij} with respect to the sequence number N
AUT_D	The authentication parameter in the group authentication
RES_D	The response parameter in the group authentication
K_{ASMED}	The session key generated in the group authentication

Each MTC that is member of the group shares with the home network the following terms: the group identifier GID, the assigned PATH, and a number of obfuscated values $O_{(i\mathcal{H}, 1)}, O_{(i\mathcal{H}, 2)}, \ldots, O_{(i\mathcal{H}, N)}, \ldots, O_{(i\mathcal{H}, M)}$. All the terms introduced by the protocol are defined in Table 1.

We distinguish *Case A* and *Case B*. In *Case A*, the MME cannot derive the needed keys to authenticate the MTC, hence the MME needs to communicate with the HSS. In *Case B*, the MME can derive the keys to authenticate the MTC without any interaction with the HSS.

The first message of the protocol is the `Attach request`, which the MTC sends to the MME, and it is exactly the same in both cases. In fact, the MTC cannot say beforehand which case applies. If this is the very first attach request that the MME receives from a member of the group or the MME cannot derive the needed keys associated to that MTC, the MME proceeds according to Case A, otherwise it follows Case B. We now describe the two cases separately. The message sequence charts for Case A and Case B are respectively depicted in Figs. 3 and 4.

Case A. This case requires that the MME communicates with the HSS to obtain the needed keys and then to authenticate MTC_i. Hence, the MME generates the `Authentication data request` message, which contains GID, PATH, NONCE,

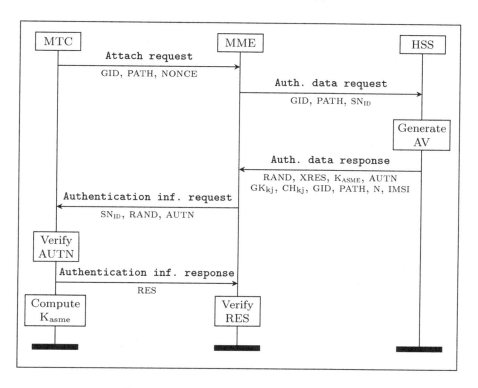

Fig. 3. Message sequence chart of Case A

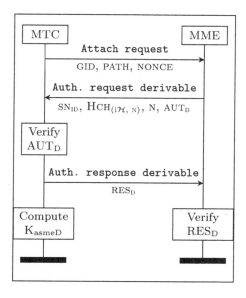

Fig. 4. Message sequence chart of Case B

and SN_{ID}. The MME then sends the message to the HSS via Diameter. The HSS checks whether GIDand PATH are valid and, according to the security policy of the group, it chooses two indexes k and j, with $j < \mathcal{H}$, such that GK_{kj} and CH_{kj} are ancestor nodes of $\text{GK}_{i\mathcal{H}}$ and $\text{CH}_{i\mathcal{H}}$ respectively. The HSS then generates an authentication vector in the same way it is generated in EPS-AKA, and sends the `Authentication data response` message to the MME. The message includes the same elements already specified in EPS-AKA plus the new elements GK_{kj}, CH_{kj}, GID, PATH, N, and IMSI. The elements GK_{kj} and CH_{kj} serve as root of two subtrees. The MME will be able to derive the values of all the leaf nodes within the subtrees without the need to communicate with the HSS. From now on, the procedure for Case A continues exactly as in EPS-AKA.

Case B. This case assumes that the MME already knows some nodes GK_{kj} and CHkj that are ancestors of $\text{GK}_{i\mathcal{H}}$ and $\text{CH}_{i\mathcal{H}}$. Hence, the MME computes $\text{GK}_{i\mathcal{H}}$ and $\text{CH}_{i\mathcal{H}}$, and from those $\text{HGK}_{(i\mathcal{H}, \text{N})}$ and the $\text{HCH}_{(i\mathcal{H}, \text{N})}$. If the MME has not previously run the group-based AKA with MTC_i, then the value of the sequence number N is the one provided in Case A by the HSS. Otherwise, it sets $\text{N} = \text{N} + 1$. The MME periodically reports the updated sequence number to the HSS to keep the synchronization of the values.

The MME computes the authentication token $\text{AUT}_{\text{D}} = f5(\text{HGK}_{(i\mathcal{H}, \text{N})},\text{NONCE}), MAC_{\text{HGK}_{(i\mathcal{H}, \text{N})}} (\text{NONCE}, \text{HCH}_{(i\mathcal{H}, \text{N})}, \text{GID}, \text{SN}_{\text{ID}}, \text{PATH})$ and sends the `Authentication request derivable` message, which contains SN_{ID}, $\text{HCH}_{(i\mathcal{H}, \text{N})}$, and AUT_{D}. The MTC de-obfuscates the value $\text{O}_{(i\mathcal{H}, \text{N})}$, and retrieves the session individual key $\text{HGK}_{(i\mathcal{H}, \text{N})} = hash(\text{K}, \text{HCH}_{(i\mathcal{H}, \text{N})}) \oplus \text{O}_{(i\mathcal{H}, \text{N})}$. Then, it sends the `Authentication response derivable` message that contains $\text{RES}_{\text{D}} = f2(\text{HGK}_{(i\mathcal{H}, \text{N})}, \text{HCH}_{(i\mathcal{H}, \text{N})})$. Both MTC and MME can compute the session key $\text{K}_{\text{ASMED}} = kdf(f5(\text{HGK}_{(i\mathcal{H}, \text{N})}, \text{NONCE}), f3(\text{HGK}_{(i\mathcal{H}, \text{N})}, \text{HCH}_{(i\mathcal{H}, \text{N})}), f4(\text{HGK}_{(i\mathcal{H}, \text{N})}, \text{HCH}_{(i\mathcal{H}, \text{N})}), \text{SN}_{\text{ID}})$.

In the proposed group-based AKA one major modification is that the IMSI is not sent by the MTC. In Case A, the HSS sends the IMSI to the MME securely via Diameter. The attach request may still contain the temporal identity GUTI due to legacy reason. However, lawful interception is always guaranteed because the combination (GID, PATH) is unique and known to the HSS. Thus, if needed, the MME can send GID and PATH of an MTC to the HSS, and obtain the corresponding IMSI.

`Authentication request derivable` has AUT_{D}, which contains the data $f5(\text{HGK}_{(i\mathcal{H}, \text{N})}, \text{NONCE})$. This data is not strictly necessary because AUT_{D} already contains a MAC for integrity check. However, we prefer to maintain the data to meet the same structure of the traditional AUTN field.

We note that MME and HSS should periodically synchronize the current value of sequence number. This prevents a corrupted MTC to successfully reuse a session individual key when moving from an MME to another. However, such attack can be easily mitigated if the HSS syncronizes the sequence number with the old MME when the new MME sends to the HSS the `Authentication data request`.

4   Security Analysis

We analyze the group-based AKA protocol in ProVerif [9], a protocol analyzer that can prove reachability and equivalence-based properties automatically. The input language of ProVerif is based on the applied pi-càlculus [6]. Authentication can be expressed as correspondence assertions [28] based on events, while privacy can be expressed as *observational equivalence* [24] property based on processes that differ only in the choice of terms. We consider threats originating from a Dolev-Yao intruder [14] who has full control of the network. The intruder can also inject messages of his choice into the public channels, and exploit the algebraic properties of cryptographic primitives due to an equational theory. Moreover, we extend the capabilities of the intruder with threats deriving from colluding corrupted principals. Differently from other works on formal analysis of AKA [1,10,26], we choose to model the communications between MME and HSS using the cryptographic primitive of probabilistic symmetric encryption rather than using ProVerif's private channels. This choice allows us to model corrupted principals by just sharing the private key with the intruder. It also increases the chance that ProVerif successfully terminates the verification, and gives the attacker more discretional power because it can observe when a communication between MME and HSS happens. As result, we achieve stronger security guarantees for the analysis of the protocol.

Table 2. Equational theory to model the proposed group-based AKA protocol

Primitive	Equation
Probabilistic symmetric enc	$sdec(senc(m, k, r), k) = m$
XOR	$xor(m1, xor(m1, m2)) = m2$
Hash	$hash(m) = d$
MAC	$MAC(m, k) = d$
Inverted hash tree	$set\_node(parent, pos) = child$ $par\_path(ch\_path(par\_path, pos)) = par\_path$

The cryptographic primitives adopted in the group-based AKA protocol are illustrated in Table 2. The theory for hash, MAC, XOR, and probabilistic symmetric key encryption are well-known in ProVerif. We introduce a novel theory in ProVerif to support inverted hash trees. The function *set_node* allows us to generate a new child node which value is given by hashing the parent's value and the position of the child node (i.e. left or right). The function *ch_path* takes in a parent's path and a position and returns the corresponding child's path. The function *par_path* takes in a child's path and returns the parent's path.

We check confidentiality of the session master keys K_{ASME} and K_{ASMED}, mutual authentication, and MTC identity privacy. The details of the formalisation in the applied pi-calculus of the requirements are in Appendix A.

Results. The results of the automatic analysis in ProVerif indicate that the protocol meets confidentiality, mutual authentication, and MTC identity privacy. Table 3 reports the execution times over an Intel Core i7 2.6 GHz machine with 12 GB RAM. Our analysis considers an unbounded number of honest MTC, HSS, and MME and an attacker in control of the network and of an unbounded number of corrupted MTCs. Note that an inverted hash tree with an unbounded number of leaves would require an unbounded number of intermediate nodes. Unfortunately, ProVerif cannot handle this scenario. We overcome this situation by fixing root and height of the tree and then generating an unbounded number of sub-trees.

5   Implementation

We choose to implement the protocol in OpenAirInterface (OAI) [7], an open-source wireless technology platform written in C. OAI is a fully-stacked EPS implementation with the goal of being used for 5G development and research. It supports MME, HSS, and a simulation of an MTC. It does not require any radio hardware since it can simulate the radio interface used in EPS via Ethernet. However, OAI supports radio hardware if needed. *OPENAIR-CN* and *Openair-interface5G* are the two main modules that constitute OAI. OPENAIR-CN is an implementation of the 3GPP specifications concerning the Evolved Packet Core Networks, in particular the MME and HSS network elements. Openair-interface5G is an implementation of a simulated MTC and provides a realistic radio stack signaling when connected to OPENAIR-CN.

5.1   Approach

Our approach to the prototype implementation is to code the group-based AKA as a patch of OAI. In doing so, we favour backward compatibility with the existing standard. It follows that, when possible, we aim to reuse the existing parameter and message structures as specified in 3GPP standards. For example, we can reuse the structure of IMSI for GID since they have a similar purpose. However, some terms have no similar counterpart in EPS so we design them from scratch. We also introduce new functions and commands that extend the functionality currently in use in EPS with ones appropriate for group-based

Table 3. Summary of the ProVerif analysis of the group-based AKA

Requirement	Result	Time
Session master key confidentiality	✓	1.8 s
Serving network authentication	✓	4.4 s
MTC authentication	✓	4.3 s
MTC identity privacy	✓	2.8 s

AKA. For example, the algorithm `traverse tree` allows both MME and HSS to find a node in the inverted hash tree. The function takes in the node's depth, the node's PATH, and an ancestor node value. Then, it traverses the subtree originating in the ancestor node according to the bit sequence in PATH: if the current bit is 0 then a byte of zeros is appended to the current node value, otherwise a byte of ones is appended to the current node value. The pseudo-code is outlined in Algorithm 1. More details regarding configuration and parameters are detailed in Appendix B.

Algorithm 1. `traverse tree`

> **input** : GK_{kj}, PATH, z=NODE DEPTH
> **output**: GK_{iz} (descendant of GK_{kj})
>
> Digest ← GK_{kj} ;
> **for** $l \leftarrow 0$ **to** NODE DEPTH-1 **do**
> | current_Bit ← bit l of PATH;
> | **if** current_Bit $= 0$ **then**
> | | Digest = (Digest ‖ 00000000);
> | **else**
> | | Digest = (Digest ‖ 11111111);
> | **end**
> | Digest ← `SHA256`(Digest);
> | Digest ← `truncate_to_128_bits`(Digest);
> **end**
> GK_{iz} ← Digest ;

5.2 Performance Analysis

We present the performance analysis of the prototype implementation of the group-based AKA in terms of latency and bandwidth consumption. The goal of the analysis is to have a quantitative evaluation of the benefit that the protocol provides with respect to the current EPS-AKA. We distinguish the analysis of the *non-access stratum* (NAS), which concerns the communication between MTCand MME, and of the *S6a* interface, which concerns the communication between MME and HSS.

Bandwidth Consumption. Our analysis considers the worst case for both EPS-AKA and group-based AKA. This is because some of the existing and new parameters can have variable sizes. Thus, we select the maximum possible value for each parameter. The bandwidth consumption for EPS-AKA concerning both NAS and S6a interface is given by the sum of the size of the parameters sent within the messages, multiplied by the number of devices. The formula of the bandwidth consumption for the group-based AKA is complicated by the inverted hash tree. Given m MTCs devices, the formula is defined in Eq. 1.

$$\textbf{BAND\_GB\_NAS} = m \times \left(\text{GID} + \frac{(\lceil \log_2 m \rceil \times 2 - 1)}{8} + 2 + \text{NONCE} \right) \\ + (m - 1) \times (\text{HCH} + \text{AUT}_\text{D} + \text{RES}_\text{D}) + \text{RAND} + \text{AUTN} + \text{RES}. \tag{1}$$

Regarding the bandwidth consumption for the S6a interface, we consider the values provided in the Authentication Information Request (AIR) and in the Authentication Information Answer (AIA) messages, which are due to the Diameter protocol. The bandwidth consumption for the group-based AKA can be computed as Eq. 2.

$$\textbf{BAND\_GB\_S6a} = \text{IMSI} + 2 \times \text{GID} + \text{RAND} + \text{XRES} + \text{AUTN} + \text{K}_\text{ASME} \\ + \text{GK}_\text{ij} + \text{CH}_\text{ij} + \mathcal{H} + \text{SN}_\text{ID} + 2 \times \left(min(\text{PATH}) + \frac{\lceil \log_2 m \rceil \times 2 - 1)}{32} \times 4 \right). \tag{2}$$

Overall, the group-based AKA consumes less bandwidth when already seven MTC devices are considered. This is described by the left picture of Fig. 5.

Latency. The latency analysis consists of the evaluation of the round-trip time (RTT) between MTC, MME, and HSS. We consider fixed locations for MTC and MME, and different geographic locations for the HSS. In so doing, we simulate different scenarios of UE attaching from different countries. Since we focus on the latency between MME and HSS, we can assume that the RTT between MTC and MME is fixed. We select three different locations from the *Wonder-Proxy* servers [27] with various distances from the MME: *Location 1* is 1 Km far; *Location 2* is 2,000 Km far; *Location 3* is 10,000 Km far. We compute the average RTT of each location by pinging 100 times the corresponding servers. Then, we run 20 instances of EPS-AKA and group-based AKA in OAI. The results are described in the right picture of Fig. 5. They show that EPS-AKA and Case A for the group-based AKA have similar values, with the latter having more latency because more amount of data is communicated. As expected, there are very small variations in Case B for the group-based AKA. This confirms that when an MTC device is running within Case B there is a significant reduction in latency.

6   Related Work

Recently, several amendments to the AKA protocol have been advanced [8,17] and new group-based AKA protocols have been proposed. Broustis et al. [11] designed three group-based AKA schemes with the goal to reduce the overall signaling between the parties. All the proposed schemes share the idea of using global values based on a shared group key and to introduce a gateway that mediates between MTC devices and MME. The use of global values and of a gateway is beneficial to the bandwidth consumption. However, none of the schemes meets

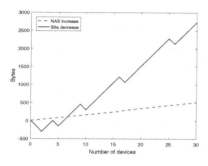 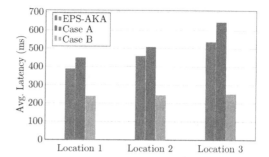

Fig. 5. On the left: The increase in NAS bandwidth consumption and the decrease in S6a bandwidth consumption when the group-based AKA is used instead of EPS AKA. On the right: latency comparison among different locations

authentication of the devices in presence of either a corrupted gateway or corrupted colluding devices [18]. Lai et al. [21] proposed *SE-AKA*, a group-based AKA protocol for LTE networks. The protocol uses public key encryption and supports key forward and backward secrecy. It reduces the communication overhead between MME and HSS to only one message exchange but increases the size of the authentication data response linearly on the size of the group, which makes the protocol not amenable for large groups. Choi et al. [13] use only symmetric cryptography for their group-based AKA protocol. The underlying idea of the protocol is to rely on a global authentication vector based on a group key shared between HSS and MTC devices. Similarly to the schemes of Broustis et al., the protocol introduces the role of a gateway, which contributes to minimizes the bandwidth consumption. However, the protocol does not guarantee any security property in presence of corrupted devices [18]. Cao et al. [12] proposed *GBAAM*, a group-based AKA that relies on the idea of using short aggregate signatures to reduce the overall signaling among the parties. The protocol benefits of pairing cryptography, which removes the need of a PKI. However, it requires each MTC device to run a classic AKA procedure to be registered with the same MME. As the devices normally require to access the network in a different geographic location than the location where they registered, this choice limits the suitability of the protocol as group-based AKA. Sun et al. [25] developed an authenticated group key agreement protocol for mobile environments. The general approach is interesting but it cannot fit the constraints of AKA in mobile telephony.

7   Conclusion

This paper demonstrates that a twenty-year-old protocol can meet modern challenges without revolutionary changes. The proposed group-based AKA is pivoted on the idea of using an inverted hash tree to manage a large number of devices efficiently. The cryptographic primitives of the protocol are based on MILE-NAGE so that the protocol can be adopted in the current standards. The implementation in OAI confirms that only minor modifications to EPS are needed to support the group-based AKA. The formal analysis of the protocol corroborates the security guarantees of the proposed solution, which proved to resist to threats due to colluding corrupted devices. The performance analysis yields promising results in term of latency and bandwidth consumption, with a remarkable gain when considering a large number of devices.

Future work includes the extension of the group-based AKA with support for secure handover among different MME and the resyncronization procedure of the sequence numbers. One approach is to use techniques from different areas, such as mobile cloud computing [29]. Another research direction is to support dynamic groups with key forward/backward secrecy: linkable group signature schemes [15,19,20] might be used on top of the protocol.

While research on areas of fundamental importance for 5G has already started (i.e., cloud security, IoT), research on 5G security is in its early stages. The results of our current implementation are promising since OAI relies on 4G network standards. We expect even better results if the group-based AKA is implemented in the future 5G architecture.

A   Formal Specification of Security Requirements

ProVerif allows for syntactical extension of the applied pi-calculus, such as *events* and *choices*, to ease the specification of security requirements. Confidentiality can be modelled as a reachability property. The secrecy of a term m is preserved if an attacker, defined as an arbitrary process, cannot construct m from any run of the protocol. More precisely, the definition of *reachability-based secrecy* says that an attacker cannot build a process A that can output the secret term m.

Authentication can be defined using *correspondence assertions*. An event e is a message emitted into a special channel that is not under the control of the attacker. To model correspondence assertions, we annotate processes with events such as $e\langle M_1, ... M_n \rangle$ and reason about the relationships ($\leadsto$) between events and their arguments in the form *"if an event $e\langle M_1, ... M_n \rangle$ has been executed, then an event $e'\langle N_1, ... N_n \rangle$ has been previously executed"*.

The applied pi-calculus supports the notion of *observation equivalence*. Informally, two processes are observational equivalent if an observer cannot distinguish the processes even if they handle different data or perform different computations. The indistinguishability characterization of the definition of observation equivalence allows us to capture privacy requirements.

Confidentiality. We check confidentiality of the session master key by proving that a fresh *secret*, which is encrypted with the key and sent in form of ciphertext on the public channel, cannot be obtained by the attacker. As soon as MTC and MME derive the session master key, each of them generates a ciphertext that encrypts the secret. They send the ciphertexts at the very end of the protocol run, accordingly the case. We specify the session master key confidentiality in ProVerif with the following query:

query attacker *(secret)*.

ProVerif is suitable to prove confidentiality as it attempts to prove that a state in which the attacker knows the secret is unreachable. It follows that the secret is known only to MTC and MME.

Authentication. We specify MTC and serving network authentication requirements as correspondence assertions. Each assertion consists of a number of events. Events normally need to agree with some arguments to capture authentication. Thus, we introduce the terms that serve as arguments in our events as follows.

- IMSI refers to the permanent subscribe identity of the MTC;
- GID refers to the group identifiers of the MME;
- SN denotes the identifiers of the MME;
- K_{ASME} denotes the session master key;
- PATH_MTC denotes the path assigned to the MTC;
- HGK_MTC refers to the session individual key derived from the GK tree and associated to the MTC;
- RAND refers to the random value generated by the HSS;
- HCH_MTC refers to the session challenge key derived from the CH tree and associated to the MTC;

Having seen the arguments, we can define the list of events needed to specify mutual group authentication between MTC and MME. The events reflect the two cases defined in the group-based AKA protocol.

- begin_mtc_A$\langle$IMSI, GID, SN, $K_{ASME}\rangle$ means that the MME with identity SN begins the authentication of the MTC with identity IMSI and group GID, and associates it with the key K_{ASME}. The event regards the case A and is emitted by the MME after the authentication data response message.
- begin_mtc_B$\langle$PATH_MTC, GID, SN, HGK_MTC$\rangle$ means that the MME with identity SN begins the authentication of the MTC with path PATH_MTC and group GID, and associates it with the key HGK_MTC. The event regards the case B and is emitted by the MME after the attach request.
- begin_mme_A$\langle$IMSI, GID, SN, RAND, $K_{ASME}\rangle$ means that the MTC with identity IMSI and group GID begins the authentication of the MME with identity SN, and associates it with the random value RAND and key K_{ASME}. The event regards the case A and is emitted by the MTC after the authentication request.
- begin_mme_B$\langle$PATH_MTC, GID, SN, HCH_MTC, $K_{ASME}\rangle$ means that the MTC with path PATH_MTC and group GID begins the authentication of the MME with identity SN, and associate it with the keys HCH_MTC and K_{ASME}. The event regards the case B and is emitted by the MTC after the authentication request derivable message.
- end_mtc_A$\langle$IMSI, GID, SN, $K_{ASME}\rangle$ means that the MTC with identity IMSI and group GID concluded the authentication of the MME with identity SN, and computed the key K_{ASME}. The event regards the case A and is emitted by the MTC after the authentication response.

- end_mtc_B⟨PATH_MTC, GID, SN, HGK_MTC⟩ means that the MTC with path PATH_MTC and group GID concluded the authentication of the MME with identity SN, and computed the key HGK_MTC. The event regards the case B and is emitted by the MTC after the authentication response derivable message.
- end_mme_A⟨IMSI, GID, SN, RAND, K$_{ASME}$⟩ means that the MME with identity SN concluded the authentication of the MTC with identity IMSI and group GID, and associates it with the random value RAND and key K$_{ASME}$. The event regards the case A and is emitted by the MME after the successful verification of RES.
- end_mme_B⟨PATH_MTC, GID, SN, HCH_MTC, K$_{ASME}$⟩ means that the MME with identity SN concluded the authentication of the MTC with path PATH_MTC and group GID, and associates it with keys HCH_MTC and K$_{ASME}$. The event regards the case B and is emitted by the MME after the successfully verification of RES$_D$.

To formalize mutual authentication we need to distinguish the authentication of the MME to MTC and the authentication of the MTC to the MME. Moreover, we need to distinguish the two cases. We formalize the authentication of the MME to MTC in Case A and Case B as follows.

Definition 1 (Serving network authentication (Case A)). *The protocol ensures serving network authentication for Case A if the correspondence assertion*

$$\text{end\_mtc\_A}\langle \text{IMSI, GID, SN, K}_{ASME}\rangle \rightsquigarrow$$
$$\text{begin\_mtc\_A}\langle \text{IMSI, GID, SN, K}_{ASME}\rangle$$

is true on every execution trace.

Definition 2 (Serving network authentication (Case B)). *The protocol ensures serving network authentication for Case B if the correspondence assertion*

$$\text{end\_mtc\_B}\langle \text{PATH\_MTC, GID, SN, HGK\_MTC}\rangle \rightsquigarrow$$
$$\text{begin\_mtc\_B}\langle \text{PATH\_MTC, GID, SN, HGK\_MTC}\rangle$$

is true on every execution trace.

In a similar way, we can formalize the authentication of the MTC to the MME in Case A and Case B.

Definition 3 (MTC authentication (Case A)). *The protocol ensures the authentication of MTC for Case A if the correspondence assertion*

$$\text{end\_mme\_A}\langle \text{IMSI, GID, SN, RAND, K}_{ASME}\rangle \rightsquigarrow$$
$$\text{begin\_mme\_A}\langle \text{IMSI, GID, SN, RAND, K}_{ASME}\rangle$$

is true on every execution trace.

Definition 4 (MTC authentication (Case B)). *The protocol ensures the authentication of MTC for Case B if the correspondence assertion*

$$\text{end\_mme\_B}\langle \text{PATH\_MTC}, \text{GID}, \text{SN}, \text{HCH\_MTC}, \text{K}_{\text{ASME}} \rangle \rightsquigarrow$$

$$\text{begin\_mme\_B}\langle \text{PATH\_MTC}, \text{GID}, \text{SN}, \text{HCH\_MTC}, \text{K}_{\text{ASME}} \rangle$$

is true on every execution trace.

Privacy. To model MTC identity privacy as equivalence property, we use the definition of labelled bisimilarity ($\approx_l$) as defined by Abadi and Fournet. We reason about the processes of MTC, MME, and HSS, which map to the corresponding roles. Each device playing the role of MTC execute the same process MTC but are instantiated with different variable values (e.g. IMSI, K). The requirement of MTC identity privacy can be conveniently specified as follows:

Definition 5 (MTC identity privacy).

$$MTC\{^{\text{IMSI}_A}/_{id}\}|MME|HSS \approx_l MTC\{^{\text{IMSI}_B}/_{id}\}|MME|HSS$$

The definition above states that two processes instantiated with two different IMSI values have to be observationally equivalent. Such equivalence means that an attacker cannot distinguish whether the MTC participating in the protocol run is the one associated with IMSI_A or IMSI_B, hence the privacy of the MTC identity is guaranteed. Note that the formulation of MTC identity privacy based on observational equivalence is more stringent than any formulation based on reachability. The latter formulation would need to assume that the attacker does not know any IMSIvalue in advance, an assumption that can be lifted up using observational equivalence.

The ProVerif code that describes the processes for MTC, MME, and HSS are respectively in Figs. 6, 7, and 8.

B   Implementation and Analysis in OAI

The configuration used by our patched version of OAI is depicted in Fig. 9. It includes three virtual machines running Linux inside a single host Intel Core i7 processor with 4GB RAM. In particular, one machine (VM1) runs the Openairinterface5G module that simulate an MTCdevice and the eNodeB base station. The other two machines (VM2 and VM3) run the OPENAIR-CN module. Note that OAI does not currently support multiple MTC device, namely the Openairinterface5G module include only a device. However, we can run multiple runs of Openairinterface5G module in different machines to instantiate several MTC devices at cost of instantiating the same number of base stations.

The communication between MTC device, MME, and HSS are performed through Ethernet interfaces. The communication between MTC device and eNodeB is done within VM1 and represents the *S1-U* interface in the 3GPP standard. The channel between VM1 and VM2 represent the *S1-MME* interface according the standard. VM3 is dedicated to the HSS, which uses a MySQL server for the storage of subscriber data.

```
let MTC (imsi_mtc: id, key_mtc: key, gid: id, path_mtc: path,
        sqn: bitstring, o_mtc: bitstring, pos: bit) =
new nonce_mtc: rand;
out(ch, (gid, path_mtc, nonce_mtc, pos));
in (ch, (case_x: int, aut_x: bitstring, sn_id: id, rand_x: rand));
if case_x=caseA then
  (let (xored_sqn: bitstring, mac_sn: bitstring)=aut_x in
   if sqn=xor(f5((key_mtc, rand_x)),xored_sqn) then
     (if mac_sn=f1((sqn, rand_x), key_mtc) then
        let res=f2((key_mtc, rand_x)) in
        let ck=f3((key_mtc, rand_x)) in
        let ik=f4((key_mtc, rand_x)) in
        let kasme=kdf((xored_sqn, ck, ik, sn_id)) in
        event beginMMEa (imsi_mtc, gid, sn_id, rand_x, kasme);
        out(ch, res);
        let knasenc_mtc = kdf_nas_enc(kasme) in
        let knasint_mtc = kdf_nas_int(kasme) in
        out(ch, senc(secret, knasenc_mtc));
        in (ch, (nasmsgmac: bitstring , mac_nas: bitstring));
        if mac_nas=nas_mac(nasmsgmac, knasint_mtc) then
        let enc_complete_msg=senc(nas_complete_msg, knasenc_mtc) in
        out (ch , (nas_complete_msg, enc_complete_msg,
                   nas_mac(enc_complete_msg, knasint_mtc)));
        event endMTCa (imsi_mtc, gid, sn_id, kasme)
      else 0)
   else  0)
else if case_x=caseB then
  let (f5_hgkmtc_nonce: bitstring, mac_hgkmtc: bitstring)=aut_x in
  let hgk_mtc=xor(h((key_mtc, rand_x)),o_mtc) in
  if f5((hgk_mtc, nonce_mtc))=f5_hgkmtc_nonce then
    if mac_hgkmtc=f1((nonce_mtc, rand_x, gid, sn_id, path_mtc),
                     bs_to_key(hgk_mtc)) then
      let res_b=f2((hgk_mtc, rand_x)) in
      let ck_b=f3((hgk_mtc, rand_x)) in
      let ik_b=f4((hgk_mtc, rand_x)) in
      let kasme_b=kdf((f5_hgkmtc_nonce, ck_b, ik_b, sn_id)) in
      event beginMMEb (path_mtc, gid, sn_id, rand_x, kasme_b);
      out(ch, res_b);
      let knasenc_mtc = kdf_nas_enc(kasme_b) in
      let knasint_mtc = kdf_nas_int(kasme_b) in
      out(ch, senc(secret, knasenc_mtc));
      in (ch, (nasmsgmac: bitstring , mac_nas: bitstring));
      if mac_nas=nas_mac(nasmsgmac, knasint_mtc) then
      let enc_complete_msg=senc(nas_complete_msg, knasenc_mtc) in
      out (ch , (nas_complete_msg, enc_complete_msg,
                 nas_mac(enc_complete_msg, knasint_mtc)));
      event endMTCb (path_mtc, gid, sn_id, hgk_mtc).
```

Fig. 6. The process of MTC in ProVerif

```
let MME_init (sn_mme: id, hss_mme: key) =
 in(ch, (gid: id, path_mtc: path, nonce_mtc: rand, =sn_mme, pos: bit));
 if (path_mtc=get_child( get_parent(path_mtc), left) && pos=left) ||
    (path_mtc=get_child( get_parent(path_mtc), right) && pos=right)  then
        (MME_a(gid, path_mtc, sn_mme, hss_mme) |
         MME_b(gid, path_mtc, nonce_mtc, sn_mme, pos)).


let MME_a (gid: id, path_mtc: path, sn_mme: id, hss_mme: key) =
 out(ch, senc( (gid, path_mtc, sn_mme), hss_mme));
 in(ch, from_hss: bitstring);
 let (=gid, GKij: bitstring, CHij: bitstring, autn: bitstring,
      xres: bitstring, rand_hss: rand, kasme: key, imsi_mtc: id,
      n: bitstring, =path_mtc)=sdec(from_hss, hss_mme) in
 let pathx=get_parent(path_mtc) in
 insert mme_keys(GKij, CHij, gid, pathx, n);
 event beginMTCa (imsi_mtc, gid, sn_mme, kasme);
 out(ch, (caseA, autn, sn_mme, rand_hss));
 in(ch, =xres);
 let knasenc_mme = kdf_nas_enc(kasme) in
 let knasint_mme = kdf_nas_int(kasme) in
 out(ch, senc(secret, knasenc_mme));
 new nasmsgmac: bitstring;
 out(ch, (nasmsgmac, nas_mac(nasmsgmac, knasint_mme)));
 in(ch, (=nas_complete_msg, enc_msg: bitstring, mac_nas: bitstring));
 if mac_nas=nas_mac(enc_msg, knasint_mme) &&
    nas_complete_msg=sdec(enc_msg, knasenc_mme) then
  out(ch, senc(secret, knasenc_mme));
  event endMMEa (imsi_mtc, gid, sn_mme, rand_hss, kasme).


let MME_b (gid: id,path_mtc: path,nonce_mtc: rand,sn_mme: id,pos: bit)=
 get mme_keys(GKij, CHij, =gid, =get_parent(path_mtc), n) in
 let GKmtc=set_node(GKij,pos) in
 let hgkmtc=hash(GKmtc, n) in
 event beginMTCb (path_mtc, gid, sn_mme, hgkmtc);
 let CHmtc=set_node(CHij,pos) in
 let hchmtc=hash(CHmtc, n) in
 let f5_hgkmtc_nonce=f5((hgkmtc, nonce_mtc)) in
 let mac_hgkmtc=f1((nonce_mtc, hchmtc, gid, sn_mme, path_mtc),
                   bs_to_key(hgkmtc)) in
 out(ch, (caseB, (f5_hgkmtc_nonce, mac_hgkmtc), sn_mme, hchmtc));
 let ck=f3((hgkmtc, hchmtc)) in
 let ik=f4((hgkmtc, hchmtc)) in
 let kasme=kdf((f5_hgkmtc_nonce, ck, ik, sn_mme)) in
 in(ch, res_d: bitstring);
 if res_d=f2((hgkmtc, hchmtc)) then
  let knasenc_mme = kdf_nas_enc(kasme) in
  let knasint_mme = kdf_nas_int(kasme) in
  out(ch, senc(secret, knasenc_mme));
  new nasmsgmac: bitstring;
  out(ch, (nasmsgmac, nas_mac(nasmsgmac, knasint_mme)));
  in(ch, (=nas_complete_msg, enc_msg: bitstring, mac_nas: bitstring));
  if mac_nas=nas_mac(enc_msg, knasint_mme) &&
     nas_complete_msg=sdec(enc_msg, knasenc_mme) then
   event endMMEb (path_mtc, gid, sn_mme, bs_to_rand(hchmtc), kasme).
```

Fig. 7. The process of MME in ProVerif

```
let HSS (sn_mme: id, mme_hss: key) =
 in(ch, from_mme: bitstring);
 let (gid: id, path_mtc: path, =sn_mme)=sdec(from_mme, mme_hss) in
 get hss_keys(=path_mtc, imsi, key_mtc, =gid, sqn, rootG, rootR, n) in
 new rand_hss: rand;
 let xored_sqn=xor(f5((key_mtc, rand_hss)),sqn)   in
 let mac_hss=f1((sqn, rand_hss), key_mtc) in
 let xres=f2((key_mtc, rand_hss)) in
 let ck=f3((key_mtc, rand_hss)) in
 let ik=f4((key_mtc, rand_hss)) in
 let kasme=kdf((xored_sqn, ck, ik, sn_mme)) in
 let autn=(xored_sqn, mac_hss) in
 out(ch, senc((gid, rootG, rootR, autn, xres, rand_hss, kasme, imsi, n,
              path_mtc), mme_hss)).
```

Fig. 8. The process of HSS in ProVerif

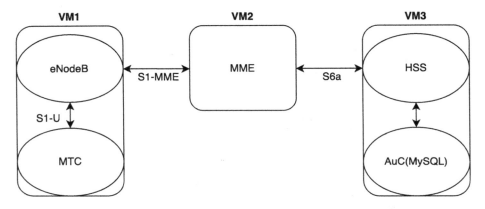

Fig. 9. Minimal network configuration needed for our patched version of OAI.

B.1 Parameters

Some terms have no similar counterpart in the existing standards so we design them from scratch. This is the case of the two auxiliary parameters TREE HEIGHT and NODE DEPTH. The first gives the height $\mathcal{H}$ of the inverted hash trees. It is used as an indicator of how many bits of the path should be used. This parameter is needed because the path is communicated in full bytes even though the size of the actual path might not be divisible by eight. We thus specify that the size of TREE HEIGHT is one byte. The parameter NODE DEPTH gives the level on which the sub-root nodes GK_{ij} and CH_{ij} are placed in the inverted hash trees. The knowledge of PATH, TREE HEIGHT, and NODE DEPTH allows the MME to deduce the structure of the inverted hash tree and to assess whether next MTC devices can be served according Case A or Case B.

To compute the bandwidth consumption at NAS level, we consider the parameters and the sizes described in Table 4. We recall Eqs. 1 and 2 concerning the

Table 4. Sizes of parameters of EPS-AKA and group-based AKA at NAS level.

Parameter	Size (bytes)	EPS-AKA	Group-based AKA	
			Case A	Case B
IMSI	9	✓	✗	✗
RAND	16	✓	✓	✗
AUTN	17	✓	✓	✗
RES	9	✓	✓	✗
GID	9	✗	✓	✓
PATH	Variable[a]	✗	✓	✓
NONCE	16	✗	✓	✓
N	6	✗	✓	✓
HCH	16	✗	✗	✓
AUT$_D$	15	✗	✗	✓
RES$_D$	9	✗	✗	✓

[a]The size of PATH is variable because it depends on the number of MTC devices considered.

bandwidth consumption for the group-based protocol for the NAS and the S6a interface.

$$\mathbf{BAND\_GB\_NAS} = m \times \left(\text{GID} + \frac{(\lceil \log_2 m \rceil \times 2 - 1)}{8} + 2 + \text{NONCE}\right)$$
$$+ (m - 1) \times (\text{HCH} + \text{AUT}_D + \text{RES}_D) + \text{RAND} + \text{AUTN} + \text{RES}.$$

$$\mathbf{BAND\_GB\_S6a} = \text{IMSI} + 2 \times \text{GID} + \text{RAND} + \text{XRES} + \text{AUTN} + K_{\text{ASME}}$$
$$\text{GK}_{ij} + \text{CH}_{ij} + \mathcal{H} + \text{SN}_{\text{ID}} + 2 \times \left(min(\text{PATH}) + \frac{\lceil \log_2 m \rceil \times 2 - 1)}{32} \times 4\right).$$

The bandwidth consumption for EPS-AKA at NAS level is

$$\mathbf{Band\_EPS\_NAS} = m \times (\text{IMSI} + \text{RAND} + \text{AUTN} + \text{RES}). \tag{3}$$

Regarding the bandwidth consumption for the S6A interface, Diameter adds to each parameter 12 bytes for header and flags. Hence, the size of parameters are bigger in S6A interface than in NAS. The values of the parameters are synthesized in Table 5. The bandwidth consumption for EPS-AKA can be computed as

$$\mathbf{Band\_EPS\_s6A} = m \times (\text{IMSI} + \text{RAND} + \text{AUTN} + \text{XRES} + K_{\text{ASME}} + \text{SN}_{\text{ID}}) \tag{4}$$

Figure 10 shows that the group-based AKA has more bandwidth consumption than the EPS-AKA at NAS level. This is because the attach request message in the group-based AKA includes the parameters PATH and NONCEin addition to

Table 5. Sizes of parameters of EPS-AKA and group-based AKA in the S6A interface.

Parameter	Size (bytes)	EPS-AKA	Group-based AKA	
			Case A	Case B
IMSI	16	✓	✓	×
RAND	28	✓	✓	×
AUTN	28	✓	✓	×
XRES	20	✓	✓	×
K_{ASME}	44	✓	✓	×
SN_{ID}	16	✓	✓	×
N	18	×	✓	×
GID	16	×	✓	×
PATH	Variable[a]	×	✓	×
CH_{ij}	28	×	✓	×
GK_{ij}	28	×	✓	×
NODE DEPTH	16	×	✓	×
TREE HEIGHT	16	×	✓	×

[a]The size of PATH is variable because it depends on the number of MTC devices considered.

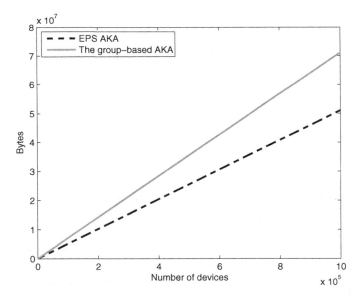

Fig. 10. Bandwidth consumption comparison between EPS AKA and the group-based AKA on the NAS.

the standard parameters. However, the bandwidth consumption rate is inverted in the S6a interface, as described in Fig. 11. The group-based AKA consumes less

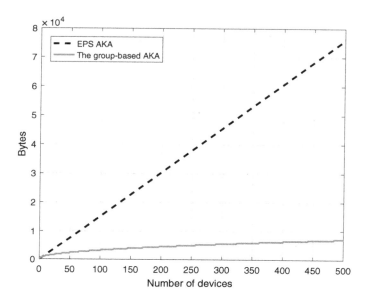

Fig. 11. Bandwidth consumption comparison between EPS AKA and group-based AKA on the S6a interface

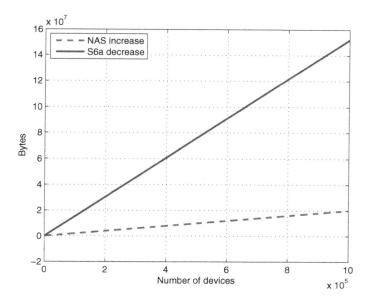

Fig. 12. Increase in NAS bandwidth consumption and decrease in S6a bandwidth consumption when the group-based AKA is used instead of EPS-AKA.

bandwidth already when more than two MTC devices are considered. Notably, when the number of MTC devices to be served are more then three, the overall bandwidth consumption of group-based AKA is less than the one of EPS-AKA. This is depicted in Fig. 12.

References

1. 3GPP: Formal analysis of the 3G authentication protocol. Technical report 33.902 (2001)
2. 3GPP: Specification of the MILENAGE algorithm set. Technical specification 35.205 (2001)
3. 3GPP: 3GPP System Architecture Evolution (SAE); Security architecture. Technical specification 33.401 (2008)
4. 3GPP: MME related interfaces based on diameter protocol. Technical specification 29.272 (2008)
5. 3GPP: Service requirements for Machine-Type Communications (MTC); Stage 1. Technical report 22.368 (2011)
6. Abadi, M., Fournet, C.: Mobile values, new names, and secure communication. In: POPL2001, pp. 104–115. ACM, New York (2001)
7. Alliance, O.S.: Openairinterface. http://www.openairinterface.org/
8. Alt, S., Fouque, P.-A., Macario-rat, G., Onete, C., Richard, B.: A cryptographic analysis of UMTS/LTE AKA. In: Manulis, M., Sadeghi, A.-R., Schneider, S. (eds.) ACNS 2016. LNCS, vol. 9696, pp. 18–35. Springer, Heidelberg (2016). doi:10.1007/978-3-319-39555-5_2
9. Blanchet, B.: An efficient cryptographic protocol verifier based on prolog rules. In: CSFW, pp. 82–96. IEEE Computer Society, Cape Breton, Canada (2001)
10. van den Broek, F., Verdult, R., de Ruiter, J.: Defeating IMSI catchers. In: 22nd ACM SIGSAC Conference on Computer and Communications Security, CCS 2015, pp. 340–351. ACM (2015)
11. Broustis, I., Sundaram, G.S., Viswanathan, H.: Group authentication: a new paradigm for emerging applications. Bell Labs Tech. J. **17**(3), 157–173 (2012)
12. Cao, J., Ma, M., Li, H.: GBAAM: group-based access authentication for MTC in LTE networks. Secur. Commun. Netw. **8**(17), 3282–3299 (2015)
13. Choi, D., Choi, H.K., Lee, S.Y.: A group-based security protocol for machine-type communications in LTE-advanced. Wirel. Netw. **21**(2), 405–419 (2014)
14. Dolev, D., Yao, A.C.: On the security of public key protocols. IEEE Trans. Inf. Theor. **29**(2), 198–208 (1983)
15. Emura, K., Hayashi, T.: A light-weight group signature scheme with time-token dependent linking. In: Güneysu, T., Leander, G., Moradi, A. (eds.) LightSec 2015. LNCS, vol. 9542, pp. 37–57. Springer, Heidelberg (2016). doi:10.1007/978-3-319-29078-2_3
16. Ericsson: Ericsson mobility report. Technical report (2015)
17. Fouque, P.A., Onete, C., Richard, B.: Achieving better privacy for the 3GPP AKA protocol. IACR Cryptology ePrint Archive **2016**, p. 480 (2016)
18. Giustolisi, R., Gehrmann, C.: Threats to 5G group-based authentication. In: SECRYPT 2016 - Proceedings of the 13th International Conference on Security and Cryptography. SciTePress (2016)
19. Hwang, J.Y., Eom, S., Chang, K.Y., Lee, P.J., Nyang, D.: Anonymity-based authenticated key agreement with full binding property. J. Commun. Netw. **18**(2), 190–200 (2016)

20. Hwang, J.Y., Lee, S., Chung, B.H., Cho, H.S., Nyang, D.: Group signatures with controllable linkability for dynamic membership. Inf. Sci. **222**, 761–778 (2013)
21. Lai, C., Li, H., Lu, R., Shen, X.S.: SE-AKA: a secure and efficient group authentication and key agreement protocol for LTE networks. Comput. Netw. **57**, 17 (2013)
22. Nokia Siemens Networks: Signaling is growing 50% faster than data traffic. Technical Report (2012)
23. Oracle: Oracle communications LTE diameter signaling index, 4th edn. White Paper (2015)
24. Ryan, M.D., Smyth, B.: Applied pi calculus. In: Formal Models and Techniques for Analyzing Security Protocols, chap. 6. IOS Press (2011)
25. Sun, H.M., He, B.Z., Chen, C.M., Wu, T.Y., Lin, C.H., Wang, H.: A provable authenticated group key agreement protocol for mobile environment. Inf. Sci. **321**, 224–237 (2015)
26. Tang, C., Naumann, D.A., Wetzel, S.: Analysis of authentication and key establishment in inter-generational mobile telephony. In: IEEE 10th International Conference on Embedded and Ubiquitous Computing (HPCC_EUC). pp. 1605–1614 (2013)
27. WonderNetwork: Wonderproxy servers. https://wonderproxy.com/servers (August 2016)
28. Woo, T.Y., Lam, S.S.: A semantic model for authentication protocols. In: 1993 IEEE Computer Society Symposium on Research in Security and Privacy, Proceedings, pp. 178–194 (1993)
29. Yang, X., Huang, X., Liu, J.K.: Efficient handover authentication with user anonymity and untraceability for mobile cloud computing. Future Gener. Comput. Syst. **62**, 190–195 (2016)

Secure and Private, yet Lightweight, Authentication for the IoT via PUF and CBKA

Christopher Huth[1(✉)], Aydin Aysu[2], Jorge Guajardo[3], Paul Duplys[1], and Tim Güneysu[4]

[1] Robert Bosch GmbH, Stuttgart, Germany
christopher.huth@de.bosch.com
[2] The University of Texas at Austin, Austin, USA
[3] Robert Bosch LLC - Research and Technology Center, Pittsburgh, USA
[4] University of Bremen & DFKI, Bremen, Germany

Abstract. The Internet of Things (IoT) is boon and bane. It offers great potential for new business models and ecosystems, but raises major security and privacy concerns. Because many IoT systems collect, process, and store personal data, a secure *and* privacy-preserving identity management is of utmost significance. Yet, strong resource limitations of IoT devices render resource-hungry public-key cryptography infeasible. Additionally, the security model of IoT enforces solutions to work under memory-leakage attacks. Existing constructions address either the privacy issue or the lightweightness, but not both. Our work contributes towards bridging this gap by combining physically unclonable functions (PUFs) and channel-based key agreement (CBKA): (i) We show a flaw in a PUF-based authentication protocol, when outsider chosen perturbation security cannot be guaranteed. (ii) We present a solution to this flaw by introducing CBKA with an improved definition. (iii) We propose a provably secure and lightweight authentication protocol by combining PUFs and CBKA.

Keywords: Cryptographic protocol · Physically unclonable function · Channel-based key agreement

1 Introduction

The Internet of Things is on its way to change your everyday life. Computing devices are miniaturized and interconnected with an expected 50 billion devices by 2020 [13]. On the one hand, the IoT creates new multi billion markets for novel services and business models, but on the other hand, it also poses new challenges for security and privacy [4, 27]. Security-wise, the ubiquitous and dynamic nature of IoT drives the need for a strong identity management and, in particular, for secure device authentication. In addition to resource constraints, keys stored in non-volatile memory have to be assumed to be leaked, since attacks on these lightweight devices are hard to prevent [18]. With respect to privacy, sensor nodes and wearables, like fitness trackers, capture highly-personal data. Also, public-key cryptography may be too expensive to be implemented on resource-constrained

© Springer International Publishing AG 2017
S. Hong and J.H. Park (Eds.): ICISC 2016, LNCS 10157, pp. 28–48, 2017.
DOI: 10.1007/978-3-319-53177-9_2

devices. In this paper, we answer how an IoT device can authenticate securely *and* privacy-friendly with said constraints.

For IoT platforms, physically unclonable functions [5,14,15,31,36] are an emerging trend which are often mentioned in the context of a lightweight solution. PUFs are already present on several products, such as small chip card microcontrollers like NXP's SmartMX2 [1] to modern high-performance FPGAs [35]. When used as key storage, PUFs benefit from uncontrollable manufacturing variations causing an intrinsically embedded key to be unique. An often mentioned security advantage of PUF over, e.g. e-fuses, is that they store no values when the device is off [17].

PUFs are included in many authentication protocols. Delvaux *et al.* [9] surveyed multiple protocols using strong PUFs, and revealed that only few can offer privacy. Moriyama *et al.* [29] propose such a PUF-based authentication protocol under complete memory leakage. Their protocol was further adapted by Aysu *et al.* [6] by reversing the generate and reproduce procedures to suit better for lightweight devices at the cost of introducing a preshared secret. But helper data of reverse fuzzy extractors could leak information when a challenge is used multiple times [8], so we encrypt the helper data with a session key.

The lightweight and secure generation of a session key or shared secret can be addressed with CBKA [24–26], which uses the inherent randomness of a wireless communication channel between two devices, while offering information-theoretic security. CBKA ensures for each execution, that a fresh session key is generated due to its common physical randomness, so storage of preshared data becomes obsolete. A possible alternative to agree on a symmetric key is Diffie-Hellman over elliptic curves (ECDH), but we want to spare devices the rather heavy computational complexity and memory footprint of calculating on elliptic curves [38].

Both technologies – PUFs and CBKA – deal with physical noise and therefore need error correction and entropy amplification. Huth *et al.* [20] propose a system for the IoT integrating PUFs and CBKA alike. Their idea is to generate a symmetric key with CBKA and authenticate it with a PUF-based protocol. The implementation overhead is small since post-processing steps can be reused for either technology.

Contribution. We summarize our contribution as follows:

- *Flaw in existing protocol.* We show the need for fuzzy extractors with outsider chosen perturbation in Aysu's protocol [6] to satisfy privacy claims, which are in conflict with lightweight and PUF-friendly fuzzy extractors.
- *Formal definition for CBKA.* We enhance their protocol, while keeping the reverse fuzzy extractor construction and possible usage of all fuzzy extractors. To prove security, we introduce a new formal definition for CBKA.
- *Protocol enhancement.* Our main contribution is a mutual authentication protocol enhancement. We integrate PUFs and CBKA, so that our protocol offers provable security and privacy under complete memory leakage assumptions and is suitable for the IoT. Summarizing, we shift digital challenges, i.e. key storage and session key generation, onto the physical domain.

Outline. First, mathematical preliminaries are introduced in Sect. 2 for notation, PUFs and fuzzy extractors. In Sect. 3, we describe our security and privacy model. Next, in Sect. 4 we show the flaw in an existing protocol. To overcome this flaw, we introduce a new formal definition for CBKA in Sect. 5. Based on our previous results, we present our main contribution in Sect. 6 – a provable secure and private mutual authentication protocol. In Sect. 7 we estimate implementation costs. We conclude this article in Sect. 8.

2   Notation and Preliminaries

We write $\mathcal{M}$ to denote a metric space with an associated distance function dis. The statistical distance between two probability distributions A and B is denoted by $\mathbf{SD}(A, B)$. U_n denotes the uniformly distributed random variable on $\{0, 1\}^n$. When A is a deterministic algorithm, $y := A(x)$ denotes the assignment to y from $A(x)$ with input x. When A is a probabilistic machine or algorithm, $y \xleftarrow{\mathsf{R}} A(x)$ denotes that y is randomly selected from A according to its distribution. When A is a set, $y \xleftarrow{\mathsf{U}} A(x)$ denotes that y is uniformly selected from A. $\tilde{H}_\infty(A)$ is the min-entropy of A and $\tilde{H}_\infty(A|B)$ indicates the conditional min-entropy of A given B. We denote an efficient algorithm as probabilistic polynomial time (PPT). We use a Truly Random Number Generator (TRNG) to derive truly random binary sequences. Furthermore, we use Symmetric Key Encryption $\mathsf{SKE} := (\mathsf{SKE.Enc}, \mathsf{SKE.Dec})$, where $\mathsf{SKE.Enc}$ uses secret key sk and plaintext m as inputs and generates ciphertext c as output. $\mathsf{SKE.Dec}$ decrypts the ciphertext c with secret key sk to generate plaintext m. A Pseudorandom Function $\mathsf{PRF} : \mathcal{K} \times \mathcal{D} \to \mathcal{R}$ inputs a secret key $sk \in \mathcal{K}$ and message $m \in \mathcal{D}$ providing an indistinguishable from random output for metric spaces $\mathcal{K}, \mathcal{D}, \mathcal{R}$.

Physically Unclonable Function. We adapt the definition by Armknecht *et al.* [3] for PUFs, which are parametrized by some thresholds δ_i, the number of iterations t, the number of inputs ℓ, the number of devices n, a negligible function $\epsilon(\cdot)$, and the security parameter λ. Here, we restate that a PUF is a probabilistic mapping $f : \mathcal{C} \to \mathcal{R}$ where $\mathcal{C}$ is a domain space and $\mathcal{R}$ is an output range of PUF f.

Requirement 1 (Intra-Distance [3]). *Whenever a single PUF is repeatedly evaluated with a fixed input, the maximum distance between the corresponding outputs is at most δ_1. That is for any created PUF $f \leftarrow \mathcal{MP}(\mathrm{param})$ and any $y \in \mathcal{C}$, it holds that $\Pr[\max(\{\mathsf{dis}(z_i, z_j)\}_{i \neq j}) \leq \delta_1 | y \in \mathcal{C}, \{z_i \leftarrow f(y)\}_{1 \leq i \leq t}] = 1 - \epsilon(\lambda)$.*

Requirement 2 (Inter-Distance I [3]). *Whenever a single PUF is evaluated on different inputs, the minimum distance among them is at least δ_2. That is for a created PUF $f \leftarrow \mathcal{MP}(\mathrm{param})$ and for any $y_1, \dots, y_\ell \in \mathcal{C}$, we have $\Pr[\min(\{\mathsf{dis}(z_i, z_j)\}_{i \neq j}) \geq \delta_2 | y_1, \dots, y_\ell \in \mathcal{C}, \{z_i \leftarrow f(y_i)\}_{1 \leq i \leq \ell}] = 1 - \epsilon(\lambda)$.*

Requirement 3 (Inter-Distance II [3]). *Whenever multiple PUFs are evaluated on a single, fixed input, the minimum distance among them is at least δ_3. That is for any created PUF $f_i \leftarrow \mathcal{MP}(\text{param})$ for $1 \leq i \leq n$ and any $y \in \mathcal{C}$, we have* $\Pr[\min(\{\text{dis}(z_i, z_j)\}_{i \neq j}) \geq \delta_3 | y \in \mathcal{C}, \{z_i \leftarrow f_i(y)\}_{1 \leq i \leq n}] = 1 - \epsilon(\lambda)$.

Requirement 4 (Min-Entropy [3]). *Whenever multiple PUFs are evaluated on multiple inputs, the min-entropy of the outputs is at least δ_4, even if the other outputs are observed. Let $z_{i,j} \leftarrow f_i(y_j)$ be the output of a PUF f_i on input y_j where $f_i \leftarrow \mathcal{MP}(\text{param})$. Then* $\Pr[\tilde{H}_\infty(z_{i,j} | \mathcal{Z}_{i,j}) \geq \delta_4 | y_1, \dots, y_\ell \in \mathcal{C}, \mathcal{Z} := \{z_{i,j} \leftarrow f_i(y_j)\}_{1 \leq i \leq n, 1 \leq j \leq \ell}, \mathcal{Z}_{i,j} := \mathcal{Z} \backslash \{z_{i,j}\}] = 1 - \epsilon(\lambda)$.

Definition 1 ([3]). *A PUF $f : \mathcal{C} \to \mathcal{R}$ has $(\mathcal{MP}, t, n, \ell, \delta_1, \delta_2, \delta_3, \epsilon)$-variance if the PUF's output has inter and intra distances as described in Requirements 1, 2 and 3, parameterized by $(\mathcal{MP}, t, n, \ell, \delta_1, \delta_2, \delta_3)$.*

Definition 2 ([3]). *A PUF $f : \mathcal{C} \to \mathcal{R}$ has $(\mathcal{MP}, n, \ell, \delta_4, \epsilon)$-min-entropy if the PUF satisfies the min-entropy requirement as described in Requirement 4.*

We define indistinguishability with a game as in [3]. The attacker is given access to all PUFs and can get any number of challenge-response pairs, except the two the attacker is choosing later. The information about all PUFs and challenge-response pairs is called state information st. The attacker cannot map a presented response back to one of two PUFs, even if the attacker chose these two PUFs and chose a challenge for each of these.

Definition 3 ([29]). *Let $\mathcal{A}$ be an adversary who can physically access PUFs f_i. Let $\mathcal{S}$ be an algorithm which only interacts with f_i via oracle access. Let $z_{i,j} \leftarrow f_i(y_j)$ be the output of a PUF $f_i : \mathcal{C} \to \mathcal{R}$ on input y_j where $f_i \leftarrow \mathcal{MP}(\text{param})$. A PUF f_i satisfies $(\mathcal{MP}, n, \ell, \epsilon)$-indistinguishability if for any distinguisher $\mathcal{D}$, the probability of distinguishing the outputs is negligibly close to ϵ such that* $|\Pr[\mathcal{D}(1^\lambda, st) \to 1 | \{st \leftarrow \mathcal{A}(1^\lambda, f_i(y_j))\}_{1 \leq i \leq n, 1 \leq j \leq \ell}] - \Pr[\mathcal{D}(1^\lambda, st) \to 1 | \{st \leftarrow \mathcal{S}^{f_i(y_j)}(1^\lambda)\}_{1 \leq i \leq n, 1 \leq j \leq \ell}]| \leq \epsilon(\lambda)$.

Extractor. Strong extractors [30] allow to extract almost all min-entropy from a non-uniform random variable. Since we deal in this paper with secrets conditioned on some side information, we here recall the definition of average-case strong extractors, which are closely related to former strong extractors. Extractors guarantee that the extracted string is uniform, even when conditioned on a seed or any other external information.

Definition 4 (Average-case Extractor [11]). *Let seed U_r be uniform on $\{0, 1\}^r$ and let X be any distribution over $\{0, 1\}^n$. Let E be any external information that may be correlated with X. A function $\text{Ext} : \{0, 1\}^n \to \{0, 1\}^\ell$ is an average-case $(n, m, \ell, \epsilon)-$strong extractor if for X with $\tilde{H}_\infty(X | E) \geq m$, we have* $\mathbf{SD}((\text{Ext}(X, U_r), U_r, E), (U_\ell, U_r, E)) \leq \epsilon$.

Definition 5 (Secure Sketch [11]). *A $(m, \tilde{m}, t)$-secure sketch for $\mathcal{M}$ is a pair of randomized procedures, "sketch" (SS) and "recover" (Rec), with the following properties:*

- *The sketching procedure SS on input $w \in \mathcal{M}$ outputs a bit string $s \in \{0, 1\}^*$. The recovery procedure Rec takes as inputs an element $w' \in \mathcal{M}$ and a bit string $s \in \{0, 1\}^*$.*
- *The* correctness *property of secure sketches guarantees that if $\mathsf{dis}(w, w') \leq t$, then $\mathsf{Rec}(w', \mathsf{SS}(w)) = w$. If $\mathsf{dis}(w, w') > t$, then no guarantee of the output of Rec can be given.*
- *The* security *property guarantees that for any distribution W over $\mathcal{M}$ with $H_\infty(W) \geq m$, we have $\tilde{H}_\infty(W|\mathsf{SS}(W)) \geq \tilde{m}$. The quantity $\tilde{m}$ is the residual min-entropy and $m - \tilde{m}$ is the entropy loss of a secure sketch.*

Definition 6 (Fuzzy Extractor [11]). *A (m, ℓ, t, ϵ)-fuzzy extractor for $\mathcal{M}$ is a pair of randomized procedures, "generate" (Gen) and "reproduce" (Rep), with the following properties:*

- *The generation procedure Gen on input $w \in \mathcal{M}$ outputs an extracted string $R \in \{0, 1\}^\ell$ and a helper string $P \in \{0, 1\}^*$. The reproduction procedure Rep takes $w' \in \mathcal{M}$ and bit string $P \in \{0, 1\}^*$ as inputs.*
- *The* correctness *property of fuzzy extractors guarantees that if $\mathsf{dis}(w, w') \leq t$ and (R, P) is output by $\mathsf{Gen}(w)$, then $\mathsf{Rep}(w', P) = R$. If $\mathsf{dis}(w, w') > t$, then no guarantee of the output of Rep can be given.*
- *The* security *property guarantees that for any distribution W over $\mathcal{M}$ of min-entropy m, with any external information E, the string R is close to uniform conditioned on P, i.e., if $H_\infty(W|E) \geq m$ and $(R, P) \leftarrow \mathsf{Gen}(w)$, then $\mathbf{SD}((R, P, E), (U_\ell, P, E)) \leq \epsilon$.*

3   Security Model

Consider the two parties, a computationally powerful verifier $\mathcal{V}$ and a resource-constrained prover $\mathcal{P}$, where $\mathcal{P}$ is equipped with a PUF. The PUF is assumed to be premeasured for challenge-response pairs during the setup phase in a secure environment. In the key generation phase, verifier and prover agree on a secret session key via CBKA. In the authentication phase, they engage in a mutual authentication test. Upon acceptance, both parties output 1, or upon rejection, they output 0, thereby ending the session. Correctness requires to always accept session if all communications have been unaltered by adversary except with negligible probability of failure. Hence, we define security and privacy as in the work of Moriyama [29] and Aysu et al. [6].

Security. Intuitively, security requires that either of the legitimate nodes reject the session, when they detect a modified message by an adversary. In this paper, we assume a secure implementation of CBKA, a secure PUF and a secure fuzzy extractor on the prover, i.e., hardware and software Trojans, side-channel and fault attacks and malware are outside the scope of this paper. Also, we assume the PUF to be tamper proof, i.e., tampering would modify its functionality, as it is standard for this security primitive. But, we do allow the adversary to issue a reveal query in the security game. This is a reasonable assumption as lightweight devices are prone to memory-leakage attacks during, e.g., the distribution chain. The adversary is also allowed to modify messages between verifier and prover at will. More formally, we consider the security game between a challenger and the adversary $\mathcal{A}$.

$$
\begin{array}{l}
\underline{\mathsf{Exp}_{\Pi,\mathcal{A}}^{\mathsf{Sec}}(k)} \\[4pt]
(pk, sk) \xleftarrow{\mathsf{R}} \mathsf{Setup}(1^k); \\[2pt]
sid^* \xleftarrow{\mathsf{R}} \mathcal{A}_1^{\mathsf{Launch,SendVerifier,SendProver,Result,Reveal}}(pk, \mathcal{R}, \mathcal{T}); \\[2pt]
b := \mathsf{Result}(sid^*); \\[2pt]
\text{Output } b
\end{array}
$$

In the defined security game, the adversary is able to issue following oracle queries $\mathcal{O} := (\mathsf{Launch}, \mathsf{SendVerifier}, \mathsf{SendProver}, \mathsf{Result}, \mathsf{Reveal})$. The queries do:

$\mathsf{Launch}(1^k)$ Launch the verifier to initiate the session.

$\mathsf{SendVerifier}(m)$ Send arbitrary message m to the verifier.

$\mathsf{SendProver}(dev, m)$ Send arbitrary message m to the prover dev, where dev is the device with PUF $f_i(\cdot)$ and $1 \leq i \leq n$.

$\mathsf{Result}(sid)$ Output whether the verifier accepts the session sid, where sid is uniquely determined by the exchanged messages.

$\mathsf{Reveal}(dev)$ Output the secret key of the prover dev contained in the non-volatile memory.

The advantage of an active adversary $\mathcal{A}$ against an authentication protocol Π is defined by probability $\mathsf{Adv}_{\Pi,\mathcal{A}}^{\mathsf{Sec}}(k)$ that $\Pr[\mathsf{Exp}_{\Pi,\mathcal{A}}^{\mathsf{Sec}}(k)]$ outputs 1 and the communication message in session sid^* is modified by the adversary $\mathcal{A}$. Note, the adversary can learn the memory content of the prover.

Definition 7 (Security, [29]). *An authentication protocol Π is secure against impersonation attack with complete memory leakage if for any PPT adversary $\mathcal{A}$, $\mathsf{Adv}_{\Pi,\mathcal{A}}^{\mathsf{Sec}}(k)$ is negligible in k (for large enough k).*

Privacy. In this paper, we use the privacy property from [29], which itself is based on the indistinguishability-based privacy model of the Juels-Weis privacy model [23]. Here, the adversary is allowed to issue the reveal query in any time to cover backward and forward privacy. However, there is a restriction that an honest protocol execution without adversarial influence is executed before and after the anonymous access. That way, prior and future tracing compromises can be locally neutralized and allow for some state update before and after the challenge is sent. The privacy model between the challenger and the adversary $\mathcal{A} := (\mathcal{A}_1, \mathcal{A}_2, \mathcal{A}_3)$ is recalled as follows.

$$\mathsf{Exp}_{\Pi,\mathcal{A}}^{\mathsf{IND}*-b}(k)$$

$(pk, sk) \xleftarrow{\mathsf{R}} \mathsf{Setup}(1^k);$

$(dev_0^*, dev_1^*, st_1) \xleftarrow{\mathsf{R}} \mathcal{A}_1^{\mathcal{O}}(pk, \mathcal{R}, \mathcal{D});$

$b \xleftarrow{\mathsf{U}} \{0,1\}, \mathcal{D}' := \mathcal{D}\backslash\{dev_0^*, dev_1^*\};$

$\pi_0 \xleftarrow{\mathsf{R}} \mathsf{Execute}(\mathcal{R}, dev_0^*); \pi_1 \xleftarrow{\mathsf{R}} \mathsf{Execute}(\mathcal{R}, dev_1^*);$

$st_2 \xleftarrow{\mathsf{R}} \mathcal{A}_2^{\mathcal{O}}(\mathcal{R}, \mathcal{D}', \mathcal{I}(dev_b^*), \pi_0, \pi_1, st_1);$

$\pi_0' \xleftarrow{\mathsf{R}} \mathsf{Execute}(\mathcal{R}, dev_0^*); \pi_1' \xleftarrow{\mathsf{R}} \mathsf{Execute}(\mathcal{R}, dev_1^*);$

$b' \xleftarrow{\mathsf{R}} \mathcal{A}_3^{\mathcal{O}}(\mathcal{R}, \mathcal{D}, \pi_0', \pi_1', st_2);$

$b' := \mathsf{Result}(sid^*);$

Output b

As in the previous security game, we allow an adversary to interact with a verifier and a prover via oracle queries $\mathcal{O}$. Upon sending two devices (dev_0^*, dev_1^*) to the challenger, a random bit b is chosen and the adversary can access the challenge device dev_b^* anonymously. Upon issuing $\mathsf{SendVerifier}(m)$, the challenger sends m to the challenge device dev_b^* and responds with its output. Also, as in the security game, the same holds true for the reveal query. We allow for re-synchronization opportunity before and after the anonymous access. The $\mathsf{Execute}$ query is the normal protocol execution between verifier and prover. The adversary can modify the transcript (π_0, π_1), but not the communication, and (π_0', π_1') are given to the adversary. Concluding, the advantage of the adversary in guessing the correct device is defined as $\mathsf{Adv}_{\Pi,\mathcal{A}}^{\mathsf{IND}*}(k) = |\Pr[\mathsf{Exp}_{\Pi,\mathcal{A}}^{\mathsf{IND}*-0}(k) \to 1] - \Pr[\mathsf{Exp}_{\Pi,\mathcal{A}}^{\mathsf{IND}*-1}(k) \to 1]|.$

Definition 8 (Privacy, [29]). *An authentication protocol Π satisfies the modified indistinguishability-based privacy under complete memory leakage if for any PPT adversary $\mathcal{A}$, $\mathsf{Adv}_{\Pi,\mathcal{A}}^{\mathsf{IND}*}(k)$ is negligible in k (for large enough k).*

4   Flaw in Existing Protocol

Recall the protocol from Aysu *et al.* [6]. The weakness here is that an attacker can decrypt the helper data, as the symmetric key sk is stored in non-volatile memory, which can leak due to their defined security model. When an attacker also queries a device with the same challenge, e.g., by jamming the further protocol so that the key, as well as the challenge, gets never updated, he is able to get multiple helper data to this one challenge. Van Herrewege *et al.* [34] and Boyen [8] pointed out that this could leak information about the PUF. In this case, only fuzzy extractors providing outsider chosen perturbation security can be used, but these reusable fuzzy extractors are expensive to implement. Schaller *et al.* [32] address this issue with an extra post-processing step by adding a small amount of noise to the PUF response. However, we overcome this issue, If we do not rely on a preshared secret to encrypt the helper data. Rather we encrypt it with a freshly generated session key, as described in Sect. 6.

Verifier $\mathcal{V}$	**Prover** $\mathcal{P}$ with $f_i(\cdot)$

Setup phase

$(sk, y_1) \xleftarrow{\text{U}} \text{TRNG}$ $\xrightarrow{\quad sk, y_1 \quad}$
$\xleftarrow{\quad z_1 \quad}$ $z_1 \xleftarrow{\text{R}} f_i(y_1)$

Authentication Phase

$holds\ database\ \{(z_1, sk, z_{old}, sk_{old})\}_i$ $holds\ (f_i(\cdot), sk, y_1)$

$m_1 \xleftarrow{\text{U}} \text{TRNG}$ $\xrightarrow{\quad m_1 \quad}$

$z_1' \xleftarrow{\text{R}} f_i(y_1)$
$(r_1, hd) := \text{FE.Gen}(z_1')$
$c := \text{SKE.Enc}(sk, hd)$

$\xleftarrow{\quad c, \dots \quad}$ $\vdots$

$hd := \text{SKE.Dec}(sk, c)$

Fig. 1. Protocol snippet by Aysu *et al.* If an adversary is able to get the secret key sk, the helper data hd can be decrypted from c by the same adversary.

The protocol snippet showing this flaw is illustrated in Fig. 1. Note, that the original protocol by Moriyama *et al.* [29] uses a forward fuzzy extractor and not a reverse one. Also in [29], the newly generated helper data gets encrypted with a fresh session key, which is not known before the authentication phase, due to previously exchanged nonces.

5   Channel-Based Key Agreement

Secure network communication relies on keys, preferably symmetric ones for efficiency reasons. ECDH is typically used in cryptographic protocols for the IoT. However, operations on an elliptic curve are computationally intense and require more energy compared to operations used for CBKA [38]. Additionally, CBKA agrees on a symmetric secret with information-theoretic security and therefore enables post-quantum security [25, 26]. This approach for key generation relies on the physical properties of the communication channel and essentially, it exploits three physical properties of multipath fading channels, namely reciprocity, temporal variation and spatial variation. These fundamental properties can be illustrated by the system model shown in Fig. 2 and are defined in Requirement 5.

Requirement 5 (Channel Observations). *Two legitimate nodes A and B generate a symmetric key from their respective channel observations* $h_{BA}(t)$ *and* $h_{AB}(t)$ *at·time t. An adversary* $\mathcal{E}$ *observes the communication between A and B so we have the following properties.*

- **Reciprocity:** *Considering the reciprocity property, it follows that the maximum distance between the channel observations of A and B at time t is at most* δ_r, *so it holds that* $\Pr\left[\max\left(|h_{BA}(t) - h_{AB}(t)|\right) \leq \delta_r\right] = 1 - \epsilon.$

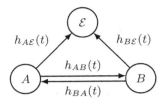

Fig. 2. Legitimate nodes A and B measure reciprocal properties of the physical channel at time t, denoted by $h_{BA}(t)$ and $h_{AB}(t)$. An adversary $\mathcal{E}$'s observations $h_{A\mathcal{E}}(t)$ and $h_{B\mathcal{E}}(t)$ are dependent on its relative position and are usually less correlated to $h_{BA}(t)$ and $h_{AB}(t)$ than $h_{BA}(t)$ is to $h_{AB}(t)$.

- **Coherence time:** *Considering the coherence time τ_c, it follows that $\{h_{ij}(t) \approx h_{ij}(t + \delta_c)\}_{i,j \in \{A,B\}, i \neq j}$ with $\delta_c \leq \tau_c$.*
- **Temporal variation:** *Temporal variation introduces randomness, and thus, for properly chosen sampling time δ_s, it holds true that $\{h_{ij}(t) \neq h_{ij}(t + \delta_s)\}_{i,j \in \{A,B\}, i \neq j}$ with $\delta_s > \tau_c$.*
- **Spatial variation:** *Spatial variation prevents adversary $\mathcal{E}$ from observing the same randomness as A and B for a sufficiently large distance with high probability, holding $\Pr\left[\{h_{ij}(t) \neq h_{i\mathcal{E}}(t)\}_{i,j \in \{A,B\}, i \neq j}\right] = 1 - \epsilon$.*

Remark 1 (spacial decorrelation). The correlation between a node and an eavesdropper for a sufficiently large distance is often modelled on Jakes model [21]. Under this assumption the decorrelation is proportional to a zero-order Bessel function, where the first zero correlation occurs at approximately $\lambda/2$, with carrier wavelength λ [7]. For instance, $\lambda/2 \approx 6.25\,\text{cm}$ for the 2.4 GHz ISM frequency band. However, in practice a distance of $\lambda/2$ might not be enough as shown by Edmann *et al.* [12] and we note that secure distance determination is outside the scope of this paper.

CBKA is usually split up in different procedures, namely *channel measurement, quantization, information reconciliation* and *privacy amplification*. Measurement of the channel estimates the channel properties at a given time t, e.g., received signal strength indicator (RSSI) values can be used for this step, as these are available on almost all modern wireless transceivers. Next, the quantization takes the channel measurement $h_{ij}(t)$ at time t and assigns a digital value to this analog estimation. After quantization, the nodes A and B have similar bit strings with ideally no bit differences. There exist different approaches to sample the channel information and transform them into a bit string, suitable for further operations [2,16,22,24,33]. To allow for some errors during channel measurement and quantization due to physical noise, a reconciliation step is required, after which nodes A and B have the exact same bit string. During this information reconciliation both nodes exchange information, causing some entropy loss. Huth *et al.* [19] surveyed several information reconciliation schemes for CBKA. As a last step, the privacy amplification [25], the entropy from the reconciled bit strings is compressed into a short key with nearly full entropy. For the notation of privacy amplification we adapt the definition of fuzzy extractors. Summarized, we define CBKA as follows:

Definition 9 (Channel-based Key Agreement). *Let A and B be two legitimate nodes, let $\mathcal{E}$ be an adversary and let C_{CR} be an authentic common randomness that can be accessed by A, B and $\mathcal{E}$. A $(m_Q, m_{IR}, t, n, \ell, \epsilon)$-channel-based key agreement is a tuple of procedures, CM, Q, IR and PA, with the following properties:*

- **Channel Measurement:** *The channel measurement procedure* CM *outputs channel observations $\{h_{ij}\}_{i,j\in\{A,B,\mathcal{E}\},i\neq j}$ with accesses to an authentic common randomness C_{CR}. The channel observations h_{ij} need to fulfill requirement 5 and if $\{h_{ij} \leftarrow \mathsf{CM}_j(C_{CR})\}_{i,j\in\{A,B,\mathcal{E}\},i\neq j}$, then it holds for the mutual information that $I(h_{BA}, h_{A\mathcal{E}}) < I(h_{AB}, h_{BA}) > I(h_{AB}, h_{B\mathcal{E}})$.*
- **Quantization:** *The quantization procedure* Q *takes a channel observation $\{h_{ij}\}_{i,j\in\{A,B,\mathcal{E}\},i\neq j}$ as input and outputs a string $\{q_j \in \{0,1\}^*\}_{j\in\{A,B,\mathcal{E}\}}$. If $\{q_j \leftarrow \mathsf{Q}_j(\mathsf{CM}_j(C_{CR}))\}_{j\in\{A,B,\mathcal{E}\}}$, then it holds that $H_\infty(q_A|(h_{A\mathcal{E}}, h_{B\mathcal{E}})) \geq m_Q \leq H_\infty(q_B|(h_{A\mathcal{E}}, h_{B\mathcal{E}}))$ and that $\mathsf{dis}(q_A, q_\mathcal{E}) > \mathsf{dis}(q_A, q_B) < \mathsf{dis}(q_B, q_\mathcal{E})$.*
- **Information Reconciliation:** *The information reconciliation procedure* IR *takes as input a quantized string $\{q_i \in \mathcal{M}\}_{i\in\{A,B\}}$ from a legitimate node and outputs a reconciled strings $\{r_i \in \{0,1\}^n\}_{i\in\{A,B\}}$. The nodes A and B exchange helper strings s_A and $s_B \in \{0,1\}^*$. The correctness property of information reconciliation guarantees that if $\mathsf{dis}(q_A, q_B) \leq t$, then $r_A = r_B$. The security property guarantees that for any distribution Q over $\mathcal{M}$ with $H_\infty(Q) \geq m_Q$, we have $H_\infty(Q|(s_A \leftarrow \mathsf{IR}_A(q_A, s_B), s_B \leftarrow \mathsf{IR}_B(q_B, s_A), h_{A\mathcal{E}}, h_{B\mathcal{E}})) \geq m_{IR}$.*
- **Privacy Amplification:** *The privacy amplification procedure* PA *is an average-case $(n, m_{IR}, \ell, \epsilon)-$strong extractor which takes an uniform seed I and a reconciled string $\{r_i \in \{0,1\}^n\}_{i\in\{A,B\}}$ from a legitimate node with minentropy m_{IR} as inputs. The output key $\{k_i \in \{0,1\}^\ell\}_{i\in\{A,B\}}$ satisfies that $\{\mathbf{SD}((\mathsf{PA}_i(r_i, I), I), (U_\ell, I)) \leq \epsilon\}_{i\in\{A,B\}}$.*
- *The correctness property of channel-based key agreement guarantees that if the requirements for procedures* CM, Q, IR *and* PA *hold and the key is generated by $\{k_i \leftarrow \mathsf{PA}_i(\mathsf{IR}_i(\mathsf{Q}_i(\mathsf{CM}_i(C_{CR}))))\}_{i\in\{A,B\}}$, then $k_A = k_B$.*
- *The security property of channel-based key agreement guarantees that for any authentic common randomness C_{CR}, if the requirements for procedures* CM, Q, IR *and* PA *hold, the key k is close to uniform conditioned on all broadcasted information, i.e., $h_{A\mathcal{E}}$, $h_{B\mathcal{E}}$, s_A and s_B.*

The quantity $m_Q - m_{IR}$ is defined as the *entropy loss* during information reconciliation IR. Note that parts of Definition 9 for CBKA are similar to Definitions 4, 5 and 6 of extractors, secure sketches and fuzzy extractors, respectively. This comes from the fact that information reconciliation of CBKA can be implemented with a secure sketch and privacy amplification can be implemented with an extractor. Reusing these modules for PUFs and CBKA allows for a lightweight implementation on resource-constrained devices [20].

The correctness property of CBKA follows directly from the correctness property of information reconciliation. One instance of information reconciliation is a secure sketch with the code-offset construction for the Hamming metric as described in the work of Dodis *et al.* [11]. Here, reconciliation is successful if the used $(n, k, 2t+1)$-code is able to correct the t Hamming errors occurring between the strings q_A and q_B. Clearly, this is always the case if t becomes not too big as required by $\mathsf{dis}(q_A, q_B) \leq t$. For an in-depth analysis of secure sketches we refer the interested reader to the seminal paper by Dodis *et al.* [11].

Additionally, we assume CBKA with an authentic (unchanged) common randomness. To further strengthen our system against an attacker that can control the wireless channel, we can use a robust fuzzy extractor for information reconciliation as defined by Dodis *et al.* [10]. As an alternative, we can introduce an out-of-band (OOB) channel to guarantee authenticity of the channel during key agreement. Mirzadeh *et al.* [28] collected and compared multiple pairing protocols using OOB channels to exclude man-in-the-middle attacks.

6   Combined Protocol with PUF and CBKA

In this section we present our main contribution – an enhanced version of the protocol by Aysu *et al.* [6]. We attenuate the digital issue, as in Sect. 4, by shifting it to the physical world.

Our protocol is assumed to start in a secure setup phase, where a first challenge-response pair (y_1, z_1) is measured. The challenge y_1 is stored on the prover $\mathcal{P}$ and the response is stored in the database hold by verifier $\mathcal{V}$.

After that, key generation phase via CBKA and authentication phase via PUF begins. A symmetric key sk is derived from the reciprocal channel between verifier $\mathcal{V}$ and prover $\mathcal{P}$ via CBKA as in Definition 9. The physical channel gets measured with CBKA.CM and is quantized with CBKA.Q. Information reconciliation CBKA.IR generates a secure sketch $s_{\mathcal{P}}$, with which the verifier $\mathcal{V}$ can also derive the same string $r_{\mathcal{P}}$ as prover $\mathcal{P}$. Privacy amplification CBKA.PA can use some public randomness m_0 to extract the entropy in $r_{\mathcal{P}}$, resulting in the session key sk. We note again, that the common randomness C_{CR} is assumed to be authentic during the key generation phase or else no guarantee can be given about security. However, the security model allows the adversary to reveal the memory content before and after the key generation phase and authentication phase.

In the actual authentication phase, the helper data hd gets encrypted with the session key sk. The generation of pseudorandom values $(s_1, \ldots, s_4)$ follow from the FE.Gen output r_1, and therefore from PUF response z_1. To update for a new response, the device chooses a new challenge y_2 and one-time pads the response z_2 with s_2. The value v_1 can be seen as a message authentication code, so that a manipulated c, m_2 or u_1 can be detected. Upon reception, the verifier decrypts the helper data hd and recovers his version of z_1 to the shared secret

r_1' via FE.Rec. Next follows the generation of the same pseudorandom values as on the prover side and use s_1' and s_3' for verification purposes. If verification of v_1 holds then the database wil get updated with the new response z_2'. If not, the verification procedure repeats with the previously old response z_{old}. If this also fails s_4' will be drawn randomly. On a successful database update, the verifier sends s_4' to the prover, who updates his challenge $y_1 := y_2$ when s_4' is valid. Our enhanced protocol is depicted in Fig. 3.

Theorem 1. *Let* CBKA *be a* $(m_Q, m_{IR}, t, n, \ell, \epsilon)$-*channel-based key agreement as in Definition 9. Let* $sk \leftarrow$ CBKA(C_{CR}) *be the output of* CBKA *for two legitimate nodes accessing an authentic common source of randomness* C_{CR}. *Let* $f_i(\cdot)$ *be a physically unclonable function, fulfilling Definitions 1, 2 and 3. Let* $z_{i,j} \leftarrow f_i(y_j)$ *be the output of a PUF* $f_i : C \rightarrow R$ *on input* y_j *where* $f_i \leftarrow \mathcal{MP}(\text{param})$. *Let* FE *be a* (m, ℓ, t, ϵ)-*fuzzy extractor as in Definition 6. Further assume that* $\mathcal{G}$ *and* $\mathcal{G}'$ *are secure pseudorandom functions. Then our protocol is secure against impersonation attacks with complete memory leakage as in Definition 7.*

Theorem 2. *Let* CBKA *be a* $(m_Q, m_{IR}, t, n, \ell, \epsilon)$-*channel-based key agreement as in Definition 9. Let* $sk \leftarrow$ CBKA(C_{CR}) *be the output of* CBKA *for two legitimate nodes accessing an authentic common source of randomness* C_{CR}. *Let* $f_i(\cdot)$ *be a physically unclonable function, fulfilling Definitions 1, 2 and 3. Let* $z_{i,j} \leftarrow f_i(y_j)$ *be the output of a PUF* $f_i : C \rightarrow R$ *on input* y_j *where* $f_i \leftarrow \mathcal{MP}(\text{param})$. *Let* FE *be a* (m, ℓ, t, ϵ)-*fuzzy extractor as in Definition 6. Further assume that* $\mathcal{G}$ *and* $\mathcal{G}'$ *are secure pseudorandom functions. Then our protocol holds the modified indistinguishability-based privacy under complete memory leakage as in Definition 8.*

The proof for Theorem 1 is given in Sect. A and the proof for Theorem 2 is stated in Sect. B.

7   Estimated Implementation Costs

As our proposed protocol in Fig. 3 is an enhancement of the original protocol in [6], there is only a marginal software and hardware overhead due to the integration of CBKA. Reference implementations of CBKA are on typical small microcontrollers as found in the IoT. However, the lightweightness of our proposed protocol comes at the cost of an expected execution time of roughly one minute.

Memory Footprint. Aysu *et al.* [6] provide two implementation results – one software implementation executed on a general purpose microcontroller and one with an additional hardware accelerator included. For the former one, they report a memory footprint of 8,104 bytes for text and 853 bytes for data on a MSP430, which offers a security of 128 bit. The data area includes global and local variables (stack, `bss` and `data`). For the latter one, they also list utilization of their

Verifier $\mathcal{V}$		Prover $\mathcal{P}$ with $f_i(\cdot)$
	Setup phase	

$y_1 \xleftarrow{\mathsf{U}} \mathsf{TRNG}$ $\xrightarrow{\;y_1\;}$ $z_1 \xleftarrow{\mathsf{R}} f_i(y_1)$
update database $(z_1, z_{old} := z_1)$ $\xleftarrow{\;z_1\;}$

Key Generation Phase and Authentication Phase

Verifier $\mathcal{V}$ and Prover $\mathcal{P}$ have access to common randomness C_{CR}
holds database $\{(z_1, z_{old})\}_i$ *holds* $(f_i(\cdot), y_1)$

$h_{\mathcal{PV}} \xleftarrow{\mathsf{R}} \mathsf{CBKA.CM}(C_{CR})$ $h_{\mathcal{VP}} \xleftarrow{\mathsf{R}} \mathsf{CBKA.CM}(C_{CR})$
$q_{\mathcal{V}} := \mathsf{CBKA.Q}(h_{\mathcal{PV}})$ $q_{\mathcal{P}} := \mathsf{CBKA.Q}(h_{\mathcal{VP}})$
                 $m_0 \xleftarrow{\mathsf{U}} \mathsf{TRNG}$
        $\xleftarrow{s_{\mathcal{P}}, m_0}$ $(r_{\mathcal{P}}, s_{\mathcal{P}}) := \mathsf{CBKA.IR}(q_{\mathcal{P}})$
$r_{\mathcal{P}} := \mathsf{CBKA.IR}(q_{\mathcal{V}}, s_{\mathcal{P}})$
$sk := \mathsf{CBKA.PA}(r_{\mathcal{P}}, m_0)$ $sk := \mathsf{CBKA.PA}(r_{\mathcal{P}}, m_0)$
$m_1 \xleftarrow{\mathsf{U}} \mathsf{TRNG}$ $\xrightarrow{\;m_1\;}$

                 $z_1 \xleftarrow{\mathsf{R}} f_i(y_1)$
                 $(r_1, hd) := \mathsf{FE.Gen}(z_1)$
                 $c := \mathsf{SKE.Enc}(sk, hd)$
                 $m_2 \xleftarrow{\mathsf{U}} \{0,1\}^k$
                 $(s_1, \ldots, s_4) := \mathcal{G}(r_1, m_1 || m_2)$
                 $y_2 \xleftarrow{\mathsf{U}} \{0,1\}^k$
                 $z_2 \xleftarrow{\mathsf{R}} f_i(y_2)$
                 $u_1 := s_2 \oplus z_2$
      $\xleftarrow{c, m_2, s_1, u_1, v_1}$ $v_1 := \mathcal{G}'(s_3, c || m_2 || u_1)$
$hd := \mathsf{SKE.Dec}(sk, c)$
$r_1' := \mathsf{FE.Rec}(z_1, hd))$
$(s_1', \ldots, s_4') := \mathcal{G}(r_1', m_1 || m_2)$
check if $(s_1 = s_1')$ **for** $1 \leq i \leq n$
then *verify* $v_1 = \mathcal{G}'(s_3', c || m_2 || u_1)$
   $z_2' := s_2' \oplus u_1$
   update database :
     $(z_1 := z_2', z_{old} := z_1)$
else $r_1' := \mathsf{FE.Rec}(z_{old}, hd))$
   $(s_1', \ldots, s_4') := \mathcal{G}(r_1', m_1 || m_2)$
$\vdots$
else $s_4' \xleftarrow{\mathsf{U}} \{0,1\}^k$ $\xrightarrow{\;s_4'\;}$
                 check if $(s_4 = s_4')$
                 update $y_1 := y_2$

Fig. 3. Detailed protocol of our proposed integration of PUF and CBKA.

hardware accelerator, which needs 3,543 lookup tables, 1,275 registers and 8 blocks of RAM on a Xilinx XC5VLX30-1FFG324. In summary, their implementation on a MSP430 with included hardware accelerator has a memory footprint of 4,920 bytes for text and 729 bytes for data on a MSP430, while also offering 128 bit of security. They note, that the hardware accelerator is about half the size as the MSP430 core. The data indicates that the protocol by Aysu *et al.* already fits into a small microcontroller.

With the implementation of Aysu *et al.* at hand, we only need to consider the additional CBKA implementation, i.e., implementation of the protocol steps CBKA.CM, CBKA.Q, CBKA.IR and CBKA.PA. The two steps of information reconciliation (CBKA.IR) and privacy amplification (CBKA.PA) form the construction of a fuzzy extractor, as described in Sect. 5. Therefore, these parts can be reused by the CBKA algorithm, resulting in only minor overhead for adapting the protocol state machine.

Channel measurements (CBKA.CM) are available if a wireless transceiver is present. However, if a wireless transceiver is present, measuring the channel results in no additional implementation cost, as every transceiver does so inherently. For example, Zenger *et al.* [37] implemented CBKA on an 8-bit Intel MCS-51, which is an SoC solution for the IoT. The authors state, that channel measurements are freely available on the given target platform. Also, their implementation offers a security of 128 bit.

The only algorithm that needs to be additionally implemented is the quantization (CBKA.Q). Zenger *et al.* report roughly 208 bytes resource overhead for their quantizer, which seems marginal compared to the original protocol implementation by Aysu *et al.*

Performance. Aysu *et al.* [6] state for their implementation of the original protocol, that it needs 111,965 to 1,730,922 clock cycles, depending on whether their proposed hardware accelerator is included. However, on their target constrained platform with a 1.846 Mhz clock, this results in an execution time on the device less than one second.

As described before, information reconciliation and privacy amplification can be reused from the implementation of Aysu *et al.*, which results in 18,597 to 690,174 additional clock cycles, depending if the hardware engine is included. This would result in a prolonged execution time of roughly half a second. Also, Zenger *et al.* report that their quantizer needs 11,876 clock cycles, which is negligible in terms of execution time.

However, regarding runtime the bottleneck is measuring the channel for CBKA, i.e. sampling enough entropy from the reciprocal channel. Here, Zenger *et al.* [37] state 60 s for a 128-bit key agreement via CBKA.

8   Conclusion

With the proliferation and increased interconnection of lightweight IoT devices, security and privacy must not fall short. In this paper, we have shown security is endangered when an existing authentication protocol is used with inexpensive, PUF-friendly fuzzy extractors. Our goal was to allow usage for these fuzzy extractors too, which offer no outsider chosen perturbation security. We achieved this with a new formal definition of CBKA and by enhancing an authentication protocol to fulfill all previously mentioned requirements. This paper shows how PUFs and CBKA can be securely integrated in the IoT, while avoiding costly public-key based solutions and associated public-key infrastructures.

A   Security Proof

We use the proof provided by the work of Moriyama [29] and Aysu *et al.* [6] as a basis for our proof. The proof for Theorem 1 is as follows.

Proof. The adversary $\mathcal{A}$ wants the verifier $\mathcal{V}$ or the prover $\mathcal{P}$ to accept the session while the communication is altered by the adversary. We concentrate only on the former case, as the verifier authentication is quite similar to that of the prover. We consider the following game transformations. Let S_i be the advantage that the adversary wins the game in Game i.

Game 0. This is the original game between the challenger and the adversary.

Game 1. The challenger randomly guesses the device dev^* with PUF $f_{i^*}(\cdot)$, where $i^* \xleftarrow{\mathsf{U}} \{1 \leq i \leq n\}$. If the adversary cannot impersonate dev^* to the verifier, the challenger aborts the game.

Game 2. Assume that ℓ is the upper bound of the sessions that the adversary can establish in the game. For $1 \leq j \leq \ell$, we evaluate or change the variables related to the session between the verifier and dev^* up to the ℓ-th session as the following.

Game 2-j-1. The challenger evaluates the output from the channel measurement and quantization of the CBKA algorithm implemented in dev^* at the j-th session. If the output does not have enough min-entropy m_Q or requirements for channel observations are violated, then the challenger aborts the game.

Game 2-j-2. The output from the information reconciliation procedure ($r_\mathcal{P}$) is changed to a random variable.

Game 2-j-3. The output from the privacy amplification procedure (sk) is changed to a random variable.

Game 2-j-4. The challenger evaluates the output from the PUF implemented in dev^* at the j-th session. If the output does not have enough min-entropy m or requirements for intra-distance and inter-distance are violated, then the challenger aborts the game.

Game 2-j-5. The output from the fuzzy extractor (r_1) is changed to a random variable.

Game 2-j-6. The output from the PRF $\mathcal{G}(r_1, \cdot)$ is derived from a truly random function in this game.

Game 2-j-7. We change the PRF $\mathcal{G}(r_{old}, \cdot)$ to a truly random function.

Game 2-j-8. We change the XORed output $u_1 := s_2 \oplus z_2$ to randomly chosen $u_1 \xleftarrow{\mathsf{U}} \{0,1\}^k$.

Game 2-j-9. The output from the PRF $\mathcal{G}'(s_3, \cdot)$ is derived from a truly random function in this game.

If the common source of randomness generates enough min-entropy, then the CBKA algorithm can output strings statistically close to uniform. Furthermore, if the PUF, that is equipped on the device generates enough min-entropy, then the fuzzy extractor can output strings statistically close to uniform. We then can set these strings as the seed for the PRF and the verifier and the prover share a common secret. So we can construct the challenge response authentication protocol with secure key update.

Lemma 1. $S_0 = n \cdot S_1$ *(where n is the number of devices, i.e. provers).*

Proof. If the adversary wins the game, there is at least one session which the verifier or prover accepts while the communication is modified by the adversary. Since the challenger randomly selects the session, the probability that the session is correctly guessed by the challenger is at least $1/n$.

Lemma 2. $|S_1 - S_{2-1-1}| \le \epsilon$ *and* $|S_{2-(j-1)-9} - S_{2-j-1}| \le \epsilon$ *for any* $2 \le j \le \ell$ *if the CBKA algorithm is secure as required in Theorem 1.*

Proof. Here, the output of the channel measurement and quantization of the CBKA algorithm has enough min-entropy and is independent from the other outputs except with negligible probability ϵ. If so, then there is no difference between these games. The property of CBKA assumed here says that even if the input to channel measurement and quantization of the CBKA algorithm is published, i.e. the authentic common randomness, the output derived from the input keeps the sufficient min-entropy property, and therefore each output is uncorrelated. Hence, the reveal query issued by the adversary is random looking by the assumption of this property.

Lemma 3. $|S_{2-j-1} - S_{2-j-2}| \le \epsilon$ *for any* $2 \le j \le \ell$ *if the CBKA.IR is an information reconciliation in a* $(m_Q, m_{IR}, t, n, \ell, \epsilon)$*-channel-based key agreement.*

Proof. Since we assumed that, always, the output from the quantization of the CBKA algorithm has enough min-entropy, the output of the information reconciliation procedure of the CBKA algorithm has enough min-entropy and is independent from the other outputs except with negligible probability ϵ. This is given by the security property of information reconciliation.

Lemma 4. $|S_{2-j-2} - S_{2-j-3}| \le \epsilon$ *for any* $2 \le j \le \ell$ *if the CBKA.PA is a privacy amplification in a* $(m_Q, m_{IR}, t, n, \ell, \epsilon)$*-channel-based key agreement.*

Proof. Since we assumed that, always, the output from the information reconciliation procedure of the CBKA algorithm has enough min-entropy, it is clear that no adversary can distinguish these games due to the randomization property of privacy amplification, meaning privacy amplification guarantees that its output is statistically close to random. This is given by the security property of privacy amplification.

Lemma 5. $|S_{2-j-3} - S_{2-j-4}| \leq \epsilon \leq j \leq \ell$ *if* f *is a secure PUF as required in Theorem 1.*

Proof. Here, the PUF's output has enough min-entropy and is independent from the other outputs except with negligible probability ϵ. If so, then there is no difference between these games. The property of the PUF assumed here says that even if the input to the PUF is published, the output derived from the input keeps the sufficient min-entropy property, and therefore each output is uncorrelated. Hence, the reveal query issued by the adversary is random looking by the assumption of this property.

Lemma 6. $|S_{2-j-4} - S_{2-j-5}| \leq \epsilon$ *for any* $2 \leq j \leq \ell$ *if the* FE *is a* (m, ℓ, t, ϵ)-*fuzzy extractor.*

Proof. Since we assumed that, always, the output from the PUF has enough min-entropy, it is clear that no adversary can distinguish these games due to the randomization property of the fuzzy extractor, meaning the fuzzy extractor guarantees that its output is statistically close to random.

Lemma 7. $\forall 1 \leq j \leq \ell$, $|S_{2-j-5} - S_{2-j-6}| \leq \mathsf{Adv}^{\mathsf{PRF}}_{\mathcal{G},\mathcal{B}}(k)$ *where* $\mathsf{Adv}^{\mathsf{PRF}}_{\mathcal{G},\mathcal{B}}(k)$ *is an advantage of* $\mathcal{B}$ *to break the security of the PRF* $\mathcal{G}$.

Proof. If there is a difference between these games, we construct an algorithm $\mathcal{B}$ which breaks the security or PRF $\mathcal{G}$. $\mathcal{B}$ can access the real PRF $\mathcal{G}(r_1, \cdot)$ or truly random function RF. $\mathcal{B}$ sets up all secret keys and simulates our protocol except the n-th session. When the adversary invokes the n-th session, $\mathcal{B}$ sends $m_1 \xleftarrow{\mathsf{U}} \{0,1\}^k$ as the output of the verifier. When $\mathcal{A}$ sends m_1^* to a device dev_i, $\mathcal{B}$ selects m_2 and issues $m_1^* \| m_2$ to the oracle instead of the normal computation of $\mathcal{G}$. Upon receiving $(s_1, \ldots, s_4)$, $\mathcal{B}$ continues the computation as the protocol specification and outputs (c, m_2, s_1, u_1, v_1) as the prover's response. When the adversary sends $(m_2^*, s_1^*, u_1^*, v_1^*)$, $\mathcal{B}$ issues $m_1 \| m_2^*$ to the oracle and obtains $(s_1', \ldots, s_6')$.

If $\mathcal{B}$ accesses the real PRF, this simulation is equivalent to Game 2-j-5. Otherwise, the oracle query issued by $\mathcal{B}$ is completely random and this distribution is equivalent to Game 2-j-6. Thus we have $|S_{2-j-5} - S_{2-j-6}| \leq \mathsf{Adv}^{\mathsf{PRF}}_{\mathcal{G},\mathcal{B}}(k)$.

Lemma 8. $\forall 1 \leq j \leq \ell$, $|S_{2-j-6} - S_{2-j-7}| \leq \mathsf{Adv}^{\mathsf{PRF}}_{\mathcal{G},\mathcal{B}}(k)$.

Proof. The proof is as the proof for Lemma 7.

Lemma 9. $\forall 1 \leq j \leq \ell$, $S_{2-j-7} = S_{2-j-8}$.

Proof. Since the PRF $\mathcal{G}(r_1, \cdot)$ is already changed to the truly random function in Game 2-j-7, s_2 is used as effectively one-time pad to encrypt z_2'. Therefore this transformation is purely conceptual change and the output distributions of these games are information theoretically equivalent.

Lemma 10. $\forall 1 \leq j \leq \ell,\ |S_{2-j-8} - S_{2-j-9}| \leq 2 \cdot \mathsf{Adv}^{\mathsf{PRF}}_{\mathcal{G}',\mathcal{B}'}(k).$

Proof. We can think that the seed input to the PRF $\mathcal{G}'$ is changed to the random variable from the previous games. Consider an algorithm $\mathcal{B}$ which interacts with PRF $\mathcal{G}'(s_3, \cdot)$ or random function RF. As in the proof for Lemma 7, $\mathcal{B}$ simulates the protocol as the challenger up to the n-th session. $\mathcal{B}$ generates (c, u_1) and issues $c\|u_1$ to the oracle. $\mathcal{B}$ generates the other variables as in the previous game and sends (c, m_2, s_1, u_1, v_1) as the prover's output after it obtains v_1 from the oracle. If the verifier receives $(c^*, m_2^*, s_1^*, u_1^*, v_1^*)$, $\mathcal{B}$ checks that $(c^*, m_2^*, s_1^*) = (c, m_2, s_1)$. If so, $\mathcal{B}$ issues $c^*\|m_2^*\|u_1^*$ to the oracle to check whether its response is identical to v_1^*.

If $\mathcal{B}$ accesses the real PRF, this simulation is equivalent to Game 2-j-8. Otherwise, $\mathcal{B}$'s simulation is identical to Game 2-j-9. Thus the difference between these games are bounded by the security of PRF $\mathcal{G}'$.

Since the above game transformation is bounded by certain assumptions; i.e. for PUF, fuzzy extractor and PRFs, we can transform Game 0 to Game 2-ℓ-9. Considering Game 2-ℓ-9 there is no advantage for the adversary to impersonate the prover. Consider the case that the server accepts the session which is not actually derived the prover. Assume that the adversary obtains (c, m_2, s_1, u_1, v_1) from the prover. To mount the man-in-the-middle attack, the adversary must modify at least one of these variables.

Even when the adversary issues the reveal query and obtains y_1 before the session, he cannot predict the response z_1. Since sk is generated after he can issue his reveal query, the session key remains secret and so hd remains encrypted. When the adversary modifies m_2, the probability that the adversary wins the security game is negligible since s_1 is chosen from the truly random function. If m_2 is not changed, the verifier only accepts s_1 since it is deterministically defined by m_1 chosen by the verifier and m_2. The first verification is passed only when the adversary reuses (c, m_2, s_1), but v_1 is also derived from another random function. Thus the adversary cannot guess it and any modified message is rejected except with negligible probability. The same argument also applies to the verifier authentication, because the prover checks the verifier with the outputs from $\mathcal{G}$ and $\mathcal{G}'$. Therefore, any adversary cannot mount the man-in-the-middle attack in our protocol and we finally have

$$\mathsf{Adv}^{\mathsf{Sec}}_{\Pi,\mathcal{A}}(1^k) \leq \frac{1}{2\ell n} \cdot \left(\mathsf{Adv}^{\mathsf{PRF}}_{\mathcal{G},\mathcal{B}}(1^k) + \mathsf{Adv}^{\mathsf{PRF}}_{\mathcal{G}',\mathcal{B}'}(1^k) \right) + \epsilon$$

if the PUF and fuzzy extractor holds its properties.

B Privacy Proof

Again, we use the proof provided by the work of Moriyama [29] and Aysu *et al.* [6] as a basis for our proof. The proof for Theorem 2 is as follows.

Proof. The proof we provide here is similar to that for Theorem 1. However, we remark that it is important to assume that our protocol satisfies security as in Theorem 1 first for privacy to hold. The reason is that if the security is broken and a malicious adversary successfully impersonates device dev_0^*, the verifier will update the secret key that is not derived by the prover any more. So the verifier does not accept this prover after the attack and the adversary easily distinguishes the prover in the privacy game. Even if the adversary honestly transmits the communication message between $\mathcal{I}(dev_0^*)$ and the verifier in the challenge phase, the authentication result is always 0 and the adversary can realize which prover is selected as the challenge prover.

We modify Game 1 such that the challenger guesses two provers which will be chosen by the adversary in the privacy game. This probability that is at least $1/n^2$, and, then, we can continue the game transformation. After that, the game transformation described in Game 2 is applied to the sessions related to dev_0^* and dev_1^*. Then the communication message (c, m_2, s_1, u_1, v_1) and (s_4') are changed to random variables. Even if the adversary can obtain the secret key of the prover within the privacy game, input to the PUF and helper data used in the challenge phase are independent from choices in the other phases. The re-synchronization allows this separation and new values are always random. Therefore, there is no information against which the adversary can distinguish the challenge prover in the privacy game, and we get:

$$\mathsf{Adv}_{\Pi,\mathcal{A}}^{\mathsf{IND}^*}(1^k) \leq \mathsf{Adv}_{\Pi,\mathcal{A}'}^{\mathsf{Sec}}(1^k) + \frac{1}{4\ell n^2} \cdot \left(\mathsf{Adv}_{\mathcal{G},\mathcal{B}}^{\mathsf{PRF}}(1^k) + \mathsf{Adv}_{\mathcal{G}',\mathcal{B}'}^{\mathsf{PRF}}(1^k) \right) + \epsilon$$

for some algorithm $(\mathcal{A}', \mathcal{B}, \mathcal{B}')$ derived from the games.

References

1. NXP strengthens SmartMX2 security chips with PUF anti-cloning technology. https://www.intrinsic-id.com/nxp-strengthens-smartmx2-security-chips-with-puf-anti-cloning-technology/. Accessed 23 Aug 2016
2. Ambekar, A., Hassan, M., Schotten, H.D.: Improving channel reciprocity for effective key management systems. In: 2012 International Symposium on Signals, Systems, and Electronics (ISSSE), pp. 1–4. IEEE (2012)
3. Armknecht, F., Moriyama, D., Sadeghi, A.-R., Yung, M.: Towards a unified security model for physically unclonable functions. In: Sako, K. (ed.) CT-RSA 2016. LNCS, vol. 9610, pp. 271–287. Springer, Heidelberg (2016). doi:10.1007/978-3-319-29485-8_16
4. Atzori, L., Iera, A., Morabito, G.: The internet of things: a survey. Comput. Netw. **54**(15), 2787–2805 (2010)
5. Aysu, A., Ghalaty, N.F., Franklin, Z., Yali, M.P., Schaumont, P.: Digital fingerprints for low-cost platforms using MEMS sensors. In: Proceedings of the Workshop on Embedded Systems Security, p. 2. ACM (2013)
6. Aysu, A., Gulcan, E., Moriyama, D., Schaumont, P., Yung, M.: End-to-end design of a PUF-based privacy preserving authentication protocol. In: Güneysu, T., Handschuh, H. (eds.) CHES 2015. LNCS, vol. 9293, pp. 556–576. Springer, Heidelberg (2015). doi:10.1007/978-3-662-48324-4_28

7. Biglieri, E., Calderbank, R., Constantinides, A., Goldsmith, A., Arogyaswami Paulraj, H., Poor, V.: MIMO Wireless Communications. Cambridge University Press, New York (2007)
8. Boyen, X.: Reusable cryptographic fuzzy extractors. In: Proceedings of the 11th ACM Conference on Computer and Communications Security, pp. 82–91. ACM (2004)
9. Delvaux, J., Peeters, R., Dawu, G., Verbauwhede, I.: A survey on lightweight entity authentication with strong PUFs. ACM Comput. Surv. **48**(2), 26: 1–26: 42 (2015)
10. Dodis, Y., Katz, J., Reyzin, L., Smith, A.: Robust fuzzy extractors and authenticated key agreement from close secrets. In: Dwork, C. (ed.) CRYPTO 2006. LNCS, vol. 4117, pp. 232–250. Springer, Heidelberg (2006). doi:10.1007/11818175_14
11. Dodis, Y., Reyzin, L., Smith, A.: Fuzzy extractors: how to generate strong keys from biometrics and other noisy data. In: Cachin, C., Camenisch, J.L. (eds.) EUROCRYPT 2004. LNCS, vol. 3027, pp. 523–540. Springer, Heidelberg (2004). doi:10.1007/978-3-540-24676-3_31
12. Edman, M., Kiayias, A., Yener, B.: On passive inference attacks against physical-layer key extraction. In: Proceedings of the Fourth European Workshop on System Security, EUROSEC 2011, New York, NY, USA, pp. 8:1–8:6. ACM (2011)
13. Evans, D.: The internet of things: how the next evolution of the internet is changing everything. CISCO white paper, vol. 1, pp. 1–11 (2011)
14. Gassend, B., Clarke, D.E., van Dijk, M., Devadas, S.: Silicon physical random functions. In: Atluri, V. (ed.) Proceedings of the 9th ACM Conference on Computer and Communications Security, CCS 2002, Washington, DC, USA, 18–22 November 2002, pp. 148–160. ACM (2002)
15. Guajardo, J., Kumar, S.S., Schrijen, G.-J., Tuyls, P.: FPGA intrinsic PUFs and their use for IP protection. In: Paillier, P., Verbauwhede, I. (eds.) CHES 2007. LNCS, vol. 4727, pp. 63–80. Springer, Heidelberg (2007). doi:10.1007/978-3-540-74735-2_5
16. Guillaume, R., Ludwig, S., Müller, A., Czylwik, A.: Secret key generation from static channels with untrusted relays. In: 2015 IEEE 11th International Conference on Wireless and Mobile Computing, Networking and Communications (WiMob), pp. 635–642 (2015)
17. Helfmeier, C., Nedospasov, D., Tarnovsky, C., Krissler, J.S., Boit, C., Seifert, J.-P.: Breaking and entering through the silicon. In: Proceedings of the 2013 ACM SIGSAC Conference on Computer and Communications Security, pp. 733–744. ACM (2013)
18. Herder, C., Meng-Day, Y., Koushanfar, F., Devadas, S.: Physical unclonable functions and applications: a tutorial. Proc. IEEE **102**(8), 1126–1141 (2014)
19. Huth, C., Guillaume, R., Strohm, T., Duplys, P., Samuel, I.A., Güneysu, T.: Information reconciliation schemes in physical-layer security: a survey. Comput. Netw. **109**, 84–104 (2016)
20. Huth, C., Zibuschka, J., Duplys, P., Güneysu, T.: Securing systems on the Internet of things via physical properties of devices and communications. In: Proceedings of 2015 IEEE International Systems Conference (SysCon 2015), pp. 8–13, April 2015
21. Jakes, W.C., Cox, D.C. (eds.): Microwave Mobile Communications. Wiley-IEEE Press, New York (1994)
22. Jana, S., Premnath, S.N., Clark, M., Kasera, S.K., Patwari, N., Krishnamurthy, S.V.: On the effectiveness of secret key extraction from wireless signal strength in real environments. In: Proceedings of the 15th Annual International Conference on Mobile Computing and Networking, pp. 321–332. ACM (2009)

23. Juels, A., Weis, S.A.: Defining strong privacy for RFID. ACM Trans. Inf. Syst. Secur. (TISSEC) **13**(1), 7 (2009)
24. Mathur, S., Trappe, W., Mandayam, N., Ye, C., Reznik, A.: Radio-telepathy: extracting a secret key from an unauthenticated wireless channel. In: Proceedings of the 14th ACM International Conference on Mobile Computing and Networking, pp. 128–139. ACM (2008)
25. Maurer, U.: Secret key agreement by public discussion from common information. IEEE Trans. Inf. Theor. **39**(3), 733–742 (1993)
26. Maurer, U., Wolf, S.: Information-theoretic key agreement: from weak to strong secrecy for free. In: Preneel, B. (ed.) EUROCRYPT 2000. LNCS, vol. 1807, pp. 351–368. Springer, Heidelberg (2000). doi:10.1007/3-540-45539-6_24
27. Medaglia, C.M., Serbanati, A.: An overview of privacy and security issues in the internet of things. In: Giusto, D., Iera, A., Morabito, G., Atzori, L. (eds.) The Internet of Things, pp. 389–395 (2010)
28. Mirzadeh, S., Cruickshank, H., Tafazolli, R.: Secure device pairing: a survey. IEEE Commun. Surv. Tutorials **16**(1), 17–40 (2014)
29. Moriyama, D., Matsuo, S., Yung, M.: PUF-based RFID authentication secure and private under memory leakage. Cryptology ePrint Archive, Report 2013/712 (2013). http://eprint.iacr.org/2013/712
30. Nishan, N., Zuckerman, D.: Randomness is linear in space. J. Comput. Syst. Sci. **52**(1), 43–52 (1996)
31. Pappu, S.R.: Physical one-way functions. Ph.D. thesis. Massachusetts Institute of Technology (2001)
32. Schaller, A., Skoric, B., Katzenbeisser, S.: Eliminating leakage in reverse fuzzy extractors. IACR Cryptology ePrint Archive 2014/741 (2014)
33. Tope, M.A., McEachen, J.C.: Unconditionally secure communications over fading channels. In: Military Communications Conference, MILCOM 2001. Communications for Network-Centric Operations: Creating the Information Force, vol. 1, pp. 54–58. IEEE (2001)
34. Van Herrewege, A., Katzenbeisser, S., Maes, R., Peeters, R., Sadeghi, A.-R., Verbauwhede, I., Wachsmann, C.: Reverse fuzzy extractors: enabling lightweight mutual authentication for PUF-enabled RFIDs. In: Keromytis, A.D. (ed.) FC 2012. LNCS, vol. 7397, pp. 374–389. Springer, Heidelberg (2012). doi:10.1007/978-3-642-32946-3_27
35. Wild, A., Güneysu, T.: Enabling SRAM-PUFs on xilinx FPGAs. In: 2014 24th International Conference on Field Programmable Logic and Applications (FPL), pp. 1–4. IEEE (2014)
36. Willers, O., Huth, C., Guajardo, J., Seidel, H.: MEMS-based gyroscopes as physical unclonable functions. Cryptology ePrint Archive, Report 2016/261 (2016). http://eprint.iacr.org/2016/261
37. Zenger, C.T., Pietersz, M., Zimmer, J., Posielek, J.-F., Lenze, T., Paar, C.: Authenticated key establishment for low-resource devices exploiting correlated random channels. Comput. Netw. **109**, 105–123 (2016)
38. Zenger, C.T., Zimmer, J., Pietersz, M., Posielek, J.-F., Paar, C.: Exploiting the physical environment for securing the internet of things. In: Proceedings of the 2015 New Security Paradigms Workshop, pp. 44–58. ACM (2015)

Lattice Cryptography

A Practical Post-Quantum Public-Key Cryptosystem Based on spLWE

Jung Hee Cheon, Kyoohyung Han, Jinsu Kim$^{(\boxtimes)}$, Changmin Lee,
and Yongha Son

Department of Mathematical Sciences, Seoul National University,
1 Gwanak-ro, Gwanak-gu, Seoul 151-747, Korea
{jhcheon,satanigh,nemokjs1,cocomi11,emsskk}@snu.ac.kr

Abstract. The Learning with Errors (LWE) problem has been widely used as a hardness assumption to construct public-key primitives. In this paper, we propose an efficient instantiation of a PKE scheme based on LWE with a sparse secret, named as spLWE. We first construct an IND-CPA PKE and convert it to an IND-CCA scheme in the quantum random oracle model by applying a modified Fujisaki-Okamoto conversion of Unruh. In order to guarantee the security of our base problem suggested in this paper, we provide a polynomial time reduction from LWE with a uniformly chosen secret to spLWE. We modify the previous attacks for LWE to exploit the sparsity of a secret key and derive more suitable parameters. We can finally estimate performance of our scheme supporting 256-bit messages: our implementation shows that our IND-CCA scheme takes $313\,\mu s$ and $302\,\mu s$ respectively for encryption and decryption with the parameters that have 128-quantum bit security.

Keywords: Practical · Post-quantum · IND-CCA · PKE · Sparse secret · LWE · Quantum random oracle model

1 Introduction

With advances in quantum computing, many people in various fields are working on making their information security systems resistant to quantum computing. The National Security Agency (NSA) has announced a plan to change its Suite B guidance [42], and the National Institute of Standards and Technology (NIST) is now beginning to prepare for the transition into quantum-resistant cryptography [41]. There have been also substantial support for post-quantum cryptography from national funding agencies including the PQCRYPTO projects [18] in Europe.

In that sense, lattice-based cryptography is a promising field to conduct practical quantum-resistant research. This is due to the seminal work of Ajtai [1] who proved a reduction from the worst-case to the average-case for some lattice problems. This means that certain problems are hard on average, as long as the related lattice problems are hard in all cases. This enables provably secure

© Springer International Publishing AG 2017
S. Hong and J.H. Park (Eds.): ICISC 2016, LNCS 10157, pp. 51–74, 2017.
DOI: 10.1007/978-3-319-53177-9_3

constructions unless all instances of related lattice problems are easy to solve. Another remarkable work in lattice-based cryptography is the introduction of Learning with Errors problem by Regev in [47]. This work shows that there exists a quantum reduction from some worst-case lattice problems (the shortest independent vectors problem, the shortest vector problem with a gap) to LWE. With a strong security guarantee, LWE makes versatile cryptographic constructions possible including fully homomorphic encryption, multi-linear map, etcetera. For more details, we refer to the recent survey [44].

In order to increase efficiency on lattice-based cryptographic schemes, ring structured problems such as Learning with Errors over the ring (RLWE) and NTRU [32,37] have received much attentions. A major advantage of using a ring structure is that one can get a relatively smaller key size and faster speed. For that reason, a lot of works about cryptographic schemes with practical implementation have been proposed in RLWE and NTRU settings: public-key encryptions [19,36,49], signatures [22,23,27], key-exchanges [5,12,51]. However, additional ring structures may give some advantages to attackers. As an example, some analyses using the ring structure have been proposed recently. In particular, some NTRU-based fully homomorphic encryptions proved valueless [16,39] and some parameters of RLWE are confirmed to be weak [30,31]. Hence, there are growing concerns about the security gap for ring-structured cryptosystems.

On the other hand, it is reported that LWE-based signatures [17,22,27] achieve good performance without the use of RLWE, and studies of practicality of LWE-based key exchange protocols have been recently started in [11]. However, less attention has been paid to practical instantiations of LWE-based cryptosystems. In this sense, proposing of a practical LWE-based public-key cryptosystem and evaluation its performance would be an interesting topic in lattice-based cryptography. However, construction of public-key cryptosystem, which satisfies both high levels of security and efficiency, is a very non-trivial and hard task. It requires the right balance between security and efficiency to constitute a complete proposal, which considers the possibility of practical use.

Our first contribution is that we are suggesting a practical post-quantum public-key cryptosystem based on spLWE that is a variant of LWE with a sparse secret vector: Based on spLWE, we propose an IND-CPA PKE inspired from [43] and convert it into an IND-CCA version in the quantum random oracle model by applying the modified Fujisaki-Okamoto conversion of Unruh [52]. We identify its practicality from our implementation on a PC. The implementation result shows that our proposal enables relatively fast encryption and decryption that take about hundreds of microseconds.

Our second contribution is that we are providing the analysis for spLWE: We proved that spLWE can be reduced from LWE, which means that the hardness of spLWE can also be based on the worst-case lattice problems. We also extend all known LWE attacks to investigate concrete hardness of spLWE. As a result, we could derive concrete parameters based on those attacks. We would like to note that we exclude the parameters which have provable security from our reduction under the consideration about practicality. Our reduction serves to guarantee the hardness of spLWE, but is not tight enough to be useful in setting concrete parameters for our scheme.

1.1 Results and Techniques

We have suggested concrete parameters for both classical and quantum security, implementation results of our scheme and a comparison table with the previous LWE-based PKE [48] and RLWE-based PKE [37] in Sect. 5.2. In 128-quantum bit security, the IND-CPA version of our encryption took about $314\,\mu s$ and the IND-CCA version of our encryption takes $313\,\mu s$ for 256-bit messages on Macbook Pro with CPU 2.6 GHz Intel Core i5 without parallelization.

To achieve this result, we chose a variant of LWE with a sparse secret. In most LWE-based encryptions, it is necessary to compute $\boldsymbol{u}^T\mathbf{A}$ or $\boldsymbol{u}^T\mathbf{A}+\mathbf{e}$ for $\boldsymbol{u}\in\mathbb{Z}_q^m$, $\boldsymbol{e}\in\mathbb{Z}_q^n$ and $\mathbf{A}\in\mathbb{Z}_q^{m\times n}$. When the vector $\boldsymbol{u}$ has low hamming weight, real computation cost is similar to that of θ-length vector. Moreover, the cost can be reduced further when restricting the non-zero components by power of two.

Unfortunately, the use of sparse secret has one drawback. It requires relatively larger dimension than that of LWE to maintain security. This is a significant factor for the performance of LWE-based schemes. A important question then arises: How large dimension is needed to maintain security? We can observe that the problem of increase in dimension can be relieved by using a small modulus q. Since the security of LWE is proportional to the size of dimension and error rate, smaller modulus leads to larger error rate. We can choose a relatively small modulus q in spLWE case from Theorem 3: The decapsulation error completely depends on inner product of secret and error vectors. We were able to identify the effect concretely from the attacks in Sect. 4.2 and Appendix for spLWE by extending all known attacks of LWE, which can be improved by exploiting the sparsity of secret: The dimension of spLWE still remains below 520. We also provide a reduction from LWE to spLWE under certain parameters in Sect. 4.1. This implies that the hardness of spLWE can be also based on the worst-case lattice problems. It can be done by generalizing the reduction of [13] from LWE to the binary LWE.

Finally, we can prove IND-CCA security of our scheme in the random oracle model. More specifically, we applied the result of the recent paper [52] to construct our PKE, which gives a slight modification of the Fujisaki-Okamoto transform in a quantum adversary setting. The modification only needs simple operations such as hashing and XOR to convert a IND-CPA PKE into IND-CCA one, and hence converting overhead is expected to be small.

1.2 Related Works

Practical instantiations and implementation results about post-quantum primitives in lattice-based cryptography have been reported mostly in the RLWE case rather than in the LWE one (e.g. [19,36,49], etc.). In particular, Peikert [43] presented efficient and practical lattice-based protocols for key transport and encryption on RLWE that are suitable for Internet standards and other open protocols. We also use the idea of KEM-based construction for improved efficiency. In our spLWE-based construction, the ciphertext size of an IND-CPA encryption scheme for ℓ-bit message is $(n \log q + 2\ell)$-bit. This is smaller than that of the known LWE-based PKEs [46,48] which have $(n \log q + \ell \log q)$-bit ciphertext size.

In the case of LWE-based PKEs [25,40,45,46,48], there are a few works on efficiency improvement. Galbraith [24] proposed variants of LWE where the entries of the random matrix are chosen to be smaller than a modulus q or binary to reduce the size of a public-key. However, there was no complete proposal which inclues attacks and parameters for practical usage. Bai et al. [7] considered LWE with binary secret to reduce the size of their signature. However, the effect on parameter and speed of their scheme was not fully investigated.

2   Preliminaries

Notations. In this paper, we use upper-case bold letters to denote matrices, and lower-case bold letters for column vectors. For a distribution $\mathcal{D}$, $a \leftarrow \mathcal{D}$ denotes choosing an element according to the distribution of $\mathcal{D}$ and $\boldsymbol{a} \leftarrow \mathcal{D}^m$ means that each component of $\boldsymbol{a}$ is sampled independently from $\mathcal{D}$. In particular, if the x_i's are independent and each x_i follows a Bernoulli distribution with ρ for a vector $\boldsymbol{x} = (x_1, \ldots, x_n)$, then we say that a vector $\boldsymbol{x}$ follows $\text{Ber}(n, \rho)$. For a given set $\mathcal{A}$, $\mathcal{U}(\mathcal{A})$ means a uniform distribution on the set $\mathcal{A}$ and $a \leftarrow \mathcal{A}$ denotes choosing an element according to the uniform distribution on $\mathcal{A}$. We denote by $\mathbb{Z}_q = \mathbb{Z}/q\mathbb{Z} = \{0, 1 \cdots, q-1\}$ and $\mathbb{T} = \mathbb{R}/\mathbb{Z}$ the additive group of real numbers modulo 1, and $\mathbb{T}_q$ the a subgroup of $\mathbb{T}$ having order q, consisting of $\{0, \frac{1}{q}, \cdots, \frac{q-1}{q}\}$. The $\langle \, , \rangle$ means the inner product of two vectors and $[\boldsymbol{x}]_i$ means the its i-th component. A function $f(\lambda)$ is called *negligible* if $f(\lambda) = o(\lambda^{-c})$ for any $c > 0$, i.e., f decrease faster than any inverse polynomial.

2.1   Security Definitions

Definition 1 (γ-spread, [52]). *A PKE is γ-spread if for every public-key generated by* Keygen *algorithm and every message* $\boldsymbol{m}$,

$$\max_{\boldsymbol{y}} Pr[\boldsymbol{y} \leftarrow \text{Enc}_{pk}(\boldsymbol{m})] \leq \frac{1}{2^\gamma}.$$

In particular, we say that a PKE is well-spread if $\gamma = \omega(\log(\lambda))$.

Definition 2 (One-way secure). *A PKE is One-Way secure if no (quantum) polynomial time algorithm (adversary) $\mathcal{A}$ can find a message $\boldsymbol{m}$ from* $\text{Enc}_{pk}(\boldsymbol{m})$, *given only public-key except with probability at most negl(λ).*

2.2   Key Encapsulation Mechanism

A *key encapsulation mechanism* (in short, KEM) is a key exchange algorithm to transmit an ephemeral key to a receiver with the receiver's public key. It differs from encryption scheme where a sender can choose a message. The sender cannot intend to make a specific ephemeral key. A KEM with ciphertext space $\mathcal{C}$ and key space $\mathcal{K}$ consists of polynomial time algorithms Setup, Keygen, Encap(may be randomized), Decap(should be deterministic).

- Params outputs public parameters.
- Keygen outputs a public encapsulation key pk and secret decapsulation key sk.
- Encap takes an encapsulation key pk and outputs a ciphertext $c \in \mathcal{C}$ and a key $k \in \mathcal{K}$.
- Decap takes a decapsulation key sk and a ciphertext c, and outputs some $k \in \mathcal{K} \cup \{\bot\}$, where $\bot$ denotes decapsulation failure.

2.3   Lattice and Lattice Reduction Algorithm

A *lattice* $L \subseteq \mathbb{R}^m$ is a set of integer linear combinations of a $\{b_1, \cdots, b_n\}$ which is a subset of independent column vectors in $\mathbb{R}^m$,

$$L = \{\sum_{i=1}^{n} a_i b_i : a_i \in \mathbb{Z}\}$$

The set of vectors $\{\mathbf{b}_1, \ldots, \mathbf{b}_n\}$, and its matrix form $\mathbf{B}$ are called a basis, and basis matrix of L respectively. Two bases matrices $\mathbf{B}_1$ and $\mathbf{B}_2$ describe the same lattice, if and only if $\mathbf{B}_2 = \mathbf{B}_1 \mathbf{U}$, where $\mathbf{U}$ is a unimodular matrix, i.e. $\det(U) = \pm 1$, $U \in \mathbb{Z}^{m \times m}$. Dimension of a lattice is defined as cardinality of a basis, i.e. $n = \dim(L)$. If $n = m$, we call lattice L to a full rank lattice. A sublattice is a subset $L' \subset L$ which is also a lattice. We define determinant (volume) of L by

$$\det(L) := \sqrt{\det(\boldsymbol{B}^T \boldsymbol{B})}$$

A length of the shortest vector in a lattice $L(\mathbf{B})$ is denoted by $\lambda_1(L(\mathbf{B}))$. More generally, the *i-th successive minima* $\lambda_i(L)$ is defined as the smallest radius r such that $\dim(\mathrm{span}(L \cap B(r))) \geq i$ where $B(r)$ is a n dimensional ball with radius r. There exist several bounds and estimations for the length of the shortest vector in a lattice.

- Minkowski's first theorem: $\lambda_1(L(\mathbf{B})) \leq \sqrt{n}(\det L(\mathbf{B}))^{1/n}$

- Gaussian heuristic: $\lambda_1(L(\mathbf{B})) \approx \sqrt{\frac{n}{2\pi e}} \det(L(\mathbf{B}))^{1/n}$ for random lattice L.

The *dual lattice* of L, denoted $\bar{L}$, is defined to be $\bar{L} = \{x \in \mathbb{R}^n : \forall v \in L, \langle x, v \rangle \in \mathbb{Z}\}$. We recall the Gram-Schmidt orthogonalization that is closely related with lattice basis reduction. The Gram-Schmidt algorithm computes orthogonal vectors $\{\mathbf{b}_1^*, \ldots, \mathbf{b}_m^*\}$ iteratively as follows:

$$\mathbf{b}_i^* = \mathbf{b}_i - \sum_{j<i} \mu_{i,j} \mathbf{b}_j^* \text{ where } \mu_{i,j} = \frac{\mathbf{b}_i \cdot \mathbf{b}_j^*}{\mathbf{b}_j^* \cdot \mathbf{b}_j^*}.$$

The goal of lattice (basis) reduction is to find a good basis for a given lattice. A basis is considered good, when the basis vectors are almost orthogonal and correspond approximately to the successive minima of the lattice. Performance of lattice reduction algorithms is evaluated by the *root Hermite factor* δ_0 defined by

$$\delta_0 = (\|\boldsymbol{v}\|/\det(L)^{1/n})^{1/n}$$

where $\boldsymbol{v}$ is the shortest vector of the reduced output basis.

2.4   Discrete Gaussian Distribution

For given $s > 0$, a *discrete Gaussian distribution* over a lattice L is defined as $D_{L,s}(x) = \rho_s(x)/\rho_s(L)$ for any $x \in L$, where

$$\rho_s(x) = \exp(-\pi\|x\|^2/s^2) \text{ and } \rho_s(L) := \sum_{x \in L} \rho_s(x).$$

We note that the standard deviation is $\sigma = s/\sqrt{2\pi}$. When $L = \mathbb{Z}$, we omit the subscript L. For a lattice L, the *smoothing parameter* $\eta_\epsilon(L)$ is defined by the smallest real number $s' > 0$ such that $\rho_{1/s'}(\tilde{L} \setminus \{\mathbf{0}\}) \le \epsilon$. We collect some useful lemmas related to a discrete Gaussian distribution and the smoothing parameter.

Lemma 1 ([9], **Lemma 2.4**).   *For any real $s > 0$ and $T > 0$, and any vector $\boldsymbol{x} \in \mathbb{R}^n$, we have*

$$Pr[|\langle \boldsymbol{x}, D_{\mathbb{Z},s}^n \rangle| \ge T \cdot s\|\boldsymbol{x}\|] < 2\exp(-\pi \cdot T^2).$$

Lemma 2 ([46], **Corollary 3.10**).   *Let L be an n-dimensional lattice, let $\boldsymbol{u}, \boldsymbol{z} \in \mathbb{R}^n$ be arbitrary vectors, and let r, α be positive real numbers. Assume that $(1/r^2 + (\|\boldsymbol{z}/\alpha\|)^2)^{-1/2} \ge \eta_\epsilon(\Lambda)$ for some $\epsilon < 1/2$. Then the distribution of $\langle \boldsymbol{z}, \boldsymbol{v} \rangle + e$ where $\boldsymbol{v} \leftarrow D_{L+\boldsymbol{u},r}$ and $e \leftarrow D_\alpha$ is within statistical distance 4ϵ of D_β for $\beta = \sqrt{(r\|\boldsymbol{z}\|)^2 + \alpha^2}$.*

Lemma 3 ([25], **Lemma 3.1**).   *For any $\epsilon > 0$ and an n-dimensional lattice Λ with basis matrix $\boldsymbol{B}$, the smoothing parameter $\eta_\epsilon(\Lambda) \le \|\tilde{\boldsymbol{B}}\| \ln(2n(1 + 1/\epsilon))/\pi$ where $\|\tilde{\boldsymbol{B}}\|$ denotes the length of the longest column vector of $\tilde{\boldsymbol{B}}$ which is the Gram-Schmidt orthogonalization of $\boldsymbol{B}$.*

2.5   Learning with Errors

For integers $n, q \ge 1$, a vector $\boldsymbol{s} \in \mathbb{Z}_q^n$, and a distribution ϕ on $\mathbb{R}$, let $A_{q,\boldsymbol{s},\phi}$ be the distribution of the pairs $(\boldsymbol{a}, b = \langle \boldsymbol{a}, \boldsymbol{s} \rangle + e) \in \mathbb{T}_q^n \times \mathbb{T}$, where $\boldsymbol{a} \leftarrow \mathbb{T}_q^n$ and $e \leftarrow \phi$.

Definition 3 (Learning with Errors (LWE)). *For integers $n, q \geq 1$, an error distribution ϕ over R, and a distribution $\mathcal{D}$ over $\mathbb{Z}_q^n$, $\mathsf{LWE}_{n,q,\phi}(\mathcal{D})$, is to distinguish (given arbitrarily many independent samples) the uniform distribution over $\mathbb{T}_q^n \times \mathbb{T}$ from $A_{q,s,\phi}$ with a fixed sample $s \leftarrow \mathcal{D}$.*

We note that a search variant of LWE is the problem of recovering s from $(\mathbf{a}, b) = (\mathbf{a}, \langle \mathbf{a}, \mathbf{s} \rangle + e) \in \mathbb{T}_q^n \times \mathbb{T}$ sampled according to $A_{q,s,\phi}$, and these are also equivalently defined on $\mathbb{Z}_q^n \times \mathbb{Z}_q$ rather than $\mathbb{T}_q^n \times \mathbb{T}$ for discrete (Gaussian) error distributions over $\mathbb{Z}_q$. Let $\mathsf{LWE}_{n,m,q,\phi}(\mathcal{D})$ denotes the case when the number of samples are bounded by $m \in \mathbb{N}$. We simply denote $\mathsf{LWE}_{n,q,\phi}$ when the secret distribution $\mathcal{D}$ is $\mathcal{U}(\mathbb{Z}_q^n)$. In many cases, ϕ is a (discrete) Gaussian distribution so we simply denote by $\mathsf{LWE}_{n,m,q,s}$ instead of $\mathsf{LWE}_{n,m,q,\phi}$. We denote binLWE by the LWE problem whose secret vector is sampled from uniform distribution over $\{0,1\}^n$. For a set $X_{n,\rho,\theta}$ which consists of the vectors $\mathbf{s} \in \mathbb{Z}^n$ whose nonzero components are in $\{\pm 1, \pm 2, \pm 4, \cdots, \pm \rho\}$, and the number of nonzero components is θ, we write $\mathsf{spLWE}_{n,m,q,s,\rho,\theta}$ as the problem $\mathsf{LWE}_{n,m,q,s}(\mathcal{U}(X_{n,\rho,\theta}))$. We also consider a variant of LWE, $\mathsf{LWE}_{n,q,\leq\alpha}$, in which the amount of noise is some unknown $\beta \leq \alpha$ as in [13]. Similarly, $\mathsf{spLWE}_{n,q,\leq\alpha,\rho,\theta}$ can be defined by the same way.

The following lemma will be used to derive some parameters from the modified attacks in section 4 and appendix.

Lemma 4 ([48]). *Given $\mathsf{LWE}_{n,m,q,s}$ samples and a vector v of length $\|v\|$ in the lattice $L = \{ \mathbf{w} \in \mathbb{Z}_q^m : \mathbf{w}^T \mathbf{A} \equiv 0 \mod q \}$, the advantage of distinguishing $\langle v, e \rangle$ from uniform random is close to $\exp(-\pi(\|v\| s/q)^2)$.*

We give some variants of LWE and some notion, which were introduced in [13] to show the reduction between binLWE and LWE.

Definition 4 ("first-is-errorless" LWE). *For integers $n, q \geq 1$ and an error distribution ϕ over $\mathbb{R}$, the first-is-errorless variant of the LWE problem is to distinguish between the following two scenarios. In the first, the first sample is uniform over $\mathbb{T}_q^n \times \mathbb{T}_q$ and the rest are uniform over $\mathbb{T}_q^n \times \mathbb{T}$. In the second, there is an unknown uniformly distributed $\mathbf{s} \in \{0, \ldots, q-1\}^n$, the first sample we get is from $A_{q,s,\{0\}}$ (where $\{0\}$ denotes the distribution that is deterministically zero) and the rest are from $A_{q,s,\phi}$.*

Definition 5 (extLWE problem). *For integers $n, m, q, t \geq 1$, a set $X \subseteq \mathbb{Z}^m$, and a distribution χ over $\frac{1}{q}\mathbb{Z}^m$, the $\mathsf{extLWE}_{n,m,q,\chi,X}$ is as follows. The algorithm gets to choose $\mathbf{x} \in X$ and then receives a tuple $(\mathbf{A}, (\mathbf{b}_i)_{i \in [t]}, (\langle \mathbf{e}_i, \mathbf{x} \rangle)_{i \in [t]}) \in \mathbb{T}_q^{n \times m} \times (\mathbb{T}_q^m)^t \times (\frac{1}{q}\mathbb{Z})^t$. Its goal is to distinguish between the following two cases. In the first, $A \in \mathbb{T}_q^{n \times m}$ is chosen uniformly, $\mathbf{e}_i \in \frac{1}{q}\mathbb{Z}^m$ are chosen from χ, and $\mathbf{b}_i = \mathbf{A}^T \mathbf{s}_i + \mathbf{e}_i \mod 1$ where $\mathbf{s}_i \in \{0, \ldots, q-1\}^n$ are chosen uniformly. The second case is identical, except that the $\mathbf{b}_i'$s are chosen uniformly in $\mathbb{T}_q^m$ independently of everything else.*

Definition 6 (Quality of a set). *A set $X \subset \mathbb{Z}^m$ is said of quality ξ if given any $\mathbf{x} \in X$, we can efficiently find a unimodular matrix $U \in \mathbb{Z}^{m \times m}$ such that if*

$U' \in \mathbb{Z}^{m \times (m-1)}$ *is the matrix obtained from* U *by removing its leftmost column then all of the columns of* U' *are orthogonal to* z *and its largest singular value is at most* ξ. *It denoted by* $Qual(X)$.

We give a lemma to show a reduction to spLWE from the standard LWE in Sect. 4.1.

Lemma 5. *The quality of a set* $X \subseteq \{0, \pm 1, \pm 2, \ldots, \pm \rho\}^m$, $\rho = 2^l$ *is bounded by* $1 + \sqrt{\rho}$.

Proof. Let $\mathbf{x} \in X$ and without loss of generality, we assume leftmost k components of $\mathbf{x}$ are nonzero, remaining entries are zero, and $|[\mathbf{x}]_i| \leq |[\mathbf{x}]_{i+1}|$ for nonzero components after reordering. We have $[\mathbf{x}]_{i+1} = \pm 2^{t_i}[\mathbf{x}]_i$ for some $t_i \leq l$. Now consider the upper bidiagonal matrix $\mathbf{U}$ whose diagonal is all 1 and whose diagonal above the main diagonal is $\mathbf{y} \in \mathbb{Z}^{m-1}$ such that $[\mathbf{x}]_{i+1} - [\mathbf{y}]_j[\mathbf{x}]_i = 0$ for $1 \leq j \leq k - 1$, and rightmost $(m - k)$ components of $\mathbf{y}$ are 0. Since $[\mathbf{x}]_{i+1} = \pm 2^{t_i}[\mathbf{x}]_i$, it follows that $[\mathbf{y}]_j$ is 2^{t_j} or -2^{t_j}. Then $\mathbf{U}$ is clearly unimodular $(\det(\mathbf{U}) = 1)$ and all the columns except the first one are orthogonal to $\mathbf{x}$. Moreover, by the triangle inequality, we can bound the norm (the largest singular value) of $\mathbf{U}$ by the sum of that of the diagonal 1 matrix and the off-diagonal matrix of which clearly have norm at most $\sqrt{\rho}$. $\square$

3   Our spLWE-Based PKE

In this section, we introduce a public key encryption scheme whose security is based on spLWE, whose ciphertext size is smaller than those of the previous works [46,48]. We use a noisy subset sum in our encryption algorithm which is proposed in the previous LWE-based encryption scheme [48], but our message encoding is different: we first construct a key encapsulation mechanism based on LWE, and conceal a message with an ephemeral key shared by KEM.

We propose two versions of one encryption scheme based on the spLWE-based KEM, where one is IND-CPA secure and the other is an IND-CCA conversion of IND-CPA by the transformation proposed in [52]. We note that these different types of schemes can be applied to various circumstances.

3.1   Our Key Encapsulation Mechanism

We use a *reconciliation* technique in [43] which is the main tool to construct our spLWE-based KEM. In our KEM, the sender generates a random number $v \in \mathbb{Z}_{2q}$ for some even integer $q > 0$, and sends $\langle v \rangle_2$ where $\langle v \rangle_2 := [\lfloor \frac{2}{q} \cdot v \rceil]_2 \in \mathbb{Z}_2$ to share $\lfloor v \rceil_2 := [\lfloor \frac{1}{q} \cdot v \rceil]_2 \in \mathbb{Z}_2$ securely. For all vectors $\boldsymbol{v} \in \mathbb{Z}_{2q}^k$, $\langle \boldsymbol{v} \rangle_2$ and $\lfloor \boldsymbol{v} \rceil_2$ are naturally defined by applying $\langle \rangle_2$ and $\lfloor \rceil_2$ component-wise, respectively. The receiver recovers $\lfloor v \rceil_2$ from $\langle v \rangle_2$ and sk using a special function named *rec*. The reconciliation function *rec* is defined as follows.

Definition 7. *For disjoint intervals* $I_0 := \{0, 1, \cdots, \lfloor \frac{q}{2} \rfloor - 1\}$, $I_1 := \{-\lfloor \frac{q}{2} \rfloor, \cdots, -2, -1\}$ *and* $E = [-\frac{q}{4}, \frac{q}{4}) \cap \mathbb{Z}$, *we define*

$$rec : \mathbb{Z}_{2q} \times \mathbb{Z}_2 \to \mathbb{Z}_2 \text{ where } rec(w, b) := \begin{cases} 0 & if \ w \in I_b + E \mod 2q, \\ 1 & otherwise. \end{cases}$$

It is naturally extended to a vector-input function $\boldsymbol{rec} : \mathbb{Z}_{2q}^k \times \mathbb{Z}_2^k \to \mathbb{Z}_2^k$ *by applying* rec *component-wise.*

The following lemmas show that $\langle v \rangle_2$ reveals no information about $\lfloor v \rceil_2$, and rec decapsulates $\lfloor v \rceil_2$ correctly when it is provided with a proper approximation of v.

Lemma 6. *If* $v \in \mathbb{Z}_{2q}$ *is uniformly random, then* $\lfloor v \rceil_2$ *is uniformly random given* $\langle v \rangle_2$.

Proof. Suppose that $\langle v \rangle_2 = b \in \mathbb{Z}_2$. It implies that v is uniform over $I_b \cup (q + I_b)$. If $v \in I_b$, then $\lfloor v \rceil_2 = 0$, and if $v \in (q + I_b)$, then $\lfloor v \rceil_2 = 1$. Therefore $\lfloor v \rceil_2$ is uniformly random over $\{0, 1\}$ given $\langle v \rangle_2$. □

Lemma 7. *For* $v, w \in \mathbb{Z}_{2q}$, *if* $|v - w| < q/4$, *then* $rec(w, \langle v \rangle_2) = \lfloor v \rceil_2$.

Proof. Let $\langle v \rangle_2 = b \in \mathbb{Z}_2$, then $v \in I_b \cup (q + I_b)$. Then $\lfloor v \rceil_2 = 0$ if and only if $v \in I_b$. Since $(I_b + E) - E = I_b + (-\frac{q}{2}, \frac{q}{2})$ and $(q + I_b)$ are disjoint (mod $2q$), we know that $v \in I_b$ if and only if $w \in I_b + E$. □

The purpose of our KEM is sharing the ephemeral key from $\mathbf{u}^T \mathbf{A} \mathbf{s} + error$ and the reconciliation function between two parties as in [43]. Here, we describe our spLWE-based KEM for k-bit sharing as follows.

- KEM.Params(λ): generate a bit-length of shared key k, a bit-length of seed y and spLWE parameters $n, m, q, s, \rho, \theta, s', \rho', \theta'$ with λ-bit security. Publish all parameters by pp.
- KEM.Keygen(pp): sample $seed_A \leftarrow \{0, 1\}^y$, $\mathbf{A} \leftarrow Gen(seed_A)$, $\mathbf{E} \leftarrow D_{\mathbb{Z}, s}^{m \times k}$ and $\mathbf{S} \leftarrow \mathcal{U}(X_{n, \rho, \theta})^k$, and compute $\mathbf{B} = \mathbf{A}\mathbf{S} + \mathbf{E} \in \mathbb{Z}_q^{m \times k}$. For a secret key sk $= \mathbf{S}$, publish a corresponding public key pk $= (seed_A, \mathbf{B})$.
- KEM.Encap(pk,pp): sample $\mathbf{u} \leftarrow X_{m, \rho', \theta'}$, $(\mathbf{e}_1, \mathbf{e}_2) \leftarrow D_{\mathbb{Z}, s'}^k \times D_{\mathbb{Z}, s'}^n$ and $\mathbf{e}_3 \in \{0, 1\}^k$. Let $\mathbf{v} = \mathbf{u}^T \mathbf{B} + \mathbf{e}_1 \in \mathbb{Z}_q^k$ and $\bar{\mathbf{v}} = 2\mathbf{v} + \mathbf{e}_3 \in \mathbb{Z}_{2q}^k$. Compute $\mathbf{c}_1 = \langle \bar{\mathbf{v}} \rangle_2 \in \mathbb{Z}_2^k$ and $\mathbf{c}_2 = \mathbf{u}^T \mathbf{A} + \mathbf{e}_2 \in \mathbb{Z}_q^n$ from $\mathbf{A} \leftarrow Gen(seed_A)$. Send a ciphertext $\mathbf{c} = (\mathbf{c}_1, \mathbf{c}_2) \in \mathbb{Z}_2^k \times \mathbb{Z}_q^n$ to the receiver, and store an ephemeral secret key $\boldsymbol{\mu} = \lfloor \bar{\mathbf{v}} \rceil_2 \in \mathbb{Z}_2^k$.
- KEM.Decap($\mathbf{c}$, sk): If q is odd, compute $\mathbf{w} = 2\mathbf{c}_2^T \mathbf{S} \in \mathbb{Z}_q^k$, and output $\boldsymbol{\mu} = \boldsymbol{rec}(\mathbf{w}, \mathbf{c}_1)$.

We would like to note that if q is even, the *doubling* process in the encapsulation phase, i.e. converting $\mathbf{v} = \mathbf{u}^T \mathbf{B} + \mathbf{e}_1$ to $\bar{\mathbf{v}} = 2\mathbf{v} + \mathbf{e}_3$, is not required.

3.2 Our KEM-Based Encryption Scheme

We now construct a public key encryption scheme based on the spLWE-based KEM in the previous section. When the message slot increases by one, the ciphertext spaces of our scheme grow only one or two bits, which is more efficient than the known LWE based encryption schemes [46,48], where the growth is about $\log q$ bits.

PKE$_1$ (IND-CPA) : With a key exchange mechanism which shares a ℓ-bit length key, it is well-known that one can convert it into a public key encryption of the ℓ-bit length message having the same security as the key exchange mechanism. This conversion only includes XOR operations after generating an ephemeral key. Note that the ciphertext space is given as $\mathbb{Z}_q^n \times \mathbb{Z}_2^{2\ell}$, which is very efficient than $\mathbb{Z}_q^{n+\ell}$, ciphertext spaces of other LWE-based schemes.

PKE$_1$ is described as follows.

- PKE$_1$.Params(λ): let ℓ be a message length, and run KEM.Params(λ) with $k = \ell$. Publish all parameters by pp.
- PKE$_1$.Keygen(pp): output a key pair (pk, sk)$\leftarrow$ KEM.Keygen(pp).
- PKE$_1$.Enc(pk, m, pp): for $c, \mu \leftarrow$ KEM.Encap(pk,pp), let $c' = m \oplus \mu$ and output a ciphertext (c, c').
- PKE$_1$.Dec((c, c'), sk): for $\mu =$ KEM.Decap(c, sk), output $m = c' \oplus \mu$.

PKE$_2$ (IND-CCA) : We can apply the transformation suggested in [52], which can improve security of the existing public key encryption schemes. As a trade-off of security, this scheme requires a more complex construction than PKE$_1$, but note that this also use light operations such as XOR or hashing, which are not serious tasks for implementation.

We specially denote the encryption phase of PKE$_1$ by PKE$_1$.Enc(pk, m, pp; r) to emphasize that a random bit-string r is used for random sampling. Here, PKE$_1$.Enc(pk, m, pp; r) becomes deterministic.

It also requires quantumly secure hash functions $G : \{0,1\}^{k_1+\ell} \to \{0,1\}^*$, $H : \{0,1\}^{k_1} \to \{0,1\}^{k_2}$ and $H' : \{0,1\}^{k_1} \to \{0,1\}^{k_3}$, where k_i will be determined later. With these parameters, our scheme has a ciphertext space $\mathbb{Z}_q^n \times \mathbb{Z}_2^{k_2+k_3+\ell}$, which also gradually increases with the growth of message slot.

PKE$_2$ is described as follows.

- PKE$_2$.Params(λ): let ℓ be a message length and $k_i > 0$ be integers such that hash functions $G : \{0,1\}^{k_1+\ell} \to \{0,1\}^*$, $H : \{0,1\}^{k_1} \to \{0,1\}^{k_2}$ and $H' : \{0,1\}^{k_1} \to \{0,1\}^{k_3}$ have λ-bit security. Let pp be an output of KEM.Params(λ) with $k = k_1$. Publish ℓ, pp and k_i.
- PKE$_2$.Keygen(pp): output a key pair (pk, sk)$\leftarrow$ KEM.Keygen(k_1).
- PKE$_2$.Enc(pk, m, pp, k_i): randomly choose $\omega \leftarrow \{0,1\}^{k_1}$, and let $c_m = H(\omega) \oplus m$. Compute $c_h = H'(\omega)$ and $(c, c') \leftarrow$ PKE$_1$.Enc(pk, ω; $G(\omega||c_m)$). Output a ciphertext (c, c', c_h, c_m).

- $\text{PKE}_2.\text{Dec}((\boldsymbol{c}, \boldsymbol{c}', \boldsymbol{c}_h, \boldsymbol{c_m}), \text{sk}, \text{pp}, k_i)$: compute $\boldsymbol{\omega} = \text{PKE}_1.\text{Dec}((\boldsymbol{c}, \boldsymbol{c}'), \text{sk})$ and $\boldsymbol{m} = H(\boldsymbol{\omega}) \oplus \boldsymbol{c_m}$. Check whether $(\boldsymbol{c}, \boldsymbol{c}') = \text{PKE}_1.\text{Enc}(\text{pk}, \boldsymbol{\omega}; G(\boldsymbol{w}||\boldsymbol{c_m}))$ and $\boldsymbol{c}_h = H'(\boldsymbol{\omega})$. If so, output $\boldsymbol{m}$, otherwise output $\perp$.

3.3 Security

In this section, we show (IND-CPA, IND-CCA) security of our encryption scheme $(\text{PKE}_1, \text{PKE}_2)$. Security of our encryption scheme is reduced to security of KEM and security of KEM comes from hardness of spLWE. Consequently, under the hardness of spLWE, PKE_1 can reach to IND-CPA security and PKE_2 achieves further quantumly IND-CCA security with the random oracle assumption. Here is a statement for security of KEM.

Theorem 1. *Assuming the hardness of* $\text{spLWE}_{n,m,q,s,\rho,\theta}$, *and* $\text{spLWE}_{n,m,q,s'}$, ρ', θ', *our KEM is IND-CPA secure.*

Proof. (Sketch) By Lemma 3, one cannot extract any information about $\boldsymbol{\mu} = \lfloor \boldsymbol{v} \rceil_2$ with $\boldsymbol{c_1}$. Moreover, even if one can know some information of $\boldsymbol{v}$, the distribution of $(\boldsymbol{c_2}, \boldsymbol{v})$ can be regarded as LWE instances as :

$$(\boldsymbol{c_2}, \boldsymbol{v}) = (\boldsymbol{u}^T \cdot \mathbf{A} + \boldsymbol{e_2}, \boldsymbol{u}^T \cdot \mathbf{B} + \boldsymbol{e_1}) = (\mathbf{C}, \mathbf{C} \cdot \mathbf{S} + \boldsymbol{e}')$$

for $\mathbf{C} = \boldsymbol{u}^{\mathbf{T}} \cdot \mathbf{A} + \boldsymbol{e_2}$ and for some $\boldsymbol{e}'$. Thus, hardness of spLWE insures that the distribution of $(\boldsymbol{c_2}, \boldsymbol{v})$ is indistinguishable from the uniform distribution over $\mathbb{Z}_q^n \times \mathbb{Z}_q^k$. $\qquad\square$

We refer [43] for the detailed IND-CPA game-based proof, where the only difference is that we assume the hardness of spLWE, not RLWE.

It is well-known in many cryptographic texts that PKE_1 has the same security level with KEM. Hence, security of PKE_1 has been demonstrated from the previous theorem. Moreover, the transformation of [52] gives quantumly IND-CCA security for PKE_2, when it is converted from an IND-CPA secure PKE with random oracle modeled hashes. When the aforementioned statements are put together, we can establish the following security theorem.

Theorem 2. *Assuming the hardness of* $\text{spLWE}_{n,m,q,s,\rho,\theta}$, $\text{spLWE}_{n,m,q,s',\rho',\theta'}$, *$PKE_1$ is IND-CPA secure, and PKE_2 is quantumly IND-CCA secure with further assumption that the function G, H and H' are modeled as random oracles.*

Proof. (Sketch) We only need to show that PKE_2 is IND-CCA secure. The transformation of [52] actually make an IND-CCA secure public key encryption from a public key encryption which is *well-spread* and *one-way*, and we briefly explain why (IND-CPA) PKE_1 is well-spread and one-way.

- Well-spreadness: Note that a ciphertext of PKE_1 is of the form

$$(\boldsymbol{c_1}, \boldsymbol{c_2}) = \left(\langle \mathbf{2}(\boldsymbol{u}^T B + \boldsymbol{e_1}) + \boldsymbol{e_3} \rangle_2, \boldsymbol{u}^T A + \boldsymbol{e_2} \right),$$

where $\boldsymbol{u} \leftarrow X_{m,\rho',\theta'}, (\boldsymbol{e_1}, \boldsymbol{e_2}) \leftarrow D_{\mathbb{Z}, s'}^k \times D_{\mathbb{Z}, s'}^n$. From hardness of spLWE, distributions of $\boldsymbol{u}^T B + \boldsymbol{e_1} \in \mathbb{Z}_q^k$ and $\boldsymbol{u}^T A + \boldsymbol{e_2} \in \mathbb{Z}_q^n$ are statistically close to uniform distributions over $\mathbb{Z}_q^k$ and $\mathbb{Z}_q^n$, and then PKE_1 is well-spread.

– One-wayness: With an oracle $\mathcal{O}$ finding $\boldsymbol{m}$ from $\mathrm{PKE}_1.\mathsf{Enc}(\mathsf{pk}, \boldsymbol{m})$ for any pk with probability ϵ, an adversary equipped with $\mathcal{O}$ wins the IND-CPA game for PKE_1 with bigger advantage than $\frac{\epsilon}{2}$: After given $\mathrm{PKE}_1.\mathsf{Enc}(\mathsf{pk}, \boldsymbol{m}_b)$, the adversary outputs the answer of $\mathcal{O}$. It can be easily shown that the advantage is bigger than $\frac{\epsilon}{2}$. $\qquad\square$

3.4 Correctness

Similar to the security case, correctness of our (IND-CPA, IND-CCA) encryption scheme is dependent on that of our spLWE-based KEM. We remark that generally, one can obtain some correctness condition for all LWE variants by examining a bound of error term in the proof below. Here, we assume $s = s', \rho = \rho'$ and $\theta = \theta'$, which is used for our parameter instantiation.

Theorem 3. *Let* $n, m, \sigma, \rho, \theta$ *be parameters in* $\mathsf{spLWE}_{n,m,q,\sigma,\rho,\theta}$, *and* ℓ *be the shared key length in* KEM. *For a per-symbol error probability* γ, *the* KEM *decapsulates correctly if*

$$q \geq 8s\rho\sqrt{\frac{2\theta}{\pi} \ln(2/\gamma)}.$$

Proof. As shown in the description of KEM.Decap, the ephemeral key is decapsulated correctly if $|\bar{\boldsymbol{v}} - \boldsymbol{w}| < q/4$ by Lemma 7. Since $\bar{\boldsymbol{v}} = 2\boldsymbol{u}^T\boldsymbol{A}\boldsymbol{S} + 2\boldsymbol{u}^T\boldsymbol{E} + 2\boldsymbol{e}_1 + \boldsymbol{e}_3$, and $\boldsymbol{w} = 2\boldsymbol{u}^T\boldsymbol{A}\boldsymbol{S} + 2\boldsymbol{e}_2\boldsymbol{S}$, it is rephrased by

$$|2\boldsymbol{u}^T \cdot \mathbf{E} - 2\boldsymbol{e}_1 \cdot \mathbf{S} + 2\boldsymbol{e}_2 + \boldsymbol{e}_3| < q/4,$$

which is equivalent to

$$|2\langle \boldsymbol{u}, [\mathbf{E}]^j\rangle + 2\langle -\boldsymbol{e}_1, [\mathbf{S}]^j\rangle + 2[\boldsymbol{e}_2]_j + [\boldsymbol{e}_3]_j| < q/4, 1 \leq j \leq \ell$$

where $\boldsymbol{u} \leftarrow X_{m,\rho',\theta'}, [\mathbf{S}]^j \leftarrow X_{n,\rho,\theta}, [\mathbf{E}]^j \leftarrow D_{\mathbb{Z},s}^m, \boldsymbol{e}_1 \leftarrow D_{\mathbb{Z},s'}^n, [\boldsymbol{e}_2]_j \leftarrow D_{\mathbb{Z},s'}, [\boldsymbol{e}_3]_j \leftarrow \{0, 1\}$. For simplicity, we ignore the small term $2[\boldsymbol{e}_2]_j + [\boldsymbol{e}_3]_j$. (This is compensated in our final choice of parameters.) By applying Lemma 1 to a $(m + n)$ dimensional vector $\boldsymbol{x} = (\boldsymbol{u}, [\mathbf{S}]^j)$ and the bound $Ts\|\boldsymbol{x}\| = q/8$, we came to have per-symbol error probability γ,

$$\gamma = 2\exp(-\pi(\frac{q}{8s\rho\sqrt{(2\theta)}})^2)$$

from $T = \frac{q}{8s\rho\sqrt{2\theta}}$. From the equation above, we get the bound on q as the statement.

4 The Hardness of spLWE

In this section, we show the hardness of spLWE via a security reduction and concrete attacks. First, we show spLWE is as hard as worst-case lattice problems to solve. For that, we provide a reduction from LWE to spLWE by generalizing the reduction [13]. Next, we also present modified attacks for spLWE, which exploit the sparsity of a secret from all known attacks for LWE and binLWE [8,14].

4.1 A Reduction from LWE to spLWE

To show our reduction for spLWE, we need extLWE^m problem whose hardness was proved in [13]. They showed that for a set X of quality ξ, there exists a reduction from $\text{LWE}_{k,m,q,s}$ to $\text{extLWE}^m_{(k+1,n,q,\beta=\sqrt{s^2\xi^2+s^2},X)}$. (Here, $n \leq m$) Based on a reduction from LWE to extLWE in [13], we prove a reduction of spLWE as shown in the diagram below. Here, ω,γ and s are constant satisfying

$$\omega = s\rho\sqrt{2\theta(2+2\sqrt{\rho}+\rho)},\ \ \gamma = \rho s\sqrt{\theta(2+2\sqrt{\rho}+\rho)},\ \ \beta \geq (\ln(2n(1+1/\epsilon))/\pi)^{1/2}/q.$$

Because $\text{Qual}(X_{n,\rho,\theta}) < 1 + \sqrt{\rho}$ by Lemma 5, extLWE $_{k+1,n,q,s\sqrt{(1+\sqrt{\rho})^2+1},X_{n,\rho,\theta}}$ is hard based on the hardness of $\text{LWE}_{k,n,q,s}$. Following theorem shows that $\text{spLWE}_{n,m,q,\leq\omega,\rho,\theta}$ problem can be hard based on the hardness of $\text{LWE}_{k,m,q,\gamma}$ and $\text{extLWE}_{n,m,q,s\sqrt{(1+\sqrt{\rho})^2+1},X_{n,\rho,\theta}}$ for the $\omega, \gamma > 0$ as above. In particular, if $\log\left(\binom{n}{\theta} \cdot (2l+2)^\theta\right) \geq k\log q + 2\log(1/\delta)$, there is a reduction from $\text{LWE}_{k,m,q,s}$ to $\text{spLWE}_{n,m,q,\leq\omega,\rho,\theta}$.

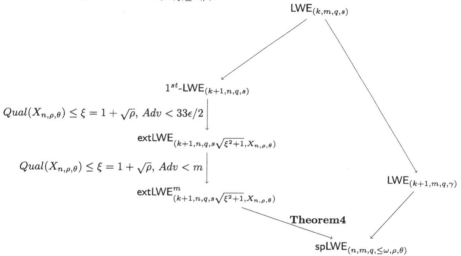

Theorem 4. *Let k, n, m, $\rho = 2^l$, θ, $q \in \mathbb{N}$, $\epsilon \in (0,1/2)$, and $\delta,\omega,\beta,\gamma > 0$ such that*

$$\beta \geq \sqrt{2\ln(2n(1+1/\epsilon))/\pi}/q \text{ where } \beta = s\sqrt{(1+\sqrt{\rho})^2+1},$$

$$\omega = \rho\beta\sqrt{2\theta},\ \ \gamma = \rho\beta\sqrt{\theta},\ \ \log\left(\binom{n}{\theta} \cdot (2l+2)^\theta\right) \geq k\log q + 2\log(1/\delta).$$

There exist (two) reductions to $\text{spLWE}_{n,m,q,\leq\omega,\rho,\theta}$ from $\text{extLWE}^m_{k,n,q,\beta,X_{n,\rho,\theta}}$, $\text{LWE}_{k,m,q,\gamma}$. An advantage of $\mathcal{A}$ for $\text{spLWE}_{n,m,q,\leq\omega,\rho,\theta}(\mathcal{D})$ is bounded as follows:

$$Adv[\mathcal{A}] \leq 2Adv[\mathcal{C}_1] + Adv[\mathcal{C}_2] + 4m\epsilon + \delta$$

for the algorithms (distinguishers) of $\text{extLWE}^m_{k,n,q,\beta,X_{n,\rho,\theta}}$, $\text{LWE}_{k,m,q,\gamma}$, $\mathcal{C}_1$ and $\mathcal{C}_2$ respectively.

Proof. The proof follows by a sequence of distribution to use hybrid argument as stated in [13]. We take into account the following six distributions:

$H_0 := \{(\mathbf{A}, \mathbf{b} = \mathbf{A}^T\mathbf{x} + \mathbf{e}) \mid \mathbf{A} \leftarrow \mathbb{T}_q^{n \times m}, \mathbf{x} \leftarrow X_{n,\rho,\theta}, \mathbf{e} \leftarrow D_{\alpha'}^m \text{ for } \alpha' = \sqrt{\beta^2\|\mathbf{x}\|^2 + \gamma^2} \leq \rho\beta\sqrt{2\theta} = \omega\}.$

$H_1 := \{(\mathbf{A}, \mathbf{A}^T\mathbf{x} - \mathbf{N}^T\mathbf{x} + \hat{\mathbf{e}} \mod 1) \mid \mathbf{A} \leftarrow \mathbb{T}_q^{n \times m}, \mathbf{x} \leftarrow X, \mathbf{N} \leftarrow D_{\frac{1}{q}\mathbb{Z},\beta}^{n \times m}, \hat{\mathbf{e}} \leftarrow D_\gamma^m\}.$

$H_2 := \{(q\mathbf{C}^T\mathbf{B} + \mathbf{N}, q\mathbf{B}^T\mathbf{C}\mathbf{x} + \hat{\mathbf{e}}) \mid \mathbf{B} \leftarrow \mathbb{T}_q^{k \times m}, \mathbf{C} \leftarrow \mathbb{T}_q^{k \times n}, \mathbf{x} \leftarrow X, \mathbf{N} \leftarrow D_{\frac{1}{q}\mathbb{Z},\beta}^{n \times m}, \hat{\mathbf{e}} \leftarrow D_\gamma^m\}.$

$H_3 := \{(q\mathbf{C}^T\mathbf{B} + \mathbf{N}, \mathbf{B}^T\mathbf{s} + \hat{\mathbf{e}}) \mid \mathbf{s} \leftarrow \mathbb{Z}_q^k, \mathbf{B} \leftarrow \mathbb{T}_q^{k \times m}, \mathbf{C} \leftarrow \mathbb{T}_q^{k \times n}, \mathbf{N} \leftarrow D_{\frac{1}{q}\mathbb{Z},\beta}^{n \times m}, \hat{\mathbf{e}} \leftarrow D_\gamma^m\}.$

$H_4 := \{(q\mathbf{C}^T\mathbf{B} + \mathbf{N}, \mathbf{u}) \mid \mathbf{u} \leftarrow \mathbb{T}^m, \mathbf{B} \leftarrow \mathbb{T}_q^{k \times m}, \mathbf{C} \leftarrow \mathbb{T}_q^{k \times n}, \mathbf{N} \leftarrow D_{\frac{1}{q}\mathbb{Z},\beta}^{n \times m}\}.$

$H_5 := \{(\mathbf{A}, \mathbf{u}) \mid \mathbf{A} \leftarrow \mathbb{T}_q^{n \times m}, \mathbf{u} \leftarrow \mathbb{T}^m\}.$

Let $\mathcal{B}_i$ be the distinguisher for the distributions between H_i and H_{i+1} for $0 \leq i \leq 4$. There are some efficient transformations from the distributions $(\mathbf{C}, \mathbf{A}, \mathbf{N}^T\mathbf{z}), (\mathbf{C}, \hat{\mathbf{A}}, \mathbf{N}^T\mathbf{z})$ to H_1, H_2, from $(\mathbf{B}, \mathbf{B}^T\mathbf{s} + \hat{\mathbf{e}}), (\mathbf{B}, \mathbf{u})$ to H_3, H_4, and from $(\mathbf{C}, \hat{\mathbf{A}}), (\mathbf{C}, \mathbf{A})$ to H_4, H_5. In fact, the samples $(\mathbf{C}, \hat{\mathbf{A}}, \mathbf{N}^T\mathbf{z}), (\mathbf{B}, \mathbf{B}^T\mathbf{s} + \hat{\mathbf{e}})$, and $(\mathbf{C}, \hat{\mathbf{A}})$ are $\mathsf{extLWE}_{k,n,q,\beta,X}^m$, $\mathsf{LWE}_{k,m,q,\gamma}$ and $\mathsf{extLWE}_{k,n,q,\beta,\{0^n\}}^m$ samples respectively. The others are uniform distribution samples in the corresponding domain. It follows that $Adv[\mathcal{B}_1], Adv[\mathcal{B}_3], Adv[\mathcal{B}_4]$ are bound by the distinguishing advantages of $\mathsf{extLWE}_{k,n,q,\beta,X}^m$, $\mathsf{LWE}_{k,m,q,\gamma}$, $\mathsf{extLWE}_{k,n,q,\beta,\{0^n\}}^m$ respectively.

Since $\|\mathbf{x}\| \leq \rho\sqrt{\theta}$, and $\beta \geq \sqrt{2\ln(2n(1 + 1/\epsilon))/\pi}/q \geq \sqrt{2}\eta_\epsilon(\mathbb{Z}^n)/q$ from Lemma 3, it follows that the statistical distance between $-\mathbf{N}^T\mathbf{x} + \hat{\mathbf{e}}$ and $D_{\alpha'}^m$ is at most $4m\epsilon$ by Lemma 2. This gives $Adv[\mathcal{B}_0] \leq 4m\epsilon$. The last $Adv[\mathcal{B}_2]$ is bound by δ from the Leftover hash lemma. To sum up, $Adv[\mathcal{A}] \leq 2Adv[\mathcal{C}_1] + Adv[\mathcal{C}_2] + 4m\epsilon + \delta$ with trivial reduction to $\mathsf{extLWE}_{k,n,q,\beta,\{0^n\}}^m$ from $\mathsf{extLWE}_{k,n,q,\beta,X}^m$. $\square$

4.2 Attacks for spLWE

There exist many attacks for LWE including a dual attack and primal attacks [4,20]. Here, we exclude a combinatorial BKW algorithm, the Arora and Ge algorithm and their variants, as they are not suitable in our case [2,6,21,28,33]. Since the analysis of traditional dual attack is based on the (discrete) Gaussian error (and secret in the LWE normal form), these traditional attacks are not directly applicable to spLWE. Therefore, we modify those attacks to analyze concrete hardness of spLWE. We also consider random guess on a sparse secret vector $\mathbf{s}$ as in appendix.

Dual (distinguish) Attack. Assume that we are given $(\mathbf{A}, \mathbf{b}) \in \mathbb{Z}_q^{m \times n} \times \mathbb{Z}_q^m$ and want to distinguish whether they are uniform random samples or spLWE samples. For a constant $c \in \mathbb{R}$ with $c \leq q$, consider a lattice $L_c(\mathbf{A})$ defined by

$$L_c(\mathbf{A}) = \left\{(\boldsymbol{x}, \boldsymbol{y}/c) \in \mathbb{Z}^m \times (\mathbb{Z}/c)^n : \boldsymbol{x}^T\mathbf{A} = \boldsymbol{y} \mod q\right\}.$$

If the samples $(\mathbf{A}, \boldsymbol{b})$ came from spLWE, for $(\boldsymbol{x}, \boldsymbol{y}) \in L_c(\mathbf{A})$, we have

$$
\begin{aligned}
\langle \boldsymbol{x}, \boldsymbol{b} \rangle &= \langle \boldsymbol{x}, \mathbf{A}\boldsymbol{s} + \boldsymbol{e} \rangle \\
&= \langle \boldsymbol{x}, \mathbf{A}\boldsymbol{s} \rangle + \langle \boldsymbol{x}, \boldsymbol{e} \rangle \\
&= c\langle \boldsymbol{y}, \boldsymbol{s} \rangle + \langle \boldsymbol{x}, \boldsymbol{e} \rangle \quad \bmod q
\end{aligned}
$$

For a sufficiently small vector $(\boldsymbol{v}, \boldsymbol{w}) \in L_c(\mathbf{A})$, the value $\langle \boldsymbol{v}, \boldsymbol{b} \rangle \bmod q$ becomes small when the samples are spLWE ones, and $\langle \boldsymbol{v}, \boldsymbol{b} \rangle \bmod q$ is uniformly distributed when $(\mathbf{A}, \boldsymbol{b})$ came from the uniform distribution. Hence, one can decide whether the samples came from spLWE distribution or uniform distribution from the size of $\langle \boldsymbol{v}, \boldsymbol{b} \rangle \bmod q$ with some success probability. We now determine how small a vector $(\boldsymbol{v}, \boldsymbol{w})$ must be found as follows. First, we estimate the length of $(\boldsymbol{v}, \boldsymbol{w}) \in L_c(\mathbf{A})$. One can easily check that

$$
\left(\begin{array}{c|c} I_m & 0 \\ \hline \dfrac{1}{c}\mathbf{A}^T & \dfrac{q}{c}I_n \end{array} \right)
$$

is a basis matrix of $L_c(\mathbf{A})$. Hence, we can figure out $\dim(L_c(\mathbf{A})) = m + n$ and $\det(L_c(\mathbf{A})) = (q/c)^n$.

Therefore, a lattice reduction algorithm with a root Hermite factor δ_0 gives $(\boldsymbol{v}, \boldsymbol{w}) \in L_c(\mathbf{A})$, such that

$$
||(\boldsymbol{v}, \boldsymbol{w})|| = \delta_0^{m+n}(q/c)^{\frac{n}{m+n}}, \tag{1}
$$

and the length is minimized when $m = \sqrt{n(\log q - \log c)/\log \delta_0} - n$.

Next, we consider the distribution of $c\langle \boldsymbol{w}, \boldsymbol{s} \rangle + \langle \boldsymbol{v}, \boldsymbol{e} \rangle \bmod q$. Here, we assume that the coefficients of sparse vector $\boldsymbol{s}$ are independently sampled by $(b_1 d_1, b_2 d_2, \ldots, b_n d_n)$ where $d_i \leftarrow \mathrm{Ber}(n, \theta/n)$, $b_i \leftarrow \{\pm 1, \pm 2, \pm 4, \ldots, \pm \rho\}$, and $\rho = 2^l$ for some $l \in \mathbb{Z}_{\geq 0}$. Since $c\langle \boldsymbol{w}, \boldsymbol{s} \rangle$ is the sum of many independent random variables, asymptotically it follows a Gaussian distribution with mean 0, and variance $(c||\boldsymbol{w}||)^2 \cdot \frac{2\theta(4^{l+1}-1)}{3n(2l+2)}$. From that $\langle \boldsymbol{v}, \boldsymbol{e} \rangle$ follows a Gaussian distribution with mean 0, variance $(\sigma||\boldsymbol{v}||)^2$, and Lemma 4, we have distinguishing advantage

$$
\exp(-\pi(s'/q)^2) \text{ where } s' = \sqrt{2\pi}\sqrt{\sigma^2||\boldsymbol{v}||^2 + c^2\frac{2\theta(4^{l+1}-1)}{3n(2l+2)}||\boldsymbol{w}||^2}. \tag{2}
$$

From above Eqs. 1 and 2 with distinguishing advantage ϵ, we need to find small δ_0 such that

$$
\delta_0 = (c/q)^{\frac{-n}{(m+n)^2}} \left(\frac{q}{M}\sqrt{\ln(1/\epsilon)/\pi}\right)^{1/(m+n)} \text{ where } M = \sqrt{2\pi}\sqrt{\sigma^2\frac{m}{m+n} + c^2\frac{2\theta(4^{l+1}-1)}{3n(2l+2)}\frac{n}{m+n}}
$$

5   Parameter Selection and Implementation Result

5.1   Parameter Selection

To deduce some appropriate parameters, we assume that the best known classical and quantum SVP (sieving) algorithm in dimension k runs in time $2^{0.292k}$ and $2^{0.265k}$ respectively [10,34]. The BKZ 2.0 lattice basis reduction algorithm gives the root Hermite factor $\delta_0 \approx (\frac{k}{2\pi e}(\pi k)^{1/k})^{1/2(k-1)}$ for block size k [15], and the iteration number of exact SVP solver is $\frac{n^3}{k^2}\log n$ [29].

We consider a direct CVP attack by sieving [35], modified dual (distinguish) and embedding attack. Moreover, since our secret key is a sparse vector, our attack can be improved if one can guess some components of secret to be zero. After that, we can apply the attack to a smaller dimensional spLWE instances. We denote the probability of the correct guessing t components from n components by $p_{n,t,\theta}$. It can be computed as $\binom{n-\theta}{t}/\binom{n}{t}$.

To sum up the previous sections, the parameters must satisfy the followings for the quantum security:

- $n \log q \cdot (2l+1)^\theta \cdot \binom{n}{\theta} > 2^{2\lambda}$ from bruteforce attack (grover algorithm), where $\binom{n}{\theta} = \frac{n!}{(\theta!)(n-\theta!)}$ (For classical security, 2λ becomes λ)
- Let $T(n, q, \theta, s, l)$ be a BKZ 2.0 running time to get root Hermite factor δ_0, which satisfies the following equation:

$$\delta_0 = \max_{1<c<q, 1\leq m\leq n}\left\{(c/q)^{\frac{-n}{(m+n)^2}}(\frac{q}{M}\sqrt{\ln(1/\epsilon)/\pi})^{1/(m+n)}\right\}$$

where

$$M = \sqrt{2\pi}\cdot\sqrt{\sigma^2\frac{m}{m+n} + c^2\frac{2\theta(4^{l+1}-1)}{3n(2l+2)}\frac{n}{m+n}}.$$

Taking into the probability $p_{n,t,\theta}$, our parameters should satisfy the following:

$$\min_t\left\{\frac{1}{p_{n,t,\theta}}\cdot T(n-t, q, \theta, s, l)\right\} > 2^\lambda \text{ where } p_{n,t,\theta} = \binom{n-\theta}{t}/\binom{n}{t}$$

- To prevent the direct CVP attack, n and θ should satisfy the following equation:

$$\min_t\left\{\frac{1}{p_{n,t,\theta}}\cdot 2^{0.265(n-t)}\right\} > 2^\lambda$$

For classical security, 0.265 becomes 0.292.
- For the correctness, $q \geq 8s\rho\sqrt{\frac{2\theta}{\pi}\ln(2/\gamma)}$ by the Lemma 7.
- The parameters k_1 and k_2 are a symmetric key length of XOR operations, and k_3 is a length of hash value. For λ-bit security, it is known that k_1 and k_2 should be λ (2λ) and k_3 should be 2λ (3λ) in classical (quantum) security model.

5.2 Implementation Result

We use C++ on a Linux-based system, with GCC compiler and apply the Eigen library (www.eigen.tuxfamily.org), which makes vector and matrix operations fast. To sample u efficiently in our encryption algorithm, we assume that there are only one non-zero element in each n/θ-size block. To follow the previous reduction and security proof, we need a sampling of discrete Gaussian distribution when we generate error vectors in key generation and encryption algorithm. We use *box-muller transformation* to generate discretized Gaussian distribution. In the case below, message space length is 32-byte and secret key is ternary vector. We used PC (Macbook Pro) with CPU 2.6 GHz Intel Core i5 without parallelization.

Table 1. Implementation result in classical hardness with 256 bit message

Parameters					IND-CPA				IND-CCA		
λ	n	q	s	θ	Setup(ms)	Enc(μs)	Dec(μs)	Cptx(byte)	Enc(μs)	Dec(μs)	Cptx(byte)
72	300	382	5	27	9.8	96	41	401	116	130	435
96	400	441	5	36	16.3	167	62	513	181	182	548
128	565	477	5	42	29.3	273	102	700	291	282	733

Table 2. Implementation result in quantum hardness with 256 bit message

Parameters					IND-CPA				IND-CCA		
λ	n	q	s	θ	Setup(ms)	Enc(μs)	Dec(μs)	Cptx(byte)	Enc(μs)	Dec(μs)	Cptx(byte)
72	300	410	5	31	9.8	96	41	401	108	130	435
96	400	477	5	42	16.0	163	56	514	186	191	548
128	565	520	5	50	129.5	314	106	770	313	302	804

We also compare our implementation with software implementation in [26], which implements LWE-based PKE [48] and Ring version PKE [37,38]. Their implementation is executed on an Intel Core 2 Duo CPU running at 3.00 GHz PC. Parameters in each row are secure in same security parameters.

The table above shows that our PKE scheme is about 20 times faster than RLWE-based PKE scheme in [37,38]. The sparsity of secret vector makes modulus size q smaller and complexity in encryption/decryption algorithm lower.

Acknowledgements. We thank Damien Stehlé for helpful discussions on the initial version of our reduction, and Duhyeong Kim for pointing out some typos in our reduction. We also thank Yongsoo Song and the ICISC reviewers for their useful comments. This work was supported by Samsung Research Funding Center of Samsung Electronics under Project Number SRFC-TB1403-00.

Table 3. Our scheme vs. LWE vs. RLWE: Time in milliseconds for encryption and decryption for a 16-byte plaintext.

Our scheme			[26]	LWE		RLWE	
(n, q, s, θ)	Enc	Dec	(n, q, s)	Enc	Dec	Enc	Dec
(150, 285, 5.0, 15)	0.027	0.011	(128, 2053, 6.77)	3.01	1.24	0.76	0.28
(300, 396, 5.0, 29)	0.063	0.019	(256, 4093, 8.87)	11.01	2.37	1.52	0.57
(400, 545, 5.0, 55)	0.109	0.026	(384, 4093, 8.35)	23.41	3.41	2.51	0.98
(560, 570, 5.0, 60)	0.223	0.04	(512, 4093, 8.0)	46.05	4.52	3.06	1.18

A   Appendix

A.1   Attacks for Search spLWE

Dual (search) Attack. In this section, we assume the Geometric Series Assumption (GSA) on q-ary lattices, introduced by Schnorr [50], and this will be used to estimate the length of last vector of BKZ 2.0 reduced basis. Let $\mathbf{B} = \{\boldsymbol{b}_1, \cdots, \boldsymbol{b}_n\}$ be a basis for an n-dimensional lattice Λ, which is reduced by the BKZ 2.0 with root Hermite factor δ_0, then the GSA says:

$$\|\boldsymbol{b}_i^*\| = \beta^{i-1} \cdot \|\boldsymbol{b}_1^*\| \text{ for some constant} 0 < \beta \leq 1,$$

where $\{\boldsymbol{b}_1^*, \cdots, \boldsymbol{b}_n^*\}$ is the Gram-schmidt orthogonalization of $\{\boldsymbol{b}_1, \cdots, \boldsymbol{b}_n\}$. From $\|\boldsymbol{b}_1\| = \delta_0^n \cdot \det(\mathbf{B})^{1/n}$, we have:

$$\det(\mathbf{B}) = \prod_{i=1}^{n} \|\boldsymbol{b}_i^*\| = \prod_{i=1}^{n} \beta^{i-1} \cdot \|\boldsymbol{b}_1^*\| = \beta^{\frac{(n-1)n}{2}} \cdot \delta_0^{n^2} \cdot \det(\mathbf{B}).$$

From the equation above, it follows that $\beta = \delta_0^{-2n^2/(n-1)n}$. Since BKZ reduced basis satisfies $\boldsymbol{b}_i = \boldsymbol{b}_i^* + \sum_{j=0}^{i-1} \mu_{ij} \cdot \boldsymbol{b}_j^*$ with $|\mu_{ij}| \leq 1/2$, one can show that,

$$\|\boldsymbol{b}_i\| \leq \|\boldsymbol{b}_1\| \cdot \sqrt{\frac{1 - \beta^{2i-2}}{4 - 4\beta^2} + \beta^{2i-2}}.$$

We now describe the dual attack against a small number of LWE instances $(\mathbf{A}, \mathbf{A}\boldsymbol{s} + \boldsymbol{e}) = (\mathbf{A}, \boldsymbol{b}) \in \mathbb{Z}^{m \times n} \times \mathbb{Z}^m$. For some constant $c \in \mathbb{N}$ with $c \leq q$, we consider a scaled lattice $\Lambda_c(\mathbf{A})$.

$$\Lambda_c(\mathbf{A}) = \{(\boldsymbol{x}, \boldsymbol{y}/c) \in \mathbb{Z}^m \times (\mathbb{Z}^n/c) : \boldsymbol{x}\mathbf{A} = \boldsymbol{y} \bmod q\}.$$

A dimension and determinant of the lattice $\Lambda_c(\mathbf{A})$ is $n + m$ and $(q/c)^n$ respectively. With the assumptions above, we can obtain vectors $\{(\boldsymbol{v}_i, \boldsymbol{w}_i)\}_{1 \leq i \leq n}$ in $\Lambda_c(\mathbf{A})$ such that,

$$\|(\boldsymbol{v}_i, \boldsymbol{w}_i)\| \leq \delta_0^{m+n} \cdot (q/c)^{\frac{n}{m+n}} \cdot \sqrt{\frac{1 - \beta^{2i-2}}{4 - 4\beta^2} + \beta^{2i-2}} \approx \delta_0^{m+n}(q/c)^{\frac{n}{m+n}} \cdot \sqrt{\frac{1}{4 - 4\beta^2}}.$$

Clearly, the element $(\boldsymbol{v}_i, \boldsymbol{w}_i)$ in $\Lambda_c(\mathbf{A})$ satisfies

$$\boldsymbol{v}_i \cdot \boldsymbol{b} = \boldsymbol{v}_i \cdot (A \cdot \boldsymbol{s} + \boldsymbol{e}) = \langle c \cdot \boldsymbol{w}_i, \boldsymbol{s} \rangle + \langle \boldsymbol{v}_i, \boldsymbol{e} \rangle = \langle (\boldsymbol{v}_i, \boldsymbol{w}_i), (\boldsymbol{e}, c \cdot \boldsymbol{s}) \rangle \bmod q.$$

If, for $1 \leq i \leq n$, $(\boldsymbol{v}_i, \boldsymbol{w}_i)$ is short enough to satisfy $\|(\boldsymbol{v}_i, \boldsymbol{w}_i)\| \cdot \|(\boldsymbol{e}, c \cdot \boldsymbol{s})\| < q/2$, the above equation hold over $\mathbb{Z}$. Then we can recover $\boldsymbol{e}$ and $\boldsymbol{s}$ by solving the system of linear equations. Since, $\|(\boldsymbol{e}, c\boldsymbol{s})\| \approx \sqrt{n \cdot \sigma^2 + c^2 \cdot \|\boldsymbol{s}\|^2}$, condition for attack is following:

$$\delta_0^{n+m} \cdot (q/c)^{\frac{n}{m+n}} \cdot \sqrt{\frac{n \cdot \sigma^2 + c^2 \cdot \|\boldsymbol{s}\|^2}{4 - 4\beta^2}} < \frac{q}{2}$$

for constant $0 < c \leq q$. To find an optimized constant c, we assume $m = n$. In this case, the size is optimized with $c = \sqrt{n \cdot \sigma^2 / \|s\|^2}$. Therefore, final condition to success attack is following:

$$2\delta_0^{4n} \cdot \sigma \cdot \|\boldsymbol{s}\| \cdot \sqrt{n} < q(1 - \beta^2).$$

Modified Embedding Attack. One can reduce the LWE problem to unique-SVP problem via Kannan's embedding technique. First, we consider a column lattice

$$\Lambda_q(\mathbf{A}') = \{\boldsymbol{y} \in \mathbb{Z}^{m+1} : \boldsymbol{y} = \mathbf{A}'\boldsymbol{x} \bmod q\} \text{ for } \mathbf{A}' = \begin{pmatrix} 1 & 0 \\ -\boldsymbol{b} & \mathbf{A} \end{pmatrix}.$$

The vector $(1, \boldsymbol{e})^T$ is in lattice $\Lambda_q(\mathbf{A}')$ and its size is approximately $\sigma\sqrt{m}$. If this value is sufficiently smaller than $\lambda_2(\Lambda_q(\mathbf{A}'))$ ($\approx \sqrt{\frac{m}{2\pi e}} q^{(m-n)/m}$), one can find the vector $(1, \boldsymbol{e})^T$ via some lattice reduction algorithms. In particular, the vector $(1, \boldsymbol{e})^T$ can be found with high probability with the BKZ algorithms in [3], if

$$\frac{\lambda_2(\Lambda_{m+1})}{\lambda_1(\Lambda_{m+1})} = \frac{\lambda_2(\Lambda_q(\mathbf{A}))}{\|(1, \boldsymbol{e})\|} \geq \tau \cdot \delta_0^m,$$

where $\tau \approx 0.4$. For spLWE case, we can obtain a much larger gap than that of the ordinary attack for LWE. We now consider a scaled lattice $\Lambda_c(\mathbf{B})$ generated by the following matrix:

$$\mathbf{B} = \begin{pmatrix} 1 & 0 & 0 \\ 0 & c\mathbf{I}_n & 0 \\ -\boldsymbol{b} & \mathbf{A} & q\mathbf{I}_m \end{pmatrix}$$

for a constant $0 < c < 1$. The vector $(1, c\boldsymbol{s}, \boldsymbol{e})^T$ is in this lattice and its size is approximately $\sqrt{m \cdot \sigma^2 + c^2 \|\boldsymbol{s}\|^2}$. Define a matrix $\mathbf{B}'$ as following,

$$\mathbf{B}' = \begin{pmatrix} c\mathbf{I}_n & 0 \\ \mathbf{A} & q\mathbf{I}_m \end{pmatrix}.$$

We have $\lambda_1(\Lambda_c(B)) = \sqrt{m \cdot \sigma^2 + c^2 \cdot ||s||^2}$ and $\lambda_1(\Lambda_c(B')) = \sqrt{\frac{n+m}{2\pi e}}$ $\cdot$ $\det(\Lambda_c(B'))^{1/(n+m)} = \sqrt{\frac{n+m}{2\pi e}} \cdot (q^m c^n)^{1/n+m}$. Therefore, it is necessary to find the root Hermite factor δ_0 such that:

$$\sqrt{\frac{n+m}{2\pi e}} \cdot (q^m c^n)^{1/n+m} \geq 0.4 \cdot \delta_0^{n+m} \cdot \sqrt{m \cdot \sigma^2 + c^2 ||s||^2} \tag{3}$$

$$\Leftrightarrow \sqrt{\frac{n+m}{2\pi e \cdot (m \cdot \sigma^2 + c^2 ||s||^2)}} \cdot (q^m c^n)^{1/n+m} \geq 0.4 \cdot \delta_0^{n+m} \tag{4}$$

The left part of inequality above is maximized when $c = \sqrt{n\sigma^2}/||s||$, so we have:

$$\sqrt{\frac{1}{2\pi e \cdot \sigma^2}} \left(q^m \cdot \left(\frac{\sigma\sqrt{n}}{||s||} \right)^n \right)^{1/(n+m)} \geq 0.4 \cdot \delta_0^{n+m}$$

A.2   Improving Lattice Attacks for spLWE

A time complexity of all attacks suggested in this paper is heavily depend on the dimension of lattices used in the attacks. Therefore, if one can reduce the dimension of lattices, one can obtain a high advantage to solve the LWE problem. In this section, we introduce two techniques to improve lattice-based attacks for spLWE instances. The first thing is a method of ignoring some components of a sparse secret and the other is a method of trading between dimension and modulus, which has been introduced in [13]. For convenience, we denote $T(m)$ as the expected time of solving m-dimensional LWE.

Ignoring Components on Secret Vectors. Most entries of a secret vector s are zero. Therefore, by ignoring some components, one can reduce the dimension of LWE. More precisely, we delete k entries of secret vector s and its corresponding column of A. For convenience, we denote it as s' and A', respectively. If the deleted components of s are zero, the following equation also holds:

$$A \cdot s + e = A' \cdot s' + e \bmod q.$$

The probability P_k that the selected k entries are zero is $\binom{n-\theta}{k}/\binom{n}{k}$. It implies that one can reduce the n-dimensional LWE to $(n-k)$-dimensional LWE with probability P_k. In other words, solving $1/P_k$ instances in $(n-k)$-dimensional LWE, one can expect to solve the n dimension LWE. Hence, in order to guarantee λ bits security, it gives:

$$T(n-k)/P_k \geq 2^\lambda. \tag{5}$$

Modulus Dimension Switching. In [13], they describe a modulus dimension switching technique for LWE instances. Using the Corollary 3.4 in [13], for n, q, θ, w that divides n and $\epsilon \in (0, 1/2)$, one can reduce a $\mathsf{LWE}_{n,q,\leq\alpha}$

instances to $\mathsf{LWE}_{n/w,q^w,\leq\beta}$ instances, where β is a constant satisfying $\beta^2 \geq \alpha^2 + (4/\pi)\ln(2n(1+1/\epsilon))\cdot\theta/q^2 \approx \alpha^2$. Along this reduction, a secret vector $s = (s_1, s_2, \cdots, s_n)$ of $\mathsf{spLWE}_{n,q,\leq\alpha,\rho,\theta}$ is changed to $s'' = (s_1 + qs_2 + \cdots + q^{w-1}s_w, \cdots, s_{n-w+1} + \cdots + q^{w-1}s_n)$ of $\mathsf{spLWE}_{n/w,q^w,\leq\beta,\rho',\theta'}$. Hence, if one can recover the s'' by solving $\mathsf{LWE}_{n/w,q^w,\leq\beta,\rho',\theta'}$ instances, one can also reveal the vector s. Let t be the number of a set $W = \{s_{wi}|s_{wi} \neq 0, 1 \leq i \leq n/w\}$ and P'_w be the probability of $t = 0$, i.e. P'_w is equal to $\dfrac{\binom{n-\theta}{n/w}}{\binom{n}{n/w}}$. When t is not zero, the expected size of $\|s''\|$ is $\sqrt{tq^w}$. In that case, applying the attacks in Sects. 4.2, A.1 and A.2 to converted n/w-dimensional LWE instances is not a good approach to obtain higher the advantage. Hence, we only consider the case $t = 0$. We can obtain the following conditions to get λ-bit security:

$$T(n/w)/P'_w \geq 2^\lambda. \tag{6}$$

By combining the ignoring k components with modulus dimension switching techniques, we can reach the final condition to obtain the λ-bit security:

$$T((n-k)/w)/(P_k P'_w) \geq 2^\lambda. \tag{7}$$

References

1. Ajtai, M.: Generating hard instances of lattice problems. In: Proceedings of the Twenty-Eighth Annual ACM Symposium on Theory of Computing, pp. 99–108. ACM (1996)
2. Albrecht, M., Cid, C., Faugere, J.C., Fitzpatrick, R., Perret, L.: Algebraic algorithms for LWE problems, Jean-Charles Faugere (2014)
3. Albrecht, M.R., Fitzpatrick, R., Göpfert, F.: On the efficacy of solving LWE by reduction to unique-SVP. In: Lee, H.S., Han, D.G. (eds.) ICISC 2013. LNCS, vol. 8565, pp. 293–310. Springer, Heidelberg (2014). doi:10.1007/978-3-319-12160-4_18
4. Albrecht, M.R., Player, R., Scott, S.: On the concrete hardness of learning with errors. J. Math. Cryptol. 9(3), 169–203 (2015)
5. Alkim, E., Ducas, L., Poppelmann, T., Schwabe, P.: Post-quantum key exchange-a new hope. Technical report, Cryptology ePrint Archive, Report 2015/1092 (2015). http://eprint.iacr.org
6. Arora, S., Ge, R.: New algorithms for learning in presence of errors. In: Aceto, L., Henzinger, M., Sgall, J. (eds.) ICALP 2011. LNCS, vol. 6755, pp. 403–415. Springer, Heidelberg (2011). doi:10.1007/978-3-642-22006-7_34
7. Bai, S., Galbraith, S.D.: An improved compression technique for signatures based on learning with errors. In: Benaloh, J. (ed.) CT-RSA 2014. LNCS, vol. 8366, pp. 28–47. Springer, Heidelberg (2014). doi:10.1007/978-3-319-04852-9_2
8. Bai, S., Galbraith, S.D.: Lattice decoding attacks on binary LWE. In: Susilo, W., Mu, Y. (eds.) ACISP 2014. LNCS, vol. 8544, pp. 322–337. Springer, Heidelberg (2014). doi:10.1007/978-3-319-08344-5_21
9. Banaszczyk, W.: Inequalities for convex bodies and polar reciprocal lattices in R^n. Discrete Comput. Geom. 13(2), 217–231 (1995)

10. Becker, A., Ducas, L., Gama, N., Laarhoven, T.: New directions in nearest neighbor searching with applications to lattice sieving. In: Proceedings of the Twenty-Seventh Annual ACM-SIAM Symposium on Discrete Algorithms, SIAM, pp. 10–24 (2016)
11. Bos, J., Costello, C., Ducas, L., Mironov, I., Naehrig, M., Nikolaenko, V., Raghunathan, A., Stebila, D.: Frodo: take off the ring! practical, quantum-secure key exchange from LWE (2016)
12. Bos, J.W., Costello, C., Naehrig, M., Stebila, D.: Post-quantum key exchange for the TLS protocol from the ring learning with errors problem. In: 2015 IEEE Symposium on Security and Privacy, pp. 553–570. IEEE (2015)
13. Brakerski, Z., Langlois, A., Peikert, C., Regev, O., Stehlé, D.: Classical hardness of learning with errors. In: Proceedings of the Forty-Fifth Annual ACM Symposium on Theory of Computing, pp. 575–584. ACM (2013)
14. Buchmann, J., Göpfert, F., Player, R., Wunderer, T.: On the hardness of LWE with binary error: revisiting the hybrid lattice-reduction and meet-in-the-middle attack. In: Pointcheval, D., Nitaj, A., Rachidi, T. (eds.) AFRICACRYPT 2016. LNCS, vol. 9646, pp. 24–43. Springer, Heidelberg (2016). doi:10.1007/978-3-319-31517-1_2
15. Chen, Y.: Réduction de réseau et sécurité concréte du chiffrement complétement homomorphe. Ph.D. thesis, ENS-Lyon, France (2013)
16. Cheon, J.H., Jeong, J., Lee, C.: An algorithm for NTRU problems and cryptanalysis of the GGH multilinear map without a low level encoding of zero. Cryptology ePrint Archive, Report 2016/139 (2016). http://eprint.iacr.org/2016/139
17. Dagdelen, Ö., Bansarkhani, R., Göpfert, F., Güneysu, T., Oder, T., Pöppelmann, T., Sánchez, A.H., Schwabe, P.: High-speed signatures from standard lattices. In: Aranha, D.F., Menezes, A. (eds.) LATINCRYPT 2014. LNCS, vol. 8895, pp. 84–103. Springer, Heidelberg (2015). doi:10.1007/978-3-319-16295-9_5
18. Daniel, A., Lejla, B. et al.: Initial recommendations of long-term secure post-quantum systems, Technical report (2015). http://pqcrypto.eu.org/docs/initial-recommendations.pdf
19. De Clercq, R., Roy, S.S., Vercauteren, F., Verbauwhede, I.: Efficient software implementation of ring-LWE encryption. In: Proceedings of the 2015 Design, Automation and Test in Europe Conference and Exhibition, pp. 339–344, EDA Consortium (2015)
20. De Meyer, L.: Security of LWE-based cryptosystems (2015)
21. Duc, A., Tramèr, F., Vaudenay, S.: Better algorithms for LWE and LWR. In: Oswald, E., Fischlin, M. (eds.) EUROCRYPT 2015. LNCS, vol. 9056, pp. 173–202. Springer, Heidelberg (2015). doi:10.1007/978-3-662-46800-5_8
22. Ducas, L., Durmus, A., Lepoint, T., Lyubashevsky, V.: Lattice signatures and bimodal gaussians. In: Canetti, R., Garay, J.A. (eds.) CRYPTO 2013. LNCS, vol. 8042, pp. 40–56. Springer, Heidelberg (2013). doi:10.1007/978-3-642-40041-4_3
23. Bansarkhani, R., Buchmann, J.: Improvement and efficient implementation of a lattice-based signature scheme. In: Lange, T., Lauter, K., Lisoněk, P. (eds.) SAC 2013. LNCS, vol. 8282, pp. 48–67. Springer, Heidelberg (2014). doi:10.1007/978-3-662-43414-7_3
24. Galbraith, S.D.: Space-efficient variants of cryptosystems based on learning with errors (2013). https://www.math.auckland.ac.nz/~sgal018/compact-LWE.pdf
25. Gentry, C., Peikert, C., Vaikuntanathan, V.: Trapdoors for hard lattices and new cryptographic constructions. In: Proceedings of the Fortieth Annual ACM Symposium on Theory of Computing, pp. 197–206. ACM (2008)

26. Göttert, N., Feller, T., Schneider, M., Buchmann, J., Huss, S.: On the design of hardware building blocks for modern lattice-based encryption schemes. In: Prouff, E., Schaumont, P. (eds.) CHES 2012. LNCS, vol. 7428, pp. 512–529. Springer, Heidelberg (2012). doi:10.1007/978-3-642-33027-8_30

27. Güneysu, T., Lyubashevsky, V., Pöppelmann, T.: Practical lattice-based cryptography: a signature scheme for embedded systems. In: Prouff, E., Schaumont, P. (eds.) CHES 2012. LNCS, vol. 7428, pp. 530–547. Springer, Heidelberg (2012). doi:10.1007/978-3-642-33027-8_31

28. Guo, Q., Johansson, T., Stankovski, P.: Coded-BKW: solving LWE using lattice codes. In: Gennaro, R., Robshaw, M. (eds.) CRYPTO 2015. LNCS, vol. 9215, pp. 23–42. Springer, Heidelberg (2015). doi:10.1007/978-3-662-47989-6_2

29. Hanrot, G., Pujol, X., Stehlé, D.: Analyzing blockwise lattice algorithms using dynamical systems. In: Rogaway, P. (ed.) CRYPTO 2011. LNCS, vol. 6841, pp. 447–464. Springer, Heidelberg (2011). doi:10.1007/978-3-642-22792-9_25

30. Chen, H., Lauter, K., Stange, K.E.: Attacks on search RLWE. Cryptology ePrint Archive, Report 2015/971 (2015). http://eprint.iacr.org/2015/971

31. Chen, H., Lauter, K., Stange, K.E.: Vulnerable galois rlwe families and improved attacks. Cryptology ePrint Archive, Report 2016/193 (2016). http://eprint.iacr.org/2016/193

32. Buhler, J.P. (ed.): ANTS 1998. LNCS, vol. 1423. Springer, Heidelberg (1998)

33. Kirchner, P., Fouque, P.-A.: An improved BKW algorithm for LWE with applications to cryptography and lattices. In: Gennaro, R., Robshaw, M. (eds.) CRYPTO 2015. LNCS, vol. 9215, pp. 43–62. Springer, Heidelberg (2015). doi:10.1007/978-3-662-47989-6_3

34. Laarhoven, T.: Search problems in cryptography, Ph.D. thesis, Eindhoven University of Technology (2015). http://www.thijs.com/docs/phd-final.pdf.8

35. Laarhoven, T.: Sieving for closest lattice vectors (with preprocessing). arXiv preprint (2016). arXiv:1607.04789

36. Liu, Z., Seo, H., Sinha Roy, S., Großschädl, J., Kim, H., Verbauwhede, I.: Efficient ring-LWE encryption on 8-Bit AVR processors. In: Güneysu, T., Handschuh, H. (eds.) CHES 2015. LNCS, vol. 9293, pp. 663–682. Springer, Heidelberg (2015). doi:10.1007/978-3-662-48324-4_33

37. Lyubashevsky, V., Peikert, C., Regev, O.: On ideal lattices and learning with errors over rings. In: Gilbert, H. (ed.) EUROCRYPT 2010. LNCS, vol. 6110, pp. 1–23. Springer, Heidelberg (2010). doi:10.1007/978-3-642-13190-5_1

38. Lyubashevsky, V., Peikert, C., Regev, O.: A toolkit for ring-LWE cryptography. In: Johansson, T., Nguyen, P.Q. (eds.) EUROCRYPT 2013. LNCS, vol. 7881, pp. 35–54. Springer, Heidelberg (2013). doi:10.1007/978-3-642-38348-9_3

39. Albrecht, M., Bai, S., Ducas, L.: A subfield lattice attack on overstretched NTRU assumptions: cryptanalysis of some FHE and graded encoding schemes. Cryptology ePrint Archive, Report 2016/127 (2016). http://eprint.iacr.org/2016/127

40. Micciancio, D., Peikert, C.: Trapdoors for lattices: simpler, tighter, faster, smaller. In: Pointcheval, D., Johansson, T. (eds.) EUROCRYPT 2012. LNCS, vol. 7237, pp. 700–718. Springer, Heidelberg (2012). doi:10.1007/978-3-642-29011-4_41

41. NIST. Technical report (2015). http://www.nist.gov/itl/csd/ct/post-quantum-crypto-workshop-2015.cfm

42. NSA. Cryptography today. Technical report (2015). https://www.nsa.gov/ia/programs/suitebcryptography/, Also at: https://www.iad.gov/iad/programs/iad-initiatives/cnsa-suite.cfm

43. Peikert, C.: Lattice cryptography for the internet. In: Mosca, M. (ed.) PQCrypto 2014. LNCS, vol. 8772, pp. 197–219. Springer, Heidelberg (2014). doi:10.1007/978-3-319-11659-4_12
44. Peikert, C., et al.: Decade of Lattice Cryptography. World Scientific, Singapore (2016)
45. Peikert, C., Waters, B.: Lossy trapdoor functions and their applications. SIAM J. Comput. **40**(6), 1803–1844 (2011)
46. Regev, O.: On lattices, learning with errors, random linear codes, and cryptography. In: Proceedings of the thirty-seventh annual ACM symposium on Theory of computing, ACM, pp. 84–93 (2005)
47. Regev, O.: On lattices, learning with errors, random linear codes, and cryptography. J. ACM (JACM) **56**(6), 34 (2009)
48. Lindner, R., Peikert, C.: Better key sizes (and attacks) for LWE-based encryption. In: Kiayias, A. (ed.) CT-RSA 2011. LNCS, vol. 6558, pp. 319–339. Springer, Heidelberg (2011). doi:10.1007/978-3-642-19074-2_21
49. Roy, S.S., Vercauteren, F., Mentens, N., Chen, D.D., Verbauwhede, I.: Compact ring-LWE cryptoprocessor. In: Batina, L., Robshaw, M. (eds.) CHES 2014. LNCS, vol. 8731, pp. 371–391. Springer, Heidelberg (2014). doi:10.1007/978-3-662-44709-3_21
50. Schnorr, C.P.: Lattice reduction by random sampling and birthday methods. In: Alt, H., Habib, M. (eds.) STACS 2003. LNCS, vol. 2607, pp. 145–156. Springer, Heidelberg (2003). doi:10.1007/3-540-36494-3_14
51. Singh, V.: A practical key exchange for the internet using lattice cryptography. IACR Cryptology ePrint Archive, p. 138 (2015)
52. Targhi, E.E., Unruh, D.: Quantum security of the fujisaki-okamoto transform. Technical report (2015)

Analysis of Error Terms of Signatures Based on Learning with Errors

Jeongsu Kim[1(✉)], Suyong Park[1], Seonggeun Kim[1], Busik Jang[1],
Sang Geun Hahn[1], Sangim Jung[2], and Dongyoung Roh[2]

[1] Department of Mathematical Sciences,
Korea Advanced Institute of Science and Technology, Daejeon, Republic of Korea
`jskorea21@kaist.ac.kr`
[2] National security research institute, Daejeon, Republic of Korea

Abstract. Lyubashevsky proposed a lattice-based digital signature scheme based on short integer solution (SIS) problem without using trapdoor matrices [12]. Bai and Galbraith showed that the hard problem in Lyubashevsky's scheme can be changed from SIS to SIS and learning with errors (LWE) [4]. Using this change, they could compress the signatures. But Bai and Galbraith's scheme had some additional rejection processes on its algorithms. These rejection processes decreased the acceptance rate of the signing algorithm. We showed mathematically that the rejection process in key generation algorithm of [4] is not necessary. Using this fact, we suggested a scheme modified from [4]'s scheme, and doubled the acceptance rate of the signing algorithm. Furthermore, our implementation results show that our scheme is two times faster than that of [4] on similar parameter settings.

Keywords: Lattice · Digital signature · Learning with errors · LWE · Discrete random variable · Discrete Gaussian distribution

1 Introduction

Lattice-based cryptography is one of the most attractive research area in post-quantum cryptography. Unlike any other post-quantum cryptography candidates, it has a worst-case/average-case reduction which was shown on the seminal work of Ajtai [1]. This feature gives lattice-based cryptography a firm theoretical background. Moreover, some lattice problems, such as SIS and LWE, are not solved efficiently yet both quantumly and classically. Therefore, they are considered as hard problems even in post-quantum settings.

Based on the hard lattice problems, several digital signatures have been proposed. Ajtai and Dwork [2] proposed the first provably secure cryptosystem based on the worst-case/average-case reduction, but the size of public keys were too big to be practical. Digital signature schemes such as GGH scheme [9] or

---

S. Jung and D. Roh—National Security Research Institute, Republic of Korea.

S. Hong and J.H. Park (Eds.): ICISC 2016, LNCS 10157, pp. 75–97, 2017.
DOI: 10.1007/978-3-319-53177-9_4

NTRUSign [10] were continuously broken and repaired because of the lack of mathematical security proof.

Lyubashevsky constructed [11] a provably secure lattice-based identification scheme based on the ideal-lattice problem. Moreover, he extended this result to make a provably secure digital signature scheme based on the general lattice problem, SIS, under Fiat-Shamir paradigm [12]. His signature schemes yield signature sizes ranging from 16,500 bits to 163,000 bits up to settings.

Bai and Galbraith modified Lyubashevsky's algorithms of [12] to show that the size of signatures can be decreased to around 11,000 bits [4]. This could be done because their cryptosystem is based on both SIS and LWE problems not only on SIS problem. This change yields a choice for more smaller standard deviation σ which has great influence on the size of the signature. But the scheme of [4] additionally requires some rejection processes on key generation algorithm and signing algorithm. The acceptance rate of the signing algorithm of [4] decreased to 40% of that of [12] due to additional rejection process on the signing algorithm.

Before we present our contribution, we review some brief notations and concepts of previous works. In [12], the secret key is a matrix $\mathbf{S} \in \mathbb{Z}^{n \times k}$, and the public key is a matrix pair $(\mathbf{A} \in \mathbb{Z}_q^{m \times n}, \mathbf{T} = \mathbf{AS})$. For a vector $\mathbf{y} \in \mathbb{Z}^{n \times 1}$, the signing algorithm of [12] computes $\mathbf{z} = \mathbf{Sc} + \mathbf{y}$ and outputs $(\mathbf{z}, \mathbf{c})$ as a signature where $\mathbf{c}$ is a length k vector of weight w with entries in $\{-1, 0, 1\}$. The verification procedure of [12] checks whether $\mathbf{Ay} = \mathbf{Az} - \mathbf{Tc}$ or not. In [4], the public key is a matrix pair $(\mathbf{A}, \mathbf{T} = \mathbf{AS} + \mathbf{E})$, and the verification algorithm checks whether $\lfloor \mathbf{Ay} \mod q \rceil_d$ and $\lfloor \mathbf{Az} - \mathbf{Tc} = \mathbf{Ay} - \mathbf{Ec} \mod q \rceil_d$ are the same ($\lfloor \mathbf{v} \rceil_d = \lfloor \mathbf{w} \rceil_d$ means that the each entry of $\mathbf{v}$ and $\mathbf{w}$ are the same except for d-least significant bits). In order to make this verification works for almost all of the signatures the signing algorithm outputs, the authors of [4] inserted some rejection processes on the key generation algorithm and the signing algorithm. First, the key generation algorithm of [4] outputs public key pairs $(\mathbf{A}, \mathbf{T} = \mathbf{AS} + \mathbf{E})$ when every entry of $\mathbf{E}$ lies in $[-\lambda\sigma, \lambda\sigma]$ where $\lambda = 7$ and σ is the standard deviation of each entry of $\mathbf{E}$. Second, the signing algorithm of [4] outputs a signature according to some conditions associated with $\lambda w \sigma$, a bound of $\|\mathbf{Ec}\|_\infty$, to satisfy $\lfloor \mathbf{Ay} \mod q \rceil_d = \lfloor \mathbf{Az} - \mathbf{Tc} = \mathbf{Ay} - \mathbf{Ec} \mod q \rceil_d$.

From the signing algorithm of [4], one can know that λ, the bounding constant of $\mathbf{E}$, should be reduced in order to have higher acceptance rate of the signing algorithm. However, we found that if λ in [4] is smaller than 4.5, then the acceptance rate of the key generation algorithm becomes less than 10%. Therefore, there should be some modification on the key generation algorithm to make λ less than 4.5.

Our Contribution. We focused on the fact that the verification algorithm of [4] checks if $\lfloor \mathbf{Ay} \mod q \rceil_d = \lfloor \mathbf{Az} - \mathbf{Tc} = \mathbf{Ay} - \mathbf{Ec} \mod q \rceil_d$. Since the sizes of the entries of $\mathbf{Ec}$ is important to make the verification works, we analyzed the size of $\|\mathbf{Ec}\|_\infty$ instead of $\|\mathbf{E}\|_\infty$. Using analysis in Sect. 3.2, we concluded that the rejection process of the key generation algorithm of [4] is not needed. Therefore, the key generation algorithm of our suggested scheme does not have the rejection process. This change allows λ to be lower than 4.5, and thus yields the higher acceptance rate of signing algorithm ($\lambda = 2.52$ on our parameter sets). From our parameter settings, we noticed that our scheme can have two times better acceptance rate of signing algorithm and similar sizes of the keys and the signature compared to [4]. Furthermore, to compare our scheme and [4] properly, we implemented both our scheme and the scheme of [4]. On similar parameter settings, we could see that our signing scheme is two times faster than that of [4].

In addition, we pointed out that the signing algorithm of [4] should be slightly modified in order not to have carry or borrow problem. Because of this modification, the acceptance rate of signing algorithm of [4] should be a little bit lower than authors of [4] have expected. This modification is presented on the Line 7 of Algorithm 2.

Road Map. This paper is organized as follows: In Sect. 2, we give some notations and information to understand this paper. In Sect. 3, we introduce our signature scheme and analysis that supports our scheme. We also give actual parameters of our scheme at the end of Sect. 3. We provide benchmark results of our signature scheme in Sect. 4. In Sect. 5, we represent an interpretation of our result.

2 Preliminaries

Since our scheme is almost the same as [4], most parts of this section are the same as the Sect. 2 of [4].

2.1 Basic Notation

For a prime number $q \in \mathbb{N}$, we let $\mathbb{Z}_q$ be the set of integers modulo q in range $(-q/2, q/2]$. We write vectors in bold face lower case as $\mathbf{v} = (v_1, \cdots, v_n)^T$, and matrices in bold face upper case as $\mathbf{A}$. For a vector $\mathbf{w}$, we define $(\mathbf{w})_i$ to be the i-th coordinate of $\mathbf{w}$. The infinity norm is $\|\mathbf{v}\|_\infty = \max\limits_{1 \leq i \leq n} |v_i|$.

For $a \in \mathbb{Z}$ and $d \in \mathbb{N}$, define $[a]_{2^d}$ to be the unique remainder in $(-2^{d-1}, 2^{d-1}]$ such that $a \equiv [a]_{2^d} \pmod{2^d}$. Also, we define $\lfloor a \rfloor_d := (a - [a]_{2^d})/2^d$ (eliminate the d-least significant bits). Define $\lfloor \mathbf{v} \rfloor_d := (\lfloor v_1 \rfloor_d, \cdots, \lfloor v_m \rfloor_d)^T$ where $\mathbf{v} = (v_1, \cdots, v_m)^T \in \mathbb{Z}^m$. If a is sampled uniformly from a finite set A, then we write $a \leftarrow A$. Also, if each entry of $m \times n$ matrix $\mathbf{A}$ is sampled uniformly from $\mathbb{Z}_q$, then we write $\mathbf{A} \leftarrow \mathbb{Z}_q^{m \times n}$.

2.2 Discrete Gaussian Random Variable

For $\sigma \in \mathbb{R}_{>0}$, define $\rho_{\mu,\sigma}(x) := \exp(-(x-\mu)^2/(2\sigma^2))$ and $\rho_{\mu,\sigma}(\mathbb{Z}) := \sum_{x=-\infty}^{\infty} \rho_{\mu,\sigma}(x)$. The discrete Gaussian distribution on $\mathbb{Z}$ with mean μ and standard deviation σ is the distribution with probability density function (pdf)

$f_{\mu,\sigma}(x) := \rho_{\mu,\sigma}(x)/\rho_{\mu,\sigma}(\mathbb{Z})$ where $x \in \mathbb{Z}$. We denote this distribution $D_{\mu,\sigma}$. If it does not make any confusion, we write $\rho_\sigma(x) := \rho_{0,\sigma}(x)$, $f_\sigma(x) := f_{0,\sigma}(x)$, and $D_\sigma := D_{0,\sigma}$. If each entry of $\mathbf{y} = (y_1, \cdots, y_n)^T \in \mathbb{Z}^n$ is independently sampled from the distribution D_σ, we write $\mathbf{y} \leftarrow D_\sigma^n$.

Remark 1. If the error terms of LWE problem are sampled from discrete Gaussian distribution with mean 0, it is very convenient to bound the errors using its standard deviation. Our scheme and the scheme in [4] use this property to bound the error terms.

2.3 Hard Problems

Definition 1. *Let $n, q \in \mathbb{N}$ and let χ and ϕ be distributions on $\mathbb{Z}$. The LWE distribution for a given vector $\mathbf{s} \in \mathbb{Z}_q^n$ is the set of pairs $(\mathbf{a}, \mathbf{a} \cdot \mathbf{s} + e)$ (mod q) where $\mathbf{a} \in \mathbb{Z}_q^n$ is sampled uniformly and where e is sampled from ϕ.*

- *The computational-LWE problem is: For a vector $\mathbf{s} \leftarrow \chi^n$ and given arbitrarily many samples from the LWE distribution for $\mathbf{s}$, to compute $\mathbf{s}$.*
- *The decisional-LWE problem is: Given arbitrarily many samples from $\mathbb{Z}_q^{n+1}$ to distinguish whether the samples are distributed uniformly or whether they are distributed as the LWE distribution for some fixed vectors $\mathbf{s} \leftarrow \chi^n$.*

(n, q, ϕ)-LWE means the computational LWE problem with parameters (n, q, ϕ). Also, (n, q, α)-LWE means that $\phi = D_{\alpha q}$. From Regev [14], it is known that computational-LWE problem can be reduced to decisional-LWE problem. Therefore, if one of the problems is hard, then so is the other. Also, from [14], we know that the LWE problems are as hard as the worst-case assumptions in general lattice when χ is a uniform distribution and when ϕ is a discrete Gaussian distribution with mean 0 and standard deviation αq for some fixed real number $0 < \alpha < 1$

Regev's Reduction [14]. Let $n, q \in \mathbb{N}$ and $0 < \alpha < 1$ be such that $\alpha q \geq 2\sqrt{n}$. Then there exists a quantum reduction from worst-case GapSVP$_{\tilde{O}(n/\alpha)}$ to (n, q, α)−LWE.

In this paper, we use the matrix variant of LWE, whose LWE distribution is defined as the pairs $(\mathbf{A}, \mathbf{AS} + \mathbf{E}$ (mod q)) where $\mathbf{S}$ and $\mathbf{E}$ are matrices. One can see that this matrix variant of LWE cannot be easier than general LWE [4]. In this paper, we set $\chi = \phi = D_\sigma$ where $\sigma = \alpha q > 2\sqrt{n}$

Remark 2. From [3], it is known that there is a reduction from general LWE problem to LWE problem with $\chi = \phi$.

Short Integer Solution (SIS) Problem asks to find nonzero small $\mathbf{s}$ such that $\mathbf{As} \equiv \mathbf{0}$ (mod q) for a given matrix $\mathbf{A} \in \mathbb{Z}_q^{m \times n}$. Ajtai's work shows that if we can solve SIS problem on average case, we can solve another lattice problems on worst case. Therefore SIS problems is also considered as a hard lattice problem.

2.4   Rejection Sampling

We need to make sure that the signatures do not leak the information of the private key. To achieve this, we use the rejection sampling lemma of [12].

Rejection Sampling Lemma (Sect. 4 of [12]). Let $f : \mathbb{Z}^n \to \mathbb{R}$ be a probability distribution. Given a subset $V \subseteq \mathbb{Z}^n$, let $h : V \to \mathbb{R}$ be a probability distribution defined on V. Let $g_\mathbf{v} : \mathbb{Z}^n \to \mathbb{R}$ be a family of probability distributions indexed by $\mathbf{v} \in V$ such that for almost all $\mathbf{v}$'s from h there exists a universal upper bound $M \in \mathbb{R}$ such that

$$\Pr[Mg_\mathbf{v}(z); z \leftarrow f] \geq 1 - negligible$$

Then the output distributions of the following two algorithms have negligible statistical difference:

1. $\mathbf{v} \leftarrow h, \mathbf{z} \leftarrow g_\mathbf{v}$, output $(\mathbf{z}, \mathbf{v})$ with probability $\min\left(\frac{f(\mathbf{z})}{Mg_\mathbf{v}(\mathbf{z})}, 1\right)$, else fail
2. $\mathbf{v} \leftarrow h, \mathbf{z} \leftarrow f$, output $(\mathbf{z}, \mathbf{v})$ with probability $\frac{1}{M}$

Remark 3. On our scheme, $\mathbf{z} = \mathbf{S}\mathbf{c} + \mathbf{y}$ where $\mathbf{S}\mathbf{c}$ is close to the discrete Gaussian distribution with mean 0 and standard deviation $\sigma_{\mathbf{S}\mathbf{c}}$ and $\mathbf{y} \leftarrow [-B, B]^n$. Also, f is a distribution function of the uniform distribution on $[-(B-U), B-U]^n$ for some constants n, B and $U = 14\sigma_{\mathbf{S}\mathbf{c}}$.

3   Our Scheme

3.1   Algorithms

We first introduce our signature scheme. Our algorithm is basically the same as [4] with some slight changes. Unlike [4], our Algorithm 1 does not have a rejection process on keys. Also, there's a correction on the Line 7 of Algorithm 2 of [4]. We will give an analysis of Algorithm 1 in Sect. 3.2, and the correction of the Line 7 of Algorithm 2 of [4] in this section.

Algorithm 1. Key generation

INPUT : n, m, k, q, σ
OUTPUT : $\mathbf{A}, \mathbf{T}$

1: $\mathbf{A} \leftarrow \mathbb{Z}_q^{m \times n}$
2: $\mathbf{S} \leftarrow D_\sigma^{n \times k}$
3: $\mathbf{E} \leftarrow D_\sigma^{m \times k}$
4: $\mathbf{T} \equiv \mathbf{A}\mathbf{S} + \mathbf{E} \pmod{q}$
5: **return** $\mathbf{A}, \mathbf{T}$

Algorithm 2. Signing

INPUT : $\mu, \mathbf{A}, \mathbf{T}, \mathbf{S}, B, U, H, F, L, M$

OUTPUT : $(\mathbf{z}, c)$

1: $\mathbf{y} \leftarrow [-B, B]^n$
2: $\mathbf{v} \equiv \mathbf{A}\mathbf{y} \pmod{q}$
3: $c = H(\lfloor \mathbf{v} \rceil_d, \mu)$
4: $\mathbf{c} = F(c)$
5: $\mathbf{z} = \mathbf{S}\mathbf{c} + \mathbf{y}$
6: $\mathbf{w} \equiv \mathbf{A}\mathbf{z} - \mathbf{T}\mathbf{c} \pmod{q}$
7: **if** $\left| [w_i]_{2^d} \right| > 2^{d-1} - L$ or $|w_i| > q/2 - L$ **then**
8:     Restart
9: **end if**
10: **return** $(\mathbf{z}, c)$ with probability $\min(g_z^n(\mathbf{z})/(M \cdot g_{y,\mathbf{S}\mathbf{c}}^n(\mathbf{z})), 1)$

Algorithm 3. Verifying

INPUT : $\mu, \mathbf{z}, c, \mathbf{A}, \mathbf{T}, B, U, d, H, F$

OUTPUT : Accept or Reject

1: $\mathbf{c} = F(c)$
2: $\mathbf{w} \equiv \mathbf{A}\mathbf{z} - \mathbf{T}\mathbf{c} \pmod{q}$
3: $c' = H(\lfloor \mathbf{w} \rceil_d, \mu)$
4: **if** $c' = c$ and $\|\mathbf{z}\|_\infty \leq B - U$ **then**
5:     **return** "Accept"
6: **else**
7:     **return** "Reject"
8: **end if**

We give brief details of the parameters and the functions above. On our parameter setting, we let $k = n$ and $L = \lambda w \sigma$ for some $\lambda \in \mathbb{R}$. The hash function H outputs a binary string of length κ. The function F maps binary strings of length κ to elements of the set $\mathcal{B}_{k,w}$ of length k vectors of weight w with entries in $\{-1, 0, 1\}$. We want F to be close to injection in the sense that

$$\Pr_{s_1, s_2, \leftarrow \{0,1\}^\kappa}(F(s_1) = F(s_2)) \leq \frac{c_1}{2^\kappa}$$

for some constant c_1. We choose parameters so that $2^\kappa \approx \#\mathcal{B}_{k,w} = 2^w \binom{k}{w}$. From the construction of F, $\mathbf{c}$ is a length k vector of weight w with entries in $\{-1, 0, 1\}$. One of the methods of constructing F is given in Sect. 4.4 of [8].

The rejection sampling process on the Line 10 of Algorithm 2 needs the distribution functions $g_{y,\mathbf{S}\mathbf{c}}$, g_z and the constant M. $g_{y,\mathbf{S}\mathbf{c}}$ is the distribution function of the original distribution of $\mathbf{z}$, which is the uniform distribution on $[-B, B]^n$ shifted by $\mathbf{S}\mathbf{c}$. g_z is the distribution function of our target distribution of rejection sampling process, which is the uniform distribution on $[-(B - U), B - U]^n$.

We let $U = 14\sqrt{w}\sigma$ to make sure that the target distribution is contained in the original distribution, and $B = Un = 14\sqrt{w}\sigma n$ to make sure that M is small (we will give some details of U on the Sect. 3.4). From the given distributions, we can calculate M using the following equation:

$$\frac{1}{M} = \left(\frac{2(B - U) + 1}{2B + 1}\right)^n = \left(\frac{2 \cdot 14\sqrt{w}\sigma(n - 1) + 1}{2 \cdot 14\sqrt{w}\sigma n + 1}\right)^n \approx \left(1 - \frac{1}{n}\right)^n \approx \frac{1}{e}.$$

Verifier accepts a signature when $\mathbf{z}$ is from the target distribution $[-(B - U),$ $B - U]^n$ and $H(\lfloor \mathbf{v} \rceil_d, \mu) = H(\lfloor \mathbf{w} \rceil_d, \mu)$. Since Algorithm 2 outputs the signature after the rejection sampling process, $\mathbf{z} \in [-(B - U), B - U]^n$ almost surely. The condition $H(\lfloor \mathbf{v} \rceil_d, \mu) = H(\lfloor \mathbf{w} \rceil_d, \mu)$ holds when $\lfloor \mathbf{v} \rceil_d = \lfloor \mathbf{w} \rceil_d$. Therefore, we check whether $\lfloor \mathbf{v} \rceil_d = \lfloor \mathbf{w} \rceil_d$ holds or not on the Line 7 of Algorithm 2. Note that

$$\mathbf{w} + \mathbf{Ec} \equiv \mathbf{Az} - \mathbf{Tc} + \mathbf{Ec} \equiv \mathbf{ASc} + \mathbf{Ay} - \mathbf{ASc} - \mathbf{Ec} + \mathbf{Ec} \equiv \mathbf{Ay} \quad (\text{mod } q)$$
$$\equiv \mathbf{v} \quad (\text{mod } q).$$

From Sect. 3.2, we can assume that $\|\mathbf{Ec}\|_\infty \leq L$. To make $\lfloor \mathbf{v} \rceil_d = \lfloor \mathbf{w} \rceil_d$, we need two conditions. From

$$\lfloor \mathbf{v} \rceil_d = \lfloor \mathbf{w} \rceil_d$$
$$\Leftrightarrow \lfloor \mathbf{w} + \mathbf{Ec} \mod q \rceil_d = \lfloor \mathbf{w} \rceil_d$$
$$\Leftrightarrow (\mathbf{w} + \mathbf{Ec} \mod q) - [\mathbf{w} + \mathbf{Ec} \mod q]_{2^d} = \mathbf{w} - [\mathbf{w}]_{2^d}$$
$$\Leftrightarrow (\mathbf{w} + \mathbf{Ec} \mod q) - \mathbf{w} = [\mathbf{w} + \mathbf{Ec} \mod q]_{2^d} - [\mathbf{w}]_{2^d},$$

we expect that two following equations hold; $(\mathbf{w} + \mathbf{Ec} \mod q) = \mathbf{w} + \mathbf{Ec}$ and $[\mathbf{w} + \mathbf{Ec} \mod q]_{2^d} = [\mathbf{w}]_{2^d} + \mathbf{Ec}$. Because the two conditions have the similar nature (one is considered in $\mathbb{Z}_q$ and the other is done in $\mathbb{Z}_{2^d}$), we will focus on the first condition. To make $(\mathbf{w} + \mathbf{Ec} \mod q) = \mathbf{w} + \mathbf{Ec}$, we expect any entries of $\mathbf{w}$ not to be too close to either $-q/2$ or $q/2$, i.e., all the entries of $\mathbf{w}$ must be in $\left(-\frac{q}{2} + L, \frac{q}{2} - L\right)$. This is because the first condition can be satisfied if either carry or borrow does not occur during the addition and subtraction. More precisely, it could be the case that $(\mathbf{w})_i = ((\mathbf{w} + \mathbf{Ec})_i \pmod{q}) - (\mathbf{Ec})_i \pm q$ when $(\mathbf{w})_i \in \left(-\frac{q}{2}, -\frac{q}{2} + L\right] \cup \left[\frac{q}{2} - L, \frac{q}{2}\right]$. However, it seems the authors of [4] or [7] assumed the first equation always hold, even though they already knew that the second condition does not hold always. Note that the second equation is guaranteed by rejection process in Line 7 of Algorithm 2 of [4, 7]. Therefore we point out that the rejection process must be fixed to make sure that the first condition always holds.

Assuming that $\mathbf{w}$ is distributed close to uniformly, the acceptance rate of Line 7 of Algorithm 2 is

$$\left(1 - \frac{2L}{2^d}\right)^m \left(1 - \frac{2L}{q}\right)^m = \left(1 - \frac{2\lambda w\sigma}{2^d}\right)^m \left(1 - \frac{2\lambda w\sigma}{q}\right)^m.$$

Compared to [4] ($\lambda = 7$), we let $\lambda = 2.52$ and therefore, we can expect the increase of the acceptance rate of the signature. On our parameter setting, the acceptance rate of Line 7 of Algorithm 2 varies from 0.676 to 0.937 while the acceptance rate of Line 7 of Algorithm 2 of [4] varies from 0.371 to 0.406.

The main difference between our algorithms and algorithms in [4] is the key generation algorithm. While we do not have a rejection process on the key generation algorithm, the key generation algorithm on [4] rejects the keys if at least one element of $\mathbf{E}$ is greater than the bound $\lambda\sigma$. This rejection algorithm allows the every entry of $\mathbf{Ec}$ to lie in $[-L, L]$ where $L = \lambda w\sigma$ ($\lambda = 7$ in [4]).

3.2   Analysis of Error Terms

Our main purpose is to remove the rejection algorithm of the keys on the scheme of [4] and to bound $\|\mathbf{Ec}\|_\infty \leq L$ where $L = \lambda w\sigma$ for some $\lambda < 7$. Note that the signature only requires a bound of $\|\mathbf{Ec}\|_\infty$ for some arbitrary $\mathbf{c} \in \mathcal{B}_{n,w}$. Therefore, in order to prove that the rejection algorithm of the keys is not needed, we need to check that the probability

$$p := \Pr\left[\mathbf{E} \leftarrow D_\sigma^{m \times n}, \mathbf{c} \leftarrow \mathcal{B}_{n,w} : \|\mathbf{Ec}\|_\infty \leq L\right]$$

is big enough so that $1 - p$ is negligible.

Since every entry of $\mathbf{E}$ can be seen as a random variable, if we let $X_1, \cdots, X_w$ be independent and identically distributed (iid) discrete Gaussian random variables with mean 0 and standard deviation σ, we can write p as

$$p = \Pr\left[|c_1 X_1 + \cdots + c_w X_w| \leq L\right]^m$$

where c_i's are nonzero entries of $\mathbf{c}$ in different coordinates. If we let $X'_w := c_w X_w$, then $X'_1, \cdots, X'_w$ are also iid discrete Gaussian random variables with mean 0 and standard deviation σ and

$$p = \Pr\left[|X'_1 + \cdots + X'_w| \leq L\right]^m.$$

Therefore, it is important to know the distribution of sum of iid discrete Gaussian random variables.

Theorem 1. *Let X and Y be independent random variables such that $X \sim D_{\mu_X, \sigma_X}$ and $Y \sim D_{\mu_Y, \sigma_Y}$. If we let $Z = X + Y$, then we can write the distribution function f_Z of Z as*

$$f_Z(z) = c_{X,Y}(z) f_{\mu_X + \mu_Y, \sqrt{\sigma_X^2 + \sigma_Y^2}}(z)$$

where $c_{X,Y}(z) \approx 1$

Proof. Consider

$$f_Z(z) = \sum_{x=-\infty}^{\infty} f_{\mu_X,\sigma_X}(x) f_{\mu_Y,\sigma_Y}(z-x)$$

$$= \frac{1}{\rho_{\mu_X,\sigma_X}(\mathbb{Z})\rho_{\mu_Y,\sigma_Y}(\mathbb{Z})} \sum_{x=-\infty}^{\infty} \exp\left(-\frac{(x-\mu_X)^2}{2\sigma_X^2}\right) \exp\left(-\frac{(z-x-\mu_Y)^2}{2\sigma_Y^2}\right)$$

$$= \frac{\exp\left(-\frac{(z-(\mu_X+\mu_Y))^2}{2(\sigma_X^2+\sigma_Y^2)}\right)}{\rho_{\mu_X,\sigma_X}(\mathbb{Z})\rho_{\mu_Y,\sigma_Y}(\mathbb{Z})} \sum_{x=-\infty}^{\infty} \exp\left(-\frac{\left(x-\frac{\sigma_X^2(z-\mu_Y)+\sigma_Y^2\mu_X}{\sigma_X^2+\sigma_Y^2}\right)^2}{2\left(\frac{\sigma_X\sigma_Y}{\sqrt{\sigma_X^2+\sigma_Y^2}}\right)^2}\right)$$

$$= \frac{\rho_{\frac{\sigma_X^2(z-\mu_Y)+\sigma_Y^2\mu_X}{\sigma_X^2+\sigma_Y^2},\frac{\sigma_X\sigma_Y}{\sqrt{\sigma_X^2+\sigma_Y^2}}}(\mathbb{Z})\rho_{\mu_X+\mu_Y,\sqrt{\sigma_X^2+\sigma_Y^2}}(\mathbb{Z})}{\rho_{\mu_X,\sigma_X}(\mathbb{Z})\rho_{\mu_Y,\sigma_Y}(\mathbb{Z})} f_{\mu_X+\mu_Y,\sqrt{\sigma_X^2+\sigma_Y^2}}(z)$$

$$= c_{X,Y}(z) f_{\mu_X+\mu_Y,\sqrt{\sigma_X^2+\sigma_Y^2}}(z)$$

where

$$c_{X,Y}(z) := \frac{\rho_{\frac{\sigma_X^2(z-\mu_Y)+\sigma_Y^2\mu_X}{\sigma_X^2+\sigma_Y^2},\frac{\sigma_X\sigma_Y}{\sqrt{\sigma_X^2+\sigma_Y^2}}}(\mathbb{Z})\rho_{\mu_X+\mu_Y,\sqrt{\sigma_X^2+\sigma_Y^2}}(\mathbb{Z})}{\rho_{\mu_X,\sigma_X}(\mathbb{Z})\rho_{\mu_Y,\sigma_Y}(\mathbb{Z})}.$$

Since $\frac{1}{\sqrt{2\pi}\sigma}\rho_{\mu,\sigma}(\mathbb{Z})$ is a Riemann approximation of 1, we can know that $c_{X,Y}(z)$ is approximately 1 □

If we let $\mu_X = \mu_Y = 0$, $\sigma_X = \sigma$ and $\sigma_Y = \sqrt{k}\sigma$ for some $k \in \mathbb{N}$, then $c_{X,Y}(z)$ becomes periodic with respect to z with period $k+1$. Therefore, there exist $u_k := \max_z\{c_{X,Y}(z)\}$ and $l_k := \min_z\{c_{X,Y}(z)\}$. We can bound the distribution function $f_{\mathbf{Ec}}$ of each entry of $\mathbf{Ec}$ as

$$l_1 \cdots l_{w-1} f_{\sqrt{w}\sigma}(z) \leq f_{\mathbf{Ec}}(z) \leq u_1 \cdots u_{w-1} f_{\sqrt{w}\sigma}(z).$$

By computation, we could not tell any differences between l_i and 1 (or u_i and 1) on 50-digit precision. Therefore, we can say that the distribution function of each entry of $\mathbf{Ec}$ is almost the same as the distribution function of a discrete Gaussian random variables with mean 0 and standard deviation $\sqrt{w}\sigma$. If we let $Z_w \sim D_{\sqrt{w}\sigma}$, then we can estimate p as

$$p \approx \Pr\left[|Z_w| \leq L\right]^m,$$

and $1 - p \leq 2^{-77}$ for our parameters. Therefore, $\|\mathbf{Ec}\|_\infty$ is sufficiently small without any restriction on the error terms.

Even when $|(\mathbf{Ec})_i|$ exceeds L, if corresponding coordinate $|(\mathbf{w})_i|$ is small, the signature can be accepted in verification. More precisely, we can write

$$
\begin{aligned}
&\Pr\left[\lfloor \mathbf{v} \rceil_d \neq \lfloor \mathbf{w} \rceil_d\right] \\
&= \Pr\left[(\mathbf{w} + \mathbf{Ec} \pmod q)) \neq \mathbf{w} + \mathbf{Ec} \text{ or } [\mathbf{w} + \mathbf{Ec} \pmod q)]_{2^d} \neq [\mathbf{w}]_{2^d} + \mathbf{Ec}\right] \\
&\leq \sum_{i=1}^{m} \Pr\left[|(\mathbf{w} + \mathbf{Ec})_i| \geq \frac{q}{2}\right] + \sum_{i=1}^{m} \Pr\left[|([\mathbf{w}]_{2^d} + \mathbf{Ec})_i| \geq 2^{d-1}\right] \\
&= m\left(\Pr\left[|(\mathbf{w} + \mathbf{Ec})_1| \geq \frac{q}{2}\right] + \Pr\left[|([\mathbf{w}]_{2^d} + \mathbf{Ec})_1| \geq 2^{d-1}\right]\right) \\
&\leq 2m \sum_{j=0}^{2^{d-1}-L} \Pr\left[(\mathbf{Ec})_1 = L + j\right] \Pr\left[(\mathbf{w})_1 \geq \frac{q}{2} - L - j\right] \\
&\quad + 2m \sum_{j=0}^{2^{d-1}-L} \Pr\left[(\mathbf{Ec})_1 = L + j\right] \Pr\left[([\mathbf{w}]_{2^d})_1 \geq 2^{d-1} - L - j\right] \\
&\quad + 2m \Pr\left[|(\mathbf{Ec})_1| > 2^{d-1} - L\right] \\
&\approx \frac{2m}{\rho_{\sqrt{w}\sigma}(\mathbb{Z})}\left(\frac{1}{q - 2L} + \frac{1}{2^d - 2L}\right) \sum_{j=0}^{2^{d-1}-L} (j + 1)\, e^{-\frac{(L+j)^2}{2w\sigma^2}}.
\end{aligned}
$$

We do not think of $\Pr\left[|(\mathbf{Ec})_1| > 2^{d-1} - L\right]$ since it is negligible compared to other terms. By computation, we can know that $\Pr\left[\lfloor \mathbf{v} \rceil_d \neq \lfloor \mathbf{w} \rceil_d\right] \leq 2^{-95}$. Therefore, on our parameter settings, the probability that a signature generated by Algorithm 2 is rejected in Algorithm 3 is negligible. Furthermore, we also analyzed the reusability of the error term $\mathbf{E}$ in Appendix A.

3.3   Security Proof

Since our scheme is based on [4], the security proof is the same. In this section, we will demonstrate the sketch of security proof.

Generally, security proof of digital signature is done by proving that if there is a forging algorithm, then one can solve some hard problems using this algorithm. Therefore, if we prove that forging algorithm of our scheme can solve decisional-LWE problem or search-SIS problem, we can say that our scheme is provably secure.

Theorem 2 *(Theorem 2 of [4]). Let q be a prime. Let parameters n, m, d, κ, B be such that*

$$(2B)^n q^{m-n} \geq (2^{d+1})^m 2^\kappa.$$

Let A be a forger against the signature scheme in the random oracle model that makes h hash queries, s sign queries, runs in time t and succeeds with probability δ. Then there is a negligible ϵ and some $0 \leq \delta' \leq \delta$ such that A can be turned into either of the following two algorithms:

1. *an algorithm, running in time approximately t and with advantage $\delta - \delta' - \epsilon$, that solves the (n, m, q, α)-decisional-LWE problem.*
2. *an algorithm, running in time approximately $2t$ and with success probability δ' $\left(\delta' \text{ over } h - \frac{1}{2^\kappa}\right)$, that solves the unbalanced $(m+n, m, q)$-search-SIS problem: Given an $m \times (n + m)$ matrix $\mathbf{A}'$ to find a length n vector $\mathbf{y}_1$ and a length m vector $\mathbf{y}_2$ such that $\|\mathbf{y}_1\|_\infty, \|\mathbf{y}_2\|_\infty \leq \max(2B, 2^{d-1}) + 2E'w$ and $\mathbf{A}' \left(\begin{smallmatrix} \mathbf{y}_1 \\ \mathbf{y}_2 \end{smallmatrix}\right) \equiv 0$ (mod q) where E' satisfies*

$$(2E')^{m+n} \geq q^m 2^\kappa.$$

We first define Game 0 as our scheme. Let Game 1 be similar to Game 0 but sample $\mathbf{z}$ and c uniformly on their distributions, and replace c with $H(\lfloor \mathbf{Az} - \mathbf{Tc}\rceil_d, \mu)$. From the rejection sampling theorem, we can prove that Game 0 and Game 1 are indistinguishable. Therefore, if A can forge Game 0, then it can also forge Game 1.

Security proofs using Game 1 to prove that a forger of the signature can solve search-SIS requires $(\mathbf{S}', \mathbf{E}')$ different from $(\mathbf{S}, \mathbf{E})$ such that $\mathbf{T} = \mathbf{AS} + \mathbf{E} = \mathbf{AS}' + \mathbf{E}'$. In order $(\mathbf{S}', \mathbf{E}')$ to be exist, n should be large enough, which leads large signature size [12]. To avoid this, we define Game 2 to be the same as Game 1 except for key generation. We set the key distributions of Game 2 be large enough so that there exist $(\mathbf{S}', \mathbf{E}')$ different from $(\mathbf{S}, \mathbf{E})$ satisfying $\mathbf{T} = \mathbf{AS} + \mathbf{E} = \mathbf{AS}' + \mathbf{E}'$. Since the only difference between Game 1 and Game 2 is the key generation, if one can distinguish Game 1 from Game 2, then he/she can know which Game he/she is in for given public keys $(\mathbf{A}, \mathbf{T})$ with non-negligible probability. However, this means there's an adversary who can solve decisional-LWE. Also, by construction of Game 2, if a forger can get a valid signature from Game 2, he/she can solve the search-SIS problem.

3.4 Parameter Selection

The starting point of the parameter selection is the well-definedness of LWE problem. Since the well-definedness of Computational-LWE problem is that there is unique $\mathbf{s}$ for each LWE instance $b = \mathbf{As} + \mathbf{e}$ (mod q). Therefore, the number of possible b should be greater than the number of possible $(\mathbf{s}, \mathbf{e})$. Since we assumed that $\chi = \phi$, the following must hold [4]:

$$q^m > (2E + 1)^{m+n}$$

where E is the bound of the distributions χ and ϕ which is computed as $E = 14\sigma$ ($\|\mathbf{s}\|_\infty, \|\mathbf{e}\|_\infty > E$ with very small probability). More specifically, our scheme let $\chi = \phi = D_\sigma = D_{\alpha q}$ and in order to satisfy the conditions of (n, m, α)-LWE problem, we let $\sigma = \alpha q > 2\sqrt{n}$.

On our scheme, we sample $\mathbf{y}$ from the uniform distribution on $[-B, B]^n$. Since we want $\mathbf{z} = \mathbf{Sc} + \mathbf{y}$ of a signature $(\mathbf{z}, c)$ does not leak the information about $\mathbf{S}$, we set the target distribution of rejection sampling process as uniform distribution $[-(B - U), B - U]^n$ where U is the bound of $\mathbf{Sc}$ chosen from the lemma below.

Lemma 1 *(Lemma 4.4 of [12]). For all $k > 0$, the following inequality holds:*

$$\Pr_{x \leftarrow D_\sigma}(|x| > k\sigma) \leq 2e^{-k^2/2}$$

We can say that the distribution of each entry of $\mathbf{Sc}$ has almost the same distribution function of a discrete Gaussian random variables with mean 0 and standard deviation $\sqrt{w}\sigma$ from Theorem 1. Also, from the lemma above, if $k = 14$, $|x| > k\sigma$ with probability 2^{-140}. Therefore, if we let $U = 14\sqrt{w}\sigma \approx 14\sigma_{\mathbf{Sc}}$, then the target distribution is contained in the original distribution almost surely. In other words, $[-(B - U), B - U]^n$ will be contained in the uniform distribution $[-B, B]^n$ shifted by $\mathbf{Sc}$ almost surely.

Since our rejection sampling process set $[-(B - U), B - U]^n$ to be the target distribution, $\mathbf{z}$ must satisfy $\|\mathbf{z}\|_\infty \leq B - U$ when Algorithm 2 outputs a signature $(\mathbf{z}, c)$. Therefore, in the verifying algorithm, we check that if $\mathbf{z}$ satisfies $\|\mathbf{z}\|_\infty \leq B - U$ or not.

Since the output of hash function should be uniformly distributed, we use following lemma when we select parameters.

Lemma 2 *(Lemma 3 of [4]). Suppose $m > n > \kappa$ and D_y be a the uniform distribution on $[-B, B]$. If the following inequality holds,*

$$\frac{2^{(d+1)m}/q^{m-n}}{(2B+1)^n} \leq \frac{1}{2^\kappa},$$

the number of possible values for $\lfloor \mathbf{Ay} \pmod{q} \rceil_d$ is at least 2^κ. Therefore, the probability that two values $\mathbf{y}_1, \mathbf{y}_2$ sampled uniformly from $[-B, B]^n$ give the same value is at most $1/2^\kappa$.

This lemma ensures that there are sufficiently large amount of possible choices for $\lfloor \mathbf{Ay} \rceil_d$.

We also consider the Hermite factors which is defined as $\delta = \frac{\|\mathbf{b_1}\|_\infty}{\mathrm{vol}(L)^{\frac{1}{n}}}$ where $\|\mathbf{b_1}\|$ is given by the shortest vector obtained from the algorithms such as LLL and BKZ. Hermite factor of lattices are often used for the security estimation. The Hermite factor of breaking LWE problem (or key) and SIS problem (or sign) are given by

$$\delta_{\text{key}} \approx \left(\frac{\Gamma\left(1 + \frac{m+n+1}{2}\right)^{\frac{1}{m+n+1}}}{\sqrt{\pi(m+n)}\tau\sigma} \cdot q^{\frac{m}{m+n+1}} \right)^{\frac{1}{m+n+1}}$$

and

$$\delta_{\text{sign}} \approx \left(\frac{\left(\max\left(2B, 2^{d-1}\right) + 2E'w\right)\sqrt{m+n}}{q^{\frac{m}{m+n}}} \right)^{\frac{1}{m+n}}$$

where $\tau = 0.4$ and E' is the bound of the distribution of entries of the error $\mathbf{E}'$ in Game 2 [4,7]. Tables 2 and 3 of [6] suggest that instances with $\delta \leq 1.0065$ should require around 2^{128} operations to solve using BKZ lattice reduction.

We calculated the sizes of the signature $(\mathbf{z}, c)$ and the public key $(\mathbf{A}, \mathbf{T})$ according to the formula $n\lceil \log_2(2B) \rceil + \kappa$ and $2mn\lceil \log_2(q) \rceil$, respectively. In case of secret key, we noticed that if one have the information of public keys $(\mathbf{A}, \mathbf{T})$, and $\mathbf{S}$, he/she can know $\mathbf{E}$ by computing $\mathbf{T} - \mathbf{AS}$. Therefore, unlike storing $(\mathbf{S}, \mathbf{E})$ as [4], we store $\mathbf{S}$ only, and the size of $\mathbf{S}$ is $n^2\lceil \log_2(14\sigma) \rceil$ bits.

In summary, we present our parameter settings on Tables 1 and 2 with some formulas of certain parameters on Table 3.

Table 1. Parameter selection for $n = 512$

	I	II	III	IV	[4]-III	[4]-IV
n	512	512	512	512	512	512
m	729	807	1024	1195	945	1014
w	19	19	19	19	19	19
d	24	24	26	27	24	26
σ	87	61	90	75	66	224
$\sigma \mathbf{s}_c$	379.22	265.89	392.30	318.20	287.69	976.39
L	4165	2920	4309	3591	8778	29792
$\mathbf{B}$	2712970	1902197	2806521	2276389	2058115	6985118
$\mathbf{U}$	5309.1	3722.5	5492.2	4454.8	4027.6	13669.5
κ	132	132	132	132	132	132
$\log_2 q$	31.81	30.90	31.84	32.57	30.84	32.66
Hermit factor (key)	1.0064	1.0064	1.0063	1.0064	1.0063	1.0060
Hermit factor (signature)	1.0059	1.0055	1.0047	1.0042	1.0048	1.0046
Signature size (bits)	11908	11396	11908	11908	11396	12420
Public key size (mb)	2.986	3.202	4.194	5.048	3.750	4.283
Secret key size (mb)	0.360	0.328	0.360	0.360	0.328	0.393
Acceptance rate of Line 7 of Algorithm 2	0.695	0.753	0.875	0.937	0.372	0.406

Parameters are selected according to the acceptance rate of Line 7 of Algorithm 2 around 0.68 to 0.94. For each n, parameters are chosen so that they satisfy the conditions on the Sect. 3.4, and admits small public key size. For $n = 512$, compared I and II to [4]-III and [4]-IV, our parameters have almost twice better acceptance rate of signing algorithm, and still have smaller public keys with similar secret keys and signatures. Furthermore, III and IV shows that the acceptance rate of Line 7 of Algorithm 2 can be increased to 87.5% and 93.7%, respectively. Also, for $n = 400$ and $n = 640$, compared to [4], the acceptance rates increased by 70.3% and 103.5%, respectively. Although the public key of V, $n = 400$, increased by 24% compared to [4]-V, since the Hermit factor of V is smaller than that of [4]-V, higher level security can be achieved.

Table 2. Parameter selection for $n = 400$ and $n = 640$

	V	[4]-V	VI	[4]-I
n	400	400	640	640
m	1015	790	812	1137
w	20	20	18	18
d	24	24	24	24
σ	59	70	64	58
$\sigma_{\mathbf{S_c}}$	250.32	313.05	271.53	246.07
L	2973	9800	2903	7308
B	1398264	1748695	2429098	2201370
U	3504.4	4382.7	3801.4	3445.0
κ	132	132	132	132
$\log_2 q$	27.50	28.71	36.14	34.34
Hermit factor (key)	1.0064	1.0071	1.0064	1.0060
Hermit factor (signature)	1.0050	1.0060	1.0048	1.0038
Signature size (bits)	8932	8932	14852	14852
Public key size (mb)	2.842	2.291	4.807	6.3672
Secret key size (mb)	0.200	0.200	0.512	0.512
Acceptance rate of Line 7 of Algorithm 2	0.676	0.397	0.755	0.371

Table 3. Formulas of certain parameters of our result

	Our signature scheme	[4]'s scheme
$\sigma_{\mathbf{S_c}}$	$\sqrt{w}\sigma$	$\sqrt{w}\sigma$ (or given in [4])
L	$\lfloor 2.52w\sigma \rfloor$	$7w\sigma$
B	$14\sigma_{\mathbf{S_c}}(n-1)$	$14\sigma_{\mathbf{S_c}}(n-1)$ (or given in [4])
U	$14\sigma_{\mathbf{S_c}}$	
Signature size	$n\lceil log_2(2B) + \kappa \rceil$	
Public key size	$2mn\lceil log_2(q) \rceil$	
Secret key size	$n^2\lceil log_2(14\sigma) \rceil$	
Acceptance rate of Line 7 of Algorithm 2	$\left(1 - \frac{2L}{2^d}\right)^m \left(1 - \frac{2L}{q}\right)^m$	$\left(1 - \frac{2L}{2^d}\right)^m$

For $n = 640$, the public key decreased by 24.5%. The sizes of the secret key and the signature remain the same as those of [4].

4   Benchmarks and Comparison

In this section we provide benchmark results of our signature scheme. All results in Table 4 were obtained on an Intel Core i7-2600 running at 3,440 MHz.

We compiled our software with gcc-5.4.0 and flags -O3 -march = sandybridge -mtune = sandybridge. Table 4 shows the average clock cycle counts of 10,000 runs for signing and verification.

Table 4. Benchmarking on a desktop computer

Signature schemes	Sign	Verify
Parameter-I	12, 390, 951	1, 460, 100
Parameter-II	12, 511, 808	1, 649, 473
Parameter-III	14, 527, 352	2, 316, 040
Parameter-IV	16, 232, 730	2, 876, 514
[4]-III	29, 189, 463	1, 937, 308
[4]-IV	28, 645, 571	2, 082, 876
RSA-3072[a]	14, 907, 968	145, 836
ECDSA-256[a]	1, 381, 500	1, 557, 880

[a]The results of RSA-3072 and ECDSA-256 are on an Intel Core i7-4770 at 3,400 MHz from eBACS [5]

Comparison with [4] and RSA. Our scheme improves the acceptance rate of signing algorithm of [4], so it would be definitely faster than that of [4]. However, we don't know exactly how faster it is than [4] unless we implement them. To compare performance, we implement our scheme as well as that of [4] and execute both of them on a same machine.

The number of clock cycle counts in all results increase as parameters n, m, and k increase, and decrease as acceptance rates increase. For example, the acceptance rate of Line 7 of Algorithm 2 of Parameter-II is twice of that of [4]-III (0.754 vs. 0.372); the number of cycles for signing of Parameter-II is below half of that of [4]-III (12,511,808 vs. 29,189,463). For another example, Parameter-III is very similar to [4]-IV except for the acceptance rate of Line 7 of Algorithm 2 (0.875 vs. 0.406); the number of cycles for signing of Parameter-III is half of [4]-IV (14,527,352 vs. 28,645,571).

In Table 4, we also compare our signature scheme with other commonly used signature schemes like RSA and ECDSA. It shows that the signature scheme of [4] was not efficient as RSA-3072 or ECDSA-256 that are believed to provide 128-bit security. However, our performance for signing is comparable with RSA-3072 mainly due to the improvement of the acceptance rate during signature generation process.

5   Conclusion

With this work, we showed that analysis of error terms can yield improvement of a signature scheme based on LWE. Since our analysis of error terms of the scheme of [4] was based on mathematical theorems, any other lattice cryptography with similar structures can use the theorems of our paper. Also, since we corrected the signing algorithm of [4] in Line 7 of Algorithm 2, we can expect more accurate analysis of this scheme from now on.

A   Appendix: Reusability of Error Terms

We have proved that $\|\mathbf{Ec}\|_\infty$ is sufficiently small for one $\mathbf{E}$ and one $\mathbf{c} \in \mathcal{B}_{n,w}$. But it is also important to check that $\|\mathbf{Ec}_i\|_\infty$ is small for one arbitrary $\mathbf{E}$ and several arbitrary $\mathbf{c}_i \in \mathcal{B}_{n,w}$.

Remark 4. The events $\|\mathbf{Ec}_i\|_\infty \leq L$ may be dependent to each other. For example, if we let $n = 3$, $w = 2$, $\mathbf{c}_1 = (1, 0, -1)^T$, and $\mathbf{c}_2 = (-1, 1, 0)^T$, then the two events $\|\mathbf{Ec}_1\|_\infty \leq L$ and $\|\mathbf{Ec}_2\|_\infty \leq L$ are dependent.

Ignorable Probability. We first define an ignorable probability with respect to $r \in \mathbb{N}$ different from a negligible probability.

Definition 2. *A probability δ_r is ignorable with respect to $r \in \mathbb{N}$ if*

$$\delta_r \leq 1 - (1 - \epsilon)^r$$

for some negligible probability ϵ.

Also, for convenience, we define abs($\mathbf{A}$) to be $(|a_{ij}|)$ where $\mathbf{A} = (a_{ij})$. We need to check that the probability

$$p := \Pr\left[\mathbf{E} \leftarrow D_\sigma^{m \times n}, \mathbf{c} \leftarrow \mathcal{B}_{n,w} : \|\mathbf{Ec}_i\|_\infty \leq L \text{ for } i = 1, \cdots, r\right]$$

for some integer $r \in \mathbb{N}$ is big enough so that $1 - p$ is ignorable with respect to r.

Before we give an analysis on p, we will define some variables we use in this section. We let $\mathbf{c}_i = (c_{i,1}, c_{i,2}, \cdots, c_{i,n})^T$ and θ_i be a permutation on the set $\{1, \cdots, n\}$ such that $c'_{i,1} := c_{i,\theta_i(1)}, c'_{i,2} := c_{i,\theta_i(2)}, \cdots, c'_{i,w} := c_{i,\theta_i(w)}$ are all the nonzero entries of $\mathbf{c}_i$. We also let $X_1, \cdots, X_n$ be iid discrete Gaussian random variables with mean 0 and standard deviation σ. Furthermore, we let $X_{i,1}, \cdots, X_{i,w}$ be distinct random variables in $\{X_1, \cdots, X_n\}$ such that $X_{i,j} := X_{\theta_i(j)}$. By construction, we can know that

$$c_{i,1} X_1 + c_{i,w} X_2 + \cdots + c_{i,n} X_n = c'_{i,1} X_{i,1} + c'_{i,2} X_{i,2} + \cdots + c'_{i,w} X_{i,w}.$$

If we let

$$\begin{aligned} p_a &:= \Pr\left[|c_{i,1} X_1 + c_{i,2} X_2 + \cdots + c_{i,n} X_n| \leq L \text{ for } i = 1, \cdots, r\right] \\ &= \Pr\left[|c'_{i,1} X_{i,1} + c'_{i,2} X_{i,2} + \cdots + c'_{i,w} X_{i,w}| \leq L \text{ for } i = 1, \cdots, r\right], \end{aligned}$$

then $p = p_a^m$. Therefore, it is enough to show that p_a is big enough. But it is not easy to give a direct analysis on p_a because of the alternative signs of c_i's entries. Instead, we think of a probability

$$p_b := \Pr\left[|c_{i,1}||X_1| + |c_{i,2}||X_2| + \cdots + |c_{i,n}||X_n| \leq L \text{ for } i = 1, \cdots, r\right]$$
$$= \Pr\left[|c'_{i,1}||X_{i,1}| + |c'_{i,2}||X_{i,2}| + \cdots + |c'_{i,w}||X_{i,w}| \leq L \text{ for } i = 1, \cdots, r\right]$$
$$= \Pr\left[|X_{i,1}| + |X_{i,2}| + \cdots + |X_{i,w}| \leq L \text{ for } i = 1, \cdots, r\right]$$

which is smaller than p_a. we also think of a probability

$$p_c := \Pr\left[|Y_{i,1}| + |Y_{i,2}| + \cdots + |Y_{i,w}| \leq L \text{ for } i = 1, \cdots, r\right]$$

where $Y_{i,j}$ are iid discrete Gaussian random variables with mean 0 and standard deviation σ for every i and j. We can show that $p_c \leq p_b$ from Theorem 4. Therefore, since $p_c \leq p_b \leq p_a$, it is enough to show that p_c is big enough so that $1 - p_c^m$ is ignorable with respect to r.

Remark 5. $p_c^m = \Pr[\| \text{abs}(\mathbf{E}_i) \text{abs}(\mathbf{c}_i)\|_\infty \leq L \text{ for } i = 1, \cdots, r]$ where $\mathbf{E}_i$'s are mutually independent $m \times n$ matrices of discrete Gaussian random variables with mean 0 standard deviation σ. Therefore, $p_c^m = \Pr[\| \text{abs}(\mathbf{E}) \text{abs}(\mathbf{c})\|_\infty \leq L]^r$.

Now, Let

$$p_* := \Pr[|Y_1| + |Y_2| + \cdots + |Y_w| \leq L]$$

where Y_j are iid discrete Gaussian random variables with mean 0 and standard deviation σ for $j = 1, \cdots w$. Then $p_c = p_*^r$, and $\Pr[\| \text{abs}(\mathbf{E}) \text{abs}(\mathbf{c})\|_\infty \leq L] = p_*^m$. If the probability

$$1 - \Pr[\| \text{abs}(\mathbf{E}) \text{abs}(\mathbf{c})\|_\infty \leq L] = 1 - p_*^m$$

is negligible, then we can finally say that the probabilities

$$1 - p = 1 - p_a^m \leq 1 - p_b^m \leq 1 - p_c^m = 1 - (p_*^m)^r = 1 - (1 - (1 - p_*^m))^r$$

are ignorable with respect to r.

In order to prove that $1 - p_*^m$ is negligible, we first check that $1 - p_*$ is negligible.

Theorem 3. *Let $Y_1, \cdots, Y_w$ be the iid discrete Gaussian random variables with mean 0 and standard deviation σ. Then*

$$\Pr[|Y_1| + \cdots + |Y_w| > L] < 2^w e^{-L^2/2\sigma^2 w}.$$

Proof. From Markov's inequality, for some $t > 0$,

$$\Pr[|Y_1| + \cdots + |Y_w| > L] = \Pr\left[e^{\frac{t}{\sigma^2}(|Y_1| + \cdots + |Y_w|)} > e^{\frac{t}{\sigma^2}L}\right]$$
$$\leq \frac{\mathrm{E}\left[e^{\frac{t}{\sigma^2}(|Y_1| + \cdots + |Y_w|)}\right]}{e^{\frac{t}{\sigma^2}L}} = \frac{\mathrm{E}\left[e^{\frac{t}{\sigma^2}|Y_1|}\right]^w}{e^{\frac{t}{\sigma^2}L}}$$

Also,

$$
\begin{aligned}
\mathrm{E}\left[e^{\frac{t}{\sigma^2}|Y_1|}\right] &= \sum_{a\in\mathbb{Z}} e^{\frac{t}{\sigma^2}|a|} f_\sigma(a) \\
&= \frac{\rho_\sigma(0)}{\rho_\sigma(\mathbb{Z})} + \sum_{a\in\mathbb{N}} 2e^{\frac{t}{\sigma^2}a} \frac{\rho_\sigma(a)}{\rho_\sigma(\mathbb{Z})} \\
&= \frac{1}{\rho_\sigma(\mathbb{Z})}\left(1 + \sum_{a\in N} 2e^{\frac{t}{\sigma^2}a} e^{-\frac{a^2}{2\sigma^2}}\right) \\
&< \frac{e^{\frac{t^2}{2\sigma^2}}}{\rho_\sigma(\mathbb{Z})}\left(2e^{-\frac{t^2}{2\sigma^2}} + \sum_{a\in\mathbb{N}} 2e^{-\frac{1}{2\sigma^2}(a-t)^2}\right) \\
&< e^{\frac{t^2}{2\sigma^2}}\left(\frac{\rho_{t,\sigma}(\mathbb{Z})}{\rho_\sigma(\mathbb{Z})} + \frac{\rho_{-t,\sigma}(\mathbb{Z})}{\rho_\sigma(\mathbb{Z})}\right)
\end{aligned}
$$

where $\rho_{\mu,\sigma}(\mathbb{Z}) := \sum_{a\in\mathbb{Z}} e^{-(a-\mu)^2/2\sigma^2}$ for $\mu, \sigma \in \mathbb{R}$. From Lemma 2.9 of [13], we know that $\frac{\rho_{\pm t,\sigma}(\mathbb{Z})}{\rho_\sigma(\mathbb{Z})} \leq 1$. Therefore, we get $\Pr[|Y_1|+\cdots+|Y_w| > L] < 2^w e^{-L^2/2\sigma^2 w}$ by letting $t = L/w$ to get a tighter upper bound using AM-GM inequality. $\qquad\square$

Since we let the bound $L = \lambda\sigma w$, we can know that

$$
1 - p_*^m = 1 - (1 - (1 - p_*))^m < 1 - (1 - 2^w e^{-L^2/2\sigma^2 w})^m = 1 - (1 - 2^w e^{-\lambda^2 w/2})^m.
$$

According to the parameters we have chosen, $1 - (1 - 2^w e^{-\lambda^2 w/2})^m < 2^{-55}$.

Actually, we can compute p_* if the parameters are chosen. Let $\mathbf{p} := (p_0, p_1, \cdots, p_L)^T$ be a vector whose each entry p_i is the probability of the absolute value of discrete Gaussian random variable with mean 0 and standard deviation σ being $i = 0, \cdots, L$. In other words, $p_0 = f_\sigma(0), p_i = 2f_\sigma(i)$ for $i = 1, \cdots, L$. If we let $Y_1, Y_2, \cdots$ be iid discrete Gaussian random variables with mean 0 and standard deviation σ, then $\mathbf{p}$ contains all of the possible probability that $|Y_j| = i \leq L$ with respect to i. If we convolute $\mathbf{p}$ to itself w times (a convolution of two vectors $\mathbf{a} = (a_0, \cdots, a_s)^T$ and $\mathbf{b} = (b_0, \cdots, b_t)^T$ is defined as $\mathbf{a} * \mathbf{b} := (a_0 b_0, \cdots, \sum_{i+j=k} a_i b_j, \cdots, a_s b_t)^T \in \mathbb{R}^{s+t+1}$),

$$
\underbrace{\mathbf{p} * \cdots * \mathbf{p}}_{w} = (p_0', p_1', \cdots, p_L', \cdots, p_{wL}')^T
$$

then we know that p_i' are the exact probability that $|Y_1| + \cdots + |Y_w| = i$ for $i = 0, \cdots, L$. Since we can calculate $\mathbf{p}$, we can calculate the probability $p_* = \sum_{i=0}^L p_i'$ that $|Y_1| + \cdots + |Y_w| \leq L$. Therefore, we can compute $1 - p_*^m$. From our parameter settings, we can know that $1 - p_*^m \leq 2^{-62}$ for $n = 512$, $1 - p_*^m \leq 2^{-66}$ for $n = 400$ and $1 - p_*^m \approx 2^{-60}$ for $n = 640$.

Since we saw that $1 - p_*^m$ is negligibly small, it is left to prove that $p_c \leq p_b$, which is directly given by Theorem 4. Before we present Theorem 4, we need a lemma below.

Lemma 3. *Let $\{p_i\}_i$ and $\{q_i\}_i$ be nonnegative absolutely convergent sequences such that $\sum_{i=0}^{\infty} p_i = \sum_{i=0}^{\infty} q_i < \infty$. If there exists $N > 0$ such that for all $i \geq N$, $p_i \leq q_i$ and for all $i < N$, $p_i > q_i$, then for any nonnegative decreasing sequence $\{w_i\}_i$,*

$$\sum_{i=0}^{m} w_i p_i \geq \sum_{i=0}^{m} w_i q_i \text{ for any } m \geq 0.$$

Proof. First, consider $C_m := \sum_{i=0}^{m}(p_i - q_i)$. If $m < N$, then it is obvious that $C_m \geq 0$. If $m \geq N$, then we know that for all $i \geq N$, $p_i - q_i \leq 0$. Therefore, $C_{N-1}, C_N, C_{N+1}, \cdots$ is a decreasing sequence which converges to 0. Since $C_{N-1} \geq 0$, $C_m \geq 0$ for all $m \geq 0$. Now consider

$$S_m := \sum_{i=0}^{m} w_i(p_i - q_i) = \sum_{i=0}^{m} w_i p_i - \sum_{i=0}^{m} w_i q_i.$$

If $m < N$, then $S_m \geq 0$. If $m \geq N$, then

$$S_m \geq w_N \sum_{i=0}^{m} (p_i - q_i) \geq 0.$$

Therefore, $S_m = \sum_{i=0}^{m} w_i p_i - \sum_{i=0}^{m} w_i q_i \geq 0$ for any $m \geq 0$. $\qquad\square$

Now, we can prove a theorem below using the previous lemma.

Theorem 4. *For any positive integer r, let $X_1, \cdots, X_n$, Y_j, and $Y_{i,j}$ be iid discrete random variables for $i = 1, \cdots, r$ and $j = 1, \cdots, w$. For each i, let $X_{i,1}, X_{i,2}, \cdots, X_{i,w}$ be distinct random variables in $\{X_1, \cdots, X_n\}$ ($X_{i_0,j_0} = X_{i_1,j_1}$ can happen when $i_0 \neq i_1$). Then*

$$\Pr\left[|X_{i,1}| + |X_{i,2}| + \cdots + |X_{i,w}| \leq L \text{ for } i = 1, \cdots, r\right]$$
$$\geq \Pr\left[|Y_{i,1}| + |Y_{i,2}| + \cdots + |Y_{i,w}| \leq L \text{ for } i = 1, \cdots, r\right]$$
$$= \Pr\left[|Y_1| + |Y_2| + \cdots + |Y_w| \leq L\right]^r$$

Proof. Using Lemma 3, we can now prove Theorem 4. Let

$$A_i := \{|X_{i,1}| + |X_{i,2}| + \cdots + |X_{i,w}| \leq L\} \text{ and}$$
$$A'_i := \{|Y_{i,1}| + |Y_{i,2}| + \cdots + |Y_{i,w}| \leq L\}.$$

Then the inequality in Theorem 4 can be represented as $\Pr[\cap_{i=1}^{r} A_i] \geq \Pr[\cap_{i=1}^{r} A'_i] = \prod_{i=1}^{r} \Pr[A'_i]$. If we show that

$$\Pr\left[\bigcap_{i=1}^{s-1} A_i \,\Bigg|\, A_s\right] \geq \Pr\left[\bigcap_{i=1}^{s-1} A_i\right]$$

for $s \geq 2$, then

$$\Pr\left[\bigcap_{i=1}^{r} A_i\right] = \Pr\left[A_r\right] \Pr\left[\bigcap_{i=1}^{r-1} A_i \,\middle|\, A_r\right] \geq \Pr\left[A_r\right] \Pr\left[\bigcap_{i=1}^{r-1} A_i\right]$$

$$\geq \cdots \geq \prod_{i=1}^{r} \Pr[A_i] = \prod_{i=1}^{r} \Pr[A_i'].$$

Therefore, it is enough to compare the probabilities $\Pr\left[\cap_{i=1}^{s-1} A_i \,\middle|\, A_s\right]$ and $\Pr\left[\cap_{i=1}^{s-1} A_i\right]$ for $s \geq 2$. If $\{X_{i,j} \mid 1 \leq i \leq s-1, 1 \leq j \leq w\} \cap \{X_{s,1}, X_{s,2}, \cdots, X_{s,w}\} = \emptyset$, then $\cap_{i=1}^{s-1} A_i$ and A_s are independent, i.e. $\Pr\left[\cap_{i=1}^{s-1} A_i \,\middle|\, A_s\right] = \Pr\left[\cap_{i=1}^{s-1} A_i\right]$. Suppose $\{X_{i,j} \mid 1 \leq i \leq s-1, 1 \leq j \leq w\} \cap \{X_{s,1}, X_{s,2}, \cdots, X_{s,w}\} \neq \emptyset$. Without loss of generality, we may assume that

$$\{X_{i,j} \mid 1 \leq i \leq s-1, 1 \leq j \leq w\} \cap \{X_{s,1}, X_{s,2}, \cdots, X_{s,w}\} = \{X_{s,1}, X_{s,2}, \cdots, X_{s,k}\}$$

for some $k \leq w$. Then the two probabilities can be represented as

$$\Pr\left[\bigcap_{i=1}^{s-1} A_i \,\middle|\, A_s\right] = \sum_{t_1=0}^{L} \Pr\left[|X_{s,1}| = t_1 \mid A_s\right] \Pr\left[\bigcap_{i=1}^{s-1} A_i \,\middle|\, A_s, |X_{s,1}| = t_1\right] \text{ and}$$

$$\Pr\left[\bigcap_{i=1}^{s-1} A_i\right] = \sum_{t_1=0}^{L} \Pr\left[|X_{s,1}| = t_1\right] \Pr\left[\bigcap_{i=1}^{s-1} A_i \,\middle|\, |X_{s,1}| = t_1\right].$$

If we let

$$p_{t_1} := \Pr\left[|X_{s,1}| = t_1 \mid A_s\right],$$
$$q_{t_1} := \Pr\left[|X_{s,1}| = t_1\right],$$
$$w'_{t_1} := \Pr\left[\bigcap_{i=1}^{s-1} A_i \,\middle|\, A_s, |X_{s,1}| = t_1\right] \text{ and}$$
$$w_{t_1} := \Pr\left[\bigcap_{i=1}^{s-1} A_i \,\middle|\, |X_{s,1}| = t_1\right],$$

then we can see that p_i and q_i are probability density functions of positive discrete random variables, and $\{w_{t_1}\}_{t_1}$ is a decreasing sequence. Note that

$$p_{t_1} = \Pr\left[|X_{s,1}| = t_1\right] \frac{\Pr\left[|X_{s,2}| + \cdots |X_{s,w}| \leq L - t_1\right]}{\Pr\left[|X_{s,1}| + \cdots |X_{s,w}| \leq L\right]}$$

$$= q_{t_1} \frac{\Pr\left[|X_{s,2}| + \cdots |X_{s,w}| \leq L - t_1\right]}{\Pr\left[|X_{s,1}| + \cdots |X_{s,w}| \leq L\right]}$$

$$l_{t_1} := \frac{\Pr\left[|X_{s,2}| + \cdots |X_{s,w}| \leq L - t_1\right]}{\Pr\left[|X_{s,1}| + \cdots |X_{s,w}| \leq L\right]}.$$

We can know that $\{l_{t_1}\}_{t_1}$ is a decreasing sequence converges to 0 and $l_0 > 1$. Therefore, there exists $N_1 > 0$ such that for all $t_1 \geq N_1$, $p_{t_1} \leq q_{t_1}$ and for all $t_1 < N_1$, $p_{t_1} \geq q_{t_1}$. If we show that $w'_{t_1} \geq w_{t_1}$ for $0 \leq t_1 \leq L$, then from the Lemma 3,

$$\Pr\left[\bigcap_{i=1}^{s-1} A_i \mid A_s\right] = \sum_{t_1=0}^{L} p_{t_1} w'_{t_1} \geq \sum_{t_1=0}^{L} p_{t_1} w_{t_1} \geq \sum_{t_1=0}^{L} q_{t_1} w_{t_1} = \Pr\left[\bigcap_{i=1}^{s-1} A_i\right].$$

Therefore, it is enough to show that $w'_{t_1} \geq w_{t_1}$ for $0 \leq t_1 \leq L$. We can also write

$$w'_{t_1} = \sum_{t_2=0}^{L-t_1} \Pr\left[|X_{s,2}| = t_2 \mid A_s, |X_{s,1}| = t_1\right] \Pr\left[\bigcap_{i=1}^{s-1} A_i \mid A_s, |X_{s,1}| = t_1, |X_{s,2}| = t_2\right] \text{ and}$$

$$w_{t_1} = \sum_{t_1=0}^{L} \Pr\left[|X_{s,2}| = t_2\right] \Pr\left[\bigcap_{i=1}^{s-1} A_i \mid |X_{s,1}| = t_1, |X_{s,2}| = t_2\right].$$

Similarly, If we let

$$p_{t_1,t_2} := \Pr\left[|X_{s,2}| = t_2 \mid A_s, |X_{s,1}| = t_1\right],$$
$$q_{t_1,t_2} := \Pr\left[|X_{s,2}| = t_2\right],$$
$$w'_{t_1,t_2} := \Pr\left[\bigcap_{i=1}^{s-1} A_i \mid A_s, |X_{s,1}| = t_1, |X_{s,2}| = t_2\right], \text{ and}$$
$$w_{t_1,t_2} := \Pr\left[\bigcap_{i=1}^{s-1} A_i \mid |X_{s,1}| = t_1, |X_{s,2}| = t_2\right],$$

then we can see that $\{p_{t_1,t_2}\}_{t_2}$ and $\{q_{t_1,t_2}\}_{t_2}$ are probability density functions of positive discrete random variables, and $\{w_{t_1,t_2}\}_{t_2}$ is a decreasing sequence. Note that

$$p_{t_1,t_2} = \Pr\left[|X_{s,2}| = t_2\right] \frac{\Pr\left[|X_{s,3}| + \cdots |X_{s,w}| \leq (L - t_1) - t_2\right]}{\Pr\left[|X_{s,2}| + \cdots |X_{s,w}| \leq L - t_1\right]}$$
$$= q_{t_1,t_2} \frac{\Pr\left[|X_{s,3}| + \cdots |X_{s,w}| \leq (L - t_1) - t_2\right]}{\Pr\left[|X_{s,2}| + \cdots |X_{s,w}| \leq L - t_1\right]}$$
$$l_{t_1,t_2} := \frac{\Pr\left[|X_{s,3}| + \cdots |X_{s,w}| \leq (L - t_1) - t_2\right]}{\Pr\left[|X_{s,2}| + \cdots |X_{s,w}| \leq L - t_1\right]}.$$

We can know that $\{l_{t_1,t_2}\}_{t_2}$ is a decreasing sequence converges to 0 and $l_{t_1,0} > 1$. Therefore, there exists $N_2 > 0$ such that for all $t_2 \geq N_2$, $p_{t_2} \leq q_{t_2}$ and for all $t_2 < N_2$, $p_{t_2} \geq q_{t_2}$. If we show that $w'_{t_1,t_2} \geq w_{t_1,t_2}$ for $0 \leq t_1 + t_2 \leq L$, then from the Lemma 3,

$$w'_{t_1} = \sum_{t_2=0}^{L-t_1} p_{t_1,t_2} w'_{t_1,t_2} \geq \sum_{t_2=0}^{L-t_1} p_{t_1,t_2} w_{t_1,t_2} \geq \sum_{t_2=0}^{L-t_1} q_{t_1,t_2} w_{t_1,t_2} = w_{t_1}.$$

Therefore, it is enough to show that $w'_{t_1,t_2} \geq w_{t_1,t_2}$ for $0 \leq t_1 + t_2 \leq L$. Using similar notations and arguments, we can know that it is enough to prove that $w'_{t_1,\cdots,t_k} \geq w_{t_1,\cdots,t_k}$ for $0 \leq t_1 + \cdots + t_k \leq L$. Since the random variables $X_{s,k+1}, X_{s,k+2}, \cdots, X_{s,w}$ are independent to the random variables defining $\cap_{i=1}^{s-1} A_i$,

$$
w'_{t_1,\cdots,t_k} = \Pr\left[\bigcap_{i=1}^{s-1} A_i \ \middle| \ A_s, |X_{s,1}| = t_1, \cdots, |X_{s,k}| = t_k\right]
$$
$$
= \Pr\left[\bigcap_{i=1}^{s-1} A_i \ \middle| \ |X_{s,1}| = t_1, \cdots, |X_{s,k}| = t_k\right]
$$
$$
= w_{t_1,\cdots,t_k}
$$

□

Since Theorem 4 is a direct proof for $p_c \leq p_b$, we can say that $1 - p$ is ignorable with respect to r. According to our parameter settings, if $r = 2^{30}$, then $1 - p \leq 1 - (p_*^m)^r \leq 2^{-30}$. In other words, the probability that $\|\mathbf{Ec}_i\|_\infty \leq L$ for $i = 1, \cdots, 2^{30}$ is at least $1 - 2^{-30}$ for $L = 2w\sigma$. We thought this was enough probability to eliminate the rejection process of the keys on Algorithm 1 of [4].

References

1. Ajtai, M.: Generating hard instances of lattice problems. In: Proceedings of the Twenty-Eighth Annual ACM Symposium on Theory of Computing, pp. 99–108. ACM (1996)
2. Ajtai, M., Dwork, C.: A public-key cryptosystem with worst-case/average-case equivalence. In: Proceedings of the Twenty-Ninth Annual ACM Symposium on Theory of Computing, pp. 284–293. ACM (1997)
3. Applebaum, B., Cash, D., Peikert, C., Sahai, A.: Fast cryptographic primitives and circular-secure encryption based on hard learning problems. In: Halevi, S. (ed.) CRYPTO 2009. LNCS, vol. 5677, pp. 595–618. Springer, Heidelberg (2009). doi:10.1007/978-3-642-03356-8_35
4. Bai, S., Galbraith, S.D.: An improved compression technique for signatures based on learning with errors. In: Benaloh, J. (ed.) CT-RSA 2014. LNCS, vol. 8366, pp. 28–47. Springer, Heidelberg (2014). doi:10.1007/978-3-319-04852-9_2
5. Bernstein, D.J., Lange, T.: eBACS: ecrypt benchmarking of cryptographic systems (2009)
6. Chen, Y., Nguyen, P.Q.: BKZ 2.0: better lattice security estimates. In: Lee, D.H., Wang, X. (eds.) ASIACRYPT 2011. LNCS, vol. 7073, pp. 1–20. Springer, Heidelberg (2011). doi:10.1007/978-3-642-25385-0_1
7. Dagdelen, Ö., Bansarkhani, R., Göpfert, F., Güneysu, T., Oder, T., Pöppelmann, T., Sánchez, A.H., Schwabe, P.: High-speed signatures from standard lattices. In: Aranha, D.F., Menezes, A. (eds.) LATINCRYPT 2014. LNCS, vol. 8895, pp. 84–103. Springer, Heidelberg (2015). doi:10.1007/978-3-319-16295-9_5
8. Ducas, L., Durmus, A., Lepoint, T., Lyubashevsky, V.: Lattice signatures and bimodal gaussians. In: Canetti, R., Garay, J.A. (eds.) CRYPTO 2013. LNCS, vol. 8042, pp. 40–56. Springer, Heidelberg (2013). doi:10.1007/978-3-642-40041-4_3

9. Goldreich, O., Goldwasser, S., Halevi, S.: Public-key cryptosystems from lattice reduction problems. In: Kaliski, B.S. (ed.) CRYPTO 1997. LNCS, vol. 1294, pp. 112–131. Springer, Heidelberg (1997). doi:10.1007/BFb0052231

10. Hoffstein, J., Howgrave-Graham, N., Pipher, J., Silverman, J.H., Whyte, W.: NTRUSign: digital signatures using the NTRU lattice. In: Joye, M. (ed.) CT-RSA 2003. LNCS, vol. 2612, pp. 122–140. Springer, Heidelberg (2003). doi:10.1007/3-540-36563-X_9

11. Lyubashevsky, V.: Lattice-based identification schemes secure under active attacks. In: Cramer, R. (ed.) PKC 2008. LNCS, vol. 4939, pp. 162–179. Springer, Heidelberg (2008). doi:10.1007/978-3-540-78440-1_10

12. Lyubashevsky, V.: Lattice signatures without trapdoors. In: Pointcheval, D., Johansson, T. (eds.) EUROCRYPT 2012. LNCS, vol. 7237, pp. 738–755. Springer, Heidelberg (2012). doi:10.1007/978-3-642-29011-4_43

13. Micciancio, D., Regev, O.: Worst-case to average-case reductions based on Gaussian measures. SIAM J. Comput. **37**(1), 267–302 (2007)

14. Regev, O.: On lattices, learning with errors, random linear codes, and cryptography. J. ACM (JACM) **56**(6), 34 (2009)

Encryption

Transforming Hidden Vector Encryption Schemes from Composite to Prime Order Groups

Kwangsu Lee[✉]

Sejong University, Seoul, Korea
kwangsu@sejong.ac.kr

Abstract. Predicate encryption is a new type of public key encryption that enables searches on encrypted data. By using predicate encryption, we can search keywords or attributes on encrypted data without decrypting ciphertexts. Hidden vector encryption (HVE) is a special kind of predicate encryption. HVE supports the evaluation of conjunctive equality, comparison, and subset operations between attributes in ciphertexts and attributes in tokens. In this paper, we construct efficient HVE schemes in prime order bilinear groups derived from previous HVE schemes in composite order bilinear groups, and prove their selective security under simple assumptions. To achieve this result, we present a conversion method that transforms HVE schemes from composite order bilinear groups into prime order bilinear groups. Our method supports any types of prime order bilinear groups and uses simple assumptions.

Keywords: Searchable encryption · Predicate encryption · Hidden vector encryption · Conversion method · Bilinear maps

1 Introduction

Searchable public key encryption is a new type of public key encryption (PKE) that enables efficient searching on encrypted data [3]. In PKE, if an agent A wants to search on encrypted data for a user B, he should first decrypt ciphertexts using the private key SK of the user B. This simple method has a problem that the agent requires the user's private key. In searchable public key encryption, a ciphertext is associated with keywords or attributes, and a user can generate a token for searching from the user's private key. That is, an agent A performs searches on encrypted data using the token TK that is related with keywords or attributes instead of using the private key SK. By using searchable public key encryption, it is possible to build interesting systems like privacy preserving mail gateway systems [3], secure audit log systems [25], network audit log systems [21], and credit card payment gateway systems [7].

Predicate encryption (PE) is a generalization of searchable public key encryption [7,14]. In PE, a ciphertext is associated with an attribute x, and a token is associated with a predicate f. At first, a sender creates a ciphertext that is

© Springer International Publishing AG 2017
S. Hong and J.H. Park (Eds.): ICISC 2016, LNCS 10157, pp. 101–125, 2017.
DOI: 10.1007/978-3-319-53177-9_5

associated with an attribute x, and an agent receives a token that corresponds to a predicate f from a receiver. If $f(x) = 1$, then the agent can decrypt ciphertexts that are related with x. Otherwise, that is $f(x) = 0$, then the agent cannot get any information except that $f(x) = 0$. That is, PE provides both *message hiding* and *attribute hiding* properties. Hidden vector encryption (HVE) is a special kind of PE [7]. In HVE, a ciphertext and a token are associated with attribute vectors $\mathbf{x}, \mathbf{y}$ respectively, and the attribute vector for the token contains a special wild card attribute. If each attribute of a ciphertext is equal with the attribute of a token except the wild card attribute, then the predicate $f_{\mathbf{y}}(\mathbf{x})$ is satisfied. HVE supports the evaluation of predicates such that conjunctive equality, conjunctive subset, and conjunctive comparison.

Many HVE schemes were originally proposed in composite order bilinear groups [7,16,22]. To improve the efficiency of HVE schemes, HVE schemes in prime order bilinear groups are required. Although many HVE schemes in prime order groups were constructed from scratch [13,18,19], we would like to easily obtain HVE schemes in prime order groups from previous schemes in composite order groups. The previous conversion methods that convert cryptographic schemes from composite order to prime order bilinear groups are Freeman's method [9] and Ducas' method [8]. The method of Ducas is that random blinding elements in ciphertexts can be eliminated in asymmetric bilinear groups of prime order since the decisional Diffie-Hellman (DDH) assumption holds in asymmetric bilinear groups. The method of Freeman is that product groups and vector orthogonality provide the subgroup decision assumption and the subgroup orthogonality property in prime order bilinear groups, respectively. The merit of this method is that it can convert many cryptographic schemes from bilinear groups of composite order to asymmetric bilinear groups of prime order. The demerits of this method are that the converted scheme only works in asymmetric bilinear groups and the security of the scheme is proven under complex assumptions.

1.1 Our Results

In this paper, we present a new conversion method that transforms HVE schemes from composite order bilinear groups into prime order bilinear groups.

Our conversion method is similar to the conversion method of Freeman [9] since it uses product groups and vector orthogonality, but ours has the following three differences. The first difference is that Freeman's method is related to the subgroup decision (SD) assumption in prime order bilinear groups, whereas our method is not related to the SD assumption. The second difference is that Freeman's method only works in asymmetric bilinear groups of prime order, whereas our method works in any bilinear groups of prime order. The third difference is that cryptographic schemes that are converted from Freeman's method use complex assumptions that depend on complex basis vectors, whereas HVE schemes that are converted from our method use simple assumptions that are independent of basis vectors.

By using our conversion method, we first convert the HVE scheme of Boneh and Waters [7] in composite order bilinear groups into an HVE scheme in symmetric bilinear groups of prime order. We then prove the converted HVE scheme is selectively secure under the decisional bilinear Diffie-Hellman (DBDH) and the parallel 3-party Diffie-Hellman (P3DH) assumptions. Next, we also convert the delegatable HVE scheme of Shi and Waters [22] and the efficient HVE scheme of Lee and Lee [16] from composite order bilinear groups to HVE schemes in symmetric bilinear groups of prime order. Finally, we show that the new P3DH assumption holds in generic group model introduced by Shoup.

1.2   Related Work

PE is closely related to functional encryption [6]. In functional encryption, a ciphertext is associated with attributes $\mathbf{x}$, and a private key is associated with a function f. The main difference between PE and functional encryption is that the computation of a predicate $f(x) \in \{0, 1\}$ is only allowed in PE whereas the computation of any function $f(x)$ is allowed in functional encryption. Identity-based encryption (IBE) is the most simple type of functional encryption, and it provide an equality function for an identity in ciphertexts [4]. Hierarchical IBE (HIBE) is an extension of IBE, and it provides a conjunctive equality function for a hierarchical identity in ciphertexts [11]. Attribute-based encryption (ABE) is also an extension of IBE, and it provides the most general function that consists of AND, OR, NOT, and threshold gates [12].

The first HVE scheme was proposed by Boneh and Waters [7]. After their construction, various HVE schemes were proposed in [8, 16, 22]. A simple HVE scheme can be constructed from a PKE scheme [3, 7, 15]. This method was introduced by Boneh et al. [3] to construct a PKE scheme with keyword search (PEKS) using trapdoor permutations. After that, Boneh and Waters showed that a searchable public key encryption for general predicates also can be constructed from this method [7]. Katz and Yerukhimovich [15] showed that it is possible to construct a PE scheme from a PKE scheme if the number of predicate is less than a polynomial number of a security parameter. The main idea of this method is to use a multiple instances of key-private PKE introduced by Bellare et al. [1]. That is, the public key of searchable public key encryption consists of the public keys of key-private PKE and each instance of public keys is mapped to each predicate. However, this method has a serious problem that the total number of predicates is limited to the polynomial value of a security parameter.

Another HVE scheme can be constructed by extremely generalizing anonymous IBE (AIBE) [7, 8, 13, 16, 19, 22]. This method was introduced by Boneh and Waters [7]. They used the IBE scheme of Boneh and Boyen [2] and composite order bilinear groups to provide the anonymity of ciphertexts. Shi and Waters constructed a delegatable HVE scheme [22]. Lee and Lee constructed an efficient HVE scheme with a constant number of pairing operations [16]. In composite order bilinear groups, the random blinding property using subgroups provides the anonymity of ciphertexts and the orthogonal property among subgroups provides the successful decryption. However, it is inefficient to use composite order bilinear groups since the group order of composite order bilinear groups should be large. To overcome this problem of inefficiency, Freeman presented a general framework that converts cryptographic schemes from composite order bilinear groups to prime order bilinear groups [9]. Ducas also showed that HVE schemes in composite order bilinear groups are easily converted to schemes in prime order bilinear groups [8]. However, these conversion methods result in asymmetric bilinear groups.

Finally, an HVE scheme can be derived from inner-product encryption (IPE) [14,18,20]. IPE is a kind of PE and it enable the evaluation of inner-product predicates between the vector of ciphertexts and the vector of tokens. Katz et al. [14] constructed the first IPE scheme under composite order bilinear groups. Okamoto and Takashima constructed an hierarchical IPE scheme using dual pairing vector spaces [18]. Park proposed an IPE scheme under prime order bilinear groups and proved its security under the well-known assumptions [20]. The main idea of converting an IPE scheme to an HVE scheme is to construct a predicate of conjunctive equality using a predicate of inner product [14].

2   Preliminaries

In this section, we define hidden vector encryption, and introduce bilinear groups of prime order and two complexity assumptions.

2.1   Hidden Vector Encryption

Let Σ be a finite set of attributes and let $*$ be a special symbol not in Σ. Define $\Sigma_* = \Sigma \cup \{*\}$. The star $*$ plays the role of a wild-card or "don't care" value. For a vector $\boldsymbol{\sigma} = (\sigma_1, \ldots, \sigma_\ell) \in \Sigma_*^\ell$, we define a predicate $f_{\boldsymbol{\sigma}}$ over Σ^ℓ as follows: For $\boldsymbol{x} = (x_1, \ldots, x_\ell) \in \Sigma^\ell$, it set $f_{\boldsymbol{\sigma}}(\boldsymbol{x}) = 1$ if $\forall i : (\sigma_i = x_i$ or $\sigma_i = *)$, it set $f_{\boldsymbol{\sigma}}(\boldsymbol{x}) = 0$ otherwise.

Definition 1 (Hidden Vector Encryption). *An HVE scheme consists of four algorithms* **Setup**, **GenToken**, **Encrypt**, *and* **Query** *which are defined as follows:*

Setup($1^\lambda, \ell$): *The setup algorithm takes as input a security parameter 1^λ and the length parameter ℓ. It outputs a public key PK and a secret key SK.*

GenToken($\boldsymbol{\sigma}, SK, PK$): *The token generation algorithm takes as input a vector $\boldsymbol{\sigma} = (\sigma_1, \ldots, \sigma_\ell) \in \Sigma_*^\ell$ that corresponds to a predicate $f_{\boldsymbol{\sigma}}$, the secret key SK and the public key PK. It outputs a token $TK_{\boldsymbol{\sigma}}$ for the vector $\boldsymbol{\sigma}$.*

Encrypt($\boldsymbol{x}, M, PK$): *The encrypt algorithm takes as input a vector $\boldsymbol{x} = (x_1, \ldots, x_\ell) \in \Sigma^\ell$, a message $M \in \mathcal{M}$, and the public key PK. It outputs a ciphertext CT for $\boldsymbol{x}$ and M.*

Query($CT, TK_{\boldsymbol{\sigma}}, PK$): *The query algorithm takes as input a ciphertext CT, a token $TK_{\boldsymbol{\sigma}}$ for a vector $\boldsymbol{\sigma}$ that corresponds to a predicate $f_{\boldsymbol{\sigma}}$, and the public key PK. It outputs M if $f_{\boldsymbol{\sigma}}(\boldsymbol{x}) = 1$ or outputs $\perp$ otherwise.*

The scheme should satisfy the following correctness property: For all $x \in \Sigma^\ell$, $M \in \mathcal{M}$, $\sigma \in \Sigma^\ell_*$, let $(PK, SK) \leftarrow \textbf{Setup}(1^\lambda, \ell)$, $CT \leftarrow \textbf{Encrypt}(x, M, PK)$, and $TK_\sigma \leftarrow \textbf{GenToken}(\sigma, SK, PK)$.

- *If $f_\sigma(x) = 1$, then $\textbf{Query}(CT, TK_\sigma, PK) = M$.*
- *If $f_\sigma(x) = 0$, then $\textbf{Query}(CT, TK_\sigma, PK) = \perp$ with all but negligible probability.*

Definition 2 (Selective Security). *The selective security of HVE is defined as the following game between a challenger $\mathcal{C}$ and an adversary $\mathcal{A}$:*

1. **Init:** *$\mathcal{A}$ submits two vectors $x_0, x_1 \in \Sigma^\ell$.*
2. **Setup:** *$\mathcal{C}$ runs the setup algorithm and keeps the secret key SK to itself, then it gives the public key PK to $\mathcal{A}$.*
3. **Query 1:** *$\mathcal{A}$ adaptively requests a polynomial number of tokens for vectors $\sigma_1, \ldots, \sigma_{q_1}$ that correspond to predicates $f_{\sigma_1}, \ldots, f_{\sigma_{q_1}}$ subject to the restriction that $f_{\sigma_i}(x_0) = f_{\sigma_i}(x_1)$ for all i. In responses, $\mathcal{C}$ gives the corresponding tokens TK_{σ_i} to $\mathcal{A}$.*
4. **Challenge:** *$\mathcal{A}$ submits two messages M_0, M_1 subject to the restriction that if there is an index i such that $f_{\sigma_i}(x_0) = f_{\sigma_i}(x_1) = 1$ then $M_0 = M_1$. $\mathcal{C}$ chooses a random coin γ and gives a ciphertext CT of (x_γ, M_γ) to $\mathcal{A}$.*
5. **Query 2:** *$\mathcal{A}$ continues to request tokens for vectors $\sigma_{q_1+1}, \ldots, \sigma_q$ that correspond to predicates $f_{\sigma_{q_1+1}}, \ldots, f_{\sigma_q}$ subject to the two restrictions as before.*
6. **Guess:** *$\mathcal{A}$ outputs a guess γ'. If $\gamma = \gamma'$, it outputs 0. Otherwise, it outputs 1.*

The advantage of $\mathcal{A}$ is defined as $\textbf{Adv}_\mathcal{A}^{HVE}(\lambda) = \left| \Pr[\gamma = \gamma'] - 1/2 \right|$ where the probability is taken over the coin tosses made by $\mathcal{A}$ and $\mathcal{C}$. We say that an HVE scheme is selectively secure if all probabilistic polynomial-time (PPT) adversaries have at most a negligible advantage in the above game.

2.2 Bilinear Groups of Prime Order

Let $\mathbb{G}$ and $\mathbb{G}_T$ be multiplicative cyclic groups of prime p order. Let g be a generator of $\mathbb{G}$. The bilinear map $e : \mathbb{G} \times \mathbb{G} \to \mathbb{G}_T$ has the following properties:

1. Bilinearity: $\forall u, v \in \mathbb{G}$ and $\forall a, b \in \mathbb{Z}_p$, $e(u^a, v^b) = e(u, v)^{ab}$.
2. Non-degeneracy: $\exists g$ such that $e(g, g)$ has order p, that is, $e(g, g)$ is a generator of $\mathbb{G}_T$.

We say that $(p, \mathbb{G}, \mathbb{G}_T, e)$ are bilinear groups if the group operations in $\mathbb{G}$ and $\mathbb{G}_T$ as well as the bilinear map e are all efficiently computable.

2.3 Complexity Assumptions

We introduce two simple assumptions under prime order bilinear groups. The decisional bilinear Diffie-Hellman assumption was introduced in [4]. The parallel 3-party Diffie-Hellman (P3DH) assumption is newly introduced in this paper.

Assumption 1 (Decisional Bilinear Diffie-Hellman, DBDH). *Let $(p, \mathbb{G}, \mathbb{G}_T, e)$ be a description of the bilinear group of prime order p. The DBDH problem is stated as follows: given a challenge tuple*

$$D = ((p, \mathbb{G}, \mathbb{G}_T, e),\ g, g^a, g^b, g^c)\ and\ T,$$

decides whether $T = T_0 = e(g,g)^{abc}$ or $T = T_1 = e(g,g)^d$ with random choices of $a, b, c, d \in \mathbb{Z}_p$. The advantage of $\mathcal{A}$ is defined as $\mathbf{Adv}_{\mathcal{A}}^{DBDH}(\lambda) = \left| \Pr\left[\mathcal{A}(D, T_0) = 1\right] - \Pr\left[\mathcal{A}(D, T_1) = 1\right] \right|$ where the probability is taken over the random choices of $a, b, c, d \in \mathbb{Z}_p$ and the random bits used by $\mathcal{A}$. We say that the DBDH assumption holds if no PPT algorithm has a non-negligible advantage in solving the above problem.

Assumption 2 (Parallel 3-party Diffie-Hellman, P3DH). *Let $(p, \mathbb{G}, \mathbb{G}_T, e)$ be a description of the bilinear group of prime order p. The P3DH problem is stated as follows: given a challenge tuple*

$$D = \big((p, \mathbb{G}, \mathbb{G}_T, e),\ (g, f), (g^a, f^a), (g^b, f^b),$$
$$(g^{ab} f^{z_1}, g^{z_1}), (g^{abc} f^{z_2}, g^{z_2})\big)\ and\ T,$$

decides whether $T = T_0 = (g^c f^{z_3}, g^{z_3})$ or $T = T_1 = (g^d f^{z_3}, g^{z_3})$ with random choices of $a, b, c, d \in \mathbb{Z}_p$ and $z_1, z_2, z_3 \in \mathbb{Z}_p$. The advantage of $\mathcal{A}$ is defined as $\mathbf{Adv}_{\mathcal{A}}^{P3DH}(\lambda) = \left| \Pr\left[\mathcal{A}(D, T_0) = 1\right] - \Pr\left[\mathcal{A}(D, T_1) = 1\right] \right|$ where the probability is taken over the random choices of $a, b, c, d, z_1, z_2, z_3$ and the random bits used by $\mathcal{A}$. We say that the P3DH assumption holds if no PPT algorithm has a non-negligible advantage in solving the above problem.

Remark 1. The P3DH problem can be modified as follows: given a challenge tuple $D = \big((p, \mathbb{G}, \mathbb{G}_T, e),\ (g, f), (g^a, f^a), (g^b, f^b), (g^{ab} f^{z_1}, g^{z_1}), (g^c f^{z_2}, g^{z_2})\big)$ and T, decides whether $T = T_0 = (g^{abc} f^{z_3}, g^{z_3})$ or $T = T_1 = (g^d f^{z_3}, g^{z_3})$. However, this modified one is the same as the original one by changing the position of the challenge tuple as $D = \big((p, \mathbb{G}, \mathbb{G}_T, e),\ (g, f), (g^a, f^a), (g^b, f^b), (g^{ab} f^{z_1}, g^{z_1}), T\big)$ and $T' = (g^c f^{z_2}, g^{z_2})$, Thus, we will use any one of challenge tuple forms for the P3DH assumption.

3   Our Techniques

The basic idea to convert HVE schemes from composite order bilinear groups to prime order bilinear groups is to use bilinear product groups that are extended from bilinear groups using the direct product operation. Bilinear product groups were widely used in dual system encryption of Waters [17,24], private linear broadcast encryption of Garg et al. [10], and the conversion method of Freeman [9]. The product groups extended from multiplicative cyclic groups represent an exponent as a vector. Thus vector operations in product groups and bilinear product groups should be defined. Definitions 3 and 4 define the vector operations in product groups and bilinear product groups, respectively.

Definition 3 (Vector Operations). *Let $\mathbb{G}$ be multiplicative cyclic groups of prime p order. Let g be a generator of $\mathbb{G}$. We define vector operations over $\mathbb{G}$ as follows:*

1. *For a vector $\boldsymbol{b} = (b_1, \ldots, b_n) \in \mathbb{Z}_p^n$, define $g^{\boldsymbol{b}} := (g^{b_1}, \ldots, g^{b_n}) \in \mathbb{G}^n$.*
2. *For a vector $\boldsymbol{b} = (b_1, \ldots, b_n) \in \mathbb{Z}_p^n$ and a scalar $c \in \mathbb{Z}_p$, define $(g^{\boldsymbol{b}})^c := (g^{b_1 c}, \ldots, g^{b_n c}) \in \mathbb{G}^n$.*
3. *For two vectors $\boldsymbol{a} = (a_1, \ldots, a_n), \boldsymbol{b} = (b_1, \ldots, b_n) \in \mathbb{Z}_p^n$, define $g^{\boldsymbol{a}} g^{\boldsymbol{b}} := (g^{a_1 + b_1}, \ldots, g^{a_n + b_n}) \in \mathbb{G}^n$.*

Definition 4 (Bilinear Product Groups). *Let $(p, \mathbb{G}, \mathbb{G}_T, e)$ be bilinear groups of prime order. Let g be a generator of $\mathbb{G}$. For integers n and m, the bilinear product groups $((p, \mathbb{G}, \mathbb{G}_T, e), g^{\boldsymbol{b}_1}, \ldots, g^{\boldsymbol{b}_m})$ of basis vectors $\boldsymbol{b}_1, \ldots, \boldsymbol{b}_m$ is defined as follows*

1. *The basis vectors $\boldsymbol{b}_1, \ldots, \boldsymbol{b}_m$ are random vectors such that $\boldsymbol{b}_i = (b_{i,1}, \ldots, b_{i,n}) \in \mathbb{Z}_p^n$.*
2. *The bilinear map $e : \mathbb{G}^n \times \mathbb{G}^n \rightarrow \mathbb{G}_T$ is defined as $e(g^{\boldsymbol{a}}, g^{\boldsymbol{b}}) := \prod_{i=1}^{n} e(g^{a_i}, g^{b_i}) = e(g, g)^{\boldsymbol{a} \cdot \boldsymbol{b}}$ where $\cdot$ is the inner product operation.*

To guarantee the correctness of cryptographic schemes in bilinear product groups, the orthogonal property of composite order bilinear groups should be implemented in bilinear product groups. The previous research [9,10,17,24] showed that the orthogonal property can be implemented in bilinear product groups. The idea is that the orthogonality between vectors can be defined using the inner-product operation such that $\boldsymbol{x} \cdot \boldsymbol{y} = 0$ since the bilinear map provides the inner-product operation. Definition 5 define the orthogonality in bilinear product groups.

Definition 5 (Orthogonality). *Let $((p, \mathbb{G}, \mathbb{G}_T, e), g^{\boldsymbol{b}_1}, \ldots, g^{\boldsymbol{b}_m})$ be bilinear product groups with n, m parameters. Let G_i, G_j be subgroups spanned by $g^{\boldsymbol{b}_i}, g^{\boldsymbol{b}_j}$, respectively. That is, $G_i = \langle g^{\boldsymbol{b}_i} \rangle$ and $G_j = \langle g^{\boldsymbol{b}_j} \rangle$. Then the two subgroups G_i and G_j are orthogonal to each other if $e(\boldsymbol{A}, \boldsymbol{B}) = 1$ for all $\boldsymbol{A} \in G_i$ and $\boldsymbol{B} \in G_j$.*

The main idea of our method that converts HVE schemes from composite order bilinear groups to prime order bilinear groups is that the previous HVE schemes [7,16,22] in composite order bilinear groups use the composite 3-party Diffie-Hellman (C3DH) assumption that is not a kind of the subgroup decision (SD) assumption.

The SD assumption is to distinguish whether $h \in \mathbb{G}$ or $h \in \mathbb{G}_1$ where $\mathbb{G}$ is a group and $\mathbb{G}_1$ is a subgroup of $\mathbb{G}$ [5]. In product groups $\mathbb{G}^n$, a subgroup G is defined as a vector space spanned by some basis vectors $\boldsymbol{b}_1, \ldots, \boldsymbol{b}_m$ such that $G = \langle g^{\boldsymbol{b}_1}, \ldots, g^{\boldsymbol{b}_m} \rangle$. If a subgroup is constructed from one basis vector, then the SD assumption is related to the DDH assumption. If a subgroup is constructed from k number of basis vectors, then the SD assumption is related to the decisional k-Linear (k-DLIN) assumption [9]. In symmetric bilinear groups of prime order, a subgroup should be constructed from two basis vectors since the DDH assumption is not valid [10,24]. If a subgroup is constructed from two basis vectors, then cryptographic schemes become complicated and there is no generic conversion method from composite order groups to prime order groups. In asymmetric bilinear groups of prime order, a subgroup can be constructed from one basis vector since the DDH assumption is valid [9,17]. If a subgroup is constructed from one basis vector, then there is a generic conversion method of Freeman, but it only works in asymmetric bilinear groups.

The C3DH assumption is defined in Assumption 3. The notable properties of the C3DH assumption are that the target value T is always an element of $\mathbb{G}_{p_1 p_2}$ in contrast to the SD assumption, and the subgroup $\mathbb{G}_{p_2}$ plays the role of random blinding. From these properties of the C3DH assumption, it is possible to use just one basis vector to construct a subgroup. Additionally, it is possible to use simple basis vectors for cryptographic schemes since ciphertexts and tokens can use different subgroups that are not orthogonal.

Assumption 3 (Composite 3-party Diffie-Hellman, C3DH). *Let* $(N, \mathbb{G}, \mathbb{G}_T, e)$ *be a description of bilinear groups of composite order* $N = p_1 \cdots p_m$ *where* p_i *is a random prime. Let* g_{p_i} *be a generator of the subgroup* $\mathbb{G}_{p_i}$. *The C3DH assumption is stated as follows: given a challenge tuple*

$$\boldsymbol{D} = \left((N, \mathbb{G}, \mathbb{G}_T, e), g_{p_1}, \ldots, g_{p_m}, g_{p_1}^a, g_{p_1}^b, g_{p_1}^{ab} R_1, g_{p_1}^{abc} R_2 \right) \ and \ T,$$

decides whether $T = T_0 = g_{p_1}^c R_3$ *or* $T = T_1 = g_{p_1}^d R_3$ *with random choices of* $a, b, c, d \in \mathbb{Z}_{p_1}$ *and* $R_1, R_2, R_3 \in \mathbb{G}_{p_2}$.

For instance, we select basis vectors $\boldsymbol{b}_{1,1} = (1,0), \boldsymbol{b}_{1,2} = (1,a), \boldsymbol{b}_2 = (a,-1)$ for the conversion from bilinear groups of composite $N = p_1 p_2$ order. For the conversion from bilinear groups of composite $N = p_1 p_2 p_3$ order, we select basis vectors $\boldsymbol{b}_{1,1} = (1,0,a_1), \boldsymbol{b}_{1,2} = (1,a_2,0), \boldsymbol{b}_2 = (a_2,-1,a_1 a_2 - a_3), \boldsymbol{b}_3 = (a_1, a_3, -1)$. Although different basis vectors were selected, the assumption for the security proof is the simple one that is independent of basis vectors.

4   Conversion 1: BW-HVE

In this section, we convert the HVE scheme of Boneh and Waters [7] in composite order bilinear groups to an HVE scheme in prime order bilinear groups and prove its selective security under the DBDH and P3DH assumptions.

4.1   Construction

Setup($1^\lambda, \ell$): It first generates the bilinear group $\mathbb{G}$ of prime order p of bit size $\Theta(\lambda)$. It chooses a random value $a \in \mathbb{Z}_p$ and sets basis vectors for bilinear product groups as $\boldsymbol{b}_{1,1} = (1,0)$, $\boldsymbol{b}_{1,2} = (1,a)$, $\boldsymbol{b}_2 = (a,-1)$. It also sets $\boldsymbol{B}_{1,1} = g^{\boldsymbol{b}_{1,1}}, \boldsymbol{B}_{1,2} = g^{\boldsymbol{b}_{1,2}}, \boldsymbol{B}_2 = g^{\boldsymbol{b}_2}$. It selects random exponents $v', \{u'_i, h'_i, w'_i\}^\ell_{i=1}, \alpha \in \mathbb{Z}_p, z_v, \{z_{u,i}, z_{h,i}, z_{w,i}\}^\ell_{i=1} \in \mathbb{Z}_p$ and outputs a secret key and a public key as

$$SK = \left(\boldsymbol{V}_k = \boldsymbol{B}^{v'}_{1,2}, \{\boldsymbol{U}_{k,i} = \boldsymbol{B}^{u'_i}_{1,2}, \ \boldsymbol{H}_{k,i} = \boldsymbol{B}^{h'_i}_{1,2}, \ \boldsymbol{W}_{k,i} = \boldsymbol{B}^{w'_i}_{1,2} \}^\ell_{i=1}, \boldsymbol{B}^\alpha_{1,2} \right),$$

$$PK = \Big(\boldsymbol{B}_{1,1}, \ \boldsymbol{B}_{1,2}, \ \boldsymbol{B}_2, \ \boldsymbol{V}_c = \boldsymbol{B}^{v'}_{1,1} \boldsymbol{B}^{z_v}_2,$$

$$\{\boldsymbol{U}_{c,i} = \boldsymbol{B}^{u'_i}_{1,1} \boldsymbol{B}^{z_{u,i}}_2, \ \boldsymbol{H}_{c,i} = \boldsymbol{B}^{h'_i}_{1,1} \boldsymbol{B}^{z_{h,i}}_2, \ \boldsymbol{W}_{c,i} = \boldsymbol{B}^{w'_i}_{1,1} \boldsymbol{B}^{z_{w,i}}_2 \}^\ell_{i=1},$$

$$\Omega = e(\boldsymbol{B}^{v'}_{1,1}, \boldsymbol{B}_{1,2})^\alpha \Big).$$

GenToken$(\boldsymbol{\sigma}, SK, PK)$: It takes as input a vector $\boldsymbol{\sigma} = (\sigma_1, \ldots, \sigma_\ell) \in \Sigma^\ell_*$, the secret key SK, and the public key PK. Let S be the set of indexes that are not wild-card fields in the vector $\boldsymbol{\sigma}$. It selects random exponents $\{r_{1,i}, r_{2,i}\}_{i \in S} \in \mathbb{Z}_p$ and outputs a token as

$$TK_{\boldsymbol{\sigma}} = \Big(\boldsymbol{K}_1 = \boldsymbol{B}^\alpha_{1,2} \prod_{i \in S} (\boldsymbol{U}^{\sigma_i}_{k,i} \boldsymbol{H}_{k,i})^{r_{1,i}} \boldsymbol{W}^{r_{2,i}}_{k,i},$$

$$\{\boldsymbol{K}_{2,i} = \boldsymbol{V}^{-r_{1,i}}_k, \ \boldsymbol{K}_{3,i} = \boldsymbol{V}^{-r_{2,i}}_k \}_{i \in S} \Big).$$

Encrypt$(\boldsymbol{x}, M, PK)$: It takes as input a vector $\boldsymbol{x} = (x_1, \ldots, x_\ell) \in \Sigma^\ell$, a message $M \in \mathcal{M}$, and the public key PK. It first chooses a random exponent $t \in \mathbb{Z}_p$ and random blinding values $z_1, \{z_{2,i}, z_{3,i}\}^\ell_{i=1} \in \mathbb{Z}_p$. Then it outputs a ciphertext as

$$CT = \Big(C_0 = \Omega^t M, \ \boldsymbol{C}_1 = \boldsymbol{V}^t_c \boldsymbol{B}^{z_1}_2,$$

$$\{\boldsymbol{C}_{2,i} = (\boldsymbol{U}^{x_i}_{c,i} \boldsymbol{H}_{c,i})^t \boldsymbol{B}^{z_{2,i}}_2, \ \boldsymbol{C}_{3,i} = \boldsymbol{W}^t_{c,i} \boldsymbol{B}^{z_{3,i}}_2 \}^\ell_{i=1} \Big).$$

Query$(CT, TK_{\boldsymbol{\sigma}}, PK)$: It takes as input a ciphertext CT and a token $TK_{\boldsymbol{\sigma}}$ of a vector $\boldsymbol{\sigma}$. It first computes

$$M \leftarrow C_0 \cdot \left(e(\boldsymbol{C}_1, \boldsymbol{K}_1) \cdot \prod_{i \in S} e(\boldsymbol{C}_{2,i}, \boldsymbol{K}_{2,i}) \cdot e(\boldsymbol{C}_{3,i}, \boldsymbol{K}_{3,i}) \right)^{-1}.$$

If $M \notin \mathcal{M}$, it outputs $\perp$ indicating that the predicate $f_{\boldsymbol{\sigma}}$ is not satisfied. Otherwise, it outputs M indicating that the predicate $f_{\boldsymbol{\sigma}}$ is satisfied.

4.2 Correctness

If $f_{\boldsymbol{\sigma}}(\boldsymbol{x}) = 1$, then the following calculation shows that **Query$(CT, TK_{\boldsymbol{\sigma}}, PK) = M$** using the orthogonality of basis vectors such that $e(g^{b_2}, g^{b_{1,2}}) = 1$.

$$e(\boldsymbol{C}_1, \boldsymbol{K}_1) \cdot \prod_{i \in S} \left(e(\boldsymbol{C}_{2,i}, \boldsymbol{K}_{2,i}) \cdot e(\boldsymbol{C}_{3,i}, \boldsymbol{K}_{3,i}) \right)$$

$$= e(V_c^t, B_{1,2}^\alpha \prod_{i \in S}(U_{k,i}^{\sigma_i} H_{k,i})^{r_{1,i}} W_{k,i}^{r_{2,i}}) \cdot$$

$$\prod_{i \in S} e((U_{c,i}^{x_i} H_{c,i})^t, V_k^{-r_{1,i}}) \cdot e(W_{c,i}^t, V_k^{-r_{2,i}})$$

$$= e(B_{1,1}^{v't}, B_{1,2}^\alpha) \cdot \prod_{i \in S} e(g^{v'}, g^{u_i'(\sigma_i - x_i)})^{t \cdot r_{1,i}} = e(B_{1,1}^{v'}, B_{1,2})^{\alpha t}.$$

Otherwise, that is $f_\sigma(x) = 0$, then the probability of $\mathbf{Query}(CT, TK_\sigma, PK) \neq \perp$ is negligible by limiting $|\mathcal{M}|$ to less than $|\mathbb{G}_T|^{1/4}$.

4.3   Security

Theorem 4. *The above HVE scheme is selectively secure under the DBDH and P3DH assumptions.*

Proof. The proof of this theorem is easily obtained from the following four Lemmas 1, 2, 3 and 4. Before presenting the four lemmas, we first introduce the following three assumptions. The HVE scheme of Boneh and Waters constructed in bilinear groups of composite order $N = p_1 p_2$, and its security was proven under the DBDH, bilinear subgroup decision (BSD), and C3DH assumptions [7]. These assumptions in composite order bilinear groups are converted to the following Assumptions 4-1, 4-2 and 4-3 using our conversion method.

Assumption 4-1. Let $((p, \mathbb{G}, \mathbb{G}_T, e), g^{b_{1,1}}, g^{b_{1,2}}, g^{b_2})$ be the bilinear product group of basis vectors $b_{1,1} = (1,0), b_{1,2} = (1,a), b_2 = (a,-1)$. The Assumption 4-1 is stated as follows: given a challenge tuple

$$D = ((p, \mathbb{G}, \mathbb{G}_T, e),\ g^{b_{1,1}}, g^{b_{1,2}}, g^{b_2}, (g^{b_{1,1}})^{c_1}, (g^{b_{1,1}})^{c_2},$$
$$(g^{b_{1,2}})^{c_1}, (g^{b_{1,2}})^{c_2}, (g^{b_{1,1}})^{c_3})\ \text{and } T,$$

decides whether $T = T_0 = e(g,g)^{c_1 c_2 c_3}$ or $T = T_1 = e(g,g)^d$ with random choices of $c_1, c_2, c_3, d \in \mathbb{Z}_p$.

Assumption 4-2. Let $((p, \mathbb{G}, \mathbb{G}_T, e), g^{b_{1,1}}, g^{b_{1,2}}, g^{b_2})$ be the bilinear product group of basis vectors $b_{1,1} = (1,0), b_{1,2} = (1,a), b_2 = (a,-1)$. The Assumption 4-2 is stated as follows: given a challenge tuple

$$D = ((p, \mathbb{G}, \mathbb{G}_T, e),\ g^{b_{1,1}}, g^{b_{1,2}}, g^{b_2})\ \text{and } T,$$

decides whether $T = T_0 = e((g^{b_{1,1}})^{c_1}(g^{b_2})^{c_3}, (g^{b_{1,2}})^{c_2})$ or $T = T_1 = e((g^{b_{1,1}})^{c_1}, (g^{b_{1,2}})^{c_2})$ with random choices of $c_1, c_2, c_3 \in \mathbb{Z}_p$.

Assumption 4-3. Let $((p, \mathbb{G}, \mathbb{G}_T, e), g^{b_{1,1}}, g^{b_{1,2}}, g^{b_2})$ be the bilinear product group of basis vectors $b_{1,1} = (1,0), b_{1,2} = (1,a), b_2 = (a,-1)$. The Assumption 4-3 is stated as follows: given a challenge tuple

$$D = ((p, \mathbb{G}, \mathbb{G}_T, e),\ g^{b_{1,1}}, g^{b_{1,2}}, g^{b_2}, (g^{b_{1,2}})^{c_1}, (g^{b_{1,2}})^{c_2},$$
$$(g^{b_{1,1}})^{c_1 c_2}(g^{b_2})^{z_1}, (g^{b_{1,1}})^{c_1 c_2 c_3}(g^{b_2})^{z_2})\ \text{and } T,$$

decides whether $T = T_0 = (g^{b_{1,1}})^{c_3}(g^{b_2})^{z_3}$ or $T = T_1 = (g^{b_{1,1}})^d(g^{b_2})^{z_3}$ with random choices of $c_1, c_2, c_3, d \in \mathbb{Z}_p$ and $z_1, z_2, z_3 \in \mathbb{Z}_p$.

Lemma 1. *The above HVE scheme is selectively secure under the Assumptions 4-1, 4-2 and 4-3.*

Proof. The proof of this lemma is directly obtained from [7] since the Assumptions 4-1, 4-2 and 4-2 in prime order bilinear groups are correspond to the DBDH, BSD, and C3DH assumptions in composite order bilinear groups. That is, the proof of [7] can be exactly simulated using the vector operations in the Definition 3 and the Assumptions 4-1, 4-2 and 4-3.

Lemma 2. *If the DBDH assumption holds, then the Assumption 4-1 also holds.*

Proof. Suppose there exists an adversary $\mathcal{A}$ that breaks the Assumption 4-1 with a non-negligible advantage. An algorithm $\mathcal{B}$ that solves the DBDH assumption using $\mathcal{A}$ is given: a challenge tuple $D = ((p, \mathbb{G}, \mathbb{G}_T, e), g, g^{c_1}, g^{c_2}, g^{c_3})$ and T where $T = T_0 = e(g, g)^{c_1 c_2 c_3}$ or $T = T_1 = e(g, g)^d$. $\mathcal{B}$ first chooses random values $a \in \mathbb{Z}_p$ and computes

$$g^{b_{1,1}} = (g, 1),\ g^{b_{1,2}} = (g, g^a),\ g^{b_2} = (g^a, g^{-1}),$$
$$(g^{b_{1,1}})^{c_1} = (g^{c_1}, 1),\ (g^{b_{1,1}})^{c_2} = (g^{c_2}, 1),\ (g^{b_{1,1}})^{c_3} = (g^{c_3}, 1),$$
$$(g^{b_{1,2}})^{c_1} = (g^{c_1}, (g^{c_1})^a),\ (g^{b_{1,2}})^{c_2} = (g^{c_2}, (g^{c_2})^a).$$

Next, it gives the tuple $D' = ((p, \mathbb{G}, \mathbb{G}_T, e), g^{b_{1,1}}, g^{b_{1,2}}, g^{b_2}, (g^{b_{1,1}})^{c_1}, (g^{b_{1,1}})^{c_2}, (g^{b_{1,2}})^{c_1}, (g^{b_{1,2}})^{c_2}, (g^{b_{1,1}})^{c_3})$ and T to $\mathcal{A}$. Then $\mathcal{A}$ outputs a guess γ'. $\mathcal{B}$ also outputs γ'. If the advantage of $\mathcal{A}$ is ϵ, then the advantage of $\mathcal{B}$ is greater than ϵ since the distribution of the challenge tuple to $\mathcal{A}$ is equal to the Assumption 4-1.

Lemma 3. *The Assumption 4-2 holds for all adversaries.*

Proof. The equation $e((g^{b_{1,1}})^{c_1}(g^{b_2})^{c_3}, (g^{b_{1,2}})^{c_2}) = e((g^{b_{1,1}})^{c_1}, (g^{b_{1,2}})^{c_2})$ holds by the orthogonality of basis vectors such that $e(g^{b_2}, g^{b_{1,2}}) = 1$. Therefore, any adversary can not break the Assumption 4-2.

Lemma 4. *If the P3DH assumption holds, then the Assumption 4-3 also holds.*

Proof. Suppose there exists an adversary $\mathcal{A}$ that breaks the Assumption 4-3 with a non-negligible advantage. An algorithm $\mathcal{B}$ that solves the P3DH assumption using $\mathcal{A}$ is given: a challenge tuple $D = ((p, \mathbb{G}, \mathbb{G}_T, e), (g, f), (g^{c_1}, f^{c_1}), (g^{c_2}, f^{c_2}), (g^{c_1 c_2} f^{z_1}, g^{z_1}), (g^{c_1 c_2 c_3} f^{z_2}, g^{z_2}))$ and T where $T = T_0 = (g^{c_3} f^{z_3}, g^{z_3})$ or $T = T_1 = (g^d f^{z_3}, g^{z_3})$. $\mathcal{B}$ first computes

$$g^{b_{1,1}} = (g, 1),\ g^{b_{1,2}} = (g, f),\ g^{b_2} = (f, g^{-1}),$$
$$(g^{b_{1,2}})^{c_1} = (g^{c_1}, f^{c_1}),\ (g^{b_{1,2}})^{c_2} = (g^{c_2}, f^{c_2}),$$
$$(g^{b_{1,1}})^{c_1 c_2}(g^{b_2})^{z_1} = (g^{c_1 c_2} f^{z_1}, (g^{z_1})^{-1}),$$
$$(g^{b_{1,1}})^{c_1 c_2 c_3}(g^{b_2})^{z_2} = (g^{c_1 c_2 c_3} f^{z_2}, (g^{z_2})^{-1}).$$

Intuitively, it sets $a = \log f$. Next, it gives the tuple $D' = ((p, \mathbb{G}, \mathbb{G}_T, e), g^{\boldsymbol{b}_{1,1}}, g^{\boldsymbol{b}_{1,2}}, g^{\boldsymbol{b}_2}, (g^{\boldsymbol{b}_{1,1}})^{c_1}, (g^{\boldsymbol{b}_{1,1}})^{c_2}, (g^{\boldsymbol{b}_{1,2}})^{c_1}, (g^{\boldsymbol{b}_{1,2}})^{c_2}, (g^{\boldsymbol{b}_{1,1}})^{c_1 c_2 c_3})$ and T to $\mathcal{A}$. Then $\mathcal{A}$ outputs a guess γ'. $\mathcal{B}$ also outputs γ'. If the advantage of $\mathcal{A}$ is ϵ, then the advantage of $\mathcal{B}$ is greater than ϵ since the distribution of the challenge tuple to $\mathcal{A}$ is equal to the Assumption 4-3.

5   Conversion 2: SW-dHVE

In this section, we convert the delegatable HVE scheme of Shi and Waters [22] to prime order bilinear groups and prove its selective security under the DBDH and P3DH assumptions.

5.1   Construction

Let Σ be a finite set of attributes and let $?, *$ be two special symbol not in Σ. Define $\Sigma_{?,*} = \Sigma \cup \{?, *\}$. The symbol $?$ denotes a delegatable field, i.e., a field where one is allowed to fill in an arbitrary value and perform delegation. The symbol $*$ denotes a wild-card field or "don't care" field.

Setup$(1^\lambda, \ell)$: It first generates the bilinear group $\mathbb{G}$ of prime order p of bit size $\Theta(\lambda)$. It chooses random values $a_1, a_2, a_3 \in \mathbb{Z}_p$ and sets basis vectors for bilinear product groups as $\boldsymbol{b}_{1,1} = (1, 0, a_1)$, $\boldsymbol{b}_{1,2} = (1, a_2, 0)$, $\boldsymbol{b}_2 = (a_2, -1, a_1 a_2 - a_3)$, $\boldsymbol{b}_3 = (a_1, a_3, -1)$.
It also sets

$$\boldsymbol{B}_{1,1} = g^{\boldsymbol{b}_{1,1}}, \ \boldsymbol{B}_{1,2} = g^{\boldsymbol{b}_{1,2}}, \ \boldsymbol{B}_2 = g^{\boldsymbol{b}_2}, \ \boldsymbol{B}_3 = g^{\boldsymbol{b}_3}.$$

It selects random exponents $v', w_1', w_2', \{u_i', h_i'\}_{i=1}^\ell, \alpha \in \mathbb{Z}_p$, $z_v, z_{w,1}, z_{w,2}$, $\{z_{u,i}, z_{h,i}\}_{i=1}^\ell \in \mathbb{Z}_p$ and outputs a secret key and a public key as

$$SK = \left(\boldsymbol{V}_k = \boldsymbol{B}_{1,2}^{v'}, \boldsymbol{W}_{k,1} = \boldsymbol{B}_{1,2}^{w_1'}, \boldsymbol{W}_{k,2} = \boldsymbol{B}_{1,2}^{w_2'}, \right.$$
$$\left. \{\boldsymbol{U}_{k,i} = \boldsymbol{B}_{1,2}^{u_i'}, \boldsymbol{H}_{k,i} = \boldsymbol{B}_{1,2}^{h_i'}\}_{i=1}^\ell, \ \boldsymbol{B}_{1,2}^\alpha \right),$$

$$PK = \left(\boldsymbol{B}_{1,1}, \ \boldsymbol{B}_{1,2}, \ \boldsymbol{B}_2, \ \boldsymbol{B}_3, \right.$$
$$\boldsymbol{V}_c = \boldsymbol{B}_{1,1}^{v'} \boldsymbol{B}_2^{z_v}, \ \boldsymbol{W}_{c,1} = \boldsymbol{B}_{1,1}^{w_1'} \boldsymbol{B}_2^{z_{w,1}}, \ \boldsymbol{W}_{c,2} = \boldsymbol{B}_{1,2}^{w_2'} \boldsymbol{B}_2^{z_{w,2}},$$
$$\left. \{\boldsymbol{U}_{c,i} = \boldsymbol{B}_{1,1}^{u_i'} \boldsymbol{B}_2^{z_{u,i}}, \ \boldsymbol{H}_{c,i} = \boldsymbol{B}_{1,1}^{h_i'} \boldsymbol{B}_2^{z_{h,i}}\}_{i=1}^\ell, \ \Omega = e(\boldsymbol{B}_{1,1}, \boldsymbol{B}_{1,2})^\alpha \right).$$

GenToken(σ, SK, PK): It takes as input an attribute vector $\sigma = (\sigma_1, \ldots, \sigma_\ell) \in \Sigma_{?,*}^\ell$ and the secret key SK.

1. Let S be the set of indexes that are not delegatable fields and wild-card fields in the vector $\boldsymbol{\sigma}$. It first selects random exponents $r_1, r_2, \{r_{3,i}\}_{i \in S} \in \mathbb{Z}_p$ and random blinding values $y_1, y_2, y_3, \{y_{4,i}\}_{i \in S} \in \mathbb{Z}_p$. Then it computes decryption components as

$$K_1 = B_{1,2}^{\alpha} W_{k,1}^{r_1} W_{k,2}^{r_2} \prod_{i \in S} (U_{k,i}^{\sigma_i} H_{k,i})^{r_{3,i}} B_3^{y_1},$$

$$K_2 = V_k^{-r_1} B_3^{y_2}, \quad K_3 = V_k^{-r_2} B_3^{y_3}, \quad \{K_{4,i} = V_k^{-r_{3,i}} B_3^{y_{4,i}}\}_{i \in S}.$$

2. Let $S_?$ be the set of indexes that are delegatable fields. It selects random exponents $\{s_{1,j}, s_{2,j}, \{s_{3,j,i}\}\} \in \mathbb{Z}_p$ and random blinding values $\{y_{1,j,u}, y_{1,j,h}, y_{2,j}, y_{3,j}, \{y_{4,j,i}\}\} \in \mathbb{Z}_p$. Next, it computes delegation components as

$$\forall j \in S_? : \quad L_{1,j,u} = U_{k,i}^{s_{3,j,j}} B_3^{y_{1,j,u}},$$

$$L_{1,j,h} = W_{k,1}^{s_{1,j}} W_{k,2}^{s_{2,j}} \prod_{i \in S} (U_{k,i}^{\sigma_i} H_{k,i})^{s_{3,j,i}} H_{k,j}^{s_{3,j,j}} B_3^{y_{1,j,h}},$$

$$L_{2,j} = V_k^{-s_{1,j}} B_3^{y_{2,j}}, \quad L_{3,j} = V_k^{-s_{2,j}} B_3^{y_{3,j}},$$

$$\{L_{4,j,i} = V_k^{-s_{3,j,i}} B_3^{y_{4,j,i}}\}_{i \in S \cup \{j\}}.$$

3. Finally, it outputs a token as

$$TK_{\boldsymbol{\sigma}} = \Big(K_1, \ K_2, \ K_3, \ \{K_{4,i}\}_{i \in S},$$

$$\{L_{1,j,u}, \ L_{1,j,h}, \ L_{2,j}, \ L_{3,j}, \ \{L_{4,j,i}\}_{i \in S \cup \{j\}} \}_{j \in S_?} \Big).$$

Delegate($\boldsymbol{\sigma}', TK_{\boldsymbol{\sigma}}, PK$): It takes as input an attribute vector $\boldsymbol{\sigma}' = (\sigma_1, \ldots, \sigma_\ell) \in \Sigma_{?,*}^{\ell}$ and a token $TK_{\boldsymbol{\sigma}}$. Without loss of generality, we assume that $\boldsymbol{\sigma}'$ fixes only one delegatable field of $\boldsymbol{\sigma}$. It is clear that we can perform delegation on multiple fields if we have an algorithm to perform delegation on one field. Suppose $\boldsymbol{\sigma}'$ fixes the k-th index of $\boldsymbol{\sigma}$.

1. If the k-th index of $\boldsymbol{\sigma}'$ is set to $*$, that is, a wild-card field, then it can perform delegation by simply removing the delegation components that correspond to k-th index.

2. Otherwise, that is, if the k-th index of $\boldsymbol{\sigma}'$ is set to some value in Σ, then it perform delegation as follows:

   (a) Let S be the set of indexes that are not delegatable fields and wild-card fields in the vector $\boldsymbol{\sigma}'$. Note that $k \in S$. It selects random exponents $\mu, y_1, y_2, y_3, \{y_{4,i}\}_{i \in S} \in \mathbb{Z}_p$ and updates the token as

   $$K_1' = K_1 (L_{1,k,u}^{\sigma_k} L_{1,k,h})^{\mu} B_3^{y_1}, \ K_2' = K_2 L_{2,k}^{\mu} B_3^{y_2}, \ K_3' = K_3 L_{3,k}^{\mu} B_3^{y_3},$$

   $$K_{4,k}' = L_{4,k,k}^{\mu} B_3^{y_{4,k}}, \ \{K_{4,i}' = K_{4,i} L_{4,k,i}^{\mu} B_3^{y_{4,i}}\}_{i \in S \setminus \{k\}}.$$

   (b) Let $S_?$ be the set of indexes that are delegatable fields in the vector $\boldsymbol{\sigma}'$. It selects random exponents $\{\tau_j, y_{1,j,u}, y_{1,j,h}, y_{2,j}, y_{3,j},$

$\{y_{4,j,i}\}_{i\in S\cup\{j\}}\}_{j\in S_?} \in \mathbb{Z}_p$ and re-randomize the delegation components of the token as

$$\forall j \in S_? : \ L'_{1,j,u} = L^{\mu}_{1,j,u}B_3^{y_{1,j,u}}, \ L'_{1,j,h} = L^{\mu}_{1,j,h}(L^{\sigma_k}_{1,k,u}L_{1,k,h})^{\tau_j}B_3^{y_{1,j,h}},$$
$$L'_{2,j} = L^{\mu}_{2,j}L^{\tau_j}_{2,j}B_3^{y_{2,j}}, \ L'_{3,j} = L^{\mu}_{3,j}L^{\tau_j}_{3,j}B_3^{y_{3,j}},$$
$$L'_{4,j,j} = L^{\mu}_{4,j,j}B_3^{y_{4,j,j}}, \ L'_{4,j,k} = L^{\tau_j}_{4,j,k}B_3^{y_{4,j,k}},$$
$$\{L'_{4,j,i} = L^{\mu}_{4,j,i}L^{\tau_j}_{4,j,k}B_3^{y_{4,j,i}}\}_{i\in S\setminus\{k\}}.$$

(c) Finally, it outputs a token as

$$TK_{\sigma'} = \Big(K'_1, \ K'_2, \ K'_3, \ \{K'_{4,i}\}_{i\in S},$$
$$\{L'_{1,j,h}, L'_{1,j,u}, \ L'_{2,j}, \ L'_{3,j}, \ \{L'_{4,j,i}\}_{i\in S\cup\{j\}}\}_{j\in S_?} \Big).$$

Encrypt(x, M, PK): It takes as input an attribute vector $x = (x_1, \ldots, x_\ell) \in \Sigma^\ell$, a message $M \in \mathcal{M} \subseteq \mathbb{G}_T$, and the public key PK. It first chooses a random exponent $t \in \mathbb{Z}_p$ and random blinding values $z_1, z_2, z_3, \{z_{4,i}\}_{i=1}^\ell \in \mathbb{Z}_p$. Then it outputs a ciphertext as

$$CT = \Big(C_0 = \Omega^t M, \ C_1 = V_c^t B_2^{z_1}, \ C_2 = W_{c,1}^t B_2^{z_2}, \ C_3 = W_{c,2}^t B_2^{z_3},$$
$$\{C_{4,i} = (U_{c,i}^{x_i} H_{c,i})^t B_2^{z_{4,i}}\}_{i=1}^\ell \Big).$$

Query(CT, TK_σ, PK): It takes as input a ciphertext CT and a token TK_σ of a vector σ. It first computes

$$M \leftarrow C_0 \cdot \Big(e(C_1, K_1) \cdot e(C_2, K_2) \cdot e(C_3, K_3) \cdot \prod_{i\in S} e(C_{4,i}, K_{4,i}) \Big)^{-1}.$$

If $M \notin \mathcal{M}$, it outputs $\bot$ indicating that the predicate f_σ is not satisfied. Otherwise, it outputs M indicating that the predicate f_σ is satisfied.

5.2 Correctness

If $f_\sigma(x) = 1$, then the following calculation shows that **Query**$(CT, TK_\sigma, PK) = M$ by the orthogonality of basis vectors such that $e(g^{b_{1,1}}, g^{b_3}) = 1, e(g^{b_{1,2}}, g^{b_2}) = 1, e(g^{b_2}, g^{b_3}) = 1$.

$$e(C_1, K_1) \cdot e(C_2, K_2) \cdot e(C_3, K_3) \cdot \prod_{i\in S} e(C_{4,i}, K_{4,i})$$
$$= e((V_c)^t, B_{1,2}^\alpha W_{k,1}^{r_1} W_{k,2}^{r_2} \prod_{i\in S}(U_{c,i}^{\sigma_i} H_{c,i})^{r_{3,i}}) \cdot e(W_{c,1}^t, V_k^{-r_1}) \cdot$$
$$e(W_{c,2}^t, V_k^{-r_2}) \cdot \prod_{i\in S} e((U_{c,i}^{x_i} H_{c,i})^t, V_k^{-r_{3,i}})$$
$$= e(B_{1,1}^{v't}, B_{1,2}^\alpha) \cdot \prod_{i\in S} e(g^{v'}, g^{u'_i(\sigma_i - x_i)})^{tr_{3,i}} = e(B_{1,1}^{v'}, B_{1,2})^{\alpha t}.$$

Otherwise, that is $f_\sigma(x) = 0$, the probability of **Query**$(CT, TK_\sigma, PK) \neq \bot$ is negligible by limiting $|\mathcal{M}|$ to less than $|\mathbb{G}_T|^{1/4}$.

5.3   Security

Theorem 5. *The above dHVE scheme is selectively secure under the DBDH and P3DH assumptions.*

Proof. The proof of this theorem is easily obtained from the following five Lemmas 5, 6, 7, 8 and 9. Before presenting the five lemmas, we first introduce the following four assumptions. The HVE scheme of Shi and Waters constructed in bilinear groups of composite order $N = p_1 p_2 p_3$, and its security was proven under the DBDH, BSD, and C3DH assumptions [22]. In composite order bilinear groups, the C3DH assumption imply the l-C3DH assumption that was introduced in [22]. However, this implication is not valid in prime order bilinear groups since the basis vectors for ciphertexts and tokens are different. Thus the C3DH assumption for ciphertexts and the C3DH assumption for tokens should be treated as differently. These assumptions in composite order bilinear groups are converted to the following Assumptions 5-1, 5-2, 5-3 and 5-4 using our conversion method.

Assumption 5-1. Let $((p, \mathbb{G}, \mathbb{G}_T, e), g^{b_{1,1}}, g^{b_{1,2}}, g^{b_2}, g^{b_3})$ be the bilinear product group of basis vectors $b_{1,1} = (1, 0, a_1), b_{1,2} = (1, a_2, 0), b_2 = (a_2, -1, a_1 a_2 - a_3), b_3 = (a_1, a_3, -1)$. The Assumption 5-1 is stated as follows: given a challenge tuple

$$D = ((p, \mathbb{G}, \mathbb{G}_T, e),\ g^{b_{1,1}}, g^{b_{1,2}}, g^{b_2}, g^{b_3}, (g^{b_{1,1}})^{c_1}, (g^{b_{1,1}})^{c_2},$$
$$(g^{b_{1,2}})^{c_1}, (g^{b_{1,2}})^{c_2}, (g^{b_{1,1}})^{c_3})\ \text{and}\ T,$$

decides whether $T = T_0 = e(g, g)^{c_1 c_2 c_3}$ or $T = T_1 = e(g, g)^d$ with random choices of $c_1, c_2, c_3, d \in \mathbb{Z}_p$.

Assumption 5-2. Let $((p, \mathbb{G}, \mathbb{G}_T, e), g^{b_{1,1}}, g^{b_{1,2}}, g^{b_2}, g^{b_3})$ be the bilinear product group of basis vectors $b_{1,1} = (1, 0, a_1), b_{1,2} = (1, a_2, 0), b_2 = (a_2, -1, a_1 a_2 - a_3), b_3 = (a_1, a_3, -1)$. The Assumption 5-2 is stated as follows: given a challenge tuple

$$D = ((p, \mathbb{G}, \mathbb{G}_T, e),\ g^{b_{1,1}}, g^{b_{1,2}}, g^{b_2}, g^{b_3})\ \text{and}\ T,$$

decides whether $T = T_0 = e((g^{b_{1,1}})^{c_1}(g^{b_2})^{c_3}, (g^{b_{1,2}})^{c_2}(g^{b_3})^{c_4})$ or $T = T_1 = e((g^{b_{1,1}})^{c_1}, (g^{b_{1,2}})^{c_2})$ with random choices of $c_1, c_2, c_3, c_4 \in \mathbb{Z}_p$.

Assumption 5-3. Let $((p, \mathbb{G}, \mathbb{G}_T, e), g^{b_{1,1}}, g^{b_{1,2}}, g^{b_2}, g^{b_3})$ be the bilinear product group of basis vectors $b_{1,1} = (1, 0, a_1), b_{1,2} = (1, a_2, 0), b_2 = (a_2, -1, a_1 a_2 - a_3), b_3 = (a_1, a_3, -1)$. The Assumption 5-3 is stated as follows: given a challenge tuple

$$D = ((p, \mathbb{G}, \mathbb{G}_T, e),\ g^{b_{1,1}}, g^{b_{1,2}}, g^{b_2}, g^{b_3}, (g^{b_{1,2}})^{c_1}, (g^{b_{1,2}})^{c_2},$$
$$(g^{b_{1,1}})^{c_1 c_2}(g^{b_2})^{z_1}, (g^{b_{1,1}})^{c_1 c_2 c_3}(g^{b_2})^{z_2})\ \text{and}\ T,$$

decides whether $T = T_0 = (g^{b_{1,1}})^{c_3}(g^{b_2})^{z_3}$ or $T = T_1 = (g^{b_{1,1}})^d(g^{b_2})^{z_3}$ with random choices of $c_1, c_2, c_3, d \in \mathbb{Z}_p$, and $z_1, z_2, z_3 \in \mathbb{Z}_p$.

Assumption 5-4. Let $((p, \mathbb{G}, \mathbb{G}_T, e), g^{\boldsymbol{b}_{1,1}}, g^{\boldsymbol{b}_{1,2}}, g^{\boldsymbol{b}_2}, g^{\boldsymbol{b}_3})$ be the bilinear product group of basis vectors $\boldsymbol{b}_{1,1} = (1, 0, a_1), \boldsymbol{b}_{1,2} = (1, a_2, 0), \boldsymbol{b}_2 = (a_2, -1, a_1 a_2 - a_3), \boldsymbol{b}_3 = (a_1, a_3, -1)$. The Assumption 5-4 is stated as follows: given a challenge tuple

$$D = ((p, \mathbb{G}, \mathbb{G}_T, e), \ g^{\boldsymbol{b}_{1,1}}, g^{\boldsymbol{b}_{1,2}}, g^{\boldsymbol{b}_2}, g^{\boldsymbol{b}_3}, (g^{\boldsymbol{b}_{1,1}})^{c_1}, (g^{\boldsymbol{b}_{1,1}})^{c_2},$$
$$(g^{\boldsymbol{b}_{1,2}})^{c_1 c_2}(g^{\boldsymbol{b}_3})^{z_1}, (g^{\boldsymbol{b}_{1,2}})^{c_1 c_2 c_3}(g^{\boldsymbol{b}_3})^{z_2}) \text{ and } T,$$

decides whether $T = T_0 = (g^{\boldsymbol{b}_{1,2}})^{c_3}(g^{\boldsymbol{b}_3})^{z_3}$ or $T = T_1 = (g^{\boldsymbol{b}_{1,2}})^d(g^{\boldsymbol{b}_3})^{z_3}$ with random choices of $c_1, c_2, c_3, d \in \mathbb{Z}_p$, and $z_1, z_2, z_3 \in \mathbb{Z}_p$.

Lemma 5. *The above dHVE scheme is selectively secure under the Assumptions 5-1, 5-2, 5-3 and 5-4.*

Proof. The proof of this lemma is directly obtained from [22] since the Assumptions 5-1, 5-2, 5-3, and 5-4 in prime order bilinear groups are correspond to the DBDH, BSD, C3DH (for ciphertexts), and C3DH (for tokens) assumptions in composite order bilinear groups.

Lemma 6. *If the DBDH assumption holds, then the Assumption 5-1 also holds.*

Proof. Suppose there exists an adversary $\mathcal{A}$ that breaks the Assumption 5-1 with a non-negligible advantage. An algorithm $\mathcal{B}$ that solves the DBDH assumption using $\mathcal{A}$ is given: a challenge tuple $D = ((p, \mathbb{G}, \mathbb{G}_T, e), g, g^{c_1}, g^{c_2}, g^{c_3})$ and T where $T = T_0 = e(g, g)^{c_1 c_2 c_3}$ or $T = T_1 = e(g, g)^d$. $\mathcal{B}$ first chooses random values $a_1, a_2, a_3 \in \mathbb{Z}_p$ and sets

$$g^{\boldsymbol{b}_{1,1}} = (g, 1, g^{a_1}), \ g^{\boldsymbol{b}_{1,2}} = (g, g^{a_2}, 1),$$
$$g^{\boldsymbol{b}_2} = (g^{a_2}, g^{-1}, g^{a_1 a_2 - a_3}), \ g^{\boldsymbol{b}_3} = (g^{a_1}, g^{a_3}, g^{-1}),$$
$$(g^{\boldsymbol{b}_{1,1}})^{c_1} = (g^{c_1}, 1, (g^{c_1})^{a_1}), \ (g^{\boldsymbol{b}_{1,1}})^{c_2} = (g^{c_2}, 1, (g^{c_2})^{a_1}), \ (g^{\boldsymbol{b}_{1,1}})^{c_3} = (g^{c_3}, 1),$$
$$(g^{\boldsymbol{b}_{1,2}})^{c_1} = (g^{c_1}, (g^{c_1})^{a_2}, 1), \ (g^{\boldsymbol{b}_{1,2}})^{c_2} = (g^{c_2}, (g^{c_2})^{a_2}, 1).$$

Next, it gives the tuple $D' = ((p, \mathbb{G}, \mathbb{G}_T, e), g^{\boldsymbol{b}_{1,1}}, g^{\boldsymbol{b}_{1,2}}, g^{\boldsymbol{b}_2}, (g^{\boldsymbol{b}_{1,1}})^{c_1}, (g^{\boldsymbol{b}_{1,1}})^{c_2}, (g^{\boldsymbol{b}_{1,2}})^{c_1}, (g^{\boldsymbol{b}_{1,2}})^{c_2}, (g^{\boldsymbol{b}_{1,1}})^{c_3})$ and T to $\mathcal{A}$. Then $\mathcal{A}$ outputs a guess γ'. $\mathcal{B}$ also outputs γ'. If the advantage of $\mathcal{A}$ is ϵ, then the advantage of $\mathcal{B}$ is greater than ϵ since the distribution of the challenge tuple to $\mathcal{A}$ is equal to the Assumption 5-1.

Lemma 7. *The Assumption 5-2 holds for all adversaries.*

Proof. The equation $e((g^{\boldsymbol{b}_{1,1}})^{c_1}(g^{\boldsymbol{b}_2})^{c_3}, (g^{\boldsymbol{b}_{1,2}})^{c_2}(g^{\boldsymbol{b}_3})^{c_4}) = e((g^{\boldsymbol{b}_{1,1}})^{c_1}, (g^{\boldsymbol{b}_{1,2}})^{c_2})$ holds by the orthogonality of basis vectors such that $e(g^{\boldsymbol{b}_{1,1}}, g^{\boldsymbol{b}_3}) = 1$, $e(g^{\boldsymbol{b}_2}, g^{\boldsymbol{b}_{1,2}}) = 1, e(g^{\boldsymbol{b}_2}, g^{\boldsymbol{b}_3}) = 1$. Therefore, any adversary can not break the Assumption 5-2.

Lemma 8. *If the P3DH assumption holds, then the Assumption 5-3 also holds.*

Proof. Suppose there exists an adversary $\mathcal{A}$ that breaks the Assumption 5-3 with a non-negligible advantage. An algorithm $\mathcal{B}$ that solves the P3DH assumption using $\mathcal{A}$ is given: a challenge tuple $D = ((p, \mathbb{G}, \mathbb{G}_T, e), (g, f),$ $(g^{c_1}, f^{c_1}), (g^{c_2}, f^{c_2}), (g^{c_1 c_2} f^{z_1}, g^{z_1}), (g^{c_1 c_2 c_3} f^{z_2}, g^{z_2}))$ and $T = T_\gamma = (T_{\gamma,1}, T_{\gamma,2})$ where $T = T_0 = (g^{c_3} f^{z_3}, g^{z_3})$ or $T = T_1 = (g^d f^{z_3}, g^{z_3})$. $\mathcal{B}$ first chooses random values $a_1, a_3 \in \mathbb{Z}_p$ and sets

$$g^{\boldsymbol{b}_{1,1}} = (g, 1, g^{a_1}), \ g^{\boldsymbol{b}_{1,2}} = (g, f, 1),$$
$$g^{\boldsymbol{b}_2} = (f, g^{-1}, f^{a_1} g^{-a_3}), \ g^{\boldsymbol{b}_3} = (g^{a_1}, g^{a_3}, g^{-1}),$$
$$(g^{\boldsymbol{b}_{1,2}})^{c_1} = (g^{c_1}, f^{c_1}, 1), \ (g^{\boldsymbol{b}_{1,2}})^{c_2} = (g^{c_2}, f^{c_2}, 1),$$
$$(g^{\boldsymbol{b}_{1,1}})^{c_1 c_2} (g^{\boldsymbol{b}_2})^{z_1} = (g^{c_1 c_2} f^{z_1}, (g^{z_1})^{-1}, (g^{c_1 c_2} f^{z_1})^{a_1} (g^{z_1})^{-a_3}),$$
$$(g^{\boldsymbol{b}_{1,1}})^{c_1 c_2 c_3} (g^{\boldsymbol{b}_2})^{z_2} = (g^{c_1 c_2 c_3} f^{z_2}, (g^{z_2})^{-1}, (g^{c_1 c_2 c_3} f^{z_2})^{a_1} (g^{z_2})^{-a_3}),$$
$$T' = (T_{\gamma,1}, T_{\gamma,2}, (T_{\gamma,1})^{a_1} (T_{\gamma,2})^{-a_3}).$$

Intuitively, it sets $a_2 = \log f$. Next, it gives the tuple $D' = ((p, \mathbb{G}, \mathbb{G}_T, e), g^{\boldsymbol{b}_{1,1}},$ $g^{\boldsymbol{b}_{1,2}}, g^{\boldsymbol{b}_2}, g^{\boldsymbol{b}_3}, (g^{\boldsymbol{b}_{1,2}})^{c_1}, (g^{\boldsymbol{b}_{1,2}})^{c_2}, (g^{\boldsymbol{b}_{1,1}})^{c_1 c_2} (g^{\boldsymbol{b}_2})^{z_1}, (g^{\boldsymbol{b}_{1,1}})^{c_1 c_2 c_3} (g^{\boldsymbol{b}_2})^{z_2})$ and T' to $\mathcal{A}$. Then $\mathcal{A}$ outputs a guess γ'. $\mathcal{B}$ also outputs γ'. If the advantage of $\mathcal{A}$ is ϵ, then the advantage of $\mathcal{B}$ is greater than ϵ since the distribution of the challenge tuple to $\mathcal{A}$ is equal to the Assumption 5-3.

Lemma 9. *If the P3DH assumption holds, then the Assumption 5-4 also holds.*

Proof. Suppose there exists an adversary $\mathcal{A}$ that breaks the Assumption 5-4 with a non-negligible advantage. An algorithm $\mathcal{B}$ that solves the P3DH assumption using $\mathcal{A}$ is given: a challenge tuple $D = ((p, \mathbb{G}, \mathbb{G}_T, e), (g, f),$ $(g^{c_1}, f^{c_1}), (g^{c_2}, f^{c_2}), (g^{c_1 c_2} f^{z_1}, g^{z_1}), (g^{c_1 c_2 c_3} f^{z_2}, g^{z_2}))$ and $T = T_\gamma = (T_{\gamma,1}, T_{\gamma,2})$ where $T_0 = (g^{c_3} f^{z_3}, g^{z_3})$ or $T_1 = (g^d f^{z_3}, g^{z_3})$. $\mathcal{B}$ first chooses random values $a_2, a_3 \in \mathbb{Z}_p$ and sets

$$g^{\boldsymbol{b}_{1,1}} = (g, 1, f), \ g^{\boldsymbol{b}_{1,2}} = (g, g^{a_2}, 1),$$
$$g^{\boldsymbol{b}_2} = (g^{a_2}, g^{-1}, g^{a_3}), \ g^{\boldsymbol{b}_3} = (f, f^{a_2} g^{-a_3}, g^{-1}),$$
$$(g^{\boldsymbol{b}_{1,1}})^{c_1} = (g^{c_1}, 1, f^{c_1}), \ (g^{\boldsymbol{b}_{1,1}})^{c_2} = (g^{c_2}, 1, f^{c_2}),$$
$$(g^{\boldsymbol{b}_{1,2}})^{c_1 c_2} (g^{\boldsymbol{b}_3})^{z_1} = (g^{c_1 c_2} f^{z_1}, (g^{c_1 c_2} f^{z_1})^{a_2} (g^{z_1})^{-a_3}, (g^{z_1})^{-1}),$$
$$(g^{\boldsymbol{b}_{1,2}})^{c_1 c_2 c_3} (g^{\boldsymbol{b}_3})^{z_2} = (g^{c_1 c_2 c_3} f^{z_2}, (g^{c_1 c_2 c_3} f^{z_2})^{a_2} (g^{z_2})^{-a_3}, (g^{z_2})^{-1}),$$
$$T' = (T_{\gamma,1}, (T_{\gamma,1})^{a_2} (T_{\gamma,2})^{-a_3}, (T_{\gamma,2})^{-1}).$$

Intuitively, it sets $a_1' = \log f, a_2' = a_2, a_3' = a_1 a_2 - a_3$ where a_1', a_2', a_3' are elements of basis vectors for the Assumption 5-4. Next, it gives the tuple $D' = (g^{\boldsymbol{b}_{1,1}}, g^{\boldsymbol{b}_{1,2}}, g^{\boldsymbol{b}_2}, g^{\boldsymbol{b}_3}, (g^{\boldsymbol{b}_{1,1}})^{c_1}, (g^{\boldsymbol{b}_{1,1}})^{c_2}, (g^{\boldsymbol{b}_{1,2}})^{c_1 c_2} \cdot$ $(g^{\boldsymbol{b}_3})^{z_1}, (g^{\boldsymbol{b}_{1,2}})^{c_1 c_2 c_3} (g^{\boldsymbol{b}_3})^{z_2})$ and T' to $\mathcal{A}$. Then $\mathcal{A}$ outputs a guess γ'. $\mathcal{B}$ also outputs γ'. If the advantage of $\mathcal{A}$ is ϵ, then the advantage of $\mathcal{B}$ is greater than ϵ since the distribution of the challenge tuple to $\mathcal{A}$ is equal to the Assumption 5-4.

6   Conversion 3: LL-HVE

In this section, we convert the HVE scheme of Lee and Lee [16] to prime order bilinear groups and prove its selective security under the DBDH and P3DH assumptions.

6.1   Construction

Setup($1^\lambda, \ell$): It generates the bilinear group $\mathbb{G}$ of prime order p of bit size $\Theta(\lambda)$. It chooses random values $a_1, a_2, a_3 \in \mathbb{Z}_p$ and sets basis vectors for bilinear product groups as $\boldsymbol{b}_{1,1} = (1, 0, a_1)$, $\boldsymbol{b}_{1,2} = (1, a_2, 0)$, $\boldsymbol{b}_2 = (a_2, -1, a_1 a_2 - a_3)$, $\boldsymbol{b}_3 = (a_1, a_3, -1)$. It also sets

$$\boldsymbol{B}_{1,1} = g^{\boldsymbol{b}_{1,1}}, \ \boldsymbol{B}_{1,2} = g^{\boldsymbol{b}_{1,2}}, \ \boldsymbol{B}_2 = g^{\boldsymbol{b}_2}, \ \boldsymbol{B}_3 = g^{\boldsymbol{b}_3}.$$

It selects random exponents $v', w'_1, w'_2, \{u'_i, h_i\}_{i=1}^{\ell}, \alpha \in \mathbb{Z}_p$, $z_v, z_{w,1}, z_{w,2}, \{z_{u,i}, z_{h,i}\}_{i=1}^{\ell} \in \mathbb{Z}_p$ and outputs a secret key and a public key as

$$SK = \Big(V_k = \boldsymbol{B}_{1,2}^{v'}, W_{k,1} = \boldsymbol{B}_{1,2}^{w'_1}, W_{k,2} = \boldsymbol{B}_{1,2}^{w'_2},$$
$$\{U_{k,i} = \boldsymbol{B}_{1,2}^{u'_i}, H_{k,i} = \boldsymbol{B}_{1,2}^{h_i}\}_{i=1}^{\ell}, \ \boldsymbol{B}_{1,2}^{\alpha}\Big),$$
$$PK = \Big(\boldsymbol{B}_{1,1}, \ \boldsymbol{B}_{1,2}, \ \boldsymbol{B}_2, \ \boldsymbol{B}_3,$$
$$V_c = \boldsymbol{B}_{1,1}^{v'} \boldsymbol{B}_2^{z_v}, \ W_{c,1} = \boldsymbol{B}_{1,1}^{w'_1} \boldsymbol{B}_2^{z_{w,1}}, \ W_{c,2} = \boldsymbol{B}_{1,1}^{w'_2} \boldsymbol{B}_2^{z_{w,2}},$$
$$\{U_{c,i} = \boldsymbol{B}_{1,1}^{u'_i} \boldsymbol{B}_2^{z_{u,i}}, \ H_{c,i} = \boldsymbol{B}_{1,1}^{h_i} \boldsymbol{B}_2^{z_{h,i}}\}_{i=1}^{\ell}, \ \Omega = e(\boldsymbol{B}_{1,1}^{v'}, \boldsymbol{B}_{1,2})^{\alpha}\Big).$$

GenToken($\boldsymbol{\sigma}, SK, PK$): It takes as input a vector $\boldsymbol{\sigma} = (\sigma_1, \ldots, \sigma_\ell) \in \Sigma_*^{\ell}$ and the secret key SK. Let S be the set of indexes that are not wild-card fields in the vector $\boldsymbol{\sigma}$. It selects random exponents $r_1, r_2, r_3 \in \mathbb{Z}_p$ and random blinding values $y_1, y_2, y_3, y_4 \in \mathbb{Z}_p$. Next it outputs a token as

$$TK_{\boldsymbol{\sigma}} = \Big(K_1 = \boldsymbol{B}_{1,2}^{\alpha} W_{k,1}^{r_1} W_{k,2}^{r_2} \prod_{i \in S} (U_{k,i}^{\sigma_i} H_{k,i})^{r_3} \boldsymbol{B}_3^{y_1}, \ K_2 = V_k^{-r_1} \boldsymbol{B}_3^{y_2},$$
$$K_3 = V_k^{-r_2} \boldsymbol{B}_3^{y_3}, \ K_4 = V_k^{-r_3} \boldsymbol{B}_3^{y_4}\Big).$$

Encrypt($\boldsymbol{x}, M, PK$): It takes as input a vector $\boldsymbol{x} = (x_1, \ldots, x_\ell) \in \Sigma^l$, a message $M \in \mathcal{M}$, and the public key PK. It first chooses a random exponent $t \in \mathbb{Z}_p$ and random blinding values $z_1, z_2, z_3, \{z_{4,i}\}_{i=1}^{\ell} \in \mathbb{Z}_p$. Then it outputs a ciphertext as

$$CT = \Big(C_0 = \Omega^t M, \ C_1 = V_c^t \boldsymbol{B}_2^{z_1}, \ C_2 = W_{c,1}^t \boldsymbol{B}_2^{z_2},$$
$$C_3 = W_{c,2}^t \boldsymbol{B}_2^{z_3}, \ \{C_{4,i} = (U_{c,i}^{x_i} H_{c,i})^t \boldsymbol{B}_2^{z_{4,i}}\}_{i=1}^{\ell}\Big).$$

Query(CT, TK_σ, PK): It takes as input a ciphertext CT and a token TK_σ of a vector σ. It first computes

$$M \leftarrow C_0 \cdot \left(e(\boldsymbol{C}_1, \boldsymbol{K}_1) \cdot e(\boldsymbol{C}_2, \boldsymbol{K}_2) \cdot e(\boldsymbol{C}_3, \boldsymbol{K}_3) \cdot e(\prod_{i \in S} C_{4,i}, \boldsymbol{K}_4) \right)^{-1}.$$

If $M \notin \mathcal{M}$, it outputs $\perp$ indicating that the predicate f_σ is not satisfied. Otherwise, it outputs M indicating that the predicate f_σ is satisfied.

6.2   Correctness

If $f_\sigma(\boldsymbol{x}) = 1$, then the following calculation shows that **Query**$(CT, TK_\sigma, PK) = M$ by the orthogonality of basis vectors such that $e(g^{\boldsymbol{b}_{1,1}}, g^{\boldsymbol{b}_3}) = 1, e(g^{\boldsymbol{b}_{1,2}}, g^{\boldsymbol{b}_2}) = 1, e(g^{\boldsymbol{b}_2}, g^{\boldsymbol{b}_3}) = 1$.

$$e(\boldsymbol{C}_1, \boldsymbol{K}_1) \cdot e(\boldsymbol{C}_2, \boldsymbol{K}_2) \cdot e(\boldsymbol{C}_3, \boldsymbol{K}_3) \cdot e(\prod_{i \in S} C_{4,i}, \boldsymbol{K}_4)$$

$$= e(\boldsymbol{V}_c^t, \boldsymbol{B}_{1,2}^\alpha \boldsymbol{W}_{k,1}^{r_1} \boldsymbol{W}_{k,2}^{r_2} \prod_{i \in S}(\boldsymbol{U}_{k,i}^{\sigma_i} \boldsymbol{H}_{k,i})^{r_3}) \cdot e(\boldsymbol{W}_{c,1}^t, \boldsymbol{V}_k^{-r_1}) \cdot$$

$$e(\boldsymbol{W}_{c,2}^t, \boldsymbol{V}_k^{-r_2}) \cdot e(\prod_{i \in S}(\boldsymbol{U}_{c,i}^{x_i} \boldsymbol{H}_{c,i})^t, \boldsymbol{V}_k^{-r_3})$$

$$= e(\boldsymbol{B}_{1,1}^{v't}, \boldsymbol{B}_{1,2}^\alpha) \cdot e(g^{v'}, \prod_{i \in S} g^{u_i'(\sigma_i - x_i)})^{tr_3} = e(\boldsymbol{B}_{1,1}^{v'}, \boldsymbol{B}_{1,2})^{\alpha t}.$$

Otherwise, that is $f_\sigma(\boldsymbol{x}) = 0$, the probability of **Query**$(CT, TK_\sigma, PK) \neq \perp$ is negligible by limiting $|\mathcal{M}|$ to less than $|\mathbb{G}_T|^{1/4}$.

6.3   Security

Theorem 6. *The above HVE scheme is selectively secure under the DBDH and P3DH assumptions.*

Proof. The proof of this theorem is easily obtained from the following five Lemmas 10, 11, 12, 13 and 14. Before presenting the five lemmas, we first introduce the following four assumptions. The HVE scheme of Lee and Lee constructed in bilinear groups of composite order $N = p_1 p_2 p_3$, and its security was proven under the DBDH, BSD, and C3DH assumptions [22]. In composite order bilinear groups, the C3DH assumption imply the C2DH assumption that was introduced in [16]. However, this implication is not valid in prime order bilinear groups since the basis vectors for ciphertexts and tokens are different. Thus the C3DH assumption for ciphertexts and the C2DH assumption for tokens should be treated as differently. These assumptions in composite order bilinear groups are converted to the following Assumptions 6-1, 6-2, 6-3 and 6-4 using our conversion method.

Assumption 6-1. Let $((p, \mathbb{G}, \mathbb{G}_T, e), g^{b_{1,1}}, g^{b_{1,2}}, g^{b_2}, g^{b_3})$ be the bilinear product group of basis vectors $b_{1,1} = (1, 0, a_1), b_{1,2} = (1, a_2, 0), b_2 = (a_2, -1, a_1 a_2 - a_3), b_3 = (a_1, a_3, -1)$. The Assumption 6-1 is stated as follows: given a challenge tuple

$$D = ((p, \mathbb{G}, \mathbb{G}_T, e), \; g^{b_{1,1}}, g^{b_{1,2}}, g^{b_2}, g^{b_3}, (g^{b_{1,1}})^{c_1}, (g^{b_{1,1}})^{c_2},$$
$$(g^{b_{1,2}})^{c_1}, (g^{b_{1,2}})^{c_2}, (g^{b_{1,1}})^{c_3}) \text{ and } T,$$

decides whether $T = T_0 = e(g, g)^{c_1 c_2 c_3}$ or $T = T_1 = e(g, g)^d$ with random choices of $c_1, c_2, c_3, d \in \mathbb{Z}_p$.

Assumption 6-2. Let $((p, \mathbb{G}, \mathbb{G}_T, e), g^{b_{1,1}}, g^{b_{1,2}}, g^{b_2}, g^{b_3})$ be the bilinear product group of basis vectors $b_{1,1} = (1, 0, a_1), b_{1,2} = (1, a_2, 0), b_2 = (a_2, -1, a_1 a_2 - a_3), b_3 = (a_1, a_3, -1)$. The Assumption 6-2 is stated as follows: given a challenge tuple

$$D = ((p, \mathbb{G}, \mathbb{G}_T, e), \; g^{b_{1,1}}, g^{b_{1,2}}, g^{b_2}, g^{b_3}) \text{ and } T,$$

decides whether $T = T_0 = e((g^{b_{1,1}})^{c_1}(g^{b_2})^{c_3}, (g^{b_{1,2}})^{c_2}(g^{b_3})^{c_4})$ or $T = T_1 = e((g^{b_{1,1}})^{c_1}, (g^{b_{1,2}})^{c_2})$ with random choices of $c_1, c_2, c_3, c_4 \in \mathbb{Z}_p$.

Assumption 6-3. Let $((p, \mathbb{G}, \mathbb{G}_T, e), g^{b_{1,1}}, g^{b_{1,2}}, g^{b_2}, g^{b_3})$ be the bilinear product group of basis vectors $b_{1,1} = (1, 0, a_1), b_{1,2} = (1, a_2, 0), b_2 = (a_2, -1, a_1 a_2 - a_3), b_3 = (a_1, a_3, -1)$. The Assumption 6-3 is stated as follows: given a challenge tuple

$$D = ((p, \mathbb{G}, \mathbb{G}_T, e), \; g^{b_{1,1}}, g^{b_{1,2}}, g^{b_2}, g^{b_3}, (g^{b_{1,2}})^{c_1}, (g^{b_{1,2}})^{c_2},$$
$$(g^{b_{1,1}})^{c_1 c_2}(g^{b_2})^{z_1}, (g^{b_{1,1}})^{c_1 c_2 c_3}(g^{b_2})^{z_2}) \text{ and } T,$$

decides whether $T = T_0 = (g^{b_{1,1}})^{c_3}(g^{b_2})^{z_3}$ or $T = T_1 = (g^{b_{1,1}})^d(g^{b_2})^{z_3}$ with random choices of $c_1, c_2, c_3, d \in \mathbb{Z}_p$ and $z_1, z_2, z_3 \in \mathbb{Z}_p$.

Assumption 6-4. Let $((p, \mathbb{G}, \mathbb{G}_T, e), g^{b_{1,1}}, g^{b_{1,2}}, g^{b_2}, g^{b_3})$ be the bilinear product group of basis vectors $b_{1,1} = (1, 0, a_1), b_{1,2} = (1, a_2, 0), b_2 = (a_2, -1, a_1 a_2 - a_3), b_3 = (a_1, a_3, -1)$. The Assumption 6-4 is stated as follows: given a challenge tuple

$$D = ((p, \mathbb{G}, \mathbb{G}_T, e), \; g^{b_{1,1}}, g^{b_{1,2}}, g^{b_2}, g^{b_3}, (g^{b_{1,2}})^{c_1}(g^{b_3})^{z_1}, (g^{b_{1,2}})^{c_2}(g^{b_3})^{z_2}) \text{ and } T,$$

decides whether $T = T_0 = (g^{b_{1,2}})^{c_1 c_2}(g^{b_3})^{z_3}$ or $T = T_1 = (g^{b_{1,2}})^d(g^{b_3})^{z_3}$ with random choices of $c_1, c_2, d \in \mathbb{Z}_p$ and $z_1, z_2, z_3 \in \mathbb{Z}_p$.

Lemma 10. *The above HVE scheme is selectively secure under the Assumptions 6-1, 6-2, 6-3 and 6-4.*

Proof. The proof of this lemma is directly obtained from [16] since the Assumptions 6-1, 6-2, 6-3, and 6-4 in prime order bilinear groups are corresponds to the DBDH, BSD, C3DH, and C2DH assumptions in composite order bilinear groups.

Lemma 11. *If the DBDH assumption holds, then the Assumption 6-1 also holds.*

Lemma 12. *The Assumption 6-2 holds for all adversaries.*

Lemma 13. *If the P3DH assumption holds, then the Assumption 6-3 also holds.*

The Assumptions 6-1, 6-2 and 6-3 are the same as the Assumptions 5-1, 5-2 and 5-3. Thus we omits the proofs of Lemmas 11, 12 and 13.

Lemma 14. *If the P3DH assumption holds, then the Assumption 6-4 also holds.*

Proof. Suppose there exists an adversary $\mathcal{A}$ that breaks the Assumption 6-4 with a non-negligible advantage. An algorithm $\mathcal{B}$ that solves the P3DH assumption using $\mathcal{A}$ is given: a challenge tuple $D = ((p, \mathbb{G}, \mathbb{G}_T, e), (g, f), (g^{c_1}, f^{c_1}), (g^{c_2}, f^{c_2}), (g^{c_1 c_2} f^{z_1}, g^{z_1}), (g^{c_3} f^{z_2}, g^{z_2}))$ and $T = T_\gamma = (T_{\gamma,1}, T_{\gamma,2})$ where $T = T_0 = (g^{c_1 c_2 c_3} f^{z_3}, g^{z_3})$ or $T = T_1 = (g^d f^{z_3}, g^{z_3})$. $\mathcal{B}$ first chooses random values $a_2, a_3 \in \mathbb{Z}_p$ and sets

$$g^{b_{1,1}} = (g, 1, f), \ g^{b_{1,2}} = (g, g^{a_2}, 1),$$
$$g^{b_2} = (g^{a_2}, g^{-1}, g^{a_3}), \ g^{b_3} = (f, f^{a_2} g^{-a_3}, g^{-1}),$$
$$(g^{b_{1,2}})^{c'_1} (g^{b_3})^{z_1} = (g^{c_1 c_2} f^{z_1}, (g^{c_1 c_2} f^{z_1})^{a_2} (g^{z_1})^{-a_3}, (g^{z_1})^{-1}),$$
$$(g^{b_{1,2}})^{c'_2} (g^{b_3})^{z_2} = (g^{c_3} f^{z_2}, (g^{c_3} f^{z_2})^{a_2} (g^{z_2})^{-a_3}, (g^{z_2})^{-1}),$$
$$T' = (T_{\gamma,1}, (T_{\gamma,1})^{a_2} (T_{\gamma,2})^{-a_3}, (T_{\gamma,2})^{-1}).$$

Intuitively, it sets $a'_1 = \log f, a'_2 = a_2, a'_3 = a_1 a_2 - a_3$ and $c'_1 = c_1 c_2, c'_2 = c_3$ where a'_1, a'_2, a'_3 are elements of basis vectors for the Assumption 6-4. Next, it gives the tuple $D' = ((p, \mathbb{G}, \mathbb{G}_T, e), g^{b_{1,1}}, g^{b_{1,2}}, g^{b_2}, g^{b_3}, (g^{b_{1,1}})^{c'_1} (g^{b_2})^{z_1}, (g^{b_{1,1}})^{c'_2} (g^{b_2})^{z_2})$ and T' to $\mathcal{A}$. Then $\mathcal{A}$ outputs a guess γ'. $\mathcal{B}$ also outputs γ'. If the advantage of $\mathcal{A}$ is ϵ, then the advantage of $\mathcal{B}$ is greater than ϵ since the distribution of the challenge tuple to $\mathcal{A}$ is equal to the Assumption 6-4.

7 Conclusion

We converted the HVE scheme of Boneh and Waters, the delegatable HVE scheme of Shi and Waters, and the efficient HVE scheme of Lee and Lee from composite order bilinear groups to prime order bilinear groups. Though we used our conversion method to HVE schemes that based on the decisional C3DH assumption, it would be possible to use our method to other scheme in composite order bilinear groups that based on the decisional C3DH assumption.

Acknowledgements. This research was supported by Next-Generation Information Computing Development Program through the National Research Foundation of Korea (NRF) funded by MSIP (NRF-2016M3C4A7937115).

A   Generic Group Model

In this section, we show that the P3DH assumption holds in the generic group model. The generic group model introduced by Shoup [23] is a tool for analyzing generic algorithms that work independently of the group representation.

A.1   Master Theorem

We generalize the master theorem of Katz et al. [14] to use prime order bilinear groups instead of composite order bilinear groups and to use multiple groups elements in the target instead of just one element.

Let $\mathbb{G}, \mathbb{G}_T$ be cyclic bilinear groups of order p where p is a large prime. The bilinear map is defined as $e : \mathbb{G} \times \mathbb{G} \rightarrow \mathbb{G}_T$. In the generic group model, a random group element of $\mathbb{G}, \mathbb{G}_T$ is represented as a random variable P_i, R_i respectively where P_i, R_i are chosen uniformly in $\mathbb{Z}_p$. We say that a random variable has degree t if the maximum degree of any variable is t. Then we can naturally define the dependence and independence of random variables as in Definition 6.

Definition 6. *Let* $P = \{P_1, \ldots, P_u\}$, $T_0 = \{T_{0,1}, \ldots, T_{0,m}\}$, $T_1 = \{T_{1,1}, \ldots, T_{1,m}\}$ *be random variables over* $\mathbb{G}$ *where* $T_{0,i} \neq T_{1,i}$ *for all* $1 \leq i \leq m$, *and let* $R = \{R_1, \ldots, R_v\}$ *be random variables over* $\mathbb{G}_T$. *We say that* T_b *is dependent on* A *if there exists constants* $\{\alpha_i\}, \{\beta_i\}$ *such that*

$$\sum_i^m \alpha_i T_{b,i} = \sum_i^u \beta_i \cdot P_i$$

where $\alpha_i \neq 0$ *for at least one* i. *We say that* T_b *is independent of* P *if* T_b *is not dependent on* P.

Let $S_1 = \{(i,j) \mid e(T_{0,i}, T_{0,j}) \neq e(T_{1,i}, T_{1,j})\}$ *and* $S_2 = \{(i,j) \mid e(T_{0,i}, P_j) \neq e(T_{1,i}, P_j)\}$. *We say that* $\{e(T_{b,i}, T_{b,j})\}_{(i,j)\in S_1} \cup \{e(T_{b,i}, P_j)\}_{(i,j)\in S_2}$ *is dependent on* $P \cup R \cup \{e(T_{b,i}, T_{b,j})\}_{(i,j)\notin S_1} \cup \{e(T_{b,i}, P_j)\}_{(i,j)\notin S_2}$ *if there exist constants* $\{\alpha_{i,j}\}, \{\alpha'_{i,j}\}, \{\beta_{i,j}\}, \{\beta'_{i,j}\}, \{\gamma_{i,j}\}, \{\delta_i\}$ *such that*

$$\sum_{(i,j)\in S_1} \alpha_{i,j} \cdot e(T_{b,i}, T_{b,j}) + \sum_{(i,j)\notin S_1} \alpha'_{i,j} \cdot e(T_{b,i}, T_{b,j}) +$$
$$\sum_{(i,j)\in S_2} \beta_{i,j} \cdot e(T_{b,i}, P_j) + \sum_{(i,j)\notin S_2} \beta'_{i,j} \cdot e(T_{b,i}, P_j)$$
$$= \sum_i^u \sum_j^u \gamma_{i,j} \cdot e(P_i, P_j) + \sum_i^v \delta_i \cdot R_i.$$

where $\alpha_{i,j} \neq 0$ *for at least one* $(i,j) \in S_1$ *or* $\beta_{i,j} \neq 0$ *for at least one* $(i,j) \in S_2$. *We say that* $\{e(T_{b,i}, T_{b,j})\}_{(i,j)\in S_1} \cup \{e(T_{b,i}, P_j)\}_{(i,j)\in S_2}$ *is independent of* $P \cup R \cup \{e(T_{b,i}, T_{b,j})\}_{(i,j)\notin S_1} \cup \{e(T_{b,i}, P_j)\}_{(i,j)\notin S_2}$ *if* $\{e(T_{b,i}, T_{b,j})\}_{(i,j)\in S_1} \cup \{e(T_{b,i}, P_j)\}_{(i,j)\in S_2}$ *is not dependent on* $P \cup R \cup \{e(T_{b,i}, T_{b,j})\}_{(i,j)\notin S_1} \cup \{e(T_{b,i}, P_j)\}_{(i,j)\notin S_2}$.

Using the above dependence and independence of random variables, we can obtain the following theorem from the master theorem of Katz et al. [14].

Theorem 7. *Let* $P = \{P_1, \ldots, P_u\}$, $T_0 = \{T_{0,1}, \ldots, T_{0,m}\}$, $T_1 = \{T_{1,1}, \ldots, T_{1,m}\}$ *be random variables over* $\mathbb{G}$ *where* $T_{0,i} \neq T_{1,i}$ *for all* $1 \leq i \leq m$, *and let* $R = \{R_1, \ldots, R_v\}$ *be random variables over* $\mathbb{G}_T$. *Consider the following experiment in the generic group model:*

An algorithm is given $P = \{P_1, \ldots, P_u\}$ and $R = \{R_1, \ldots, R_v\}$. A random bit b is chosen, and the adversary is given $T_b = \{T_{b,1}, \ldots, T_{b,m}\}$. The algorithm outputs a bit b', and succeeds if $b' = b$. The algorithm's advantage is the absolute value of the difference between its success probability and $1/2$.

Let $S_1 = \{(i,j) \mid e(T_{0,i}, T_{0,j}) \neq e(T_{1,i}, T_{1,j})\}$ and $S_2 = \{(i,j) \mid e(T_{0,i}, P_j) \neq e(T_{1,i}, P_j)\}$. If T_b is independent of P for all $b \in \{0,1\}$, and $\{e(T_{b,i}, T_{b,j})\}_{(i,j) \in S_1} \cup \{e(T_{b,i}, P_j)\}_{(i,j) \in S_2}$ is independent of $P \cup R \cup \{e(T_{b,i}, T_{b,j})\}_{(i,j) \notin S_1} \cup \{e(T_{b,i}, P_j)\}_{(i,j) \notin S_2}$ for all $b \in \{0,1\}$, then any algorithm $\mathcal{A}$ issuing at most q instructions has an advantage at most $O(q^2 t/p)$.

Note that this theorem that is a slight modification of that of Katz et al. [14] still holds in prime order bilinear groups since the dependent equation of an adversary can be used to distinguish the target T_b of the assumption. Additionally, it still holds when the target consists of multiple group elements since the adversary can only make a dependent equation in Definition 6.

A.2   Analysis of P3DH Assumption

To analyze the P3DH assumption in the generic group model, we only need to show the independence of T_0, T_1 random variables. Using the notation of previous section, the P3DH assumption can be written as follows

$$P = \{1, X, A, XA, B, XB, AB + XZ_1, Z_1, C + XZ_2, Z_2\}, \quad R = \{1\}$$
$$T_0 = \{ABC + XZ_3, Z_3\}, \quad T_1 = \{D + XZ_3, Z_3\}.$$

The T_1 has a random variable D that does not exist in P. Thus the independence of T_1 is easily obtained. Therefore, we only need to consider the independence of T_0. First, T_0 is independent of P since T_0 contains Z_3 that does not exist in P. For the independence of $\{e(T_{0,i}, T_{0,j})\}_{(i,j) \in S_1} \cup \{e(T_{0,i}, P_j)\}_{(i,j) \in S_2}$, we should define two sets S_1, S_2. We obtain that $S_1 = \{(1,1), (1,2), (2,1), (2,2)\}$. However, $e(T_{0,i}, T_{0,j})$ contains Z_3^2 because of Z_3 in T_0, and Z_3^2 can not be obtained from the right part of the equation in Definition 6. Thus, the constants $\alpha_{i,j}$ should be zero for all (i,j). From this, we obtain the simple equations as follows

$$\sum_{(i,j) \in S_2} \beta_{i,j} \cdot e(T_{b,i}, P_j) + \sum_{(i,j) \notin S_2} \beta'_{i,j} \cdot e(T_{b,i}, P_j)$$
$$= \sum_{i}^{u} \sum_{j}^{u} \gamma_{i,j} \cdot e(P_i, P_j) + \sum_{i}^{v} \delta_i \cdot R_i.$$

The set S_2 is defined as $\{(i,j) \mid \forall i,j\}$ because of D in T_1. However, Z_3 in T_0 should be removed to construct a dependent equation since Z_3 does not exists in P, R. To remove Z_3 from the left part of the above simple equation, two random variables Y, XY should be paired with $T_{0,i}$ for some $Y \in P$. If Z_3 is remove in the left part of the above simple equation, then the left part has at least a degree 3 and it contains ABC. To have a degree 3 in the right part of the above simple equation, $AB + XZ_1, Z_1$ should be used. However, the right part of the above equation can not contain ABC since C, XC do not exist in P. Therefore, the independence of T_0 is obtained.

References

1. Bellare, M., Boldyreva, A., Desai, A., Pointcheval, D.: Key-privacy in public-key encryption. In: Boyd, C. (ed.) ASIACRYPT 2001. LNCS, vol. 2248, pp. 566–582. Springer, Heidelberg (2001). doi:10.1007/3-540-45682-1_33
2. Boneh, D., Boyen, X.: Efficient selective-ID secure identity-based encryption without random oracles. In: Cachin, C., Camenisch, J.L. (eds.) EUROCRYPT 2004. LNCS, vol. 3027, pp. 223–238. Springer, Heidelberg (2004). doi:10.1007/978-3-540-24676-3_14
3. Boneh, D., Crescenzo, G., Ostrovsky, R., Persiano, G.: Public key encryption with keyword search. In: Cachin, C., Camenisch, J.L. (eds.) EUROCRYPT 2004. LNCS, vol. 3027, pp. 506–522. Springer, Heidelberg (2004). doi:10.1007/978-3-540-24676-3_30
4. Boneh, D., Franklin, M.: Identity-based encryption from the weil pairing. In: Kilian, J. (ed.) CRYPTO 2001. LNCS, vol. 2139, pp. 213–229. Springer, Heidelberg (2001). doi:10.1007/3-540-44647-8_13
5. Boneh, D., Goh, E.-J., Nissim, K.: Evaluating 2-DNF formulas on ciphertexts. In: Kilian, J. (ed.) TCC 2005. LNCS, vol. 3378, pp. 325–341. Springer, Heidelberg (2005). doi:10.1007/978-3-540-30576-7_18
6. Boneh, D., Sahai, A., Waters, B.: Functional encryption: definitions and challenges. In: Ishai, Y. (ed.) TCC 2011. LNCS, vol. 6597, pp. 253–273. Springer, Heidelberg (2011). doi:10.1007/978-3-642-19571-6_16
7. Boneh, D., Waters, B.: Conjunctive, subset, and range queries on encrypted data. In: Vadhan, S.P. (ed.) TCC 2007. LNCS, vol. 4392, pp. 535–554. Springer, Heidelberg (2007). doi:10.1007/978-3-540-70936-7_29
8. Ducas, L.: Anonymity from asymmetry: new constructions for anonymous HIBE. In: Pieprzyk, J. (ed.) CT-RSA 2010. LNCS, vol. 5985, pp. 148–164. Springer, Heidelberg (2010). doi:10.1007/978-3-642-11925-5_11
9. Freeman, D.M.: Converting pairing-based cryptosystems from composite-order groups to prime-order groups. In: Gilbert, H. (ed.) EUROCRYPT 2010. LNCS, vol. 6110, pp. 44–61. Springer, Heidelberg (2010). doi:10.1007/978-3-642-13190-5_3
10. Garg, S., Kumarasubramanian, A., Sahai, A., Waters, B.: Building efficient fully collusion-resilient traitor tracing and revocation schemes. In: Proceedings of the 17th ACM Conference on Computer and Communications Security, pp. 121–130. ACM (2010)
11. Gentry, C., Silverberg, A.: Hierarchical ID-based cryptography. In: Zheng, Y. (ed.) ASIACRYPT 2002. LNCS, vol. 2501, pp. 548–566. Springer, Heidelberg (2002). doi:10.1007/3-540-36178-2_34
12. Goyal, V., Pandey, O., Sahai, A., Waters, B.: Attribute-based encryption for fine-grained access control of encrypted data. In: Proceedings of the 13th ACM Conference on Computer and Communications Security, pp. 89–98. ACM (2006)
13. Iovino, V., Persiano, G.: Hidden-vector encryption with groups of prime order. In: Galbraith, S.D., Paterson, K.G. (eds.) Pairing 2008. LNCS, vol. 5209, pp. 75–88. Springer, Heidelberg (2008). doi:10.1007/978-3-540-85538-5_5

14. Katz, J., Sahai, A., Waters, B.: Predicate encryption supporting disjunctions, polynomial equations, and inner products. In: Smart, N. (ed.) EUROCRYPT 2008. LNCS, vol. 4965, pp. 146–162. Springer, Heidelberg (2008). doi:10.1007/978-3-540-78967-3_9
15. Katz, J., Yerukhimovich, A.: On black-box constructions of predicate encryption from trapdoor permutations. In: Matsui, M. (ed.) ASIACRYPT 2009. LNCS, vol. 5912, pp. 197–213. Springer, Heidelberg (2009). doi:10.1007/978-3-642-10366-7_12
16. Lee, K., Lee, D.H.: Improved hidden vector encryption with short ciphertexts and tokens. Des. Codes Crypt. **58**(3), 297–319 (2011)
17. Lewko, A., Waters, B.: New techniques for dual system encryption and fully secure HIBE with short ciphertexts. In: Micciancio, D. (ed.) TCC 2010. LNCS, vol. 5978, pp. 455–479. Springer, Heidelberg (2010). doi:10.1007/978-3-642-11799-2_27
18. Okamoto, T., Takashima, K.: Hierarchical predicate encryption for inner-products. In: Matsui, M. (ed.) ASIACRYPT 2009. LNCS, vol. 5912, pp. 214–231. Springer, Heidelberg (2009). doi:10.1007/978-3-642-10366-7_13
19. Park, J.H.: Efficient hidden vector encryption for conjunctive queries on encrypted data. IEEE Trans. Knowl. Data Eng. **23**(10), 1483–1497 (2011)
20. Park, J.H.: Inner-product encryption under standard assumptions. Des. Codes Crypt. **58**(3), 235–257 (2011)
21. Shi, E., Bethencourt, J., Chan, T.H., Song, D., Perrig, A.: Multi-dimensional range query over encrypted data. In: 2007 IEEE Symposium on Security and Privacy (SP 2007), pp. 350–364. IEEE (2007)
22. Shi, E., Waters, B.: Delegating capabilities in predicate encryption systems. In: Aceto, L., Damgård, I., Goldberg, L.A., Halldórsson, M.M., Ingólfsdóttir, A., Walukiewicz, I. (eds.) ICALP 2008. LNCS, vol. 5126, pp. 560–578. Springer, Heidelberg (2008). doi:10.1007/978-3-540-70583-3_46
23. Shoup, V.: Lower bounds for discrete logarithms and related problems. In: Fumy, W. (ed.) EUROCRYPT 1997. LNCS, vol. 1233, pp. 256–266. Springer, Heidelberg (1997). doi:10.1007/3-540-69053-0_18
24. Waters, B.: Dual system encryption: realizing fully secure IBE and HIBE under simple assumptions. In: Halevi, S. (ed.) CRYPTO 2009. LNCS, vol. 5677, pp. 619–636. Springer, Heidelberg (2009). doi:10.1007/978-3-642-03356-8_36
25. Waters, B.R., Balfanz, D., Durfee, G., Smetters, D.K.: Building an encrypted and searchable audit log. In: NDSS, vol. 4, pp. 5–6 (2004)

Lossy Key Encapsulation Mechanism and Its Applications

Yamin Liu[1,2(✉)], Xianhui Lu[1,2,3], Bao Li[1,2,3], and Haiyang Xue[1,2]

[1] Data Assurance and Communication Security Research Center,
Chinese Academy of Sciences, Beijing, China
[2] State Key Laboratory of Information Security,
Institute of Information Engineering, Chinese Academy of Sciences, Beijing, China
{liuyamin,luxianhui,libao,xuehaiyang}@iie.ac.cn
[3] University of Chinese Academy of Sciences, Beijing, China

Abstract. We introduce a new notion, lossy key encapsulation mechanism (lossy KEM), which enhances the notion of key encapsulation mechanism with lossiness, and can be more efficient than lossy trapdoor functions. We show that lossy KEM can be constructed from lossy trapdoor functions, lossy trapdoor relations, and entropic projective hashing. Using lossy KEM as a building block, several previous constructions of lossy encryption and deterministic public key encryption can be generalized and improved in efficiency.

Keywords: Lossy key encapsulation mechanism · Lossy encryption · Deterministic public key encryption

1 Introduction

Lossy Primitives. Lossy primitives became important building blocks of various cryptosystems in the last decades. The first lossy primitive, lossy trapdoor function (LTDF), was introduced by Peikert and Waters in 2008 [20]. LTDF is useful in building plenty of cryptographic schemes, e.g., oblivious transfer, collision-resistant hash, leakage-resilient encryption, chosen ciphertext-secure encryption, and deterministic public-key encryption (DPKE). LTDF can be constructed from various number-theoretic assumptions and lattice-based assumptions [15,24], and from dual projective hashing [23].

In 2009, Bellare *et al.* introduced lossy encryption [6], which implies indistinguishability against chosen plaintext attacks (IND-CPA) and security against selective-opening attacks (SOA). Lossy encryption can be constructed from lossy trapdoor functions [6], from smooth projective hashing [17], and also from various concrete number-theoretic and lattice-based assumptions [17].

Xue *et al.* introduced the notion of lossy trapdoor relations (LTDR) in 2014 [25], which is a relaxation of LTDF for it does not require the recovery of the pre-image, thus is generally more efficient. It was shown in [25] that LTDR is useful in constructing lossy encryption, and adaptive trapdoor relation, which is

© Springer International Publishing AG 2017
S. Hong and J.H. Park (Eds.): ICISC 2016, LNCS 10157, pp. 126–144, 2017.
DOI: 10.1007/978-3-319-53177-9_6

a building block for chosen-ciphertext security. And in [25] LTDR is constructed from several concrete assumptions such as discrete logarithm related assumptions and subgroup membership assumptions.

Typically, lossy primitives works in two computationally indistinguishable modes: the injective mode and the lossy mode. In the injective mode an output is usually mapped from one pre-image, and this makes the primitives information-theoretically invertible. While in the lossy mode, an output corresponds to various pre-images, thus it statistically loses some information of the input.

Hybrid Encryption. Hybrid encryption, proposed by Cramer and Shoup in [11,13], is the combination of an asymmetric key encapsulation mechanism (KEM) and a symmetric data encapsulation mechanism (DEM). The KEM takes a public key and a randomness as input, outputs the first part of the ciphertext, and generates the encryption of a random encapsulated key via a key derivation function (KDF); the DEM encrypts the plaintext with the encapsulated key, and outputs the second part of the ciphertext. Given the secret key of the KEM part and the ciphertext, both the encapsulated key and the plaintext can be recovered.

A hybrid encryption scheme is essentially a public key encryption scheme. Compared with general-purpose public-key encryption, hybrid encryption enjoys the advantage of unrestricted message space, and is usually more efficient, as pointed out in [13]. Regarding to security, by a composition theorem, it is proved that a secure KEM plus a secure DEM can yield a secure hybrid encryption [13]. Thus, the KEM-DEM paradigm allows us to separate the design of the two parts. In many cases a simple one-time pad is enough for the DEM part, and we can focus on the KEM part.

However, whether deterministic public key encryption (DPKE), which is a promising solution to the issues of searchable encryption and randomness-subversion [1–3,8,9,16,21,23], can benefit from the KEM-DEM paradigm is a long-pending problem. Since in DPKE the encryption algorithm is deterministic, there is no randomness for generating the encapsulated key in the KEM. In [3] a hybrid encryption style DPKE was proposed, with an LTDF playing the KEM part, and a one-time pad playing the DEM part. Since an LTDF statistically hides the information of its pre-image in the lossy mode, it can cooperate with a powerful KDF, the universal computational extractor for statistically unpredictable sources $UCE[S^{sup}]$, which is a strong primitive introduced by Bellare *et al.* in [4,5] and is an important tool in the DPKE construction of [3].

Motivated by the usefulness of previous lossy primitives and the advantage of hybrid encryption, it is interesting to enhance the notion of KEM with lossiness, which is a natural match of the newly proposed primitive $UCE[S^{sup}]$, as stated in [3]. Also, it is natural to generalize the KEM usage of LTDF in [3] to embrace more efficient constructions from other primitives.

1.1   Our Contributions: Lossy KEM

Definition. We define a new lossy primitive called lossy key encapsulation mechanism, which extends the usage of several lossy primitives in some scenarios, e.g. LTDF and LTDR, to the form of KEM.

Originally, the syntax of KEM requires that the encapsulation algorithm generate a ciphertext C and an encapsulated key K out of an input randomness r. Generally, looking inside, the encapsulation algorithm can be decomposed into two subroutines: one generates a binary relation (C, tK), where C is the ciphertext, and tK is the material for producing the encapsulated key K and is usually obtained by applying an injective map on r; the other is the key derivation function, which takes tK as input and outputs K. Typically the relation (C, tK) is one-way, i.e., given a random C and the public key, it is hard to find tK. Also the decapsulation algorithm can be decomposed into two subroutines: the first one recovers tK from C with the secret key, and the other is the KDF. Note that this viewpoint on KEM was implicit in [22] by Wee, with the relation being injective, that is, there exists at most one tK corresponding to C.

The syntax of lossy KEM is similar to that of the original KEM. However, akin to previous lossy primitives, lossy KEM also works in two modes, an injective mode for functionality and a lossy mode for the security proof. In the injective mode, the key material tK can be recovered from the ciphertext C with the secret key, thus K can be recovered; while in the lossy mode, the ciphertext C statistically hides the information of tK and the encapsulated key K. The injective mode and the lossy mode should be computationally indistinguishable given the public key. We show that lossy KEM implies IND-secure KEM, just like lossy encryption implies IND-CPA secure encryption.

Constructions. Then we show the general ideas of constructing lossy KEM from two previous lossy primitives, i.e., LTDF, LTDR, and from entropic projective hashing [18]. Details of the constructions are in Sect. 4.

- Given an LTDF f, the lossy KEM on input r generates the relation $(C = f(r), tK = r)$, derives the key $K = h(tK)$, and outputs (C, K), where the KDF h is randomly chosen from a family of pairwise independent hash functions. The KDF can also be other suitable primitives. Note that the KEM usage of LTDF in the DPKE construction of [3] is just the case, with the KDF being picked from a family of UCE[S^{sup}]-secure hash functions. The lossiness of the KEM follows from that of the LTDF, i.e., in the lossy mode, $C = f(r)$ statistically hides the information of r.
- Given an LTDR (f, H), where H is a publicly computable injective map, the lossy KEM on input r generates the relation $(C = f(r), tK = H(r))$, derives the key $K = h(tK)$ and outputs (C, K), where the KDF h is also randomly chosen from a family of pairwise independent hash functions.
- Given an entropic projective hashing $(H, \Lambda, R, X, L, \Pi, S, \alpha)$, where H is the private evaluation algorithm, Λ is the public evaluation algorithm, X is a language and L is a subset of X. With a public key $x \in X$, the lossy KEM on

input $r \in R$ generates the relation $(C = \alpha(r) \in S, tK = H(r, x) \in \Pi)$, derives the key $K = h(tK)$, and outputs (C, K), where α is a projective map, and h is randomly chosen from a family of pairwise independent hash functions. If $x \in L$ then the lossy KEM is working in the injective mode, otherwise if $x \in X \backslash L$ then the lossy KEM is working in the lossy mode.

Applications. The new lossy primitive lossy KEM is useful in constructing lossy encryption and deterministic public key encryption.

- With lossy KEM, we generalize constructions of lossy encryption based on LTDF and LTDR in [6] and [25] respectively, and the construction of lossy encryption from smooth projective hashing in [17].
- Moreover, we generalize the deterministic public key encryption based on LTDF in [3]. Generally, if we choose a lossy KEM constructed from LTDR, then we can get better efficiency, compared to [3].

Organization. In Sect. 2, some notations and definitions are introduced. In Sect. 3, the definition of lossy KEM is given. In Sect. 4, several constructions of lossy KEM are shown. In Sect. 5, we construct a lossy encryption from lossy KEM. In Sect. 6, we construct a DPKE from lossy KEM. Section 7 is the conclusion.

2   Preliminaries

Notations. Let λ be the security parameter. For a string x, $|x|$ denotes its length. For a finite set S, $|S|$ denotes its size. Vectors are denoted by bold-face characters. For a vector $\mathbf{x}$, $|\mathbf{x}|$ denotes the number of its components. $x \xleftarrow{\$} S$ means that x is chosen from the set S uniformly at random. For a randomized algorithm A, $x \xleftarrow{\$} A(\cdot)$ means that x is assigned the output of A. An algorithm is efficient if it runs in polynomial time in its input length. A function $f(\lambda)$ is negligible if it decreases faster than any polynomial, and is denoted as $f(\lambda) \leq \epsilon(\lambda)$. The min-entropy of a random variable X is denoted as $\mathbf{H}_\infty(X) = -\log(\max_x P_X(x))$, wherein $P_X(x) = \Pr[X = x]$. Given a random variable Y, the conditional min-entropy of X is $\tilde{\mathbf{H}}_\infty(X|Y) = -\log(\mathbf{E}_{y \leftarrow Y} \max_x \Pr[X = x|Y = y])$ [14]. The statistical distance between two random variables X and Y is $\Delta(X, Y) = \frac{1}{2} \sum_x |P_X(x) - P_Y(x)|$, X and Y are statistically close if $\Delta(X, Y)$ is negligible, and is denoted as $X \overset{s}{\approx} Y$. X and Y are computationally indistinguishable if no efficient algorithm can tell them apart given only oracle access, and is denoted as $X \overset{c}{\approx} Y$. PPT is the short form of probabilistic polynomial time. $\perp$ is the empty symbol.

2.1 Key Encapsulation Mechanism

Here we recall the definition and security notion of KEM. In the definition we also use an alternative description, for the sake of better description of lossy KEM in subsequent sections. We believe that the alternative description is still without loss of generality and gives better understanding of KEM. We use the alternative description in some occasions if necessary. xue2014lossy A key encapsulation mechanism KEM is a triple of algorithms (KEM.Kg, KEM.Enc, KEM.Dec):

- Key generation: $(pk, sk) \xleftarrow{\$} \mathsf{KEM.Kg}(\lambda)$.
- Encapsulation: $(C, K) \leftarrow \mathsf{KEM.Enc}(pk, r)$. KEM.Enc can be decomposed into two subroutines, Rg and KDF.
  - Relation generation: $(C, tK) \leftarrow \mathsf{KEM.Enc.Rg}(pk, r)$, where tK is induced by an injective function of r.
  - Key derivation: $K \leftarrow \mathsf{KEM.Enc.KDF}(tK)$, where $\mathsf{KDF} : \{0,1\}^* \to \{0,1\}^*$ is a key derivation function (usually a pairwise independent hash function with its key specified in pk and sk).
- Decapsulation: $K \leftarrow \mathsf{KEM.Dec}(sk, C)$. Similarly, KEM.Dec can also be decomposed into two subroutines, Inv and KDF.
  - Inversion: $tK \leftarrow \mathsf{KEM.Dec.Inv}(sk, C)$;
  - Key derivation: $K \leftarrow \mathsf{KEM.Dec.KDF}(tK)$.

The IND security of KEM is described by the following game, where A is the adversary, $\mathsf{RSp}(\lambda)$ is the randomness space, KEM.kl is the length of the encapsulated key. $b' \stackrel{?}{=} b$ is a predicate denoting whether the two bits are equal, 1 is true and 0 is false.

$\mathsf{Game}^{\mathsf{ind}}_{\mathsf{KEM}, \mathsf{A}}(\lambda)$

$\quad (pk, sk) \xleftarrow{\$} \mathsf{KEM.Kg}(\lambda); r \xleftarrow{\$} \mathsf{RSp}(\lambda); (C, K_0) \leftarrow \mathsf{KEM.Enc}(pk, r);$

$\quad K_1 \xleftarrow{\$} \{0,1\}^{\mathsf{KEM.kl}}; b \xleftarrow{\$} \{0,1\}; b' \xleftarrow{\$} \mathsf{A}(pk, C, K_b); \text{Return } (b' \stackrel{?}{=} b)$

The advantage of A in winning the game is defined as $\mathsf{Adv}^{\mathsf{ind}}_{\mathsf{KEM}, \mathsf{A}}(\lambda) = 2 \Pr[\mathsf{Game}^{\mathsf{ind}}_{\mathsf{KEM},\mathsf{A}}(\lambda)] - 1$, where $\mathsf{Game}^{\mathsf{ind}}_{\mathsf{KEM},\mathsf{A}}(\lambda)$ is the abbreviation for "$\mathsf{Game}^{\mathsf{ind}}_{\mathsf{KEM}, \mathsf{A}}(\lambda) \Rightarrow 1$". The kind of abbreviation will be used throughout the paper. We say that KEM is IND secure if for all PPT adversary A, $\mathsf{Adv}^{\mathsf{ind}}_{\mathsf{KEM}, \mathsf{A}}(\lambda)$ is negligible.

2.2 Lossy Primitives

Here is a brief recap of the definitions of previous lossy primitives in literatures [6, 20, 25].

Lossy Trapdoor Functions. A collection of (m, l)-lossy trapdoor functions is a 4-tuple of PPT algorithms $\mathsf{F} = (\mathsf{F.Ig}, \mathsf{F.Lg}, \mathsf{F.Ev}, \mathsf{F.Inv})$ described below.

- Sampling the injective mode: $(\sigma_I, \tau) \xleftarrow{\$} \mathsf{F.Ig}(\lambda)$, where σ_I is a function index, and τ is a trapdoor.
- Sampling the lossy mode: $(\sigma_L, \bot) \xleftarrow{\$} \mathsf{F.Lg}(\lambda)$. In the lossy mode, the function is irreversible, thus there is no trapdoor.
- Evaluation: $y \leftarrow \mathsf{F.Ev}(\sigma, x)$, where σ is a function index, $x \in \{0,1\}^m$. There are:
  - injective mode: if σ is produced by $\mathsf{F.Ig}(\cdot)$, then the function $\mathsf{F.Ev}(\cdot)$ is injective.
  - lossy mode: if σ is produced by $\mathsf{F.Lg}(\cdot)$, then the size of the image of $\mathsf{F.Ev}(\cdot)$ is at most 2^{m-l}, i.e., there are many pre-images corresponding to an image.
- Inversion: $x \leftarrow \mathsf{F.Inv}(\tau, y)$, i.e., the function can be inverted in the injective mode with the trapdoor.

The function indices σ_I and σ_L respectively produced in the injective mode and the lossy mode should be computationally indistinguishable.

Lossy Trapdoor Relations. A collection of (m, l)-lossy trapdoor relations is a 4-tuple of PPT algorithms $\mathsf{F} = (\mathsf{F.Ig}, \mathsf{F.Lg}, \mathsf{F.Ev}, \mathsf{F.Inv})$ described below.

- Sampling the injective mode: $(\sigma_I, \tau, H) \xleftarrow{\$} \mathsf{F.Ig}(\lambda)$, where σ_I is a function index, τ is a trapdoor, and H is a publicly computable injective map.
- Sampling the lossy mode: $(\sigma_L, \bot, H) \xleftarrow{\$} \mathsf{F.Lg}(\lambda)$. Also, there is no trapdoor in the lossy mode of LTDR.
- Encapsulation: $(y, z) \leftarrow \mathsf{F.Ev}(\sigma, H, x)$, where $x \in \{0,1\}^m$, $y = f(\sigma, x)$ for a function f parameterized by σ, $z = H(x)$, and there are:
  - injective mode: if σ is produced by $\mathsf{F.Ig}(\cdot)$, then the function $f(\sigma, \cdot)$ is injective.
  - lossy mode: if σ is produced by $\mathsf{F.Lg}(\cdot)$, then the size of the image of $f(\sigma, \cdot)$ is at most 2^{m-l}.
- Decapsulation: $z \leftarrow \mathsf{F.Inv}(\tau, H, y)$, where $z = H(x)$. That is, the relation (y, z) can be recovered in the injective mode given the trapdoor.

Also, the function indices σ_I and σ_L respectively produced in the injective mode and the lossy mode should be computationally indistinguishable. LTDR is generally more efficient than LTDF since it does not require the recovery of the pre-image x but a publicly computable injective map of it, i.e., $z = H(x)$, as shown in [25].

Lossy Encryption. A lossy public key encryption LE is a 4-tuple of algorithms, $(\mathsf{LE.Kg}, \mathsf{LE.LKg}, \mathsf{LE.Enc}, \mathsf{LE.Dec})$.

- Key generation: $(pk_I, sk) \xleftarrow{\$} \mathsf{LE.Kg}(\lambda)$.

- Lossy key generation: $(pk_L, \perp) \xleftarrow{\$} \mathsf{LE.LKg}(\lambda)$.
- Encryption: $C \leftarrow \mathsf{LE.Enc}(pk, m, r)$, where m is the plaintext, and r is the randomness.
- Decryption: $m \leftarrow \mathsf{LE.Dec}(sk, C)$.

And the algorithms should satisfy the following addition properties:

1. Correctness: for all (pk_I, sk) generated by $\mathsf{LE.Kg}$, all m and r, there is $m = \mathsf{LE.Dec}(sk, C)$ where $C \leftarrow \mathsf{LE.Enc}(pk_I, m, r)$.
2. Lossiness: for all pk_L generated by $\mathsf{LE.LKg}$, and any pair of distinct messages (m_0, m_1), the respective distributions of the ciphertexts of m_0 and m_1 are statistically close, i.e., $\mathsf{LE.Enc}(pk_L, m_0, R) \stackrel{s}{\approx} \mathsf{LE.ENC}(pk_L, m_1, R)$, where R is the randomness space.
3. Indistinguishability: The public keys pk_I and pk_L respectively generated by $\mathsf{LE.Kg}$ and $\mathsf{LE.LKg}$ are computationally indistinguishable.

2.3 Entropic Projective Hashing

Cramer and Shoup introduced smooth projective hashing (SPH) in [12]. SPH is a family of keyed hash functions defined over a "hard" language, and is useful in building many cryptographic primitives such as chosen-ciphertext secure encryption, leakage-resilient encryption, lossy encryption. In [18] Kiltz et al. generalized the smoothness property of SPH to "κ-entropic". A κ-entropic projective hashing $\mathsf{P} = (H, \Lambda, R, X, L, \Pi, S, \alpha)$ is explained below:

- Hard language (X, L): X is a language and L is a subset of X. For any $x \in L$ there is a witness w, and for $x \in X \backslash L$ there is no witness. By assumption, it is hard to distinguish $x \in L$ and $x' \in X \backslash L$ efficiently.
- Key Projection α: The hash function is keyed by $r \in R$. There is also a projective map $\alpha : R \mapsto S$, given a hash key $r \in R$, generates a projective key $s = \alpha(r) \in S$. Both r and s can be used to evaluate the hash value, in the private evaluation algorithm H and public evaluation algorithm Λ respectively.
- Private evaluation H: Given the hash key r, and a hash input $x \in X$, the hash value $\pi = H(r, x) \in \Pi$ is efficiently computable.
- Public evaluation Λ: The public evaluation algorithm Λ only works for $x \in L$. For any hash key $r \in R$, the action of $H(r, \cdot)$ on L is completed determined by $\alpha(r)$. That is, for any $x \in L$ with witness w, Λ correctly computes the hash value with w and $\alpha(r)$, i.e., $\Lambda(\alpha(r), x, w) = H(r, x)$. It is also called the projective property.
- κ-entropic property: The property is defined for $x \in X \backslash L$. P is ϵ-almost κ-entropic if for all $x \in X \backslash L$, there is $\Pr[\tilde{\mathbf{H}}_\infty(H(r, x)) | \alpha(r) \geq \kappa] \geq 1 - \epsilon$. That is, the hash value of an input $x \in X \backslash L$ cannot be determined given the projective key in the information-theoretic sense.

P is smooth if the two distributions over $X \backslash L \times S \times \Pi$, defined as $Z_1 = (x, s = \alpha(r), \pi = H(r, x))$ and $Z_2 = (x, s = \alpha(r), \pi')$ where $r \in R$ and $\pi' \xleftarrow{\$} \Pi$, are statistically close [12]. That is, for $x \in X \backslash L$, the hash value $H(r, x)$ is nearly uniformly distributed in its range Π given only the projective key $\alpha(r)$. Obviously smoothness is stronger than the κ-entropic property. However, κ-entropic is enough in many scenarios. And as shown in [18], the κ-entropic property can be converted into smoothness with a pairwise independent hash.

3 Lossy Key Encapsulation Mechanism

In this section we define the notion of lossy key encapsulation mechanism. The definition combines those of KEM and lossy encryption.

Definition 1 (Lossy Key Encapsulation Mechanism). *A lossy key encapsulation mechanism* LKE *is a 4-tuple of algorithms,* (LKE.Kg, LKE.LKg, LKE.Enc, LKE.Dec).

- *Key generation:* $(pk_I, sk) \xleftarrow{\$} \mathsf{LKE.Kg}(\lambda)$.
- *Lossy key generation:* $(pk_L, \perp) \xleftarrow{\$} \mathsf{LKE.LKg}(\lambda)$.
- *Encapsulation:* $(C, K) \leftarrow \mathsf{LKE.Enc}(pk, r)$, *where* pk *is generated by either* LKE.Kg *or* LKE.LKg. LKE.Enc *can be decomposed into two subroutines,* LRg *and* KDF.
  - *Lossy relation generation:* $(C, tK) \leftarrow \mathsf{LKE.Enc.LRg}(pk, r)$, *where* C *is the image of* r, *and* tK *is induced by an injective function from* r.
  - *Key derivation:* $K \leftarrow \mathsf{LKE.Enc.KDF}(tK)$, *where* $\mathsf{KDF} : \{0, 1\}^* \rightarrow \{0, 1\}^*$ *is a key derivation function with its key specified in* pk *and* sk.
- *Decapsulation:* $K \leftarrow \mathsf{LKE.Dec}(sk, C)$. *Similarly,* LKE.Dec *can also be decomposed into two subroutines,* Inv *and* KDF.
  - *Inversion:* $tK \leftarrow \mathsf{LKE.Dec.Inv}(sk, C)$;
  - *Key derivation:* $K \leftarrow \mathsf{LKE.Dec.KDF}(tK)$;

We require the following properties for the algorithms:

1. *Correctness: for all* (pk, sk) *generated by* LKE.Kg, *there is* $K = \mathsf{LKE.Dec}(sk, C)$ *where* $(C, K) \leftarrow \mathsf{LKE.Enc}(pk, r)$.
2. *Lossiness: for all* pk *generated by* LKE.LKg, $(C, K) \leftarrow \mathsf{LKE.Enc}(pk, r)$, C *statistically hides the information of* r *and consequently the information of* tK, *thus* K *can not be recovered. In detail, denote the size of the set of all* $r's$ *as* $2^{\mathsf{LKE.il}}$ *and the size of the set of all* $C's$ *as* $2^{\mathsf{LKE.cl}}$, *then* $\mathsf{LKE.cl} < \mathsf{LKE.il}$. *We call* $\delta = \mathsf{LKE.il} - \mathsf{LKE.cl}$ *the lossiness of* LKE, *and there is* $\tilde{\mathbf{H}}_\infty(tK|C) \geq \delta$.
3. *Indistinguishability: No polynomial time algorithm can distinguish the public keys generated by* LKE.Kg *and* LKE.LKg. *We further describe the requirement by the following game:*

$$\mathsf{Game}_{\mathsf{LKE, A}}^{\mathsf{loss}}(\lambda)$$

$$(pk_0, sk) \xleftarrow{\$} \mathsf{LKE.Kg}(\lambda); (pk_1, \perp) \xleftarrow{\$} \mathsf{LKE.LKg}(\lambda);$$

$$b \xleftarrow{\$} \{0, 1\}; b' \xleftarrow{\$} \mathsf{A}(\lambda, pk_b); \ Return \ (b' \stackrel{?}{=} b)$$

The advantage of the adversary A *in winning the game, defined as* $\mathsf{Adv}_{\mathsf{LKE, A}}^{\mathsf{loss}}(\lambda) = 2 \Pr[\mathsf{Game}_{\mathsf{LKE, A}}^{\mathsf{loss}}(\lambda)] - 1$, *is negligible.*

Akin to the case that lossy encryption implies IND-CPA secure encryption [6], lossy KEM also implies IND-secure KEM. With a generalized leftover hash lemma proposed by Dodis *et al.* in [19], we prove that a lossy KEM is IND secure with the key derivation function KDF being chosen from a family of pairwise independent hash functions.

Lemma 1 (Generalized Leftover Hash Lemma [19]). *Let X, Y be random variables such that $X \in D$ and $\tilde{\mathbf{H}}_\infty(X|Y) \geq \delta$. Let $\mathcal{H}$ be a family of pairwise independent hash function from D to $\{0,1\}^k$. Then for $h \overset{\$}{\leftarrow} \mathcal{H}$, and $k \leq \delta - 2\log(1/\epsilon)$ there is $\Delta((Y, h, h(X)), (Y, h, U_k)) \leq \epsilon$.*

Theorem 1. *Assume that the key derivation function KDF is randomly chosen from a family of pairwise independent hash functions mapping D to $\{0,1\}^k$, where D is the set of all $tK's$ and $k \leq \delta - 2\log(1/\epsilon)$, then a lossy KEM LKE with lossiness δ is also IND secure. Specifically, let A be an IND adversary, then we could construct a lossy KEM adversary B, such that for A, B, there is $\mathsf{Adv}_{\mathsf{LKE},\,\mathsf{A}}^{\mathsf{ind}}(\cdot) \leq 2\mathsf{Adv}_{\mathsf{LKE},\,\mathsf{B}}^{\mathsf{loss}}(\cdot)$.*

Proof. We prove the theorem via a sequence of games. Let A be an IND adversary attacking the IND security of the lossy KEM, and Game_0 be the original IND game. Denote the probability of A in winning Game_i as $\Pr[\mathsf{G}_i^\mathsf{A}(\cdot)]$, then $\mathsf{Adv}_{\mathsf{LKE},\,\mathsf{A}}^{\mathsf{ind}}(\cdot) = 2\Pr[\mathsf{G}_0^\mathsf{A}(\cdot) - 1]$.

Game_1: Replace the key generation algorithm $\mathsf{LKE.Kg}(\cdot)$ with $\mathsf{LKE.LKg}(\cdot)$. Then we can construct a lossy KEM adversary B invoking A as follows:

> $\mathsf{B}(\lambda, pk_b)$
>
> $r \overset{\$}{\leftarrow} \mathsf{RSp}(\lambda); (C, tK) \leftarrow \mathsf{LKE.Enc.LRg}(pk, r);$
>
> $K_0 \leftarrow \mathsf{LKE.Enc.KDF}(tK); K_1 \overset{\$}{\leftarrow} \{0,1\}^k; d \overset{\$}{\leftarrow} \{0,1\};$
>
> $d' \overset{\$}{\leftarrow} \mathsf{A}(pk_b, \mathbf{C}, K_d); \text{If } (d' = d) \text{ return } 0, \text{ otherwise return } 1.$

If $b = 0$, i.e., B receives a normal public key, then B is simulating Game_0 for A. Else, if $b = 1$, i.e., B receives a lossy public key, then B is simulating Game_1. Hence, $\Pr[\mathsf{G}_0^\mathsf{A}(\cdot)] - \Pr[\mathsf{G}_1^\mathsf{A}(\cdot)] \leq \mathsf{Adv}_{\mathsf{LKE},\,\mathsf{B}}^{\mathsf{loss}}(\cdot)$.

In Game_1, LKE is working in the lossy mode, thus the ciphertext C statistically hides the information of tK, i.e., $\tilde{\mathbf{H}}_\infty(tK|C) \geq \delta$. With Lemma 1 there is $\Delta((C, \mathsf{KDF}, \mathsf{KDF}(tK)), (C, \mathsf{KDF}, U_k)) \leq \epsilon$, i.e., K_0 and K_1 are statistically close, thus the probability of A in winning the game is $\Pr[\mathsf{G}_\mathsf{A}^1(\cdot)] = 1/2$.

By summing up there is $\mathsf{Adv}_{\mathsf{LKE},\,\mathsf{A}}^{\mathsf{ind}}(\cdot) \leq 2\mathsf{Adv}_{\mathsf{LKE},\,\mathsf{B}}^{\mathsf{loss}}(\cdot)$, which is negligible since LKE is assumed to be lossy. □

4   Constructions of Lossy KEM

Here we show constructions of lossy KEM from lossy trapdoor functions, lossy trapdoor relations, and entropic projective hashing. The constructions are direct and simple.

4.1 Lossy KEM from LTDF

Given a collection of lossy trapdoor functions $F = (F.Ig, F.Lg, F.Ev, F.Inv)$, and a family of pairwise independent hash functions $\mathcal{H}$, we could construct a lossy KEM $LK = (LK.Kg, LK.LKg, LK.Enc, LK.Dec)$ as follows:

- Key generation $(pk_I, sk) \overset{\$}{\leftarrow} LK.Kg(\lambda)$: $(\sigma_I, \tau) \overset{\$}{\leftarrow} F.Ig(\lambda)$; $h \overset{\$}{\leftarrow} \mathcal{H}$; $(pk_I, sk) \leftarrow ((\sigma_I, h), (\tau, h))$.
- Lossy key generation $(pk_L, \perp) \overset{\$}{\leftarrow} LK.LKg(\lambda)$: $(\sigma_L, \perp) \overset{\$}{\leftarrow} F.Lg(\lambda)$; $h \overset{\$}{\leftarrow} \mathcal{H}$; $(pk_L, \perp) \leftarrow ((\sigma_L, h), \perp)$.
- Encapsulation $(C, K) \leftarrow LK.Enc(pk, r)$: $C \leftarrow F.Ev(\sigma, r), tK \leftarrow r, K \leftarrow h(tK)$.
- Decapsulation $K \leftarrow LK.Dec(sk, C)$: $r \leftarrow F.Inv(\tau, C), tK \leftarrow r, K \leftarrow h(tK)$.

Theorem 2. *Assume that F is a collection of (m, l)-lossy trapdoor functions, and $\mathcal{H}$ is a family of pairwise independent hash functions, then LK is a lossy KEM with lossiness $\delta = l$.*

Proof. – Correctness: follows from the injective mode of F, i.e., for all (σ_I, τ) produced by $F.Ig$, and $C \leftarrow F.Ev(\sigma_I, r)$, there is $r = F.Inv(\tau, C)$, thus $K \leftarrow h(r)$ can be recovered.
- Lossiness: follows from the lossy mode of F, i.e., for all $(\sigma_L, \perp)$ produced by $F.Lg$, and $C \leftarrow F.Ev(\sigma_L, r)$, the size of the set of all C's is at most 2^{m-l}, i.e., C statistically loses at least l bits information of r. Since $tK = r$, it means that $\tilde{H}_\infty(tK|C) \geq l$. Thus $K = h(r)$ can not be recovered. And the lossiness of LK is l.
- Indistinguishability: follows from the indistinguishability of the injective mode and the lossy mode of F.

$\square$

4.2 Lossy KEM from LTDR

Given a collection of lossy trapdoor relations $F = (F.Ig, F.Lg, F.Ev, F.Inv)$ and and a family of pairwise independent hash functions $\mathcal{H}$, we could construct a lossy KEM $LK = (LK.Kg, LK.LKg, LK.Enc, LK.Dec)$ as follows:

- Key generation $(pk_I, sk) \overset{\$}{\leftarrow} LK.Kg(\lambda)$: $(\sigma_I, H, \tau) \overset{\$}{\leftarrow} F.Ig(\lambda)$; $h \overset{\$}{\leftarrow} \mathcal{H}$; $(pk_I, sk) \leftarrow ((\sigma_I, H, h), (\tau, H, h))$.
- Lossy key generation $(pk_L, \perp) \overset{\$}{\leftarrow} LK.LKg(\lambda)$: $(\sigma_L, H, \perp) \overset{\$}{\leftarrow} F.Lg(\lambda)$; $h \overset{\$}{\leftarrow} \mathcal{H}$; $(pk_L, \perp) \leftarrow ((\sigma_L, H, h), \perp)$.
- Encapsulation $(C, K) \leftarrow LK.Enc(pk, r)$: $(C, H(r)) \leftarrow F.Ev(\sigma, H, r), tK \leftarrow H(r), K \leftarrow h(tK)$.
- Decapsulation $K \leftarrow LK.Dec(sk, C)$: $H(r) \leftarrow F.Inv(\tau, H, C), tK \leftarrow H(r), K \leftarrow h(H(r))$.

Theorem 3. *Assume that F is a collection of (m, l)-lossy trapdoor relations, and $\mathcal{H}$ is a family of pairwise independent hash functions, then LK is a lossy KEM with lossiness $\delta = l$.*

Proof. – Correctness: follows from the injective mode of F, i.e., for all (σ_I, τ) produced by F.Ig, and $(C, H(r)) \leftarrow$ F.Ev(σ_I, H, r), there is $H(r) =$ F.Inv(τ, H, C), thus $K \leftarrow h(H(r))$ can be recovered.
- Lossiness: follows from the lossy mode of F, i.e., for all $(\sigma_L, \perp)$ produced by F.Lg, and $C \leftarrow$ F.Ev(σ_L, H, r), the size of the set of all C's is at most 2^{m-l}, i.e., C statistically loses at least l bits information of r and $H(r)$. Since $tK = H(r)$, there is $\tilde{\mathbf{H}}_\infty(tK|C) \geq l$. Thus $K = h(H(r))$ can not be recovered. And the lossiness of LK is l.
- Indistinguishability: follows from the indistinguishability of the injective mode and the lossy mode of F.

$\square$

4.3 Lossy KEM from Entropic Projective Hashing

In [23] Wee defined dual projective hashing, which is similar to smooth projective hashing, for the purpose of constructing lossy trapdoor function and deterministic public key encryption. Here we show that lossy KEM can be directly constructed from the weaker primitive, entropic projective hashing, without making a detour from lossy trapdoor functions, in a similar way with the lossy encryption constructed from smooth projective hashing in [17].

Given a κ-entropic projective hashing $\mathsf{P} = (H, \Lambda, R, X, L, \Pi, S, \alpha)$ and a family of pairwise independent hash functions $\mathcal{H}$, we construct a lossy KEM LK = (LK.Kg, LK.LKg, LK.Enc, LK.Dec) as follows:

- Key generation $(pk_I, sk) \overset{\$}{\leftarrow}$ LK.Kg(λ): $(x, w) \overset{\$}{\leftarrow} L$; $h \overset{\$}{\leftarrow} \mathcal{H}$; $(pk_I, sk) \leftarrow ((x, h), (x, w, h))$.
- Lossy key generation $(pk_L, \perp) \overset{\$}{\leftarrow}$ LK.LKg(λ): $(x', \perp) \overset{\$}{\leftarrow} X \backslash L$; $h \overset{\$}{\leftarrow} \mathcal{H}$; $(pk_L, \perp) \leftarrow ((x', h), \perp)$.
- Encapsulation $(C, K) \leftarrow$ LK.Enc(pk, r): $C \leftarrow \alpha(r), tK \leftarrow H(r, x), K \leftarrow h(tK)$.
- Decapsulation $K \leftarrow$ LK.Dec(sk, C): $tK \leftarrow \Lambda(\alpha(r), x, w), K \leftarrow h(tK)$.

Theorem 4. *Assume that* P *is a κ-entropic projective hashing, and* $\mathcal{H}$ *is a family of pairwise independent hash functions, then* LK *is a lossy KEM with lossiness κ.*

Proof. – Correctness: Follows from the projective property of P, i.e., for all $x \in L$ with witness w, and $C = \alpha(r)$, there is $tK = \Lambda(\alpha(r), x, w) = H(r, x)$, thus $K = h(tK)$ can be recovered.
- Lossiness: Follows from the entropic property of P, since for all $x' \in X \backslash L$, given $C = \alpha(r)$, $tK = H(r, x')$ can not be determined by C, and with overwhelming probability there is $\tilde{\mathbf{H}}_\infty(H(r, x')|\alpha(r)) \geq \kappa$. It means that $H(\cdot, x')$ is an injective function of r in the case of $x' \in X \backslash L$, and C statistically hides the information of tK, with lossiness κ.
- Indistinguishability: Follows from the indistinguishability of $x \in L$ and $x' \in X \backslash L$.

$\square$

5   Lossy Encryption from Lossy KEM

A natural and immediate application of lossy KEM is to construct lossy encryption, with a proper randomness extractor, e.g., a pairwise-independent hash, being the key derivation function. In detail, given a lossy KEM LKE = (LKE.Kg, LKE.LKg, LKE.Enc, LKE.Dec), with its encapsulated key length being k; let the KDF h of LKE be chosen from a family of pairwise-independent hash functions $\mathcal{H}$ with proper i/o length, and the description of h be specified in the public key and secret key. Then we construct a lossy encryption scheme LE = (LE.Kg, LE.LKg, LE.Enc, LE.Dec) encrypting messages from $\{0,1\}^k$ as follows:

LE.Kg(1^λ)	LE.LKg(1^λ)
$(pk_I, sk) \xleftarrow{\$} $ LKE.Kg(1^λ)	$(pk_L, \bot) \xleftarrow{\$} $ LKE.LKg(1^λ)
$(PK_I, SK) \leftarrow (pk_I, sk)$	$PK_L \leftarrow pk_L$
Return (PK_I, SK)	Return $(PK_L, \bot)$
LE.Enc(PK, m, r)	LE.Dec(SK, C)
$(C_1, tK) \leftarrow$ LKE.Enc.Rg(pk, r)	$(C_1, C_2) \leftarrow C$
$K \leftarrow h(tK)$	$tK \leftarrow$ LKE.Dec.Inv(SK, C_1)
$C_2 \leftarrow m \oplus K$	$K \leftarrow h(tK)$
Return (C_1, C_2)	$m \leftarrow C_2 \oplus K$
	Return m

The construction is a generalization of the lossy encryptions from lossy trapdoor functions and lossy trapdoor relations proposed in [6,25]; if LKE is constructed from entropic projective hashing, then it also generalizes the lossy encryption from smooth projective hashing in [17]; thus it is obvious that LE satisfies the properties of lossy encryption.

Theorem 5. *Assume that* LKE *is a lossy KEM with lossiness* δ, *and* $\mathcal{H}$ *is a family of pairwise independent hash functions mapping D to* $\{0,1\}^k$, *where D is the set of all tK's and* $k \leq \delta - 2\log(1/\epsilon)$. *Then* LE *is a lossy encryption.*

Proof. – The correctness and indistinguishability of LE follow readily from those properties of LKE.

– As to the lossiness, i.e., for all PK_L generated by LE.LKg, the encryption of any pair of distinct messages (m_0, m_1) should be statistically close, it mainly follows from the lossy mode of the lossy KEM. In the lossy mode, there is $\tilde{\mathbf{H}}_\infty(tK|C_1) \geq \delta$. With Lemma 1 we know that K is statistically close to the uniform distribution on $\{0,1\}^k$. Consequently, C_2 statistically hides the information of the plaintext. Thus, the ciphertext distributions of two distinct messages are statistically close.

$\square$

6   Deterministic Public Key Encryption from Lossy KEM

Another application of lossy KEM is the construction of deterministic public key encryption scheme. Firstly we recall some definitions.

6.1   Deterministic Public Key Encryption

A deterministic PKE scheme DE = (DE.Kg, DE.Enc, DE.Dec) is defined below:

1. (probabilistic) Key generation: $(PK, SK) \xleftarrow{\$} DE.Kg(\lambda)$;
2. (deterministic) Encryption: $C \leftarrow DE.Enc(PK, M)$;
3. (deterministic) Decryption: $M \leftarrow DE.Dec(SK, C)$.

We use the IND-style definition of PRIV security from [2]. A PRIV adversary $A = (A_1, A_2)$ of the DPKE scheme is a pair of PPT algorithms:

- Message generator A_1: $(\mathbf{m}_0, \mathbf{m}_1) \leftarrow A_1(\lambda)$; it is required that
  i. $|\mathbf{m}_0| = |\mathbf{m}_1| \leq v(\lambda)$ for a certain polynomial v, and $|\mathbf{m}_0[i]| = |\mathbf{m}_1[i]|$ for every $1 \leq i \leq |\mathbf{m}_0|$, and
  ii. For $i \neq j$, $1 \leq i, j \leq |\mathbf{m}_0|$, there is $\mathbf{m}_b[i] \neq \mathbf{m}_b[j]$ for $b = 0$ and $b = 1$ respectively.
- Guesser A_2: $b' \leftarrow A_2(\lambda, PK, \mathbf{c}_b)$.

To make the security of DPKE schemes achievable, we should further stipulate that the adversary A have *high min-entropy*. That is, the function $\mathsf{Guess}_A(\lambda) = \Pr[\mathbf{m}_b[i] = m : (\mathbf{m}_0, \mathbf{m}_1) \xleftarrow{\$} A_1(\lambda)]$ is negligible for all $b \in \{0, 1\}, 1 \leq i \leq |\mathbf{m}_b|, m \in \{0, 1\}^*$.

The IND-style PRIV security is described by the following game:

$$\mathsf{Game}^{\mathsf{priv}}_{\mathsf{DE}, A}(\lambda)$$

$$(pk, sk) \xleftarrow{\$} DE.Kg(\lambda); b \xleftarrow{\$} \{0, 1\}; (\mathbf{m}_0, \mathbf{m}_1) \xleftarrow{\$} A_1(\lambda);$$

$$\text{For } i = 1 \text{ to } |\mathbf{m}_0| \text{ do } \mathbf{c}[i] \leftarrow DE.Enc(pk, \mathbf{m}_b[i]);$$

$$b' \xleftarrow{\$} A_2(\lambda, pk, \mathbf{c}); \text{ Return } (b' \overset{?}{=} b)$$

The advantage of the adversary A in winning the game is defined as $\mathsf{Adv}^{\mathsf{priv}}_{\mathsf{DE}, A}(\lambda) = 2 \Pr[\mathsf{Game}^{\mathsf{priv}}_{\mathsf{DE}, A}(\lambda)] - 1$.

We say that DE is PRIV secure if $\mathsf{Adv}^{\mathsf{priv}}_{\mathsf{DE}, A}(\cdot)$ is negligible for all PPT adversary A with high min-entropy.

6.2   Universal Computational Extractor

In [3] Bellare and Hoang solved the long-pending open problem of constructing full PRIV secure DPKE in the standard model with the "UCE + LTDF" method, where UCE stands for universal computational extractor studied in [4,5,10].

A family of hash functions H=(H.Kg,H.Ev)is UCE[S] secure if it is indistinguishable with a random oracle of the same input and output length for any PPT adversary pair (S, D), where S is called the source and D is called the distinguisher. S interacts with an oracle HASH and outputs a leakage L describing the interaction. The oracle HASH is decided by a bit $b \in \{0, 1\}$. If $b = 0$ then HASH is a random oracle [7]; otherwise, HASH is a function from H. The distinguisher D receives the leakage L and outputs a guess bit about HASH. Here is the formal definition of the UCE security and the oracle HASH.

$$\text{Game}^{\text{uce}}_{H,S,D}(1^\lambda)$$
$$b \xleftarrow{\$} \{0,1\}; hk \xleftarrow{\$} \text{H.Kg}(1^\lambda);$$
$$L \xleftarrow{\$} S^{\text{HASH}}(1^\lambda); b' \xleftarrow{\$} D(1^\lambda, hk, L);$$
$$\text{Return } (b' \stackrel{?}{=} b)$$

$$\text{HASH}(x, 1^l)$$
$$\text{If } T[x, l] = \bot \text{ then}$$
$$\text{If } b = 0 \text{ then } T[x, l] \xleftarrow{\$} \{0, 1\}^l$$
$$\text{Else } T[x, l] \leftarrow \text{H.Ev}(1^\lambda, hk, x, 1^l)$$
$$\text{Return } T[x, l]$$

However, to make UCE security meaningful, the source S should be restricted to a certain type. In this paper we use statistically unpredictable sources, i.e., the HASH queries of S is hard to guess for a statistical predictor P given the leakage of S. Since the unpredictability of S is the property of S and is unrelated to the property of H, here the oracle HASH is the random oracle.

$$\text{Game}^{\text{pred}}_{S,P}(1^\lambda)$$
$$Q \leftarrow \emptyset; L \xleftarrow{\$} S^{\text{HASH}}(1^\lambda);$$
$$Q' \xleftarrow{\$} P(1^\lambda, L); \text{Return } (Q' \cap Q \neq \emptyset)$$

$$\text{HASH}(x, 1^l)$$
$$\text{If } T[x, l] = \bot \text{ then } T[x, l] \xleftarrow{\$} \{0, 1\}^l;$$
$$Q \leftarrow Q \cup x; \text{Return } T[x, l]$$

We say that a hash family H is UCE[S^{sup}] secure if $\text{Adv}^{\text{uce}}_{H,S,D} = 2 \Pr[\text{Game}^{\text{uce}}_{H,S,D}(1^\lambda)] - 1$ is negligible for all PPT adversaries (S, D), where S is statistically unpredictable for all computationally unbounded predictor P, with $\text{Adv}^{\text{pred}}_{S,P}(1^\lambda) = \Pr[\text{Game}^{\text{pred}}_{S,P}(1^\lambda)]$ being negligible.

6.3 DPKE from Lossy KEM

We generalize the "UCE + LTDF" method for constructing full PRIV-secure DPKE in the standard model proposed in [3] to a "UCE + lossy KEM" way. Given a lossy KEM LKE = (LKE.Kg, LKE.LKg, LKE.Enc, LKE.Dec), with its input length denoted as LKE.il, ciphertext length denoted as LKE.cl, and encapsulated key length denoted as LKE.kl; and a UCE[S^{sup}] secure hash function family H=(H.Kg, H.Ev) with variable input/output length, we construct a deterministic public key encryption DE = (DE.Kg, DE.LKg, DE.Enc, DE.Dec) as follows:

DE.Kg(λ)	DE.Enc(PK, m)	DE.Dec(λ)
$(pk, sk) \xleftarrow{\$} \text{LKE.Kg}(\lambda)$	$r \leftarrow \text{H.Ev}(hk, m, 1^{\text{LKE.il}})$	$(C_1, C_2) \leftarrow C$
$hk \xleftarrow{\$} \text{H.Kg}(\lambda)$	$(C_1, tK) \leftarrow \text{LKE.Enc.Rg}(pk, r)$	$tK \leftarrow \text{LKE.Dec.Inv}(sk, C_1)$
$PK \leftarrow (pk, hk)$	$K \leftarrow \text{H.Ev}(hk, tK, 1^{\text{LKE.kl}})$	$K \leftarrow \text{H.Ev}(hk, tK, 1^{\text{LKE.kl}})$
$SK \leftarrow (sk, hk)$	$C_2 \leftarrow m \oplus K$	$m \leftarrow C_2 \oplus K$
Return (PK, SK)	Return (C_1, C_2)	Return m

Then we prove the PRIV security of DE with the following theorem, which is similar to the Theorem 3.2 of [3], since the construction is a generalization of the DE1 scheme in [3].

Theorem 6. *Assume that* LKE *is a lossy KEM,* H *is a* UCE[S^{sup}] *secure hash family with variable output length, then the deterministic public key encryption* DE *is PRIV secure. Specifically, let* $\mathsf{A} = (\mathsf{A}_1, \mathsf{A}_2)$ *be a PRIV adversary with high min-entropy, then we could construct a lossy KEM adversary* B, *a pair of UCE adversary* (S, D), *such that for* A, B *and an arbitrary statistical predictor* P,

$$\text{Adv}^{\text{priv}}_{\text{DE},\mathsf{A}}(\cdot) \leq 2\text{Adv}^{\text{loss}}_{\text{LKE},\mathsf{B}}(\cdot) + 2\text{Adv}^{\text{uce}}_{\text{H},\mathsf{S},\mathsf{D}}(\cdot) + 3v^2/2^{\text{LKE.il}},$$

$$\text{Adv}^{\text{pred}}_{\mathsf{S},\mathsf{P}}(\cdot) \leq qv\text{Guess}_{\mathsf{A}}(\cdot) + 3v^2/2^{1+\text{LKE.il}} + qv/2^{\delta},$$

where v *bounds the size of message vectors output by* A, δ *is the lossiness of* LKE, *and* q *bounds the output size of* P.

Proof. Let Game_0 be the original PRIV game. We prove the theorem via a sequence of games. Denote the probability of A in winning Game_i as $\Pr[\mathsf{G}^{\mathsf{A}}_i(\cdot)]$. Thus the advantage of A is $\text{Adv}^{\text{priv}}_{\text{DE},\mathsf{A}}(\cdot) = 2\Pr[\mathsf{G}^{\mathsf{A}}_0(\cdot)] - 1$.

Game_1: Replace $\text{LKE.Kg}(\cdot)$ with $\text{LKE.LKg}(\cdot)$. We can construct a lossy KEM adversary B simulating a PRIV game for the adversary $\mathsf{A} = (\mathsf{A}_1, \mathsf{A}_2)$ as follows:

$\mathsf{B}(\lambda, pk)$

$\quad (\mathbf{m}_0, \mathbf{m}_1) \xleftarrow{\$} \mathsf{A}_1(\lambda); hk \xleftarrow{\$} \text{H.Kg}(\lambda); PK \leftarrow (pk, hk); b \xleftarrow{\$} \{0, 1\};$

$\quad$ For $i = 1$ to $|\mathbf{m}_0|$ do

$\quad\quad r \leftarrow \text{H.Ev}(hk, \mathbf{m}_b[i], 1^{\text{LKE.il}}); (\mathbf{C}_1[i], tK) \leftarrow \text{LKE.Enc.Rg}(pk, r);$

$\quad\quad \mathbf{K}[i] \leftarrow \text{H.Ev}(hk, tK, 1^{\text{LKE.kl}}); \mathbf{C}_2[i] \leftarrow \mathbf{m}_b[i] \oplus \mathbf{K}[i];$

$\quad \mathbf{C} \leftarrow (\mathbf{C}_1, \mathbf{C}_2); b' \xleftarrow{\$} \mathsf{A}_2(\lambda, PK, \mathbf{C});$ Return $(b' \overset{?}{=} b)$

If pk is generated by $\text{LKE.Kg}(\cdot)$ then B is simulating Game_0 for A; otherwise B is simulating Game_1. Thus $\Pr[\mathsf{G}^{\mathsf{A}}_0(\cdot)] - \Pr[\mathsf{G}^{\mathsf{A}}_1(\cdot)] \leq \text{Adv}^{\text{loss}}_{\text{LKE},\mathsf{B}}(\cdot)$.

Game_2: Replace the hash function $\text{H}(hk, \cdot, \cdot)$ with a random oracle. We construct a UCE adversary (S, D) as follows.

$S(\lambda)$

$(pk, \perp) \xleftarrow{\$} \mathsf{LKE.Kg}(\lambda); PK \leftarrow pk;$

$b \xleftarrow{\$} \{0,1\}; (\mathbf{m}_0, \mathbf{m}_1) \xleftarrow{\$} \mathsf{A}_1(\lambda);$

For $i = 1$ to $|\mathbf{m}_0|$ do

$\quad r \leftarrow \mathsf{HASH}(\mathbf{m}_b[i], 1^{\mathsf{LKE.il}});$

$\quad (\mathbf{C}_1[i], tK) \leftarrow \mathsf{LKE.Enc.Rg}(pk, r);$

$\quad \mathbf{K}[i] \leftarrow \mathsf{HASH}(tK, 1^{\mathsf{LKE.kl}}); \mathbf{C}_2[i] \xleftarrow{\$} \mathbf{m}_b[i] \oplus \mathbf{K}[i];$

$\mathbf{C} \leftarrow (\mathbf{C}_1, \mathbf{C}_2); \mathrm{Return}\ (b, PK, \mathbf{C})$

$\mathsf{D}(\lambda, hk, L)$

$(b, PK, \mathbf{C}) \leftarrow L;$

$b' \xleftarrow{\$} \mathsf{A}_2(\lambda, PK, \mathbf{C});$

$\mathrm{Return}\ (b' \overset{?}{=} b)$

We can see that if HASH is H.Ev, then (S, D) are simulating Game_1, otherwise they are simulating Game_2. Thus, $\Pr[\mathsf{G}_1^A(\cdot)] - \Pr[\mathsf{G}_2^A(\cdot)] \leq \mathsf{Adv}_{\mathsf{H,S,D}}^{\mathsf{uce}}(\cdot)$.

Game_3: identical to Game_2, except that the random oracle now picks a fresh value for every query, regardless of possible repetitions. Now the random oracle in Game_3 is as follows:

$$\mathsf{HASH}(x, l)$$

$$y \xleftarrow{\$} \{0,1\}^l; \mathrm{Return}\ y$$

Let v be a polynomial that bounds $|\mathbf{m}|$. Since the components of $\mathbf{m}$ are distinct, Game_2 and Game_3 are different only if:

1. some tK is repeated due to repeated r, which happens with probability at most $v^2/2^{1+\mathsf{LKE.il}}$.
2. some tK is coincided with $\mathbf{m}_b[i]$ for some i, the probability is bounded by $v^2/2^{\mathsf{LKE.il}}$.

Hence $\Pr[\mathsf{G}_2^A(\cdot)] - \Pr[\mathsf{G}_3^A(\cdot)] \leq 3v^2/2^{1+\mathsf{LKE.il}}$. Finally, $\Pr[\mathsf{G}_3^A(\cdot)] = 1/2$ since the challenge for A_2 is independent of the challenge bit now.

Thus, by summing up there is $\mathsf{Adv}_{\mathsf{DE,A}}^{\mathsf{priv}}(\cdot) \leq 2\mathsf{Adv}_{\mathsf{LKE,B}}^{\mathsf{loss}}(\cdot) + 2\mathsf{Adv}_{\mathsf{H,S,D}}^{\mathsf{uce}} + 3v^2/2^{\mathsf{LKE.il}}$.

Now we should prove the statistical unpredictability of S. The leakage of S is $L = (b, PK, \mathbf{C})$. Let P be a statistical predictor with maximum output size q, and the task of P is finding any $\mathbf{m}_b[i]$ or intermediate value tK. In the original unpredictability game, S is interacting with a normal random oracle. However, if we replace the random oracle with the one defined in Game_3, then L contains no information of $\mathbf{m}_b$ or any tK. Thus, the guessing probability as to $\mathbf{m}_b$ is bounded by $qv\mathsf{Guess}_A(\cdot)$, and the guessing probability as to tK is bounded by $qv/2^\delta$, where δ is the lossiness of LKE. By summing up, there is $\mathsf{Adv}_{\mathsf{S,P}}^{\mathsf{pred}}(\cdot) \leq 3v^2/2^{1+\mathsf{LKE.il}} + qv\mathsf{Guess}_A(\cdot) + qv/2^\delta$, which is negligible. $\square$

Let the lossy KEM be a "LTDF + UCE" combination, then we get the DPKE scheme in [3] as a special case. However, if we construct the lossy KEM with

"LTDR + UCE" or "entropic projective hash + UCE" then we can get better efficiency with the same security, since generally LTDR is considered to be more efficient than LTDF, as stated in [25].

7 Conclusion

In this paper, we abstract the KEM usage of several lossy primitives and introduce a new lossy primitive lossy KEM. Lossy KEM can be constructed from previous lossy primitives such as LTDF and LTDR, and from entropic projective hashing. With lossy KEM, we generalize previous constructions of lossy encryption and DPKE, and get better efficiency.

Acknowledgments. We are grateful to anonymous reviewers for their helpful comments. The authors are supported by the National Natural Science Foundation of China. Specifically, Yamin Liu is supported by No. 61502480, Xianhui Lu is supported by No. 61572495 and No. 61272534, Bao Li is supported by No. 61379137, and Haiyang Xue is supported by No. 61602473.

References

1. Bellare, M., Boldyreva, A., O'Neill, A.: Deterministic and efficiently searchable encryption. In: Menezes, A. (ed.) CRYPTO 2007. LNCS, vol. 4622, pp. 535–552. Springer, Heidelberg (2007). doi:10.1007/978-3-540-74143-5_30
2. Bellare, M., Fischlin, M., O'Neill, A., Ristenpart, T.: Deterministic encryption: definitional equivalences and constructions without random oracles. In: Wagner, D. (ed.) CRYPTO 2008. LNCS, vol. 5157, pp. 360–378. Springer, Heidelberg (2008). doi:10.1007/978-3-540-85174-5_20
3. Bellare, M., Hoang, V.T.: Resisting randomness subversion: fast deterministic and hedged public-key encryption in the standard model. In: Oswald, E., Fischlin, M. (eds.) EUROCRYPT 2015. LNCS, vol. 9057, pp. 627–656. Springer, Heidelberg (2015). doi:10.1007/978-3-662-46803-6_21
4. Bellare, M., Hoang, V.T., Keelveedhi, S.: Instantiating random oracles via UCEs. In: Canetti, R., Garay, J.A. (eds.) CRYPTO 2013. LNCS, vol. 8043, pp. 398–415. Springer, Heidelberg (2013). doi:10.1007/978-3-642-40084-1_23
5. Bellare, M., Hoang, V.T., Keelveedhi, S.: Instantiating random oracles via UCEs. In: Cryptology ePrint Archive (2013)
6. Bellare, M., Hofheinz, D., Yilek, S.: Possibility and impossibility results for encryption and commitment secure under selective opening. In: Joux, A. (ed.) EUROCRYPT 2009. LNCS, vol. 5479, pp. 1–35. Springer, Heidelberg (2009). doi:10.1007/978-3-642-01001-9_1
7. Bellare, M., Rogaway, P.: Random oracles are practical: a paradigm for designing efficient protocols. In: Proceedings of the 1st ACM Conference on Computer and Communications Security, pp. 62–73. ACM (1993)
8. Boldyreva, A., Fehr, S., O'Neill, A.: On notions of security for deterministic encryption, and efficient constructions without random oracles. In: Wagner, D. (ed.) CRYPTO 2008. LNCS, vol. 5157, pp. 335–359. Springer, Heidelberg (2008). doi:10.1007/978-3-540-85174-5_19

9. Brakerski, Z., Segev, G.: Better security for deterministic public-key encryption: the auxiliary-input setting. In: Rogaway, P. (ed.) CRYPTO 2011. LNCS, vol. 6841, pp. 543–560. Springer, Heidelberg (2011). doi:10.1007/978-3-642-22792-9_31

10. Brzuska, C., Farshim, P., Mittelbach, A.: Indistinguishability obfuscation and UCEs: the case of computationally unpredictable sources. In: Garay, J.A., Gennaro, R. (eds.) CRYPTO 2014. LNCS, vol. 8616, pp. 188–205. Springer, Heidelberg (2014). doi:10.1007/978-3-662-44371-2_11

11. Cramer, R., Shoup, V.: A practical public key cryptosystem provably secure against adaptive chosen ciphertext attack. In: Krawczyk, H. (ed.) CRYPTO 1998. LNCS, vol. 1462, pp. 13–25. Springer, Heidelberg (1998). doi:10.1007/BFb0055717

12. Cramer, R., Shoup, V.: Universal hash proofs and a paradigm for adaptive chosen ciphertext secure public-key encryption. In: Knudsen, L.R. (ed.) EUROCRYPT 2002. LNCS, vol. 2332, pp. 45–64. Springer, Heidelberg (2002). doi:10.1007/3-540-46035-7_4

13. Cramer, R., Shoup, V.: Design and analysis of practical public-key encryption schemes secure against adaptive chosen ciphertext attack. SIAM J. Comput. **33**(1), 167–226 (2003)

14. Dodis, Y., Reyzin, L., Smith, A.: Fuzzy extractors: how to generate strong keys from biometrics and other noisy data. In: Cachin, C., Camenisch, J.L. (eds.) EUROCRYPT 2004. LNCS, vol. 3027, pp. 523–540. Springer, Heidelberg (2004). doi:10.1007/978-3-540-24676-3_31

15. Freeman, D.M., Goldreich, O., Kiltz, E., Rosen, A., Segev, G.: More constructions of lossy and correlation-secure trapdoor functions. In: Nguyen, P.Q., Pointcheval, D. (eds.) PKC 2010. LNCS, vol. 6056, pp. 279–295. Springer, Heidelberg (2010). doi:10.1007/978-3-642-13013-7_17

16. Fuller, B., O'Neill, A., Reyzin, L.: A unified approach to deterministic encryption: new constructions and a connection to computational entropy. J. Cryptol. **28**(3), 671–717 (2015)

17. Hemenway, B., Libert, B., Ostrovsky, R., Vergnaud, D.: Lossy encryption: constructions from general assumptions and efficient selective opening chosen ciphertext security. In: Lee, D.H., Wang, X. (eds.) ASIACRYPT 2011. LNCS, vol. 7073, pp. 70–88. Springer, Heidelberg (2011). doi:10.1007/978-3-642-25385-0_4

18. Kiltz, E., Pietrzak, K., Stam, M., Yung, M.: A new randomness extraction paradigm for hybrid encryption. In: Joux, A. (ed.) EUROCRYPT 2009. LNCS, vol. 5479, pp. 590–609. Springer, Heidelberg (2009). doi:10.1007/978-3-642-01001-9_34

19. Naor, M., Segev, G.: Public-key cryptosystems resilient to key leakage. In: Halevi, S. (ed.) CRYPTO 2009. LNCS, vol. 5677, pp. 18–35. Springer, Heidelberg (2009). doi:10.1007/978-3-642-03356-8_2

20. Peikert, C., Waters, B.: Lossy trapdoor functions and their applications. SIAM J. Comput. **40**(6), 1803–1844 (2011)

21. Raghunathan, A., Segev, G., Vadhan, S.: Deterministic public-key encryption for adaptively chosen plaintext distributions. In: Johansson, T., Nguyen, P.Q. (eds.) EUROCRYPT 2013. LNCS, vol. 7881, pp. 93–110. Springer, Heidelberg (2013). doi:10.1007/978-3-642-38348-9_6

22. Wee, H.: Efficient chosen-ciphertext security via extractable hash proofs. In: Rabin, T. (ed.) CRYPTO 2010. LNCS, vol. 6223, pp. 314–332. Springer, Heidelberg (2010). doi:10.1007/978-3-642-14623-7_17

23. Wee, H.: Dual projective hashing and its applications — lossy trapdoor functions and more. In: Pointcheval, D., Johansson, T. (eds.) EUROCRYPT 2012. LNCS, vol. 7237, pp. 246–262. Springer, Heidelberg (2012). doi:10.1007/978-3-642-29011-4_16

24. Xue, H., Li, B., Lu, X., Jia, D., Liu, Y.: Efficient lossy trapdoor functions based on subgroup membership assumptions. In: Abdalla, M., Nita-Rotaru, C., Dahab, R. (eds.) CANS 2013. LNCS, vol. 8257, pp. 235–250. Springer, Heidelberg (2013). doi:10.1007/978-3-319-02937-5_13
25. Xue, H., Lu, X., Li, B., Liu, Y.: Lossy trapdoor relation and its applications to lossy encryption and adaptive trapdoor relation. In: Chow, S.S.M., Liu, J.K., Hui, L.C.K., Yiu, S.M. (eds.) ProvSec 2014. LNCS, vol. 8782, pp. 162–177. Springer, Heidelberg (2014). doi:10.1007/978-3-319-12475-9_12

Expanded Framework for Dual System Encryption and Its Application

Minqian Wang[1,2] and Zhenfeng Zhang[1,2(✉)]

[1] Trusted Computing and Information Assurance Laboratory,
Institute of Software, Chinese Academy of Sciences, Beijing, China
{wangminqian,zfzhang}@tca.iscas.ac.cn
[2] University of Chinese Academy of Sciences, Beijing, China

Abstract. Recently, Attrapadung (Eurocrypt 2014) proposed a generic framework that abstracts the concept of dual system encryption techniques. We expand their framework by proposing an extended perfect security for pair encoding scheme, which implies a new approach to employ dual system encryption methodology to obtain full security of attribute-based encryption (ABE) system via a generic construction.

Using this expanded framework, we obtain a fully secure ciphertext-policy ABE (CP-ABE) construction in composite order groups with short public parameters. Compared with previous works that either have public parameter size scaling linear with the number of attributes or require parameterized assumptions, our CP-ABE system achieves the advantages of an exponential improvement in terms of public parameter size and static assumptions relied on simultaneously.

Keywords: Attribute-based encryption · Dual system encryption · Full security

1 Introduction

Attribute-based encryption (ABE), initially developed from fuzzy identity-based encryption [27], enables flexible and fine-grained access control of encrypted data. Instead of encrypting to a targeted individual recipient, a sender is able to specify in a general way about who can view the message. In ABE for *predicate R* which is a boolean function $R : \mathbb{X} \times \mathbb{Y} \rightarrow \{0, 1\}$, a private key issued by an authority is associated with a descriptive value $X \in \mathbb{X}$, while a ciphertext encrypting a message M is associated with a value $Y \in \mathbb{Y}$. A key for X can decrypt a ciphertext for Y if and only if $R(X, Y) = 1$. Generally, either one of the values for encryption and secret key is a set of attributes, and the other is an access policy over a universe of attributes. Goyal et al. [15] clarified the concept of ABE into two forms: Key-Policy ABE (KP-ABE) if the access policy is for secret key, and Ciphertext-Policy ABE (CP-ABE) if the access policy is for encryption.

The crucial security requirement for ABE is collusion resistance, namely that any group of users holding secret keys can learn nothing about the plaintext if

© Springer International Publishing AG 2017
S. Hong and J.H. Park (Eds.): ICISC 2016, LNCS 10157, pp. 145–160, 2017.
DOI: 10.1007/978-3-319-53177-9_7

none of them is individually authorized to decrypt the ciphertext. Some intuitive and elegant constructions of ABE in bilinear groups [15,29] were only proven secure in the selective security model: a weakened model where the attacker is required to declare the target he intends to attack before seeing the public parameters. In 2009, Waters [28] introduced the dual system encryption methodology to prove full security for (hierarchical) identity-based encryption. Later, dual system encryption technique was extended to the ABE setting and employed in almost all fully secure ABE constructions [2,16,18,22–24] up to now.

Generic Framework for Dual System Encryption of [2]. In 2014, Attrapadung [2] proposed a generic framework that abstracts the concept of dual system encryption techniques. The framework of [2] introduces a new primitive called *pair encoding* schemes for predicates, and provides a generic construction that compiles any secure pair encoding into a fully secure ABE[1] scheme. The security of encodings comes into two flavors: an information-theoretical notion named *perfectly master-key hiding*, which captures the traditional dual system approach, and a computational notion named *doubly selectively master-key hiding*, which generalizes the techniques used to prove selective security for ABE inside the dual system encryption methodology.

The framework of [2] is claimed to be a "toolbox" for checking whether "classical" dual system techniques can be applied or not to a candidate ABE scheme (either existing or newly designed). More precisely, if the pair encoding extracted from ABE scheme is not perfectly master-key hiding, the dual system encryption techniques cannot be applied in a classical way, hence we should turn to doubly selective security. Proving this security for encoding essentially resurrects the selective proof techniques for ABE and requires a reduction to computational assumptions that needed in both KP-ABE and CP-ABE settings. However, state of art technique for proving selective security of CP-ABE [29] inevitably introduces an undesirable *parameterized q-type assumption* which means that the number of terms in the assumption is parameterized by a value q that depends on the behavior of the attacker. This leads to questions:

If the underlying pair encoding scheme does not satisfy perfect security, is it possible not to reduce the security of ABE to parameterized assumptions? *Is there any other property of pair encoding that can also imply fully secure ABE besides the security proposed by [2]?*

Most recently, Kowalczyk and Lewko [16] presented a KP-ABE scheme with short public parameters whose size grows only logarithmically with the bound on the number of attribute-uses in the access policies, and employed dual system encryption to prove full security under *standard* decisional linear assumption (DLIN). When checking the pair encoding scheme extracted from [16], we can conclude that it does not satisfy perfectly master-key hiding property (details are given in Sect. 4.1). However, it obtained full security not relied on parameterized assumption. In other words, the framework given in [2] does not capture the approach that utilized in [16].

---

[1] In our paper, we use "attribute-based encryption" to refer to *public-index predicate encryption*, which is a subclass of functional encryption categorized in [6]. In [2], the same class was referred as "functional encryption" (FE).

Our Contribution. In this work, we expand the framework of [2] by proposing an *extended perfect security* for pair encoding scheme, which implies a new way to employ dual system encryption methodology to obtain full security of ABE system. Via this expanded framework, we present a fully secure CP-ABE construction in composite order groups. Our scheme greatly reduces the size of public parameters. In Table 1 we summarize the comparison between our work and the existing schemes with comparative security guarantee. Our CP-ABE system achieves the advantages of short public parameters that grow logarithmically with the number of attributes and static assumptions relied on simultaneously, compared with previous works that either have public parameter size scaling linear with the number of attributes or require parameterized assumptions.

Table 1. Summary of existing CP-ABE schemes with full security. Here, n denotes the universe size, k is the maximum number of times an attribute may be used, m is the size of attribute set for a secret key, and $\ell \leq kn$ is the number of rows in the share-generating matrix of the access structure. PP, CT, SK sizes are given in terms of group elements. Note that $AY15$ [3] achieves large universe, we restrict the attribute universe to $[n]$ for comparison.

Reference	Security	PP size	SK size	CT size	Group	Assumption
LOS+10 [18]	Full	$O(kn)$	$O(km)$	$O(\ell)$	Composite	Static
OT10 [23]	Full	$O(kn)$	$O(km)$	$O(\ell)$	Prime	Static
LW12 [22]	Full	$O(n)$	$O(m)$	$O(\ell)$	Composite/prime	Non-static
AY15 [3]	Full	$O(1)$	$O(m)$	$O(\ell)$	Composite	Non-static
Ours	Full	$O(k \log n)$	$O(km)$	$O(\ell)$	Composite	Static

Approach. Dual system encryption is implemented by designing a "semifunctional space" where the "delayed parameters" and "key isolation" mechanisms [22] help us to carry out an information-theoretic argument or similar selective techniques. In this work, we essentially intermix the computational and information-theoretical dual system approaches together. Specifically, we use computational steps to increase the entropy available for the follow-up information-theoretic argument. We formalize this kind of computational dispose as "extended perfect security" for pair encoding scheme. Then, we compile the pair encoding scheme with this new security to an ABE construction via the generic construction given in [2]. It is worth noting that if the extended perfect security can be proven under static assumption, the full security of ABE will not be forced to reduce to parameterized assumptions any more.

1.1 Other Related Works

There have been a body of ABE constructions which are shown to be selectively secure, like [15, 21, 25, 26, 29]. Fully secure constructions in the standard model were provided by Lewko et al. [18], Okamoto and Takashima [23] and Lewko and Waters [22]. Subsequently, [17,21,24] presented fully secure unbounded ABE constructions. Another interesting direction in ABE is building ABE systems with multiple authorities [7,8,20]. Recent results give ABE for circuits [13,14], but the underlying cryptographic tools such as multilinear maps [12] used in them seem inefficient. Dual system encryption proof techniques have also been further studied in the works of [1,9–11,30] to simplify the design and analysis of ABE constructions.

1.2   Organization

In Sect. 2, we give the relevant background on ABE system and composite order bilinear groups, as well as the complexity assumptions. Section 3 recalls the framework of [2]. We present our extended security for pair encoding and the new theorem for proving full security of ABE in Sect. 4. A concrete CP-ABE construction is given in Sect. 5. Finally the conclusion is given.

2   Preliminaries

Notations. For $n \in \mathbb{N}$, we define $[n] \triangleq \{1, 2, \ldots, n\}$. When S is a set, we denote by $s \xleftarrow{\$} S$ the fact that the variable s is picked uniformly at random from S. We treat a vector as a row vector. Denote $M \in \mathbb{Z}_N^{d \times n}$ be $d \times n$ matrix in $\mathbb{Z}_N$. Denote the transpose of M as $M^\top$. Let G be a group of order p. For $g \in G$ and $\boldsymbol{a} = (a_1, \ldots, a_n) \in \mathbb{Z}_p^n$, we denote $g^{\boldsymbol{a}} = (g^{a_1}, \ldots, g^{a_n})$. For $g^{\boldsymbol{a}}, g^{\boldsymbol{b}} \in G^n$, we denote $e(g^{\boldsymbol{a}}, g^{\boldsymbol{b}}) = e(g, g)^{\boldsymbol{a}\boldsymbol{b}^\top}$.

2.1   Background for ABE

ABE Definition. An attribute-based encryption (ABE) system for predicate $R(\cdot, \cdot)$ consists of four algorithms:

Setup($\lambda, \mathcal{U}$) → (PP, MSK): takes as input a security parameter λ and the attribute universe $\mathcal{U}$. It outputs the public parameters PP and a master secret key MSK.

KeyGen(MSK, PP, X) → SK: takes as input the master secret key MSK, the public parameters PP and a key attribute $X \in \mathbb{X}$. It outputs a private key SK.

Encrypt(PP, M, Y) → CT: takes as input the public parameters PP, the message M and a ciphertext attribute $Y \in \mathbb{Y}$. It outputs a ciphertext CT.

Decrypt(PP, CT, SK) → M: takes as input the public parameters PP, a ciphertext CT and a private key SK. It outputs the message M or $\perp$.

Correctness. For all message M, $X \in \mathbb{X}$, $Y \in \mathbb{Y}$ such that $R(X, Y) = 1$. If KeyGen(MSK, PP, X) → SK and Encrypt(PP, M, Y) → CT where (PP, MSK) is generated from Setup($\lambda, \mathcal{U}$), Decrypt(PP, CT, SK) → M.

Security Model for ABE. The full security for ABE system is described by a game between a challenger and an adversary as following:

Setup. The challenger runs the Setup algorithm and sends the public parameters PP to the adversary.

Phase 1. The adversary adaptively queries the challenger for private keys corresponding to attributes $X_1, \ldots, X_{q_1}$. Each time, the challenger responds with a private key obtained by running KeyGen(MSK, PP, X_k).

Challenge. The adversary declares two equal length messages M_0 and M_1 and attribute Y^* which should satisfy that $R(X_k, Y^*) = 0$ for $k = 1, \ldots, q_1$. The challenger flips a random coin $b \in \{0, 1\}$ and runs Encrypt(PP, M_b, Y^*), producing CT. It sends CT to the adversary.

Phase 2. The adversary adaptively queries the challenger for private keys corresponding to attributes $X_{q_1+1}, \ldots, X_q$, with the added restriction that none of these satisfies $R(X_k, Y^*) = 1$. Each time, the challenger responds with a private key obtained by running KeyGen(MSK, PP, X_k).

Guess. The adversary outputs a guess b' for b.

Definition 1. *An attribute-based encryption system is fully secure if all polynomial time adversaries have at most a negligible advantage in this security game, where the advantage of an adversary is defined to be $Adv = |Pr[b' = b] - \frac{1}{2}|$.*

2.2 Composite Order Bilinear Groups

We define bilinear groups (G, G_T) of composite order $N = p_1 p_2 p_3$, where p_1, p_2, p_3 are three distinct primes, with an efficiently computable bilinear map $e : G \times G \to G_T$ which has the "bilinear" property: $e(u^a, v^b) = e(u, v)^{ab}$ and the "non-degenerate" property: $e(g, g) \neq 1 \in G_T$ whenever $g \neq 1 \in G$.

Let $\mathcal{G}$ denote a group generator which takes a security parameter λ and outputs $(G, G_T, e, N, p_1, p_2, p_3)$. We let G_{p_i} denote the subgroup of order p_i of G with generator g_i for $i = 1, 2, 3$, and $G_{p_i p_j}$ $(i \neq j)$ denote the subgroup of order $p_i p_j$ in G. Any element h in G can be expressed as $g_1^{a_1} g_2^{a_2} g_3^{a_3}$ where a_i is uniquely determined modulo p_i. Note that these subgroups G_{p_i} (for $i = 1, 2, 3$) are "orthogonal" to each other under the bilinear map e: if $h_i \in G_{p_i}$, and $h_j \in G_{p_j}$ for $i \neq j$, then $e(h_i, h_j) = 1 \in G_T$.

Definition 2 (Subgroup Decision Assumptions (SD)^2). *Subgroup Decision Problem 1,2,3 are defined as follows.* $(G, G_T, e, N, p_1, p_2, p_3) \leftarrow \mathcal{G}(\lambda)$.

(SD1). Given $g_1 \xleftarrow{\$} G_{p_1}, Z_3 \xleftarrow{\$} G_{p_3}$, and $T \in G$, decide if $T = T_1 \xleftarrow{\$} G_{p_1 p_2}$ or $T = T_2 \xleftarrow{\$} G_{p_1}$.

---

[2] The Subgroup Decision Assumptions were introduced in [19]. Strictly speaking, the $SD3$ assumption is not an instantiation of general subgroup decision assumptions, while it was classified into them in framework [2]. Our work follows [2] and inherits the same notation here.

(SD2). Let $g_1, Z_1 \xleftarrow{\$} G_{p_1}, Z_2, W_2 \xleftarrow{\$} G_{p_2}, Z_3, W_3 \xleftarrow{\$} G_{p_3}$. Given g_1, Z_1Z_2, Z_3, W_2W_3 and $T \in G$, decide if $T = T_1 \xleftarrow{\$} G_{p_1p_2p_3}$ or $T = T_2 \xleftarrow{\$} G_{p_1p_3}$.

(SD3). Let $g_1 \xleftarrow{\$} G_{p_1}, g_2, W_2, Y_2 \xleftarrow{\$} G_{p_2}, Z_3 \xleftarrow{\$} G_{p_3}$ and $\alpha, s \xleftarrow{\$} \mathbb{Z}_N$. Given $g_1, g_2, Z_3, g_1^\alpha Y_2, g_1^s W_2$ and $T \in G_T$, decide if $T = T_1 = e(g, g)^{\alpha s}$ or $T = T_2 \xleftarrow{\$} G_T$.

We define the advantage of an adversary $\mathcal{A}$ against Problem i for $\mathcal{G}$ as the distance $Adv_{\mathcal{A}}^{SDi}(\lambda) = |Pr[\mathcal{A}(D, T_1) = 1] - Pr[\mathcal{A}(D, T_2) = 1]|$, where D denotes the given elements in each assumption excluding T. We say that Assumption SDi holds for $\mathcal{G}$ if $Adv_{\mathcal{A}}^{SDi}(\lambda)$ is negligible in λ for any polynomial time algorithm $\mathcal{A}$.

3   Pair Encoding Scheme

In this section, we recall the framework of [2] briefly, including the syntax and security definition of pair encoding scheme, and the generic construction for ABE from pair encoding.

3.1   Pair Encoding

We recall the definition of pair encoding schemes given in [2]. A pair encoding scheme for predicate R consists of four deterministic algorithms P = (Param, Enc1, Enc2, Pair):

- Param(κ) $\rightarrow$ n. It takes as input an index κ and outputs n, which specifies the number of common variables in Enc1, Enc2. For default notation, let $\boldsymbol{h} = (h_1, ..., h_n)$ denote the common variables.
- Enc1(X, N) $\rightarrow$ ($\boldsymbol{k} = (k_1, ..., k_{m_1}); m_2$). It takes as inputs $X \in \mathbb{X}, N \in \mathbb{N}$, and outputs a sequence of polynomials $\{k_i\}_{i \in [1,m_1]}$ with coefficients in $\mathbb{Z}_N$, and $m_2 \in \mathbb{N}$ that specifies the number of its own variables. Each polynomial k_i is a linear combination of monomials $\alpha, r_j, h_k r_j$, where $\alpha, r_1, ..., r_{m_2}, h_1, ..., h_n$ are variables.
- Enc2(Y, N) $\rightarrow$ ($\boldsymbol{c} = (c_1, ..., c_{w_1}); w_2$). It takes as inputs $Y \in \mathbb{Y}, N \in \mathbb{N}$, and outputs a sequence of polynomials $\{c_i\}_{i \in [1,w_1]}$ with coefficients in $\mathbb{Z}_N$, and $w_2 \in \mathbb{N}$ that specifies the number of its own variables. Each polynomial c_i is a linear combination of monomials $s, s_j, h_k s, h_k s_j$, where $s, s_1, ..., s_{w_2}, h_1, ..., h_n$ are variables.
- Pair(X, Y, N) $\rightarrow$ $\boldsymbol{E}$. It takes as inputs X, Y, N, and output $\boldsymbol{E} \in \mathbb{Z}_N^{m_1 \times w_1}$.

Correctness. For $(\boldsymbol{k}; m_2) \leftarrow$ Enc1(X, N), $(\boldsymbol{c}; w_2) \leftarrow$ Enc2(Y, N), $\boldsymbol{E} \leftarrow$ Pair(X, Y, N), we have that if $R(X, Y) = 1$, then $\boldsymbol{k}\boldsymbol{E}\boldsymbol{c}^\top = \alpha s$.

3.2   Security of Pair Encoding

The framework of [2] described two types of security notion for pair encoding:

Perfect Security. The security notion is referred as *perfectly master-key hiding*: for $N \in \mathbb{N}$, if $R(X, Y) = 0$, let $n \leftarrow \mathsf{Param}(\kappa), (\boldsymbol{k}; m_2) \leftarrow \mathsf{Enc1}(X, N), (\boldsymbol{c}; w_2) \leftarrow \mathsf{Enc2}(Y, N)$, then the two distributions are identical:

$$\{\boldsymbol{c}(\boldsymbol{s}, \boldsymbol{h}),\ \boldsymbol{k}(0, \boldsymbol{r}, \boldsymbol{h})\} \quad \text{and} \quad \{\boldsymbol{c}(\boldsymbol{s}, \boldsymbol{h}),\ \boldsymbol{k}(\alpha, \boldsymbol{r}, \boldsymbol{h})\}.$$

Computational Security. The computational security states that the following two distributions are computationally indistinguishable:

$$\{g_2^{\boldsymbol{c}(\boldsymbol{s}, \boldsymbol{h})},\ g_2^{\boldsymbol{k}(0, \boldsymbol{r}, \boldsymbol{h})}\} \quad \text{and} \quad \{g_2^{\boldsymbol{c}(\boldsymbol{s}, \boldsymbol{h})},\ g_2^{\boldsymbol{k}(\alpha, \boldsymbol{r}, \boldsymbol{h})}\}.$$

This notion is reminiscent of *selective security* for ABE. Hence, two flavors are defined as *selectively secure* and *co-selectively secure master-key hiding* to dispose which kind of query (for X or Y) comes first.

3.3   Generic Construction of ABE from Pair Encoding

From a pair encoding scheme P, an ABE(P) scheme can be achieved via a generic construction given in [2].

$\mathsf{Setup}(1^\lambda, \kappa)$: Run $(G, G_T, e, N, p_1, p_2, p_3) \leftarrow \mathcal{G}(\lambda)$. Pick $g_1 \xleftarrow{\$} G_{p_1}, Z_3 \xleftarrow{\$} G_{p_3}$. Obtain $n \leftarrow \mathsf{Param}(\kappa)$. Pick $\boldsymbol{h} \xleftarrow{\$} \mathbb{Z}_N^n$ and $\alpha \in \mathbb{Z}_N$. The public parameter is $\mathrm{PP} = (g_1, e(g_1, g_1)^\alpha, g_1^{\boldsymbol{h}}, Z_3)$. The master secret key is $\mathrm{MSK} = \alpha$.

$\mathsf{KeyGen}(X, \mathrm{MSK}, \mathrm{PP})$: Upon input $X \in \mathbb{X}$, run $(\boldsymbol{k}; m_2) \leftarrow \mathsf{Enc1}(X, N)$. Parse $\mathrm{MSK} = \alpha$. Pick $\boldsymbol{r} \xleftarrow{\$} \mathbb{Z}_N^{m_2}, \boldsymbol{R}_3 \xleftarrow{\$} G_{p_3}^{m_1}$. Output the secret key SK:

$$K = g_1^{\boldsymbol{k}(\alpha, \boldsymbol{r}, \boldsymbol{h})} \cdot \boldsymbol{R}_3 \in G^{m_1}.$$

$\mathsf{Encrypt}(Y, M, \mathrm{PP})$: Upon input $Y \in \mathbb{Y}$, run $(\boldsymbol{c}; w_2) \leftarrow \mathsf{Enc2}(Y, N)$. Pick $\boldsymbol{s} = (s, s_1, \ldots, s_{w_2}) \xleftarrow{\$} \mathbb{Z}_N^{w_2+1}$. Output a ciphertext $\mathrm{CT} = (C, C_0)$, where

$$C = g_1^{\boldsymbol{c}(\boldsymbol{s}, \boldsymbol{h})} \in G^{w_1}, \qquad C_0 = e(g_1, g_1)^{\alpha s} M \in G_T.$$

Note that C can be computed from $g_1^{\boldsymbol{h}}$ and $\boldsymbol{s}$.

$\mathsf{Decrypt}(\mathrm{CT}, \mathrm{SK})$: Parse X, Y from SK, CT. When $R(X, Y) = 1$, run $\boldsymbol{E} \leftarrow \mathsf{Pair}(X, Y)$. Compute $e(g_1, g_1)^{\alpha s} \leftarrow e(\boldsymbol{K}^{\boldsymbol{E}}, C)$, and $M \leftarrow C_0 / e(g_1, g_1)^{\alpha s}$.

Correctness. For $R(X, Y) = 1$, we have

$$e(\boldsymbol{K}^{\boldsymbol{E}}, C) = e((g_1^{\boldsymbol{k}} \cdot \boldsymbol{R}_3)^{\boldsymbol{E}}, g_1^{\boldsymbol{c}}) = e(g_1, g_1)^{\boldsymbol{k} \boldsymbol{E} \boldsymbol{c}^\top} = e(g_1, g_1)^{\alpha s},$$

where the last equality comes from the correctness of the pair encoding scheme.

Security. The framework of [2] proved that the above construction of ABE is fully secure when the underlying pair encoding scheme satisfies either perfect security or computational security. The security theorem for the generic construction is as follows.

Theorem 1. *Suppose that a pair encoding scheme P for predicate R is perfectly master-key hiding (or selectively and co-selectively master-key hiding) in $\mathcal{G}$, and the Subgroup Decision Assumption 1, 2, 3 hold in $\mathcal{G}$. Also, suppose that R is domain-transferable[3]. Then the construction of attribute-based encryption for predicate R is fully secure.*

4   New Security for Pair Encoding and Security Theorem for Expanded Framework

In this section, we firstly check that the pair encoding extracted from ABE scheme in [16] is not perfectly secure. Secondly, we propose a new security definition for pair encoding scheme. Eventually, we present the security theorem for ABE from the new extended security of pair encoding via the generic construction in [2].

4.1   Pair Encoding Scheme of KP-ABE in [16]

Recently, Kowalczyk and Lewko [16] presented a KP-ABE scheme that supports LSSS access policy.[4] The KP-ABE construction supports a polynomially sized attribute universe $\mathcal{U}$ where attributes are non-empty subsets $K \subseteq [k]$ for some fixed k. The encoding of each attribute in scheme corresponds to an element g^{A_k}, where $A_k := \sum_{j \in K} a_j$. For security, Kowalczyk *et al.* employed dual system encryption approach to prove full security under standard DLIN and Subgroup Decision Assumptions. The pair encoding scheme extracted from KP-ABE [16] is shown as follows.

- $\mathsf{Param}(|\mathcal{U}|) \;\to\; 2k$ where $k \;=\; \lceil \log |\mathcal{U}| \rceil$. Denote $\boldsymbol{h} \;=\; (\boldsymbol{a}, \boldsymbol{b}) \;=\; (a_1, \ldots, a_k, b_1, \ldots, b_k)$.
- $\mathsf{Enc1}((A, \pi), N) \;\to\; (\{k_{1,i}, k_{2,i}, k_{3,i}\}_{i \in [1,m]})$: For LSSS $A \in \mathbb{Z}_N^{m \times k}$, and $\pi : [1, m] \to \mathcal{U}$ where π is injective.

$$k_{1,i} = A_i \boldsymbol{\alpha}^\top + r_i \sum_{j \in \pi[i]} a_j, \qquad k_{2,i} = r_i, \qquad k_{3,i} = r_i \sum_{j \in \pi[i]} b_j$$

where $\boldsymbol{\alpha} = (\alpha, v_2, \ldots, v_k)$ and $\boldsymbol{r} = (r_1, \ldots, r_m, v_2, \ldots, v_k)$.
- $\mathsf{Enc2}(Y, N) \to (c_1, \{c_{2,y}, c_{3,y}\}_{y \in Y})$: For $Y \subseteq \mathcal{U}$,

$$c_1 = s, \qquad c_{2,y} = s \sum_{j \in y} a_j + s_i \sum_{j \in y} b_j, \qquad c_{3,y} = s_i$$

where $\boldsymbol{s} = \{s, s_1, \ldots, s_{|Y|}\}$.

---

[3] Informally speaking, R is domain-transferable [2] if $R_N(X, Y) = R_p(X, Y)$ for any prime $p | N$ with high probability.

[4] We give the definition of access structure and linear secret share scheme (LSSS) in Appendix A.

This encoding scheme is not perfectly master-key hiding (defined in Sect. 3.2). We take an instance to illustrate here. Assume access structure includes attributes x_1, x_2, x_3 which correspond to attribute encodings a_1, a_2, a_3 (and parallel b_1, b_2, b_3) in exponent respectively, while $Y = (y_1, y_2, y_3)$ that corresponds to elements with $(a_1 + a_2, a_2 + a_3, a_1 + a_2 + a_3)$ (and parallel $(b_1 + b_2, b_2 + b_3, b_1 + b_2 + b_3)$) in exponent. It is obvious that $R(X, Y) = 0$ since there is no interaction between attribute sets for encryption and secret key. Now we will show how to compute α from the pair encoding scheme. Firstly from $k_{2,i} = r_i$ and $k_{3,i} = r_i b_i$, we can compute b_i for $i = 1, 2, 3$, thus $b_1 + b_2, b_2 + b_3, b_1 + b_2 + b_3$ are obtained. From these with $c_{3,y_i} = s_i$ and c_{2,y_i} for $i = 1, 2, 3$, we know $s(a_1 + a_2), s(a_2 + a_3), s(a_1 + a_2 + a_3)$. Since we know $c_1 = s$, each a_i for $i = 1, 2, 3$ can be computed. Finally, we can compute $A_i \boldsymbol{\alpha}^\top$ for all i from $k_{1,i} = A_i \boldsymbol{\alpha}^\top + r_i a_i$, and extract α.

4.2 Extended Perfect Security of Pair Encoding

Inspired by the security reduction of Kowalczyk and Lewko [16], we formalize a new security definition for pair encoding scheme. The new security captures the intuitive that constructs a computational indistinguishability between the pair encoding scheme and a perfectly secure one, and uses the latter to implement the information-theoretic argument. Hence, we name it "extended perfectly master-key hiding".

Extended Perfect Security. Let $\mathsf{P}' = (\mathsf{Param}', \mathsf{Enc1}', \mathsf{Enc2}', \mathsf{Pair}')$ is a perfectly master-key hiding pair encoding scheme for predicate R. The pair encoding scheme $\mathsf{P} = (\mathsf{Param}, \mathsf{Enc1}, \mathsf{Enc2}, \mathsf{Pair})$ for predicate R is P'-*extended perfectly master-key hiding*(P'-ePMH) if all polynomial time adversary $\mathcal{A}$ have at most a negligible advantage in the following game where $R(X, Y) = 0$:

$$\mathsf{Exp}_{\mathcal{G}, b, \mathcal{A}}(\lambda) : (G, G_T, e, N, p_1, p_2, p_3) \leftarrow \mathcal{G}(\lambda),$$

$$g_1 \xleftarrow{\$} G_{p_1}, g_2 \xleftarrow{\$} G_{p_2}, g_3 \xleftarrow{\$} G_{p_3}, \ \alpha = 0 \text{ or } \alpha \xleftarrow{\$} \mathbb{Z}_N,$$

$$n \leftarrow \mathsf{Param}(\kappa), \boldsymbol{h} \xleftarrow{\$} \mathbb{Z}_N^n; \ n' \leftarrow \mathsf{Param}'(\kappa), \boldsymbol{h}' \xleftarrow{\$} \mathbb{Z}_N^{n'},$$

$$b' \leftarrow \mathcal{A}^{\mathcal{O}_1(\cdot), \mathcal{O}_2(\cdot)}(g_1, g_2, g_3),$$

where the oracles $\mathcal{O}_1, \mathcal{O}_2$ can be queried once and are defined as:

$\mathcal{O}_1(X):$ if $b = 0$, run $(\boldsymbol{k}; m_2) \leftarrow \mathsf{Enc1}(X, p_2)$, $\boldsymbol{r} \xleftarrow{\$} \mathbb{Z}_{p_2}^{m_2}$, return $g_2^{\boldsymbol{k}(\alpha, \boldsymbol{r}, \boldsymbol{h})}$;

       if $b = 1$, run $(\boldsymbol{k}'; m_2') \leftarrow \mathsf{Enc1}'(X, p_2)$, $\boldsymbol{r}' \xleftarrow{\$} \mathbb{Z}_{p_2}^{m_2'}$, return $g_2^{\boldsymbol{k}'(\alpha, \boldsymbol{r}', \boldsymbol{h}')}$.

$\mathcal{O}_2(Y):$ if $b = 0$, run $(\boldsymbol{c}; w_2) \leftarrow \mathsf{Enc2}(Y, N)$, $\boldsymbol{s} \xleftarrow{\$} \mathbb{Z}_{p_2}^{w_2 + 1}$, return $g_2^{\boldsymbol{c}(\boldsymbol{s}, \boldsymbol{h})}$;

       if $b = 1$, run $(\boldsymbol{c}'; w_2') \leftarrow \mathsf{Enc2}'(Y, N)$, $\boldsymbol{s}' \xleftarrow{\$} \mathbb{Z}_{p_2}^{w_2' + 1}$, return $g_2^{\boldsymbol{c}'(\boldsymbol{s}', \boldsymbol{h}')}$.

We define the advantage of $\mathcal{A}$ in the security game as $\mathsf{Adv}_{\mathcal{A}}(\lambda) = |Pr[\mathsf{Exp}_{\mathcal{G}, 0, \mathcal{A}}(\lambda) = 1] - Pr[\mathsf{Exp}_{\mathcal{G}, 1, \mathcal{A}}(\lambda) = 1]|$.

4.3 Security Theorem of ABE Construction

We obtain a CP-ABE construction from a pair encoding scheme via the *same* generic construction in [2]. For security, we employ the dual system encryption mechanism which designs a "semi-functional" space. Indeed, the property of "delayed parameters" and "key isolation" [22] helps us in this work to essentially intermix the computational and information-theoretical dual system approaches. Specifically, we use a computational steps before the information-theoretic argument in the semi-functional space to increase the entropy available for the latter, and this kind of computational processing is implied by the extended perfect security of pair encoding scheme.

Theorem 2. *Suppose that a pair encoding scheme P for predicate R is extended perfectly master-key hiding, and the Subgroup Decision Assumption 1,2,3 hold in $\mathcal{G}$. Suppose also that R is domain-transferable. Then the construction $ABE(P)$ in $\mathcal{G}$ for predicate R is fully secure.*

Semi-functional Algorithms. We define some semi-functional types which will be used in the proof only, and the underlying pair encoding can be perfectly, extended perfectly or computationally secure.

$\mathsf{SFSetup}(1^\lambda, \kappa)$: This is exactly the same as $\mathsf{Setup}(1^\lambda, \kappa)$ except that it additionally outputs a generator $g_2 \xleftarrow{\$} G_{p_2}$ and $\hat{\boldsymbol{h}} \xleftarrow{\$} \mathbb{Z}_N^n$. We call $\hat{\boldsymbol{h}}$ a semi-functional parameter.

$\mathsf{SFEncrypt}(Y, M, \mathrm{PP}, g_2, \hat{\boldsymbol{h}})$: Upon inputs Y, M, PP, g_2 and $\hat{\boldsymbol{h}}$, first run $(\boldsymbol{c}; w_2) \leftarrow \mathsf{Enc2}(Y, N)$. Pick $\boldsymbol{s} = (s, s_1, \ldots, s_{w_2}) \xleftarrow{\$} \mathbb{Z}_N^{w_2+1}$, $\hat{\boldsymbol{s}} \in \mathbb{Z}_N^{w_2+1}$. Output a ciphertext $\mathrm{CT} = (\boldsymbol{C}, C_0)$ as

$$C = g_1^{\boldsymbol{c}(\boldsymbol{s},\boldsymbol{h})} g_2^{\boldsymbol{c}(\hat{\boldsymbol{s}},\hat{\boldsymbol{h}})} \in G^{w_1}, \quad C_0 = e(g_1, g_1)^{\alpha s} M \in G_T.$$

$\mathsf{SFEncrypt}(X, \mathrm{MSK}, \mathrm{PP}, g_2, type, \hat{\alpha}, \hat{\boldsymbol{h}})$: Upon inputs $X, \mathrm{MSK}, \mathrm{PP}, g_2$ and $type \in \{1, 2, 3\}$, $\hat{\alpha} \in \mathbb{Z}_N$, first run $(\boldsymbol{k}; m_2) \leftarrow \mathsf{Enc1}(X, N)$. Pick $\boldsymbol{r}, \hat{\boldsymbol{r}} \xleftarrow{\$} \mathbb{Z}_N^{m_2}$, $\boldsymbol{R}_3 \xleftarrow{\$} G_{p_3}^{m_1}$. Output the secret key SK:

$$\boldsymbol{K} = \begin{cases} g_1^{\boldsymbol{k}(\alpha,\boldsymbol{r},\boldsymbol{h})} \cdot g_2^{\boldsymbol{k}(0,\hat{\boldsymbol{r}},\hat{\boldsymbol{h}})} \cdot \boldsymbol{R}_3 & \text{if } type = 1 \\ g_1^{\boldsymbol{k}(\alpha,\boldsymbol{r},\boldsymbol{h})} \cdot g_2^{\boldsymbol{k}(\hat{\alpha},\hat{\boldsymbol{r}},\hat{\boldsymbol{h}})} \cdot \boldsymbol{R}_3 & \text{if } type = 2 \\ g_1^{\boldsymbol{k}(\alpha,\boldsymbol{r},\boldsymbol{h})} \cdot g_2^{\boldsymbol{k}(\hat{\alpha},0,0)} \cdot \boldsymbol{R}_3 & \text{if } type = 3 \end{cases}$$

Security Proof Structure. We use a sequence of games in the following order, where each game is defined as follows.

$\mathsf{G}_{\mathrm{real}}$ is the actual security game, and each of the following game is defined exactly as its previous game in the sequence except the specified modification that is defined in Fig. 1. For notational purpose, let $\mathsf{G}_{0,5} = \mathsf{G}_0$. In the diagram, we also write the underlying assumptions used for indistinguishability between adjacent games. We stress that the (P'-ePMH) property is employed twice: once for $\alpha = 0$ and the other for random $\alpha \in \mathbb{Z}_N$. PMH' in the figure represents the perfect security of the encoding P'.

$\mathsf{G}_{\mathrm{res}}$: The restriction becomes $R_{p_2}(X_j, Y^*) = 0$. (Instead of $R_N(X_j, Y^*) = 0$)

G_0:   Modify $\mathsf{SFSetup}(1^\lambda, \kappa) \to (\mathrm{PP}, \mathrm{MSK}, g_2, \hat{\boldsymbol{h}})$

   Modify $\mathrm{CT} \leftarrow \mathsf{SFEncrypt}(Y, M_b, \mathrm{PP}, \mathrm{MSK}, g_2, \hat{\boldsymbol{h}})$

$\mathsf{G}_{k,1}$: Modify $\hat{\alpha}_j \xleftarrow{\$} \mathbb{Z}_N, \mathrm{SK}_j \leftarrow \begin{cases} \mathsf{SFKeyGen}(X_j, \mathrm{MSK}, \mathrm{PP}, g_2, 3, \hat{\alpha}_j, \mathbf{0}) & \text{if } j < k \\ \mathsf{SFKeyGen}(X_j, \mathrm{MSK}, \mathrm{PP}, g_2, 1, 0, \hat{\boldsymbol{h}}) & \text{if } j = k \\ \mathsf{KeyGen}(X_j, \mathrm{MSK}, \mathrm{PP}) & \text{if } j > k \end{cases}$

$\mathsf{G}_{k,2}$: Modify $\mathrm{SK}_j \leftarrow \mathsf{SFKeyGen}(X_j, \mathrm{MSK}, \mathrm{PP}, g_2, 1, 0, \hat{\boldsymbol{h}}')$ if $j = k$

   Modify $\mathrm{CT} \leftarrow \mathsf{SFEncrypt}(Y, M_b, \mathrm{PP}, \mathrm{MSK}, g_2, \hat{\boldsymbol{h}}')$

$\mathsf{G}_{k,3}$: Modify $\mathrm{SK}_j \leftarrow \mathsf{SFKeyGen}(X_j, \mathrm{MSK}, \mathrm{PP}, g_2, 2, \hat{\alpha}_j, \hat{\boldsymbol{h}}')$ if $j = k$

$\mathsf{G}_{k,4}$: Modify $\mathrm{SK}_j \leftarrow \mathsf{SFKeyGen}(X_j, \mathrm{MSK}, \mathrm{PP}, g_2, 2, \hat{\alpha}_j, \hat{\boldsymbol{h}})$ if $j = k$

   Modify $\mathrm{CT} \leftarrow \mathsf{SFEncrypt}(Y, M_b, \mathrm{PP}, \mathrm{MSK}, g_2, \hat{\boldsymbol{h}})$

$\mathsf{G}_{k,5}$: Modify $\hat{\alpha}_j \xleftarrow{\$} \mathbb{Z}_N, \mathrm{SK}_j \leftarrow \begin{cases} \mathsf{SFKeyGen}(X_j, \mathrm{MSK}, \mathrm{PP}, g_2, 3, \hat{\alpha}_j, \mathbf{0}) & \text{if } j \le k \\ \mathsf{KeyGen}(X_j, \mathrm{MSK}, \mathrm{PP}) & \text{if } j > k \end{cases}$

$\mathsf{G}_{\mathrm{fin}}$: Modify $M \xleftarrow{\$} \mathcal{M}$, $\mathrm{CT} \leftarrow \mathsf{SFEncrypt}(Y, M, \mathrm{PP}, \mathrm{MSK}, g_2, \hat{\boldsymbol{h}})$.

Fig. 1. The sequence of games in the security proof.

5 Concrete Construction

We present a CP-ABE scheme where ciphertexts are associated with LSSS access structures. Our CP-ABE scheme is a "small universe" construction which supports a polynomially sized attribute universe $\mathcal{U}$ where attributes are non-empty subsets $K \subseteq [k]$ for some fixed k. The public parameter size of our scheme grows only logarithmically with the bound on the number of attribute-uses in the access policies. The encoding scheme P is given below:

- $\mathsf{Param}(|\mathcal{U}|) \to 2k + 1$ where $k = \lceil \log |\mathcal{U}| \rceil$. Denote $\boldsymbol{h} = (\boldsymbol{a}, \boldsymbol{b}, \phi) = (a_1, \dots, a_k, b_1, \dots, b_k, \phi)$.
- $\mathsf{Enc1}(X, N) \to (k_1, k_2, \{k_{3,x}, k_{4,x}\}_{x \in X})$: For $X \subseteq \mathcal{U}$,

$$k_1 = \alpha + \phi r, \quad k_2 = r, \quad k_{3,x} = r \sum_{j \in x} a_j + r_i \sum_{j \in x} b_j, \quad k_{4,x} = r_i$$

where $\boldsymbol{r} = \{r, r_1, \dots, r_{|X|}\}$.

- Enc2$((A, \pi), N) \rightarrow (c_1, \{c_{2,i}, c_{3,i}, c_{4,i}\}_{i \in [1,m]})$: For LSSS $A \in \mathbb{Z}_N^{m \times k}$, and π : $[1, m] \rightarrow \mathcal{U}$ where π is injective,

$$c_1 = s, \quad c_{2,i} = \phi A_i v^\top + s_i \sum_{j \in \pi[i]} a_j, \quad c_{3,i} = s_i, \quad c_{4,i} = s_i \sum_{j \in \pi[i]} b_j,$$

where $v = (s, v_2, \ldots, v_k)$ and $s = (s_1, \ldots, s_m, v_2, \ldots, v_k)$.

Correctness. When $R((A, \pi), S) = 1$, let $I = \{i \in [1, m] | \pi(i) \in S\}$, we have reconstruction coefficients $\{\omega_i\}_{i \in I}$ such that $\sum_{i \in I} \omega_i A_i v^\top = s$. Therefore,

$$k_1 c_1 - \sum_{i \in I} \omega_i (k_2 c_{2,i} - k_{3,\pi(i)} c_{3,i} + k_{4,\pi(i)} c_{4,i}) = \alpha s + \phi r s - \sum_{i \in I} \phi \omega_i A_i v^\top r = \alpha s.$$

5.1 Security Proof

Note that the above pair encoding scheme is not perfectly secure, which can be illustrated using a similar approach to Sect. 4.1. We prove the extended perfectly master-key hiding security for it under the DLIN assumption introduced by [5].

Decisional Linear Assumption (DLIN). Let $\mathbb{G} = (p, G, G_T, e) \leftarrow \mathcal{G}$ where p is a prime. Let $g \xleftarrow{\$} G, y_1, y_2, c_1, c_2 \xleftarrow{\$} \mathbb{Z}_p$. Given $\mathbb{G}, g, g^{y_1}, g^{y_2}, g^{y_1 c_1}, g^{y_2 c_2}$. The assumption states that it is hard for any polynomial-time adversary to distinguish whether $T = g^{c_1 + c_2}$ or $T \leftarrow G$.

Theorem 3. *Our pair encoding scheme for CP-ABE is extended perfectly master-key hiding under the DLIN.*

Proof Overview. Firstly, we define pair encoding scheme P$'$ and prove that it satisfies perfect security. Secondly, we prove the computational indistinguishability between P and P$'$. The detailed proof is given in the full version.

The encoding scheme P$'$ is defined as follows. It can be observed that the difference between P and P$'$ reside in the public parameters and the corresponding elements for attributes: one is the subset-sum form, while the other is fresh randomness.

- Param$(|\mathcal{U}|) \rightarrow 2|\mathcal{U}|$. Denote $h = (a, b, \phi) = ((a_u)_{u \in \mathcal{U}}, (b_u)_{u \in \mathcal{U}}, \phi)$.
- Encl$(X, N) \rightarrow (k_1, k_2, \{k_{3,x}, k_{4,x}\}_{x \in X})$: For $X \subseteq \mathcal{U}$,

$$k_1 = \alpha + \phi r, \quad k_2 = r, \quad k_{3,x} = r a_x + r_i b_x, \quad k_{4,x} = r_i$$

where $r = \{r, r_1, \ldots, r_{|X|}\}$.

- Enc2$((A, \pi), N) \rightarrow (c_1, \{c_{2,i}, c_{3,i}, c_{4,i}\}_{i \in [1,m]})$: For LSSS $A \in \mathbb{Z}_N^{m \times k}$, and π : $[1, m] \rightarrow \mathcal{U}$ where π is injective,

$$c_1 = s, \quad c_{2,i} = \phi A_i v^\top + s_i a_{\pi(i)}, \quad c_{3,i} = s_i, \quad c_{4,i} = s_i b_{\pi(i)},$$

where $v = (s, v_2, \ldots, v_k)$ and $s = (s_1, \ldots, s_m, v_2, \ldots, v_k)$.

Lemma 1. *The pair encoding* P' *is perfectly master-key hiding.*

Proof. When $R(X, Y) = 0$, we have that (A, π) does not accept S. For $j = 1, \ldots, m$, we consider two cases. If $\pi(j) \notin S$, then $a_{\pi(j)}, b_{\pi(j)}$ does not appear anywhere. If $\pi(j) \in S$, we can compute $b_{\pi(j)}$ from $c_{3,j}$ and $c_{4,j}$, and compute $a_{\pi(j)}$ from $k_{3,j}$ and $k_{4,j}$. Since we know s_j, $\phi A_j \boldsymbol{v}^\top$ for these A_j are obtained. Now from the property of LSSS, there exists $\boldsymbol{w}$ with $w_1 \neq 0$ such that $\boldsymbol{w}$ is orthogonal to these A_j where $\pi(j) \in Y$. Thus, $\phi A_j \boldsymbol{v}^\top = \phi A_j (\boldsymbol{v}^\top + z \boldsymbol{w}^\top)$ for any unknown $z \in \mathbb{Z}_N$. Therefore, $\phi A_i \boldsymbol{v}^\top$ does not leak the information on ϕs, and the perfect master-key hiding is satisfied.

Lemma 2. $\{g_2^{\boldsymbol{k}(\alpha, \boldsymbol{r}, \boldsymbol{h})}, g_2^{\boldsymbol{c}(\boldsymbol{s}, \boldsymbol{h})}\}$ *and* $\{g_2^{\boldsymbol{k}(\alpha, \boldsymbol{r}, \boldsymbol{h}')}, g_2^{\boldsymbol{c}(\boldsymbol{s}, \boldsymbol{h}')}\}$ *are computationally indistinguishable under the DLIN.*

Proof. (sketch) It can be observed that the difference between the two pair encoding scheme is the $\sum_{j \in x} a_j$ (and $\sum_{j \in x} b_j$) in P is replaced by a fresh randomness a_x (and b_x) in P'. The proof is essentially based on the conclusion ("bilinear entropy expansion lemma" in [16]) that $2(2^k - 1)$ group elements formed as $\{g^{t_K}, g^{t_K A_K}\}$ where $g^{\sum_{j \in K} a_j} = g^{A_K}$ and $\{t_K\}$ are $2^k - 1$ random exponents, are computationally indistinguishable from $2(2^k - 1)$ uniformly random group elements under the DLIN assumption.

6   Conclusion

In this work, we expand the framework of [2] by proposing an extended perfect security for pair encoding scheme, which provides a new way to employ dual system encryption methodology to obtain full security of ABE system via the generic construction from [2].

Using this expanded framework, we obtain a fully secure CP-ABE construction in composite order groups which greatly reduce the public parameters. Compared with previous works, our CP-ABE system achieves the advantages of short public parameters that grow logarithmically with the number of attributes and static assumptions relied on simultaneously.

Acknowledgement. We would like to thank the anonymous reviewers for their valuable comments. This work is supported by the National Natural Science Foundation of China (No. U1536205) and the National Basic Research Program of China (No. 2013CB338003).

A   Linear Secret Sharing Schemes

Here we present the definition of access structure and linear secret sharing schemes introduced in [4], adapted to match our ABE setting.

Definition 3 (Access Structure). *Let $\mathcal{U}$ be the attribute universe. An access structure on $\mathcal{U}$ is a collection $\mathbb{A}$ of non-empty sets of attributes, i.e. $\mathbb{A} \subseteq 2^{\mathcal{U}} \backslash \{\}$. The sets in $\mathbb{A}$ are called the authorized sets and the sets not in $\mathbb{A}$ are called the unauthorized sets.*

Additionally, an access structure is called monotone if $\forall B, C \in \mathbb{A} : if\ B \in \mathbb{A}$ and $B \subseteq C$, then $C \in \mathbb{A}$.

Definition 4 (Linear Secret Sharing Schemes (LSSS)). *Let p be a prime and $\mathcal{U}$ the attribute universe. A secret sharing scheme Π realizing access structures on $\mathcal{U}$ is linear over $\mathbb{Z}_p$ if*

1. *The shares of a secret $s \in \mathbb{Z}_p$ for each attribute form a vector over $\mathbb{Z}_p$.*
2. *For each access structure $\mathbb{A}$ on $\mathcal{U}$, there exists an $\ell \times n$ matrix A called the share-generating matrix, and a function ρ, that labels the rows of A with attributes from $\mathcal{U}$, i.e. $\rho : [\ell] \to \mathcal{U}$, which satisfy the following: During the generation of the shares, we consider the column vector $\boldsymbol{v} = (s, v_2, \ldots, v_n)$, where $v_2, \ldots, v_n \leftarrow \mathbb{Z}_p$. Then the vector of ℓ shares of the secret s according to Π is equal to $A\boldsymbol{v}$. The share $(A\boldsymbol{v})_j$ where $j \in [\ell]$ belongs to attribute $\rho(j)$. We will refer to the pair (A, ρ) as the policy of the access structure $\mathbb{A}$.*

According to [4], each secret sharing scheme should satisfy the *reconstruction requirement* (each authorized set can reconstruct the secret) and the *security requirement* (any unauthorized set cannot reveal any partial information about the secret).

For our composite order group construction, we will employ LSSS matrices over $\mathbb{Z}_N$, where N is a product of three distinct primes p_1, p_2 and p_3. Let S denote an authorized set for the access structure $\mathbb{A}$, and I be the set of rows whose labels are in S, i.e. $I = \{i | i \in [\ell] \wedge \rho(i) \in S\}$. The reconstruction requirement asserts that the vector $(1, 0, \ldots, 0)$ is in the span of rows of A indexed by I modulo N. This means that there exist constants $\{\omega_i\}_{i \in I}$ such that, for any valid shares $\{\lambda_i = (A\boldsymbol{v})\}_{i \in I}$ of a secret s according to Π, we have $\sum_{i \in I} \omega_i \lambda_i = s$. Furthermore, these constants $\{\omega_i\}_{i \in I}$ can be found in time polynomial in the size of the share-generating matrix A.

On the other hand, for unauthorized sets S', no such $\{\omega_i\}$ exist. However, in our security proof for composite order system, we will further assume that for an unauthorized set, the corresponding rows of A do not include the vector $(1, 0, \ldots, 0)$ in their span *modulo* p_2. We may assume this because if an adversary can produce an access matrix A over $\mathbb{Z}_N$ and an unauthorized set over $\mathbb{Z}_N$ that is authorized over $\mathbb{Z}_{p_2}$, this can be used to produce a non-trivial factor of the group order N, which would violate our subgroup decision assumptions.

References

1. Agrawal, S., Chase, M.: A study of pair encodings: predicate encryption in prime order groups. In: Kushilevitz, E., Malkin, T. (eds.) TCC 2016. LNCS, vol. 9563, pp. 259–288. Springer, Heidelberg (2016). doi:10.1007/978-3-662-49099-0_10

2. Attrapadung, N.: Dual system encryption via doubly selective security: framework, fully secure functional encryption for regular languages, and more. In: Nguyen, P.Q., Oswald, E. (eds.) EUROCRYPT 2014. LNCS, vol. 8441, pp. 557–577. Springer, Heidelberg (2014). doi:10.1007/978-3-642-55220-5_31

3. Attrapadung, N., Yamada, S.: Duality in ABE: converting attribute based encryption for dual predicate and dual policy via computational encodings. In: Nyberg, K. (ed.) CT-RSA 2015. LNCS, vol. 9048, pp. 87–105. Springer, Heidelberg (2015). doi:10.1007/978-3-319-16715-2_5

4. Beimel, A.: Secure schemes for secret sharing and key distribution. Technion-Israel Institute of technology, Faculty of computer science (1996)

5. Boneh, D., Boyen, X., Shacham, H.: Short group signatures. In: Franklin, M. (ed.) CRYPTO 2004. LNCS, vol. 3152, pp. 41–55. Springer, Heidelberg (2004). doi:10.1007/978-3-540-28628-8_3

6. Boneh, D., Sahai, A., Waters, B.: Functional encryption: definitions and challenges. In: Ishai, Y. (ed.) TCC 2011. LNCS, vol. 6597, pp. 253–273. Springer, Heidelberg (2011). doi:10.1007/978-3-642-19571-6_16

7. Chase, M.: Multi-authority attribute based encryption. In: Vadhan, S.P. (ed.) TCC 2007. LNCS, vol. 4392, pp. 515–534. Springer, Heidelberg (2007). doi:10.1007/978-3-540-70936-7_28

8. Chase, M., Chow, S.S.: Improving privacy and security in multi-authority attribute-based encryption. In: Proceedings of the 16th ACM Conference on Computer and Communications Security, pp. 121–130. ACM (2009)

9. Chase, M., Meiklejohn, S.: Déjà Q: using dual systems to revisit q-type assumptions. In: Nguyen, P.Q., Oswald, E. (eds.) EUROCRYPT 2014. LNCS, vol. 8441, pp. 622–639. Springer, Heidelberg (2014). doi:10.1007/978-3-642-55220-5_34

10. Chen, J., Gay, R., Wee, H.: Improved dual system ABE in prime-order groups via predicate encodings. In: Oswald, E., Fischlin, M. (eds.) EUROCRYPT 2015. LNCS, vol. 9057, pp. 595–624. Springer, Heidelberg (2015). doi:10.1007/978-3-662-46803-6_20

11. Chen, J., Wee, H.: Fully, (Almost) tightly secure IBE and dual system groups. In: Canetti, R., Garay, J.A. (eds.) CRYPTO 2013. LNCS, vol. 8043, pp. 435–460. Springer, Heidelberg (2013). doi:10.1007/978-3-642-40084-1_25

12. Garg, S., Gentry, C., Halevi, S.: Candidate multilinear maps from ideal lattices. In: Johansson, T., Nguyen, P.Q. (eds.) EUROCRYPT 2013. LNCS, vol. 7881, pp. 1–17. Springer, Heidelberg (2013). doi:10.1007/978-3-642-38348-9_1

13. Garg, S., Gentry, C., Halevi, S., Sahai, A., Waters, B.: Attribute-based encryption for circuits from multilinear maps. In: Canetti, R., Garay, J.A. (eds.) CRYPTO 2013. LNCS, vol. 8043, pp. 479–499. Springer, Heidelberg (2013). doi:10.1007/978-3-642-40084-1_27

14. Gorbunov, S., Vaikuntanathan, V., Wee, H.: Attribute-based encryption for circuits. J. ACM (JACM) 62(6), 45 (2015)

15. Goyal, V., Pandey, O., Sahai, A., Waters, B.: Attribute-based encryption for fine-grained access control of encrypted data. In: Proceedings of the 13th ACM Conference on Computer and Communications Security, pp. 89–98. ACM (2006)

16. Kowalczyk, L., Lewko, A.B.: Bilinear entropy expansion from the decisional linear assumption. In: Gennaro, R., Robshaw, M. (eds.) CRYPTO 2015. LNCS, vol. 9216, pp. 524–541. Springer, Heidelberg (2015). doi:10.1007/978-3-662-48000-7_26

17. Lewko, A.: Tools for simulating features of composite order bilinear groups in the prime order setting. In: Pointcheval, D., Johansson, T. (eds.) EUROCRYPT 2012. LNCS, vol. 7237, pp. 318–335. Springer, Heidelberg (2012). doi:10.1007/978-3-642-29011-4_20

18. Lewko, A., Okamoto, T., Sahai, A., Takashima, K., Waters, B.: Fully secure functional encryption: attribute-based encryption and (hierarchical) inner product encryption. In: Gilbert, H. (ed.) EUROCRYPT 2010. LNCS, vol. 6110, pp. 62–91. Springer, Heidelberg (2010). doi:10.1007/978-3-642-13190-5_4

19. Lewko, A., Waters, B.: New techniques for dual system encryption and fully secure HIBE with short ciphertexts. In: Micciancio, D. (ed.) TCC 2010. LNCS, vol. 5978, pp. 455–479. Springer, Heidelberg (2010). doi:10.1007/978-3-642-11799-2_27

20. Lewko, A., Waters, B.: Decentralizing attribute-based encryption. In: Paterson, K.G. (ed.) EUROCRYPT 2011. LNCS, vol. 6632, pp. 568–588. Springer, Heidelberg (2011). doi:10.1007/978-3-642-20465-4_31

21. Lewko, A., Waters, B.: Unbounded HIBE and attribute-based encryption. In: Paterson, K.G. (ed.) EUROCRYPT 2011. LNCS, vol. 6632, pp. 547–567. Springer, Heidelberg (2011). doi:10.1007/978-3-642-20465-4_30

22. Lewko, A., Waters, B.: New proof methods for attribute-based encryption: achieving full security through selective techniques. In: Safavi-Naini, R., Canetti, R. (eds.) CRYPTO 2012. LNCS, vol. 7417, pp. 180–198. Springer, Heidelberg (2012). doi:10.1007/978-3-642-32009-5_12

23. Okamoto, T., Takashima, K.: Fully secure functional encryption with general relations from the decisional linear assumption. In: Rabin, T. (ed.) CRYPTO 2010. LNCS, vol. 6223, pp. 191–208. Springer, Heidelberg (2010). doi:10.1007/978-3-642-14623-7_11

24. Okamoto, T., Takashima, K.: Fully secure unbounded inner-product and attribute-based encryption. In: Wang, X., Sako, K. (eds.) ASIACRYPT 2012. LNCS, vol. 7658, pp. 349–366. Springer, Heidelberg (2012). doi:10.1007/978-3-642-34961-4_22

25. Ostrovsky, R., Sahai, A., Waters, B.: Attribute-based encryption with non-monotonic access structures. In: Proceedings of the 14th ACM Conference on Computer and Communications Security, pp. 195–203. ACM (2007)

26. Rouselakis, Y., Waters, B.: Practical constructions and new proof methods for large universe attribute-based encryption. In: Proceedings of the 2013 ACM SIGSAC Conference on Computer & Communications Security, pp. 463–474. ACM (2013)

27. Sahai, A., Waters, B.: Fuzzy identity-based encryption. In: Cramer, R. (ed.) EURO-CRYPT 2005. LNCS, vol. 3494, pp. 457–473. Springer, Heidelberg (2005). doi:10.1007/11426639_27

28. Waters, B.: Dual system encryption: realizing fully secure IBE and HIBE under simple assumptions. In: Halevi, S. (ed.) CRYPTO 2009. LNCS, vol. 5677, pp. 619–636. Springer, Heidelberg (2009). doi:10.1007/978-3-642-03356-8_36

29. Waters, B.: Ciphertext-policy attribute-based encryption: an expressive, efficient, and provably secure realization. In: Catalano, D., Fazio, N., Gennaro, R., Nicolosi, A. (eds.) PKC 2011. LNCS, vol. 6571, pp. 53–70. Springer, Heidelberg (2011). doi:10.1007/978-3-642-19379-8_4

30. Wee, H.: Dual system encryption via predicate encodings. In: Lindell, Y. (ed.) TCC 2014. LNCS, vol. 8349, pp. 616–637. Springer, Heidelberg (2014). doi:10.1007/978-3-642-54242-8_26

Adaptively Secure Broadcast Encryption with Dealership

Kamalesh Acharya[✉] and Ratna Dutta

Department of Mathematics, Indian Institute of Technology Kharagpur,
Kharagpur 721302, India
kamaleshiitkgp@gmail.com, ratna@maths.iitkgp.ernet.in

Abstract. In this paper, we put forward first *adaptively chosen plaintext attack* (CPA) secure *broadcast encryption with dealership* (BED) scheme in standard model. We achieve adaptive security in the standard model under reasonable assumption in contrast to semi-static security of Gritti et al. and selective security in random oracle model by Acharya et al. Our scheme also achieves *privacy* in form of hiding the group of subscribed users from broadcaster and supports *maximum number of accountability* under reasonable assumptions. Unlike the scheme of Gritti et al., our scheme does not need to rely on users' response to detect the dishonest dealer like recently proposed scheme of Acharya et al.

Keywords: Broadcast encryption with dealership · Chosen plaintext attack · Maximum number of accountability · Privacy · Adaptive security

1 Introduction

Broadcast encryption is a mechanism in which a group of subscribed users recover a common message. Broadcast encryption has been studied extensively [2,4,5,7–10,15,16] since its introduction in 1994 by Fiat and Naor [11], with a major focus on obtaining constructions with short parameters and adaptive security in the standard model.

Broadcast encryption with dealership (BED) and its security issues were first formulated by Gritti et al. [13] in 2015. In a BED, instead of broadcaster, a dealer selects a set of users and generates a group token hiding the group. A broadcaster implicitly verifies the group size and if the verification succeeds, it generates a ciphertext using this group token. A user of the group decrypts the ciphertext and recovers the message. This creates business opportunity for dealers who buy products (e.g. T.V. channels) in a bulk and resell to users in a rate so that user and dealer both get profit.

Dealership can have a profound impact on modelling the modern business strategies. For instance, consider the following applications:

- Let a broadcaster sells each access of a channel at \$ 30. A dealer gets 10 access at a discount rate of \$ 200 and sells each at \$ 25. Then both the subscriber and the dealer get benefit. A user may have the flexibility to choose a particular dealer depending on his attributes such as location, offer price etc.

© Springer International Publishing AG 2017
S. Hong and J.H. Park (Eds.): ICISC 2016, LNCS 10157, pp. 161–177, 2017.
DOI: 10.1007/978-3-319-53177-9_8

- A broadcaster employs several dealers in different cities to promote some products. Dealers convince the customers and sell the products. Eventually, the sell of the products increases and dealers get commission from the broadcaster.

In a BED, it is crucial for the dealer to hide the identities of the users. Otherwise, the broadcaster can directly approach to the users and provide a rate cheaper than the dealer. Eventually, the dealer will have no role in the BED system. The dealer should not be able to involve more than k users while he is paying for k users. Otherwise, business of the broadcaster will be ruined. Illegal users including the dealer should be unable to recover messages. Otherwise, the business of the dealer will be damaged. Designing BED construction which achieves adaptive security in standard model with the aforementioned security attributes is a challenging task.

Gritti et al. [13] has combined the broadcast encryption scheme of Gentry et al. [12] with the membership encryption of Guo et al. [14] to develop the first BED. The scheme is secure under reasonable assumptions. Acharya et al. [1] has pointed out a flaw in privacy proof and proposed a scheme using [8] which solves the problem, moreover in their scheme the broadcaster does not need to wait for user's response to detect the dishonest behaviour of a dealer. But their scheme is selectively secure in random oracle model.

A proof in the random oracle model can serve only as a heuristic argument, as all parties gets a black box access to a truly random function. In *selective security* model, the adversary commits target recipient set before the setup phase. In *semi-static security* model, the adversary commits a set G of user indices before the setup phase like selective security model, but it can select any subset of G as target set in the challenge generation phase. These two security models do not capture the powers of several types of attackers. Adaptive security introduced by Gentry et al. [12], on the other hand is known as full security of broadcast encryption. Here target recipient set is not fixed initially and the adversary can fix the target recipient set after seeing the public parameter and compromised private keys.

In this work, we obtain the first adaptively CPA secure broadcast encryption in dealership framework, where a broadcaster need not to wait for user's response to detect a dishonest dealer. The starting point of our construction is the identity based broadcast encryption scheme of Ren et al. [17]. We extend this work to support dealership. Our BED scheme is secure under the q-weaker Decisional Augmented Bilinear Diffie-Hellman Exponent assumption. The scheme is also secure on *privacy* issue under the hardness of the discrete logarithm problem and achieves *maximum number of accountability* under the $(N + 1 + j)$-Diffie-Hellman Exponent assumption.

More interestingly, dealer can involve new set of users without changing the existing public key and secret key. Like other broadcast schemes, revoked users will be unable to recover messages in our scheme.

2 Preliminaries

Notation: Let $[m]$ denotes integers from 1 to m and $[a, b]$ denotes integers from a to b. We use the notation $x \in_R S$ to denote x is a random element of S and λ to represent bit size of prime integer p. Let $\epsilon : \mathbb{N} \to \mathbb{R}$ be a function, where $\mathbb{N}$ and $\mathbb{R}$ are the sets of natural and real number respectively. The function ϵ is said to be a *negligible function* if $\exists\, d \in \mathbb{N}$ such that $\epsilon(\lambda) \le \frac{1}{\lambda^d}$. Let $|G|$ denotes the number of elements of group G.

We define broadcast encryption with dealership and its CPA security definition following [13]. For privacy and maximum number of accountability, we follow [1].

2.1 Broadcast Encryption with Dealership

Syntax of Bed: A broadcast encryption with dealership scheme Bed = (Bed.Setup, Bed.KeyGen, Bed.GroupGen, Bed.Verify, Bed.Encrypt, Bed.Decrypt) consists of four probabilistic polynomial time (PPT) algorithms - Bed.Setup, Bed.KeyGen, Bed.GroupGen, Bed.Encrypt and two deterministic polynomial time algorithms - Bed.Verify, Bed.Decrypt. Formally, Bed is described as follows:

- (PP, MK)←Bed.Setup(N, λ): Taking as input the total number of users N in the system and security parameter λ, the private key generation centre (PKGC) constructs the public parameter PP and a master key MK. It makes PP public and keeps MK secret to itself.

- (sk_i)←Bed.KeyGen(PP, MK, i): The PKGC takes as input PP, MK and a subscribed user i and generates a secret key sk_i of user i and sends sk_i to user i through a secure communication channel between them.
- ($P(G), k$)←Bed.GroupGen(PP, G): Selecting a set of subscribed users G, the dealer generates a group token $P(G)$ using PP. It outputs a threshold value k, where $|G| \le k$ together with $P(G)$. The dealer sends G to each subscribed user $u \in G$ through a secure communication channel between them. Subscribed users keep G secret to themselves.
- ($0 \vee 1$)←Bed.Verify($P(G)$, PP, k): Using $P(G)$, PP, k, the broadcaster implicitly verifies group size $|G| \le k$ and sets

$$\text{Bed.Verify}(P(G), \text{PP}, k) = \begin{cases} 1, & \text{if } |G| \le k \\ 0, & \text{otherwise.} \end{cases}$$

If the verification fails i.e., Bed.Verify($P(G)$, PP, k) = 0, the broadcaster aborts.
- (C)←Bed.Encrypt($P(G)$, PP, M): The broadcaster takes as input $P(G)$, PP, a message M and produces a ciphertext C.
- (M)←Bed.Decrypt(PP, sk_i, C, G): A subscribed user i with secret key sk_i outputs the message M using PP, C and subscribed user set G.

Correctness: The correctness of the scheme Bed lies in the fact that the message M can be retrieved from the ciphertext C by any subscribed user in G. Suppose (PP, MK)←Bed.Setup(N, λ), ($P(G), k$)←Bed.GroupGen(PP, G). Then for every subscribed user $i \in G$,

$$\text{Bed.Decrypt}\Big(\text{PP}, \text{Bed.KeyGen}(\text{PP}, \text{MK}, i), \text{Bed.Encrypt}\big(P(G), \text{PP}, M\big), G\Big) = M.$$

2.2 Security Framework

⟨I⟩ **Privacy:** Preserving privacy of the subscribed user set G selected by the dealer is of crucial importance. Otherwise, the broadcaster can directly approach to the subscribed users, thereby can damage the business of the dealer. Our privacy model grantees that no information of G is revealed from group token $P(G)$.

The privacy of G of the protocol Bed is described using a game between an adversary $\mathcal{A}$ and a challenger $\mathcal{C}$ as follows:

Setup: The challenger $\mathcal{C}$ runs Bed.Setup(N, λ) to generate the public para-meter PP and master key MK. It sends PP to $\mathcal{A}$.

Challenge: The adversary $\mathcal{A}$ selects two sets of users G_0, G_1 of same size and submits G_0, G_1 to $\mathcal{C}$. The challenger $\mathcal{C}$ chooses $b \in_R \{0,1\}$, generates a group token $P(G_b)$ by running Bed.GroupGen(PP, G_b) and sends $P(G_b)$ to $\mathcal{A}$.

Guess: The adversary $\mathcal{A}$ outputs a guess $b' \in \{0,1\}$ of b and wins if $b' = b$.

We define the advantage of the adversary $\mathcal{A}$ in the above privacy game as $Adv_{\mathcal{A}}^{\text{Bed}-\text{P}} = |Pr(b' = b) - \frac{1}{2}|$. The probability is taken over random bits used by $\mathcal{C}$ and $\mathcal{A}$.

Definition 1. *The BED scheme* Bed *is said to be* (T, ϵ)-*secure under group privacy issue, if* $Adv_{\mathcal{A}}^{\text{Bed}-\text{P}} \leq \epsilon$ *for every PPT adversary* $\mathcal{A}$ *with running time at most* T.

⟨II⟩ **Maximum Number of Accountability:** Maximum number of account-ability ensures that the encrypted content can be decrypted by preselected maximum number of users. The security game between an adversary $\mathcal{A}$ and a challenger $\mathcal{C}$ addressing maximum number of accountability of the protocol Bed is described as follows:

Setup: The challenger $\mathcal{C}$ runs Bed.Setup(N, λ) and generates public parame-ter PP and master key MK. It sends PP to $\mathcal{A}$.

Challenge: The challenger $\mathcal{C}$ sends an integer k to $\mathcal{A}$.

Guess: The adversary $\mathcal{A}$ computes $P(G^*)$, with $|G^*| > k$ by running Bed.GroupGen(PP, G^*) and sends $(P(G^*), G^*)$ to $\mathcal{C}$.

Win: The challenger $\mathcal{C}$ outputs $(P(G^*), G^*)$ if Bed.Verify$(P(G^*), PP, k) = 1$; otherwise $\mathcal{C}$ aborts.

We define the advantage of the adversary $\mathcal{A}$ in the above game as $Adv_{\mathcal{A}}^{\text{Bed-M}} = |\left(Pr(\text{Bed.Verify}(P(G^*), PP, k)) = 1\right) - \frac{1}{2}|$ where $k < |G^*|$. The probability is taken over random bits used by $\mathcal{C}$ and $\mathcal{A}$.

Definition 2. *The BED scheme* Bed *is said to be* (T, ϵ)-*secure under maximum number of accountability, if* $Adv_{\mathcal{A}}^{\text{Bed}-\text{M}} \leq \epsilon$ *for every PPT adversary* $\mathcal{A}$ *with running time at most* T.

⟨II⟩**Indistinguishability of Bed under CPA**: We describe the adaptive security of the scheme Bed as an indistinguishability game played between a challenger $\mathcal{C}$ and an adversary $\mathcal{A}$.

Setup: The challenger $\mathcal{C}$ generates $(\mathsf{PP}, \mathsf{MK}) \leftarrow \mathsf{Bed.Setup}(N, \lambda)$. It keeps the master key MK secret to itself and sends public parameter PP to $\mathcal{A}$.

Phase 1: Receiving key generation queries for users $i_1, \ldots, i_m$, the adversary $\mathcal{A}$ generates $sk_i \leftarrow \mathsf{Bed.KeyGen}(\mathsf{PP}, \mathsf{MK}, i)$ for user $i \in \{i_1, \ldots, i_m\}$ and sends to $\mathcal{C}$.

Challenge: The adversary $\mathcal{A}$ sends a set G to $\mathcal{C}$ where indices of G has not been queried before. It also sends two messages M_0, M_1 to $\mathcal{C}$. The challenger $\mathcal{C}$ selects $b \in_R \{0, 1\}$ and generates $(C^*) \leftarrow \mathsf{Bed.Encrypt}(P(G), \mathsf{PP}, M_b)$, where $(P(G), k) \leftarrow \mathsf{Bed.GroupGen}(\mathsf{PP}, G)$. Finally, $\mathcal{C}$ sends C^* to $\mathcal{A}$.

Phase 2: This is identical to Phase 1 key generation queries with a restriction that queried user indices does not lie in G.

Guess: The adversary $\mathcal{A}$ outputs a guess $b' \in \{0, 1\}$ of b and wins if $b' = b$.

Let t be the number of corrupted users and N be the total number of users. Adversary $\mathcal{A}$ is allowed to get reply up to t key generation queries. The adversary $\mathcal{A}$'s advantage in the above security game is defined as

$$Adv_{\mathcal{A}}^{\mathsf{Bed-IND}}(t, N) = |Pr(b' = b) - Pr(b' \neq b)|$$
$$= |2Pr(b' = b) - 1|$$
$$= |Pr[b' = 1|b = 1] - Pr[b' = 1|b = 0]|.$$

The probability is taken over random bits used by $\mathcal{C}$ and $\mathcal{A}$.

Definition 3. *Let* $Adv^{\mathsf{Bed-IND}}(t, N) = \max_{\mathcal{A}} \left[Adv_{\mathcal{A}}^{\mathsf{Bed-IND}}(t, N) \right]$, *where maximum is taken over all PPT algorithm running in* $poly(\lambda)$ *(polynomial of* λ*) time. The BED scheme Bed is said to be* (t, N)*- secure if* $Adv^{\mathsf{Bed-IND}} = \epsilon(\lambda)$, *where* $\epsilon(\lambda)$ *is a negligible function in security parameter* λ.

This indistinguishability model is usual security model of broadcast encryption where no information of plaintext is revealed from a ciphertext.

2.3 Complexity Assumptions

Definition 4 (Bilinear Map). *Let* $\mathbb{G}$ *and* $\mathbb{G}_1$ *be two multiplicative cyclic groups of prime order* p. *Let* g *be a generator of* $\mathbb{G}$. *A function* $e : \mathbb{G} \times \mathbb{G} \longrightarrow \mathbb{G}_1$ *is said to be bilinear mapping if it has the following properties:*

1. $e(u^a, v^b) = e(u, v)^{ab}$, $\forall u, v \in \mathbb{G}$ *and* $\forall a, b \in \mathbb{Z}_p$.
2. *The function is non-degenerate, i.e.,* $e(g, g)$ *is a generator of* $\mathbb{G}_1$.
3. e *is efficiently computable.*

The tuple $\mathbb{S} = (p, \mathbb{G}, \mathbb{G}_1, e)$ *is called a prime order bilinear group system.*

⟨i⟩ The Discrete Logarithm (DL) Assumption:
   Input: $\langle Z = (g^\alpha, g)\rangle$, where $\alpha \in_R \mathbb{Z}_p$, g is a generator of $\mathbb{G}$.
   Output: α.

Definition 5 *The* DL *assumption holds with* (T, ϵ) *if for every PPT adversary* $\mathcal{A}$ *with running time at most* T, *the advantage of solving the above problem is at most* ϵ, *i.e.,*

$$Adv_\mathcal{A}^{\mathsf{DL}} = |Pr[\mathcal{A}(Z) = \alpha]| \le \epsilon(\lambda),$$

where $\epsilon(\lambda)$ *is a negligible function in security parameter* λ.

⟨ii⟩ The $(l + i)$-Diffie-Hellman Exponent $((l + i)$-DHE$)$ $(i > 0)$ Assumption [6]:
   Input: $\langle Z = (\mathbb{S}, g, g^\alpha, \ldots, g^{\alpha^l})\rangle$, where g is generator of $\mathbb{G}$, $\alpha \in_R \mathbb{Z}_p$.
   Output: $g^{\alpha^{l+i}}$.

Definition 6. *The* $(l + i)$-DHE *$(i > 0)$ assumption holds with* (T, ϵ) *if for every PPT adversary* $\mathcal{A}$ *with running time at most* T, *the advantage of solving the above problem is at most* ϵ, *i.e.,*

$$Adv_\mathcal{A}^{(l+i)-\mathsf{DHE}} = |Pr[\mathcal{A}(Z) = g^{\alpha^{l+i}}]| \le \epsilon(\lambda),$$

where $\epsilon(\lambda)$ *is a negligible function in security parameter* λ.

⟨iii⟩   The l-weaker Decisional Augmented Bilinear Diffie-Hellman Exponent $(l$-wDABD HE$)$ Assumption [17]:
   Input: $\langle Z = (\mathbb{S}, h, h^{\alpha^{l+2}}, \ldots, h^{\alpha^{2l}}, g, g^\alpha, \ldots, g^{\alpha^l}), K\rangle$, where g is a generator of $\mathbb{G}$, $h \in_R \mathbb{G}, \alpha \in_R \mathbb{Z}_p$, K is either $e(g, h)^{\alpha^{l+1}}$ or a random element $X \in \mathbb{G}_1$.
   Output: 0 if $K = e(g, h)^{\alpha^{l+1}}$; 1 otherwise.

Definition 7. *The* l-wDABDHE *assumption holds with* (T, ϵ) *if for every PPT adversary* $\mathcal{A}$ *with running time at most* T, *the advantage of solving the above problem is at most* ϵ, *i.e.,*

$$Adv_\mathcal{A}^{l-\mathsf{wDABDHE}} = |Pr[\mathcal{A}(Z, K = e(g, h)^{\alpha^{l+1}}) = 1] - Pr[\mathcal{A}(Z, K = X) = 1]|$$
$$\le \epsilon(\lambda),$$

where $\epsilon(\lambda)$ *is a negligible function in security parameter* λ.

3   Our **Bed** Construction

Our broadcast encryption with dealership Bed = (Bed.Setup, Bed. KeyGen, Bed. GroupGen, Bed.Verify, Bed.Encrypt, Bed.Decrypt) is described as follows:

- $(\mathsf{PP}, \mathsf{MK}) \leftarrow$ Bed.Setup(N, λ): Using the security parameter λ and public identity ID = $\{ID_1, ID_2, \ldots, ID_N\} \in (\mathbb{Z}_p)^N$ of a group of N users, the PKGC generates the public parameter PP and a master key MK as follows:

1. Selects a bilinear group system $\mathbb{S} = (p, \mathbb{G}, \mathbb{G}_1, e)$, where $\mathbb{G}, \mathbb{G}_1$ are groups of prime order p and $e : \mathbb{G} \times \mathbb{G} \to \mathbb{G}_1$ is a bilinear mapping.
2. Picks $\alpha \in_R \mathbb{Z}_p$, and sets PP, MK as
   $$\text{PP} = (\mathbb{S}, l_0, l_0^\alpha, \ldots, l_0^{\alpha^N}, g, g^\alpha, \ldots, g^{\alpha^N}, g^{\alpha^{N+1}}, e(g,g), e(g,l_0), \text{ID}), \quad \text{MK} = (\alpha),$$ where g is generators of $\mathbb{G}$, l_0 is random non-identity element of $\mathbb{G}$.
3. Keeps MK secret to itself and makes PP public.

Note that the public identity of the user i is $ID_i \in \mathbb{Z}_p$ for $i \in [N]$.

- $(sk_i) \leftarrow \text{Bed.KeyGen}(\text{PP}, \text{MK}, i)$: The PKGC selects $h_i \in_R \mathbb{G}$, $r_i \in_R \mathbb{Z}_p$ for each user $i \in [N]$ and generates a secret key $sk_i = (d_{1,i}, d_{2,i}, d_{3,i}, \text{label}_i)$, where

$$d_{1,i} = (h_i g^{r_i})^{\frac{1}{\alpha(\alpha + ID_i)}}, d_{2,i} = r_i,$$
$$d_{3,i} = (h_i l_0^{d_{2,i}})^{\frac{1}{\alpha}}, \text{label}_i = (h_i, h_i^\alpha, \ldots, h_i^{\alpha^N}).$$

It sends sk_i to user i through a secure communication channel between them.
- $(P(G), k) \leftarrow \text{Bed.GroupGen}(\text{PP}, G)$: The dealer selects a group of k' users $G = \{i_1, i_2, \ldots, i_{k'}\} \subseteq [N]$ and performs the following using PP:

1. Generates a polynomial $F(x) = \prod_{i_j \in G} (x + ID_{i_j}) = \sum_{i=0}^{k'} F_i x^i$, where F_i's are function of ID_j for $j \in G$.
2. Selects $t_1 \in_R \mathbb{Z}_p$ and generates the group token $P(G) = (w_1, w_2, w_3, w_4, w_5)$ by setting

$$w_1 = \prod_{i=0}^{k'} (g^{\alpha^{i+1}})^{t_1 F_i} = g^{\alpha \sum_{i=0}^{k'} \alpha^i t_1 F_i} = g^{\alpha F(\alpha) t_1},$$

$$w_2 = \prod_{i=0}^{k'} (g^{\alpha^{N-k+i+1}})^{t_1 F_i} = g^{\alpha^{N-k+1} \sum_{i=0}^{k'} \alpha^i t_1 F_i} = g^{\alpha^{N-k+1} F(\alpha) t_1},$$

$$w_3 = (g^\alpha)^{-t_1} = g^{-t_1 \alpha}, w_4 = e(g,g)^{-t_1}, w_5 = e(g,l_0)^{t_1}.$$

3. Selects a threshold value k on the group size G where $k \geq k' = |G|$.
4. Delivers G to each subscribed user through a secure communication channel between the user and the dealer. The subscribed users keep G secret to themselves.
5. Publishes $P(G)$ together with the threshold value k.
- $(0 \vee 1) \leftarrow \text{Bed.Verify}(P(G), \text{PP}, k)$: Taking as input the group token $P(G) = (w_1, w_2, w_3, w_4, w_5)$, the threshold value k, and $g^{\alpha^k}, g^{\alpha^N}$, extracted from PP, the broadcaster sets

$$\text{Bed.Verify}(P(G), \text{PP}, k) = \begin{cases} 1, & \text{if } e(w_1, g^{\alpha^N}) = e(w_2, g^{\alpha^k}) \\ 0, & \text{otherwise.} \end{cases}$$

Notice that, $e(w_1, g^{\alpha^N}) = e(g^{\alpha F(\alpha) t_1}, g^{\alpha^N}) = e(g, g)^{\alpha^{N+1} t_1 F(\alpha)}$

and, $e(w_2, g^{\alpha^k}) = e(g^{\alpha^{N-k+1} F(\alpha) t_1}, g^{\alpha^k}) = e(g, g)^{\alpha^{N+1} t_1 F(\alpha)}.$

If the verification fails i.e., $\text{Bed.Verify}(P(G), \text{PP}, k) = 0$, the broadcaster aborts. We point down here that only two components namely w_1, w_2 of $P(G)$ are used during this verification process.

- $(C) \leftarrow$ Bed.Encrypt$(P(G), \mathsf{PP}, M)$: Using PP and $P(G) = (w_1, w_2, w_3, w_4, w_5)$ with Bed.Verify$(P(G), \mathsf{PP}, k) = 1$ and selecting $r \in_R \mathbb{Z}_p$, the broadcaster computes ciphertext C for message $M \in \mathbb{G}_1$ as

$$
\begin{aligned}
C = (C_1, C_2, C_3, C_M) &= \left(w_1^r, w_3^r, w_4^r, M w_5^r \right) \\
&= \left(g^{\alpha F(\alpha) t_1 r}, g^{-t_1 r \alpha}, e(g,g)^{-t_1 r}, M e(g, l_0)^{t_1 r} \right) \\
&= \left(g^{\alpha F(\alpha) s}, g^{-s\alpha}, e(g,g)^{-s}, M e(g, l_0)^s \right) \text{ where } t_1 r = s \text{ (say)}.
\end{aligned}
$$

Finally, it broadcasts the ciphertext C. Note that this encryption process utilizes three components w_3, w_4, w_5 of $P(G)$, together with w_1 which has already been used in combination with w_2 and passed the verification in procedure Bed.Verify successfully.

- $(K) \leftarrow$ Bed.Decrypt$(\mathsf{PP}, sk_i, \mathsf{Hdr}, G)$: Using the secret key sk_i, the public parameter PP, the ciphertext $C = (C_1, C_2, C_3, C_M)$ and the set of subscribed users G, a subscribed user i recovers the message M as follows:

$$
\left[e(C_1, d_{1,i}) e\left(C_2, (h_i g^{d_{2,i}})^{A_{i,G,\alpha}} \right) \right]^{\left\{ \frac{1}{\prod_{j \in G, j \neq i} ID_j} \right\}} C_3^{d_{2,i}} = e(g, h_i)^s,
$$

$$
\left[e(C_1, d_{3,i}) e\left(C_2, (h_i l_0^{d_{2,i}})^{B_{G,\alpha}} \right) \right]^{\left\{ \frac{1}{\prod_{j \in G} ID_j} \right\}} = e(g, h_i l_0^{r_i})^s,
$$

$$
K = \left\{ \frac{e(g, h_i l_0^{r_i})^s}{e(g, h_i)^s} \right\}^{\frac{1}{d_{2,i}}} = e(g, l_0)^s, \quad M = \frac{C_M}{K}.
$$

$$
\text{where} \quad A_{i,G,\alpha} = \frac{1}{\alpha} \left\{ \prod_{j \in G, j \neq i} (\alpha + ID_j) - \prod_{j \in G, j \neq i} ID_j \right\},
$$

$$
B_{G,\alpha} = \frac{1}{\alpha} \left\{ \prod_{j \in G} (\alpha + ID_j) - \prod_{j \in G} ID_j \right\}.
$$

Note that $(h_i g^{d_{2,i}})^{A_{i,G,\alpha}}$, $(h_i l_0^{d_{2,i}})^{B_{G,\alpha}}$ can be computed using $g^{\alpha^i}, h^{\alpha^i}, d_{2,i}$ values, without the knowledge of α as $A_{i,G,\alpha}, B_{G,\alpha}$ are polynomials in α (does not contain $\frac{1}{\alpha}$ term).

Correctness: The correctness of decryption procedure follows as:

$$
\left[e(C_1, d_{1,i}) e\left(C_2, (h_i g^{d_{2,i}})^{A_{i,G,\alpha}} \right) \right]^{\left\{ \frac{1}{\prod_{j \in G, j \neq i} ID_j} \right\}}
$$

$$
= \left[e\left(g^{s\alpha \prod_{j \in G} (\alpha + ID_j)}, (h_i g^{r_i})^{\frac{1}{\alpha(\alpha + ID_i)}} \right) \right.
$$

$$
\left. \times e(g^{-\alpha s}, h_i g^{r_i})^{\frac{1}{\alpha} \left\{ \prod_{j \in G, j \neq i} (\alpha + ID_j) - \prod_{j \in G, j \neq i} ID_j \right\}} \right]^{\left\{ \frac{1}{\prod_{j \in G, j \neq i} ID_j} \right\}}
$$

$$= \left[e(g, h_i g^{r_i})^{s\left\{\prod_{j\in G, j\neq i}(\alpha+ID_j)\right\}}\right.$$

$$\left. \times e(g, h_i g^{r_i})^{-s\left\{\prod_{j\in G, j\neq i}(\alpha+ID_j)-\prod_{j\in G, j\neq i}ID_j\right\}}\right]^{\left\{\frac{1}{\prod_{j\in G, j\neq i}ID_j}\right\}}$$

$$= \left[e(g, h_i g^{r_i})^{s\prod_{j\in G, j\neq i}ID_j}\right]^{\left\{\frac{1}{\prod_{j\in G, j\neq i}ID_j}\right\}} = e(g, h_i g^{r_i})^s,$$

Therefore, $\left[e(C_1, d_{1,i})e(C_2, h_i g^{d_{2,i}})^{A_{i,G,\alpha}}\right]^{\left\{\frac{1}{\prod_{j\in G, j\neq i}ID_j}\right\}} C_3^{d_{2,i}}$

$$= e(g, h_i g^{r_i})^s e(g, g)^{-s r_i} = e(g, h_i)^s,$$

Similarly, $\left[e(C_1, d_{3,i})e\left(C_2, (h_i l_0^{d_{2,i}})^{B_{G,\alpha}}\right)\right]^{\left\{\frac{1}{\prod_{j\in G}ID_j}\right\}}$

$$= \left[e\left(g^{s\alpha \prod_{j\in G}(\alpha+ID_j)}, (h_i l_0^{r_i})^{\frac{1}{\alpha}}\right)\right.$$

$$\left. \times e(g^{-\alpha s}, h_i l_0^{r_i})^{\frac{1}{\alpha}\left\{\prod_{j\in G}(\alpha+ID_j)-\prod_{j\in G}ID_j\right\}}\right]^{\left\{\frac{1}{\prod_{j\in G}ID_j}\right\}}$$

$$= \left[e(g, h_i l_0^{r_i})^{s\left\{\prod_{j\in G}(\alpha+ID_j)\right\}}\right.$$

$$\left. \times e(g, h_i l_0^{r_i})^{-s\left\{\prod_{j\in G}(\alpha+ID_j)-\prod_{j\in G}ID_j\right\}}\right]^{\left\{\frac{1}{\prod_{j\in G}ID_j}\right\}}$$

$$= \left[e(g, h_i l_0^{r_i})^{s\prod_{j\in G}ID_j}\right]^{\left\{\frac{1}{\prod_{j\in G}ID_j}\right\}} = e(g, h_i l_0^{r_i})^s,$$

Hence, $K = \left\{\frac{e(g, h_i l_0^{r_i})^s}{e(g, h_i)^s}\right\}^{\frac{1}{d_{2,i}}} = \left\{\frac{e(g, h_i)^s e(g, l_0^{r_i})^s}{e(g, h_i)^s}\right\}^{\frac{1}{r_i}} = e(g, l_0)^s,$

$$M = \frac{C_M}{K}.$$

Remark 1. The dealer needs to use secure communication channel to intimate subscribed users about the subscribed user set. The dealer has to use these secure channels between him and the subscribed user each time a new group token is generated on group membership change. It is essential to remove the reuse of secure communication channel for dynamic group of users. This can be done by using a suitable public key encryption as follows:

The dealer generates (public key, secret key) pair (p_i, s_i) for each user $i \in [N]$ in Bed.Setup phase and sends s_i to user i. Let at some time $u_1, u_2, \ldots, u_{k'}$ be the subscribed user indices. In a network of N users, to represent an user's index, at most $s = \log_2 N$ bits are required. We need an encryption scheme $\mathcal{E}$ with message space of at least $(N + 2)s$ bits. In time of group token generation, the delear also generates y as

$$y = \left(\left[\mathcal{E}_{p_i}(u_1 || \dots || u_{k'} || k' || Y) \right]_{i=1}^{k'}, \left[\mathcal{E}_{\hat{p}_i}(R_i) \right]_{i=1}^{k-k'}, Y \right).$$

Here each of $u_1, \dots, u_{k'}, k', Y$ is of s bits, if not, fill up the left side with zeros; R_i are random messages, $\hat{p}_i$ are random key values for $i \in [1, k - k']$, $||$ denotes concatenation of bits. User i decrypts the ciphertext using secret key s_i. If it gets decrypted value whose last s bits matches with Y, then it recovers the subscribed user set.

Remark 2. Here w_3, w_4, w_5 are not involved in verification. So the dealer can generate valid w_1, w_2 components to pass verification and some random w_3, w_4, w_5. But in that case subscribed user will unable to recover exact w_5^r and thereby will unable to retrieve the desire message M. User will complain to the broadcaster who in tern inform the dealer that group token is wrongly provided.

4   Security

Theorem 1. *(Privacy). Our* Bed *described in Sect. 3 is computationally secure as per the group privacy issue as described in Sect. 2.2 under the hardness of the discrete logarithm problem.*

Proof. The privacy of Bed is described using a game between a challenger $\mathcal{C}$ and an adversary $\mathcal{A}$ as follows:

Setup: The challenger $\mathcal{C}$ selects $\alpha \in_R \mathbb{Z}_p$ and generates the public parameter PP and the master key MK as, PP $= (\mathbb{S}, l_0, l_0^{\alpha}, \dots, l_0^{\alpha^N}, g, g^{\alpha}, \dots, g^{\alpha^N}, g^{\alpha^{N+1}},$ $e(g, g), e(g, l_0), \mathsf{ID})$, MK $= (\alpha)$, by calling Bed.Setup(N, λ). Here l_0 is random non-identity element of $\mathbb{G}$, g is generator of group $\mathbb{G}$, ID $= \{ID_1, ID_2, \dots, ID_N\} \in (\mathbb{Z}_p)^N$ is the set of public identities of N users. It keeps MK secret to itself and hands PP to $\mathcal{A}$.

Challenge: The adversary $\mathcal{A}$ selects two sets of users G_0, G_1 of same size and submits G_0, G_1 to $\mathcal{C}$. The challenger $\mathcal{C}$ chooses G_b, $b \in_R \{0, 1\}$ and generates a group token $P(G_b)$ by running Bed.GroupGen(PP, G_b) as

$$P(G_b) = (w_1, w_2, w_3, w_4, w_5)$$
$$= (g^{\alpha F(\alpha) t_1}, g^{\alpha^{N-k+1} F(\alpha) t_1}, g^{-t_1 \alpha}, e(g, g)^{-t_1}, e(g, l_0)^{t_1}) \text{ where } t_1 \in \mathbb{Z}_p.$$

Guess: The adversary $\mathcal{A}$ outputs a guess $b' \in \{0, 1\}$ of b and wins if $b' = b$.

The adversary $\mathcal{A}$ can predict G_b from $P(G_b)$, if it can predict the random number t_1 chosen by the challenger $\mathcal{C}$. As $\mathcal{A}$ possesses G_0, G_1, he can compute $P(G_0)$ if he can know t_1. If $P(G_0)$ matches with $P(G_b)$, $\mathcal{A}$ predicts $b = 0$, else $b = 1$. Therefore, prediction of b is same as predicting t_1 from $P(G_b)$ i.e., computing t_1 from $w_3 = g^{-\alpha t_1}$ where g^{α} is available to $\mathcal{A}$ trough PP. So, security depends on the hardness of the discrete logarithm problem. Hence the theorem.

Theorem 2. *(Maximum number of accountability). Our proposed BED scheme* Bed *described in Sect. 3 is secure as per maximum number of accountability security model as described in Sect. 2.2 under the* $(N+1+j)$*-Diffie-Hellman Exponent* $((N+1+j)$-DHE$)$ *hardness assumption.*

Proof. Assume that there is a PPT adversary $\mathcal{A}$ that breaks the maximum number of accountability of our Bed scheme with non-negligible advantage. We construct an algorithm $\mathcal{C}$ that attempts to solve an instance of the $(N+1+j)$-DHE $(j > 0)$ problem using $\mathcal{A}$ as a sub-routine. $\mathcal{C}$ is given an instance of the $(N+1+j)$-DHE problem $\langle Z = (\mathbb{S}, g, g^\alpha, g^{\alpha^2}, \ldots, g^{\alpha^{N+1}})\rangle$, where $\mathbb{S}$ is a bilinear group system, g is a generator of the group $\mathbb{G}$, $\alpha \in_R \mathbb{Z}_p$. Now $\mathcal{C}$ plays the role of the challenger in the security game and interacts with $\mathcal{A}$ as follows:

Setup: The challenger $\mathcal{C}$ takes $x \in_R \mathbb{Z}_p$ and sets $l_0^{\alpha^i} = (g^{\alpha^i})^x, i \in [0, N]$. It sets $\mathsf{PP} = (\mathbb{S}, l_0, l_0^\alpha, \ldots, l_0^{\alpha^N}, g, g^\alpha, \ldots, g^{\alpha^{N+1}}, e(g,g), e(g,l_0), \mathsf{ID})$, where $\mathsf{ID} = \{ID_1, ID_2, \ldots, ID_N\} \in (\mathbb{Z}_p)^N$ is the set of public identities of N users. The challenger $\mathcal{C}$ implicitly sets $\mathsf{MK} = (\alpha)$ and hands PP to $\mathcal{A}$.

Challenge: The challenger $\mathcal{C}$ submits a threshold value $k \in [N]$ on the group size to $\mathcal{A}$.

Guess: The adversary $\mathcal{A}$ selects $t_1 \in_R \mathbb{Z}_p$ and computes $P(G^*)$ by running Bed.GroupGen(PP, G^*) (where $|G^*| = \hat{k} > k$) as $P(G^*) = (\hat{w}_1, \hat{w}_2, \hat{w}_3, \hat{w}_4, \hat{w}_5) = (g^{\alpha\hat{F}(\alpha)t_1}, g^{\alpha^{N-k+1}\hat{F}(\alpha)t_1}, g^{-t_1\alpha}, e(g,g)^{-t_1}, e(g,l_0)^{t_1})$. The adversary $\mathcal{A}$ sends $(P(G^*), G^*)$ to $\mathcal{C}$.

If the adversary $\mathcal{A}$ outputs a valid $P(G^*)$ for a group G^* of size $\hat{k} > k$ i.e., Bed.Verify$(P(G^*), \mathsf{PP}, k) = 1$, then

$$\hat{F}(x) = \prod_{i_j \in G^*} (x + ID_{i_j}) = \sum_{i=0}^{\hat{k}} \hat{F}_i x^i \text{ is a } \hat{k} \ (>k) \text{ degree polynomial. Notice}$$

that $\hat{w}_2 = g^{\alpha^{N-k+1}\hat{F}(\alpha)t_1} = \prod_{i=0}^{\hat{k}} (g^{\alpha^{N-k+i+1}})^{t_1\hat{F}_i}$.

Therefore if $\mathcal{A}$ wins against maximum number of accountability game then it can compute $g^{\alpha^{N+2}}, \ldots, g^{\alpha^{N+1+\hat{k}-k}}$ i.e., it can solve the $(N+1+j)$-DHE $(1 \leq j \leq \hat{k} - k)$ problem. This completes the proof.

Theorem 3. *Our proposed scheme* Bed *described in Sect. 3 achieves adaptive semantic (indistinguishability against CPA) security as per the message indistinguishability security game of Sect. 2.2 under the q-weaker Decisional Augmented Bilinear Diffie-Hellman Exponent (q-*wDABDHE*) $(q \geq 2N)$ hardness assumption where N is total number of users.*

Proof. Let a PPT adversary $\mathcal{A}$ breaks the adaptive semantic security of our proposed Bed scheme with a non-negligible advantage. We construct a PPT distinguisher $\mathcal{C}$ that attempts to solve the q-wDABDHE problem using $\mathcal{A}$ as a subroutine. Let $\mathcal{C}$ be given a q-wDABDHE $(q \geq 2N)$ instance $\langle Z, X \rangle$ with $Z = (\mathbb{S}, \hat{g}, \hat{g}^{\alpha^{q+2}}, \ldots, \hat{g}^{\alpha^{2q}}, g, g^\alpha, \ldots, g^{\alpha^q})$, where g is generator of group $\mathbb{G}$, $\hat{g} \in_R$

$\mathbb{G}, \alpha \in_R \mathbb{Z}_p$, X is either $e(\hat{g}, g)^{\alpha^{q+1}}$ or a random element of $\mathbb{G}_1$. We describe below the interaction of $\mathcal{A}$ with the distinguisher $\mathcal{C}$ who attempts to output 0 if $X = e(\hat{g}, g)^{\alpha^{q+1}}$ and 1 otherwise.

Setup: The challenger $\mathcal{C}$ chooses $b_{0,j} \in_R \mathbb{Z}_p, j \in [0, N-1]$ and sets the polynomials $P^0(x), Q^0(x)$ as $P^0(x) = \sum\limits_{j=0}^{N-1} b_{0,j} x^j, Q^0(x) = xP^0(x) + 1$.

Using $g, g^\alpha, \ldots, g^{\alpha^q}$ $(q \geq 2N)$, $\mathcal{C}$ computes $l_0^{\alpha^i}, i \in [0, N]$ as

$$l_0^{\alpha^i} = g^{\alpha^i} \prod_{j=0}^{N-1} (g^{\alpha^{j+i+1}})^{b_{0,j}} = g^{\alpha^i(1+\alpha P^0(\alpha))} = g^{\alpha^i Q^0(\alpha)}.$$

It sets $\mathsf{PP} = (\mathbb{S}, l_0, l_0^\alpha, \ldots, l_0^{\alpha^N}, g, g^\alpha, \ldots, g^{\alpha^N}, g^{\alpha^{N+1}}, e(g, g), e(g, l_0), \mathsf{ID})$, where $\mathsf{ID} = \{ID_1, ID_2, \ldots, ID_N\} \in (\mathbb{Z}_p)^N$ is the set of public identities of N users. $\mathcal{C}$ implicitly sets $\mathsf{MK} = (\alpha)$. As $Q^0(x)$ is random, the distribution of PP is identical to that in the original scheme.

Phase 1: The adversary $\mathcal{A}$ issues m key generation queries on $\{ID_{i_j}\}_{j=1}^m$. The challenger $\mathcal{C}$ generates the private key sk_i for users $i \in \{i_1, \ldots, i_m\} \subseteq [N]$ as follows. It chooses

$b_{i,j}, b_i \in_R \mathbb{Z}_p, j \in [0, N-2]$, sets $P^i(x) = \sum\limits_{j=0}^{N-2} b_{i,j} x^j, Q^i(x) = x(x + ID_i)P^i(x) + b_i$ and computes

$$d_{1,i} = \prod_{j=0}^{N-2} (g^{\alpha^j})^{b_{i,j}} = g^{\sum\limits_{j=0}^{N-2} b_{i,j}\alpha^j} = g^{P^i(\alpha)},$$

$$d_{2,i} = -Q^i(-ID_i) = ID_i(-ID_i + ID_i)P^i(-ID_i) - b_i = -b_i,$$

$$d_{3,i} = \prod_{j=0}^{N-1} (g^{\alpha^j})^{-b_i b_{0,j}} \prod_{j=0}^{N-2} \{(g^{\alpha^{j+1}})^{b_{i,j}} (g^{\alpha^j})^{b_{i,j}ID_i}\}$$

$$= \prod_{j=0}^{N-1} g^{-b_i b_{0,j}\alpha^j} \prod_{j=0}^{N-2} g^{\{b_{i,j}(\alpha+ID_i)\alpha^j\}}$$

$$= g^{-b_i \sum\limits_{j=0}^{N-1} b_{0,j}\alpha^j} g^{\{(\alpha+ID_i)\sum\limits_{j=0}^{N-2} b_{i,j}\alpha^j\}} = g^{-b_i P^0(\alpha)+(\alpha+ID_i)P^i(\alpha)},$$

$$h_i^{\alpha^k} = (g^{\alpha^k})^{b_i} \prod_{j=0}^{N-2} \{(g^{\alpha^{k+j+2}})^{b_{i,j}} (g^{\alpha^{k+j+1}})^{b_{i,j}ID_i}\}$$

$$= g^{\alpha^k\left(\alpha(\alpha+ID_i)P^i(\alpha)+b_i\right)} = g^{\alpha^k Q^i(\alpha)}.$$

The challenger sets $\mathsf{label}_i = (h_i^{\alpha^k}, k \in [0, N])$ and sends $sk_i = (d_{1,i}, d_{2,i}, d_{3,i}, \mathsf{label}_i)$ to the adversary $\mathcal{A}$. As $b_i, Q^i(x)$ are random, $d_{2,i}, \mathsf{label}_i$

have identical distribution to those in the original scheme. It is left to show that $d_{1,i}, d_{3,i}$ follow the original distribution.

$$d_{1,i} = g^{P^i(\alpha)} = g^{\frac{Q^i(\alpha)-b_i}{\alpha(\alpha+ID_i)}}$$

$$= g^{\frac{Q^i(\alpha)+d_{2,i}}{\alpha(\alpha+ID_i)}} = (h_i g^{d_{2,i}})^{\frac{1}{\alpha(\alpha+ID_i)}},$$

$$\text{Now, } -b_i P^0(\alpha) + (\alpha + ID_i)P^i(\alpha)$$

$$= \frac{1}{\alpha}\Big\{ -b_i \alpha P^0(\alpha) + Q^i(\alpha) - b_i \Big\}$$

$$= \frac{1}{\alpha}\Big\{ -b_i(Q^0(\alpha) - 1) + Q^i(\alpha) - b_i \Big\}$$

$$= \frac{1}{\alpha}\Big\{ -b_i Q^0(\alpha) + Q^i(\alpha) \Big\}$$

$$\Rightarrow d_{3,i} = g^{-b_i P^0(\alpha)+(\alpha+ID_i)P^i(\alpha)}$$

$$= g^{\frac{1}{\alpha}\big\{ -b_i Q^0(\alpha)+Q^i(\alpha) \big\}}$$

$$= \Big(g^{Q^i(\alpha)} g^{-b_i Q^0(\alpha)}\Big)^{\frac{1}{\alpha}} = (h_i l_0^{d_{2,i}})^{\frac{1}{\alpha}}.$$

Thus $d_{1,i}, d_{3,i}$ are identical to original scheme.

Challenge: The adversary $\mathcal{A}$ sends a set of user indices G to $\mathcal{C}$, where identities of users of G has not been queried before. It also sends two equal length messages M_0, M_1. The challenger $\mathcal{C}$ sets $\lambda(x) = \prod\limits_{j \in G}(x + ID_j) = \sum\limits_{i=0}^{|G|} \lambda_i x^i$, where λ_i are function of ID_j for $j \in G$ and computes $\prod\limits_{i=0}^{|G|}(\hat{g}^{\alpha^{q+2+i}})^{\lambda_i} = (\hat{g}^{\alpha^{q+2}})^{\sum\limits_{i=0}^{|G|}\lambda_i \alpha^i} = (\hat{g}^{\alpha^{q+2}})^{\prod\limits_{i \in G}(\alpha+ID_i)}$. Note that $\hat{g}^{\alpha^i}, i \in [q+2, 2q], q \geq 2N$ are available to $\mathcal{C}$ through the given instance $\langle Z, X \rangle$.

Extracting g^{α^i} from the given instance $\langle Z, X \rangle$, $\mathcal{C}$ computes $\prod\limits_{i=0}^{N-1}(g^{\alpha^i})^{b_{0,i}} = g^{\sum\limits_{i=0}^{N-1}b_{0,i}\alpha^i} = g^{P^0(\alpha)}$ and sets the challange ciphertext for $M_b, b \in \{0,1\}$ as,

$$C^* = \Big((\hat{g}^{\alpha^{q+2}})^{\prod\limits_{i \in G}(\alpha+ID_i)}, \hat{g}^{-\alpha^{q+2}}, X^{-1}, M_b X e(\hat{g}^{\alpha^{q+2}}, g^{P^0(\alpha)})\Big)$$

$$= (C_1, C_2, C_3, C_{M_b}).$$

If $X = e(\hat{g}, g)^{\alpha^{q+1}}$, we have

$$C_1 = (\hat{g}^{\alpha^{q+2}})^{\prod\limits_{i \in G}(\alpha+ID_i)} = (g^{\log_g \hat{g}^{\alpha^{q+2}}})^{\prod\limits_{i \in G}(\alpha+ID_i)}$$

$$= (g^{\alpha\alpha^{q+1}\log_g \hat{g}})^{\prod\limits_{i \in G}(\alpha+ID_i)} = (g^{\alpha})^{s\prod\limits_{i \in G}(\alpha+ID_i)},$$

$$C_2 = \hat{g}^{-\alpha^{q+2}} = g^{(-\log_g \hat{g})\alpha^{q+2}} = g^{-\alpha\alpha^{q+1}\log_g \hat{g}} = g^{-\alpha s},$$

$$C_3 = X^{-1} = e(\hat{g}, g)^{-\alpha^{q+1}} = e(g^{\log_g \hat{g}}, g)^{-\alpha^{q+1}}$$

$$= e(g,g)^{-\alpha^{q+1}\log_g \hat{g}} = e(g,g)^{-s},$$

$$C_{M_b} = M_b X e(\hat{g}^{\alpha^{q+2}}, g^{P^0(\alpha)}) = M_b e(\hat{g}, g)^{\alpha^{q+1}} e(\hat{g}^{\alpha^{q+2}}, g^{P^0(\alpha)})$$

$$= M_b e(\hat{g}^{\alpha^{q+1}}, g) e(\hat{g}^{\alpha^{q+1}}, g^{\alpha P^0(\alpha)}) = M_b e(\hat{g}^{\alpha^{q+1}}, g^{\alpha P^0(\alpha)+1})$$

$$= M_b e(\hat{g}^{\alpha^{q+1}}, g^{Q^0(\alpha)}) = M_b e(g^s, l_0) = M_b e(g, l_0)^s$$

where s is implicitly set as $s = \alpha^{q+1}\log_g \hat{g}$.

Thus distribution of C^* is similar to our real construction from $\mathcal{A}$'s point of view.

$\mathcal{C}$ returns C^* to $\mathcal{A}$.

Phase 2: This is similar to Phase 1 key generation queries. The adversary $\mathcal{A}$ sends key generation queries for $\{i_{m+1}, \ldots, i_t\} \subseteq [N]$ with a restriction that $i_j \notin G$ and receives back secret keys $\{sk_{i_j}\}_{j=m+1}^{t}$ simulated in the same manner by $\mathcal{C}$ as in Phase 1.

Guess: Finally, $\mathcal{A}$ outputs a guess $b' \in \{0,1\}$ of b to $\mathcal{C}$ and wins if $b' = b$. If $b' = b$, $\mathcal{C}$ outputs 0, indicating that $X = e(\hat{g}, g)^{\alpha^{q+1}}$; otherwise, it outputs 1, indicating that X is a random element of $\mathbb{G}_1$.

The simulation of $\mathcal{C}$ is perfect when $X = e(\hat{g}, g)^{\alpha^{q+1}}$. Therefore, we have $Pr[\mathcal{C}(Z, X = e(\hat{g}, g)^{\alpha^{q+1}}) = 0] = \frac{1}{2} + Adv_{\mathcal{A}}^{\mathsf{Bed-IND}}$,

where $Adv_{\mathcal{A}}^{\mathsf{Bed-IND}}$ is the advantage of the adversary $\mathcal{A}$ in the above indistinguishability game. On the other hand, M_b is completely hidden from the adversary $\mathcal{A}$ when $X = R$ is random, thereby $Pr[\mathcal{C}(Z, X = R) = 0] = \frac{1}{2}$.

Hence, the advantage of the challenger $\mathcal{C}$ in solving q-wDABDHE is

$$Adv_{\mathcal{C}}^{q-\mathsf{wDABDHE}}(t, N) = |Pr[\mathcal{C}(Z, X = e(\hat{g}, g)^{\alpha^{q+1}}) = 0] - Pr[\mathcal{C}(Z, X = R) = 0]|$$

$$= \frac{1}{2} + Adv_{\mathcal{A}}^{\mathsf{Bed-IND}} - \frac{1}{2} = Adv_{\mathcal{A}}^{\mathsf{Bed-IND}}.$$

Therefore, if $\mathcal{A}$ has non-negligible advantage in correctly guessing b', then $\mathcal{C}$ predicts $X = e(\hat{g}, g)^{\alpha^{q+1}}$ or random element of $\mathbb{G}_1$ (i.e., solves q-wDABDHE ($q \geq 2N$) instance given to $\mathcal{C}$) with non-negligible advantage. Hence the theorem follows.

5   Efficiency

We have compared our Bed construction with the existing works in Tables 1 and 2. We note down the following points:

- Our scheme achieves adaptive security, while [13] is semi-static and [1] is selective.
- Like [13], our scheme is secure in standard model whereas [1] is secure in random oracle model.

Table 1. Comparative summaries of storage, communication bandwith and security of BED schemes.

Scheme	|PP|	|PK|	|SK|	$\|P(G)\|$	|CT|	SM	RO	SA
[13]*	$(2N+4)\|\mathbb{G}\|+1\|\mathbb{G}_1\|$	$N\|\mathbb{Z}_p\|+N\|\mathbb{G}\|$	$(N+1)\|\mathbb{G}\|$	$5\|\mathbb{G}\|+1\|\mathbb{G}_1\|$	$2\|\mathbb{G}\|+1\|\mathbb{G}_1\|$	Semi-static	No	N-DBDHE
[1]	$(N+2)\|\mathbb{G}\|+1\|\mathbb{G}_1\|$	0	$1\|\mathbb{G}\|$	$3\|\mathbb{G}\|+1\|\mathbb{G}_1\|$	$2\|\mathbb{G}\|+1\|\mathbb{G}_1\|$	Selective	Yes	GDDHE
Our Bed	$(2N+3)\|\mathbb{G}\|+2\|\mathbb{G}_1\|$	0	$(N+3)\|\mathbb{G}\|+1\|\mathbb{Z}_p\|$	$3\|\mathbb{G}\|+2\|\mathbb{G}_1\|$	$2\|\mathbb{G}\|+2\|\mathbb{G}_1\|$	Adaptive	No	$q-$wDABDHE

\|PP\| = public parameter size, \|PK\| = public key size, \|SK\| = secret key size, $\|P(G)\|$ = group token size, \|CT\| = ciphertext size, N = total number of users, $\|\mathbb{G}\|$ = bit size of an element of $\mathbb{G}$, $\|\mathbb{G}_1\|$ = bit size of an element of $\mathbb{G}_1$, $\|\mathbb{Z}_p\|$ = bit size of an element of $\mathbb{Z}_p$, SM = security model, RO = random oracle, SA = security assumption, N-DBDHE = N- decisional bilinear diffie-hellman exponent, GDDHE = general decisional diffie-hellman exponent, q-wDABDHE = q-weaker decisional augmented bilinear diffie-hellman exponent, $q \geq 2N$.

Table 2. Comparative summary of computation cost of parameter generation, encryption and decryption algorithm for BED schemes.

Scheme	PP		SK		$P(G)$				Enc			Dec			
	$\#E_\mathbb{G}$	$\#\mathrm{pr}$	$\#E_\mathbb{G}$	$\#I_\mathbb{G}$	$\#E_\mathbb{G}$	$\#E_{\mathbb{G}_1}$	$\#I_\mathbb{G}$	$\#I_{\mathbb{G}_1}$	$\#E_\mathbb{G}$	$\#E_{\mathbb{G}_1}$	$\#\mathrm{pr}$	$\#E_\mathbb{G}$	$\#E_{\mathbb{G}_1}$	$\#\mathrm{pr}$	$\# I_{\mathbb{G}_1}$
[13]*	$2N+3$	1	$N+2$	1	$k'+4$	1	0	0	2	1	2	0	0	2	1
[1]	$N+1$	1	1	0	$2k'+3$	1	1	0	2	1	0	$k'-1$	1	2	1
Our Bed	$2N+1$	2	$N+4$	0	$2k'+3$	2	1	1	2	2	0	$4k'-2$	4	4	1

PP = public parameter, SK = secret key, $P(G)$ = group token, Enc = encryption, Dec = decryption, N = total number of users, k' = number of users selected by the dealer, $\#E_\mathbb{G}$ = number of exponentiations in $\mathbb{G}$, $\#E_{\mathbb{G}_1}$ = number of exponentiations in $\mathbb{G}_1$, $\#\mathrm{pr}$ = number of pairings, $\#I_\mathbb{G}$ = number of inversions in $\mathbb{G}$, $\#I_{\mathbb{G}_1}$ = number of inversions in $\mathbb{G}_1$.
*In scheme [13], broadcaster need's users response to detect a cheating dealer and has a flaw in security proof as pointed by [1].

- All the schemes are semantically secure under same type assumptions. Note that security of N-DBDHE, GDDHE, q-wDABDHE $(q \geq 2N)$ follows from (P, Q, f)-General Decisional Diffie-Hellman Exponent $((P, Q, f)$- GDDHE) problem of Boneh et al. [3].
- Unlike [13], our construction does not require any public key. Except secret key size of [1], other parameter sizes asymptotically matches with [1].
- Computation costs asymptotically matches (in big-O approximation) with existing schemes except decryption cost of [13] and secret key generation of [1]. At the expense of the computation cost, we achieve adaptive security.

6   Conclusion

We have proposed the first adaptively CPA secure BED scheme which supports privacy, maximum number of accountability and compares well with existing schemes. Our security analysis is in the standard model under reasonable assumptions.

A   General Decisional Diffie-Hellman Exponent Problem [3]

We give an overview of General Decisional Diffie-Hellman Exponent problem in symmetric case. Let $\mathbb{S} = (p, \mathbb{G}, \mathbb{G}_1, e)$ is a bilinear group system. Let g be generator of group $\mathbb{G}$ and set $g_1 = e(g, g)$. Let $P, Q \in \mathbb{F}_p[X_1, \ldots, X_n]^s$ be two s tuple of n variate polynomials over $\mathbb{F}_p$. We write $P = (p_1, \ldots, p_s), Q = (q_1, \ldots, q_s)$ and impose that $p_1 = 1, q_1 = 1$. For a set Ω, a function $h : \mathbb{F}_p \to \Omega$ and a vector $(x_1, \ldots, x_n) \in \mathbb{F}_p{}^n$ we write,

$$h(P(x_1, \ldots, x_n)) = (h(p_1(x_1, \ldots, x_n)), \ldots, h(p_s(x_1, \ldots, x_n))) \in \Omega^s.$$

We use similar notation for the s-tuple Q. A polynomial $f \in \mathbb{F}_p[X_1, \ldots, X_n]$ depends on P, Q if there exists $a_{i,j}, b_i (1 \leq i \leq s) \in \mathbb{Z}_p$ such that

$$f = \sum_{1 \leq i,j \leq s} a_{i,j} p_i p_j + \sum_{1 \leq i,j \leq s} b_i q_i.$$

Otherwise, f is independent of P, Q. The (P, Q, f)-General Decisional Diffie-Hellman Exponent $((P, Q, f)$-GDDHE) problem is defined as follows:

Definition 8 $((P, Q, f)$-GDDHE:$)$ Given $H(x_1, \ldots, x_n) = (g^{P(x_1, \ldots, x_n)},$ $g_1^{Q(x_1, \ldots, x_n)})$ and $T \in \mathbb{G}_1$, decide whether $T = g_1^{f(x_1, \ldots, x_n)}$.

Boneh et al. [3] have proved that (P, Q, f)-GDDHE is intractable, if f does not depend on P, Q.

Hardness of l-wDABDHE assumption: Let us consider $h = g^{\beta}$. If we formulate l-wDABDHE problem as the (P, Q, f)-GDDHE problem then

$$P = (1, \alpha, \alpha^2, \ldots, \alpha^l, \beta, \beta\alpha^{l+2}, \ldots, \beta\alpha^{2l})$$

$$Q = (1)$$

$$f = (\beta\alpha^{l+1})$$

Following the technique of [8], it is easy to show that f does not depend on P, Q. So, cryptographic hardness of l-wDABDHE assumption follows.

References

1. Acharya, K., Dutta, R.: Secure and efficient construction of broadcast encryption with dealership. In: Chen, L., Han, J. (eds.) ProvSec 2016. LNCS, vol. 10005, pp. 277–295. Springer, Heidelberg (2016). doi:10.1007/978-3-319-47422-9_16
2. Barth, A., Boneh, D., Waters, B.: Privacy in encrypted content distribution using private broadcast encryption. In: Crescenzo, G., Rubin, A. (eds.) FC 2006. LNCS, vol. 4107, pp. 52–64. Springer, Heidelberg (2006). doi:10.1007/11889663_4
3. Boneh, D., Boyen, X., Goh, E.-J.: Hierarchical identity based encryption with constant size ciphertext. In: Cramer, R. (ed.) EUROCRYPT 2005. LNCS, vol. 3494, pp. 440–456. Springer, Heidelberg (2005). doi:10.1007/11426639_26

4. Boneh, D., Gentry, C., Waters, B.: Collusion resistant broadcast encryption with short ciphertexts and private keys. In: Shoup, V. (ed.) CRYPTO 2005. LNCS, vol. 3621, pp. 258–275. Springer, Heidelberg (2005). doi:10.1007/11535218_16
5. Boneh, D., Waters, B., Zhandry, M.: Low overhead broadcast encryption from multilinear maps. In: Garay, J.A., Gennaro, R. (eds.) CRYPTO 2014. LNCS, vol. 8616, pp. 206–223. Springer, Heidelberg (2014). doi:10.1007/978-3-662-44371-2_12
6. Camacho, P.: Fair exchange of short signatures without trusted third party. In: Dawson, E. (ed.) CT-RSA 2013. LNCS, vol. 7779, pp. 34–49. Springer, Heidelberg (2013). doi:10.1007/978-3-642-36095-4_3
7. Chor, B., Fiat, A., Naor, M.: Tracing traitors. In: Desmedt, Y.G. (ed.) CRYPTO 1994. LNCS, vol. 839, pp. 257–270. Springer, Heidelberg (1994). doi:10.1007/3-540-48658-5_25
8. Delerablée, C.: Identity-based broadcast encryption with constant size ciphertexts and private keys. In: Kurosawa, K. (ed.) ASIACRYPT 2007. LNCS, vol. 4833, pp. 200–215. Springer, Heidelberg (2007). doi:10.1007/978-3-540-76900-2_12
9. Delerablée, C., Paillier, P., Pointcheval, D.: Fully collusion secure dynamic broadcast encryption with constant-size ciphertexts or decryption keys. In: Takagi, T., Okamoto, E., Okamoto, T., Okamoto, T. (eds.) Pairing 2007. LNCS, vol. 4575, pp. 39–59. Springer, Heidelberg (2007). doi:10.1007/978-3-540-73489-5_4
10. Dodis, Y., Fazio, N.: Public key broadcast encryption for stateless receivers. In: Feigenbaum, J. (ed.) DRM 2002. LNCS, vol. 2696, pp. 61–80. Springer, Heidelberg (2003). doi:10.1007/978-3-540-44993-5_5
11. Fiat, A., Naor, M.: Broadcast encryption. In: Stinson, D.R. (ed.) CRYPTO 1993. LNCS, vol. 773, pp. 480–491. Springer, Heidelberg (1994). doi:10.1007/3-540-48329-2_40
12. Gentry, C., Waters, B.: Adaptive security in broadcast encryption systems (with Short Ciphertexts). In: Joux, A. (ed.) EUROCRYPT 2009. LNCS, vol. 5479, pp. 171–188. Springer, Heidelberg (2009). doi:10.1007/978-3-642-01001-9_10
13. Gritti, C., Susilo, W., Plantard, T., Liang, K., Wong, D.S.: Broadcast encryption with dealership. Int. J. Inf. Secur. **15**(3), 271–283 (2016)
14. Guo, F., Mu, Y., Susilo, W., Varadharajan, V.: Membership encryption and its applications. In: Boyd, C., Simpson, L. (eds.) ACISP 2013. LNCS, vol. 7959, pp. 219–234. Springer, Heidelberg (2013). doi:10.1007/978-3-642-39059-3_15
15. Lewko, A., Sahai, A., Waters, B.: Revocation systems with very small private keys. In: 2010 IEEE Symposium on Security and Privacy, pp. 273–285. IEEE (2010)
16. Phan, D.-H., Pointcheval, D., Shahandashti, S.F., Strefler, M.: Adaptive cca broadcast encryption with constant-size secret keys and ciphertexts. Int. J. Inf. Secur. **12**(4), 251–265 (2013)
17. Ren, Y., Wang, S., Zhang, X.: Non-interactive dynamic identity-based broadcast encryption without random oracles. In: Chim, T.W., Yuen, T.H. (eds.) ICICS 2012. LNCS, vol. 7618, pp. 479–487. Springer, Heidelberg (2012)

Implementation and Algorithms

A New Algorithm for Residue Multiplication Modulo $2^{521} - 1$

Shoukat Ali$^{(\boxtimes)}$ and Murat Cenk

Institute of Applied Mathematics, Middle East Technical University,
Dumlupınar Blv. No:1, 06800 Ankara, Turkey
shoukat.1983@gmail.com, mcenk@metu.edu.tr

Abstract. We present a new algorithm for residue multiplication modulo the Mersenne prime $p = 2^{521} - 1$ based on the Toeplitz matrix-vector product. For this modulus, our algorithm yields better result in terms of the total number of operations than the previously known best algorithm of Granger and Scott presented in Public Key Cryptography (PKC) 2015. We have implemented three versions of our algorithm to provide an extensive comparison — according to the best of our knowledge — with respect to the well-known algorithms and to show the robustness of our algorithm for this 521-bit Mersenne prime modulus. Each version is having less number of operations than its counterpart. On our machine, Intel Pentium CPU G2010 @ 2.80 GHz machine with gcc 5.3.1 compiler, we find that for each version of our algorithm modulus p is more efficient than modulus $2p$. Hence, by using Granger and Scott code, constant-time variable-base scalar multiplication, for modulus p we find $1,251,502$ clock cycles for P-521 (NIST and SECG curve) and $1,055,105$ cycles for E-521 (Edwards curve). While, on the same machine the clock cycles counts of Granger-Scott code (modulus $2p$) for P-521 and E-521 are $1,332,165$ and $1,148,871$ respectively.

Keywords: Residue multiplication · Toeplitz matrix-vector product · Mersenne prime · Elliptic curve cryptography

1 Introduction

In elliptic curve cryptography (ECC), the scalar multiplication is a vital operation and used for key generation, key exchange using Diffie-Hellman and digital signature. For cryptographic sizes, a scalar multiplication requires several hundreds of modular multiplications and the cost of other primitive operations is negligible with respect to this operation. Therefore, a good amount of research has focused on improving the efficiency of modular multiplication.

In modular multiplication, the reduction requires special attention and Solinas, therefore, constructed a group of modulus, Generalized Mersenne Numbers (GMN), to speedup the modular reduction. This explains why his four recommended moduli are fully part of the standards such as NIST [5] and SECG [3]. However, the Solinas primes are not the only special primes. Mersenne primes,

© Springer International Publishing AG 2017
S. Hong and J.H. Park (Eds.): ICISC 2016, LNCS 10157, pp. 181–193, 2017.
DOI: 10.1007/978-3-319-53177-9_9

Crandall primes, and Montgomery primes are some of the other examples. The reduction modulo Mersenne prime is optimal because the cost of reduction is equivalent to modular addition due to the constant term 1. It is not the case that the focus has been entirely on the design of new special primes. That is why, the researchers have also devised techniques of replacing the expensive division operation with less expensive operation(s). Barrett reduction and Montgomery multiplication are some examples of these techniques.

In general, the use of schoolbook multiplication is recommended for ECC sizes because the cost of overheads in other techniques outweighs the saving of the multiplication operation. Karatsuba technique has been used well for binary fields and for prime fields the bit-length is perceived not to be sufficient to make the cost of 25% saved multiplication worth more than the addition overhead. However, Bernstein et al. [1] have used two levels of refined Karatsuba followed by schoolbook multiplication in an ingenious way on the modulus of size 414-bit. They have achieved a good efficiency by splitting the operands into limbs of size less than the word-size (32-bit) of the machine in order to postpone the carry and avoid overflow in double precision. In addition, Granger and Scott proposed an efficient algorithm for residue multiplication modulo the Mersenne prime $2^{521} - 1$ in [6]. They achieved a good efficiency because of the modulus form and found out that residue multiplication can take as many word-by-word multiplication as squaring with very little extra addition as overhead.

In this paper, we propose a new algorithm for residue multiplication modulo the Mersenne prime $2^{521} - 1$ that is cheaper in terms of the total number of operations than the recently proposed algorithm of Granger and Scott [6]. Although our technique has 9 (single precision) multiplications more than that of the one in [6], the number of (single precision) additions is 47 less. So, even if one takes the ratio of multiplication to addition 1 : 4 — in the literature it is generally taken 1 : 3 — still our technique has less total number of operations. We have achieved this efficiency based on the representation and structure of residue multiplication modulo the Mersenne prime $2^{521} - 1$ as Toeplitz matrix-vector product. Toeplitz matrices have the great properties of (1) partitioning of a Toeplitz matrix results into Toeplitz matrices, (2) addition and subtraction of Toeplitz matrices is also a Toeplitz matrix, (3) addition and subtraction require only computation of first row and first column, and (4) Toeplitz matrix-vector product can be performed efficiently. Using these four properties, we have achieved a better efficiency, less number of operations, than the multiplication algorithm in [6]. It should be noted that unlike the algorithm in [6] which is modulus $2p$, we worked modulus p and better implementation results are obtained. We have implemented and tested three versions of our algorithm to show its robustness for the Mersenne prime $2^{521} - 1$ modulus and to provide a comprehensive comparison in terms of the number of the operations with respect to the well-known efficient algorithms.

The rest of the paper is organized as follows. In Sect. 2, we briefly introduce the Toeplitz matrix-vector product (TMVP), some previous work, and the formula that we use for our multiplication algorithm. Next, we show how the residue multiplication modulo 521-bit Mersenne prime can be represented as

TMVP and present our algorithmic technique with its arithmetic cost in detail in Sect. 3. The pseudo-code of our algorithm, the details of modulus p, the three versions of our algorithm along with their implementation results, and the arithmetic cost comparison of our algorithm with respect to the well-known algorithm are all discussed in Sect. 4. Then, in Sect. 5 we report the implementation results of the scalar multiplication in ECC both for modulus p and $2p$. Finally, we conclude our paper in Sect. 6.

2   Algorithms for Toeplitz Matrix-Vector Product

It can be observed from the work in [6] that residue multiplication modulo $2^{521}-1$ can be presented by Toeplitz matrix-vector product (TMVP). A Toeplitz matrix or diagonal-constant matrix is a matrix in which each descending diagonal from left to right is constant i.e. an $n \times n$ Toeplitz matrix is of the following form:

$$\begin{bmatrix} a_0 & a_1 & a_2 & \cdots & \cdots & \cdots & a_{n-1} \\ a_n & a_0 & a_1 & \ddots & \ddots & \ddots & a_{n-2} \\ a_{n+1} & a_n & a_0 & \ddots & \ddots & \ddots & a_{n-3} \\ \vdots & \ddots & \ddots & \ddots & \ddots & \ddots & \vdots \\ \vdots & & \ddots & \ddots & \ddots & \ddots & \vdots \\ \vdots & & & \ddots & a_n & a_0 & a_1 \\ a_{2(n-1)} & \cdots & \cdots & \cdots & a_{n+1} & a_n & a_0 \end{bmatrix}$$

One of the techniques for TMVP is to use the schoolbook method and for size n the time complexity is $\mathcal{O}(n^2)$. In the literature, there are algorithms better than the schoolbook. For example, a leading study on this subject for multiplication over $\mathbb{F}_2$ can be found in [4]. For a TMVP of size 3 we have

$$\begin{bmatrix} a_0 & a_1 & a_2 \\ a_3 & a_0 & a_1 \\ a_4 & a_3 & a_0 \end{bmatrix} \times \begin{bmatrix} b_0 \\ b_1 \\ b_2 \end{bmatrix} = \begin{bmatrix} m_3 + m_4 + m_6 \\ m_2 - m_4 + m_5 \\ m_1 - m_2 - m_3 \end{bmatrix} \tag{1}$$

where

$$m_1 = (a_4 + a_3 + a_0)b_0, \qquad m_2 = a_3(b_0 - b_1), \qquad m_3 = a_0(b_0 - b_2),$$
$$m_4 = a_1(b_1 - b_2), \qquad m_5 = (a_0 + a_3 + a_1)b_1, \qquad m_6 = (a_2 + a_0 + a_1)b_2$$

Using the m_i for $i = 1, \ldots, 6$ the total cost of (1) will be $6\mathbf{M} + 8\mathbf{A} + 6\mathbf{A}_d$ where $\mathbf{M}$ is the cost of a single precision/word multiplication, $\mathbf{A}$ is the cost of a single precision/word addition and $\mathbf{A}_d$ is the cost of a double precision/word addition. The cost of single precision addition is 8 because one can take common either $(a_3 + a_0)$ between m_1 and m_5 or $(a_0 + a_1)$ between m_5 and m_6. One can say that for all those machines where the ratio of multiplication to addition is greater than or equal to 1 : 3 this observation is worth to try. For larger bitlength, we can use this technique recursively and for size n it results in a time complexity of $\mathcal{O}(n^{1.63})$ which is better than schoolbook.

3   Multiplication Modulo $2^{521} - 1$ Using TMVP

Suppose F and G are two large integers of 521-bit and we are working on a 64-bit machine. As performed in [6] the partitioning of operands F, G results in nine limbs where each limb comprises of at most 58-bit stored in a 64-bit word. One can represent F, G as follows.

$$F = f_0 + 2^{58}f_1 + 2^{116}f_2 + 2^{174}f_3 + 2^{232}f_4 + 2^{290}f_5 + 2^{348}f_6 + 2^{406}f_7 + 2^{464}f_8$$
$$G = f_0 + 2^{58}g_1 + 2^{116}g_2 + 2^{174}g_3 + 2^{232}g_4 + 2^{290}g_5 + 2^{348}g_6 + 2^{406}g_7 + 2^{464}g_8$$

Note that the limbs f_8 and g_8 are 57-bit. We are interested to work with modulus $p = 2^{521} - 1$ to have the result directly as 521-bit residue. One has also the choice of modulus $2p$ where the residue will be at most 522-bit as in [6] and then a final reduction has to be performed to obtain the correct 521-bit residue. We believe modulus p is an efficient approach for two reasons (i) final reduction is not required and (ii) when modular multiplication is performed thousands of times. Let $Z = FG \bmod (2^{521} - 1)$. Then, the limbs will be $Z = [Z_0, Z_1, Z_2, Z_3, Z_4, Z_5, Z_6, Z_7, Z_8]$ where

$$
\begin{aligned}
Z_0 &= f_0g_0 + 2f_8g_1 + 2f_7g_2 + 2f_6g_3 + 2f_5g_4 + 2f_4g_5 + 2f_3g_6 + 2f_2g_7 + 2f_1g_8,\\
Z_1 &= f_1g_0 + f_0g_1 + 2f_8g_2 + 2f_7g_3 + 2f_6g_4 + 2f_5g_5 + 2f_4g_6 + 2f_3g_7 + 2f_2g_8,\\
Z_2 &= f_2g_0 + f_1g_1 + f_0g_2 + 2f_8g_3 + 2f_7g_4 + 2f_6g_5 + 2f_5g_6 + 2f_4g_7 + 2f_3g_8,\\
Z_3 &= f_3g_0 + f_2g_1 + f_1g_2 + f_0g_3 + 2f_8g_4 + 2f_7g_5 + 2f_6g_6 + 2f_5g_7 + 2f_4g_8,\\
Z_4 &= f_4g_0 + f_3g_1 + f_2g_2 + f_1g_3 + f_0g_4 + 2f_8g_5 + 2f_7g_6 + 2f_6g_7 + 2f_5g_8,\\
Z_5 &= f_5g_0 + f_4g_1 + f_3g_2 + f_2g_3 + f_1g_4 + f_0g_5 + 2f_8g_6 + 2f_7g_7 + 2f_6g_8,\\
Z_6 &= f_6g_0 + f_5g_1 + f_4g_2 + f_3g_3 + f_2g_4 + f_1g_5 + f_0g_6 + 2f_8g_7 + 2f_7g_8,\\
Z_7 &= f_7g_0 + f_6g_1 + f_5g_2 + f_4g_3 + f_3g_4 + f_2g_5 + f_1g_6 + f_0g_7 + 2f_8g_8,\\
Z_8 &= f_8g_0 + f_7g_1 + f_6g_2 + f_5g_3 + f_4g_4 + f_3g_5 + f_2g_6 + f_1g_7 + f_0g_8
\end{aligned}
$$

In the above expression, the constant 2 appears as a result of the reduction. There are two important points to take into account (i) the summation of f_ig_j and $2f_mg_n$ should not cause overflow in double precision and (ii) each Z_i contains the carry to be propagated.

The above expression in matrix-vector form will be

$$
\begin{bmatrix}
f_0 & 2f_8 & 2f_7 & 2f_6 & 2f_5 & 2f_4 & 2f_3 & 2f_2 & 2f_1 \\
f_1 & f_0 & 2f_8 & 2f_7 & 2f_6 & 2f_5 & 2f_4 & 2f_3 & 2f_2 \\
f_2 & f_1 & f_0 & 2f_8 & 2f_7 & 2f_6 & 2f_5 & 2f_4 & 2f_3 \\
f_3 & f_2 & f_1 & f_0 & 2f_8 & 2f_7 & 2f_6 & 2f_5 & 2f_4 \\
f_4 & f_3 & f_2 & f_1 & f_0 & 2f_8 & 2f_7 & 2f_6 & 2f_5 \\
f_5 & f_4 & f_3 & f_2 & f_1 & f_0 & 2f_8 & 2f_7 & 2f_6 \\
f_6 & f_5 & f_4 & f_3 & f_2 & f_1 & f_0 & 2f_8 & 2f_7 \\
f_7 & f_6 & f_5 & f_4 & f_3 & f_2 & f_1 & f_0 & 2f_8 \\
f_8 & f_7 & f_6 & f_5 & f_4 & f_3 & f_2 & f_1 & f_0
\end{bmatrix}
\times
\begin{bmatrix}
g_0 \\ g_1 \\ g_2 \\ g_3 \\ g_4 \\ g_5 \\ g_6 \\ g_7 \\ g_8
\end{bmatrix}
\tag{2}
$$

3.1 Proposed Technique

By using (1) the above TMVP (2) can be represented as follows:

$$\begin{bmatrix} A_0 & 2A_2 & 2A_1 \\ A_1 & A_0 & 2A_2 \\ A_2 & A_1 & A_0 \end{bmatrix} \times \begin{bmatrix} B_0 \\ B_1 \\ B_2 \end{bmatrix} = \begin{bmatrix} M_3 + M_4 + M_6 \\ M_2 - M_4 + M_5 \\ M_1 - M_2 - M_3 \end{bmatrix}$$

where the sub-matrices A_i for $i = 0, 1, 2$ are of size 3×3 and are not independent whereas the vectors B_i are of size 3×1. Here, for simplicity we use the schoolbook matrix-vector product technique for size 3 and later we discuss other options. For a Toeplitz matrix, one needs the first row and first column to represent it. Therefore, from here onwards, we show a Toeplitz matrix just by its first row and first column and leave the other entries blank. In other words, a computer programmer can use one-dimensional array rather a two-dimensional array for Toeplitz matrix. Similarly, by a word we mean 64-bit and a double-word 128-bit. From (1) we have

$$M_1 = (A_2 + A_1 + A_0)B_0, \qquad M_2 = A_1(B_0 - B_1)$$
$$M_3 = A_0(B_0 - B_2), \qquad M_4 = 2A_2(B_1 - B_2)$$
$$M_5 = (A_0 + A_1 + 2A_2)B_1, \qquad M_6 = (2(A_2 + A_1) + A_0)B_2$$

Computing M_2:

$$B_0 - B_1 = \begin{bmatrix} g_0 \\ g_1 \\ g_2 \end{bmatrix} - \begin{bmatrix} g_3 \\ g_4 \\ g_5 \end{bmatrix} = \begin{bmatrix} g_0 - g_3 \\ g_1 - g_4 \\ g_2 - g_5 \end{bmatrix} = \begin{bmatrix} U_1 \\ U_2 \\ U_3 \end{bmatrix}$$

$$A_1(B_0 - B_1) = \begin{bmatrix} f_3 & f_2 & f_1 \\ f_4 & & \\ f_5 & & \end{bmatrix} \times \begin{bmatrix} U_1 \\ U_2 \\ U_3 \end{bmatrix}$$

Hence, the total cost of M_2 is 9**M**+3**A**+6 **A**$_d$

Computing M_4:

$$B_1 - B_2 = \begin{bmatrix} g_3 \\ g_4 \\ g_5 \end{bmatrix} - \begin{bmatrix} g_6 \\ g_7 \\ g_8 \end{bmatrix} = \begin{bmatrix} g_3 - g_6 \\ g_4 - g_7 \\ g_5 - g_8 \end{bmatrix} = \begin{bmatrix} U_7 \\ U_8 \\ U_9 \end{bmatrix}$$

$$2A_2(B_1 - B_2) = \begin{bmatrix} 2f_6 & 2f_5 & 2f_4 \\ 2f_7 & & \\ 2f_8 & & \end{bmatrix} \times \begin{bmatrix} U_7 \\ U_8 \\ U_9 \end{bmatrix}$$

Hence, the total cost of M_4 is $9\mathbf{M} + 3\mathbf{A} + 6\mathbf{A}_d + 5\text{-}\textbf{shift}$ where the shifts are due to multiplication of f_i by 2 for $i = 4, \ldots, 8$. Note that, some of the elements of $2A_2$ appear in different places therefore, it is computed once and used in different places.

Computing M_3:

$$B_0 - B_2 = \begin{bmatrix} g_0 \\ g_1 \\ g_2 \end{bmatrix} - \begin{bmatrix} g_6 \\ g_7 \\ g_8 \end{bmatrix} = \begin{bmatrix} g_0 - g_6 \\ g_1 - g_7 \\ g_2 - g_8 \end{bmatrix} = \begin{bmatrix} U_4 \\ U_5 \\ U_6 \end{bmatrix}$$

$$A_0(B_0 - B_2) = \begin{bmatrix} f_0 \ 2f_8 \ 2f_7 \\ f_1 \\ f_2 \end{bmatrix} \times \begin{bmatrix} U_4 \\ U_5 \\ U_6 \end{bmatrix}$$

where $2f_8$ and $2f_7$ have already been computed by M_4. Hence, the total cost of M_3 is $9\mathbf{M} + 3\mathbf{A} + 6\mathbf{A}_d$.

Computing M_1:

$$A_2 + A_1 = \begin{bmatrix} f_6 \ f_5 \ f_4 \\ f_7 \\ f_8 \end{bmatrix} + \begin{bmatrix} f_3 \ f_2 \ f_1 \\ f_4 \\ f_5 \end{bmatrix} = \begin{bmatrix} f_6 + f_3 \ f_5 + f_2 \ f_4 + f_1 \\ f_7 + f_4 \\ f_8 + f_5 \end{bmatrix} = \begin{bmatrix} S_1 \ S_2 \ S_3 \\ S_4 \\ S_5 \end{bmatrix}$$

$$(A_2 + A_1) + A_0 = \begin{bmatrix} S_1 \ S_2 \ S_3 \\ S_4 \\ S_5 \end{bmatrix} + \begin{bmatrix} f_0 \ 2f_8 \ 2f_7 \\ f_1 \\ f_2 \end{bmatrix} = \begin{bmatrix} S_6 \ S_7 \ S_8 \\ S_9 \\ S_{10} \end{bmatrix}$$

$$(A_2 + A_1 + A_0)B_0 = \begin{bmatrix} S_6 \ S_7 \ S_8 \\ S_9 \\ S_{10} \end{bmatrix} \times \begin{bmatrix} g_0 \\ g_1 \\ g_2 \end{bmatrix}$$

Again $2f_8$ and $2f_7$ are used but already computed by M_4. Hence, the total cost of M_1 is $9\mathbf{M} + 10\mathbf{A} + 6\mathbf{A}_d$.

Computing M_6: For the sub-matrices addition, we have

$$2(A_2 + A_1) + A_0 = (A_2 + A_1 + A_0) + (A_2 + A_1)$$

and we have already computed both the parenthesized expressions on the right-hand side so

$$(A_2 + A_1 + A_0) + (A_2 + A_1) = \begin{bmatrix} S_6 \ S_7 \ S_8 \\ S_9 \\ S_{10} \end{bmatrix} + \begin{bmatrix} S_1 \ S_2 \ S_3 \\ S_4 \\ S_5 \end{bmatrix} = \begin{bmatrix} S_{11} \ S_{12} \ S_{13} \\ S_{14} \\ S_{15} \end{bmatrix}$$

$$((A_2 + A_1 + A_0) + (A_2 + A_1))B_2 = \begin{bmatrix} S_{11} \ S_{12} \ S_{13} \\ S_{14} \\ S_{15} \end{bmatrix} \times \begin{bmatrix} g_6 \\ g_7 \\ g_8 \end{bmatrix}$$

Hence, the total cost of M_6 is $9\mathbf{M} + 5\mathbf{A} + 6\mathbf{A}_d$.

Computing M_5: Here, for the addition of submatrices one has to compute $S_{16} = S_6 + f_6$ only. While the other four elements have already been computed i.e. two by M_1 and two by M_6 as shown below

$$(A_0 + A_1) + 2A_2 = \begin{bmatrix} f_0 + f_3 \ 2f_8 + f_2 \ 2f_7 + f_1 \\ f_1 + f_4 \\ f_2 + f_5 \end{bmatrix} + \begin{bmatrix} 2f_6 \ 2f_5 \ 2f_4 \\ 2f_7 \\ 2f_8 \end{bmatrix} = \begin{bmatrix} S_{16} \ S_{15} \ S_{14} \\ S_8 \\ S_7 \end{bmatrix}$$

$$(A_0 + A_1 + 2A_2)B_1 = \begin{bmatrix} S_{16} \ S_{15} \ S_{14} \\ S_8 \\ S_7 \end{bmatrix} \times \begin{bmatrix} g_3 \\ g_4 \\ g_5 \end{bmatrix}$$

Hence, the total cost of M_5 is $9\mathbf{M} + 1\mathbf{A} + 6\mathbf{A}_d$.

Final Computation: At last, we have to compute

$$\begin{bmatrix} M_3 + M_4 + M_6 \\ M_2 - M_4 + M_5 \\ M_1 - M_2 - M_3 \end{bmatrix}$$

where each M_i is a 3×1 vector and the elements are of double-word size so the total cost is $18\,\mathbf{A}_d$. Finally, the overall cost of the whole method is $54\mathbf{M} + 25\mathbf{A} + 54\mathbf{A}_d + 5\text{-shift}$.

Note that, one can take $M_1 = (A_2 + (A_1 + A_0))B_0, M_5 = ((A_0 + A_1) + 2A_2)B_1, M_6 = ((2A_2 + (A_1 + A_0)) + A_1)B_2$ where M_2, M_3, M_4 remain unchanged and $2A_2$ is computed once. But we found the total cost as $54\mathbf{M} + 29\mathbf{A} + 54\mathbf{A}_d + 5\text{-shift}$ which is not efficient.

4 Algorithms and Comparison

Algorithm 1 presents the pseudocode of our algorithm that we discussed in detail in Sect. 3.1. A main advantage of our algorithm is the opportunity to use any combination of M_i for $i = 1, \ldots, 6$ for efficient implementation. For an extensive comparison of the arithmetic cost and to show the robustness of our algorithm for the 521-bit Mersenne prime, we have implemented three versions of our algorithm (i) Hybrid version, (ii) Recursive version, and (iii) Mixed version. These versions also provide the choice of selecting the optimal implementation on the underlying machine using a particular compiler/interpreter. These versions are discussed in detail in the following sections.

4.1 Residue Representation

The work with modulus $2p$ has been discussed in detail in [6]. In this section, we explain the case of working modulus p that we are interested in. We are performing the same carry propagation technique as in [6] so that one can easily switch, with few changes, from p to $2p$ and vice versa.

Through testing we find that if either of the inputs (F or G) is $2^{521} - 2$ and the other in $[2^{521} - 17, 2^{521} - 2]$, then the output limbs are in $[0, 2^{59} - 1] \times [0, 2^{58} - 1]^7 \times [0, 2^{57} - 1]$ where $[0, 2^{59} - 1]$ is the range of the least significant limb z_0 and $[0, 2^{57} - 1]$ is the range of the most significant limb z_8. While for all the other values, the carry propagation results into unique residue modulo p with input and output limbs in $[0, 2^{58} - 1]^8 \times [0, 2^{57} - 1]$. Therefore, we leave the output of our multiplication algorithm in the *reduced limb form* i.e. $[0, 2^{59} - 1] \times [0, 2^{58} - 1]^7 \times [0, 2^{57} - 1]$.

Working with modulus p also requires some changes in squaring algorithm and again through testing we find that if the operand is in $[2^{521} - 5, 2^{521} - 2]$, then the output will be in $[0, 2^{59} - 1] \times [0, 2^{58} - 1]^7 \times [0, 2^{57} - 1]$. So, in case of scalar multiplication in ECC the intermediate results are in the *reduced limb form* as in [6].

4.2   Implementation Results

For implementation we use Ubuntu 16.04 LTS on an Intel Pentium CPU G2010 @ 2.80 GHz desktop machine with 4 GB RAM and the Turbo Boost being disabled. There are two cores and from BIOS one can change the number of cores. Therefore, we have tested our programs both with one core and two cores. We find testing on two cores a better choice especially in case of scalar multiplication in ECC.

We have implemented our multiplication algorithm in C language using gcc 5.3.1. For the clock cycles count, we use the technique proposed by Paoloni in his white paper [7]. All the three versions of our algorithm are tested on the same set of 10^3 (random) integers by calling the function twice in 10^3 iterations loop. The values are read limb-by-limb from separate files for each operand. We find 164 as the minimum mean cycles count for the multiplication function, gmul(), of Scott which is more than the report cycles of 155 in [6].

Hybrid Version: For this version first we apply (1) for the matrix-vector decomposition to obtain M_i for $i = 1, \ldots, 6$ then use schoolbook matrix-vector product to compute each M_i. This version[1] is already explained in detail in Sect. 3.1 and the pseudo-code is given as Algorithm 1. After testing and running multiple times we find the minimum mean clock cycles count as 179 and 181 at -O3 for modulus p and $2p$ respectively.

Mixed Version: Rather applying (1) individually on each M_i $i = 1, \ldots, 6$ one can further exploit the formula to find the common expressions (having same result) on the matrix elements of M_i. Unfortunately, the vectors do not have common expressions. Which implies that one has to exploit the m_i for $i = 1, 5, 6$ of each M_i at second level. From (1) we know that within an M_i there is one intra-common expression — involving two elements — between two m_i and therefore, one has to exploit the third one for inter-common expression with other M_i. For example, for M_2 we have $m_1 = (f_3 + f_4 + f_5)U_1, m_5 = (f_2 + f_3 + f_4)U_2, m_6 = (f_1 + f_2 + f_3)U_3$ and by taking $f_3 + f_4$ as intra-common, leaves $f_1 + f_2 + f_3$ for inter-common.

The total number of single precision addition can be reduced if one finds inter-common expression among more than two M_i for $i = 1, \ldots, 6$. However, in this particular case we find commonality between two M_i only. There are two candidate groups $\{M_2, M_3, M_4\}$ and $\{M_1, M_5, M_6\}$ for inter-common expression. For our implementation we have taken $\{M_2, M_3\}$ and $\{M_5, M_6\}$ for applying (1) at second level to exploit the inter-common expression while using

---

[1] https://github.com/Shoukat-Ali/521-bit-Mersenne-Prime/blob/master/hybrid.c.

schoolbook for M_4 and M_1. Instead of two M_i one may take either $\{M_2, M_3, M_4\}$ or $\{M_1, M_5, M_6\}$ for inter-common expression but that will not reduce the total number of single precision addition because there is no inter-common expression among more than two M_i. Since at the second level all the elements of the Toeplitz sub-matrix are independent therefore, it is impossible to find inter-common expression involving more than two matrix elements.

Based on the arithmetic cost, we have tested three implementations of this version: (i) computing M_2, M_3, M_4 by applying (1) through a function call (ii) in-lining the computation of M_2, M_3, M_4 rather making a call, and (iii) computing M_2, M_3 and M_5, M_6 through function calls as discussed above. We find (ii) as the optimal implementation[2] and the minimum mean cycles count as 195 and 197 at -O3 for modulus p and $2p$ respectively.

Recursive Version: Instead of applying schoolbook for the computation of M_i for $i = 1, \ldots, 6$ one may re-apply (1). For this version we have tested three implementations: (i) function calls (ii) in-lining rather making calls, and (iii) using the Mixed version exploitation for $\{M_2, M_3\}$ and $\{M_5, M_6\}$ where M_1, M_4 are computed by another function calls. To make things clear about how it differs from Mixed version. Here, we specify that for all M_i we apply (1) no matter how the inter-common expressions are exploited. We find (i) as the optimal implementation[3] and the minimum mean cycles count as 193 and 194 at -O3 for modulus p and $2p$ respectively.

4.3   Arithmetic Cost

According to the best of our knowledge we provide a table of the arithmetic cost of the well-known algorithms and the three versions of our multiplication algorithm. The idea is to provide an extensive comparison and to show the robustness of our algorithm for 521-bit Mersenne prime modulus. For the Karatsuba 3-way we use the formula in [8]. We use the Toom-3 formula in [2] and find that the recursive version is not useful because with respect to Schoolbook it trades **4M** with **18A** plus some shifts and a division by 3. In addition, we couldn't find any common (sub-)expression between two levels using the Bodrato's formula therefore, recursive Toom-3 is not useful for this bit-length. The number of operations are given in Table 1 which precludes the cost of shifts, division by small constant(s), and carry propagation. From the table it is evident that for the 521-bit Mersenne prime modulus and 64-bit limb our technique is a good alternative with respect to the well-known existing multiplication algorithms.

---

[2] https://github.com/Shoukat-Ali/521-bit-Mersenne-Prime/blob/master/mixed_inline.c.

[3] https://github.com/Shoukat-Ali/521-bit-Mersenne-Prime/blob/master/recursive_v1.c.

Algorithm 1. (Hybrid version) Multiplication

Input: $F = [f_0, \ldots\ldots, f_8], G = [g_0, \ldots\ldots, g_8] \in [0, 2^{59} - 1] \times [0, 2^{58} - 1]^7 \times [0, 2^{57} - 1]$
Output: $Z = [z_0, \ldots\ldots, z_8] \in [0, 2^{59} - 1] \times [0, 2^{58} - 1]^7 \times [0, 2^{57} - 1]$ where $Z \equiv FG$
$(\bmod\ 2^{521} - 1)$

$T_5 \leftarrow 2f_8,$ $\qquad c \leftarrow 2f_7,$ $\qquad T_1[3] \leftarrow 2f_6,$ $\qquad T_1[4] \leftarrow 2f_5$
$T_1[0] \leftarrow g_0 - g_3,$ $\qquad\qquad T_1[1] \leftarrow g_1 - g_4,$ $\qquad T_1[2] \leftarrow g_2 - g_5$
$X_0 \leftarrow (f_3 \cdot T_1[0]) + (f_2 \cdot T_1[1]) + (f_1 \cdot T_1[2])$
$X_1 \leftarrow (f_4 \cdot T_1[0]) + (f_3 \cdot T_1[1]) + (f_2 \cdot T_1[2])$
$X_2 \leftarrow (f_5 \cdot T_1[0]) + (f_4 \cdot T_1[1]) + (f_3 \cdot T_1[2])$
$T_1[0] \leftarrow g_3 - g_6,$ $\qquad\qquad T_1[1] \leftarrow g_4 - g_7,$ $\qquad T_1[2] \leftarrow g_5 - g_8$
$X_6 \leftarrow (T_1[3] \cdot T_1[0]) + (T_1[4] \cdot T_1[1]) + (2f_4 \cdot T_1[2])$
$X_7 \leftarrow (c \cdot T_1[0]) + (T_1[3] \cdot T_1[1]) + (T_1[4] \cdot T_1[2])$
$X_8 \leftarrow (T_5 \cdot T_1[0]) + (c \cdot T_1[1]) + (T_1[3] \cdot T_1[2])$
$T_1[0] \leftarrow g_0 - g_6,$ $\qquad\qquad T_1[1] \leftarrow g_1 - g_7,$ $\qquad T_1[2] \leftarrow g_2 - g_8$
$X_3 \leftarrow (f_0 \cdot T_1[0]) + (T_5 \cdot T_1[1]) + (c \cdot T_1[2])$
$X_4 \leftarrow (f_1 \cdot T_1[0]) + (f_0 \cdot T_1[1]) + (T_5 \cdot T_1[2])$
$X_5 \leftarrow (f_2 \cdot T_1[0]) + (f_1 \cdot T_1[1]) + (f_0 \cdot T_1[2])$

$T_6[0] \leftarrow f_4 + f_1,$ $\qquad\qquad T_6[1] \leftarrow f_5 + f_2,$ $\qquad T_6[2] \leftarrow f_6 + f_3$
$T_6[3] \leftarrow f_7 + f_4,$ $\qquad\qquad T_6[4] \leftarrow f_8 + f_5$
$T_1[0] \leftarrow T_6[0] + c,$ $\qquad\quad T_1[1] \leftarrow T_6[1] + T_5,$ $\qquad T_1[2] \leftarrow T_6[2] + f_0$
$T_1[3] \leftarrow T_6[3] + f_1,$ $\qquad\quad T_1[4] \leftarrow T_6[4] + f_2$
$T_6[0] \leftarrow T_1[0] + T_6[0],$ $\quad T_6[1] \leftarrow T_1[1] + T_6[1],$ $\qquad T_6[2] \leftarrow T_1[2] + T_6[2]$
$T_6[3] \leftarrow T_1[3] + T_6[3],$ $\quad T_6[4] \leftarrow T_1[4] + T_6[4]$
$T_5 \leftarrow T_1[2] + f_6$

$C \leftarrow (T_1[2] \cdot g_2) + (T_1[3] \cdot g_1) + (T_1[4] \cdot g_0) - X_2 - X_5$
$c \leftarrow C \bmod 2^{57}$
$C \leftarrow (T_6[0] \cdot g_8) + (T_6[1] \cdot g_7) + (T_6[2] \cdot g_6) + X_3 + X_6 + (C \gg 57)$
$z_0 \leftarrow C \bmod 2^{58}$
$C \leftarrow (T_6[1] \cdot g_8) + (T_6[2] \cdot g_7) + (T_6[3] \cdot g_6) + X_4 + X_7 + (C \gg 58)$
$z_1 \leftarrow C \bmod 2^{58}$
$C \leftarrow (T_6[2] \cdot g_8) + (T_6[3] \cdot g_7) + (T_6[4] \cdot g_6) + X_5 + X_8 + (C \gg 58)$
$z_2 \leftarrow C \bmod 2^{58}$
$C \leftarrow (T_6[3] \cdot g_5) + (T_6[4] \cdot g_4) + (T_5 \cdot g_3) + X_0 - X_6 + (C \gg 58)$
$z_3 \leftarrow C \bmod 2^{58}$
$C \leftarrow (T_6[4] \cdot g_5) + (T_5 \cdot g_4) + (T_1[0] \cdot g_3) + X_1 - X_7 + (C \gg 58)$
$z_4 \leftarrow C \bmod 2^{58}$
$C \leftarrow (T_5 \cdot g_5) + (T_1[0] \cdot g_4) + (T_1[1] \cdot g_3) + X_2 - X_8 + (C \gg 58)$
$z_5 \leftarrow C \bmod 2^{58}$
$C \leftarrow (T_1[0] \cdot g_2) + (T_1[1] \cdot g_1) + (T_1[2] \cdot g_0) - X_0 - X_3 + (C \gg 58)$
$z_6 \leftarrow C \bmod 2^{58}$
$C \leftarrow (T_1[1] \cdot g_2) + (T_1[2] \cdot g_1) + (T_1[3] \cdot g_0) - X_1 - X_4 + (C \gg 58)$
$z_7 \leftarrow C \bmod 2^{58}$
$c \leftarrow c + (C \gg 58)$
$z_8 \leftarrow c \bmod 2^{57}$
$z_0 \leftarrow z_0 + (c \gg 57)$
Return Z

Table 1. Number of operations for modular multiplication

Technique	Arithmetic cost
Karatsuba 3-way recursive [8]	$36\mathbf{M} + 54\mathbf{A} + 93\mathbf{A}_d$
Recursive version[b] (this paper)	$36\mathbf{M} + 73\mathbf{A} + 54\mathbf{A}_d$
Toom-3 plus Schoolbook [2]	$45\mathbf{M} + 30\mathbf{A} + 76\mathbf{A}_d$
Granger-Scott[a] [6]	$45\mathbf{M} + 72\mathbf{A} + 52\mathbf{A}_d$
Mixed version[b] (this paper)	$45\mathbf{M} + 48\mathbf{A} + 54\mathbf{A}_d$
Karatsuba 3-way plus Schoolbook [8]	$54\mathbf{M} + 18\mathbf{A} + 75\mathbf{A}_d$
Hybrid version (this paper)	$54\mathbf{M} + 25\mathbf{A} + 54\mathbf{A}_d$

[a]The cost of **MUL** algorithm
[b]The cost of the optimal implementation in terms of cycles count

5   Scalar Multiplication and Timings

We use the same desktop computer with the same options as we did for the testing of the different versions of our multiplication algorithm. For scalar multiplication on NIST curve P-521 and Edwards curve E-521 we use the same code of Granger-Scott available at http://indigo.ie/~mscott/ws521.cpp and http://indigo.ie/~mscott/ed521.cpp. But for clock cycles count we use the technique — using rdtscp() for second call — suggested by Paoloni in his white paper in [7].

We run the clock cycles measurement loop of Scott in a loop of 40 iterations in order to obtain consistent cycles count. We have also checked other numbers of iterations but on our machine 40 iterations return consistent cycles count. In the Scott's programs we have replaced their multiplication algorithm by different versions of our multiplication algorithm and changes are made according to the modulus. For modulus p we have amended both ws521.cpp and ed521.cpp according to our needs that include scr(), gsqr(), gsqr2(), and gmuli().

From the results of the clock cycles count of the different versions of our algorithm with respect to the multiplication algorithm in [6], one would also expect higher number of clock cycles for scalar multiplication using our algorithm. While measuring the clock cycles and playing with gcc compiler we observed a strange behavior that when either the multiplication algorithm in [6] or our algorithm (Hybrid version) is called consecutively more than 2 times in a loop then our algorithm starts to take less and less number of cycles. Therefore, we find the cycles counts for scalar multiplication using each version of our algorithm to be less than the Granger-Scott algorithm. Since compiler optimization/behavior is not our domain so, we don't know why gcc behaves like this. For each version of our multiplication algorithm we have used the optimal implementation on our machine. But we report the cycles counts using the Hybrid version of our algorithm[4,5] which shows the least number among the different versions. Using the command openssl speed ecdh on our machine where the installed version is 1.0.2g. For

---

[4] https://github.com/Shoukat-Ali/521-bit-Mersenne-Prime/blob/master/ed521.cpp
[5] https://github.com/Shoukat-Ali/521-bit-Mersenne-Prime/blob/master/ws521.cpp

the NIST P-521 it reports 1745.1 operations per second which is approximately $1,604,493$ cycles count. The clock cycles counts are given in Table 2. Although the number of clock cycles counts with CACHE_SAFE (defined for cache safety) is more than without CACHE_SAFE option but we prefer the former choice. So, through testing with CACHE_SAFE on our machine we find the fixed window of width 4 as the optimal choice both for Granger-Scott and our algorithm. Hence, the cycles counts are for windows of width 4 with CACHE_SAFE.

Table 2. Clock Cycles counts of scalar multiplication operation; GS stands for Granger-Scott algorithm, p and $2p$ stand for modulus p and $2p$ implementation of the Hybrid version our algorithm respectively

openSSL	P-521	E-521
$\approx 1,604,493$	$GS = 1,332,165$	$GS = 1,148,871$
	$2p = 1,270,130$	$2p = 1,073,127$
	$p = 1,251,502$	$p = 1,055,105$

We have executed the scalar multiplication programs both for P-521 and E-521 multiple times in order to obtain the least cycles counts. In case of P-521 for Granger-Scott algorithm we find $1,332,165$ as the minimum mean cycles count. While for both modulus $2p$ and p of the Hybrid version of our algorithm we find $1,270,130$ and $1,251,502$ cycles respectively. Similarly, in E-521 for Granger-Scott algorithm we find $1,148,871$ as the minimum mean cycles count. However, for the modulus $2p$ and p of the Hybrid version of our algorithm we find $1,073,127$ and $1,055,105$ cycles respectively. Hence, the experimental results support our observation and intuition for multiple calls (in thousands or more) and modulus choice.

We have also tested the same (reported) programs on an Intel Core i7 − 2670QM CPU @ 2.20 GHz with Turbo Boost and Hyper-Threading being enabled. Again the clock cycles counts of the programs using our multiplication algorithm (Hybrid version) are less than Granger-Scott algorithm and the minimum clock cycles is found for modulus p. In this testing we find that for P-521 the minimum mean clock cycles counts are $GS = 1,063,370$ and $p = 1,001,180$ with window of size 5 and 4 respectively. On the other hand, for E-521 we have $GS = 893,371$ and $p = 847,145$ with window of size 4.

6   Conclusion

In this paper we have proposed a new algorithm for residue mutliplication modulo the Mersenne prime $2^{521} − 1$ using the Toeplitz Matrix-Vector Product (TMVP) approach. Our algorithm takes less number of operations than Granger-Scott algorithm [6] in total. To show the robustness of our algorithm for the 521-bit Mersenne prime modulus we have implemented three versions of our algorithm and provide a comprehensive comparsion — according to the best of our knowledge — in terms of the arithmetic cost with respect to the well-known efficient algorithms. We have tested the three versions of our algorithm individually and also as part of the scalar multiplication in elliptic curve cryptography (ECC). We have computed the clock cycles of all the programs at optimization level three i.e. -O3. In spite of the less number of operations, the implementation results — minimum mean clock cycles count — of the three versions of our multiplication algorithm depict a different story with respect to Granger-Scott multiplication algorithm. But for scalar multiplication all the three versions of our algorithm report less number of clock cycles count. We have covered the details of modulus p which shows better implementation results than the modulus $2p$, discussed in [6]. That is why, we have reported the implementation results of both modulus p and $2p$.

Acknowledgments. We are very thankful to Michael Scott for answering our questions related to implementation. This work is supported by TÜBİTAK under Grant No. BIDEB-114C052 and EEEAG-115R289.

References

1. Bernstein, D.J., Chuengsatiansup, C., Lange, T.: Curve41417: Karatsuba revisited. In: Batina, L., Robshaw, M. (eds.) CHES 2014. LNCS, vol. 8731, pp. 316–334. Springer, Heidelberg (2014). doi:10.1007/978-3-662-44709-3_18
2. Bodrato, M.: Towards optimal toom-cook multiplication for univariate and multivariate polynomials in characteristic 2 and 0. In: Carlet, C., Sunar, B. (eds.) WAIFI 2007. LNCS, vol. 4547, pp. 116–133. Springer, Heidelberg (2007). doi:10. 1007/978-3-540-73074-3_10
3. Certicom Research. SEC 2: recommended elliptic curve domain parameters. In: Proceeding of Standards for Efficient Cryptography, Version 2.0, 27 January 2010
4. Fan, H., Hasan, M.A.: A new approach to subquadratic space complexity parallel multipliers for extended binary fields. IEEE Trans. Comput. **56**(2), 224–233 (2007)
5. FIPS PUB 186-4: Federal information processing standards publication. Digital Signature Standard (DSS), Information Technology Laboratory, National Institute of Standards and Technology (NIST), Gaithersburg, MD 20899-8900, July 2013
6. Granger, R., Scott, M.: Faster ECC over $\mathbb{F}_{2^{521}-1}$. In: Katz, J. (ed.) PKC 2015. LNCS, vol. 9020, pp. 539–553. Springer, Heidelberg (2015). doi:10.1007/978-3-662-46447-2_24
7. Paoloni, G.: How to benchmark code execution times on Intel IA-32 and IA-64 instruction set architectures, p. 123. Intel Corporation, September 2010
8. Weimerskirch, A., Paar, C.: Generalizations of the Karatsuba algorithm for efficient implementations. In: IACR Cryptology ePrint Archive 2006, p. 224 (2006)

Enhancing Data Parallelism of Fully Homomorphic Encryption

Paulo Martins[(✉)] and Leonel Sousa

INESC-ID, Instituto Superior Técnico,
Universidade de Lisboa, Rua Alves Redol, 9, 1000-029 Lisboa, Portugal
paulo.sergio@netcabo.pt, las@inesc-id.pt

Abstract. With Fully Homomorphic Encryption (FHE), it is possible to produce encryptions of the addition and multiplication of encrypted values without access to the private-key. Since homomorphic multiplication is the most burdensome operation of FHE, every possible improvement to it has a significant impact on the performance of the homomorphic evaluation of arbitrary functions. In this paper, we propose an optimized homomorphic multiplication algorithm and apply it to the NTT-based Fast Lattice library (NFLlib), which is a library designed for the implementation of Lattice-based Cryptography (LBC). When implemented with AVX2 Single Instruction Multiple Data (SIMD) extensions on a i7-4770k CPU, the proposed algorithm produces a normalized speed-up of 1.93 when compared with the fastest AVX2 implementation of the state of the art. Furthermore, when extended to decryption, the new method achieves a normalized speed-up of 2.0 when compared with related art.

Keywords: Homomorphic Encryption · Data parallelism · Ring learning with errors

1 Introduction

The use of embedded systems is becoming ubiquitous, as more sensors and actuators are incorporated into everyday electronics and on the general infrastructure. Since these devices often have limited computational resources, it would be beneficial to offload parts of their computation to a third party. However, the processed data may be private, which means that the third party should not have access to it. This problem can be solved with Homomorphic Encryption (HE), which enables the direct processing of encrypted data [14].

With HE schemes, the computation is not described based on sequential programs but using arithmetic circuits, where signals pass through a cascade of logic gates. This type of description is similar to how Boolean circuits are represented. For the Fan-Vercauteren (FV) scheme [6], the homomorphic addition of values, which when the plaintext is instantiated with binary fields corresponds to the evaluation of XOR gates, is implemented as the addition of two elements in a polynomial ring. In contrast, homomorphic multiplications, corresponding to

© Springer International Publishing AG 2017
S. Hong and J.H. Park (Eds.): ICISC 2016, LNCS 10157, pp. 194–207, 2017.
DOI: 10.1007/978-3-319-53177-9_10

AND gates, are dependent not only of multiplications and additions of elements in polynomial rings, but also of scaling and division of large numbers.

The NFLlib library [1] provides a way to efficiently perform arithmetic over rings of the form $\mathfrak{R}_q = \mathbb{Z}_q[x]/(x^n+1)$, where n is a power of two, with which it is possible to implement schemes like FV. The value of q is chosen as a product of primes satisfying $q_i = 1 \bmod 2n$ ($q = \prod_{i=0}^{h_1-1} q_i$) mainly by two reasons: (i) it is possible to represent numbers modulo q by their remainders modulo $q_i, \forall i$, using the Chinese Remainder Theorem CRT; (ii) due to the form of the q_i, it is possible to transform polynomials using the Number Theoretic Transform NTT, enabling multiplications of polynomials to be done coefficient-wise. This representation of elements of $\mathfrak{R}_q$ is very suitable to parallelization. Aguilar-Melchor et al. have used SIMD extensions to improve the performance of NFLlib. However, they faced problems when testing their library for the FV scheme, and stated that "The relatively small gain on the homomorphic multiplication can be explained by the fact that the (...) procedure is essentially constituted of operations independent of NFLlib, such as divisions and rounding" [1].

Herein, we propose algorithmic improvements to homomorphic mutliplication, namely by changing the underlying computation so that most of it can be performed directly using the CRT representation. Due to the way the cryptosystem was constructed, the decryption operation depends on similar operations but to a lesser extent. Thus, the proposed techniques naturally extend to the decryption procedure, also improving the performance in that case. It should be also noticed that other cryptosystems rely on similar operations, such as the ones proposed in [3,11], and thus the techniques herein presented can be easily extended to those settings.

2   Background

This work adopts the polynomial ring $\mathfrak{R} = \mathbb{Z}[x]/(\Phi_m(x))$, where $\Phi_m(x)$ is a cyclotomic ring with degree $n = \varphi(m)$ (φ denotes Euler's totient function) [7]. Typically m is set to $m = 2n$, with n a power of two, which leads to $\Phi_m(x) = x^n + 1$. The expansion factor of $\mathfrak{R}$ is

$$\delta_{\mathfrak{R}} = \max\{\|ab\|/(\|a\|\|b\|) : a, b \in \mathfrak{R}\} \tag{1}$$

where $\|a\|$ corresponds to the infinity norm, i.e. for $a \in \mathfrak{R}$ with $a = \sum_{i=0}^{n-1} a[i]x^i$, $\|a\| = \max_i|a[i]|$. Also, $\mathfrak{R}_q$ is used to describe the ring $\mathbb{Z}_q[x]/(\Phi(x))$, where $\mathbb{Z}_q$ is the ring $\mathbb{Z}/(q\mathbb{Z})$. Let $q > 1$ be an integer, $\mathbb{Z}_q$ denotes the set of integers in $(-q/2, q/2]$. Similarly, R_q denotes the set of polynomials in $\mathfrak{R}$ with coefficients in $\mathbb{Z}_q$.

For $a \in \mathbb{Z}$, the notation $[a]_q$ represents the unique integer in $\mathbb{Z}_q$ with $[a]_q = a \pmod q$, and $a \bmod q$, without parenthesis, is used to denote $a - \lfloor a/q \rfloor q$. For $a \in \mathbb{Q}$, $b = \lfloor a \rceil$ is used to denote the closest integer $b \in \mathbb{Z}$ to a, with ties broken upward. $\langle a, b \rangle$ is used to denote the inner product of two vectors $a, b \in \mathfrak{R}^l$. Often, $f(a)$, for $f : \mathbb{Z}_q \to \mathbb{Z}_{q'}$ and $a \in \mathbb{Z}_q^l$, will be used to denote the result of applying f to all entries of vector a. Furthermore, fixed an integer w, let $l_{w,q} = \lfloor \log_w(q) \rfloor + 1$.

A polynomial in R_q can be rewritten in base w as $\sum_{i=0}^{l_{w,q}-1} a_i w^i$, where the $a_i \in \mathfrak{R}$ have coefficients in $(-w/2, w/2]$. Moreover, the functions $\mathrm{Decomp}_{w,q}$ and $\mathrm{Powers}_{w,q}$ are defined as:

$$\mathrm{Decomp}_{w,q}(a) = ([a_i]_w)_{i=0}^{l_{w,q}-1}; \ \mathrm{Powers}_{w,q}(a) = ([aw^i]_q)_{i=0}^{l_{w,q}-1} \tag{2}$$

Note that

$$\langle \mathrm{Decomp}_{w,q}(a), \mathrm{Powers}_{w,q}(b) \rangle = ab (\mathrm{mod} q) \tag{3}$$

Finally, let χ_{key} be a distribution in $\mathfrak{R}[x]$ with coefficients drawn at random from $\{-1, 0, 1\}$, and χ_{err} a discrete Gaussian distribution with mean 0.

2.1   Fan-Vercauteren Scheme

This paper is focused on the homomorphic multiplication of ciphertexts of the FV scheme [6]. This scheme is supported on [2]. An explanation on how to select parameters ensuring both security and correctness of the homomorphic evaluation of circuits can be found in [6,11]. A private-key is generated as $s \leftarrow \chi_{key}$, and the corresponding public-key is computed as $(b = [-(as + e)]_q, a)$, where $a \leftarrow R_q$ is drawn uniformly at random from R_q, and $e \leftarrow \chi_{err}$. The homomorphic multiplication is supported on an evaluation key:

$$\gamma = ([\mathrm{Powers}_{w,q}(s^2) - (e + as)]_q, a) \tag{4}$$

where $e \leftarrow \chi_{err}^{l_{w,q}}$, and $a \leftarrow R_q^{l_{w,q}}$ is drawn uniformly at random from $R_q^{l_{w,q}}$. To encrypt a message $m \in R_t$, $u \leftarrow \chi_{key}$ and $e_1, e_2 \leftarrow \chi_{err}$ are randomly chosen and c is computed ($\Delta = \lfloor q/t \rfloor$):

$$c = ([\Delta m + bu + e_1]_q, [au + e_2]_q) \tag{5}$$

Decryption is correctly performed as long as $\|v\| < \Delta/2$ for $[c_0 + c_1 s]_q = \Delta m + v$ and is computed as

$$m = \left[\left\lfloor \frac{t}{q} [c_0 + c_1 s]_q \right\rceil \right]_t \tag{6}$$

Given two ciphertexts $c_1 = (c_{1,0}, c_{1,1})$ and $c_2 = (c_{2,0}, c_{2,1})$, encrypting messages m_1 and m_2, their homomorphic addition is computed as $c_{add} = ([c_{1,0} + c_{2,0}]_q, [c_{1,1} + c_{2,1}]_q)$. This operation adds the plaintexts in $\mathfrak{R}_t$, and roughly adds the underlying noise terms. Homomorphic multiplications proceed in two steps. In the first step, Eq. (7) is computed.

$$c_{mult} = \left(\left[\left\lfloor \frac{t}{q} c_{1,0} c_{2,0} \right\rceil \right]_q, \left[\left\lfloor \frac{t}{q} (c_{1,1} c_{2,0} + c_{1,0} c_{2,1}) \right\rceil \right]_q, \left[\left\lfloor \frac{t}{q} c_{1,1} c_{2,1} \right\rceil \right]_q \right) \tag{7}$$

According to [6, Lemma 2], if $[c_{i,0} + c_{i,1} s]_q = \Delta m_i + v_i$ and $\|v_i\| < E < \Delta/2$, where the v_i correspond to the error terms, then:

$$\left[c_{mult,0} + c_{mult,1} s + c_{mult,2} s^2 \right]_q = \Delta [m_1 m_2]_t + v_3 \tag{8}$$

with $\|v_3\| < 2\delta_{\Re}tE(\delta_{\Re} + 1) + 8t^2\delta_{\Re}^2$. In a second step, to convert $\boldsymbol{c_{mult}}$ to a vector of dimension two, the relinearization procedure of Eq. (9) is applied.

$$c_3 = \Big([c_{mult,0} + \langle \text{Decomp}_{w,q}(c_{mult,2}), \boldsymbol{\gamma_0} \rangle]_q,$$

$$[c_{mult,1} + \langle \text{Decomp}_{w,q}(c_{mult,2}), \boldsymbol{\gamma_1} \rangle]_q \Big) \quad (9)$$

This procedure is underpinned by the fact that

$$[c_{3,0} + c_{3,1}s]_q = [c_{mult,0} + c_{mult,1}s + c_{mult,2}s^2 - \langle \text{Decomp}_{w,q}(c_{mult,2}), e \rangle]_q \tag{10}$$

and therefore the noise introduced by relinearisation is bounded by $l_{w,q}B_{err}w\delta_{\Re}/2$, where B_{err} is a value that bounds the norm of χ_{err} with high probability. c_3 can be deciphered by applying the original decryption procedure to produce m_1m_2.

2.2   Chinese Residue Theorem and Number Theoretic Transform

Throughout the paper we will be working with moduli q that are composite and square-free with factorization $q = q_0 \ldots q_{h_1-1}$. The CRT states that there is an isomorphism:

$$\text{CRT}_q : \Re_q \to \Re_{q_0} \times \ldots \times \Re_{q_{h_1-1}},$$
$$a \to (a_0, \ldots, a_{h_1-1}) = ([a]_{q_0}, \ldots, [a]_{q_{h_1-1}}) \tag{11}$$

In particular, the CRT is an invertible map such that $\text{CRT}_q(a + b) = \text{CRT}_q(a) + \text{CRT}_q(b)$ and $\text{CRT}_q(ab) = \text{CRT}_q(a) \cdot \text{CRT}_q(b)$, where the operation "$\cdot$" denotes coefficient-wise modular multiplication.

Multiplication of a and b ($a, b \in \Re_{q_i}$) for $\Phi_m(x) = x^n + 1$, corresponds to the negative wrapped convolution of the coefficients of a and b. In particular if $c = ab$, then the coefficients of c are computed as:

$$c[j] = \left[\sum_{k=0}^{n-1} (-1)^{\lfloor \frac{j-k}{n} \rfloor} a[k]b[j-k \bmod n] \right]_{q_i}, \forall j \in [0, n) \tag{12}$$

There is a faster multiplication algorithm than the direct evaluation of Eq. (12), whose complexity is $\mathcal{O}(n^2)$. An instantiation of the Fast Fourier Transform (FFT), popularized by Cooley and Tukey [4], in a finite field, denoted NTT, allows for the same multiplication to take place in quasi-linear time $\mathcal{O}(n \log n)$. The values of q_i are chosen such that there exists $\phi_i^{2n} = 1(\bmod q_i)$, and $\phi_i^j \neq 1(\bmod q_i), \forall j \in [0, 2n)$, namely by choosing primes q_i that satisfy $q_i = 1 \bmod 2n$. Let $\omega = \phi^2$, the NTT_{q_i} and $\text{NTT}_{q_i}^{-1}$ functions are defined as:

$$A[j] = \text{NTT}_{q_i}(a)[j] = \left[\sum_{k=0}^{n-1} a[k]\omega^{jk} \right]_{q_i}, \forall j \in [0, n) \tag{13}$$

$$a[j] = \text{NTT}_{q_i}^{-1}(A)[j] = \left[n^{-1} \sum_{k=0}^{n-1} A[k]\omega^{-jk} \right]_{q_i}, \forall j \in [0, n) \tag{14}$$

where $\left[x^{-1}\right]_{q_i}$ denotes the modular multiplicative inverse of x, i.e. $\left[xx^{-1}\right]_{q_i} = 1$.

Furthermore, let $\bar{a}, \bar{b}$ and $\bar{c}$ be defined as $\bar{a}[j] = a[j]\phi_i^j$, $\bar{b}[j] = b[j]\phi_i^j$ and $\bar{c}[j] = c[j]\phi_i^j$, $\forall_j$. Then $\bar{c} = \mathrm{NTT}_{q_i}^{-1}(\mathrm{NTT}_{q_i}(\bar{a}) \cdot \mathrm{NTT}_{q_i}(\bar{b}))$ [12].

These two approaches can be combined, namely by representing polynomials in the CRT and the NTT domains, which enable very efficient implementations of addition and multiplication: one can add and multiply the polynomials coefficient-wise, while for instance exploiting SIMD extensions. This is the approach followed by NFLlib. However, some operations such as $\mathrm{Decomp}_{l,w}$ require the polynomials to be represented in the "natural" domain.

2.3   Mixed Radix System

The Mixed Radix System (MRS) is a representation system that will be used in this paper to optimize the homomorphic multiplication operation. A polynomial $a \in R_q$, with $q = q_0 \ldots q_{h_1-1}$ as in the previous section, is represented by polynomials $\hat{a}_i$ (herein denoted as mixed radix digits) with coefficients in $(-q_i/2, q_i/2]$ such that:

$$a = \hat{a}_0 + \hat{a}_1 q_0 + \hat{a}_2 q_0 q_1 + \ldots + \hat{a}_{h-1} q_0 q_1 \ldots q_{h_1-2} \tag{15}$$

There is a direct relation, described in Eq. (16), between the polynomials $\hat{a}_i$ and the polynomials $a_i = [a]_{q_i}$ obtained through CRT remaindering.

$$\hat{a}_0 = a_0, \quad \hat{a}_1 = \left[(a_1 - \hat{a}_0)q_0^{-1}\right]_{q_1}$$

$$\ldots \tag{16}$$

$$\hat{a}_{h_1-1} = \left[((((a_{h_1-1} - \hat{a}_0)q_0^{-1} - \hat{a}_1)q_1^{-1} - \ldots)q_{h_1-3}^{-1} - \hat{a}_{h_1-2})q_{h_1-2}^{-1}\right]_{q_{h_1-1}}$$

It can be seen that after computing the $\hat{a}_i$ polynomials, Eq. (15) gives us a way to invert CRT remaindering.

3   Homomorphic Multiplication Algorithm

A straightforward algorithm for homomorphic multiplication, the Naive Homomorphic Multiplication (NHM), is presented in Fig. 1(a). Assuming the ciphertexts to be multiplied, $\boldsymbol{c_1}, \boldsymbol{c_2}$, are represented in the CRT and NTT domains, one would first reverse this representation[1], so that following operations can be implemented in a different ring:

$$c_{i,j} := \mathrm{CRT}_q^{-1}(\mathrm{NTT}_q^{-1}(c_{i,j})), \forall i \in \{1, 2\}, j \in \{0, 1\} \tag{17}$$

As depicted in Fig. 1(a), by the label in the middle gray box, this representation is used to implement arithmetic in $\mathfrak{R}$. Thus one can now compute

$$\boldsymbol{c'_{mult}} := (tc_{1,0}c_{2,0}, t(c_{1,1}c_{2,0} + c_{1,0}c_{2,1}), tc_{1,1}c_{2,1}) \tag{18}$$

---

[1] := is used to denote imperative assignment.

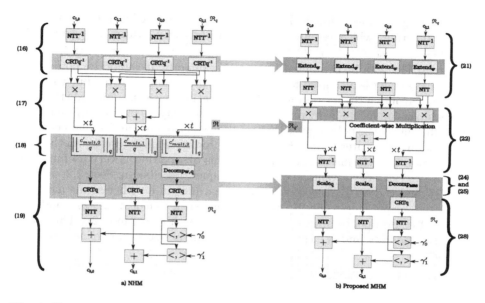

Fig. 1. Homomorphic multiplication algorithms for FV with highlighted differences: (a) Naive Homomorphic Multiplication (NHM); (b) MRS-based Homomorphic Multiplication (MHM)

without modular reductions. A scaling operation would follow in the algorithm:

$$c_{mult} := \left[\left\lfloor \frac{c'_{mult}}{q} \right\rceil \right]_q \tag{19}$$

Afterwards, Eq. (9) would be evaluated, and since it is reduced modulo q, it can be evaluated in $\mathfrak{R}_q$ by computing:

$$c_3 := \left([\mathrm{NTT}_q(\mathrm{CRT}_q(c_{mult,0})) + \langle \mathrm{NTT}_q(\mathrm{CRT}_q(\mathrm{Decomp}_{w,q}(c_{mult,2}))), \gamma_0 \rangle]_q , \right.$$
$$\left. [\mathrm{NTT}_q(\mathrm{CRT}_q(c_{mult,1})) + \langle \mathrm{NTT}_q(\mathrm{CRT}_q(\mathrm{Decomp}_{w,q}(c_{mult,2}))), \gamma_1 \rangle]_q \right)$$
$$\tag{20}$$

where it is assumed that γ is represented in the CRT and NTT domain.

3.1 Proposed MRS-based Homomorphic Multiplication Algorithm

The proposed MRS-based Homomorphic Multiplication (MHM) Algorithm is depicted in Fig. 1(b). The main contributions of this proposal are the introduction of functions Extend_{qr}, Scale_q and Decomp_{MRS}. The Extend_{qr} function maps polynomials from a ring $\mathfrak{R}_q$ to a larger ring $\mathfrak{R}_{q'}$, through a process that exploits the MRS, which is quite suitable to parallelization. Functions Scale_q and Decomp_{MRS} compute the scaling of polynomials and polynomial digit decomposition, respectively. They also exploit the MRS, enabling data parallelism.

Analysing the algorithm in Fig. 1(b), firstly, instead of computing the full CRT_q^{-1} function, which requires costly multi-precision arithmetic, we simply extend the representation of $\text{NTT}_q^{-1}(c_{i,j})$ to a ring with a larger dynamic range, so that Eq. (18) can be computed in that ring directly. It should be noted that in [8] a larger ring is also used for a similar cryptographic scheme, but with the purpose of avoiding the bit-decomposition operation, with the downside that the lattice dimension has to be increased to provide security. In our case, if we bound the coefficients of the polynomials that result from (18), one can see that choosing a new moduli q' greater than this value will produce similar results whether the computation is performed in $\mathfrak{R}$ or in $\mathfrak{R}_{q'}$. This observation is very useful, since it means we can take advantage of the techniques described in Sect. 2.2, namely the CRT and the NTT, to compute expression (18) in an efficient manner. We choose the second ring to be $\mathfrak{R}_{q'}$ with $q' = qr$, such that $q' > 2t\delta_{\mathfrak{R}}q^2$, and r is a square-free product of primes $r = r_0 \ldots r_{h_2-1}$, with $r_i = 1 \bmod 2n$. Thus both CRT remaindering and NTTs are applicable. Furthermore, we define Extend_{qr} as follows:

$$\text{Extend}_{qr} : \mathfrak{R}_{q_0} \times \ldots \times \mathfrak{R}_{q_{h_1-1}} \to \mathfrak{R}_{q_0} \times \ldots \times \mathfrak{R}_{q_{h_1-1}} \times \mathfrak{R}_{r_0} \times \ldots \times \mathfrak{R}_{r_{h_2-1}}$$

$$(a_0, \ldots, a_{h_1-1}) \to (a_0, \ldots, a_{h_1-1}, [\hat{a}_0 + \hat{a}_1 q_0 + \ldots + \hat{a}_{h-1} q_0 \ldots q_{h_1-2}]_{r_0},$$
$$[\hat{a}_0 + \hat{a}_1 q_0 + \ldots + \hat{a}_{h-1} q_0 \ldots q_{h_1-2}]_{r_1}, \ldots,$$
$$[\hat{a}_0 + \hat{a}_1 q_0 + \ldots + \hat{a}_{h-1} q_0 \ldots q_{h_1-2}]_{r_{h_2-1}})$$

$$(21)$$

where the $\hat{a}_i$ correspond to the mixed radix digits of a in Eq. (16). Thus, (17) can be replaced by

$$c_{i,j} := \text{NTT}_{qr}(\text{Extend}_{qr}(\text{NTT}_q^{-1}(c_{i,j}))), \forall i \in \{1,2\}, j \in \{0,1\} \qquad (22)$$

and the operations of Eq. (18) are now implemented using Eq. (23) with coefficient-wise additions and multiplications.

$$\boldsymbol{c'_{mult}} := \text{NTT}_{qr}^{-1}((tc_{1,0} \cdot c_{2,0}, t(c_{1,1} \cdot c_{2,0} + c_{1,0} \cdot c_{2,1}), tc_{1,1} \cdot c_{2,1})) \qquad (23)$$

Additionally, we propose an enhancement to Eq. (19) that allows for an efficient implementation of the scaling operation. Concretely, if we consider the mixed radix digits of a polynomial $a \in \mathfrak{R}_{q'}$, $(\hat{a}_0, \ldots, \hat{a}_{h_1+h_2-1})$, after dividing it by q and rounding to the closest integer, only the highest order digits remain:

$$\left[\left[\left\lfloor \frac{a}{q} \right\rceil\right]\right]_q = \left[\left[\left\lfloor \frac{\sum_{i=0}^{h_1-1} \hat{a}_i \prod_{0 \le j < i} q_j + q \sum_{i=0}^{h_2-1} \hat{a}_{h_1+i} \prod_{0 \le j < i} r_j}{q} \right\rceil\right]\right]_q =$$

$$[\hat{a}_{h_1} + \hat{a}_{h_1+1} r_0 + \ldots + \hat{a}_{h_1+h_2-1} r_0 \ldots r_{h_2-2}]_q \qquad (24)$$

since $\left|\sum_{i=0}^{h_1-1}\hat{a}_i\prod_{0\leq j<i}q_j\right| < q/2$. According to Eqs. (19) and (24) is rewritten for $c_{mult,0}$ and $c_{mult,1}$ as the implementation of function Scale_q:

$$\text{Scale}_q : \mathfrak{R}_{q_0}\times\ldots\times\mathfrak{R}_{q_{h_1-1}}\times\mathfrak{R}_{r_0}\times\ldots\times\mathfrak{R}_{r_{h_2-1}}\to\mathfrak{R}_{q_0}\times\ldots\times\mathfrak{R}_{q_{h_1-1}}$$

$$c'_{mult,i}\to\left(\left[\widehat{c'_{mult,i_{h_1}}}+\widehat{c'_{mult,i_{h_1+1}}}r_0+\ldots+\widehat{c'_{mult,i_{h_1+h_2+1}}}r_0\ldots r_{h_2-2}\right]_{q_0},\right.$$

$$\left[\widehat{c'_{mult,i_{h_1}}}+\widehat{c'_{mult,i_{h_1+1}}}r_0+\ldots+\widehat{c'_{mult,i_{h_1+h_2+1}}}r_0\ldots r_{h_2-2}\right]_{q_1},$$

$$\ldots$$

$$\left.\left[\widehat{c'_{mult,i_{h_1}}}+\widehat{c'_{mult,i_{h_1+1}}}r_0+\ldots+\widehat{c'_{mult,i_{h_1+h_2+1}}}r_0\ldots r_{h_2-2}\right]_{q_{h_1-1}}\right)$$

$$(25)$$

It should be noted that $c'_{mult,i}$ is inputted in the CRT domain, and therefore the computation of the mixed radix digits $\widehat{c'_{mult,i_j}}$ is very efficient. Moreover, we redefine the Decomp function to exploit the MRS for digit decomposition of polynomials:

$$\text{Decomp}_{MRS}(c_{mult,2}) = (\widehat{c'_{mult,2_{h_1}}},\ldots,\widehat{c'_{mult,2_{h_1+h_2-1}}})\qquad(26)$$

which is also computed very efficiently from the CRT values of $c'_{mult,2}$. For this definition to be valid, the evaluation key also has to be redefined as:

$$\boldsymbol{\gamma}' = ([\text{Powers}_{MRS}(s^2)-(\boldsymbol{e}+\boldsymbol{a}s)]_q,\boldsymbol{a})\in R^{h_2}\qquad(27)$$

where s, e and $\boldsymbol{a}$ are as defined in Sect. 2.1, and

$$\text{Powers}_{MRS}(s^2) = (s^2,s^2r_0,s^2r_0r_1,\ldots,s^2r_0r_1\ldots r_{h_2-2})\qquad(28)$$

Finally, since $c_{mult,0}$ and $c_{mult,1}$ are already in the CRT domain, Eq. (20) is redefined as:

$$\boldsymbol{c_3}:=([\text{NTT}_q(c_{mult,0})+\langle\text{NTT}_q(\text{CRT}_q(\text{Decomp}_{MRS}(c_{mult,2}))),\boldsymbol{\gamma'_0}\rangle]_q,$$
$$\left[\text{NTT}_q(c_{mult,1})+\langle\text{NTT}_q(\text{CRT}_q(\text{Decomp}_{MRS}(c_{mult,2}))),\boldsymbol{\gamma'_1}\rangle\right]_q)\qquad(29)$$

The polynomials in $\text{Decomp}_{MRS}(c_{mult,2})$ have coefficients with small values, and therefore the computation of the CRT_q remaindering function is very simple, corresponding in general to a single addition or subtraction by q_i for each channel. $\boldsymbol{c_3}$ now satisfies:

$$[c_{3,0}+c_{3,1}s]_q = [c_{mult,0}+c_{mult,1}s+c_{mult,2}s^2-\langle\text{Decomp}_{MRS}(c_{mult,2}),\boldsymbol{e}\rangle]_q$$

$$(30)$$

which corresponds to an encryption of the product of the values encrypted by c_1 and c_2 (cf. Eq. (8)). The noise increase due to the new relinearisation procedure is bounded by $h_2B_{err}\max_i r_i\delta_{\mathfrak{R}}/2$ (due to the way the Decomp function was redefined, one needs to update the bound on the relinearisation noise term referred in Sect. 2.1, by replacing $l_{w,q}$ with h_2 and w by $\max_i r_i$).

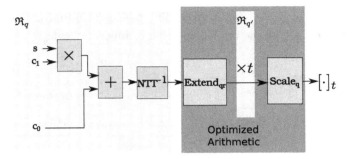

Fig. 2. MRS-based decryption algorithm for FV

3.2   Decryption Algorithm

One can see from Eq. (6) that some of the operations involved in decryption are similar to the ones that were optimized in Sect. 3.1. Herein, we propose the exploitation of functions Extend_{qr} and Scale_q to implement also the decryption procedure, as described in Fig. 2. In particular, one starts by computing the value of $[c_0 + c_1 s]_q$ over $\mathfrak{R}_q$. Afterwards, the NTT transform is inverted, and $[c_0 + c_1 s]_q$ is extended to a larger ring $\mathfrak{R}_{q'}$ with $q' = qr$. Unlike for homomorphic multiplication, q' is only slighter larger than q, and it has to satisfy $q' \geq qt$. Thus r will typically consist of a small prime. Then, it is possible to compute $u = t[c_0 + c_1 s]_q$. Furthermore, if r is chosen as a single small prime, the Scale_q function in this case corresponds solely to the computation of the MRS digits. In particular, for the polynomial u, the function will compute $\hat{u}_0, \hat{u}_1, \ldots, \hat{u}_{h_1}$ and output $\hat{u}_{h_1}$, as per Eq. (24). Finally, a reduction modulo t is applied.

4   Implementation Details and Experimental Results

The proposed algorithms were programmed and run on an Intel Core i7-4770k CPU, operated at 3.5GHz, and featuring 32GB of main memory. This processor has both SSE4.2 and AVX2 SIMD extensions [10], enabling the processing of 128 and 256 bits simultaneously, which we have exploited to accelerate the execution of the proposed algorithms (Figs. 1(b) and 2). Furthermore, we have used the NFLlib library [1] for the implementation of ring arithmetic, corresponding to the operations in $\mathfrak{R}_q$ or $\mathfrak{R}_{q'}$ in Figs. 1 and 2. We have exploited one set of parameters provided by the library where the q_i and the r_i are 30-bits wide, and a lazy modular reduction algorithm is used for computing the NTT [1]. The 30-bit CRT remainders map nicely into the SIMD registers, allowing one to operate on 4 remainders at a time when using SSE4.2, or 8 when using AVX2.

A core operation that is featured in functions Extend_{qr}, Scale_q and Decomp_{MRS} is the computation of the mixed radix digits. These values were computed as described in Eq. (16) using SIMD extensions to process multiple polynomial coefficients at the same time. Moreover, the required modular

Algorithm 1. Optimized Modular Multiplication Algorithm

Require: $a, b \in [0, q_i)$
Require: $b' = \lfloor (b\beta)/q_i \rfloor$
Ensure: $c = a \times b \bmod q_i \in [0, q_i)$
  $s := \lfloor (ab')/\beta \rfloor$
  $c := ab - sq_i \bmod \beta$
  if $c \geq q_i$ **then**
    $c := c - q_i$
  end if
  return c

Table 1. Average execution time for a single homomorphic multiplication. The values inside parenthesis in the SEQ column refer to the speed-up of the proposed sequential MHM when compared with the NHM

Platform	L	n	$\log_2 w$	$\log_2 q$	Naive	SEQ	SSE4.2	AVX2	Notes
i7-4770k	1	4096	32	120	1.46 s	9.31 ms (157)	7.67 ms	7.39 ms	
Xeon E5-2666 v3	1	4096	32	124	-	-	-	17.2 ms	In [1]
i7-2600	1	4096	32	127	-	148 ms	-	-	In [11]
i7-4770k	10	8192	32	300	14.0 s	78.8 ms (178)	60.3 ms	54.5 ms	
i7-4770k	31	16384	70	810	186 s	977 ms (190)	711 ms	597 ms	
i7-4770k	44	32768	205	1230	1609 s	4.01 s (401)	2.85 s	2.59 s	

inverses were pre-computed. Expression (15) that appears both in functions Extend_{qr} and Scale_q, but computed modulo r_i or q_i, was implemented using Horner's rule [5].

Operations inside each channel q_i were implemented with representation on $[0, q_i)$, and their values are only converted to $(-q_i/2, q_i/2]$ when used in other channels (for instance, when using the value $\hat{a}_i$ in channel q_j in Eq. (16)). After importing a value $z_i \in (-q_i/2, q_i/2]$ from channel q_i to a channel q_j, its value is mapped to $[0, q_j)$, by adding or subtracting a multiple of q_j. This solution ensures mathematical correctness and enables a more efficient arithmetic while numbers are used strictly inside a channel.

Furthermore, since in all modular multiplications of the functions Extend_{qr}, Scale_q and Decomp_{MRS} one of the operands is known beforehand, an optimized multiplication algorithm was adopted. This technique was based on the modular multiplication algorithm used in NFLlib for the computation of the NTT. For a multiplication $c = a \times b \bmod q_i$, with $c, a, b \in [0, q_i)$, the value of $b' = \lfloor (b\beta)/q_i \rfloor$ was pre-computed for $\beta = 2^{32}$, and c was evaluated as described in Algorithm 1. The value of β was selected to be $\beta = 2^{32}$ because we have adopted 32-bit lanes for the SIMD registers.

Several versions of the homomorphic multiplication algorithm were implemented, compiled with g++ 4.9.2 [13] with the -O3 flag, and tested on the Intel Core i7-4770k CPU. The first is an implementation of the NHM, where the NFLlib [1] was used for the computations over $\mathfrak{R}_q$ without SIMD extensions,

Table 2. Average execution time for the decryption operation

Platform	L	n	$\log_2 w$	$\log_2 q$	Naive	SEQ	SSE4.2	AVX2	Notes
i7-4770k	1	4096	32	120	1.28 ms	577 μs	403 μs	373 μs	
Xeon E5-2666 v3	1	4096	32	124	-	-	-	900 μs	In [1]
i7-2600	1	4096	32	127	-	16 ms	-	-	In [11]
i7-4770k	10	8192	32	300	11.5 ms	4.21 ms	2.56 ms	2.16 ms	
i7-4770k	31	16384	70	810	146 ms	45.2 ms	23.6 ms	18.0 ms	
i7-4770k	44	32768	205	1230	692 ms	187 ms	90.0 ms	66.7 ms	

and a naive polynomial arithmetic was used for the implementation of arithmetic modulo $\mathfrak{R}$ in the middle gray box of Fig. 1(a), namely by implementing polynomial multiplication as described in Eq. (12) but over $\mathbb{Z}$ using GMP 6.0.0 [9]. The other three implementations refer to different instances of the MHM, which was depicted in Fig. 1(b): one where no SIMD extensions are used (SEQ), a second one where SSE4.2 is applied, and a third one with AVX2. The execution times of a single homomorphic multiplication for the NHM, the proposed MHM and related art can be found in Table 1. The value of L corresponds to the maximum level of homomorphic multiplications that can be performed for $t = 2$ with the defined values of n (the degree of the polynomial of the underlying ring), w (a parameter of the Decomp and Powers functions when Decomp$_{MRS}$ is not used), and $\log_2 q$ (an approximation of the logarithm of the underlying modulus). Furthermore, the results were verified for $\sigma_{err} = 8$ (corresponding to the standard deviation of the distribution χ_{err}).

Observing the results in Table 1, one can conclude that the proposed algorithm is much faster than the naive implementation. For the sequential MHM a speed-up of 157 is achieved when compared with the NHM for the first set of parameters. This speed-up is mainly due to the exploitation of the CRT and the NTT. Number processing is split into multiple channels whose bit-width is exactly tailored for the word-length of a given processor, which leads to an increased performance when compared with the use of general multi-precision arithmetic libraries, such as GMP [9]. Whereas the use of a v-lane SIMD engine could ideally result on a v-fold speed-up, this is difficult to achieve in practice. Beyond the fact that programs do not always use SIMD instructions, the i7-4770k is a powerful super-scalar processor which features several levels of pipeline that lead to the exploitation of instruction-level parallelism even for sequential programs. Thus, in practice more modest speed-ups are obtained from the SIMD extensions than one would expect theoretically, as it can be seen in Fig. 3(a). Nevertheless, speed-ups of up to 1.64 were obtained when comparing the AVX2 implementation of MHM with the sequential one.

Finally, it can be seen that the AVX2 implementation of the proposed MHM algorithm is faster than the related art. By taking into consideration that the frequency of operation of the Xeon E5-2666 v3 CPU is 2.9 GHz, whereas that of the i7-4770k is 3.5 GHz, one gets a normalized acceleration of 1.93 for the

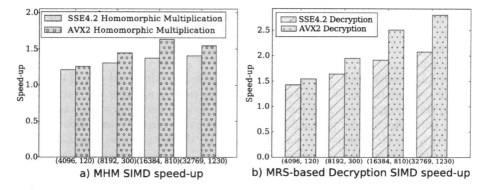

Fig. 3. Speed-up of (a) The SIMD Versions of MHM when compared with the sequential MHM execution, and of (b) The SIMD MRS-based decryption when compared with the Sequential MRS-based Decryption. The values on the x-axis refer to $(n, \log_2 q)$

AVX2 MHM implementation when compared with that in [1] (both processors are based on the Haswell microarchitecture). One can conclude that the speed-up achieved with the proposed algorithm is due to the adoption of the Extend and Scale functions. The usage of the MRS is very important not only to reduce the overhead of converting polynomials from one ring to a larger one, and for scaling numbers, but also for the exploitation of SIMD parallelism.

Similarly, several decryption algorithms were implemented and tested on the Intel Core i7-4770k CPU. The obtained average execution times are presented in Table 2, for parameters that are similar to those of Table 1. The advantages that are brought forth by the proposed Extend_{qr} and Scale_q functions are confirmed with the results in Table 2. In particular, they make decryption more suitable to SIMD parallelization, and the AVX2 implementation achieves speed-ups of up to 2.8 when compared with the sequential implementation, as presented in Fig. 3(b). Furthermore, when compared with [1], and by taking into account the different frequencies of operation of the Xeon E5-2666 v3 CPU (2.9 GHz) and the i7-4770k (3.5 GHz), one obtains a normalized speed-up of 2.0.

Since other homomorphic cryptosystems rely on similar operations, namely the ones proposed in [3,11], the techniques herein proposed can be extended to those settings. In particular, for [3], the Decomp_{MRS} method could be applied to the homomorphic multiplication operation. Moreover, since [11] has a similar structure to FV, the techniques herein proposed would be directly applicable to the homomorphic multiplication and decryption operations.

5   Conclusions

FHE has been a major advance in cryptography since it allows to protect sensitive data, even while it is being processed. While theoretically feasible, most HE schemes are burdensome and hard to implement in practice. From the results presented in this paper, one can conclude that whereas SIMD extensions may play an important role in bringing FHE to practical implementations, it is also important to design the underlying algorithms in ways that expose more data parallelism.

We have considered the use of the MRS to reduce the overhead of converting the representation of polynomials from one ring to a larger one, as well as scaling their magnitude. This has resulted in very efficient algorithms and arithmetic, suitable to data parallelism and SIMD processing. When implemented with AVX2 SIMD extensions on a i7-4770k CPU, the proposed methods and techniques produced a normalized speed-up of 1.93 when compared with the fastest AVX2 implementation of the state of the art. Furthermore, we have shown that these techniques can readily be extended to the decryption operation, producing a relative speed-up of 2.0 when compared with related art. Finally, these techniques can be extended to other FHE schemes, such as [3,11].

Acknowledgments. This work was partially supported by the ARTEMIS Joint Undertaking under grant agreement nr. 621429 and by national funds through Fundação para a Ciência e a Tecnologia (FCT) with reference UID/CEC/50021/2013, and through the PhD grant with reference SFRH/BD/103791/2014.

References

1. Aguilar-Melchor, C., Barrier, J., Guelton, S., Guinet, A., Killijian, M.-O., Lepoint, T.: NFLlib: NTT-based fast lattice library. In: RSA Conference Cryptographers' Track, San Francisco, United States, February 2016
2. Brakerski, Z.: Fully homomorphic encryption without modulus switching from classical gapSVP. Cryptology ePrint Archive, Report 2012/078 (2012). http://eprint.iacr.org/2012/078
3. Brakerski, Z., Gentry, C., Vaikuntanathan, V.: (Leveled) fully homomorphic encryption without bootstrapping. In: Proceedings of the 3rd Innovations in Theoretical Computer Science Conference, ITCS 2012, pp. 309–325. ACM, New York (2012)
4. Cooley, J.W., Tukey, J.W.: An algorithm for the machine calculation of complex Fourier series. Math. Comput. **19**, 297–301 (1965). http://cr.yp.to/bib/entries.html#1965/cooley
5. Cormen, T.H., Stein, C., Rivest, R.L., Leiserson, C.E.: Introduction to Algorithms, 2nd edn. McGraw-Hill Higher Education, New York (2001)
6. Fan, J., Vercauteren, F.: Somewhat practical fully homomorphic encryption. Cryptology ePrint Archive, Report 2012/144 (2012). http://eprint.iacr.org/
7. Garrett, P.B.: Making, Breaking Codes: Introduction to Cryptology, 1st edn. Prentice Hall PTR, Upper Saddle River (2000)
8. Gentry, C., Halevi, S., Smart, N.P.: Homomorphic evaluation of the AES circuit. Cryptology ePrint Archive, Report 2012/099 (2012). http://eprint.iacr.org/2012/099
9. Granlund, T., GMP development team: GNU MP: The GNU Multiple Precision Arithmetic Library, 6.0.0 edn. (2014). http://gmplib.org/
10. Intel. Intel intrinsics guide (2016)

11. Lepoint, T., Naehrig, M.: A comparison of the homomorphic encryption schemes FV and YASHE. Cryptology ePrint Archive, Report 2014/062 (2014). http://eprint.iacr.org/

12. Pöppelmann, T., Güneysu, T.: Towards efficient arithmetic for lattice-based cryptography on reconfigurable hardware. In: Hevia, A., Neven, G. (eds.) LATIN-CRYPT 2012. LNCS, vol. 7533, pp. 139–158. Springer, Heidelberg (2012). doi:10.1007/978-3-642-33481-8_8

13. Stallman, R.M., Community, G.D.: Collection, Using The Gnu Compiler: A Gnu Manual For Gcc Version 4.9.2. CreateSpace, Paramount, CA (2015)

14. Vaikuntanathan, V.: Computing blindfolded: new developments in fully homomorphic encryption. In: Proceedings of the 2011 IEEE 52nd Annual Symposium on Foundations of Computer Science, FOCS 2011, pp. 5–16. IEEE Computer Society, Washington, DC (2011)

An Improvement of Optimal Ate Pairing on KSS Curve with Pseudo 12-Sparse Multiplication

Md. Al-Amin Khandaker[1(✉)], Hirotaka Ono[1], Yasuyuki Nogami[1],
Masaaki Shirase[2], and Sylvain Duquesne[3]

[1] Graduate School of Natural Science and Technology, Okayama University,
Okayama, Japan
{khandaker,hirotaka.ono}@s.okayama-u.ac.jp,
yasuyuki.nogami@okayama-u.ac.jp
[2] Future University Hakodate, Hakodate, Japan
shirase@fun.ac.jp
[3] Université Rennes I, Rennes, France
sylvain.duquesne@univ-rennes1.fr

Abstract. Acceleration of a pairing calculation of an Ate-based pairing such as Optimal Ate pairing depends not only on the optimization of Miller algorithm's loop parameter but also on efficient elliptic curve arithmetic operation and efficient final exponentiation. Some recent works have shown the implementation of Optimal Ate pairing over Kachisa-Schaefer-Scott (KSS) curve of *embedding degree* 18. Pairing over KSS curve is regarded as the basis of next generation security protocols. This paper has proposed a *pseudo 12-sparse multiplication* to accelerate Miller's loop calculation in KSS curve by utilizing the property of rational point groups. In addition, this papers has showed an enhancement of the elliptic curve addition and doubling calculation in Miller's algorithm by applying implicit mapping of its sextic twisted isomorphic group. Moreover this paper has implemented the proposal with recommended security parameter settings for KSS curve at 192 bit security level. The simulation result shows that the proposed *pseudo 12-sparse multiplication* gives more efficient Miller's loop calculation of an Optimal Ate pairing operation along with recommended parameters than pairing calculation without sparse multiplication.

Keywords: KSS curve · Sparse multiplication · Optimal Ate pairing

1 Introduction

From the very beginning of the cryptosystems that utilizes elliptic curve pairing; proposed independently by Sakai et al. [18] and Joux [10], has unlocked numerous novel ideas to researchers. Many researchers tried to find out security protocol that exploits pairings to remove the need of certification by a trusted authority. In this consequence, several ingenious pairing based encryption scheme such as ID-based encryption scheme by Boneh and Franklin [5] and group signature authentication by Nakanishi et al. [16] has come into the focus. In such outcome,

© Springer International Publishing AG 2017
S. Hong and J.H. Park (Eds.): ICISC 2016, LNCS 10157, pp. 208–219, 2017.
DOI: 10.1007/978-3-319-53177-9_11

Ate-based pairings such as Ate [6], Optimal-ate [22], twisted Ate [14], R-ate [13], and χ-Ate [17] pairings and their applications in cryptosystems have caught much attention since they have achieved quite efficient pairing calculation. But it has always been a challenge for researchers to make pairing calculation more efficient for being used practically as pairing calculation is regarded as quite time consuming operation.

Bilinear pairing operation consist of two predominant parts, named as Miller's loop and final exponentiation. Finding pairing friendly curves [8] and construction of efficient extension field arithmetic are the ground work for any pairing operation. Many research has been conducted for finding pairing friendly curves [3,7] and efficient extension field arithmetic [2]. Some previous work on optimizing the pairing algorithm on pairing friendly curve such Optimal Ate pairing by Matsuda et al. [14] on Barreto-Naehrig (BN) curve [4] is already carried out. The previous work of Mori et al. [15] has showed the *pseudo 8-sparse multiplication* to efficiently calculate Miller's algorithm defined over BN curve. Apart from it, Aranha et al. [1] has improved Optimal Ate pairing over KSS curve for 192 bit security level by utilizing the relation $t(\chi) - 1 \equiv \chi + 3p(\chi) \bmod r(\chi)$ where $t(\chi)$ is the Frobenius trace of KSS curve, χ is an integer also known as *mother parameter*, $p(\chi)$ is the prime number and $r(\chi)$ is the order of the curve. This paper has exclusively focused on efficiently calculating the Miller's loop of Optimal Ate pairing defined over KSS curve [11] for 192-bit security level by applying *pseudo 12-sparse multiplication* technique along with other optimization approaches. The parameter settings recommended in [1] for 192 bit security on KSS curve is used in the simulation implementation. But in the recent work, Kim et al. [12] has suggested to update the key sizes associated with pairing-based cryptography due to the new development of discrete logarithm problem over finite field. The parameter settings of [1] doesn't end up at the 192 bit security level according to [12]. However the parameter settings of [1] is primarily adapted in this paper in order to show the resemblance of the proposal with the experimental result.

In general, pairing is a bilinear map from two rational point groups $\mathbb{G}_1$ and $\mathbb{G}_2$ to a multiplicative group $\mathbb{G}_3$ [21]. When KSS pairing-friendly elliptic curve of embedding degree $k = 18$ is chosen for Ate-based pairing, then the bilinear map is denoted by $\mathbb{G}_1 \times \mathbb{G}_2 \rightarrow \mathbb{G}_3$, where $\mathbb{G}_1 \subset E(\mathbb{F}_p)$, $\mathbb{G}_2 \subset E(\mathbb{F}_{p^{18}})$ and $\mathbb{G}_3 \subset \mathbb{F}_{p^{18}}^*$ and p denotes the characteristic and E is the curve defined over corresponding extension field $\mathbb{F}_{p^k}$. Rational point in $\mathbb{G}_2 \subset E(\mathbb{F}_{p^{18}})$ has a special vector representation where out of 18 $\mathbb{F}_p$ coefficients 3 continuous $\mathbb{F}_p$ coefficients are non-zero and the others are zero. By utilizing such representation along with the sextic twisted isomorphic sub-field property of $\mathbb{F}_{p^{18}}$, this paper has computed the elliptic curve doubling and elliptic curve addition in the Miller's algorithm as $\mathbb{F}_{p^3}$ arithmetic without any explicit mapping from $\mathbb{F}_{p^{18}}$ to $\mathbb{F}_{p^3}$.

Finally this paper proposes *pseudo 12-sparse multiplication* in affine coordinates for line evaluation in the Miller's algorithm by considering the fact that multiplying or dividing the result of Miller's loop calculation by an arbitrary non-zero $\mathbb{F}_p$ element does not change the result as the following final exponentiation cancels the effect of multiplication or division. Following the division by a non-zero $\mathbb{F}_p$ element, one of the 7 non-zero $\mathbb{F}_p$ coefficients (which is a combination of 1 $\mathbb{F}_p$ and 2 $\mathbb{F}_{p^3}$ coefficients) becomes 1 that yields calculation efficiency. The calculation overhead caused from the division is canceled by isomorphic mapping with a quadratic and cubic residue in $\mathbb{F}_p$. This paper doesn't end up by giving only the theoretic proposal of improvement of Optimal Ate pairing by pseudo 12-sparse multiplication. In order to evaluate the theoretic proposal, this paper shows some experimental results with recommended parameter settings.

2　Fundamentals

This section briefly reviews the fundamentals of KSS curve [11], towering extension field with irreducible binomials [2], sextic twist, pairings and sparse multiplication [15].

2.1　KSS Curve

Kachisa-Schaefer-Scott (KSS) curve [11] is a non supersingular pairing friendly elliptic curve of embedding degree 18. The equation of KSS curve defined over $\mathbb{F}_{p^{18}}$ is given as follows:

$$E : y^2 = x^3 + b, \quad b \in \mathbb{F}_p \tag{1}$$

together with the following parameter settings,

$$p(\chi) = (\chi^8 + 5\chi^7 + 7\chi^6 + 37\chi^5 + 188\chi^4 + 259\chi^3 + 343\chi^2 + 1763\chi + 2401)/21, \tag{2a}$$

$$r(\chi) = (\chi^6 + 37\chi^3 + 343)/343, \tag{2b}$$

$$t(\chi) = (\chi^4 + 16\chi + 7)/7, \tag{2c}$$

where $b \neq 0$, $x, y \in \mathbb{F}_{p^{18}}$ and characteristic p (prime number), Frobenius trace t and order r are obtained systematically by using the integer variable χ, such that $\chi \equiv 14 \pmod{42}$.

2.2　Towering Extension Field

In extension field arithmetic, higher level computations can be improved by towering. In towering, higher degree extension field is constructed as a polynomial of lower degree extension fields. Since KSS curve is defined over $\mathbb{F}_{p^{18}}$, this paper has represented extension field $\mathbb{F}_{p^{18}}$ as a tower of sub-fields to improve arithmetic operations. In some previous works, such as Bailey et al. [2] explained tower of extension by using irreducible binomials. In what follows, let $(p-1)$ be divisible by 3 and c is a certain quadratic and cubic non residue in $\mathbb{F}_p$. Then for KSS-curve [11], where $k = 18$, $\mathbb{F}_{p^{18}}$ is constructed as tower field with irreducible binomial as follows:

$$\begin{cases} \mathbb{F}_{p^3} &= \mathbb{F}_p[i]/(i^3 - c), \\ \mathbb{F}_{p^6} &= \mathbb{F}_{p^3}[v]/(v^2 - i), \\ \mathbb{F}_{p^{18}} &= \mathbb{F}_{p^6}[\theta]/(\theta^3 - v). \end{cases} \tag{3}$$

Here isomorphic sextic twist of KSS curve defined over $\mathbb{F}_{p^{18}}$ is available in the base extension field $\mathbb{F}_{p^3}$.

2.3   Sextic Twist

Let z be a certain quadratic and cubic non residue $z \in \mathbb{F}_{p^3}$. The sextic twisted curve E' of KSS curve E defined in Eq. (1) and their isomorphic mapping ψ_6 are given as follows:

$$E' : y^2 = x^3 + bz, \quad b \in \mathbb{F}_p$$
$$\psi_6 : E'(\mathbb{F}_{p^3})[r] \longmapsto E(\mathbb{F}_{p^{18}})[r] \cap \mathrm{Ker}(\pi_p - [p]),$$
$$(x, y) \longmapsto (z^{-1/3}x, z^{-1/2}y) \tag{4}$$

where $\mathrm{Ker}(\cdot)$ denotes the kernel of the mapping. Frobenius mapping π_p for rational point is given as

$$\pi_p : (x, y) \longmapsto (x^p, y^p). \tag{5}$$

The order of the sextic twisted isomorphic curve $\#E'(\mathbb{F}_{p^3})$ is also divisible by the order of KSS curve E defined over $\mathbb{F}_p$ denoted as r. Extension field arithmetic by utilizing the sextic twisted sub-field curve $E'(\mathbb{F}_{p^3})$ based on the isomorphic twist can improve pairing calculation. In this paper, $E'(\mathbb{F}_{p^3})[r]$ shown in Eq. (4) is denoted as $\mathbb{G}_2'$.

Isomorphic mapping between $\mathbf{E}(\mathbb{F}_p)$ and $\hat{\mathbf{E}}(\mathbb{F}_p)$ Let us consider $\hat{E}(\mathbb{F}_p)$ is isomorphic to $E(\mathbb{F}_p)$ and $\hat{z}$ as a quadratic and cubic residue in $\mathbb{F}_p$. Mapping between $E(\mathbb{F}_p)$ and $\hat{E}(\mathbb{F}_p)$ is given as follows:

$$\hat{E} : y^2 = x^3 + b\hat{z},$$
$$\hat{E}(\mathbb{F}_p)[r] \longmapsto E(\mathbb{F}_p)[r],$$
$$(x, y) \longmapsto (\hat{z}^{-1/3}x, \hat{z}^{-1/2}y),$$
$$\textbf{where } \hat{z}, \hat{z}^{-1/2}, \hat{z}^{-1/3} \in \mathbb{F}_p. \tag{6}$$

2.4   Pairings

As described earlier bilinear pairing requires two rational point groups to be mapped to a multiplicative group. In what follows, Optimal Ate pairing over KSS curve of embedding degree $k = 18$ is described as follows.

Optimal Ate Pairing. Let us consider the following two additive groups as $\mathbb{G}_1$ and $\mathbb{G}_2$ and multiplicative group as $\mathbb{G}_3$. The Ate pairing α is defined as follows:

$$\mathbb{G}_1 = E(\mathbb{F}_{p^k})[r] \cap \mathrm{Ker}(\pi_p - [1]),$$
$$\mathbb{G}_2 = E(\mathbb{F}_{p^k})[r] \cap \mathrm{Ker}(\pi_p - [p]).$$

$$\alpha : \mathbb{G}_2 \times \mathbb{G}_1 \longrightarrow \mathbb{F}'_{p^k}/(\mathbb{F}^*_{p^k})^r. \tag{7}$$

where $\mathbb{G}_1 \subset E(\mathbb{F}_p)$ and $\mathbb{G}_2 \subset E(\mathbb{F}_{p^{18}})$ in the case of KSS curve.

Let $P \in \mathbb{G}_1$ and $Q \in \mathbb{G}_2$, Ate pairing $\alpha(Q, P)$ is given as follows.

$$\alpha(Q, P) = f_{t-1,Q}(P)^{\frac{p^k-1}{r}}, \tag{8}$$

where $f_{t-1,Q}(P)$ symbolize the output of Miller's algorithm. The bilinearity of Ate pairing is satisfied after calculating the final exponentiation. It is noted that improvement of final exponentiation is not the focus of this paper. Several works [19, 20] have been already done for efficient final exponentiation.

The previous work of Aranha et al. [1] has mentioned about the relation $t(\chi) - 1 \equiv \chi + 3p(\chi) \bmod r(\chi)$ for Optimal Ate pairing. Exploiting the relation, Optimal Ate pairing on the KSS curve is defined by the following representation.

$$(Q, P) = (f_{\chi,Q} \cdot f^p_{3,Q} \cdot l_{[\chi]Q,[3p]Q})^{\frac{p^{18}-1}{r}}, \tag{9}$$

where χ is the mother parameter. The calculation procedure of Optimal Ate pairing is shown in Algorithm 1. In what follows, the calculation steps from 1 to 5 shown in Algorithm 1 is identified as Miller's loop. Steps 3 and 5 are line evaluation along with elliptic curve doubling and addition. These two steps are key steps to accelerate the loop calculation. As an acceleration technique *pseudo 12-sparse multiplication* is proposed in this paper.

2.5 Sparse Multiplication

In the previous work, Mori et al. [15] has substantiated the pseudo 8-sparse multiplication for BN curve. Adapting affine coordinates for representing rational points, we can apply Mori's work in the case of KSS curve. The doubling phase and addition phase in Miller's loop can be carried out efficiently by the following calculations. Let $P = (x_P, y_P)$, $T = (x, y)$ and $Q = (x_2, y_2) \in E'(\mathbb{F}_{p^3})$ be given in affine coordinates, and let $T + Q = (x_3, y_3)$ be the sum of T and Q.

Step 3: Elliptic curve doubling phase ($T = Q$)

$$A = \frac{1}{2y}, B = 3x^2, C = AB, D = 2x, x_3 = C^2 - D,$$
$$E = Cx - y, y_3 = E - Cx_3, F = C\overline{x}_P,$$
$$l_{T,T}(P) = y_P + Ev + F\theta = y_P + Ev - Cx_P\theta, \tag{10}$$

where $\overline{x}_P = -x_P$ will be pre-computed. Here $l_{T,T}(P)$ denotes the tangent line at the point T.

Step 5: Elliptic curve addition phase ($T \neq Q$)

$$A = \frac{1}{x_2 - x}, B = y_2 - y, C = AB, D = x + x_2, x_3 = C^2 - D,$$
$$E = Cx - y, y_3 = E - Cx_3, F = C\overline{x}_P,$$
$$l_{T,Q}(P) = y_P + Ev + F\theta = y_P + Ev - Cx_P\theta, \tag{11}$$

where $\overline{x}_P = -x_P$ will be pre-computed. Here $l_{T,Q}(P)$ denotes the tangent line between the point T and Q.

Analyzing Eqs. (10) and (11), we get that E and Cx_P are calculated in $\mathbb{F}_{p^3}$. After that, the basis element 1, v and θ identifies the position of y_P, E and Cx_P in $\mathbb{F}_{p^{18}}$ vector representation. Therefore vector representation of $l_{\psi_6(T),\psi_6(T)}(P) \in \mathbb{F}_{p^{18}}$ consists of 18 coefficients. Among them at least 11 coefficients are equal to zero. In the other words, only 7 coefficients $y_P \in \mathbb{F}_p$, $Cx_P \in \mathbb{F}_{p^3}$ and $E \in \mathbb{F}_{p^3}$ are perhaps to be non-zero. $l_{\psi_6(T),\psi_6(Q)}(P) \in \mathbb{F}_{p^{18}}$ also has the same vector structure. Thus, the calculation of multiplying $l_{\psi_6(T),\psi_6(T)}(P) \in \mathbb{F}_{p^{18}}$ or $l_{\psi_6(T),\psi_6(Q)}(P) \in \mathbb{F}_{p^{18}}$ is called sparse multiplication. In the above mentioned instance especially called 11-sparse multiplication. This sparse multiplication accelerates Miller's loop calculation as shown in Algorithm 1. This paper comes up with pseudo 12-sparse multiplication.

Algorithm 1. Optimal Ate pairing on KSS curve

Input: $\chi, P \in \mathbb{G}_1, Q \in \mathbb{G}_2'$
Output: (Q, P)
1   $f \leftarrow 1, T \leftarrow Q$
2   **for** $i = \lfloor \log_2(\chi) \rfloor$ **downto** 1 **do**
3     $f \leftarrow f^2 \cdot l_{T,T}(P), \ T \leftarrow [2]T$
4   **if** $\chi[i] = 1$ **then**
5      $f \leftarrow f \cdot l_{T,Q}(P), \ T \leftarrow T + Q$

6   $f_1 \leftarrow f_{3,Q}^p, \ f \leftarrow f \cdot f_1$
7   $Q_1 \leftarrow [\chi]Q, \ Q_2 \leftarrow [3p]Q$
8   $f \leftarrow f \cdot l_{Q_1,Q_2}(P)$
9   $f \leftarrow f^{\frac{p^{18}-1}{r}}$
10 **return** f

---

3   Improved Optimal Ate Pairing for KSS Curve

In this section we describe the main proposal. Before going to the details, at first we give an overview of the improvement procedure of Optimal Ate pairing in KSS curve. The following two ideas are proposed in order to efficiently apply 12-sparse multiplication on Optimal Ate pairing on KSS curve.

1. In Eqs. (10) and (11) among the 7 non-zero coefficients, one of the non-zero coefficients is $y_P \in \mathbb{F}_p$. And y_P remains uniform through Miller's loop calculation. Thereby dividing both sides of those Eqs. (10) and (11) by y_P, the coefficient becomes 1 which results in a more efficient sparse multiplication by $l_{\psi_6(T),\psi_6(T)}(P)$ or $l_{\psi_6(T),\psi_6(Q)}(P)$. This paper calls it *pseudo 12-sparse multiplication*.

2. Division by y_P in Eqs. (10) and (11) causes a calculation overhead for the other non-zero coefficients in the Miller's loop. To cancel this additional cost in Miller's loop, the map introduced in Eq. (6) is applied.

It is to be noted that this paper doesn't focus on making final exponentiation efficient in Miller's algorithm since many efficient algorithms are available. From Eqs. (10) and (11) the above mentioned ideas are introduced in details.

3.1 Pseudo 12-Sparse Multiplication

As said before y_P shown in Eq. (10) is a non-zero elements in $\mathbb{F}_p$. Thereby, dividing both sides of Eq. (10) by y_P we obtain as follows:

$$y_P^{-1} l_{T,T}(P) = 1 + E y_P^{-1} v - C(x_P y_P^{-1})\theta. \tag{12}$$

Replacing $l_{T,T}(P)$ by the above $y_P^{-1} l_{T,T}(P)$, the calculation result of the pairing does not change, since *final exponentiation* cancels $y_P^{-1} \in \mathbb{F}_p$. One of the non-zero coefficients becomes 1 after the division by y_P, which results in more efficient vector multiplications in Miller's loop. This paper calls it *pseudo* $12 - sparse\ multiplication$. Algorithm 2 introduces the detailed calculation procedure of pseudo 12-sparse multiplication.

Algorithm 2. Pseudo 12-sparse multiplication

Input: $a, b \in \mathbb{F}_{p^{18}}$
   $a = (a_0 + a_1\theta + a_2\theta^2) + (a_3 + a_4\theta + a_5\theta^2)v,\ b = 1 + b_1\theta + b_3 v$
   where $a_i, b_j, c_i \in \mathbb{F}_{p^3} (i = 0, \cdots, 5, j = 1, 3)$
Output: $c = ab = (c_0 + c_1\theta + c_2\theta^2) + (c_3 + c_4\theta + c_5\theta^2)v \in \mathbb{F}_{p^{18}}$
1 $c_1 \leftarrow a_0 \times b_1, c_5 \leftarrow a_2 \times b_3, t_0 \leftarrow a_0 + a_2, S_0 \leftarrow b_1 + b_3$
2 $c_3 \leftarrow t_0 \times S_0 - (c_1 + c_5)$
3 $c_2 \leftarrow a_1 \times b_1, c_6 \leftarrow a_3 \times b_3, t_0 \leftarrow a_1 + a_3$
4 $c_4 \leftarrow t_0 \times S_0 - (c_2 + c_6)$
5 $c_5 \leftarrow c_5 + a_4 \times b_1, c_6 \leftarrow c_6 + a_5 \times b_1$
6 $c_7 \leftarrow a_4 \times b_3, c_8 \leftarrow a_5 \times b_3$
7 $c_0 \leftarrow c_6 \times i$
8 $c_1 \leftarrow c_1 + c_7 \times i$
9 $c_2 \leftarrow c_2 + c_8 \times i$
10 $c \leftarrow c + a$
11 return $c = (c_0 + c_1\theta + c_2\theta^2) + (c_3 + c_4\theta + c_5\theta^2)v$

3.2 Line Calculation in Miller's Loop

The comparison of Eqs. (10) and (12) shows that the calculation cost of Eq. (12) is little bit higher than Eq. (10) for $E y_P^{-1}$. The cancellation process of $x_P y_P^{-1}$ terms by utilizing isomorphic mapping is introduced next. The $x_P y_P^{-1}$ and y_P^{-1} terms are pre-computed to reduce execution time complexity. The map introduced in Eq. (6) can find a certain isomorphic rational point $\hat{P}(x_{\hat{P}}, y_{\hat{P}}) \in \hat{E}(\mathbb{F}_p)$ such that

$$x_{\hat{P}} y_{\hat{P}}^{-1} = 1. \tag{13}$$

Here the twist parameter z of Eq. (4) is considered to be $\hat{z} = (x_P y_P^{-1})^6$ of Eq. (6), where $\hat{z}$ is a quadratic and cubic residue in $\mathbb{F}_p$ and $\hat{E}$ denotes the KSS curve defined by Eq. (6). From the isomorphic mapping Eq. (4), such z is obtained by solving the following equation considering the input $P(x_P, y_P)$.

$$z^{1/3} x_P = z^{1/2} y_P, \tag{14}$$

Afterwards the $\hat{P}(x_{\hat{P}}, y_{\hat{P}}) \in \hat{E}(\mathbb{F}_p)$ is given as

$$\hat{P}(x_{\hat{P}}, y_{\hat{P}}) = (x_P^3 y_P^{-2}, x_P^3 y_P^{-2}). \tag{15}$$

As the x and y coordinates of $\hat{P}$ are the same, $x_{\hat{P}} y_{\hat{P}}^{-1} = 1$. Therefore, corresponding to the map introduced in Eq. (6), first mapping not only P to $\hat{P}$ shown above but also Q to $\hat{Q}$ shown below.

$$\hat{Q}(x_{\hat{Q}}, y_{\hat{Q}}) = (x_P^2 y_P^{-2} x_Q, x_P^3 y_P^{-3} y_Q). \tag{16}$$

When we define a new variable $L = (x_P^{-3} y_P^2) = y_{\hat{P}}^{-1}$, the line evaluations, Eqs. (10) and (11) become the following calculations. In what follows, let $\hat{P} = (x_{\hat{P}}, y_{\hat{P}}) \in E(\mathbb{F}_p)$, $T = (x, y)$ and $Q = (x_2, y_2) \in E'(\mathbb{F}_{p^3})$ be given in affine coordinates and let $T + Q = (x_3, y_3)$ be the sum of T and Q.

Step 3: Doubling phase ($T = Q$)

$$A = \tfrac{1}{2y}, B = 3x^2, C = AB, D = 2x, x_3 = C^2 - D,$$
$$E = Cx - y, y_3 = E - Cx_3,$$
$$\hat{l}_{T,T}(P) = y_P^{-1} l_{T,T}(P) = 1 + ELv - C\theta, \tag{17}$$

where $L = y_{\hat{P}}^{-1}$ will be pre-computed.

Step 5: Addition phase ($T \neq Q$)

$$A = \tfrac{1}{x_2 - x}, B = y_2 - y, C = AB, D = x + x_2, x_3 = C^2 - D,$$
$$E = Cx - y, y_3 = E - Cx_3,$$
$$\hat{l}_{T,Q}(P) = y_P^{-1} l_{T,Q}(P) = 1 + ELv - C\theta, \tag{18}$$

where $L = y_{\hat{P}}^{-1}$ will be pre-computed.

As we compare the above equation with to Eqs. (10) and (11), the third term of the right-hand side becomes simple since $x_{\hat{P}} y_{\hat{P}}^{-1} = 1$.

In the above procedure, calculating $\hat{P}$, $\hat{Q}$ and L by utilizing x_P^{-1} and y_P^{-1} will create some computational overhead. In spite of that, calculation becomes efficient as it is performed in isomorphic group together with pseudo 12-sparse multiplication in the Miller's loop. Improvement of Miller's loop calculation is presented by experimental results in the next section.

4 Cost Evaluation and Experimental Result

This section shows some experimental results with evaluating the calculation costs in order to the signify efficiency of the proposal. It is to be noted here that in the following discussions "Previous method" means Optimal Ate pairing with no use the sparse multiplication, "11-sparse multiplication" means Optimal Ate pairing with 11-sparse multiplication and "Proposed method" means Optimal Ate pairing with Pseudo 12-sparse multiplication.

4.1 Parameter Settings and Computational Environment

In the experimental simulation, this paper has considered the 192 bit security level for KSS curve. Table 1 shows the parameters settings suggested in [1] for 192 bit security over KSS curve. However this parameter settings does not necessarily comply with the recent suggestion of key size by Kim et al. [12] for 192 bit security level. The sole purpose to use this parameter settings in this paper is to compare the literature with the experimental result.

To evaluate the operational cost and to compare the execution time of the proposal based on the recommended parameter settings, the following computational environment is considered. Table 2 shows the computational environment.

4.2 Cost Evaluation

Let us consider m, s, a and i to denote the times of multiplication, squaring, addition and inversion $\in \mathbb{F}_p$. Similarly, $\tilde{m}, \tilde{s}, \tilde{a}$ and $\tilde{i}$ denote the number of multiplication, squaring, addition and inversion $\in \mathbb{F}_{p^3}$ and $\hat{m}, \hat{s}, \hat{a}$ and $\hat{i}$ to denote the count of multiplication, squaring, addition and inversion $\in \mathbb{F}_{p^{18}}$ respectively. Tables 3 and 4 show the calculation costs with respect to operation count.

Table 1. Parameters

Security level	χ	$p(\chi)$ [bit]	c Eq. (3)	b Eq. (1)
192-bit	$-2^{64} - 2^{51} + 2^{46} + 2^{12}$	508	2	2

Table 2. Computing environment

CPU	Core i5 6600
Memory	8.00 GB
OS	Ubuntu 16.04 LTS
Library	GMP 6.1.0 [9]
Compiler	gcc 5.4.0
Programming language	C

Table 3. Operation count of line evaluation

$E(\mathbb{F}_{p^{18}})$ Operations	Previous method	11-sparse multiplication	Proposed method
Precomputation	-	$\tilde{a}$	$6\tilde{m} + 2\tilde{i}$
Doubling + $l_{T,T}(P)$	$9\hat{a} + 6\hat{m} + 1\hat{i}$	$7\tilde{a} + 6\tilde{m} + 1\tilde{i}$	$7\tilde{a} + 6\tilde{m} + 1\tilde{i}$
Addition + $l_{T,Q}(P)$	$8\hat{a} + 5\hat{m} + 1\hat{i}$	$6\tilde{a} + 5\tilde{m} + 1\tilde{i}$	$6\tilde{a} + 5\tilde{m} + 1\tilde{i}$

Table 4. Operation count of multiplication

$\mathbb{F}_{p^{18}}$ Operations	Previous method	11-sparse multiplication	Proposed method
Vector Multiplication	$30\tilde{a} + 18\tilde{m} + 8a$	$1\hat{a} + 11\tilde{a} + 10\tilde{m} + 3a + \mathbf{18m}$	$1\hat{a} + 11\tilde{a} + 10\tilde{m} + 3a$

Table 5. Calculation time of Optimal Ate pairing at the 192-bit security level

Operation	Previous method	11-sparse multiplication	Proposed method
Doubling+ $l_{T,T}(P)$ [μs]	681	44	44
Addition+ $l_{T,Q}(P)$ [μs]	669	39	37
Multiplication [μs]	119	74	65
Miller's Algorithm [ms]	524	142	140

By analyzing the Table 4 we can find that 11-sparse multiplication requires 18 more multiplication in $\mathbb{F}_p$ than pseudo 12-sparse multiplication.

4.3 Experimental Result

Table 5 shows the calculation times of Optimal Ate pairing respectively. In this execution time count, the time required for final exponentiation is excluded. The results (time count) are the averages of 10000 iterations on PC respectively. According to the experimental results, pseudo 12-sparse contributes to a few percent acceleration of 11-sparse.

5   Conclusion and Future Works

This paper has proposed pseudo 12-sparse multiplication for accelerating Optimal Ate pairing on KSS curve. According to the calculation costs and experimental results shown in this paper, the proposed method can calculate Optimal Ate pairing more efficiently. As a future work we would like to evaluate the efficiency in practical case by implementing it in some pairing based protocols.

Acknowledgment. This work is partially supported by the Strategic Information and Communications R&D Promotion Programme (SCOPE) of Ministry of Internal Affairs and Communications, Japan.

References

1. Aranha, D.F., Fuentes-Castañeda, L., Knapp, E., Menezes, A., Rodríguez-Henríquez, F.: Implementing pairings at the 192-bit security level. In: Abdalla, M., Lange, T. (eds.) Pairing 2012. LNCS, vol. 7708, pp. 177–195. Springer, Heidelberg (2013). doi:10.1007/978-3-642-36334-4_11
2. Bailey, D.V., Paar, C.: Efficient arithmetic in finite field extensions with application in elliptic curve cryptography. J. Crypt. **14**(3), 153–176 (2001). http://dx.doi.org/10.1007/s001450010012
3. Barreto, P.S.L.M., Lynn, B., Scott, M.: Constructing elliptic curves with prescribed embedding degrees. In: Cimato, S., Persiano, G., Galdi, C. (eds.) SCN 2002. LNCS, vol. 2576, pp. 257–267. Springer, Heidelberg (2003). doi:10.1007/3-540-36413-7_19
4. Barreto, P.S.L.M., Naehrig, M.: Pairing-friendly elliptic curves of prime order. In: Preneel, B., Tavares, S. (eds.) SAC 2005. LNCS, vol. 3897, pp. 319–331. Springer, Heidelberg (2006). doi:10.1007/11693383_22
5. Boneh, D., Lynn, B., Shacham, H.: Short signatures from the Weil pairing. In: Boyd, C. (ed.) ASIACRYPT 2001. LNCS, vol. 2248, pp. 514–532. Springer, Heidelberg (2001). doi:10.1007/3-540-45682-1_30
6. Cohen, H., Frey, G., Avanzi, R., Doche, C., Lange, T., Nguyen, K., Vercauteren, F.: Handbook of Elliptic and Hyperelliptic Curve Cryptography. CRC Press, Boca Raton (2005)
7. Dupont, R., Enge, A., Morain, F.: Building curves with arbitrary small MOV degree over finite prime fields. J. Crypt. **18**(2), 79–89 (2005)
8. Freeman, D., Scott, M., Teske, E.: A taxonomy of pairing-friendly elliptic curves. J. Crypt. **23**(2), 224–280 (2010)
9. Granlund, T.: The GMP development team: GNU MP: The GNU Multiple Precision Arithmetic Library, 6.1.0 edn. (2015). http://gmplib.org/
10. Joux, A.: A one round protocol for tripartite Diffie–Hellman. In: Bosma, W. (ed.) ANTS 2000. LNCS, vol. 1838, pp. 385–393. Springer, Heidelberg (2000). doi:10.1007/10722028_23
11. Kachisa, E.J., Schaefer, E.F., Scott, M.: Constructing Brezing-Weng pairing-friendly elliptic curves using elements in the cyclotomic field. In: Galbraith, S.D., Paterson, K.G. (eds.) Pairing 2008. LNCS, vol. 5209, pp. 126–135. Springer, Heidelberg (2008). doi:10.1007/978-3-540-85538-5_9
12. Kim, T., Barbulescu, R.: Extended tower number field sieve: A new complexity for medium prime case. Technical report, IACR Cryptology ePrint Archive, 2015: 1027 (2015)
13. Lee, E., Lee, H.S., Park, C.M.: Efficient and generalized pairing computation on abelian varieties. IEEE Trans. Inf. Theor. **55**(4), 1793–1803 (2009)
14. Matsuda, S., Kanayama, N., Hess, F., Okamoto, E.: Optimised versions of the ate and twisted ate pairings. In: Galbraith, S.D. (ed.) Cryptography and Coding 2007. LNCS, vol. 4887, pp. 302–312. Springer, Heidelberg (2007). doi:10.1007/978-3-540-77272-9_18
15. Mori, Y., Akagi, S., Nogami, Y., Shirase, M.: Pseudo 8–sparse multiplication for efficient ate–based pairing on Barreto–Naehrig curve. In: Cao, Z., Zhang, F. (eds.) Pairing 2013. LNCS, vol. 8365, pp. 186–198. Springer, Heidelberg (2014). doi:10.1007/978-3-319-04873-4_11
16. Nakanishi, T., Funabiki, N.: Verifier-local revocation group signature schemes with backward unlinkability from bilinear maps. In: Roy, B. (ed.) ASIACRYPT 2005. LNCS, vol. 3788, pp. 533–548. Springer, Heidelberg (2005). doi:10.1007/11593447_29

17. Nogami, Y., Akane, M., Sakemi, Y., Katou, H., Morikawa, Y.: Integer variable chi-based ate pairing. In: Proceedings of the Second International Conference on Pairing-Based Cryptography - Pairing 2008, Egham, UK, pp. 178–191, 1–3 September 2008. http://dx.doi.org/10.1007/978-3-540-85538-5_13

18. Sakai, R., Kasahara, M.: ID based cryptosystems with pairing on elliptic curve. IACR Cryptology ePrint Archive 2003, p. 54 (2003)

19. Scott, M., Benger, N., Charlemagne, M., Perez, L.J.D., Kachisa, E.J.: On the final exponentiation for calculating pairings on ordinary elliptic curves. In: Shacham, H., Waters, B. (eds.) Pairing 2009. LNCS, vol. 5671, pp. 78–88. Springer, Heidelberg (2009). doi:10.1007/978-3-642-03298-1_6

20. Shirase, M., Takagi, T., Okamoto, E.: Some efficient algorithms for the final exponentiation of η_T pairing. In: Dawson, E., Wong, D.S. (eds.) ISPEC 2007. LNCS, vol. 4464, pp. 254–268. Springer, Heidelberg (2007). doi:10.1007/978-3-540-72163-5_20

21. Silverman, J.H., Cornell, G., Artin, M.: Arithmetic Geometry. Springer, Heidelberg (1986)

22. Vercauteren, F.: Optimal pairings. IEEE Trans. Inf. Theor. **56**(1), 455–461 (2010)

Signatures (and Protocol)

Revisiting the Cubic UOV Signature Scheme

Dung H. Duong[1,2(✉)], Albrecht Petzoldt[1], Yacheng Wang[3],
and Tsuyoshi Takagi[1,2]

[1] Institute of Mathematics for Industry, Kyushu University, 744 Motooka,
Nishi-ku, Fukuoka 819-0395, Japan
{duong,petzoldt,takagi}@imi.kyushu-u.ac.jp
[2] JST, CREST, 4-1-8 Honcho, Kawaguchi, Saitama 332-0012, Japan
[3] Graduate School of Mathematics, Kyushu University, Fukuoka, Japan
ma216004@math.kyushu-u.ac.jp

Abstract. As recently been emphasized by NSA and NIST, there is an increasing need for cryptographic schemes being secure against quantum computer attacks. Especially in the area of digital signature schemes, multivariate cryptography is one of the main candidates for this. At Inscrypt 2015, Nie et al. proposed a new multivariate signature scheme called CUOV [20], whose public key consists both of quadratic and cubic polynomials. However, the scheme was broken by an attack of Hashimoto [15]. In this paper we take a closer look on the CUOV scheme and its attack and propose two new multivariate signature schemes called CSSv and SVSv, which are secure against Hashimoto's attack and all other known attacks on multivariate schemes. Especially our second construction SVSv is very efficient and outperforms current multivariate signature schemes such as UOV and Rainbow in terms of key and signature size.

Keywords: Post-quantum cryptography · Multivariate cryptography · Signature schemes

1 Introduction

The currently most widely used public key cryptosystems are the number theory based schemes RSA [24], DSA [18] and ECC [17]. However, these schemes will become insecure as soon as large enough quantum computers arrive [25]. Therefore, one needs alternatives to those classical public key schemes, based on hard mathematical problems not affected by quantum computer attacks (so called post quantum cryptosystems). The increasing importance of research in this field has recently been emphasized by a number of authorities, including the American National Security Agency (NSA), who recommended governmental organizations to switch their security infrastructures from schemes such as RSA and ECC to post-quantum cryptosystems [13], and the National Institute of Standards and Technology (NIST), which is preparing to develop standards for these schemes [5].

According to [5], multivariate cryptography is one of the main candidates for this standardization. Multivariate schemes are in general very fast and require

© Springer International Publishing AG 2017
S. Hong and J.H. Park (Eds.): ICISC 2016, LNCS 10157, pp. 223–238, 2017.
DOI: 10.1007/978-3-319-53177-9_12

only modest computational resources, which makes them attractive for the use on low cost devices like smart cards and RFID chips [2,4]. Since the late 1980's, many multivariate schemes both for encryption and signatures were proposed. One of the first was the Matsumoto-Imai cryptosystem [19], which was later extended to schemes such as Sflash [23] and HFE [22]. However, due to some flaws in the design (low rank of the private polynomials, low degree of regularity, ...), many of these schemes have been broken by direct, rank and differential attacks [11,21]. Another research direction led to the development of SingleField signature schemes such as UOV [16] and Rainbow [7]. These two schemes have withstood (for suitable parameters) cryptanalysis for nearly 20 years now and therefore are considered to provide high security. While the signature generation of UOV is very efficient, it has a very large public key. To deal with this, Ding and Schmidt [7] proposed the Rainbow signature scheme, which can be seen as a multi-layer version of UOV with smaller keys and shorter signatures. However, the multi-layer structure of Rainbow enables a number of new attacks [1,8] which makes the parameter choice of Rainbow to be a challenging task. Furthermore, this shows that one has to be very careful when designing new multivariate schemes on the basis of UOV and Rainbow.

At Inscrypt 2015, Nie et al. proposed a new idea of using cubic polynomials in the public key in a way that the key sizes are not too large and the signing process is efficient (CUOV) [20]. The use of cubic polynomials in the public key increases the degree of regularity of the system and hence increases the security against direct attacks. In addition, several attacks such as differential attacks are also not applicable against the scheme. Furthermore, the CUOV scheme has shorter signatures and a smaller private key than UOV and Rainbow. However, the scheme was broken by a newly developed attack of Hashimoto [15].

In this paper we revisit the CUOV scheme of Nie et al. [20] and analyze why it can be broken by Hashimoto's attack. Furthermore, we identify a number of components not relevant for the security of the scheme. By omitting these unnecessary components, we propose our first improved multivariate signature scheme, called CSSv (see Sect. 3). By our modifications, in addition to avoiding Hashimoto's attack, we make the signature generation much more stringent and reduce the number of cubic polynomials in the public key from 3 to 1, thus reducing the public key size by up to 40%. We show that the resulting scheme resists not only Hashimoto's attack, but also all other known attacks on multivariate cryptosystems, including direct and rank attacks (Sect. 3.2). Based on our construction of CSSv, we then propose a second new multivariate signature scheme called SVSv (Sect. 4). While, as in the case of CUOV, the public key of CSSv consists of both cubic and quadratic polynomials, the public key of SVSv is completely quadratic, which decreases the key sizes further without weakening the security of the construction (Sect. 4.2). The scheme provides shorter signatures than Rainbow and reduces both public and private key size significantly (by 24% and 79% respectively compared to Rainbow).

2   The Cubic Unbalanced Oil and Vinegar Signature Scheme (CUOV)

In this section we recall the CUOV scheme of [20]. Before we come to the description of the scheme itself, we start with a short overview of the basic concepts of multivariate cryptography.

2.1   Multivariate Cryptography

The basic objects of multivariate cryptography are systems of multivariate quadratic polynomials over a finite field K. The security of multivariate schemes is based on the *MQ-Problem* which asks for a solution of a given system of multivariate quadratic polynomials over the field K. The MQ-Problem is proven to be NP-hard even for quadratic polynomials over the field GF(2) [12].

To build a public key cryptosystem on the basis of the MQ-Problem, one starts with an easily invertible quadratic map $\mathcal{F} : K^n \to K^m$ (*central map*). To hide the structure of $\mathcal{F}$ in the public key, one composes it with two invertible affine (or linear) maps $\mathcal{T} : K^m \to K^m$ and $\mathcal{S} : K^n \to K^n$. The *public key* is therefore given by $\mathcal{P} = \mathcal{T} \circ \mathcal{F} \circ \mathcal{S} : K^n \to K^m$. The *private key* consists of $\mathcal{T}, \mathcal{F}$ and $\mathcal{S}$.

In this paper we consider multivariate signature schemes. For these schemes, we require $n \geq m$, which ensures that every message has a signature.

Signature Generation: To generate a signature for a message (or its hash value) $\mathbf{d} \in K^m$, one computes recursively $\mathbf{w} = \mathcal{T}^{-1}(\mathbf{d}) \in K^m$, $\mathbf{y} = \mathcal{F}^{-1}(\mathbf{w}) \in K^n$ and $\mathbf{z} = \mathcal{S}^{-1}(\mathbf{y})$. $\mathbf{z} \in K^n$ is the signature of the message $\mathbf{d}$. Here, $\mathcal{F}^{-1}(\mathbf{w})$ means finding one (of possibly many) pre-image of $\mathbf{w}$ under the central map $\mathcal{F}$.

Signature Verification: To check the authenticity of a signature $\mathbf{z} \in K^n$, the verifier simply computes $\mathbf{d}' = \mathcal{P}(\mathbf{z})$. If the result is equal to the message $\mathbf{d}$, the signature is accepted, otherwise rejected.

2.2   The CUOV Scheme

In [20], Nie et al. proposed a new multivariate signature scheme called Cubic Unbalanced Oil and Vinegar (CUOV). The scheme can be described as follows.

Let K be a finite field with q elements and $o, v \in \mathbb{N}$. The number of variables in the scheme is given by $n = o + v$, the number of equations is o.

Key Generation: The *central map* $\mathcal{F}$ of the CUOV scheme has the form $\mathcal{F} = \bar{\mathcal{F}} \circ (\hat{\mathcal{F}} \times \mathrm{id}_v) : K^n \to K^o$. Here, $\hat{\mathcal{F}} : K^n \to K^o$ consists of one quadratic and $o - 1$ affine polynomials of the form

$$\begin{cases} \hat{f}^{(1)} = \sum_{i=1}^{o} \sum_{j=o+1}^{n} a_{ij}^{(1)} \cdot y_i y_j + \sum_{i=o+1}^{n} \sum_{j=i}^{n} a_{ij}^{(1)} \cdot y_i y_j + \sum_{i=1}^{n} b_i^{(1)} \cdot y_i + c^{(1)}, \\ \hat{f}^{(2)} = \sum_{i=1}^{n} b_i^{(2)} \cdot y_i + c^{(2)}, \\ \qquad \cdots \\ \hat{f}^{(o)} = \sum_{i=1}^{n} b_i^{(o)} \cdot y_i + c^{(o)}, \end{cases}$$

$$(1)$$

where the coefficients $a_{ij}^{(k)}, b_j^{(k)}, c^{(k)}$ are random elements of K with $i \in \{1, \dots, v\}, j \in \{1, \dots, n\}$ and $k \in \{1, \dots, o\}$ and

$$\hat{\mathcal{F}} \times \mathrm{id}_v : K^n \to K^n$$

$$(y_1, \dots, y_o, y_{o+1}, \dots, y_n) \mapsto (\hat{f}^{(1)}, \dots, \hat{f}^{(o)}, \underbrace{y_{o+1}, \dots, y_n}_{\text{vinegar variables}}).$$

Note that $\hat{f}^{(1)}$ has the form of an oil and vinegar polynomial with o oil and v vinegar variables (cf. [16]).

The map $\bar{\mathcal{F}}$ is a map from $K^o \times K^v$ to K^o, $(x_1, \dots, x_o, y_{o+1}, \dots, y_n) \mapsto (\bar{f}^{(1)}, \dots, \bar{f}^{(o)})$ of the form

$$\begin{cases} \bar{f}^{(1)} = r_1 \cdot (x_1 + x_1 \cdot x_2) + g_1(y_{o+1}, \dots, y_n), \\ \bar{f}^{(2)} = r_2 \cdot x_1 \cdot x_2 + g_2(y_{o+1}, \dots, y_n), \\ \bar{f}^{(3)} = r_3 \cdot (x_1 + x_2) \cdot x_3 + g_3(y_{o+1}, \dots, y_n), \\ \quad \dots \\ \bar{f}^{(o)} = r_o \cdot (x_{o-2} + x_{o-1}) \cdot x_o + g_o(y_{o+1}, \dots, y_n). \end{cases} \quad (2)$$

Here $r_1, \dots, r_o$ are random elements in $K \backslash \{0\}$, g_1, g_2, g_3 are random cubic polynomials in the v vinegar variables $y_{o+1}, \dots, y_n$, whereas $g_4, \dots, g_o$ are random quadratic maps.

Due to the structure of $\hat{\mathcal{F}}$ and $\bar{\mathcal{F}}$, the *central map* $\mathcal{F} = (f^{(1)}, \dots, f^{(o)})$ of the CUOV scheme consists of three cubic polynomials $f^{(1)}, f^{(2)}, f^{(3)}$ and $(o-3)$ quadratic polynomials $f^{(4)}, \dots, f^{(o)}$.

To hide the structure of $\mathcal{F}$ in the public key, we choose randomly an invertible affine map $\mathcal{S} : K^n \to K^n$. The *public key* is given by $\mathcal{P} = \mathcal{F} \circ \mathcal{S} : K^n \to K^o$ and consists of three cubic polynomials $p^{(1)}, p^{(2)}, p^{(3)}$ and $(o-3)$ quadratic polynomials $p^{(4)}, \dots, p^{(o)}$. The *private key* consists of the polynomials $\hat{f}^{(1)}, \dots, \hat{f}^{(o)}$ and $g_1, \dots, g_o$, the invertible affine map $\mathcal{S}$ and the field elements $r_1, \dots, r_o$.[1] The key generation process is illustrated in Algorithm 1.

Signature Generation: To generate a signature $\mathbf{z} \in K^n$ for a message (hash value) $\mathbf{d} = (d_1, \dots, d_o) \in K^o$, the signer performs the following steps.

(1) Choose random values for the vinegar variables $y_{o+1}, \dots, y_n$ and substitute them into the polynomials $\hat{f}^{(1)}, \dots, \hat{f}^{(o)}$ and $g_1, \dots, g_o$.
(2) Compute x_1 by $x_1 = \frac{1}{r_1} \cdot (d_1 - g_1) - \frac{1}{r_2} \cdot (d_2 - g_2)$, $x_2 = \frac{1}{r_2 \cdot x_1} \cdot (d_2 - g_2)$ and recursively $x_i = \frac{1}{r_i \cdot (x_{i-2} + x_{i-1})} \cdot (d_i - g_i)$ $(i = 3, \dots, o)$. If any of the denominators in these equations happens to be zero, choose other values for the vinegar variables $y_{o+1}, \dots, y_n$.
(3) Solve the linear system given by the last $o - 1$ equations of (1) to obtain for $y_2, \dots, y_o$ univariate linear representations in y_1. If this fails, choose other values for the vinegar variables $y_{o+1}, \dots, y_n$.

---

[1] In contrast to the standard construction of multivariate cryptography (see above), Nie et al. did not use a second affine map $\mathcal{T}$. The reason for this is that $\mathcal{T}$ would turn the public key into a completely cubic map and therefore increase the key size drastically.

Algorithm 1. Key Generation of CUOV [20]

Input: Finite field K with q elements and integers o, v
Output: CUOV key pair $((\mathcal{F}, \mathcal{S}), \mathcal{P})$
1: Choose randomly o polynomials $\hat{f}^{(i)}$ in $n = o + v$ variables as shown in (1).
2: Choose 3 random cubic polynomials g_1, g_2, g_3 in v variables.
3: Choose $o - 3$ random quadratic polynomials $g_4, \ldots, g_o$ in v variables.
4: Choose random elements $r_1, \ldots, r_o \in K \backslash \{0\}$.
5: Define $\bar{f}^{(1)}(x_1, \ldots, x_o, y_{o+1}, \ldots, y_n), \ldots, \bar{f}^{(o)}(x_1, \ldots, x_o, y_{v+1}, \cdots, y_n)$ as shown in (2)
6: The central map is $\mathcal{F} = (f^{(1)}, \ldots, f^{(o)}) : K^n \to K^o$. where for each $i = 1, \ldots, o$ we have $f^{(i)} = \bar{f}^{(i)}(\hat{f}^{(1)}, \ldots, \hat{f}^{(o)}, y_{v+1}, \ldots, y_n)$
7: Choose randomly an invertible affine map $\mathcal{S} : K^n \to K^n$.
8: $\mathcal{P} = \mathcal{F} \circ \mathcal{S} : K^n \to K^o$
9: **return** $((\mathcal{F}, \mathcal{S}), \mathcal{P})$

---

(4) Substitute the linear relations found in the previous step into $\hat{f}^{(1)}$ and solve the resulting linear equation for y_1.
(5) Compute a signature $\mathbf{z} \in K^n$ for $\mathbf{d}$ by $\mathbf{z} = \mathcal{S}^{-1}(y_1, \ldots, y_n)$.

Signature Verification: To check the authenticity of a signature $\mathbf{z} \in K^n$, the verifier simply computes $\mathbf{d}' = \mathcal{P}(\mathbf{z}) \in K^o$. If the result is equal to the message $\mathbf{d}$, the signature is accepted, otherwise rejected.

2.3 The Attack of Hashimoto [15]

In the case of the CUOV scheme we have

$$\bar{f}^{(1)} - \frac{r_1}{r_2} \cdot \bar{f}^{(2)} = r_1 \cdot x_1 + \underbrace{(g_1(y_{o+1}, \ldots, y_n) - \frac{r_1}{r_2} \cdot g_2(y_{o+1}, \ldots, y_n))}_{\text{cubic map in } y_{o+1}, \ldots, y_n}. \quad (3)$$

By denoting

$$D_c p^{(i)}(\mathbf{z}) = p^{(i)}(\mathbf{z} + \mathbf{c}) - p^{(i)}(\mathbf{z}) \quad (4)$$

for $p^{(i)}$ being the i-th component of the CUOV public key, some fixed vector $\mathbf{c} \in K^n$ and Q_i being the coefficient matrix of the corresponding quadratic form $(i = 1, 2)$, Hashimoto showed that, due to Eq. (3), there exists an (easy to find) linear combination $Q_1 + \beta \cdot Q_2$ of rank at most v. By using this fact, Hashimoto could identify (the linear representations of) the vinegar variables $y_{o+1}, \ldots, y_n$, compute an equivalent central map and therefore forge signatures.

3 Our First Improved Scheme

In this section we take a closer look at the CUOV signature scheme and Hashimoto's attack. We analyze which properties make the scheme insecure and develop a strategy to avoid these weaknesses. Furthermore, we identify some components of CUOV which are not relevant for the security of the scheme. By removing them from the scheme, we can make the signature generation process much more stringent and reduce the public key size of the scheme. We denote our improved scheme by CSSv (Cubic Signature Scheme with Vinegar).

By studying Hashimoto's attack closely, we find that it works mainly due to the fact that, in the case of CUOV, we have a linear combination of the central polynomials $\bar{f}^{(i)}$ which is the sum of a quadratic form $\mathcal{X}$ in $y_1, \ldots, y_n$ and a cubic polynomial $\mathcal{G}$ in $y_{o+1}, \ldots, y_n$ (c.f. Eq. (3)). By taking the differential (Eq. (4)), the quadratic terms of $\mathcal{X}$ vanish, and there remain only quadratic terms in the variables $y_{o+1}, \ldots, y_n$. For the attacker this means that Hashimoto's attack works if and only if there exists an (easy to find) relation of the public polynomials of the form

$$\mathcal{Y} = \sum_{i=1}^{o} a_i \cdot p^{(i)} = \mathcal{X} + \mathcal{G},$$

with $\mathcal{X}$ being a quadratic map of rank n and $\mathcal{G}$ being a cubic map of rank v.

To prevent Hashimoto's attack, we therefore have to design our scheme in a way that such a relation does not exist. In the CSSv scheme, this is achieved by reducing the number of cubic polynomials from 3 to 1 and introducing an additional affine map $\mathcal{T}$ (see Sect. 3.2).

Furthermore, we identified the following components of CUOV not relevant for the security of the scheme. By omitting them, we can make the signature generation process much more straightforward and reduce the key sizes significantly.

1. The use of the coefficients r_i in Eq. (2) is unnecessary, since these factors can easily be included into the maps $\hat{f}^{(1)}, \ldots, \hat{f}^{(o)}$.
2. Instead of using an oil and vinegar polynomial for $\hat{f}^{(1)}$, we can easily switch to a random quadratic one. In this case we have to solve in step (4) of the signing process a univariate quadratic polynomial.
3. Taking the sum $x_{i-2} + x_{i-1}$ in equations $3, \ldots, o$ of (2) does not bring extra security into the scheme since the result is still a linear combination of $y_1, \ldots, y_n$.
4. The summation $(x_1 + x_1 \cdot x_2)$ in the first component of (2) is unnecessary, too, since $\hat{f}^{(1)}$ was chosen as a random polynomial.

3.1   The CSSv Signature Scheme

In this subsection we propose our first improved scheme CSSv, which is obtained by applying our strategy to prevent Hashimoto's attack and removing the above identified unnecessary components from the CUOV scheme of Nie et al. [20]. Our scheme can be described as follows.

Key Generation: Let K be a finite field with q elements and $o, v \in \mathbb{N}$. We set $n = o + v$. As in the case of the CUOV scheme (see previous section), the *central map* $\mathcal{F}$ of the CSSv scheme has the form $\mathcal{F} = \bar{\mathcal{F}} \circ (\hat{\mathcal{F}} \times \mathrm{id}_v) : K^n \to K^o$, with id_v being the identity map in K^v. The map $\hat{\mathcal{F}} = (\hat{f}^{(1)}, \dots, \hat{f}^{(o)})$ has the form

$$
\begin{cases}
\hat{f}^{(1)} = \sum_{i=1}^{n} \sum_{j=i}^{n} a_{ij}^{(1)} \cdot y_i y_j + \sum_{i=1}^{n} b_i^{(1)} \cdot y_i + c^{(1)} \\
\hat{f}^{(2)} = \sum_{i=1}^{n} b_i^{(2)} \cdot y_i + c^{(2)} \\
\cdots \\
\hat{f}^{(o)} = \sum_{i=1}^{n} b_i^{(o)} \cdot y_i + c^{(o)}
\end{cases}
\tag{5}
$$

with a random quadratic polynomial $\hat{f}^{(1)}$ and affine maps $\hat{f}^{(2)}, \dots, \hat{f}^{(o)}$ in the variables $y_1, \dots, y_n$.

The map $\bar{\mathcal{F}} : K^o \times K^v \to K^o, (x_1, \dots, x_o, y_{o+1}, \dots, y_n) \mapsto (\bar{f}^{(1)}, \dots, \bar{f}^{(o)})$ is given by

$$
\begin{cases}
\bar{f}^{(1)} = x_1 + g_1(y_{o+1}, \dots, y_n) \\
\bar{f}^{(2)} = x_1 \cdot x_2 + g_2(y_{o+1}, \dots, y_n) \\
\cdots \\
\bar{f}^{(o)} = x_{o-1} \cdot x_o + g_o(y_{o+1}, \dots, y_n).
\end{cases}
\tag{6}
$$

Here we choose randomly a cubic polynomial g_2 and $(o-1)$ quadratic polynomials $g_1, g_3, \dots, g_o$ in the v variables $y_{o+1}, \dots, y_n$.

The *central map* $\mathcal{F} = (f^{(1)}, \dots, f^{(o)})$ therefore consists of one cubic polynomial $f^{(2)}$ and $(o - 1)$ quadratic polynomials $f^{(1)}, f^{(3)}, \dots, f^{(o)}$ in the variables $y_1, \dots, y_n$. In order to hide the structure of $\mathcal{F}$ in the public key, we choose two invertible affine maps $\mathcal{S} : K^n \to K^n$ and $\mathcal{T} : K^o \to K^o$. While the map $\mathcal{S}$ is chosen completely at random, the matrix T representing the map $\mathcal{T}$ has the form

$$
T = \begin{pmatrix} \star_{1 \times 1} & \star_{1 \times 1} & \star_{1 \times (o-2)} \\ \star_{(o-1) \times 1} & 0_{(o-1) \times 1} & \star_{(o-1) \times (o-2)} \end{pmatrix} \in K^{o \times o}.
\tag{7}
$$

The *public key* has the form $\mathcal{P} = (p^{(1)}, \dots, p^{(o)}) = \mathcal{T} \circ \mathcal{F} \circ \mathcal{S} : K^n \to K^o$, the *private key* consists of $\hat{\mathcal{F}}, g_1, \dots, g_o, \mathcal{S}$ and $\mathcal{T}$. Due to the special form of the map $\mathcal{T}$, the public key consists of one cubic polynomial $p^{(1)}$ and $(o - 1)$ quadratic polynomials $p^{(2)}, \dots, p^{(o)}$ in n variables. The key generation process is illustrated in Algorithm 2.

Signature Generation: In order to generate a signature for a message (or hash value) $\mathbf{d} \in K^o$, the signer performs the following steps.

1. Compute $\mathbf{w} = \mathcal{T}^{-1}(\mathbf{d}) \in K^o$.
2. Choose random values for the vinegar variables $y_{o+1}, \dots, y_n$ and substitute them into the polynomials $\hat{f}^{(1)}, \dots, \hat{f}^{(o)}$ and $g_1, \dots, g_o$.
3. Compute $x_1 = w_1 - g_1$ and recursively $x_i = \frac{1}{x_{i-1}} \cdot (w_i - g_i)$ $(i = 2, \dots, o)$. If one of the x_i $(i = 1, \dots, o - 1)$ occurs to be 0, choose other values for the vinegar variables $y_{o+1}, \dots, y_n$.
4. Solve the linear system given by the last $o - 1$ equations of (5) to obtain univariate linear representations of $y_2, \dots, y_o$ in the single variable y_1. If this fails, choose other values for the vinegar variables $y_{o+1}, \dots, y_n$.

Algorithm 2. Key Generation of CSSv

Input: Finite field K with q elements and integers o, v
Output: CSSv key pair $((\mathcal{F}, \mathcal{S}, \mathcal{T}), \mathcal{P})$
 1: Choose randomly 1 quadratic polynomial $\hat{f}^{(1)}$ and $(o-1)$ affine maps $\hat{f}^{(2)}, \ldots, \hat{f}^{(o)}$
    in the $n = o + v$ variables $y_1, \ldots, y_n$.
 2: Choose 1 random cubic polynomial g_2 in the v variables $y_{o+1}, \ldots, y_n$
 3: Choose $o - 1$ random quadratic polynomials $g_1, g_3, g_4, \ldots, g_o$ in the v variables
    $y_{o+1}, \ldots, y_n$
 4: Define $\bar{f}^{(1)}(x_1, \ldots, x_o, y_{o+1}, \ldots, y_n), \ldots, \bar{f}^{(o)}(x_1, \cdots, x_o, y_{o+1}, \ldots, y_n)$ as in (6)
 5: The central map is $\mathcal{F} = (f^{(1)}, \cdots, f^{(o)}) : K^n \to K^o$ where for each $i = 1, \ldots, o$ we
    have $f^{(i)} = \bar{f}^{(i)}(\hat{f}^{(1)}, \ldots, \hat{f}^{(o)}, y_{o+1}, \ldots, y_n)$
 6: Choose a randomly invertible affine map $\mathcal{S} : K^n \to K^n$
 7: Choose a randomly invertible affine map $\mathcal{T} : K^o \to K^o$ as in (7)
 8: $\mathcal{P} = \mathcal{T} \circ \mathcal{F} \circ \mathcal{S} : K^n \to K^o$
 9: **return** $((\mathcal{F}, \mathcal{S}, \mathcal{T}), \mathcal{P})$

---

5. Substitute these relations into the first equation of (5) to get a univariate quadratic equation in the variable y_1, and solve it. If the equation has no solution, choose other values for the vinegar variables $y_{o+1}, \ldots, y_n$.
6. Compute a signature $\mathbf{z} \in K^n$ of the message $\mathbf{d}$ by $\mathbf{z} = \mathcal{S}^{-1}(y_1, \ldots, y_n)$.

Signature Verification: To check if $\mathbf{z} \in K^n$ is indeed a valid signature for a message $\mathbf{d} \in K^o$, the verifier simply computes $\mathbf{d}' = \mathcal{P}(\mathbf{z})$. If $\mathbf{d}' = \mathbf{d}$ holds, the signature is accepted, otherwise it is rejected.

3.2 Security

Rank Attacks. There are two main types of rank attacks: The MinRank attack [1,6] and the HighRank attack [14]. The goal of the MinRank attack is to find a linear combination of the matrices associated to the homogeneous quadratic parts of the public polynomials of low rank. The idea is that such a linear combination corresponds to a central polynomial.

In the case of the CSSv scheme, the matrices associated to the central polynomials have rank $\geq v + 2$ ($v + 1$ if q even and v odd). Recovering such a central polynomial by solving a MinRank Problem has a complexity of at least q^{v+2}. By choosing the parameter v in an appropriate way, it is therefore easy to prevent attacks of the MinRank type.

The HighRank attack tries to find (the linear representations of) the variables which appear the fewest times in the central polynomials. However, since all the variables $y_1, \ldots, y_n$ appear in every component of the central map, the HighRank attack is not applicable against CSSv.

Direct Attacks. The most straightforward method to attack a multivariate cryptosystem is the direct attack. For this type of attack, one tries to solve the equation $\mathcal{P}(\mathbf{z}) = \mathbf{d}$ directly as an instance of the MQ-Problem. The most efficient and popular tool for this are Gröbner bases methods such as the F_4 algorithm [10]. The complexity of this algorithm can be estimated by

$$O\left(m \cdot \binom{n + d_{reg} - 1}{d_{reg}}^{\omega}\right),$$

where d_{reg} is the so called degree of regularity of the system and $2 < \omega \leq 3$ is the linear algebra constant.

In order to estimate the security of our scheme against direct attacks, we have to study the degree of regularity of the public systems. To do this, we carried out a number of experiments with MAGMA [3] (see Table 2 in the appendix of this paper). As our experiments showed, the public systems of CSSv behave, for $v = \frac{o}{2}$, very similar to random systems. On the other hand we found that, for smaller values of v, the public systems are significantly easier to solve.[2] In our parameter selection (see Sect. 5), we therefore choose $o = 2 \cdot v$ and the value of o in such a way, that the complexity of a direct attack against our scheme is beyond the proposed levels of security. As we found, this choice also prevents the MinRank attack against our scheme.

Linearization Equations Attack. The Linearization Equations attack was first successfully used by Patarin [21] to break the Matsumoto-Imai cryptosystem [19]. The idea of this attack is to look for equations of the form

$$\sum_{i=1}^{n} \sum_{j=1}^{m} \alpha_{ij} \cdot z_i \cdot d_j + \sum_{i=1}^{n} \beta_i \cdot z_i + \sum_{j=1}^{m} \gamma_j \cdot d_j + \delta \qquad (8)$$

fulfilled by the message/signature pairs $(\mathbf{d}, \mathbf{z})$ of a cryptosystem. By substituting a given message $\mathbf{d}^{\star}$ into (8), one obtains a linear equation in the components z_i of the signature which helps to forge a signature $\mathbf{z}^{\star}$ for the message $\mathbf{d}^{\star}$.

However since, in the case of the CSSv scheme, the maps $\hat{f}^{(1)}, \ldots, \hat{f}^{(o)}$ and $g_1, \ldots, g_o$ are chosen completely at random, there should not exist any linearization equations for our scheme.

Differential Attacks. In a differential attack one looks for symmetries or invariants of the differential

$$\mathcal{G}(\mathbf{x}, \mathbf{y}) = \mathcal{P}(\mathbf{x} + \mathbf{y}) - \mathcal{P}(\mathbf{x}) - \mathcal{P}(\mathbf{y}) + \mathcal{P}(\mathbf{0})$$

of the public key of a multivariate cryptosystem. Differential attacks were successfully applied to attack multivariate BigField Schemes such as Sflash [9] and PMI [11]. However, differential properties have also been found for SingleField Schemes such as SimpleMatrix [26]. However, while the structure of the map $\bar{\mathcal{F}}$ looks similar to the central map of the SimpleMatrix scheme [26], the differential properties are efficiently destroyed by the use of the random quadratic maps $g_1, \ldots, g_o$.

---

[2] Our experiments showed that the same holds for the original CUOV scheme. In our comparison (see Table 1) we therefore changed the parameters compared to [20] to cover this fact.

Hashimoto's Attack. To simplify the description, let us assume here that the affine map $\mathcal{S}$ is the identity map, i.e. we have $\mathcal{P} = \mathcal{T} \circ \mathcal{F}$.[3] As shown above, Hashimoto's attack relies on the fact that there exists an (easy to find) relation of the public polynomials $p^{(1)}, \ldots, p^{(o)}$ of the form

$$\mathcal{Y} = \sum_{i=1}^{o} a_i \cdot p^{(i)} = \mathcal{X} + \mathcal{G}, \tag{9}$$

with $\mathcal{X}$ being a quadratic form in the variables $z_1, \ldots, z_n$ and $\mathcal{G}$ being a cubic polynomial in $z_{o+1}, \ldots, z_n$. Since the only quadratic terms in the public key of CSSv are contained in $p^{(1)}$, we have $a_1 \neq 0$. But this implies that $\mathcal{Y}$ also contains cubic terms in the variables $z_1, \ldots, z_o$. Furthermore, since $p^{(1)}$ is the only cubic polynomial in $\mathcal{P}$ and the structure of the central polynomials is efficiently hidden by the use of the affine map $\mathcal{T}$, we can not remove these terms from $\mathcal{Y}$ without recovering $\mathcal{T}$ (i.e. solving a MinRank problem). Therefore, finding a relation of the form (9) is infeasible, which means that Hashimoto's attack is not applicable to our scheme.

4   Our Second Improved Scheme

In this section we propose, based on the idea of the CSSv scheme, a second signature scheme, which we call the Simple Vector Signature Scheme with Vinegar (SVSv)[4]. Our goal here is to get rid off the cubic equations in the private and public polynomials and therefore to reduce the size of the public key further.

4.1   Construction

Key generation: Let K be a finite field with q elements, $o, v, r \in \mathbb{N}$ and set $n = o + v + r$.[5] As in the case of the CUOV and the CSSv scheme, the *central map* of the SVSv scheme has the form $\mathcal{F} = \bar{\mathcal{F}} \circ (\hat{\mathcal{F}} \times \mathrm{id}_v)$, where id_v is the identity map in K^v. The map $\hat{\mathcal{F}} = (\hat{f}^{(1)}, \ldots, \hat{f}^{(o)}) : K^n \to K^o$ consists of o randomly chosen affine polynomials in the n variables $y_1, \ldots, y_n$. The map $\bar{\mathcal{F}} : K^o \times K^{v+r} \to K^o$ is given by

$$\begin{cases} \bar{f}^{(1)} &= x_1^2 + g_1(y_{o+1}, \ldots, y_n) \\ \bar{f}^{(2)} &= x_1 \cdot x_2 + g_2(y_{o+1}, \ldots, y_{o+v}) \\ \quad \ldots \\ \bar{f}^{(o)} &= x_{o-1} \cdot x_o + g_o(y_{o+1}, \ldots, y_{o+v}) \end{cases} \tag{10}$$

---

[3] By doing so, we do not have to distinguish between a quadratic form of rank v and a quadratic form in v variables.

[4] The design of our scheme is inspired by the SimpleMatrix scheme [26]. Hence the name.

[5] The reason for using the parameter r is to ensure that all components of the central map have the same rank (see Sect. 3.2). For the case of $(q \bmod 2) = (v \bmod 2) = 0$, we use $r = 2$, otherwise $r = 1$.

where $g_1, \ldots, g_o$ are randomly chosen quadratic polynomials in the vinegar variables $y_{o+1}, \ldots, y_n$. Therefore, in contrast to the CUOV and CSSv scheme, all the components of the central map of the SVSv scheme are quadratic polynomials. To hide the structure of $\mathcal{F}$ in the public key, we combine it with two randomly chosen invertible affine maps $\mathcal{T} : K^o \to K^o$ and $\mathcal{S} : K^n \to K^n$. The *public key* is given by $\mathcal{P} = \mathcal{T} \circ \mathcal{F} \circ \mathcal{S} : K^n \to K^o$ and consists of o quadratic polynomials in n variables. The *private key* consists of the o affine polynomials $\hat{f}^{(1)}, \ldots, \hat{f}^{(o)}$ in n variables, the o quadratic polynomials $g_1, \ldots, g_o$ in $v + r$ variables and the two affine maps $\mathcal{S}$ and $\mathcal{T}$. The key generation is illustrated in Algorithm 3.

Algorithm 3. Key Generation of SVSv

Input: Finite field K with q elements and integers o, v, r
Output: SVSv key pair $((\mathcal{F}, \mathcal{S}, \mathcal{T}), \mathcal{P})$
 1: Choose randomly o affine polynomials $\hat{f}^{(i)}$ in the $n = o + v$ variables $y_1, \ldots, y_n$
 2: Choose a random quadratic polynomial g_1 in the $v + r$ variables $y_{o+1}, \ldots, y_n$
 3: Choose $o - 1$ random quadratic polynomials $g_2, \ldots, g_o$ in the v variables $y_{o+1}, \ldots, y_{o+v}$
 4: Define polynomials $\bar{f}^{(1)}(x_1, \ldots, x_o, y_{o+1}, \ldots, y_n), \ldots, \bar{f}^{(o)}(x_1, \ldots, x_o, y_{o+1}, \ldots, y_n)$ as shown in (10)
 5: The central map is $\mathcal{F} = (f^{(1)}, \ldots, f^{(o)}) : K^n \to K^o$ where, for each $i = 1, \ldots, o$, we have $f^{(i)} = \bar{f}^{(i)}(\hat{f}^{(1)}, \ldots, \hat{f}^{(o)}, y_{o+1}, \ldots, y_n)$
 6: Choose randomly invertible affine maps $\mathcal{S} : K^n \to K^n$ and $\mathcal{T} : K^o \to K^o$
 7: $\mathcal{P} = \mathcal{T} \circ \mathcal{F} \circ \mathcal{S} : K^n \to K^o$
 8: **return** $((\mathcal{F}, \mathcal{S}, \mathcal{T}), \mathcal{P})$

Signature Generation: To generate a signature for a message $\mathbf{d} = (d_1, \ldots, d_o) \in K^o$, the signer performs the following steps.

(1) Compute the pre-image $\mathbf{w} = \mathcal{T}^{-1}(\mathbf{d})$.
(2) Choose random values for the vinegar variables $y_{o+1}, \ldots, y_n$ and substitute them into the polynomials $\hat{f}^{(1)}, \ldots, \hat{f}^{(o)}$ and $g_1, \ldots, g_o$. We obtain the values of $x_1, \ldots, x_o$ as follows:
  (a) Compute $x_1 = \sqrt{w_1 - g_1} = \begin{cases} (w_1 - g_1)^{1/2} & q = 1 \bmod 2 \\ (w_1 - g_1)^{q/2} & q = 0 \bmod 2 \end{cases}$. If $x_1 = 0$ holds, we choose other values for the vinegar variables $y_{o+1}, \ldots, y_n$.
  (b) Inductively, for $i = 2, \ldots, o$, x_i can be obtained by $x_i = (w_i - g_i)/x_{i-1}$. If x_i occurs to be 0, we choose other values for the vinegar variables $y_{o+1}, \ldots, y_n$.
(3) Having found $(x_1, \ldots, x_o)$, we solve the linear system given by $\hat{f}^{(1)}, \ldots, \hat{f}^{(o)}$ for $(y_1, \ldots, y_o)$. If there is no solution, we go back to Step (2).
(4) From a solution $(y_1, \ldots, y_n)$, a signature $\mathbf{z} \in K^n$ for $\mathbf{d}$ is easily obtained by computing $\mathbf{z} = \mathcal{S}^{-1}(y_1, \ldots, y_n)$.

Signature Verification: To check the authenticity of a signature $\mathbf{z} \in K^n$, one simply computes $\mathbf{d}' = \mathcal{P}(\mathbf{z})$. If the result is equal to the message $\mathbf{d}$, the signature is accepted, otherwise rejected.

4.2   Security

Rank Attacks. Similar to our analysis in Sect. 3.2, we study here the security of our scheme against the MinRank and the HighRank attack.

In the case of the SVSv scheme, the rank of all matrices $G_1, \ldots, G_o$ associated to the homogeneous quadratic parts of the central map components is $v+2$ ($v+1$ in the case of even q and odd v).

In order to ensure that all the matrices G_i have the same rank, we use the parameter r of our scheme. For odd q and $r = 0$, the rank of G_1 would be 1 less than the rank of the other matrices G_i ($i = 2, \ldots, o$). In order to avoid this, we increase the number of variables in g_1 by 1. In the case of even q, the situation is a bit more complicated, since the rank of the matrices G_i is always even. In this case, we choose $r = 1$ if v is odd and $r = 2$ otherwise.

The complexity of a MinRank attack against our scheme is therefore greater or equal to q^{v+2}. By choosing the parameter v in an appropriate way, we therefore can easily defend our scheme against the MinRank attack.

Since, similar to the case of CSSv, every component of the central map of SVSv contains all the variables $y_1, \ldots, y_n$, the HighRank is not applicable against our scheme.

Direct Attacks. In order to estimate the security of our scheme against direct attacks, we carried out a number of experiments with MAGMA [3] (see Table 3 in the appendix of this paper).

As our experiments showed, the public systems of SVSv behave, for $o = 2 \cdot v$, very similar to random systems, whereas, for smaller values of v, the SVSv systems are significantly easier to solve. In our parameter selection (see next section), we therefore choose $o = 2 \cdot v$ and the value of o in such a way that the complexity of a direct attack against the scheme is beyond the proposed levels of security. As we find, this parameter choice also prevents the MinRank attack.

Hashimoto's attack [15]. Again, let us assume that the affine map $\mathcal{S}$ is the identity map, i.e. $\mathcal{P} = \mathcal{T} \circ \mathcal{F}$. In order to make Hashimoto's attack work, we have to find a relation of the public polynomials of the form

$$\mathcal{Y} = \sum_{i=1}^{o} a_i \cdot p^{(i)} = \mathcal{X} + \mathcal{G}$$

with a quadratic map $\mathcal{X}$ in $z_1, \ldots, z_n$ and a cubic map $\mathcal{G}$ in $z_{o+1}, \ldots, z_n$. In order to get cubic terms in $\mathcal{Y}$, the coefficients a_i have to be polynomials itself. However, this implies that $\mathcal{Y}$ also contains cubic terms in the variables $z_1, \ldots, z_o$. Removing them requires to reconstruct the map $\mathcal{T}$ (i.e. solving a MinRank problem) which, as shown above, is infeasible.

Other Attacks. Similar to the CSSv scheme (see previous section), Linearization Equations Attacks are not applicable to SVSv due to the random choice of the maps $\hat{f}^{(1)}, \ldots, \hat{f}^{(o)}$ and $g_1, \ldots, g_o$. Furthermore, the use of the vinegar maps $g_1, \ldots, g_o$ efficiently destroys the differential properties of the central map $\mathcal{F}$ and therefore prevents differential attacks.

5   Parameters and Efficiency

In Table 1, we compare our CSSv and SVSv with the original CUOV [20], UOV [16] and Rainbow [7] signature schemes in terms of key and signature size. As can be seen from the table, our schemes provide, for the same security level, shorter signatures and smaller public keys than CUOV, UOV and Rainbow. In particular, SVSv achieves a reduction of the public key size of up to 55%, 79% and 24% compared to CUOV, UOV and Rainbow respectively. Regarding the private key size, the reduction factors are 13%, 93% and 79% respectively.

The signature generation process of both the CSSv and the SVSv scheme can be implemented very efficiently. Besides solving systems of linear equations, the signature generation of CSSv requires only the solution of a univariate quadratic equation; see Step 5 of the Signature Generation in Sect. 3.1. In the case of the

Table 1. Comparison of key sizes and signature lengths for parameters at 80-bit, 100-bit and 128-bit security level

Security level (bit)	Scheme parameters	Hash length (bit)	Signature length (bit)	Public key size (KB)	Private key size (KB)
80	$UOV(2^8, 28, 56)$	224	672	99.9	93.5
	$Rainbow(2^8, 17, 13, 13)$	208	344	25.1	19.1
	$CUOV(2^8, 26, 13)$	208	312	47.6	6.5
	Our CSSv$(2^8, 26, 13)$	**208**	**312**	**29.7**	**6.9**
	Our SVSv$(2^8, 26, 13, 1)$	**208**	**320**	**21.9**	**6.0**
100	$UOV(2^8, 35, 70)$	280	840	193.8	179.5
	$Rainbow(2^8, 26, 16, 17)$	264	472	59.0	45.0
	$CUOV(2^8, 34, 17)$	272	408	106.8	12.7
	Our CSSv$(2^8, 34, 17)$	**272**	**408**	**66.1**	**13.1**
	Our SVSv$(2^8, 34, 17, 1)$	**272**	**416**	**47.5**	**11.3**
128	$UOV(2^8, 45, 90)$	360	1080	409.4	375.9
	$Rainbow(2^8, 36, 21, 22)$	344	632	136.1	102.5
	$CUOV(2^8, 44, 22)$	352	528	232.0	24.8
	Our CSSv$(2^8, 44, 22)$	**352**	**528**	**142.6**	**24.6**
	Our SVSv$(2^8, 44, 22, 2)$	**352**	**544**	**103.8**	**21.4**

Table 2. Comparison of execution time for parameters at 80-bit security level

Scheme parameters	Key generation [s]	Signature generation [s]	Signature verification [s]
$UOV(2^8, 28, 56)$	6.186	0.421	1.685
$Rainbow(2^8, 17, 13, 13)$	3.824	0.370	0.808
$SVSv(2^8, 26, 13)$	**1.638**	**0.081**	**0.292**
$CSSv(2^8, 26, 13)$	2.128	0.141	0.453
$CUOV(2^8, 26, 13)$	6.041	0.248	1.076

SVSv scheme, we need to compute the square root of a finite field element, which is just a 2-power in fields of even characteristic; see Step 2(a) of the Signature Generation in Sect. 4.1. Table 2 compares the execution time in second ([s]) of our schemes with those of UOV, Rainbow and CUOV at a security level of 80 bit. The experiments were performed by using a straightforward MAGMA [3] implementation (version 2.19-7) on a processor Intel(R) Core(TM) i5-4300U CPU @ 2.50 GHz with 8 GB RAM in Windows 7 Professional. Here, we use MAGMA commands `IsConsistent()` for solving linear systems, `Factorization()` for solving univariate quadratic equations, `Sqrt()` for computing square-root of numbers over finite fields and `Cputime()` for computing the execution time.

In the signature generation process of both the CSSv and the SVSv scheme we require all variables $x_1, \ldots, x_{o-1}$ to be different from zero. However this holds, in the case of $q = 256$, with a high probability of $\left(\frac{255}{256}\right)^{o-1}$. For the parameter sets proposed in Table 1, this probability is at least 84.5%. Therefore, the probability of finding a signature in the first try (without choosing other values for the vinegar variables) is very high.

6   Conclusion

In this paper we revisited the recently proposed multivariate signature scheme CUOV of Nie et al. [20] and the attack of Hashimoto against this scheme. We carefully analyzed which design properties make the scheme insecure and proposed two new multivariate signature schemes called CSSv and SVSv which avoid Hashimoto's attack. We showed that our schemes are secure not only against Hashimoto's attack, but also against all known attacks on multivariate cryptosystems, including direct, rank and differential attacks. Especially the SVSv scheme is very efficient and outperforms current multivariate constructions such as UOV and Rainbow in terms of key and signature size.

Acknowledgments. The first and second author thank the Japanese Society for the Promotion of Science (JSPS) for financial support under grant KAKENHI 16K17644 and 15F15350.

A   Experiments with MAGMA

In this section we present the results of our experiments with the direct attack against the CSSv and SVSv schemes. For our experiments we created, for $K = GF(256)$ and different values of o and v, public systems of CSSv and SVSv in MAGMA [3] code. We then fixed v (resp. $v + r$ in the case of SVSv) of the variables to create determined systems and solved these using the F4 algorithm [10] integrated in MAGMA. Tables 2 and 3 show the degree of regularity of the corresponding systems. For each of the parameter sets listed in the table we performed 10 experiments.

As the experiments show, the public systems of both CSSv and SVSv behave, for $o = 2 \cdot v$, very similar to random systems. On the other hand, for smaller values of v, the public systems are significantly easier to solve.

Table 3. Experiments with the direct attack against CSSv

	o	8	9	10	1	12	13	14	15
CSSv with $v = \frac{o}{3}$	v	-	3	-	-	4	-	-	5
	d_{reg}	-	8	-	-	9	-	-	11
CSSv with $v = \frac{o}{2}$	v	4	-	5	-	6	-	7	-
	d_{reg}	11	-	13	-	15	-	17	-
Random system[a]	d_{reg}	11	12	13	14	15	16	17	18

[a]Determined system with 1 cubic and $(o - 1)$ quadratic equations

Table 4. Experiments with the direct attack against the SVSv scheme

	o	8	9	10	11	12	13	14	15
SVSv with $v = \frac{o}{3}$	(v, r)	-	(3, 1)	-	-	(4, 2)	-	-	(5,1)
	d_{reg}	-	8	-	-	9	-	-	11
SVSv with $v = \frac{o}{2}$	(v, r)	(4, 2)	-	(5, 1)	-	(6, 2)	-	(7, 1)	-
	d_{reg}	10	-	12	-	14	-	16	-
Random system	d_{reg}	10	11	12	13	14	15	16	17

References

1. Billet, O., Gilbert, H.: Cryptanalysis of rainbow. In: Prisco, R., Yung, M. (eds.) SCN 2006. LNCS, vol. 4116, pp. 336–347. Springer, Heidelberg (2006). doi:10.1007/11832072_23
2. Bogdanov, A., Eisenbarth, T., Rupp, A., Wolf, C.: Time-area optimized public-key engines: $\mathcal{MQ}$-cryptosystems as replacement for elliptic curves? In: Oswald, E., Rohatgi, P. (eds.) CHES 2008. LNCS, vol. 5154, pp. 45–61. Springer, Heidelberg (2008). doi:10.1007/978-3-540-85053-3_4
3. Bosma, W., Cannon, J., Playoust, C.: The magma algebra system I: the user language. J. Symbolic Comput. **24**(3), 235–265 (1997)
4. Chen, A.I.-T., Chen, M.-S., Chen, T.-R., Cheng, C.-M., Ding, J., Kuo, E.L.-H., Lee, F.Y.-S., Yang, B.-Y.: SSE implementation of multivariate PKCs on modern ×86 CPUs. In: Clavier, C., Gaj, K. (eds.) CHES 2009. LNCS, vol. 5747, pp. 33–48. Springer, Heidelberg (2009). doi:10.1007/978-3-642-04138-9_3
5. Chen, L., Jordan, S., Liu, Y.-K., Moody, D., Peralta, R., Perlner, R., Smith-Tone, D.: Report on post-quantum cryptography. National Institute of Standards and Technology Internal Report, 8105 (2016)
6. Coppersmith, D., Stern, J., Vaudenay, S.: Attacks on the birational permutation signature schemes. In: Stinson, D.R. (ed.) CRYPTO 1993. LNCS, vol. 773, pp. 435–443. Springer, Heidelberg (1994). doi:10.1007/3-540-48329-2_37
7. Ding, J., Schmidt, D.: Rainbow, a new multivariable polynomial signature scheme. In: Ioannidis, J., Keromytis, A., Yung, M. (eds.) ACNS 2005. LNCS, vol. 3531, pp. 164–175. Springer, Heidelberg (2005). doi:10.1007/11496137_12

8. Ding, J., Yang, B.-Y., Chen, C.-H.O., Chen, M.-S., Cheng, C.-M.: New differential-algebraic attacks and reparametrization of rainbow. In: Bellovin, S.M., Gennaro, R., Keromytis, A., Yung, M. (eds.) ACNS 2008. LNCS, vol. 5037, pp. 242–257. Springer, Heidelberg (2008). doi:10.1007/978-3-540-68914-0_15

9. Dubois, V., Fouque, P.-A., Shamir, A., Stern, J.: Practical cryptanalysis of SFLASH. In: Menezes, A. (ed.) CRYPTO 2007. LNCS, vol. 4622, pp. 1–12. Springer, Heidelberg (2007). doi:10.1007/978-3-540-74143-5_1

10. Faugere, J.-C.: A new efficient algorithm for computing Gröbner bases (f4). J. Pure Appl. Algebra **139**(1), 61–88 (1999)

11. Fouque, P.-A., Granboulan, L., Stern, J.: Differential cryptanalysis for multivariate schemes. In: Cramer, R. (ed.) EUROCRYPT 2005. LNCS, vol. 3494, pp. 341–353. Springer, Heidelberg (2005). doi:10.1007/11426639_20

12. Garey, M.R., Johnson, D.S.: A Guide to the Theory of NP-Completeness. WH Freemann, New York (1979)

13. Goodin, D.: NSA preps quantum-resistant algorithms to head off cryptoapocalypse

14. Goubin, L., Courtois, N.T.: Cryptanalysis of the TTM cryptosystem. In: Okamoto, T. (ed.) ASIACRYPT 2000. LNCS, vol. 1976, pp. 44–57. Springer, Heidelberg (2000). doi:10.1007/3-540-44448-3_4

15. Hashimoto, Y.: On the security of cubic UOV

16. Kipnis, A., Patarin, J., Goubin, L.: Unbalanced oil and vinegar signature schemes. In: Stern, J. (ed.) EUROCRYPT 1999. LNCS, vol. 1592, pp. 206–222. Springer, Heidelberg (1999). doi:10.1007/3-540-48910-X_15

17. Koblitz, N.: Elliptic curve cryptosystems. Math. Comput. **48**(177), 203–209 (1987)

18. Kravitz, D.W.: Digital signature algorithm, 27 July 1993. US Patent 5,231,668

19. Matsumoto, T., Imai, H.: Public quadratic polynomial-tuples for efficient signature-verification and message-encryption. In: Barstow, D., et al. (eds.) EUROCRYPT 1988. LNCS, vol. 330, pp. 419–453. Springer, Heidelberg (1988). doi:10.1007/3-540-45961-8_39

20. Nie, X., Liu, B., Xiong, H., Lu, G.: Cubic unbalance oil and vinegar signature scheme. In: Lin, D., Wang, X.F., Yung, M. (eds.) Inscrypt 2015. LNCS, vol. 9589, pp. 47–56. Springer, Heidelberg (2016). doi:10.1007/978-3-319-38898-4_3

21. Patarin, J.: Cryptanalysis of the matsumoto and imai public key scheme of eurocrypt 88. In Annual International Cryptology Conference, pp. 248–261. Springer, 1995

22. Patarin, J.: Hidden fields equations (HFE) and isomorphisms of polynomials (IP): two new families of asymmetric algorithms. In: Maurer, U. (ed.) EUROCRYPT 1996. LNCS, vol. 1070, pp. 33–48. Springer, Heidelberg (1996). doi:10.1007/3-540-68339-9_4

23. Patarin, J., Courtois, N., Goubin, L.: FLASH, a fast multivariate signature algorithm. In: Naccache, D. (ed.) CT-RSA 2001. LNCS, vol. 2020, pp. 298–307. Springer, Heidelberg (2001). doi:10.1007/3-540-45353-9_22

24. Rivest, R.L., Shamir, A., Adleman, L.: A method for obtaining digital signatures and public-key cryptosystems. Commun. ACM **21**(2), 120–126 (1978)

25. Shor, P.W.: Polynomial-time algorithms for prime factorization and discrete logarithms on a quantum computer. SIAM Rev. **41**(2), 303–332 (1999)

26. Tao, C., Diene, A., Tang, S., Ding, J.: Simple matrix scheme for encryption. In: Gaborit, P. (ed.) PQCrypto 2013. LNCS, vol. 7932, pp. 231–242. Springer, Heidelberg (2013). doi:10.1007/978-3-642-38616-9_16

Network Coding Signature Schemes Against Related-Key Attacks in the Random Oracle Model

Jinyong Chang[1], Honglong Dai[1], Maozhi Xu[1($\boxtimes$)], and Rui Xue[2]

[1] School of Mathematics, Peking University,
Beijing 100871, People's Republic of China
{changjinyong,daihonglong}@pku.edu.cn, mzxu@math.pku.edu.cn
[2] State Key Laboratory of Information Security, Institute of Information Engineering,
Chinese Academy of Sciences, Beijing 100093, People's Republic of China
xuerui@iie.ac.cn

Abstract. In this paper, we consider the related-key attack (RKA) on the network coding signature (NCS) scheme, which is widely used to protect network coding against pollution attacks. In particular, based on the original security model proposed by Boneh et al. in PKC 2009, we first give the definition of RKA security for general NCS schemes. Then, by presenting a concrete pollution attack on the random-model (RO) based NCS scheme of Boneh et al., we prove that their scheme is not RKA secure in a "weaker" sense (w.r.t. linear functions). Lastly, we show that a slight modification of it yields a "stronger" RKA secure (w.r.t. d-order polynomial functions) NCS scheme under the d-co-computational Diffie-Hellman (d-co-CDH) assumption of bilinear groups.

Keywords: Network coding signature · Related-key attack · Co-CDH assumption · Bilinear groups

1 Introduction

Network coding is an attractive paradigm which offers an interesting alternative to traditional routing mechanisms. Instead of merely storing and forwarding the packets in transmission, the outgoing packets contain vectors that are calculated as linear combinations of vectors conveyed by incoming packets, which is proven capable of achieving maximized throughput, enhanced robustness, and lower energy consumption for communication networks [3,10].

Unfortunately, network coding is highly sensitive to pollution attacks, where malicious nodes inject invalid packets in the network in order to prevent target nodes from recovering the original file. The problem is particularly acute because errors introduced into even a single packet can propagate and pollute multiple packets making their way to the destination.

Network coding signature (NCS) scheme is a useful tool to provide cryptographic protection against pollution attacks [3]. In [3], Boneh et al. proposed an

© Springer International Publishing AG 2017
S. Hong and J.H. Park (Eds.): ICISC 2016, LNCS 10157, pp. 239–253, 2017.
DOI: 10.1007/978-3-319-53177-9_13

efficient NCS scheme, which is suitably homomorphic and has constant public-key size, in the random oracle (i.e. not standard) model. Until now, their result has been cited nearly 200 times and their scheme has been widely used in network coding such as [5, 8].

Related-Key Attack. Related-Key Attack (RKA) is a new-type attack on many cryptographic schemes or primitives, which is formalized by Bellare and Kohno [2]. Informally, RKA refers to that, given physical access to a hardware device, an adversary can use fault injection techniques to tamper with and induce modifications to the internal state of the cryptographic hardware device, such as a signing key for a signature scheme or a decryption key for an encryption scheme [1, 9]. Hence, in recent years, RKA-security has been widely considered for kinds of cryptographic primitives, such as public-key encryption [9], pseudorandom functions [2], protocols [4], authentication encryption [6], signatures [7] etc.

Our Contributions. In this paper, we consider the RKA security for the NCS schemes. As far as we know, this is the first time to "bring" RKA into the NCS schemes. In particular, our contributions include the following three aspects:

- We first define the model of Φ-RKA security for NCS schemes, where Φ is a function family from the signing key space to itself, describing which operations is allowed to manipulate the signing key for an adversary.
- Second, by presenting a practical pollution attack, we prove that the random-oracle based scheme proposed by Boneh, Freeman, Katz, and Waters in [3] (BFKW-NCS scheme, for short), is not Φ_{lin}-RKA secure, where Φ_{lin} consists of linear functions of secret key.
- Finally, we show that a slight modification of the original BFKW-NCS scheme yields $\Phi_{d\text{-poly}}$-RKA secure NCS scheme under the d-co-CDH assumption, where $\Phi_{d\text{-poly}}$ consists of d-order polynomial functions of signing key.

Since $\Phi_{\text{lin}} \subset \Phi_{d\text{-poly}}$ for $d > 0$, we remark that the RKA security in the latter sense is "stronger" than that in the former one.

Organizations. The remainder of the paper is organized as follows. In Sect. 2, we review some standard notions and present the definition of NCS scheme as well as its RKA security. In Sect. 3, we describe the related-key attack on BFKW scheme and then modify it into one that is RKA secure w.r.t. some function families. Discussion of efficiency can be found in Sect. 4. Finally, we conclude our results in Sect. 5.

2 Preliminaries

Basic Notation. In this paper, we always denote by λ the security parameter of algorithms and by 1^λ its unary form. For $n \in \mathbb{N}$, $[n]$ denote the set $\{1, 2, \cdots, n\}$. If S is a set, then denote by $|S|$ the number of elements in it and by $s \xleftarrow{\$} S$ uniformly randomly choosing s from S. If $\mathbf{v} \in S^n$, then let v_i denote its ith component. If p is a prime number, then $\mathbb{F}_p$ is the finite field $\{0, 1, \cdots, p-1\}$.

PPT means probabilistic polynomial time. A function $negl(\lambda)$ is negligible if for any integer $c > 0$, there is a $\lambda_0 \in \mathbb{Z}$ such that for all $\lambda > \lambda_0$, we have $negl(\lambda) < \lambda^{-c}$. $(a \overset{?}{=} b)$ is a predicate function, which returns 1 if and only if $a = b$.

2.1 Bilinear Groups and Complexity Assumptions

Let GenBiGroup be a PPT algorithm, which takes 1^λ as input, and outputs

$$\mathcal{G} := (p, \mathbb{G}_1, \mathbb{G}_2, \mathbb{G}_T, e, \varphi)$$

with the following properties:

- p is a prime number satisfying $p \geq 2^\lambda$.
- $\mathbb{G}_1, \mathbb{G}_2, \mathbb{G}_T$ are cyclic groups satisfying

$$|\mathbb{G}_1| = |\mathbb{G}_2| = |\mathbb{G}_T| = p.$$

- $e : \mathbb{G}_1 \times \mathbb{G}_2 \to \mathbb{G}_T$ is a map, which can be efficiently computable and satisfying:
  - **Non-Degeneracy:** If $\mathbb{G}_1 = \langle g \rangle$, $\mathbb{G}_2 = \langle h \rangle$, then $\mathbb{G}_T = \langle e(g, h) \rangle$.
  - **Bilinearity:** For all $g \in \mathbb{G}_1$, $h \in \mathbb{G}_2$, and $a, b \in \mathbb{Z}$, it holds that $e(g^a, h^b) = e(g, h)^{ab}$.
  - $\varphi : \mathbb{G}_2 \to \mathbb{G}_1$ is an isomorphism, which can also be efficiently computable.

d-Co-Computational Diffie-Hellman Assumption. We introduce the d-co-computational Diffie-Hellman (d-co-CDH) problem on $\mathcal{G}$. In particular, it is a problem of computing $g^x \in \mathbb{G}_1$ for an adversary $\mathcal{A}$, when given the description of $\mathcal{G}$, $g \in \mathbb{G}_1$, and $(h, h^x, \cdots, h^{x^d}) \in \mathbb{G}_2^{d+1}$, where $x \in \{0, 1, \cdots, p-1\}$. Define the advantage $\mathrm{Adv}_{\mathcal{G}, \mathcal{A}}^{d\text{-co-CDH}}(1^\lambda)$ of $\mathcal{A}$ as follows:

$$\Pr\left[\omega = g^x : x \overset{\$}{\leftarrow} [p-1], \ \omega \leftarrow \mathcal{A}(\mathcal{G}, g, h, h^x, \cdots, h^{x^d})\right].$$

The d-co-CDH assumption over $\mathcal{G}$ says that the advantage $\mathrm{Adv}_{\mathcal{G}, \mathcal{A}}^{d\text{-co-CDH}}(1^\lambda)$ is negligible for any PPT adversary $\mathcal{A}$.

Note that the 1-co-CDH assumption is just the co-CDH assumption in [3].

2.2 Network Coding Signature Scheme

Definition 1. *A network coding signature (NCS) scheme Π is defined by three PPT algorithms* Setup, Sign, Verify *[3]. Concretely,*

- Setup: *Take as inputs the security parameter 1^λ, and a positive integer N, which denotes the length of a vector to be signed. Output a prime p, and a public/private key-pair* (PK, SK).

- **Sign:** Take as inputs the secret key SK, an identifier $id \xleftarrow{\$} \mathcal{I} := \{0,1\}^\lambda$, and an m-dimensional subspace $V \subset \mathbb{F}_p^N$, where $0 < m < N$ and V is described by properly augmented basis vectors $\boldsymbol{v}_1, \cdots, \boldsymbol{v}_m \in \mathbb{F}_p^N$.[1] Output a signature σ (for V)[2].
- **Verify:** Take as inputs the public key PK, an identifier id, a vector $\boldsymbol{y} \in \mathbb{F}_p^N$, and a signature σ. Output 1 (accept) or 0 (reject).

The correctness requires that, for any $(p, PK, SK) \leftarrow \text{Setup}(1^\lambda, N)$, all $id \in \mathcal{I}$, and $V \subset \mathbb{F}_p^N$, if $\sigma \leftarrow \text{Sign}(SK, id, V)$, then

$$\text{Verify}(PK, id, \mathbf{y}, \sigma) = 1,$$

for all $\mathbf{y} \in V$.

Related-Key Attack Security. We define the following game $\text{Exp}_{\Pi, \mathcal{A}}^{\Phi\text{-RKA}}(1^\lambda)$ between a challenger $\mathcal{C}$ and an adversary $\mathcal{A}$, where Φ is a function family from the secret-key space $\mathcal{SK}$ to $\mathcal{SK}$ (i.e. $\Phi = \{\phi : \mathcal{SK} \to \mathcal{SK}\}$).

- **Initialization.** The challenger $\mathcal{C}$ runs $\text{Setup}(1^\lambda, N)$ to obtain the parameter p and the public/private key-pair (PK, SK). Give p and PK to $\mathcal{A}$.
- **Queries.** Proceeding adaptively, the adversary $\mathcal{A}$ submits ξth query (ϕ_ξ, V_ξ), where $\phi_\xi \in \Phi$ and $V_\xi \subset \mathbb{F}_p^N$ is a vector subspace, described by properly augmented basis vectors $\mathbf{v}_1^{(\xi)}, \cdots, \mathbf{v}_{m_\xi}^{(\xi)} \in \mathbb{F}_p^N$. Then the challenger $\mathcal{C}$ chooses $id_\xi \xleftarrow{\$} \mathcal{I}$, runs

$$\sigma^{(\xi)} \leftarrow \text{Sign}(\phi_\xi(SK), id_\xi, V_\xi),$$

and returns $id_\xi, \sigma^{(\xi)}$ to $\mathcal{A}$.[3]
- **Output.** Finally, $\mathcal{A}$ outputs an identifier id^*, a vector $\mathbf{y}^* \in \mathbb{F}_p^N$, and a signature σ^*.

We call the adversary $\mathcal{A}$ wins the game if

$$\text{Verify}(PK, id^*, \mathbf{y}^*, \sigma^*) = 1,$$

and one of the following cases holds:

---

[1] The properly augmented basis $\{\mathbf{v}_i\}_{i=1}^m$ of V means that for $1 \le i \le m$,

$$\mathbf{v}_i = \{v_{i,1}, \cdots, v_{i,N-m}, \overbrace{0, \cdots 0, \underset{\underbrace{}_{m}}{1}, 0 \cdots, 0}^{i}\}.$$

[2] We remark that the signing algorithm Sign may sign subspaces with *different* dimensions.

[3] We remark that, in this situation, the signature $\sigma^{(\xi)}$ should be a valid one under the public key $PK^{(\xi)}$ that is corresponding to $\phi_\xi(SK)$. That is,

$$\text{Verify}(PK^{(\xi)}, id_\xi, \mathbf{y}^{(\xi)}, \sigma^{(\xi)}) = 1,$$

for all $\mathbf{y}^{(\xi)} \in V_\xi$.

1. $id^* \neq id_\xi$ for all ξ and $\mathbf{y}^* \neq \mathbf{0}$ (type 1 forgery),
2. $id^* = id_{\xi_0}$ for some ξ_0, $\phi_{\xi_0}(\mathsf{SK}) = \mathsf{SK}$, and $\mathbf{y}^* \notin V_{\xi_0}$ (type 2 forgery),
3. $id^* = id_{\xi_0}$ for some ξ_0, $\phi_{\xi_0}(\mathsf{SK}) \neq \mathsf{SK}$, and $\mathbf{y}^* \neq \mathbf{0}$ (type 3 forgery).

The advantage $\mathrm{Adv}_{\Pi,\mathcal{A}}^{\Phi\text{-RKA}}(1^\lambda)$ is defined to be the probability that $\mathcal{A}$ wins the game $\mathrm{Exp}_{\Pi,\mathcal{A}}^{\Phi\text{-RKA}}(1^\lambda)$. The NCS scheme Π is Φ-RKA secure if and only if, for any PPT adversary $\mathcal{A}$, its advantage $\mathrm{Adv}_{\Pi,\mathcal{A}}^{\Phi\text{-RKA}}(1^\lambda)$ is negligible in λ.

Obviously, the security becomes stronger along with richer function families. The following two families are two classical ones and used in our paper. **Linear Functions.** Assume that $(G, +)$ is an additive group. The class Φ_{lin} of linear functions over G is defined as follows. $\Phi_{\mathrm{lin}} := \{\phi_\Delta | \Delta \in G\}$, where $\phi_\Delta(k) := k + \Delta$ for a key $k \in G$.

Polynomial Functions. Assume that F is a finite field. The class of d-order polynomial functions is defined as follows. $\Phi_{d\text{-poly}} := \{\phi_f | f \in F_d[x]\}$, where $F_d[x]$ is the set of polynomials over F with degree at most d, and $\phi_f(k) := f(k)$ for a key $k \in F$.

2.3   Homomorphic Network Coding Signature Scheme

A homomorphic network coding signature (HNCS) scheme Π' is defined by the four PPT algorithms $\mathsf{Setup}', \mathsf{Sign}', \mathsf{Combine}', \mathsf{Verify}'$. Concretely,

- Setup': Same as Setup.
- Sign': Take as inputs SK, an identifier $id \xleftarrow{\$} \mathcal{I} := \{0,1\}^\lambda$, an integer $m < N$, which indicates the dimension of the space being signed, and a vector $\mathbf{v} \in \mathbb{F}_p^N$. Output a signature σ (for $\mathbf{v}$).
- $\mathsf{Combine}'$: Take as inputs the public key PK, an identifier id, $((\beta_1, \sigma_1), \cdots, (\beta_\ell, \sigma_\ell))$, where $\beta_i \in \mathbb{F}_p$, for $1 \leq i \leq \ell$. Output a signature σ.
- Verify': Take as inputs the public key PK, an identifier id, an integer $m < N$, a vector $\mathbf{y} \in \mathbb{F}_p^N$, and a signature σ. Output 1 (accept) or 0 (reject).

Lemma 1 ([3]). *Given a HNCS scheme Π', it is easy to construct a NCS scheme Π as follows:*

- $\mathsf{Setup}(1^\lambda, N) := \mathsf{Setup}'(1^\lambda, N)$.
- $\mathsf{Sign}(\mathsf{SK}, id, V)$: *For $i = 1, \cdots, m$, run*

$$\sigma_i \leftarrow \mathsf{Sign}'(\mathsf{SK}, id, m, \mathbf{v}_i),$$

where $\{\mathbf{v}_i\}$ is a properly augmented basis of $V \subset \mathbb{F}_p^N$. Return the signature $\sigma = (\sigma_1, \cdots, \sigma_m)$.
- $\mathsf{Verify}(\mathsf{PK}, id, \mathbf{y}, \sigma)$: *Parse σ as $(\sigma_1, \cdots, \sigma_m)$ and run*

$$b \leftarrow \mathsf{Verify}'(\mathsf{PK}, id, m, \mathbf{y},$$
$$\mathsf{Combine}'(\mathsf{PK}, id, \{(y_{N-m+i}, \sigma_i)\}_{i=1}^m)).$$

Output the bit b.

Hence, it is sufficient to construct a HNCS scheme when one wants to obtain a NCS scheme.

3 RKA Secure NCS in the Random Oracle Model

In this section, we discuss the RKA security of the RO-based NCS scheme proposed by Boneh, Freeman, Katz, and Waters in [3] (i.e. BFKW-NCS). More precisely, we will present a concrete related-key attack on the original BFKW-NCS scheme. Then a slight modification yields a RKA secure NCS scheme with richer function family.

3.1 BFKW's Homomorphic Network Coding Signature Scheme

First, we recall Boneh et al.'s homomorphic network coding signature (called BFKW-HNCS) scheme $\Pi_1' = (\text{Setup}_1', \text{Sign}_1', \text{Combine}_1', \text{Verify}_1')$ as follows.

- Setup_1': Take as inputs 1^λ, and a positive integer N. Run $\mathcal{G} \leftarrow \text{GenBiGroup}(1^\lambda)$. Parse $\mathcal{G}$ as $(p, \mathbb{G}_1, \mathbb{G}_2, \mathbb{G}_T, e, \varphi)$. Then choose

$$g_1, \cdots, g_N \overset{\$}{\leftarrow} \mathbb{G}_1 \backslash \{1\}, \quad h \overset{\$}{\leftarrow} \mathbb{G}_2 \backslash \{1\}, \quad x \overset{\$}{\leftarrow} \mathbb{F}_p.$$

  Let $u = h^x$, and $H : \mathbb{Z} \times \mathbb{Z} \rightarrow \mathbb{G}_1$ be a hash function. Finally, output the public key $\text{PK} = (\mathcal{G}, g_1, \cdots, g_N, h, u, H)$ and the secret key $\text{SK} = x$.
- Sign_1': Take as inputs the secret key $\text{SK} = x$, an identifier $id \in \{0,1\}^\lambda$, an integer $m < N$, which indicates the dimension of the space being signed, and a vector $\mathbf{v} := (v_1, \cdots, v_N) \in \mathbb{F}_p^N$. Denote $n := N - m$ and output

$$\sigma := \left(\prod_{i=1}^{m} H(id, i)^{v_{n+i}} \prod_{j=1}^{n} g_j^{v_j} \right)^x.$$

- $\text{Combine}_1'$: Take as inputs the public key PK, an identifier id, $((\beta_1, \sigma_1), \cdots, (\beta_\ell, \sigma_\ell))$, where $\beta_i \in \mathbb{F}_p$ for $1 \leq i \leq \ell$. Output $\sigma = \prod_{i=1}^{\ell} \sigma_i^{\beta_i}$.
- Verify_1': Take as input the public key PK, an identifier id, an integer $m < N$, which indicates the dimension of the space being signed, a vector $\mathbf{y} \in \mathbb{F}_p^N$, and a signature σ. Define $n := N - m$ and output

$$\left(e \left(\prod_{i=1}^{m} H(id, i)^{y_{n+i}} \prod_{j=1}^{n} g_j^{y_j}, u \right) \overset{?}{=} e(\sigma, h) \right).$$

The correctness of this scheme can be easily verified.

According to Lemma 1, we know that there exists a NCS (i.e. BFKW-NCS) scheme Π_1 based on this HNCS scheme. For completeness, we present Π_1 in the Section Appendix.

3.2 Related-Key Attack on the BFKW-NCS Scheme

In this subsection, we will show that the BFKW-NCS scheme Π_1 is not Φ_{lin}-RKA secure by providing a simple and efficient attack.

Concretely, an adversary $\mathcal{A}$ submits *only one* query $(\phi_\Delta, \{\mathbf{v}\})^4$ to $\mathcal{C}$ (in $\text{Exp}_{\Pi_1, \mathcal{A}}^{\Phi_{\text{lin}}\text{-RKA}}(1^\lambda))$, where $\Delta \ (\neq 0) \in \mathbb{F}_p$, $\phi_\Delta(x) := x + \Delta$, and $\mathbf{v} \in \mathbb{F}_p^N$. Given the identifier id and the signature σ from $\mathcal{C}$, $\mathcal{A}$ computes

$$\sigma^* = \frac{\sigma}{\left(H(id, 1) \cdot \prod_{j=1}^{N-1} g_j^{v_j} \right)^\Delta},$$

and outputs $(id^*, \mathbf{y}^*, \sigma^*) := (id, \mathbf{v}, \sigma^*)$.

Next, we prove that the adversary $\mathcal{A}$ is able to win the game $\text{Exp}_{\Pi_1, \mathcal{A}}^{\Phi_{\text{lin}}\text{-RKA}}(1^\lambda))$ with probability 1. Now that $\mathcal{A}$ chose ϕ_Δ as the modification function of secret key x, the corresponding public key PK' equals to $(\mathcal{G}, g_1, \cdots, g_N, h, u', H)$, where $u' = u \cdot h^\Delta$. In addition, since σ is a valid signature for $\{\mathbf{v}\}$ with respect to PK', we have

$$\text{Verify}_1(\text{PK}', id, \mathbf{v}, \sigma) = 1.$$

That is,

$$
\begin{aligned}
e\left(\sigma, h\right) &= e\left(\prod_{i=1}^{m} H(id, i)^{v_{n+i}} \prod_{j=1}^{n} g_j^{v_j}, u' \right) \\
&= e\left(H(id, 1)^{v_N} \prod_{j=1}^{N-1} g_j^{v_j}, u' \right) \\
&= e\left(\left(H(id, 1)^{v_N} \prod_{j=1}^{N-1} g_j^{v_j} \right)^{x+\Delta}, h \right),
\end{aligned}
$$

where the second equation holds because $m = 1$ and $n = N - 1$. According to the nondegeneracy of e, we know that

$$\sigma = \left(H(id, 1) \cdot \prod_{j=1}^{N-1} g_j^{v_j} \right)^{x+\Delta},$$

which further implies that

$$\sigma^* = \left(H(id, 1) \cdot \prod_{j=1}^{N-1} g_j^{v_j} \right)^x.$$

---

[4] Here, we remark that the submitted subspace $\{\mathbf{v}\}$ is 1-dimensional and the last element $v_N = 1$ since $\mathbf{v}$ is the properly augmented basis. Hence, it is obvious that $m = 1$ and $n = N - m = N - 1$.

Therefore, it clearly holds that

$$
e\left(\prod_{i=1}^{m} H(id,i)^{y^*_{n+i}} \prod_{j=1}^{n} g_j^{y^*_j}, u\right) = e\left(H(id,1)^{y^*_N} \prod_{j=1}^{N-1} g_j^{y^*_j}, u\right)
$$
$$
= e\left(H(id,1)^{v_N} \prod_{j=1}^{N-1} g_j^{v_j}, u\right)
$$
$$
= e\left(\sigma^*, h\right),
$$

where the second equation holds because $\mathbf{y}^* = \mathbf{v}$. That is,

$$
\mathtt{Verify}_1(\mathtt{PK}, id^*, \mathbf{y}^*, \sigma^*) = 1.
$$

Moreover, since $id^* = id$, $\Delta \neq 0$, and $\mathbf{y}^* \neq \mathbf{0}$, the output $(id^*, \mathbf{y}^*, \sigma^*)$ of $\mathcal{A}$ is a type 3 forgery.

We would like to remark that this attack is outside the security model considered in [3].

3.3   Improved BFKW-NCS Scheme and Its RKA Security

Improved BFKW-HNCS Scheme. According to Lemma 1, it is sufficient to present the modified BFKW-HNCS scheme. In fact, we only slightly modify the original BFKW-HNCS Π'_1 (in Sect. 3.1) into the following $\Pi'_2 = (\mathtt{Setup}'_2, \mathtt{Sign}'_2, \mathtt{Combine}'_2, \mathtt{Verify}'_2)$.

- $\mathtt{Setup}'_2$: Same as $\mathtt{Setup}'_1$.
- $\mathtt{Sign}'_2$: Take as inputs the secret key $\mathtt{SK} = x$, an identifier $id \in \{0,1\}^\lambda$, an integer $m < N$, which indicates the dimension of the space being signed, and a vector $\mathbf{v} := (v_1, \cdots, v_N) \in \mathbb{F}_p^N$. Denote $n := N - m$ and compute

$$
\sigma := \left(\prod_{i=1}^{m} H(id,i,h^x)^{v_{n+i}} \prod_{j=1}^{n} g_j^{v_j}\right)^x.
$$

- $\mathtt{Combine}'_2$: Same as $\mathtt{Combine}'_1$.
- $\mathtt{Verify}'_2$: Take as input the public key $\mathtt{PK}$, an identifier id, an integer $m < N$, which indicates the dimension of the space being signed, a vector $\mathbf{y} \in \mathbb{F}_p^N$, and a signature σ. Define $n := N - m$ and output

$$
\left(e\left(\prod_{i=1}^{m} H(id,i,u)^{y_{n+i}} \prod_{j=1}^{n} g_j^{y_j}, u\right) \stackrel{?}{=} e\left(\sigma, h\right)\right).
$$

The correctness of this scheme can be easily verified. Let Π_2 be the NCS scheme constructed from Π'_2. Since the differences between Π_1 and Π_2 are very small, we omit it here.

RKA Security of Π_2. First, we would like to give some underlying intuition about the design of Π_2 and explain why this modification makes it achieving the RKA security. From the concrete related-key attack presented in Sect. 3.2, we know that any RKA adversary $\mathcal{A}$ can easily recover a signature σ^* under the public key $\mathsf{PK} = (\mathcal{G}, g_1, \cdots, g_N, h, u, H)$ from the signature σ (for the same vector $\mathbf{v}$) under the public key $\mathsf{PK}' = (\mathcal{G}, g_1, \cdots, g_N, h, u', H)$, where $u' = u \cdot h^{\Delta}$. The reason lies in that the public key "changes" from PK to PK' when the secret key $\mathsf{SK} = x$ is modified into $\mathsf{SK}' = x + \Delta$. As a result, the signatures σ^* and σ for the same vector $\mathbf{v}$ have the same base number and hence it is not hard to compute σ^* from σ if $\mathcal{A}$ knows the difference Δ between SK and SK'.

In order to obtain a RKA secure NCS scheme, we modify the input of hash function H. More precisely, H takes an extra input h^x, which corresponds to a recalculated value u in the public key PK. Now, in related-key attack, if the secret key $\mathsf{SK} = x$ is modified into another one SK', then the corresponding hash values will be independent according to the randomness of H, which results in the base numbers of the signatures σ^* and σ (for $\mathbf{v}$) irrelevant. Hence, the obtained signature σ becomes useless when the adversary intends to compute a valid forgery.

Next, we formally prove the RKA security of Π_2. In particular, we consider the function family $\Phi_{d\text{-poly}}$ and prove that Π_2 achieves the $\Phi_{d\text{-poly}}$-RKA security under the d-co-CDH assumption. That is,

Theorem 1. *Under the d-co-CDH assumption over $\mathcal{G}$, the improved BFKW-NCS scheme Π_2 is $\Phi_{d\text{-poly}}$-RKA secure in the random oracle model.*

More precisely, for any PPT adversary $\mathcal{A}$, attacking on the $\Phi_{d\text{-poly}}$-RKA security of Π_2 and making q_S RKA signing oracle queries, and q_H random oracle queries to H, there exists a PPT algorithm $\mathcal{B}$, attacking on d-co-CDH problem over $\mathcal{G}$, such that

$$Adv_{\Pi_2, \mathcal{A}}^{\Phi_{d\text{-poly}}\text{-}RKA}(1^\lambda) \leq Adv_{\mathcal{G}, \mathcal{B}}^{d\text{-}co\text{-}CDH}(1^\lambda) - \frac{q_S^2 + q_S q_H}{2^\lambda} - \frac{1}{p}. \tag{1}$$

Proof. We follow the proof outline of Theorem 6 in [3]. First, we describe the construction of $\mathcal{B}$. In particular, given the description of $\mathcal{G} = (p, \mathbb{G}_1, \mathbb{G}_2, \mathbb{G}_T, e, \varphi)$, $g \in \mathbb{G}_1$, and $(h, z_1, \cdots, z_d) \in \mathbb{G}_2^{d+1}$, with $z_1 = h^x, \cdots, z_d = h^{x^d}$, $\mathcal{B}$ intends to output an element $\omega \in \mathbb{G}_1$ satisfying $\omega = g^x$. Now, he simulates the following environment for $\mathcal{A}$:

- **Initialization.** $\mathcal{B}$ chooses $s_1, t_1, \cdots, s_N, t_N \xleftarrow{\$} \mathbb{F}_p$, and sets $g_j := g^{s_j}\varphi(h)^{t_j}$ for $j = 1, \cdots, N$. Return the public key $\mathsf{PK} = (\mathcal{G}, g_1, \cdots, g_N, h, z_1, H)$ to $\mathcal{A}$, where H is the random oracle simulated by $\mathcal{B}$. In addition, $\mathcal{B}$ also initializes an empty list HL.
- **Hash Queries.** When $\mathcal{A}$ submits (id, i, u) to $\mathcal{B}$ for its hash value, $\mathcal{B}$ does as follows.
  1. If there exists (id, i, u) in HL, then return the corresponding value $H(id, i, u)$ to $\mathcal{A}$.

2. Else, choose $\varsigma_i, \tau_i \xleftarrow{\$} \mathbb{F}_p$, set

$$H(id, i, u) := g^{\varsigma_i} \varphi(h)^{\tau_i},$$

and add $((id, i, u), H(id, i, u))$ to HL. Finally, return $H(id, i, u)$ to $\mathcal{A}$.

- **Signing Queries.** When $\mathcal{A}$ submits the ξth query (ϕ_ξ, V_ξ), where, for $1 \leq \xi \leq q_S$, $\phi_\xi \in \Phi_{d\text{-poly}}$ is described by $(a_{\xi 0}, \cdots, a_{\xi d}) \in \mathbb{F}_p^{d+1}$ (i.e. $\phi_\xi(x) := a_{\xi 0} + a_{\xi 1} x + \cdots + a_{\xi d} x^d$), and V_ξ is described by properly augmented basis vectors $\mathbf{v}_1^{(\xi)}, \cdots, \mathbf{v}_{m_\xi}^{(\xi)} \in \mathbb{F}_p^N$, $\mathcal{B}$ does the following:

  1. Choose $id_\xi \xleftarrow{\$} \{0, 1\}^\lambda$.
  2. Check if $(id_\xi, *, *)$ has already been queried to hash oracle, where $*$ denotes an arbitrary value. If it is, then abort. (The simulation has failed.)
  3. Let

  $$n_\xi := N - m_\xi, \quad \varsigma_i^{(\xi)} := -\sum_{j=1}^{n_\xi} s_j v_{ij}^{(\xi)},$$

  for $i = 1, \cdots, m_\xi$. Set

  $$\mathbf{s}^{(\xi)} := (s_1, \cdots, s_{n_\xi}, \varsigma_1^{(\xi)}, \cdots, \varsigma_{m_\xi}^{(\xi)}).$$

  4. Choose $\tau_i^{(\xi)} \xleftarrow{\$} \mathbb{F}_p$ for $i = 1, \cdots, m_\xi$, and set

  $$\mathbf{t}^{(\xi)} := (t_1, \cdots, t_{n_\xi}, \tau_1^{(\xi)}, \cdots, \tau_{m_\xi}^{(\xi)}).$$

  5. Set

  $$H(id_\xi, i, h^{a_{\xi 0}} \cdots z_d^{a_{\xi d}}) := g^{\varsigma_i^{(\xi)}} \varphi(h)^{\tau_i^{(\xi)}},$$

  for $i = 1, \cdots, m_\xi$. Then add

  $$\left((id_\xi, i, h^{a_{\xi 0}} z_1^{a_{\xi 1}} \cdots z_d^{a_{\xi d}}), H(id_\xi, i, h^{a_{\xi 0}} z_1^{a_{\xi 1}} \cdots z_d^{a_{\xi d}}) \right)$$

  to HL.
  6. Compute $\sigma_i^{(\xi)} := \varphi(z_1)^{\mathbf{v}_i^{(\xi)} \cdot \mathbf{t}^{(\xi)}}$ for $1 \leq i \leq m_\xi$.
  7. Return id_ξ and $\sigma^{(\xi)} := (\sigma_1^{(\xi)}, \cdots, \sigma_{m_\xi}^{(\xi)})$ to $\mathcal{A}$.

- **Output.** When $\mathcal{A}$ outputs an identifier id^*, a nonzero vector $\mathbf{y}^* \in \mathbb{F}_p^N$, and a signature $\sigma^* = (\sigma_1^*, \cdots, \sigma_m^*)$, $\mathcal{B}$ first checks if

$$\texttt{Verify}(\text{PK}, id^*, \mathbf{y}^*, \sigma^*) = 1.$$

  - If it is not, then output **Fail**.
  - Else, he continues to check if id^* is one of the identifiers chosen on some signature query.
    * If it is not (i.e. type 1 forgery), for each $i \in [m]$, run hash query about (id^*, i, z_1) to get the value $H(id^*, i, z_1)$. Set $\mathbf{s} := (s_1, \cdots, s_n, \varsigma_1, \cdots, \varsigma_m)$ and $\mathbf{t} := (t_1, \cdots, t_n, \tau_1, \cdots, \tau_m)$, and output

$$\omega = \left(\frac{\prod_{i=1}^m (\sigma_i^*)^{y_{n+i}^*}}{\varphi(z_1)^{\mathbf{t} \cdot \mathbf{y}^*}} \right)^{1/(\mathbf{s} \cdot \mathbf{y}^*)}. \tag{2}$$

* Else, assume that $id^* = id_{\xi_0}$. Now, continue to check if $\phi_{\xi_0}(\mathsf{SK}) = \mathsf{SK}$.
  • If it is, and $\mathbf{y}^* \notin V_{\xi_0}$ (i.e. type 2 forgery), let $\mathbf{s} := \mathbf{s}^{(\xi_0)}$ and $\mathbf{t} := \mathbf{t}^{(\xi_0)}$
    be the vectors defined in the ξ_0th signing query and output (2).
  • Else (i.e. type 3 forgery), for $i \in [m]$, $\mathcal{B}$ runs hash query (id_{ξ_0}, i, z_1)
    to get $H(id_{\xi_0}, i, z_1)$. Still set

$$\mathbf{s} := (s_1, \cdots, s_n, \varsigma_1, \cdots, \varsigma_m),$$

and

$$\mathbf{t} := (t_1, \cdots, t_n, \tau_1, \cdots, \tau_m),$$

and output (2).

This ends the description of $\mathcal{B}$. We first observe that the elements $g_1 \cdots, g_N$ are random ones in $\mathbb{G}_1$ and the answers to all hash queries are uniformly random in $\mathbb{G}_1$. Thus, the public key PK simulated by $\mathcal{B}$ is distributed identically to the public key produced in the real algorithm Setup_2.

Next, we prove that, given the public key PK and hash queries, $\mathcal{B}$ correctly simulated the signatures if he does not abort. In fact, it suffices to show that, in the ξth signing query, for each $\mathbf{v}_i^{(\xi)}$,

$$\left(\prod_{i=1}^{m} H(id_\xi, i, h^{a_{\xi 0}} \cdots z_d^{a_{\xi d}})^{v_{i,n+i}^{(\xi)}} \cdot \prod_{j=1}^{n} g_j^{v_{i,j}^{(\xi)}} \right)^x = \varphi(z_1)^{\mathbf{v}_i^{(\xi)} \cdot \mathbf{t}^{(\xi)}}.$$

According to the simulation of $\mathcal{B}$, we know that

$$\left(\prod_{i=1}^{m_\xi} H(id_\xi, i, h^{a_{\xi 0}} z_1^{a_{\xi 1}} \cdots z_d^{a_{\xi d}})^{v_{i,n_\xi+i}^{(\xi)}} \cdot \prod_{j=1}^{n_\xi} g_j^{v_{i,j}^{(\xi)}} \right)^x$$

$$= \left(\prod_{i=1}^{m_\xi} \left(g^{\varsigma_i^{(\xi)}} \varphi(h)^{\tau_i^{(\xi)}} \right)^{v_{i,n_\xi+i}^{(\xi)}} \prod_{j=1}^{n_\xi} \left(g^{s_j} \varphi(h)^{t_j} \right)^{v_{i,j}^{(\xi)}} \right)^x$$

$$= \left(g^{\mathbf{s}^{(\xi)} \cdot \mathbf{v}_i^{(\xi)}} \varphi(h)^{\mathbf{t}^{(\xi)} \cdot \mathbf{v}_i^{(\xi)}} \right)^x$$

$$= \varphi(h)^{x \mathbf{v}_i^{(\xi)} \cdot \mathbf{t}^{(\xi)}}$$

$$= \varphi(z_1)^{\mathbf{v}_i^{(\xi)} \cdot \mathbf{t}^{(\xi)}}.$$

where the third equation holds since $\mathbf{s}^{(\xi)} \perp V_\xi$.

Now we analyze the probability that $\mathcal{B}$ aborts while interacting with the adversary $\mathcal{A}$. $\mathcal{B}$ aborts the simulation only if there exists an identifier that has been included in some query to the hash oracle or signing oracle. When responding to $\mathcal{A}$'s signing queries, $\mathcal{B}$ chooses the identifier id independently. Therefore, the probability that $\mathcal{B}$ responds to two different signing queries by choosing the same identifier is at most $q_S^2/2^\lambda$. While the probability that the identifier randomly chosen by $\mathcal{B}$ has already been requested to the hash oracle is at most $q_S q_H/2^\lambda$.

Finally, if $\mathcal{A}$ outputs a valid forgery $(id^*, \mathbf{y}^*, \sigma^*)$ (i.e. $\mathtt{Verify}_2(\mathsf{PK}, id^*, \mathbf{y}^*, \sigma^*) = 1$), then we have

$$e\left(\prod_{i=1}^{m}(\sigma_i^*)^{y_{n+i}^*}, h\right) = e\left(\prod_{i=1}^{m} H(id^*, i, z_1)^{y_{n+i}^*} \prod_{j=1}^{n} g_j^{y_j^*}, z_1\right)$$

$$= e\left(g^{\mathbf{s} \cdot \mathbf{y}^*} \varphi(h)^{\mathbf{t} \cdot \mathbf{y}^*}, z_1\right)$$

$$= e\left(g^{x(\mathbf{s} \cdot \mathbf{y}^*)} \varphi(z_1)^{\mathbf{t} \cdot \mathbf{y}^*}, h\right),$$

where the second equation holds according to the last part of $\mathcal{B}$'s simulation. Now, since the bilinear function e is non-degenerated, we have

$$\prod_{i=1}^{m}(\sigma_i^*)^{y_{n+i}^*} = g^{x(\mathbf{s} \cdot \mathbf{y}^*)} \varphi(z_1)^{\mathbf{t} \cdot \mathbf{y}^*}.$$

Therefore, if $\mathbf{s} \cdot \mathbf{y}^* \neq 0$, the element ω output by $\mathcal{B}$ equals g^x.

Next, we show that, in the following three cases, the event $\mathbf{s} \cdot \mathbf{y}^* = 0$ occurs with negligible probability.

- **Case 1.** If $\mathcal{A}$'s output is a type 1 forgery (i.e. id^* is not one of the identifiers chosen in the signing oracle queries), then the only possible "leakage" of ς_i for this id^* are the values $H(id^*, i, z_1)$ for $i = 1, \cdots, m$. However, from the simulation of $\mathcal{B}$, we know that ς_i's are uniform in $\mathbb{F}_p$ and independent of $\mathcal{A}$'s view since, for the "new" id^*, the items τ_i's in $(H(id^*, 1, z_1), \cdots, H(id^*, m, z_1))$ are chosen randomly, which "mask" the information of ς_i's. In addition, by Lemma 7 of [3][5], we know that $s_1, \cdots, s_N$ are still uniform in $\mathbb{F}_p$ and independent of $\mathcal{A}$'s view. Hence, $\mathbf{s} = (s_1, \cdots, s_n, \varsigma_1, \cdots, \varsigma_m)$ is random in $\mathbb{F}_p^N$. It follows that, for a nonzero vector $\mathbf{y}^*$, the probability that $\mathbf{s} \cdot \mathbf{y}^* = 0$ equals $1/p$.
- **Case 2.** If $\mathcal{A}$'s output is a type 2 forgery (i.e. the id^* is just the identifier of $\mathcal{A}$'s ξ_0th signing oracle queries, $\phi_{\xi_0}(\mathsf{SK}) = \mathsf{SK}$ and $\mathbf{y}^* \notin V_{\xi_0}$), then still according to the Lemma 7 in [3], from $\mathcal{A}$'s view, the variables $s_1, \cdots, s_N$ are uniform in $\mathbb{F}_p$ and hence $\mathbf{s} = (s_1, \cdots, s_n, \varsigma_1, \cdots, \varsigma_m)$ is uniformly random in $V_{\xi_0}^{\perp}$. For the similar reason as in the analysis of [3], we know that an uniform distribution on $\mathbf{s} \in V_{\xi_0}^{\perp}$ produces an uniform one on $\mathbf{s} \cdot \mathbf{y}^* \in \mathbb{F}_p$ when $\mathbf{y}^* \notin V_{\xi_0}^{\perp}$. Therefore, the event $\mathbf{s} \cdot \mathbf{y}^* = 0$ occurs with probability $1/p$.
- **Case 3.** If $\mathcal{A}$'s output is a type 3 forgery (i.e. the id^* is just the identifier of $\mathcal{A}$'s ξ_0th signing oracle queries and $\phi_{\xi_0}(\mathsf{SK}) \neq \mathsf{SK}$), then the two values $H(id_{\xi_0}, i, h^{a_{\xi_0 0}} z_1^{a_{\xi_0 1}} \cdots z_d^{a_{\xi_0 d}})$ and $H(id_{\xi_0}, i, z_1)$ should be mutual independent since $\mathcal{B}$ runs the "new" hash query on (id_{ξ_0}, i, z_1). Similar to Case 1, the only "leakage" of ς_i's in $\mathbf{s}$ comes from the values $H(id_{\xi_0}, i, z_1)$ for $1 \leq i \leq m$. However, the τ_i's in $H(id_{\xi_0}, i, z_1)$ are chosen randomly and hence independent of $\mathcal{A}$'s view, which "mask" the information of ς_i's. Therefore, for $\mathbf{y}^* \neq \mathbf{0}$, the probability that $\mathbf{s} \cdot \mathbf{y}^* = 0$ equals $1/p$ for the same reason as Case 1.

---

[5] Performing a completely similar analysis, we know that Lemma 7 of [3] still holds in the RKA case.

Putting all the facts together, we know that (1) holds. This ends the proof of Theorem 1.

4   Discussion of Efficiency

In this section, we briefly discuss the efficiency of our proposed scheme. Note that the algorithms $\mathtt{Setup}'_2$ and $\mathtt{Combine}'_2$ are same as those of the original BFKW-NCS scheme. While the only change we made is "adding" the item h^x into the input of hash function H, which is computed in $\mathtt{Sign}'_2$ and $\mathtt{Verify}'_2$, the communication and computation costs are exactly same as that of the BFKW-NCS scheme.

5   Conclusions

We consider the RKA security of the practical network coding signature scheme for the first time. Based on the RKA security model proposed in this paper, we show that BFKW-NCS scheme can not achieve weaker RKA security. However, a slight modification of it can achieve a stronger one under the d-co-CDH assumption.

Acknowledgement. This work is supported by National Natural Science Foundation of China (No. 61602061; No. 61672059; No. 61272499; No. 61472016; No. 61472414; No. 61402471), the Strategic Priority Research Program of Chinese Academy of Sciences (No. XDA06010701), the Foundation of Institute of Information Engineering for Cryptography, and the Project of College Students' Innovation and Entrepreneurship of Shanxi (No. 2016431).

Appendix

The BFKW-NCS scheme $\Pi_1 = (\mathtt{Setup}_1, \mathtt{Sign}_1, \mathtt{Verify}_1)$ constructed from BFKW-HNCS scheme $\Pi'_1 = (\mathtt{Setup}'_1, \mathtt{Sign}'_1, \mathtt{Combine}'_1, \mathtt{Verify}'_1)$ is as follows.

- $\mathtt{Setup}_1$: Take as inputs 1^λ, and N. Run the algorithm $\mathtt{GenBiGroup}(1^\lambda)$ to obtain $\mathcal{G}$. Parse $\mathcal{G}$ as $(p, \mathbb{G}_1, \mathbb{G}_2, \mathbb{G}_T, e, \varphi)$. Then choose

$$h \xleftarrow{\$} \mathbb{G}_2 \backslash \{1\}, \ g_1, \cdots, g_N \xleftarrow{\$} \mathbb{G}_1 \backslash \{1\}, \ \text{and} \ x \xleftarrow{\$} \mathbb{F}_p.$$

Let $u = h^x$ and define $H : \mathbb{Z} \times \mathbb{Z} \to \mathbb{G}_1$ as a hash function. Finally, output p, $\mathtt{PK} = (\mathcal{G}, g_1, \cdots, g_N, h, u, H)$ and $\mathtt{SK} = x$.

- $\mathtt{Sign}_1$: Take as inputs $\mathtt{SK} = x$, $id \in \{0,1\}^{\lambda}$, and $V := \mathrm{span}\{\mathbf{v}_1, \cdots, \mathbf{v}_m\} \subset \mathbb{F}_p^N$, where $\{\mathbf{v}_i\}$ is a properly augmented basis of V. Compute

$$\sigma_1 = \left(\prod_{i=1}^{m} H(id, \; i)^{v_{1,n+i}} \prod_{j=1}^{n} g_j^{v_{1,j}} \right)^x ,$$

$$\vdots$$

$$\sigma_m = \left(\prod_{i=1}^{m} H(id, \; i)^{v_{m,n+i}} \prod_{j=1}^{n} g_j^{v_{m,j}} \right)^x .$$

Output id and $\sigma = (\sigma_1, \cdots, \sigma_m)$.
- $\mathtt{Verify}_1$: Take as inputs $\mathtt{PK}$, id, $\mathbf{y} \in \mathbb{F}_p^N$, and σ. Parse σ as $\sigma_1, \cdots, \sigma_m$ and define $n := N - m$. Then compute

$$\sigma' = \prod_{i=1}^{m} \sigma_i^{y_{n+i}} .$$

Finally, output

$$\left(e \left(\prod_{i=1}^{m} H(id, i)^{y_{n+i}} \prod_{j=1}^{n} g_j^{y_j}, u \right) \stackrel{?}{=} e \left(\sigma', h \right) \right) .$$

References

1. Bellare, M., Cash, D., Miller, R.: Cryptography secure against related-key attacks and tampering. In: International Conference on the Theory and Application of Cryptology and Information Security, pp. 486–503. Springer, Heidelberg (2011)
2. Bellare, M., Kohno, T.: A theoretical treatment of related-key attacks: RKA-PRPs, RKA-PRFs, and applications. In: Biham, E. (ed.) EUROCRYPT 2003. LNCS, vol. 2656, pp. 491–506. Springer, Heidelberg (2003). doi:10.1007/3-540-39200-9_31
3. Boneh, D., Freeman, D., Katz, J., Waters, B.: Signing a linear subspace: signature schemes for network coding. In: Jarecki, S., Tsudik, G. (eds.) PKC 2009. LNCS, vol. 5443, pp. 68–87. Springer, Heidelberg (2009). doi:10.1007/978-3-642-00468-1_5
4. Cui, H., Mu, Y., Au, M.H.: Proof of retrievability with public verifiability resilient against related-key attacks. IET Inf. Secur. **9**(1), 43–49 (2015)
5. Dong, J., Curtmola, R., Nita-Rotaru, C.: Practical defenses against pollution attacks in wireless network coding. ACM Trans. Inf. Syst. Secur. (TISSEC) **14**(1), 7 (2011)
6. Lu, X., Li, B., Jia, D.: KDM-CCA security from RKA secure authenticated encryption. In: Oswald, E., Fischlin, M. (eds.) EUROCRYPT 2015. LNCS, vol. 9056, pp. 559–583. Springer, Heidelberg (2015). doi:10.1007/978-3-662-46800-5_22
7. Morita, H., Schuldt, J.C.N., Matsuda, T., Hanaoka, G., Iwata, T.: On the security of the schnorr signature scheme and DSA against related-key attacks. In: Kwon, S., Yun, A. (eds.) ICISC 2015. LNCS, vol. 9558, pp. 20–35. Springer, Heidelberg (2016). doi:10.1007/978-3-319-30840-1_2

8. Oggier, F., Datta, A.: Byzantine fault tolerance of regenerating codes. In: 2011 IEEE International Conference on Peer-to-Peer Computing (P2P), pp. 112–121. IEEE (2011)

9. Wee, H.: Public key encryption against related key attacks. In: Fischlin, M., Buchmann, J., Manulis, M. (eds.) PKC 2012. LNCS, vol. 7293, pp. 262–279. Springer, Heidelberg (2012). doi:10.1007/978-3-642-30057-8_16

10. Zhao, F., Kalker, T., Médard, M., Han, K.J.: Signatures for content distribution with network coding. In: 2007 IEEE International Symposium on Information Theory, pp. 556–560. IEEE (2007)

New Realizations of Efficient and Secure Private Set Intersection Protocols Preserving Fairness

Sumit Kumar Debnath$^{(\boxtimes)}$ and Ratna Dutta

Department of Mathematics, Indian Institute of Technology Kharagpur,
Kharagpur 721302, India
sd.iitkgp@gmail.com, ratna@maths.iitkgp.ernet.in

Abstract. *Private Set Intersection (PSI)* is a useful cryptographic primitive for developing practical privacy preserving techniques for Big Data. PSI allows entities to securely extract intersection of the large data sets they own, without revealing any other crucial information for their input sets. Fairness is a critical issue for both mutual Private Set Intersection (mPSI) and its cardinality variant, namely mutual Private Set Intersection Cardinality (mPSI-CA). Achieving *fairness* over *prime* order groups with *linear complexity* in *malicious model* remains an interesting challenge for both mPSI and mPSI-CA. None of the prior works achieve all the aforementioned properties together. We address these issues using an off-line *semi-trusted* third party, called *arbiter*. Arbiter is semi-trusted in the sense that he cannot get access to the private information of the parties but follow the protocol honestly. In this work, we propose a construction of fair and efficient mPSI with linear communication and computation overheads using prime order groups. Our mPSI employs (Distributed) ElGamal encryption and the verifiable encryption of Cramer-Shoup. A concrete security analysis is provided against malicious parties under Decisional Diffie-Hellman (DDH) assumption. We further extend our mPSI to mPSI-CA retaining all the security properties of mPSI. On a more positive note, our mPSI-CA is the *first* in its kind with *linear complexity* preserving *fairness*.

Keywords: mPSI · mPSI-CA · Malicious adversary · Fairness · Semi-trusted arbiter

1 Introduction

In everyday life, dependence on the availability of electronic information increases rapidly. As a consequence, there is a strong need for efficient cryptographic techniques that allow secret sharing of information. Among these, Private Set Intersection (PSI) emerged as an object of fundamental interest for many real life applications. It is a two-party protocol that enables only the involved parties to compute *secretly* the intersection of their respective private input sets and not more than that. If only one of the parties learns the intersection, the protocol is called a *one-way* PSI. On the other hand, if both the

S. Hong and J.H. Park (Eds.): ICISC 2016, LNCS 10157, pp. 254–284, 2017.
DOI: 10.1007/978-3-319-53177-9_14

parties learn the intersection, the protocol is known as *mutual* PSI (mPSI). *Private Set Intersection Cardinality* (PSI-CA) is another related primitive whereby two parties learn cardinality rather than the content of the intersection of their respective input sets. When both the parties obtain the cardinality of the intersection, the protocol is termed as *mutual* PSI-CA (mPSI-CA). PSI protocols and its variants have found several practical applications, particularly in privacy preserving location-based services, data mining, social networks, testing of fully sequenced human genomes, collaborative botnet detection, on-line gaming etc. For instance, suppose two real estate companies want to detect the customers (e.g., homeowners) who are double dealing, i.e. have signed exclusive contracts with both the companies to assist them in selling their house. mPSI is a proper choice for this situation.

Efficiency and fairness are two main challenges in designing mPSI protocols apart from establishing security in against malicious adversaries. Efficiency is measured by communication and computation complexities. In contrast, fairness ensures that either both the involved parties receive the intersection of their private input sets at the completion of the protocol or none receive the intersection. An mPSI protocol can be obtained by two instantiations of an one-way PSI protocol [13]. However, this approach does not prevent a player from unfairly aborting the protocol, thereby unable to maintain fairness. Most of the fair cryptographic protocols achieve their fairness in the optimistic way by using an off-line *trusted* third party, called *arbiter* [9, 18, 19]. An arbiter gets involved in the protocol only if a corrupted player prematurely aborts the protocol in order to recover the output for an honest party. However, it is practically infeasible to find a fully trusted third party in real life. Achieving optimistic fairness in PSI protocol is not an easy task. Generic construction for optimistic fair protocols is not available in the literature. Besides, *fully* trusted arbiter gets access to some private information which is highly undesirable.

Our Contributions: In this work, we give new efficient construction of mPSI and mPSI-CA preserving fairness. We note that the work of [18] is the only fair optimistic mPSI protocol with linear computation and communication overhead that achieves security in the standard model against malicious adversaries. However, the system of [18] has composite order group setting where group operations are slow as compared to prime order group. In this paper, we present a fair mPSI in prime order groups with *linear* complexity in the random oracle model (ROM) against *malicious* adversaries. Furthermore, constructions for fair mPSI-CA with *linear* complexity in the *standard model* against *malicious* adversaries over *prime* order group have remained elusive. We extend our mPSI by combining it with two permutations and propose the *first* fair mPSI-CA scheme in prime order groups that withstands malicious adversary and has linear complexity. We integrate ElGamal encryption [21], distributed ElGamal encryption [5], Cramer-Shoup cryptosystem [10] and blend zero-knowledge proofs for discrete logarithm to build the proposed mPSI and mPSI-CA. More precisely, our proposed constructions have the following salient features:

- Our mPSI is proven to be secure against both the malicious parties under the DDH assumption in prime order groups. Fairness is arguably hardest part to achieve for mPSI. We achieve fairness in the optimistic way by using an off-line arbiter. While most of the prior works use fully trusted arbiter, our mPSI uses only *semi-trusted* arbiter who does not have access to the private information of any of the parties, but follows the protocol honestly.
- We emphasize that our mPSI protocol outperforms the existing mPSI protocols in terms of both communication and computation overhead. [9,18,19,33,34]. The mPSI constructions of [9,19,34] attain quadratic computation complexities. The mPSI of [19] has the additional restriction that the party constructing the polynomial should have more number of inputs than the other party, whereas our protocol does not have any such restriction. The mPSI of [33,34] do not preserve fairness. To the best of our knowledge, [18,19] are the most efficient fair mPSI protocols. Specifically, the mPSI of [18] requires approximately $156(v + w)$ exponentiations and $77(v+w)$ group elements over *composite* order groups, where v, w are sizes of the input sets of the participants. In contrast, our mPSI requires only $39v+72w+27$ exponentiations and $21v+31w+26$ group elements over *prime* order groups. Further, the security analysis in [18] is in hybrid model. Note that any modular operation over composite order group is more expensive than the operation over prime order group. Compared to ours, the mPSI of [19] needs more exponentiations and group elements, approximately $11w + 96v + 12wv$ and $7w + 53v + 2wv + 5$.
- Furthermore, we extend our mPSI to mPSI-CA by employing two random permutations. As an outcome, we develop the *first fair* mPSI-CA construction which demonstrates linear communication and computation complexity. Our scheme is proven to be secure against malicious adversaries without using random oracles. Prior to this work, there are only two mPSI-CA protocols [9,34], both of which in composite order group and attain quadratic computational overhead. The mPSI-CA of [9] can be modified to achieve fairness using an optimistic fair exchange scheme, where the trusted third party certifies the inputs. This approach does not work in general cases to achieve fairness where inputs are not certified by a trusted authority. In real life applications, it is infeasible to force the participants to use the same inputs in two different instances. We emphasize that our mPSI-CA achieves fairness using only a semi-trusted arbiter.
- Finally, the communication cost of our constructions can be further reduced by transforming interactive zero-knowledge proofs with its non-interactive variant using Fiat-Shamir technique [22]. However, in this case we can ensure the security of our scheme in the random oracle model (ROM) [3].

Related Works: The concept of PSI was introduced by Agrawal et al. [1]. In the subsequent years, there has been a sequence of works on constructing one-way PSI [1,11,13,14,16,20,23,24,26–28,30–32,35,36]. These works employed several existing ideas and advances such as Oblivious Polynomial Evaluations (OPE), Oblivious Pseudorandom Function (OPRF), Unpredictable function (UPF), Additively Homomorphic Encryption (AHE), Garbled Circuit (GC), Bloom filter (BF) etc. The first one-way PSI-CA dates back to the work of Agrawal et al. [1]. Following this work, a variety of solutions are provided with improved efficiency and security level [1,9,12,16,17,24,29,34].

The work of Kissner and Song [34] combined OPE with AHE and presented the first mPSI protocol. Their construction can support more than two players in the communication system. Following this work, another construction of mPSI was proposed by Camenisch and Zaverucha [9] which also relies on OPE. In their construction the inputs need to be certified by a trusted party in order to achieve fairness using an optimistic fair exchange protocol. Later, Kim et al. [33] came up with an mPSI protocol coupling prime representation technique with threshold AHE. Although the proposed protocol does not achieve fairness, it provides linear complexity and is secure in the ROM against semi-honest adversaries. In the subsequent year, Dong et al. [19] sketched the first fair optimistic mPSI protocol secure in the standard model against malicious adversaries. However, the scheme has quadratic computation overhead. Very recently, in the work of [18], the authors used two-way OPRF (mOPRF) to construct a fair optimistic mPSI protocol with linear computation and communication overhead. The work of [18] is basically the extended work of [15].

Kissner and Song [34] introduced the concept of mPSI-CA and gave the first construction of this primitive based on OPE, where more than two players can be involved. Fairness is not addressed in this work. Later, Camenisch and Zaverucha [9] obtained a fair mPSI-CA protocol for certified sets based on OPE. Both the constructions [9,34] are over composite order group and have quadratic computation overhead.

2 Preliminaries

Throughout the paper the notations represented by Table 1 are to be used.

Definition 1. Negligible Function: *A function* $\epsilon : \mathbb{N} \to \mathbb{R}$ *is said to be negligible function of* κ *if for each constant* $c > 0$, *we have* $\epsilon(\kappa) = o(\kappa^{-c})$ *for all sufficiently large* κ.

Table 1. Notations

$a \leftarrow S$	a is output of the procedure S
κ	Security parameter
$x \hookleftarrow X$	Variable x is chosen uniformly at random from set X
$\{\mathcal{X}_t\}_{t \in \mathcal{N}} \equiv^c \{\mathcal{Y}_t\}_{t \in \mathcal{N}}$	The distribution ensemble $\{\mathcal{X}_t\}_{t \in \mathcal{N}}$ is computationally indistinguishable from the distribution ensemble $\{\mathcal{Y}_t\}_{t \in \mathcal{N}}$
π	Zero-knowledge proof of knowledge for discrete logarithm
$\widehat{\pi}$	Zero-knowledge argument for shuffle
$\wedge_{j=1}^{w}(X_j)$	$X_1 \wedge \ldots \wedge X_w$
$\wedge_{j=1}^{w}(X_j)(Y_j)(Z_j)$	$\wedge_{j=1}^{w}(X_j) \wedge_{j=1}^{w}(Y_j) \wedge_{j=1}^{w}(Z_j)$

Definition 2. *A functionality $\mathcal{F}_\Pi$, computed by two parties A and B with inputs X_A and X_B respectively by running a protocol Π, is defined as $\mathcal{F}_\Pi : X_A \times X_B \to Y_A \times Y_B$, where Y_A and Y_B are the outputs of A and B respectively after completion of the protocol Π between A and B.*

Definition 3. Decisional Diffie-Hellman (DDH) Assumption [4]: *Let the algorithm gGen generates a modulus n and a generator g of a multiplicative group $\mathbb{G}$ of order n on the input 1^κ. Suppose $a, b, c \hookleftarrow \mathbb{Z}_n$. Then the DDH assumption states that no PPT algorithm $\mathcal{A}$ can distinguish between the two distributions $\langle g^a, g^b, g^{ab} \rangle$ and $\langle g^a, g^b, g^c \rangle$ i.e., $|Prob[\mathcal{A}(g, g^a, g^b, g^{ab}) = 1] - Prob[\mathcal{A}(g, g^a, g^b, g^c) = 1]|$ is negligible function of κ.*

2.1 Security Model

Informally, the basic security requirements of any multi-party protocol are

(a) *Correctness.* At the end of the protocol an honest party should receive the correct output.
(b) *Privacy.* After completion of the protocol, no party should learn more than its prescribe output.
(c) *Fairness.* A dishonest party should receive its output if and only if the honest party also receives its output.

In this work, we focus on the *malicious* model where the adversary can behave arbitrarily. A protocol is said to be secure if any adversary in the real protocol can be simulated by an adversary in the ideal world. The security framework of mPSI is formally described below following [19].

The real world: The protocol has three participants – party A, party B and an arbiter Ar. All the participants have access to the public parameters of the protocol including the functionality $\mathcal{F}_{\mathsf{mPSI}} : (X, Y) \to (X \cap Y, X \cap Y)$, the security parameter κ, Ar's public key pk_{Ar} and other cryptographic parameters to be used. Party A has a private input X, party B has a private input Y and Ar has an input $\in \{\circ, \perp\}$. The adversary $\mathcal{C}$ can corrupt upto two parties in the protocol and can behave arbitrarily. At the end of the execution, an honest party outputs whatever prescribed in the protocol, a corrupted party outputs nothing, and an adversary outputs its view which consists of the transcripts available to the adversary. The joint output of $A, B, Ar, \mathcal{C}$ in the real world is denoted by $\mathsf{REAL}_{\mathsf{mPSI}, \mathcal{C}}(X, Y)$.

The ideal process: In the ideal process, there is an incorruptible trusted party T who can compute the ideal functionality $\mathcal{F}_{\mathsf{mPSI}}$, and parties $\bar{A}, \bar{B}$ and $\bar{A}r$. Party $\bar{A}$ has input X, $\bar{B}$ has input Y and $\bar{A}r$ has an input $\in \{\circ, \perp\}$. The interaction is as follows:

(i) $\bar{A}$ sends $\overline{X}$ or $\perp$ to T, following it $\bar{B}$ sends $\overline{Y}$ or $\perp$ to T; and then $\bar{A}r$ sends two messages $b_A \in \{\circ, \perp\} \cup X_A$ and $b_B \in \{\circ, \perp\} \cup Y_B$ to T, where X_A and Y_B are two arbitrary sets. The inputs $\overline{X}$ and $\overline{Y}$ may be different from X and Y respectively if the party is malicious.

(ii) T sends private delayed output to $\bar{A}$ and $\bar{B}$. T's reply to $\bar{A}(\bar{B})$ depends on $\bar{A}$ and $\bar{B}$'s messages and $b_A(b_B)$. Response of T to $\bar{A}(\bar{B})$ is as follows:

   (a) If $b_A(b_B) = \circ$, and T has received $\overline{X} \neq \perp$ from $\bar{A}$ and $\overline{Y} \neq \perp$ from $\bar{B}$, then T sends $\overline{X} \cap \overline{Y}$ to $\bar{A}(\bar{B})$.
   (b) Else if $b_A(b_B) = \circ$, but T has received $\perp$ from either $\bar{A}$ or $\bar{B}$, then T sends $\perp$ to $\bar{A}(\bar{B})$.
   (c) Else $b_A(b_B) \neq \circ$, then T sends $b_A(b_B)$ to $\bar{A}(\bar{B})$.

In the ideal process, if $\bar{A}$, $\bar{B}$ and $\bar{A}r$ are honest then they behave as follows: $\bar{A}$ and $\bar{B}$ send their inputs to T and $\bar{A}r$ sends $b_A = \circ$ and $b_B = \circ$. The ideal process adversary $\mathcal{SIM}$ gets the inputs of the corrupted parties and may replace them and gets T's response to corrupted parties. The joint output of $\bar{A}, \bar{B}, \bar{A}r, \mathcal{SIM}$ in the ideal process is denoted by $\mathsf{IDEAL}_{\mathcal{F}_{\mathsf{mPSI}}, \mathcal{SIM}}(X, Y)$. The security definition in terms of simulatability is

Definition 4. Simulatability: *Let* $\mathcal{F}_{\mathsf{mPSI}} : ((X, |Y|), (Y, |X|)) \rightarrow (X \cap Y, X \cap Y)$ *be the functionality for* mPSI *protocol. Then the protocol* mPSI *is said to securely compute* $\mathcal{F}_{\mathsf{mPSI}}$ *in malicious model if for every real world adversary* $\mathcal{C}$, *there exists an ideal world adversary* $\mathcal{SIM}$ *such that the joint distribution of all outputs of the ideal world is computationally indistinguishable from the outputs in the real world, i.e.,* $\mathsf{IDEAL}_{\mathcal{F}_{\mathsf{mPSI}}, \mathcal{SIM}}(X, Y) \equiv^c \mathsf{REAL}_{\mathsf{mPSI}, \mathcal{C}}(X, Y).$

Note that the security framework for mPSI-CA is same as the security framework of mPSI except that each $X \cap Y$ will be $|X \cap Y|$ and each of X_A, Y_B will be the set $\mathbb{N} \cup \{0\}$.

2.2   Homomorphic Encryption [6]

We describe below *multiplicatively* homomorphic encryption schemes the ElGamal encryption [21] and the distributed ElGamal encryption [5] which are semantically secure provided DDH problem is hard in underlying group.

ElGamal encryption: The ElGamal encryption [21] is a multiplicatively homomorphic encryption $\mathcal{EL} = (\mathcal{EL}.\mathsf{Setup}, \mathcal{EL}.\mathsf{KGen}, \mathcal{EL}.\mathsf{Enc}, \mathcal{EL}.\mathsf{Dec})$ which works as follows:

$\mathcal{EL}.\mathsf{Setup}(1^\kappa)$ – On input 1^κ, a trusted third party outputs a public parameter $\mathsf{par} = (\mathsf{p}, \mathsf{q}, \mathsf{g})$, where p, q are primes such that q divides $p - 1$ and g is a generator of the unique cyclic subgroup $\mathbb{G}$ of $\mathbb{Z}_p^*$ of order q.
$\mathcal{EL}.\mathsf{KGen}(\mathsf{par})$ – User A_i chooses $a_i \leftarrowtail \mathbb{Z}_q$, computes $y_{A_i} = g^{a_i}$, reveals $epk_{A_i} = y_{A_i}$ as his public key and keeps $esk_{A_i} = a_i$ secret to himself.
$\mathcal{EL}.\mathsf{Enc}(m, epk_{A_i}, \mathsf{par}, r)$ – Encryptor encrypts a message $m \in \mathbb{G}$ using the public key $epk_{A_i} = y_{A_i}$ by computing ciphertext tuple $\mathsf{eE}_{epk_{A_i}}(m) = (\alpha, \beta) = (g^r, my^r_{A_i})$, where $r \leftarrowtail \mathbb{Z}_q$.
$\mathcal{EL}.\mathsf{Dec}(\mathsf{eE}_{epk_{A_i}}(m), esk_{A_i})$ – On receiving ciphertext tuple $\mathsf{eE}_{epk_{A_i}}(m) = (\alpha, \beta) = (g^r, my^r_{A_i})$, decryptor A_i decrypts it using the secret key $esk_{A_i} = a_i$ by computing $\frac{\beta}{(\alpha)^{a_i}} = \frac{m(g^{a_i})^r}{(g^r)^{a_i}} = m$.

Distributed ElGamal encryption [5]: The distributed ElGamal encryption $\mathcal{DEL} = (\mathcal{DEL}.\mathsf{Setup}, \mathcal{DEL}.\mathsf{KGen}, \mathcal{DEL}.\mathsf{Enc}, \mathcal{DEL}.\mathsf{Dec})$ is executed between two parties A_1 and A_2 as follows:

$\mathcal{DEL}.\mathsf{Setup}(1^\kappa)$ – Same as the ElGamal encryption.

$\mathcal{DEL}.\mathsf{KGen}(\mathsf{par})$ – Each participant $A_i, i = 1, 2$ selects $a_i \hookleftarrow \mathbb{Z}_q$, publishes $y_{A_i} = g^{a_i}$ along with a zero-knowledge proof $\mathsf{PoK}\{a_i | y_{A_i} = g^{a_i}\}$. Then, each of A_1, A_2 publishes the public key for the $\mathcal{DEL}$ as $pk = h = g^{a_1 + a_2}$, while the secret key for $\mathcal{DEL}$ is $sk = a_1 + a_2$. Note that sk is not known to anyone under the hardness of DLP in $\mathbb{G}$.

$\mathcal{DEL}.\mathsf{Enc}(m, pk, \mathsf{par}, r)$ – Encryptor encrypts a message $m \in \mathbb{G}$ using public key $pk = h = g^{a_1 + a_2}$ and computes the ciphertext tuple $\mathsf{dE}_{pk}(m) = (\alpha, \beta) = (g^r, mh^r)$, where $r \hookleftarrow \mathbb{Z}_q$.

$\mathcal{DEL}.\mathsf{Dec}(\mathsf{dE}_{pk}(m), a_1, a_2)$ – Given a ciphertext $\mathsf{dE}_{pk}(m) = (\alpha, \beta) = (g^r, mh^r)$, each participant A_i publishes $\alpha_i = \alpha^{a_i}$ and proves the correctness of the proof $\mathsf{PoK}\{a_i | y_{A_i} = g^{a_i} \wedge \alpha_i = \alpha^{a_i}\}$ to A_j, where $i, j \in \{1, 2\}$ and $i \neq j$. If proofs are valid, then each of A_1, A_2 recovers the message m as $\frac{\beta}{\alpha_1 \alpha_2} = \frac{\beta}{(\alpha)^{(a_1 + a_2)}} = \frac{mh^r}{g^{r(a_1 + a_2)}} = \frac{mh^r}{h^r} = m$.

2.3   Verifiable Encryption [6]

We describe below a CCA2-secure verifiable encryption scheme $\mathcal{VE} = (\mathcal{VE}.\mathsf{Setup}, \mathcal{VE}.\mathsf{KGen}, \mathcal{VE}.\mathsf{Enc}, \mathcal{VE}.\mathsf{Dec})$ which is a variant of Cramer-Shoup cryptosystem [10] over prime order group [19].

$\mathcal{VE}.\mathsf{Setup}(1^\kappa)$ – On input 1^κ, a trusted third party outputs a public parameter $\mathsf{ppar} = (\mathsf{par}, \widetilde{g}, \mathcal{H})$, where $\mathsf{par} = (p, q, g), p, q$ are primes such that q divides $p - 1$ and $g, \widetilde{g}$ are generators of the unique cyclic subgroup $\mathbb{G}$ of $\mathbb{Z}_p^*$ of order q, $\mathcal{H} : \{0, 1\}^* \to \mathbb{Z}_q$ is an one-way hash function.

$\mathcal{VE}.\mathsf{KGen}(\mathsf{par}, \widetilde{g})$ – User U chooses $u_1, u_2, v_1, v_2, w_1 \hookleftarrow \mathbb{Z}_q$, computes $a = g^{u_1} \widetilde{g}^{u_2}$, $b = g^{v_1} \widetilde{g}^{v_2}$, $c = g^{w_1}$, publishes $vpk_U = (a, b, c)$ as his public key and keeps $vsk_U = (u_1, u_2, v_1, v_2, w_1)$ secret to himself.

$\mathcal{VE}.\mathsf{Enc}(m, vpk_U, \mathsf{ppar}, z, L, \mathcal{H})$ – To encrypt a message $m \in \mathbb{G}$ using public key $vpk_U = (a, b, c)$, encryptor picks $z \hookleftarrow \mathbb{Z}_q$ and sets $e_1 = g^z, e_2 = \widetilde{g}^z, e_3 = c^z m$, constructs a label $L \in \{0, 1\}^*$ using information that are available to both encryptor and decryptor, computes $\rho = \mathcal{H}(e_1, e_2, e_3, L)$, sets $e_4 = a^z b^{z\rho}$, and computes the ciphertext $\mathsf{vE}_{vpk_U}(m) = (e_1, e_2, e_3, e_4)$.

$\mathcal{VE}.\mathsf{Dec}(\mathsf{vE}_{vpk_U}(m), vsk_U, L, \mathcal{H})$ – Decryptor U, on receiving ciphertext $\mathsf{vE}_{vpk_U}(m) = (e_1, e_2, e_3, e_4)$, computes $\rho = \mathcal{H}(e_1, e_2, e_3, L)$ and then verifies $e_1^{u_1} e_2^{u_2} (e_1^{v_1} e_2^{v_2})^\rho = e_4$ using secret key $vsk_U = (u_1, u_2, v_1, v_2, w_1)$. If the verification succeeds, then he recovers the message m by computing $e_3/(e_1)^{w_1} = c^z m/g^{zw_1} = g^{zw_1} m/g^{zw_1} = m$.

2.4   Zero-Knowledge Proof of Knowledge [2]

Zero-Knowledge proof [2] is a two-party protocol, where prover ($\mathcal{P}$) wants to convince the verifier ($\mathcal{V}$) about the truth of the claim that he knows some secret values, and the verifier wants to check that the claim is true. A zero-knowledge proof protocol π for relation R should satisfy the following three properties:

(a) *Completeness.* Completeness, also known as *proof of knowledge*, means that an honest prover convinces the verifier that he knows the secret values.
(b) *Soundness.* Soundness indicates that a cheating prover, who does not know the actual secret values, will succeed to convince the verifier with negligible probability. In other words, if the success-probability of the prover is non-negligible, then there exists a *knowledge extractor* that can extract the secret values.
(c) *Zero-knowledge.* Zero-knowledge ensures that the verifier does not obtain any useful information about the secret values of the prover.

Zero-Knowledge Proof for Discrete Logarithm [8]: We follow the notations introduced by [7] for the various zero-knowledge proofs of knowledge of discrete logarithms and proofs of validity of statements about discrete logarithms. We describe below a general construction of interactive zero-knowledge proofs of knowledge, denoted by $\pi = \mathsf{PoK}\{(\alpha_1, ..., \alpha_l) \mid \bigwedge_{i=1}^{M} X_i = f_i(\alpha_1, ..., \alpha_l)\}$, where the prover $\mathcal{P}$ wants to prove the knowledge of $(\alpha_1, ..., \alpha_l)$ to the verifier $\mathcal{V}$ by sending the commitments to $X_i = f_i(\alpha_1, ..., \alpha_l), i = 1, ..., M$ such that extracting $(\alpha_1, ..., \alpha_l)$ from $X_1, ..., X_M$ is infeasible for anyone. For each $i = 1, ..., M, f_i$ is publicly computable linear function from $\mathcal{X}^l$ to $\mathcal{Y}$, where $\mathcal{X}$ is *additive* set and $\mathcal{Y}$ is *multiplicative* set. This proof system satisfies soundness property under the hardness of DDH assumption. For example, let us consider

$$\mathsf{PoK}\{(\alpha_1, \alpha_2) \mid X_1 = g^{\alpha_1} = f_1(\alpha_1, \alpha_2) \wedge X_2 = g^{\alpha_2} h^{\alpha_1} = f_2(\alpha_1, \alpha_2)\} \quad (1)$$

The Eq. 1 denotes the zero-knowledge proof of knowledge of integers α_1, α_2 such that $X_1 = g^{\alpha_1}$ and $X_2 = g^{\alpha_2} h^{\alpha_1}$ hold, where $\alpha_1, \alpha_2 \in \mathbb{Z}_q$ and X_1, X_2, g, h are the elements of a cyclic group of order $\mathbb{G}$ of order q with generator g. The prover is proving the knowledge of (α_1, α_2) to the verifier, which are not known to the verifier while all other parameters are known to the verifier. To prove the knowledge of (α_1, α_2), the prover interacts with the verifier as follows:

1. The prover chooses $v_1, v_2 \hookleftarrow \mathbb{Z}_q$ and sends the commitments $\overline{X}_1 = g^{v_1} = f_1(v_1, v_2), \overline{X}_2 = g^{v_2} h^{v_1} = f_2(v_1, v_2)$ to the verifier.
2. The verifier chooses $c \hookleftarrow \mathbb{Z}_q$ and gives c as challenge to the prover.
3. The prover sets $r_1 = v_1 + c\alpha_1, r_2 = v_2 + c\alpha_2$ and sends the response (r_1, r_2) to the verifier.
4. The verifier checks whether the relations $f_1(r_1, r_2) = g^{r_1} = \overline{X}_1 X_1^c$ and $f_2(r_1, r_2) = g^{r_2} h^{r_1} = \overline{X}_2 X_2^c$ hold. If both hold, then the verifier accepts it, otherwise rejects it.

Lemma 1. *If Exp is the total number of exponentiations computed and GE is the total number of group elements sent for verification of the proof system π, then: (a) $Exp = M + 2\sum_{i=1}^{M}(number\ of\ exponentiations\ to\ compute X_i)$, and (b) $GE = M + l + 1$.*

• **Non-interactive Version:** Using Fiat-Shamir method [22], the proof system represtend by Eq. 1 can be converted to non-interactive zero-knowledge proof as follows:

1. The prover chooses $v_1, v_2 \hookleftarrow \mathbb{Z}_q$ and computes $\overline{X}_i = f_i(v_1, v_2), i = 1, 2$. Further, the prover computes $c = \widehat{H}(X_1\|X_2\|\overline{X}_1\|\overline{X}_2)$, where $\widehat{H} : \{0, 1\}^* \to \mathbb{Z}_q$ is a hash function. Finally, the prover sets $r_j = v_j - c\alpha_j$ for each $j = 1, 2$ and sends (c, r_1, r_2) to the verifier.
2. The verifier computes $\widetilde{X}_i = f_i(r_1, r_2) \cdot X_i^c = f_i(r_1 + c\alpha_1, r_2 + c\alpha_2) = f_i(v_1, v_2)$ for $i = 1, 2$ and checks whether the relation $c = \widehat{H}(X_1\|X_2\|\widetilde{X}_1\|\widetilde{X}_2)$ holds. If this holds, then the verifier accepts it, otherwise rejects it.

Note that in this case, Exp remains unchanged but GE reduces to $l + 1$.

Zero-Knowledge Argument for Shuffle [25]: We briefly discuss the zero-knowledge argument for shuffle of [25] which we use in our mPSI-CA. Let p, q be two primes such that q divide $p - 1$, $\mathbb{G}$ be a subgroup of $\mathbb{Z}_p^*$ of order q, $g_0(\neq 1)$ be an element of $\mathbb{G}$, $x \hookleftarrow \mathbb{Z}_q$ be a private key and $m_0 = g_0^x \bmod p$ be a public key used for re-encryption in shuffling. Let $\{\tau_u\}_{u=-4}^v$ be $v + 5$ elements of $\mathbb{G}$ that are uniformly and randomly generated so that neither $\mathcal{P}$ nor $\mathcal{V}$ can generate non-trivial integers $a, \{a_u\}_{u=-4}^v$ satisfying $g_0^a \prod_{u=-4}^v \tau_u^{a_u} \equiv 1 \bmod p$ with non-negligible probability.

The prover $\mathcal{P}$ chooses $\{A_{0i} \hookleftarrow \mathbb{Z}_q\}_{i=1}^v$ and a permutation matrix $(A_{ji})_{j,i=1,...,v}$ of order $v \times v$ corresponding to a permutation $\phi \in \Sigma_v$, where Σ_v denotes the set of all possible permutations over the set $\{1, ..., v\}$ and the permutation matrix $(A_{ji})_{j,i=1,...,v}$ is defined as $A_{ji} = 1 \bmod q$ if $\phi(j) = i, 0$ otherwise. The prover $\mathcal{P}$ shuffles v ElGamal ciphertexts $\{(g_i, m_i)\}_{i=1}^v$, yelding ciphertexts $\{(g_i', m_i')\}_{i=1}^v$ as

$$(g_i', m_i') = \left(\prod_{u=0}^v g_u^{A_{ui}}, \prod_{u=0}^v m_u^{A_{ui}}\right) = (g_0^{A_{0i}} g_{\phi^{-1}(i)}, m_0^{A_{0i}} m_{\phi^{-1}(i)}) \bmod p. \quad (2)$$

The zero-knowledge argument of [25] for the correctness of a shuffle is denoted by $\widehat{\pi} = \mathsf{PoKArg}\{(\phi \in \Sigma_v, A_{01}, ..., A_{0v} \in \mathbb{Z}_q)|\{(g_i', m_i') = (g_0^{A_{0i}} g_{\phi^{-1}(i)}, m_0^{A_{0i}} m_{\phi^{-1}(i)})\}_{i=1}^v\}$. The prover $\mathcal{P}$ wants to prove the knowledge of the permutation $\phi \in \Sigma_v$ and randomness $\{A_{0i} \in \mathbb{Z}_q\}_{i=1}^v$ to the verifier $\mathcal{V}$ such that Eq. 2 holds for each $i = 1, ..., v$. Note that decryption of the ciphertexts (g_i', m_i') and $(g_{\phi^{-1}(i)}, m_{\phi^{-1}(i)})$ give same message. This proof system satisfies soundness property under the hardness of DDH assumption. For verification process see [25].

Lemma 2. *If Exp is the total number of exponentiations computed and GE is the total number of group elements sent for verification of the proof system represented by $\widehat{\pi}$, then (a) Exp $= 15v + 22$, (b) GE $= 4v + 16$. In particular, commitment generation requires $9v + 12$ Exp and verification process requires $6v + 10$ Exp.*

For the distributed ElGamal encryption $\mathcal{DEL}$ presented in the Sect. 2.2, the zero-knowledge argument for shuffle will be of the form $\mathsf{PoKArg}\{(\phi \in \Sigma_v, \rho_1, ..., \rho_v \in \mathbb{Z}_q)|\{C_i' = C_{\phi^{-1}(i)}\mathcal{DEL}.\mathsf{Enc}(g^0, pk, \mathsf{par}, \rho_i)\}_{i=1}^v\}$, where ciphertexts $\{C_i = (g_i, m_i)\}_{i=1}^v$ are shuffled to $\{C_i' = (g_i', m_i')\}_{i=1}^v$.

3   Protocol

3.1   The mPSI

Our mPSI protocol consists of

- a **Setup** algorithm to generate global parameter by a trusted third party, public/private key generation of participants A, B and an arbiter Ar,
- an **mPSI Protocol** executed between two parties A, B with their private input sets X, Y respectively to compute $X \cap Y$, and
- a **Dispute Resolution Protocol** involving an off-line arbiter Ar. The arbiter Ar takes part into the Dispute Resolution protocol only when a corrupted player prematurely aborts the protocol and resolve the dispute without knowing the private information of A and B.

The **Setup** algorithm is represented by Fig. 1.

Setup(1^κ) – We use the ElGamal encryption $\mathcal{EL}$, the distributed ElGamal encryption $\mathcal{DEL}$ and the verifiable encryption $\mathcal{VE}$ over prime order group as described in the sections 2.2 and 2.3.

- A trusted third party generates $\mathsf{ppar} = (\mathsf{par}, \widetilde{g}, \mathcal{H}) \leftarrow \mathcal{VE}.\mathsf{Setup}(1^\kappa)$, where $\mathsf{par} = (p, q, g)$, chooses a collision resistant hash function $\overline{H} : \{0,1\}^* \to \mathbb{G}$, $\tau_i, \iota_j \xleftarrow{} \mathbb{G}$ for $i = -4, ..., v; j = -4, ..., w$, where $\mathbb{G} = <g>$ is the cyclic subgroup of $\mathbb{Z}_p^*$ of order q. Finally, the trusted third party publishes all these as global parameter gpar i.e., $\mathsf{gpar} = (\mathsf{ppar}, \overline{H}, \{\tau_i\}_{i=-4}^v, \{\iota_j\}_{j=-4}^w)$. Note that $\{\tau_i\}_{i=-4}^v, \{\iota_j\}_{j=-4}^w$ are to be used in zero-knowledge arguments for shuffle.
- Each of A, B generates

$$(epk_A = y_A = g^{a_1}, esk_A = a_1) \leftarrow \mathcal{EL}.\mathsf{KGen}(\mathsf{par}), \text{ where } a_1 \xleftarrow{} \mathbb{Z}_q,$$
$$(epk_B = y_B = g^{a_2}, esk_B = a_2) \leftarrow \mathcal{EL}.\mathsf{KGen}(\mathsf{par}), \text{ where } a_2 \xleftarrow{} \mathbb{Z}_q.$$

They publish the public keys epk_A, epk_B through the trusted third party who acts as certifying authority in this case. Parties A, B keeps the respcetive secret keys esk_A, esk_B to themselves.
- Arbiter Ar generates

$$(vpk_{Ar} = (a = g^{u_1}\widetilde{g}^{u_2}, b = g^{v_1}\widetilde{g}^{v_2}, c = g^{w_1}), vsk_{Ar} = (u_1, u_2, v_1, v_2, w_1))$$
$$\leftarrow \mathcal{VE}.\mathsf{KGen}(\mathsf{par}, \widetilde{g}), \text{ where } u_1, u_2, v_1, v_2, w_1 \xleftarrow{} \mathbb{Z}_q$$

and publishes the public key vpk_{Ar} through the trusted third party who works as certifying authority in this case.
- Let $pk = h = epk_A \cdot epk_B = g^{a_1+a_2}$ and $sk = a_1 + a_2$. Then (pk, sk) pair serves as the public-secret key pair for $\mathcal{DEL}$. Note that the secret key $sk = a_1 + a_2$ for $\mathcal{DEL}$ is not known to anyone. However, the public key pk for $\mathcal{DEL}$ is publicly computable from epk_A and epk_B.

Fig. 1. Setup algorithm of our mPSI

mPSI Protocol: The 5 round mPSI protocol is an interactive protocol between party A with private set $X = \{x_1, ..., x_v\}$ and party B with private set $Y = \{y_1, ..., y_w\}$, where $(\text{gpar}, epk_A, epk_B, pk = epk_A \cdot epk_B)$ is their common input. Initially, both parties have secret shares of an ElGamal encryption scheme and they compute hash of their private sets X, Y to get $S_A = \{\overline{H}(x_1), ..., \overline{H}(x_v)\}$, $S_B = \{\overline{H}(y_1), ..., \overline{H}(y_w)\}$ respectively and uses these as their input sets. Then they encrypt their own inputs and rerandomize the peer's encryptions so that they arrive at the same randomness analogous to a Diffe-Hellman exchange. They also exchange some auxiliary group elements which bind some of these random coins. Essentially, in each round, a transcript $R_i(i = 1, ..., 5)$ containing some messages with zero-knowledge proofs is genetrated and sent by one party, which is then verified by the other party. To verify the correctness of $R_i(i = 1, ..., 5)$, corresponding party verifies the associated zero-knowledge proofs using a similar technique presented in Sect. 2.4. Finally, a set of group elements is arrived at and then both parties check whether a function applied to their individual elements is a memeber of this and if so, then these are the elements in the intersection. A high level overview of mPSI protocol is given in Fig. 2. To get the intersection $X \cap Y$, A and B proceed in 6 steps as follows:

Step 1. Party A

(i) chooses $r_{x_1}, ..., r_{x_v} \leftarrow \mathbb{Z}_q$, computes $S_A = \{\overline{H}(x_1), ..., \overline{H}(x_v)\}$, encrypts each member $\overline{H}(x_i) \in S_A$ with the public key $pk = h = g^{a_1+a_2}$ to get

$$\mathsf{dE}_{pk}(\overline{H}(x_i)) = (c_{x_i}, d_{x_i}) = (g^{r_{x_i}}, \overline{H}(x_i)h^{r_{x_i}}) \leftarrow \mathcal{DEL}.\mathsf{Enc}(\overline{H}(x_i), pk, \mathsf{par}, r_{x_i});$$

(ii) generates the proof

$$\pi_1 = \mathsf{PoK}\big\{(r_{x_1}, ..., r_{x_v})| \wedge_{i=1}^v (c_{x_i} = g^{r_{x_i}})\big\};$$

(iii) sends $R_1 = \big\langle \{\mathsf{dE}_{pk}(\overline{H}(x_i))\}_{i=1}^v, \pi_1\big\rangle$ to B.

Step 2. On receiving $R_1 = \big\langle \{\mathsf{dE}_{pk}(\overline{H}(x_i))\}_{i=1}^v, \pi_1\big\rangle$ from A, party B verifies the validity of the proof π_1. If verification fails, then B aborts. Otherwise, B does the following:

(i) chooses $r_{y_1}, ..., r_{y_w} \leftarrow \mathbb{Z}_q$, computes $S_B = \{\overline{H}(y_1), ..., \overline{H}(y_w)\}$, encrypts each $\overline{H}(y_j) \in S_B$ with the public key $pk = h = g^{a_1+a_2}$ and generates

$$\mathsf{dE}_{pk}(\overline{H}(y_j)) = (c_{y_j}, d_{y_j}) = (g^{r_{y_j}}, \overline{H}(y_j)h^{r_{y_j}}) \leftarrow \mathcal{DEL}.\mathsf{Enc}(\overline{H}(y_j), pk, \mathsf{par}, r_{y_j});$$

(ii) selects $r, r_{g_1}, \alpha \leftarrow \mathbb{Z}_q$ and computes $\widehat{g} = g^\alpha$,

$$\mathsf{dE}_{pk}(\widehat{g}^r) = (c_{\widehat{g}}, d_{\widehat{g}}) = (g^{r_{g_1}}, \widehat{g}^r h^{r_{g_1}}) \leftarrow \mathcal{DEL}.\mathsf{Enc}(\widehat{g}^r, pk, \mathsf{par}, r_{g_1}),$$

$$\mathsf{dE}_{pk}((\overline{H}(y_j))^r) = (\widehat{c}_{y_j}, \widehat{d}_{y_j}) = ((c_{y_j})^r, (d_{y_j})^r) \text{ for } 1 \le j \le w,$$

$$\mathsf{dE}_{pk}((\overline{H}(x_i))^r) = (\widehat{c}_{x_i}, \widehat{d}_{x_i}) = ((c_{x_i})^r, (d_{x_i})^r) \text{ for } 1 \le i \le v;$$

(iii) constructs proof

$$\pi_2 = \mathsf{PoK}\big\{(r_{y_1}, ..., r_{y_w}, r, r_{g_1})| \wedge_{j=1}^w (c_{y_j} = g^{r_{y_j}})(\widehat{c}_{y_j} = (c_{y_j})^r)(\widehat{d}_{y_j} = (d_{y_j})^r)$$
$$\wedge_{i=1}^v (\widehat{c}_{x_i} = (c_{x_i})^r)(\widehat{d}_{x_i} = (d_{x_i})^r) \wedge (c_{\widehat{g}} = g^{r_{g_1}}) \wedge (d_{\widehat{g}} = \widehat{g}^r h^{r_{g_1}})\big\}\big\};$$

Common input: $\mathsf{gpar}, epk_A, epk_B, pk = epk_A \cdot epk_B, vpk_{Ar}$

A's private input:
$X = \{x_1, ..., x_v\}, esk_A = a_1$
$r_{x_1}, ..., r_{x_v} \hookleftarrow \mathbb{Z}_q$
for $1 \leq i \leq v$, $\mathsf{dE}_{pk}(\overline{H}(x_i)) = (c_{x_i}, d_{x_i})$
$R_1 = \langle \{\mathsf{dE}_{pk}(\overline{H}(x_i))\}_{i=1}^v, \pi_1 \rangle$

$\xrightarrow{R_1}$

B's private input:
$Y = \{y_1, ..., y_w\}, esk_B = a_2$

$r_{y_1}, ..., r_{y_w}, r, r_{\hat{g}}, \alpha \hookleftarrow \mathbb{Z}_q, \hat{g} = g^\alpha$,
$\mathsf{dE}_{pk}(\hat{g}^r) = (c_{\hat{g}}, d_{\hat{g}})$
for $1 \leq j \leq w$, $\mathsf{dE}_{pk}(\overline{H}(y_j)) = (c_{y_j}, d_{y_j})$
and $\mathsf{dE}_{pk}((\overline{H}(y_j))^r) = (c'_{y_j}, d'_{y_j})$

$\xleftarrow{R_2}$ for $1 \leq i \leq v$, $\mathsf{dE}_{pk}((\overline{H}(x_i))^r) = (\hat{c}_{x_i}, \hat{d}_{x_i})$

$\alpha_1, ..., \alpha_v, r_1, ..., r_w, z_1, ..., z_w, r', r_{\bar{g}}, \beta \hookleftarrow \mathbb{Z}_q$
$\bar{g} = g^\beta$ and $\mathsf{dE}_{pk}(\bar{g}^{r'}) = (c_{\bar{g}}, d_{\bar{g}})$
for $1 \leq i \leq v$, $\mathsf{dE}_{pk}((\overline{H}(x_i))^{rr'}) = (\bar{c}_{x_i}, \bar{d}_{x_i})$,
$C_{x_i} = \bar{c}_{x_i} c_{\bar{g}} c_{\hat{g}}$ and $\mathsf{eE}_{epk_B}((C_{x_i})^{a_1})$
for $1 \leq j \leq w$, $\mathsf{dE}_{pk}((\overline{H}(y_j))^{rr'}) = (\bar{c}_{y_j}, \bar{d}_{y_j})$,
$C_{y_j} = \bar{c}_{y_j} c_{\bar{g}} c_{\hat{g}}$, $\bar{u}_{y_j} = (C_{y_j})^{a_1} g^{r_j}$, $\mathsf{vE}_{vpk_{Ar}}(g^{r_j})$
$R_3 = \langle \{\mathsf{dE}_{pk}((\overline{H}(x_i))^{rr'}), \mathsf{eE}_{epk_B}((C_{x_i})^{a_1})\}_{i=1}^v,$
$\{\mathsf{dE}_{pk}((\overline{H}(y_j))^{rr'}), \mathsf{vE}_{vpk_{Ar}}(g^{r_j}), \bar{u}_{y_j}\}_{j=1}^w,$
$\bar{g}, \mathsf{dE}_{pk}(\bar{g}^{r'}), \pi_3 \rangle$

$R_2 = \langle \{\mathsf{dE}_{pk}(\overline{H}(y_j)), \mathsf{dE}_{pk}((\overline{H}(y_j))^r)\}_{j=1}^w,$
$\{\mathsf{dE}_{pk}((\overline{H}(x_i))^r)\}_{i=1}^v, \mathsf{dE}_{pk}(\hat{g}^r), \hat{g}, \pi_2 \rangle$

$\xrightarrow{R_3}$

for $1 \leq i \leq v$, $C_{x_i} = \bar{c}_{x_i} c_{\bar{g}} c_{\hat{g}}$ and
$s_{x_i} = (C_{x_i})^{a_2}$
for $1 \leq j \leq w$, $C_{y_j} = \bar{c}_{y_j} c_{\bar{g}} c_{\hat{g}}$ and
$s_{y_j} = (C_{y_j})^{a_2}$

$\xleftarrow{R_4}$ $R_4 = \langle \{s_{x_i}\}_{i=1}^v, \{s_{y_j}\}_{j=1}^w, \pi_4 \rangle$

for $1 \leq i \leq v$, $\frac{d_{x_i} d_{\bar{g}} d_{\hat{g}}}{(C_{x_i})^{a_1} s_{x_i}} = \bar{g}^{r'} \hat{g}^r (\overline{H}(x_i))^{rr'}$
for $1 \leq j \leq w$, $\frac{d_{y_j} d_{\bar{g}} d_{\hat{g}}}{(C_{y_j})^{a_1} s_{y_j}} = \bar{g}^{r'} \hat{g}^r (\overline{H}(y_j))^{rr'}$
$X \cap Y = \{x_i \in X | \bar{g}^{r'} \hat{g}^r (\overline{H}(x_i))^{rr'} \in \Gamma_Y\}$
where $\Gamma_Y = \{\bar{g}^{r'} \hat{g}^r (\overline{H}(y_j))^{rr'}\}_{j=1}^w$
$R_5 = \langle \{(g^{r_j})\}_{j=1}^w, \pi_5 \rangle$

$\xrightarrow{R_5}$

for $1 \leq i \leq v$,
$(C_{x_i})^{a_1} \leftarrow \mathcal{EL}.\mathsf{Dec}(\mathsf{eE}_{epk_B}((C_{x_i})^{a_1}), a_2)$
$\frac{d_{x_i} d_{\bar{g}} d_{\hat{g}}}{(C_{x_i})^{a_1} s_{x_i}} = \bar{g}^{r'} \hat{g}^r (\overline{H}(x_i))^{rr'}$
for $1 \leq j \leq w$,
$\frac{\bar{u}_{y_j}}{g^{r_j}} = (C_{y_j})^{a_1}$, $\frac{d_{y_j} d_{\bar{g}} d_{\hat{g}}}{(C_{y_j})^{a_1} s_{y_j}} = \bar{g}^{r'} \hat{g}^r (\overline{H}(y_j))^{rr'}$
$X \cap Y = \{y_j \in Y | \bar{g}^{r'} \hat{g}^r (\overline{H}(y_j))^{rr'} \in \Gamma_X\}$,
where $\Gamma_X = \{\bar{g}^{r'} \hat{g}^r (\overline{H}(x_i))^{rr'}\}_{i=1}^v$

Fig. 2. Communication flow of our mPSI

(iv) sends $R_2 = \langle \{\mathsf{dE}_{pk}(\overline{H}(y_j)), \mathsf{dE}_{pk}((\overline{H}(y_j))^r)\}_{j=1}^w, \{\mathsf{dE}_{pk}((\overline{H}(x_i))^r)\}_{i=1}^v,$
$\mathsf{dE}_{pk}(\widehat{g}^r), \widehat{g}, \pi_2 \rangle$ to A.

Step 3. Party A, on receiving $R_2 = \langle \{\mathsf{dE}_{pk}(\overline{H}(y_j)), \mathsf{dE}_{pk}((\overline{H}(y_j))^r)\}_{j=1}^w,$
$\{\mathsf{dE}_{pk}((\overline{H}(x_i))^r)\}_{i=1}^v, \mathsf{dE}_{pk}(\widehat{g}^r), \widehat{g}, \pi_2 \rangle$ from B, checks the validity of the proof
π_2. Party A aborts if the verification fails, else dose the following:

(i) selects $r', r_{g_2}, \beta \hookleftarrow \mathbb{Z}_q$ and computes $\bar{g} = g^{\beta}$

$$\mathsf{dE}_{pk}(\bar{g}^{r'}) = (c_{\bar{g}}, d_{\bar{g}}) = (g^{r_{g_2}}, \bar{g}^{r'} h^{r_{g_2}}) \leftarrow \mathcal{DEL}.\mathsf{Enc}(\bar{g}^{r'}, pk, par, r_{g_2}),$$

$$\mathsf{dE}_{pk}((\overline{H}(x_i))^{rr'}) = (\bar{c}_{x_i}, \bar{d}_{x_i}) = ((\widehat{c}_{x_i})^{r'}, (\widehat{d}_{x_i})^{r'}) = ((c_{x_i})^{rr'}, (d_{x_i})^{rr'}), 1 \le i \le v,$$

$$\mathsf{dE}_{pk}((\overline{H}(y_j))^{rr'}) = (\bar{c}_{y_j}, \bar{d}_{y_j}) = ((\widehat{c}_{y_j})^{r'}, (\widehat{d}_{y_j})^{r'}) = ((c_{y_j})^{rr'}, (d_{y_j})^{rr'}), 1 \le j \le w;$$

(ii) chooses $\alpha_1, ..., \alpha_v \hookleftarrow \mathbb{Z}_q$ and for each $i = 1, ..., v$, computes $(C_{x_i})^{a_1} = (\bar{c}_{x_i} c_{\bar{g}} c_{\bar{g}})^{a_1}$ with his secret key $esk_A = a_1$ and encrypts $(C_{x_i})^{a_1}$ using B's public key $epk_B = y_B$ to generate $\mathsf{eE}_{epk_B}((C_{x_i})^{a_1})$

$$= (u_{x_i}, \bar{u}_{x_i}) = (g^{\alpha_i}, (C_{x_i})^{a_1}(y_B)^{\alpha_i}) \leftarrow \mathcal{EL}.\mathsf{Enc}((C_{x_i})^{a_1}, y_B, par, \alpha_i);$$

(iii) generates a label $L \in \{0, 1\}^*$ using a session ID which has been agreed by all parities beforehand and the hash of past communication;

(iv) chooses $r_1, ..., r_w, z_1, ..., z_w \hookleftarrow \mathbb{Z}_q$, for each $j = 1, ..., w$, computes $\bar{u}_{y_j} = (C_{y_j})^{a_1} g^{r_j} = (\bar{c}_{y_j} c_{\bar{g}} c_{\bar{g}})^{a_1} g^{r_j}$ and generates $\mathsf{vE}_{vpk_{Ar}}(g^{r_j}) = (t_{1j}, t_{2j}, t_{3j}, t_{4j})$

$$= (g^{z_j}, \widetilde{g}^{z_j}, c^{z_j} g^{r_j}, a^{z_j} b^{z_j \rho_j}) \leftarrow \mathcal{VE}.\mathsf{Enc}(g^{r_j}, vpk_{Ar}, gpar, z_j, L, \mathcal{H}),$$

where $vpk_{Ar} = (a, b, c)$ is the arbiter Ar's public key and $\rho_j = \mathcal{H}(t_{1j}, t_{2j}, t_{3j}, L)$;

(v) constructs proof

$$\pi_3 = \mathsf{PoK}\big\{(a_1, r', r_1, ..., r_w, z_1, ..., z_w, \alpha_1, ..., \alpha_v, r_{g_2})|(y_A = g^{a_1})$$
$$\wedge_{j=1}^w (\bar{c}_{y_j} = (\widehat{c}_{y_j})^{r'})(\bar{d}_{y_j} = (\widehat{d}_{y_j})^{r'})(\bar{u}_{y_j} = (C_{y_j})^{a_1} \cdot g^{r_j}) \wedge (d_{\bar{g}} = \bar{g}^r h^{r_{g_2}})$$
$$\wedge_{j=1}^w (t_{1j} = g^{z_j})(t_{2j} = \widetilde{g}^{z_j})(t_{3j} = c^{z_j} g^{r_j})(t_{4j} = a^{z_j} b^{z_j \rho_j}) \wedge (c_{\bar{g}} = g^{r_{g_2}})$$
$$\wedge_{i=1}^v (\bar{c}_{x_i} = (\widehat{c}_{x_i})^{r'})(\bar{d}_{x_i} = (\widehat{d}_{x_i})^{r'})(u_{x_i} = g^{\alpha_i})(\bar{u}_{x_i} = (C_{x_i})^{a_1}(y_B)^{\alpha_i})\big\};$$

(vi) sends $R_3 = \big\langle\{\mathsf{dE}_{pk}((\overline{H}(x_i))^{rr'}), \mathsf{eE}_{epk_B}((C_{x_i})^{a_1})\}_{i=1}^v, \{\mathsf{dE}_{pk}((\overline{H}(y_j))^{rr'}),$
$\mathsf{vE}_{vpk_{Ar}}(g^{r_j}), \bar{u}_{y_j}\}_{j=1}^w, \mathsf{dE}_{pk}(\bar{g}^{r'}), \bar{g}, \pi_3\big\rangle$ to B.

Step 4. On receiving $R_3 = \big\langle\{\mathsf{dE}_{pk}((\overline{H}(x_i))^{rr'}), \mathsf{eE}_{epk_B}((C_{x_i})^{a_1})\}_{i=1}^v, \{\mathsf{dE}_{pk}$ $((\overline{H}(y_j))^{rr'}), \mathsf{vE}_{vpk_{Ar}}(g^{r_j}), \bar{u}_{y_j}\}_{j=1}^w, \mathsf{dE}_{pk}(\bar{g}^{r'}), \bar{g}, \pi_3\big\rangle$, party B verifies the validity of the proof π_3. If the verification fails, then B aborts. Otherwise, B proceeds as follows:

(i) extracts $\{\bar{c}_{x_i}\}_{i=1}^v, \{\bar{c}_{y_j}\}_{j=1}^w, c_{\bar{g}}$ from $\{\mathsf{dE}_{pk}((\overline{H}(x_i))^{rr'})\}_{i=1}^v, \{\mathsf{dE}_{pk}$ $((\overline{H}(y_j))^{rr'})\}_{j=1}^w, \mathsf{dE}_{pk}(\bar{g}^{r'})$ respectively in R_3 and computes $\{s_{x_i} = (C_{x_i})^{a_2} = (\bar{c}_{x_i} c_{\bar{g}} c_{\bar{g}})^{a_2}\}_{i=1}^v, \{s_{y_j} = (C_{y_j})^{a_2} = (\bar{c}_{y_j} c_{\bar{g}} c_{\bar{g}})^{a_2}\}_{j=1}^w$ using his secret key $esk_B = a_2$ and $c_{\bar{g}}$ computed in *Step* 2;

(ii) constructs the proof

$$\pi_4 = \mathsf{PoK}\big\{(a_2)|(y_B = g^{a_2}) \wedge_{i=1}^v (s_{x_i} = (C_{x_i})^{a_2}) \wedge_{j=1}^w (s_{y_j} = (C_{y_j})^{a_2})\big\};$$

(iii) sends $R_4 = \big\langle\{s_{x_i}\}_{i=1}^v, \{s_{y_j}\}_{j=1}^w, \pi_4\big\rangle$ to A.

Step 5. Party A, on receiving $R_4 = \langle \{s_{x_i}\}_{i=1}^{v}, \{s_{y_j}\}_{j=1}^{w}, \pi_4 \rangle$ from B, checks the validity of the proof π_4. Party A aborts if the verification does not succeed, else extracts $d_{\bar{g}}$ from $\mathsf{dE}_{pk}(\bar{g}^r)$ in R_2, does the following using his secret key $esk_A = a_1$ and $\{C_{x_i}, \bar{d}_{x_i}\}_{i=1}^{v}, \{C_{y_j}, \bar{d}_{y_j}\}_{j=1}^{w}, d_{\bar{g}}$ computed in *Step* 3:

(i) computes

$$\frac{\bar{d}_{x_i} d_{\widehat{g}} d_{\bar{g}}}{(C_{x_i})^{a_1} s_{x_i}} = \frac{\bar{d}_{x_i} d_{\widehat{g}} d_{\bar{g}}}{(\bar{c}_{x_i} c_{\widehat{g}} c_{\bar{g}})^{(a_1+a_2)}} = \frac{(d_{x_i})^{rr'} d_{\widehat{g}} d_{\bar{g}}}{((c_{x_i})^{rr'} c_{\widehat{g}} c_{\bar{g}})^{a_1+a_2}}$$

$$= \frac{\bar{g}^{r'} \widehat{g}^r (\overline{H}(x_i))^{rr'} g^{(r_{x_i} rr' + r_{g_2} + r_{g_1})(a_1+a_2)}}{g^{(r_{x_i} rr' + r_{g_2} + r_{g_1})(a_1+a_2)}} = \bar{g}^{r'} \widehat{g}^r (\overline{H}(x_i))^{rr'}, 1 \le i \le v,$$

and $$\frac{\bar{d}_{y_j} d_{\widehat{g}} d_{\bar{g}}}{(C_{y_j})^{a_1} s_{y_j}} = \frac{\bar{d}_{y_j} d_{\widehat{g}} d_{\bar{g}}}{(\bar{c}_{y_j} c_{\widehat{g}} c_{\bar{g}})^{(a_1+a_2)}} = \frac{(d_{y_j})^{rr'} d_{\widehat{g}} d_{\bar{g}}}{((c_{y_j})^{rr'} c_{\widehat{g}} c_{\bar{g}})^{a_1+a_2}}$$

$$= \frac{\bar{g}^{r'} \widehat{g}^r (\overline{H}(y_j))^{rr'} g^{(r_{y_j} rr' + r_{g_2} + r_{g_1})(a_1+a_2)}}{g^{(r_{y_j} rr' + r_{g_2} + r_{g_1})(a_1+a_2)}} = \bar{g}^{r'} \widehat{g}^r (\overline{H}(y_j))^{rr'}, 1 \le j \le w;$$

(ii) sets $X \cap Y = \{x_i \in X | \bar{g}^{r'} \widehat{g}^r (\overline{H}(x_i))^{rr'} \in \{\bar{g}^{r'} \widehat{g}^r (\overline{H}(y_j))^{rr'}\}_{j=1}^{w}\}$;

(iii) constructs the proof

$$\pi_5 = \mathsf{PoK}\{(z_1, ..., z_w) | \wedge_{j=1}^{w} (t_{1j} = g^{z_j})(t_{2j} = \widetilde{g}^{z_j})(t_{3j} = c^{z_j} g^{r_j})(t_{4j} = a^{z_j} b^{z_j \rho_j})\};$$

(iv) sends $R_5 = \langle \{(g^{r_j})\}_{j=1}^{w}, \pi_5 \rangle$ to B. Note that A constructs the proof π_5 to prove that $g^{r_j} \in R_5$ was encrypted in *Step* 3 to generate $\mathsf{vE}_{vpk_{Ar}}(g^{r_j})$ for $j = 1, ..., w$ using Ar's public key.

Step 6. On receiving $R_5 = \langle \{(g^{r_j})\}_{j=1}^{w}, \pi_5 \rangle$ from A, party B verifies the validity of the proof π_5. If the verification of the proof succeeds, then B

(i) for each $i = 1, ..., v$, decrypts $\mathsf{eE}_{epk_B}((C_{x_i})^{a_1})$ received in *Step* 3 using his secret key $esk_B = a_2$ to get $(C_{x_i})^{a_1} \leftarrow \mathcal{EL}.\mathsf{Dec}(\mathsf{eE}_{epk_B}((C_{x_i})^{a_1}), esk_B)$, extracts $\bar{d}_{x_i}, d_{\bar{g}}$ from $\mathsf{dE}_{pk}((\overline{H}(x_i))^{rr'}), \mathsf{dE}_{pk}(\bar{g}^{r'})$ respectively in R_3, uses s_{x_i} computed in *Step* 4 and $d_{\widehat{g}}$ computed in *Step* 2 to generate

$$\frac{\bar{d}_{x_i} d_{\widehat{g}} d_{\bar{g}}}{(C_{x_i})^{a_1} s_{x_i}} = \frac{\bar{d}_{x_i} d_{\widehat{g}} d_{\bar{g}}}{(\bar{c}_{x_i} c_{\widehat{g}} c_{\bar{g}})^{(a_1+a_2)}} = \frac{(d_{x_i})^{rr'} d_{\widehat{g}} d_{\bar{g}}}{((c_{x_i})^{rr'} c_{\widehat{g}} c_{\bar{g}})^{a_1+a_2}}$$

$$= \frac{\bar{g}^{r'} \widehat{g}^r (\overline{H}(x_i))^{rr'} g^{(r_{x_i} rr' + r_{g_2} + r_{g_1})(a_1+a_2)}}{g^{(r_{x_i} rr' + r_{g_2} + r_{g_1})(a_1+a_2)}} = \bar{g}^{r'} \widehat{g}^r (\overline{H}(x_i))^{rr'};$$

(ii) for each $j = 1, ..., w$, extracts $\bar{d}_{y_j}, d_{\bar{g}}$ from $\mathsf{dE}_{pk}((\overline{H}(y_j))^{rr'}), \mathsf{dE}_{pk}(\bar{g}^{r'})$ from in R_3 respectively, uses $\bar{u}_{y_j}$ obtained from R_3, s_{y_j} computed in *Step* 4 and $d_{\widehat{g}}$ computed in *Step* 2 to generate

$$\frac{\bar{u}_{y_j}}{g^{r_j}} = \frac{(C_{y_j})^{a_1} \cdot g^{r_j}}{g^{r_j}} = (C_{y_j})^{a_1},$$

and $$\frac{\bar{d}_{y_j} d_{\widehat{g}} d_{\bar{g}}}{(C_{y_j})^{a_1} s_{y_j}} = \frac{\bar{d}_{y_j} d_{\widehat{g}} d_{\bar{g}}}{(\bar{c}_{y_j} c_{\widehat{g}} c_{\bar{g}})^{(a_1+a_2)}} = \frac{(d_{y_j})^{rr'} d_{\widehat{g}} d_{\bar{g}}}{((c_{y_j})^{rr'} c_{\widehat{g}} c_{\bar{g}})^{a_1+a_2}}$$

$$= \frac{\bar{g}^{r'} \widehat{g}^r (\overline{H}(y_j))^{rr'} g^{(r_{y_j} rr' + r_{g_2} + r_{g_1})(a_1+a_2)}}{g^{(r_{y_j} rr' + r_{g_2} + r_{g_1})(a_1+a_2)}} = \bar{g}^{r'} \widehat{g}^r (\overline{H}(y_j))^{rr'};$$

(iii) sets $X \cap Y = \{y_j \in Y | \bar{g}^{r'} \hat{g}^r (\overline{H}(y_j))^{rr'} \in \{\bar{g}^r \hat{g}^r (\overline{H}(x_i))^{rr'}\}_{i=1}^v\}$.

If the verification of π_5 does not succeed or B does not get $R_5 = \langle \{(g^{r_j})\}_{j=1}^w, \pi_5 \rangle$ from A i.e., if A prematurely aborts, then B sends a dispute resolution request to the arbiter Ar.

We describe the Dispute Resolution Protocol in Fig. 3.

The arbiter Ar, on receiving a dispute resolution request from B, interacts with A and B in the following way:

Step 1. Party B sends all the messages sent and received in Step 1-3 of the mPSI protocol to the arbiter Ar. As Ar knows the session ID, after receiving the messages from B, the arbiter Ar computes the label L and then verifies the consistency between messages and the label L. If the verification fails or if the transcript ends before the end of *Step* 3 of the mPSI protocol then Ar aborts so that neither party gets any advantage. Otherwise, Ar continues with the following steps.

Step 2. Similar to *Step* 4 of the mPSI protocol, B sends $R_4 = \langle \{s_{x_i} = (C_{x_i})^{a_2}\}_{i=1}^v, \{s_{y_j} = (C_{y_j})^{a_2}\}_{j=1}^w, \pi_4 \rangle$ to Ar, where π_4 is same the as π_4 of the mPSI protocol.

Step 3. The arbiter Ar, on receiving $R_4 = \langle \{s_{x_i} = (C_{x_i})^{a_2}\}_{i=1}^v, \{s_{y_j} = (C_{y_j})^{a_2}\}_{j=1}^w, \pi_4 \rangle$ from B, verifies the validity of the proof π_4. If the verification does not succeed then Ar aborts, there by neither party gets any advantage. Otherwise, Ar decrypts $\{\mathsf{vE}_{vpk_{Ar}}(g^{r_j})\}_{j=1}^w$ and sends $\{g^{r_j}\}_{j=1}^w$ to B so that B can compute $X \cap Y$ using the similar technique as described in *Step* 6 of our mPSI protocol. The arbiter Ar also forwards $\langle \{s_{x_i}\}_{i=1}^v, \{s_{y_j}\}_{j=1}^w \rangle$ to A who in turns can compute $X \cap Y$ using the similar technique as explained in *Step* 5 of our mPSI protocol.

Fig. 3. Dispute resolution protocol of our mPSI

Remark 1. In *Step* 3 of mPSI protocol, A encrypts each g^{r_j} to get $\mathsf{vE}_{pk_{Ar}}(g^{r_j})$ for $1 \leq j \leq w$, using the public key pk_{Ar} of Ar and a label $L \in \{0,1\}^*$. Note that the label L used by Ar should be same as the label L used by A. Party A generates label L using the following two inputs –

(i) a session ID which has been agreed by all parities beforehand,

(ii) the hash of past communication.

As Ar knows the session ID, after receiving all the messages from B in the *Step* 1 of dispute resolution protocol Ar can compute the label L. Due to the session ID, Ar can verify the identities of A, B and that the protocol execution is within a certain time window. As only B can raise a dispute resolution request to Ar, party A uses the hash of past communication as an input of L to ensure that B cannot get any advantage by modifying messages.

Correctness: To prove the correctness of our protocol we need to show that $X \cap Y = \{x_i \in X | \bar{g}^{r'} \hat{g}^r (\overline{H}(x_i))^{rr'} \in \{\bar{g}^{r'} \hat{g}^r (\overline{H}(y_1))^{rr'}, ..., \bar{g}^{r'} \hat{g}^r (\overline{H}(y_w))^{rr'}\}\}$ and $X \cap Y = \{y_j \in Y | \bar{g}^{r'} \hat{g}^r (\overline{H}(y_j))^{rr'} \in \{\bar{g}^{r'} \hat{g}^r (\overline{H}(x_1))^{rr'}, ..., \bar{g}^{r'} \hat{g}^r (\overline{H}(x_v))^{rr'}\}\}$. Let $x_i \in X$ and $\bar{g}^{r'} \hat{g}^r (\overline{H}((x_i))^{rr'} \in \{\bar{g}^{r'} \hat{g}^r (\overline{H}(y_1))^{rr'}, ..., \bar{g}^{r'} \hat{g}^r (\overline{H}(y_w))^{rr'}\}$. Then there exists $y_j \in Y$ such that $\bar{g}^{r'} \hat{g}^r (\overline{H}(x_i))^{rr'} = \bar{g}^{r'} \hat{g}^r (\overline{H}(y_j))^{rr'}$. i.e., $x_i = y_j \in Y$

i.e., $x_i \in X \cap Y$. On the other hand $x_i \in X \cap Y$ implies there exists y_j such that $x_i = y_j$ i.e., $\bar{g}^{r'} \hat{g}^r (\overline{H}(x_i))^{rr'} = \bar{g}^{r'} \hat{g}^r (\overline{H}(y_j))^{rr'}$. Thus the first equality holds. Similarly it can be shown that the second equality holds.

3.2 The mPSI-CA

Similar to the mPSI, our mPSI-CA also consists of a **Setup** algorithm, an **mPSI-CA Protocol** and a **Dispute Resolution Protocol**.
Setup(1^κ) : Similar to the Setup algorithm of the mPSI.

mPSI-CA Protocol: Our mPSI-CA protocol is also an interactive protocol between parties A and B consisting 5 rounds. Two random permutations ϕ and ψ are to be used by B and A respectively. Let the parties A, B have private input sets $X = \{x_1, ..., x_v\}, Y = \{y_1, ..., y_w\}$ respectively and (gpar, $epk_A, epk_B, pk = epk_A \cdot epk_B = h$) be their common input. Then the parties A and B interact to get the cardinality $|X \cap Y|$ of $X \cap Y$ as follows:
Step 1. Party A proceeds as follows:

(i) chooses $r_{x_1}, ..., r_{x_v} \leftarrowtail \mathbb{Z}_q$ and encrypts each member $x_i \in X$ with the public key $pk = h = g^{a_1+a_2}$ to get

$$\mathsf{dE}_{pk}(x_i) = (c_{x_i}, d_{x_i}) = (g^{r_{x_i}}, x_i h^{r_{x_i}}) \leftarrow \mathcal{DEL}.\mathsf{Enc}(x_i, pk, \mathsf{par}, r_{x_i});$$

(ii) generates the proof $\pi_1 = \mathsf{PoK}\{(r_{x_1}, ..., r_{x_v})| \wedge_{i=1}^v (c_{x_i} = g^{r_{x_i}})\}$;
(iii) sends $R_1 = \langle \{\mathsf{dE}_{pk}(x_i)\}_{i=1}^v, \pi_1 \rangle$ to B.

Step 2. Party B, on receiving $R_1 = \langle \{\mathsf{dE}_{pk}(x_i)\}_{i=1}^v, \pi_1 \rangle$ from A, verifies the validity of the proof π_1. If verification fails, then B aborts. Otherwise, B does the following:

(i) chooses $r_{y_1}, ..., r_{y_w} \leftarrowtail \mathbb{Z}_q$ and encrypts each $y_j \in Y$ with the public key $pk = h = g^{a_1+a_2}$ to get

$$\mathsf{dE}_{pk}(y_j) = (c_{y_j}, d_{y_j}) = (g^{r_{y_j}}, y_j h^{r_{y_j}}) \leftarrow \mathcal{DEL}.\mathsf{Enc}(y_j, pk, \mathsf{par}, r_{y_j});$$

(ii) selects a random permutation $\phi \in \Sigma_v, \alpha_1, ..., \alpha_v \leftarrowtail \mathbb{Z}_q$ and computes for each $i = 1, ..., v, \mathsf{dE}_{pk}(\bar{x}_i) = (\mathsf{dE}_{pk}(x_{\phi^{-1}(i)}))(\mathcal{DEL}.\mathsf{Enc}(1, pk, \mathsf{par}, \alpha_i)) = (c'_{x_i}, d'_{x_i}) = (c_{x_{\phi^{-1}(i)}} g^{\alpha_i}, d_{x_{\phi^{-1}(i)}} h^{\alpha_i})$;
(iii) chooses $r, r_{g_1}, \alpha \leftarrowtail \mathbb{Z}_q$ and computes $\hat{g} = g^\alpha$

$$\mathsf{dE}_{pk}(\hat{g}^r) = (c_{\hat{g}}, d_{\hat{g}}) = (g^{r_{g_1}}, \hat{g}^r h^{r_{g_1}}) \leftarrow \mathcal{DEL}.\mathsf{Enc}(\hat{g}^r, pk, \mathsf{par}, r_{g_1}),$$
$$\mathsf{dE}_{pk}((y_j)^r) = (c'_{y_j}, d'_{y_j}) = ((c_{y_j})^r, (d_{y_j})^r) \text{ for } 1 \le j \le w,$$
$$\mathsf{dE}_{pk}((\bar{x}_i)^r) = (\hat{c}_{x_i}, \hat{d}_{x_i}) = ((c'_{x_i})^r, (d'_{x_i})^r) \text{ for } 1 \le i \le v;$$

(iv) constructs proof

$$\pi_2 = \mathsf{PoK}\{(r_{y_1}, ..., r_{y_w}, r, r_{g_2})| \wedge_{j=1}^w (c_{y_j} = g^{r_{y_j}})(c'_{y_j} = (c_{y_j})^r)(d'_{y_j} = (d_{y_j})^r)$$
$$\wedge_{i=1}^v (\hat{c}_{x_i} = (c'_{x_i})^r)(\hat{d}_{x_i} = (d'_{x_i})^r) \wedge (c_{\hat{g}} = g^{r_{g_1}}) \wedge (d_{\hat{g}} = \hat{g}^r h^{r_{g_1}})\},$$
$$\hat{\pi}_2 = \mathsf{PoK}\{(\phi \in \Sigma_v, \{\alpha_i\}_{i=1}^v)| \{\mathsf{dE}_{pk}(\bar{x}_i) = \mathsf{dE}_{pk}(x_{\phi^{-1}(i)})\mathcal{DEL}.\mathsf{Enc}(1, pk, \mathsf{par}, \alpha_i)\}_{i=1}^v\};$$

(v) sends $R_2 = \langle \{\mathsf{dE}_{pk}(y_j), \mathsf{dE}_{pk}((y_j)^r)\}_{j=1}^w, \{\mathsf{dE}_{pk}(\bar{x}_i), \mathsf{dE}_{pk}((\bar{x}_i)^r)\}_{i=1}^v, \mathsf{dE}_{pk}$ $(\widehat{g^r}), \widehat{g}, \pi_2, \widehat{\pi}_2 \rangle$ to A.

Step 3. On receiving $R_2 = \langle \{\mathsf{dE}_{pk}(y_j), \mathsf{dE}_{pk}((y_j)^r)\}_{j=1}^w, \{\mathsf{dE}_{pk}(\bar{x}_i), \mathsf{dE}_{pk}((\bar{x}_i)^r)\}$ $_{i=1}^v, \mathsf{dE}_{pk}(\widehat{g^r}), \widehat{g}, \pi_2, \widehat{\pi}_2 \rangle$ from B, party A verifies the validity of the proofs $\pi_2, \widehat{\pi}_2$. If at least one of the verifications fails then A aborts. Otherwise, proceeds as follows:

(i) selects a random permutation $\psi \in \Sigma_w, \beta_1, ..., \beta_w \hookleftarrow \mathbb{Z}_q$ and computes for each $j = 1, ..., w$, $\mathsf{dE}_{pk}((\bar{y}_j)^r) = (\mathsf{dE}_{pk}((y_{\psi^{-1}(j)})^r))(\mathcal{DEL}.$ $\mathsf{Enc}(1, pk, \mathsf{par}, \beta_j)) = (\widehat{c}_{y_j}, \widehat{d}_{y_j}) = (c'_{y_{\psi^{-1}(j)}} g^{\beta_j}, d'_{y_{\psi^{-1}(j)}} h^{\beta_j})$;

(ii) selects $r', r_{g_2}, \beta \hookleftarrow \mathbb{Z}_q$ and computes $\bar{g} = g^\beta$

$$\mathsf{dE}_{pk}(\bar{g}^{r'}) = (c_{\bar{g}}, d_{\bar{g}}) = (g^{r_{g_2}}, \bar{g}^{r'} h^{r_{g_2}}) \leftarrow \mathcal{DEL}.\mathsf{Enc}(\bar{g}^{r'}, pk, \mathsf{par}, r_{g_2}),$$

$$\mathsf{dE}_{pk}((\bar{x}_i)^{rr'}) = (\bar{c}_{x_i}, \bar{d}_{x_i}) = ((\widehat{c}_{x_i})^{r'}, (\widehat{d}_{x_i})^{r'}) = ((c'_{x_i})^{rr'}, (d'_{x_i})^{rr'})$$

$$= ((c_{x_{\phi^{-1}(i)}} g^{\alpha_i})^{rr'}, (d_{x_{\phi^{-1}(i)}} h^{\alpha_i})^{rr'}) \text{ for } i = 1, ..., v,$$

$$\mathsf{dE}_{pk}((\bar{y}_j)^{rr'}) = (\bar{c}_{y_j}, \bar{d}_{y_j}) = ((\widehat{c}_{y_j})^{r'}, (\widehat{d}_{y_j})^{r'}) = ((c'_{y_{\psi^{-1}(j)}} g^{\beta_j})^{r'}, (d'_{y_{\psi^{-1}(j)}} h^{\beta_j})^{r'})$$

$$= ((c_{y_{\psi^{-1}(j)}} g^{\beta_j})^{rr'}, (d_{y_{\psi^{-1}(j)}} h^{\beta_j})^{rr'}) \text{ for } j = 1, ..., w;$$

(iii) chooses $\sigma_1, ..., \sigma_v \hookleftarrow \mathbb{Z}_q$ and for each $i = 1, ..., v$, computes $(C_{x_i})^{a_1} = (\bar{c}_{x_i} c_{\bar{g}} c_{\widehat{g}})^{a_1}$ using his secret key $esk_A = a_1$ and encrypts $(C_{x_i})^{a_1}$ using B's public key $epk_B = y_B$ to generate $\mathsf{eE}_{epk_B}((C_{x_i})^{a_1})$

$$= (u_{x_i}, \bar{u}_{x_i}) = (g^{\sigma_i}, (C_{x_i})^{a_1}(y_B)^{\sigma_i}) \leftarrow \mathcal{EL}.\mathsf{Enc}((C_{x_i})^{a_1}, y_B, \mathsf{par}, \sigma_i);$$

(iv) generates a label $L \in \{0, 1\}^*$ using a session ID which has been agreed by all parities beforehand and the hash of past communication;

(v) chooses $r_1, ..., r_w, z_1, ..., z_w \hookleftarrow \mathbb{Z}_q$, for each $j = 1, ..., w$ computes $\bar{u}_{y_j} = (C_{y_j})^{a_1} g^{r_j} = (\bar{c}_{y_j} c_{\bar{g}} c_{\widehat{g}})^{a_1} g^{r_j}$ and generates $\mathsf{vE}_{vpk_{Ar}}(g^{r_j}) = (t_{1j}, t_{2j}, t_{3j}, t_{4j})$

$$= (g^{z_j}, \widetilde{g}^{z_j}, c^{z_j} g^{r_j}, a^{z_j} b^{z_j \rho_j}) \leftarrow \mathcal{VE}.\mathsf{Enc}(g^{r_j}, vpk_{Ar}, \mathsf{gpar}, z_j, L, \mathcal{H}),$$

where $vpk_{Ar} = (a, b, c)$ is the arbiter Ar's public key and $\rho_j = \mathcal{H}(t_{1j}, t_{2j}, t_{3j}, L)$;

(vi) constructs proof

$$\pi_3 = \mathsf{PoK}\{(a_1, r', r_1, ..., r_w, z_1, ..., z_w, \sigma_1, ..., \sigma_v, r_{g_2}) | (y_A = g^{a_1}) \wedge (c_{\bar{g}} = g^{r_{g_2}})$$
$$\wedge_{j=1}^w (\bar{c}_{y_j} = (\widehat{c}_{y_j})^{r'})(\bar{d}_{y_j} = (\widehat{d}_{y_j})^{r'})(\bar{u}_{y_j} = (C_{y_j})^{a_1} \cdot g^{r_j}) \wedge (d_{\bar{g}} = \bar{g}^r h^{r_{g_2}})$$
$$\wedge_{j=1}^w (t_{1j} = g^{z_j})(t_{2j} = \widetilde{g}^{z_j})(t_{3j} = c^{z_j} g^{r_j})(t_{4j} = a^{z_j} b^{z_j \rho_j})$$
$$\wedge_{i=1}^v (\bar{c}_{x_i} = (\widehat{c}_{x_i})^{r'})(\bar{d}_{x_i} = (\widehat{d}_{x_i})^{r'})(u_{x_i} = g^{\sigma_i})(\bar{u}_{x_i} = (C_{x_i})^{a_1}(y_B)^{\sigma_i})\},$$
$$\widehat{\pi}_3 = \mathsf{PoK}\{(\psi \in \Sigma_w, \{\beta_i\}_{i=1}^v) | \{\mathsf{dE}_{pk}((\bar{y}_j)^r) = \mathsf{dE}_{pk}((y_{\psi^{-1}(j)})^r)\mathcal{DEL}.\mathsf{Enc}(1, pk, \mathsf{par}, \beta_j)\}_{j=1}^w\};$$

(vii) sends $R_3 = \langle \{\mathsf{dE}_{pk}((\bar{x}_i)^{rr'}), \mathsf{eE}_{epk_B}((C_{x_i})^{a_1})\}_{i=1}^v, \{\mathsf{dE}_{pk}((\bar{y}_j)^{rr'}), \mathsf{dE}_{pk}$ $((\bar{y}_j)^r), \mathsf{vE}_{vpk_{Ar}}(g^{r_j}), \bar{u}_{y_j}\}_{j=1}^w, \mathsf{dE}_{pk}(\bar{g}^{r'}), \bar{g}, \pi_3, \widehat{\pi}_3 \rangle$ to B.

Step 4. On receiving $R_3 = \langle \{dE_{pk}((\bar{x}_i)^{rr'}), eE_{epk_B}((C_{x_i})^{a_1})\}_{i=1}^v, \{dE_{pk}((\bar{y}_j)^{rr'}),$
$dE_{pk}((\bar{y}_j)^r), vE_{vpk_{A_r}}(g^{r_j}), \bar{u}_{y_j}\}_{j=1}^w, dE_{pk}(\bar{g}^{r'}), \bar{g}, \pi_3, \hat{\pi}_3 \rangle$ from A, party B checks the proofs $\pi_3, \hat{\pi}_3$. If the verification of at least one of the proofs fails then B aborts, else dose the following:

(i) extracts $\{\bar{c}_{x_i}\}_{i=1}^v, \{\bar{c}_{y_j}\}_{j=1}^w, c_{\bar{g}}$ from $\{dE_{pk}((\bar{x}_i)^{rr'})\}_{i=1}^v, \{dE_{pk}((\bar{y}_j)^{rr'})\}_{j=1}^w,$
$dE_{pk}(\bar{g}^{r'})$ respectively in R_3 and computes $\{s_{x_i} = (C_{x_i})^{a_2} = (\bar{c}_{x_i} c_{\bar{g}} c_{\hat{g}})^{a_2}\}_{i=1}^v,$
$\{s_{y_j} = (C_{y_j})^{a_2} = (\bar{c}_{y_j} c_{\bar{g}} c_{\hat{g}})^{a_2}\}_{j=1}^w$ using his secret key $esk_B = a_2$ and $c_{\hat{g}}$ computed in *Step* 2;
(ii) constructs the proof
$$\pi_4 = \mathsf{PoK}\{(a_2)|(y_B = g^{a_2}) \wedge_{i=1}^v (s_{x_i} = (C_{x_i})^{a_2})(s_{y_j} = (C_{y_j})^{a_2})\};$$
(iii) sends $R_4 = \langle \{s_{x_i}\}_{i=1}^v, \{s_{y_j}\}_{j=1}^w, \pi_4 \rangle$ to A.

Step 5. Party A, on receiving $R_4 = \langle \{s_{x_i}\}_{i=1}^v, \{s_{y_j}\}_{j=1}^w, \pi_4 \rangle$ from B, checks the validity of the proof π_4. Party A aborts if the verification does not succeed, else extracts $d_{\hat{g}}$ from $dE_{pk}(\hat{g}^r)$ in R_2, does the following using his secret key $esk_A = a_1$ and $\{C_{x_i}, \bar{d}_{x_i}\}_{i=1}^v, \{C_{y_j}, \bar{d}_{y_j}\}_{j=1}^w, d_{\hat{g}}$ computed in *Step* 3:

(i) computes for $i = 1, ..., v$,

$$\frac{\bar{d}_{x_i} d_{\hat{g}} d_{\bar{g}}}{(C_{x_i})^{a_1} s_{x_i}} = \frac{\bar{d}_{x_i} d_{\hat{g}} d_{\bar{g}}}{(\bar{c}_{x_i} c_{\hat{g}} c_{\bar{g}})^{(a_1+a_2)}} = \frac{(d_{x_{\phi^{-1}(i)}})^{rr'} d_{\hat{g}} d_{\bar{g}} h^{\alpha_i}}{((c_{x_{\phi^{-1}(i)}})^{rr'} c_{\hat{g}} c_{\bar{g}} g^{\alpha_i})^{a_1+a_2}}$$

$$= \frac{\bar{g}^{r'} \hat{g}^r (x_{\phi^{-1}(i)})^{rr'} g^{((r_{x_{\phi^{-1}(i)}}+\alpha_i)rr'+r_{g_2}+r_{g_1})(a_1+a_2)}}{g^{((r_{x_{\phi^{-1}(i)}}+\alpha_i)rr'+r_{g_2}+r_{g_1})(a_1+a_2)}} = \bar{g}^{r'} \hat{g}^r (x_{\phi^{-1}(i)})^{rr'}$$

and for $j = 1, ..., w$,

$$\frac{\bar{d}_{y_j} d_{\hat{g}} d_{\bar{g}}}{(C_{y_j})^{a_1} s_{y_j}} = \frac{\bar{d}_{y_j} d_{\hat{g}} d_{\bar{g}}}{(\bar{c}_{y_j} c_{\hat{g}} c_{\bar{g}})^{(a_1+a_2)}} = \frac{(d_{y_{\psi^{-1}(j)}})^{rr'} d_{\hat{g}} d_{\bar{g}} h^{\alpha_j}}{((c_{y_{\psi^{-1}(j)}})^{rr'} c_{\hat{g}} c_{\bar{g}} g^{\alpha_j})^{a_1+a_2}}$$

$$= \frac{\bar{g}^{r'} \hat{g}^r (y_{\psi^{-1}(j)})^{rr'} g^{((r_{y_{\psi^{-1}(j)}}+\alpha_j)rr'+r_{g_2}+r_{g_1})(a_1+a_2)}}{g^{((r_{y_{\phi^{-1}(j)}}+\alpha_j)rr'+r_{g_2}+r_{g_1})(a_1+a_2)}} = \bar{g}^{r'} \hat{g}^r (y_{\psi^{-1}(j)})^{rr'}$$

(ii) sets the cardinality of $X \cap Y$ as

$$|X \cap Y| = |\{\bar{g}^{r'} \hat{g}^r (x_{\phi^{-1}(i)})^{rr'}\}_{i=1}^v \cap \{\bar{g}^{r'} \hat{g}^r (y_{\psi^{-1}(j)})^{rr'}\}_{j=1}^w|;$$

(iii) constructs the proof

$$\pi_5 = \mathsf{PoK}\{(z_1, ..., z_w)| \wedge_{j=1}^w (t_{1j} = g^{z_j})(t_{2j} = \tilde{g}^{z_j})(t_{3j} = c^{z_j} g^{r_j})(t_{4j} = a^{z_j} b^{z_j \rho_j})\};$$

(iv) sends $R_5 = \langle \{(g^{r_j})\}_{j=1}^w, \pi_5 \rangle$ to B.

Step 6. On receiving $R_5 = \langle \{(g^{r_j})\}_{j=1}^w, \pi_5 \rangle$ from A, party B verifies the validity of the proof π_5. If the verification of the proof succeeds, then B

(i) for each $i = 1, ..., v$, decrypts $\mathsf{eE}_{pk_B}((C_{x_i})^{a_1})$ received in *Step* 3 using his secret key $sk_B = a_2$ to get $(C_{x_i})^{a_1} \leftarrow \mathcal{EL}.\mathsf{Dec}(\mathsf{eE}_{epk_B}((C_{x_i})^{a_1}), esk_B)$, extracts $\bar{d}_{x_i}, d_{\bar{g}}$ from $\mathsf{dE}_{pk}((x_i)^{rr'}), \mathsf{dE}_{pk}(\bar{g}^{r'})$ respectively in R_3, uses s_{x_i} computed in *Step* 4 and $d_{\widehat{g}}$ computed in *Step* 2 to generate

$$
\frac{\bar{d}_{x_i} d_{\widehat{g}} d_{\bar{g}}}{(C_{x_i})^{a_1} s_{x_i}} = \frac{\bar{d}_{x_i} d_{\widehat{g}} d_{\bar{g}}}{(\bar{c}_{x_i} c_{\widehat{g}} c_{\bar{g}})^{(a_1 + a_2)}} = \frac{(d_{x_{\phi^{-1}(i)}})^{rr'} d_{\widehat{g}} d_{\bar{g}} h^{\alpha_i}}{((c_{x_{\phi^{-1}(i)}})^{rr'} c_{\widehat{g}} c_{\bar{g}} g^{\alpha_i})^{a_1 + a_2}}
$$

$$
= \frac{\bar{g}^{r'} \widehat{g}^r (x_{\phi^{-1}(i)})^{rr'} g^{((r_{x_{\phi^{-1}(i)}} + \alpha_i) rr' + r_{g_2} + r_{g_1})(a_1 + a_2)}}{g^{((r_{x_{\phi^{-1}(i)}} + \alpha_i) rr' + r_{g_2} + r_{g_1})(a_1 + a_2)}} = \bar{g}^{r'} \widehat{g}^r (x_{\phi^{-1}(i)})^{rr'}
$$

(ii) for each $j = 1, ..., w$, extracts $\bar{d}_{y_j}, d_{\bar{g}}$ from $\mathsf{dE}_{pk}((y_j)^{rr'}), \mathsf{dE}_{pk}(\bar{g}^{r'})$ from in R_3 respectively, uses $\bar{u}_{y_j}$ obtained from R_3, s_{y_j} computed in *Step* 4 and $d_{\widehat{g}}$ computed in *Step* 2 to generate

$$
\frac{\bar{u}_{y_j}}{g^{r_j}} = \frac{(C_{y_j})^{a_1} \cdot g^{r_j}}{g^{r_j}} = (C_{y_j})^{a_1},
$$

and $\dfrac{\bar{d}_{y_j} d_{\widehat{g}} d_{\bar{g}}}{(C_{y_j})^{a_1} s_{y_j}} = \dfrac{\bar{d}_{y_j} d_{\widehat{g}} d_{\bar{g}}}{(\bar{c}_{y_j} c_{\widehat{g}} c_{\bar{g}})^{(a_1 + a_2)}} = \dfrac{(d_{y_{\psi^{-1}(j)}})^{rr'} d_{\widehat{g}} d_{\bar{g}} h^{\alpha_j}}{((c_{y_{\psi^{-1}(j)}})^{rr'} c_{\widehat{g}} c_{\bar{g}} g^{\alpha_j})^{a_1 + a_2}}$

$$
= \frac{\bar{g}^{r'} \widehat{g}^r (y_{\psi^{-1}(j)})^{rr'} g^{((r_{y_{\psi^{-1}(j)}} + \alpha_j) rr' + r_{g_2} + r_{g_1})(a_1 + a_2)}}{g^{((r_{y_{\phi^{-1}(j)}} + \alpha_j) rr' + r_{g_2} + r_{g_1})(a_1 + a_2)}} = \bar{g}^{r'} \widehat{g}^r (y_{\psi^{-1}(j)})^{rr'};
$$

(iii) sets the cardinality as

$$
|X \cap Y| = |\{\bar{g}^{r'} \widehat{g}^r (x_{\phi^{-1}(i)})^{rr'}\}_{i=1}^v \cap \{\bar{g}^{r'} \widehat{g}^r (y_{\psi^{-1}(j)})^{rr'}\}_{j=1}^w|.
$$

If the verification of π_5 does not succeed or A does not send $R_5 = \langle \{(g^{r_j})\}_{j=1}^w, \pi_5 \rangle$ i.e., if A prematurely aborts, then B sends a dispute resolution request to the arbiter Ar.

Dispute Resolution Protocol: This is analogous to the Dispute Resolution Protocol of the mPSI except that each $X \cap Y$ will be replaced by $|X \cap Y|$.

4   Security

Theorem 1. *If the encryption schemes $\mathcal{EL}$, $\mathcal{DEL}$ and $\mathcal{VE}$ are semantically secure and the associated proof protocols are zero knowledge proof under the DDH assumption, then the protocol mPSI presented in Sect. 3.1 is a secure computation protocol for the functionality $\mathcal{F}_{mPSI} : ((X, |Y|), (Y, |X|)) \rightarrow (X \cap Y, X \cap Y)$ in the security model described in Sect. 2.1.*

Proof. Let us consider $\mathcal{C}$ as the real world adversary that breaks the security of our mPSI protocol among three parties A with private input set X, B with private input set Y and Ar with no input set. Also let there be an incorruptible trusted party T, parties $\bar{A}, \bar{B}, \bar{A}r$ and simulator $\mathcal{SIM}$ in the ideal process. In real world, the global parameter $\overline{gpar} = (\mathsf{ppar}, \overline{H})$, where $\mathsf{ppar} = (\mathsf{par}, \tilde{g}, \mathcal{H})$, $\mathsf{par} = (p, q, g)$ is generated by a trusted party who certifies the public key pk_A, pk_B, pk_{Ar} of A, B, Ar respectively. In contrast, in ideal process simulator $\mathcal{SIM}$ does those things. We denote the joint output of $A, B, Ar, \mathcal{C}$ in the real world as $\mathsf{REAL}_{\mathsf{mPSI}, \mathcal{C}}(X, Y)$ and the joint output of $\bar{A}, \bar{B}, \bar{A}r, \mathcal{SIM}$ in the ideal process as $\mathsf{IDEAL}_{\mathcal{F}_{\mathsf{mPSI}}, \mathcal{SIM}}(X, Y)$. We consider two cases: (case I) when the adversary corrupts two parties among the three parties and (case II) when the adversary corrupts only one party among the three parties.

- **Case I (When the adversary $\mathcal{C}$ corrupts two parties)**

1. **A and Ar are corrupted.** Let $\mathcal{Z}$ be a distinguisher who controls $\mathcal{C}$, feeds the input of the honest party B, and also sees the output of B. Now we will present a series of games $Game_0, ..., Game_4$ to prove that $\mathcal{Z}$'s view in the real world ($\mathcal{C}$'s view $+B$'s output) and its view in the ideal world ($\mathcal{C}$'s view $+ \bar{B}$'s output) are indistinguishable. For each $i = 0, ..., 3$, $Game_{i+1}$ modifies $Game_i$ slightly such that $\mathcal{Z}$'s views in $Game_i$ and $Game_{i+1}$ remain indistinguishable. The probability that $\mathcal{Z}$ distinguishes the view of $Game_i$ from the view of real protocol, is denoted by $Pr[Game_i]$ and S_i is considered as simulator in $Game_i$.

$Game_0$: This game is same as real world protocol, where the simulator S_0 has full knowledge of B and interacts with $\mathcal{C}$. Hence,

$$Prob[\mathsf{REAL}_{\mathsf{mPSI}, \mathcal{C}}(X, Y)] = Prob[Game_0].$$

$Game_1$: $Game_1$ is same as $Game_0$ except that
(a) the simulator S_1 maintains a list χ_A and records all queries the adversary made to the random oracle $\overline{H}$.
(b) if the proof π_1 is valid then the simulator S_1 runs the extractor algorithm for π_1 with $\mathcal{C}$ to extract the exponents $\{r_{x_1}, ..., r_{x_v}\}$. The simulator S_1 extracts $\overline{H}(x_i) = \frac{d_{x_i}}{h^{r_{x_i}}}$ by extracting $d_{x_i} = \overline{H}(x_i)h^{r_{x_i}}$ from $\mathsf{dE}_{pk}(\overline{H}(x_i))$ in R_1, h from $pk = epk_A \cdot epk_B$ and using the exponent r_{x_i} for $1 \le i \le v$. The simulator S_1 then extracts x_i from $\overline{H}(x_i)$ utilizing the list χ_A for $i = 1, ..., v$. In this way S_1 extracts the private input set $X = \{x_1, ..., x_v\}$ of A.
$\mathcal{Z}$'s views in $Game_0$ and $Game_1$ are indistinguishable because of simulation soundness of the proof π_1. Therefore,

$$|Prob[Game_1] - Prob[Game_0]| \le \epsilon_1(\kappa), \text{ where } \epsilon_1(\kappa) \text{ is a negligible function.}$$

$Game_2$: In this game the simulator S_2 has the knowledge of extracted set $X = \{x_1, ..., x_v\}$, input set $Y = \{y_1, ..., y_w\}$ and secret key $esk_B = a_2$ of B. Note that Y is same as S_B in some order and S_2 has the knowledge of that. $Game_2$ is same as $Game_1$ except that
(a) if the verification of the proof π_5 succeeds then S_3 outputs $X \cap Y$ as the final output of B making use of the extracted X,

(b) if the verification of the proof π_5 does not succeed or $\mathcal{C}$ aborts prematurely in mPSI protocol then the following cases arise:

$\diamond$ if $\mathcal{C}$ sends $\{g_1, ..., g_w\} \subset \mathbb{G}$ to S_3 in dispute resolution protocol then S_3 does the following:

- for each $i = 1, ..., v$, decrypts $\mathsf{eE}_{epk_B}((C_{x_i})^{a_1})$ using $esk_B = a_2$ to get $(C_{x_i})^{a_1}$, extracts $\bar{d}_{x_i}, \bar{c}_{x_i}$ from $\mathsf{dE}_{pk}((x_i)^{rr'})$ and $c_{\bar{g}}, d_{\bar{g}}$ from $\mathsf{dE}_{pk}(\bar{g}^{r'})$ in R_3, and uses $c_{\widehat{g}}, d_{\widehat{g}}$ computed in *Step 2* to compute
$$\frac{\bar{d}_{x_i} d_{\bar{g}} d_{\widehat{g}}}{(C_{x_i})^{a_1}(\bar{c}_{x_i} c_{\bar{g}} c_{\widehat{g}})^{a_2}} = \bar{g}^{r'} \widehat{g}^{r}(\overline{H}(x_i))^{rr'};$$

- for each $j = 1, ..., w,$, computes $\dfrac{\bar{d}_{y_j} d_{\bar{g}} d_{\widehat{g}}}{\frac{\bar{u}_{y_j}}{g_j}(\bar{c}_{y_j} c_{\bar{g}} c_{\widehat{g}})^{a_2}} = \widehat{y}_j$ by extracting $\bar{d}_{y_j}, \bar{c}_{y_j}$ from $\mathsf{dE}_{pk}((\overline{H}(y_j))^{rr'})$ and $c_{\bar{g}}, d_{\bar{g}}$ from $\mathsf{dE}_{pk}(\bar{g}^{r'})$ in R_3, using $\bar{u}_{y_j}$ obtained from R_3 and $c_{\widehat{g}}, d_{\widehat{g}}$ computed in *Step 2*;

- outputs $\{y_j \in Y | \widehat{y}_j \in \{\bar{g}^{r'} \widehat{g}^{r}(\overline{H}(x_1))^{rr'}, ..., \bar{g}^{r'} \widehat{g}^{r}(\overline{H}(x_v))^{rr'}\}\}$ as the final output of B.

$\diamond$ if $\mathcal{C}$ aborts in dispute resolution protocol then S_3 outputs $\perp$ as the final output of B.

By the simulation soundness property of the proof π_5, $\mathcal{Z}$'s views in $Game_2$ and $Game_3$ are indistinguishable. Hence,

$$|Prob[Game_2] - Prob[Game_1]| \leq \epsilon_2(\kappa), \text{ where } \epsilon_2(\kappa) \text{ is a negligible function.}$$

$Game_3$: $Game_3$ is same as $Game_2$ except that S_3 does the following after extracting $X = \{x_1, ..., x_v\}$:

(a) computes $X \cap Y$,

(b) constructs a set $\overline{Y} = \{\bar{y}_1, ..., \bar{y}_w\}$ by including all the elements of $X \cap Y$ together with $w - |X \cap Y|$ many random elements chosen from $\mathbb{G}$,

(c) chooses $r, \alpha \hookleftarrow \mathbb{Z}_q$,

(d) computes $\widehat{g} = g^{\alpha}$ and the tuple $\langle \{\mathsf{dE}_{pk}(\overline{H}(\bar{y}_j)), \mathsf{dE}_{pk}((\overline{H}(\bar{y}_j))^r)\}_{j=1}^{w}, \{\mathsf{dE}_{pk}((\overline{H}(x_i))^r)\}_{i=1}^{v}, \mathsf{dE}_{pk}(\widehat{g}^r) \rangle$,

(e) sends the tuple $\langle \{\mathsf{dE}_{pk}(\overline{H}(\bar{y}_j)), \mathsf{dE}_{pk}((\overline{H}(\bar{y}_j))^r)\}_{j=1}^{w}, \{(\mathsf{dE}_{pk}((\overline{H}(x_i))^r)\}_{i=1}^{v}, \mathsf{dE}_{pk}(\widehat{g}^r), \widehat{g} \rangle$ as $\langle \{\mathsf{dE}_{pk}(\overline{H}(y_j)), \mathsf{dE}_{pk}((\overline{H}(y_j))^r)\}_{j=1}^{w}, \{\mathsf{dE}_{pk}((\overline{H}(x_i))^r)\}_{i=1}^{v}, \mathsf{dE}_{pk}(\widehat{g}^r), \widehat{g} \rangle$ to $\mathcal{C}$ and simulates π_2.

As the encryption $\mathcal{DEL}$ is semantically secure, $\langle \{\mathsf{dE}_{pk}(\overline{H}(y_j)), \mathsf{dE}_{pk}((\overline{H}(y_j))^r)\}_{j=1}^{w}, \{\mathsf{dE}_{pk}((\overline{H}(x_i))^r)\}_{i=1}^{v}, \mathsf{dE}_{pk}(\widehat{g}^r), \widehat{g} \rangle$ is identically distributed in $Game_3$ and $Game_2$. The zero-knowledge (simulatability) of π_2 and indistinguishability of the tuple $\langle \{\mathsf{dE}_{pk}(\overline{H}(y_j)), \mathsf{dE}_{pk}((\overline{H}(y_j))^r)\}_{j=1}^{w}, \{\mathsf{dE}_{pk}((\overline{H}(x_i))^r)\}_{i=1}^{v}, \mathsf{dE}_{pk}(\widehat{g}^r), \widehat{g} \rangle$ make the views of $\mathcal{Z}$'s in $Game_2$ and $Game_3$ indistinguishable. Therefore, there exists a negligible function $\epsilon_3(\kappa)$ such that

$$|Prob[Game_3] - Prob[Game_2]| \leq \epsilon_3(\kappa).$$

$Game_4$: This game is same as $Game_3$ except that during the setup phase S_4 chooses $a_2 \hookleftarrow \mathbb{Z}_q$ and in *Step 4* simulates π_4, instead of proving it. By the zero-knowledge (simulatability) of π_4 the views of $\mathcal{Z}$'s in $Game_3$ and $Game_4$ are indistinguishable. Consequently,

$$|Prob[Game_4] - Prob[Game_3]| \leq \epsilon_4(\kappa), \text{ where } \epsilon_4(\kappa) \text{ is a negligible function.}$$

Let us construct the ideal world adversary $\mathcal{SIM}$ that uses $\mathcal{C}$ as subroutine, simulates the honest party B and controls $\bar{A}, \bar{A}r$ and incorporates all steps from $Game_4$.

(i) First $\mathcal{SIM}$ plays the role of trusted party by generating the global parameter $\overline{\text{gpar}} = (\text{ppar}, \overline{H})$. $\mathcal{SIM}$ then plays the role of honest party B by choosing $\bar{a}_2 \hookleftarrow \mathbb{Z}_q$ and publishing $g^{\bar{a}_2}$ as the public key $epk_B = y_B$. $\mathcal{SIM}$ also acts as certifying authority to obtain respective public keys epk_A, vpk_{Ar} of A, Ar. $\mathcal{SIM}$ then invokes $\mathcal{C}$.

(ii) The simulator $\mathcal{SIM}$ maintains a list χ_A and records all queries the adversary made to the random oracle $\overline{H}$.

(iii) On receiving $R_1 = \langle \{\text{dE}_{pk}(\overline{H}(x_i))\}_{i=1}^v, \pi_1 \rangle$ from $\mathcal{C}$, $\mathcal{SIM}$ verifies the proof π_1. If the verification does not succeed, then $\mathcal{SIM}$ instructs $\bar{A}$ to send $\perp$ to T, $\bar{A}r$ to send $b_B = \circ$ to T and terminates the execution. Otherwise, $\mathcal{SIM}$ runs the extractor algorithm for π_1 with $\mathcal{C}$ to extract $\{r_{x_1}, ..., r_{x_v}\}$. Utilizing $\{r_{x_1}, ..., r_{x_v}\}$ and the list χ_A, $\mathcal{SIM}$ extracts the input set $X = \{x_1, ..., x_v\}$ by extracting $\{d_{x_i} = \overline{H}(x_i)h^{r_{x_i}}\}_{i=1}^v$ from $\{\text{dE}_{pk}(\overline{H}(x_i))\}_{i=1}^v$ in R_1 and h from $pk = epk_A \cdot epk_B$. $\mathcal{SIM}$ then instructs $\bar{A}$ to send X to T, $\bar{A}r$ to send $b_A = \circ$ to T and receives $X \cap S_B = X \cap Y$ from T.

(iv) $\mathcal{SIM}$ constructs a set $\overline{Y} = \{\bar{y}_1, ..., \bar{y}_w\}$ by including all the elements of $X \cap Y$ together with $w - |X \cap Y|$ many random elements chosen from $\mathbb{G}$. $\mathcal{SIM}$ then chooses $r, \alpha \hookleftarrow \mathbb{Z}_q$, computes $\hat{g} = g^\alpha$, the tuple $\langle \{\text{dE}_{pk}(\overline{H}(\bar{y})_j), \text{dE}_{pk}((\overline{H}(\bar{y}_j))^r)\}_{j=1}^w, \{\text{dE}_{pk}((\overline{H}(x_i))^r)\}_{i=1}^v, \text{dE}_{pk}(\hat{g}^r)\rangle$, sends $\langle \{\text{dE}_{pk}(\overline{H}(\bar{y}_j)), \text{dE}_{pk}((\overline{H}(\bar{y}_j))^r)\}_{j=1}^w, \{(\text{dE}_{pk}((\overline{H}(x_i))^r)\}_{i=1}^v, \text{dE}_{pk}(\hat{g}^r), \hat{g}\rangle$ as $\langle \{\text{dE}_{pk}(\overline{H}(y_j)), \text{dE}_{pk}((\overline{H}(y_j))^r)\}_{j=1}^w, \{\text{dE}_{pk}((\overline{H}(x_i))^r)\}_{i=1}^v, \text{dE}_{pk}(\hat{g}^r), \hat{g}\rangle$ to $\mathcal{C}$ and simulates π_2.

(v) On receiving the transcript $R_3 = \langle \{\text{dE}_{pk}((\overline{H}(x_i))^{rr'}), \text{eE}_{epk_B}((C_{x_i})^{a_1})\}_{i=1}^v, \{\text{dE}_{pk}((\overline{H}(\bar{y}_j))^{rr'}), \text{vE}_{vpk_{Ar}}(g^{r_j}), \bar{u}_{\bar{y}_j}\}_{j=1}^w, \text{dE}_{pk}(\hat{g}^r), \bar{g}, \pi_3 \rangle$ from $\mathcal{C}$, $\mathcal{SIM}$ verifies the validity of the proof π_3. If the verification fails then $\mathcal{SIM}$ instructs $\bar{A}$ to send $\perp$ to T, $\bar{A}r$ to send $b_B = \circ$ to T and terminates the execution. Otherwise, $\mathcal{SIM}$ computes $\{s_{x_i} = (C_{x_i})^{\bar{a}_2}\}_{i=1}^v, \{s_{y_j} = (C_{\bar{y}_j})^{\bar{a}_2}\}_{j=1}^w$, sends it to $\mathcal{C}$ and simulates the proof π_4. $\mathcal{SIM}$ then executes following steps according to $\mathcal{C}$'s reply.

(vi) If $\mathcal{C}$ instructs A to send $\{g_1, ..., g_w\} \subset \mathbb{G}$, then $\mathcal{SIM}$ verifies the validity of the proof π_5. If the verification succeeds then $\mathcal{SIM}$ instructs $\bar{A}r$ to send $b_B = \circ$. If verification fails or $\mathcal{C}$ instructs A to abort in mPSI protocol then the following cases arise:

$\diamond$ if $\mathcal{C}$ instructs Ar to send $\{g_1, ..., g_w\} \subset \mathbb{G}$ in dispute resolution protocol, then $\mathcal{SIM}$ does the following:

- for each $i = 1, ..., v$, decrypts $\mathsf{eE}_{epk_B}((C_{x_i})^{a_1})$ using $esk_B = a_2$ to get $(C_{x_i})^{a_1}$, extracts $\bar{d}_{x_i}, \bar{c}_{x_i}$ from $\mathsf{dE}_{pk}((\overline{H}(x_i))^{rr'})$ and $c_{\bar{g}}, d_{\bar{g}}$ from $\mathsf{dE}_{pk}(\bar{g}^{r'})$ in R_3 and uses $c_{\widehat{g}}, d_{\widehat{g}}$ computed in $Step\ 2$ to compute
$$\frac{\bar{d}_{x_i} d_{\bar{g}} d_{\widehat{g}}}{(C_{x_i})^{a_1}(\bar{c}_{x_i} c_{\bar{g}} c_{\widehat{g}})^{\bar{a}_2}} = \bar{g}^{r'}\widehat{g}^r(\overline{H}(x_i))^{rr'};$$

- for each $j = 1, ..., w$,, computes $\frac{\bar{d}_{\bar{y}_j} d_{\bar{g}} d_{\widehat{g}}}{\frac{\bar{u}_{\bar{y}_j}}{\bar{g}_j}(\bar{c}_{\bar{y}_j} c_{\bar{g}} c_{\widehat{g}})^{\bar{a}_2}} = \tilde{y}_j$ by extracting $\bar{d}_{\bar{y}_j}, \bar{c}_{\bar{y}_j}$ from $\mathsf{dE}_{pk}((\overline{H}(\bar{y}_j))^{rr'})$ and $c_{\bar{g}}, d_{\bar{g}}$ from $\mathsf{dE}_{pk}(\bar{g}^{r'})$ in R_3, using $\bar{u}_{\bar{y}_j}$ obtained from R_3 and $c_{\widehat{g}}, d_{\widehat{g}}$ computed in $Step\ 2$;

- instructs $\bar{A}r$ to send $b_B = \{\bar{y}_j \in \overline{Y} | \tilde{y}_j \in \{\bar{g}^{r'}\widehat{g}^r(\overline{H}(x_i))^{rr'}\}_{i=1}^v\}$ to T, outputs whatever $\mathcal{C}$ outputs and terminates.

  ⋄ if $\mathcal{C}$ instructs Ar to abort in dispute resolution protocol $\mathcal{SIM}$ instructs $\bar{A}r$ to send $b_B = \perp$ to T. Then $\mathcal{SIM}$ outputs whatever $\mathcal{C}$ outputs and terminates.

(vii) If $\mathcal{C}$ instructs both A and Ar to abort, then $\mathcal{SIM}$ instructs $\bar{A}r$ to send $b_B = \perp$ to T, outputs whatever $\mathcal{C}$ outputs and terminates.

Thus the ideal world adversary $\mathcal{SIM}$ provides $\mathcal{C}$ the same simulation as the simulator S_4 in $Game_4$. Hence $Prob[\mathsf{IDEAL}_{\mathcal{F}_{\mathsf{mPSI}}, \mathcal{SIM}}(X, Y)] = Prob[Game_4]$ and

$$|Prob[\mathsf{IDEAL}_{\mathcal{F}_{\mathsf{mPSI}}, \mathcal{SIM}}(X, Y)] - Prob[\mathsf{REAL}_{\mathsf{mPSI}, \mathcal{C}}(X, Y)]|$$
$$= |Prob[Game_4] - Prob[Game_0]| \leq \Sigma_{i=1}^4 |Prob[Game_i] - Prob[Game_{i-1}]|$$
$$\leq \Sigma_{i=1}^4 \epsilon_i(\kappa) = \rho(\kappa), \text{ where } \rho(\kappa) \text{ is a negligible function.}$$

Therefore we have $\mathsf{IDEAL}_{\mathcal{F}_{\mathsf{mPSI}}, \mathcal{SIM}}(X, Y) \equiv^c \mathsf{REAL}_{\mathsf{mPSI}, \mathcal{C}}(X, Y)$.

2. **B and Ar are corrupted.** Let us consider $\mathcal{Z}$ as a distinguisher who controls $\mathcal{C}$, feeds the input of the honest party A, and also sees the output of B. Now we argue that $\mathcal{Z}$'s view in the real world ($\mathcal{C}$'s view + A's output) and its view in the ideal world ($\mathcal{C}$'s view + $\bar{A}$'s output) are indistinguishable. To prove that a series of games $Game_0, ..., Game_5$ is presented, where each $Game_{i+1}$ modifies $Game_i$ slightly such that $\mathcal{Z}$'s views in $Game_i$ and $Game_{i+1}$ remain indistinguishable, for $i = 0, .., 4$. Let us denote the probability that $\mathcal{Z}$ distinguishes the view of $Game_i$ from the view of real protocol by $Pr[Game_i]$. We consider S_i as simulator in $Game_i$.

$Game_0$: This game is same as real world protocol, where the simulator S_0 has full knowledge of A and interacts with $\mathcal{C}$. Hence,

$$Prob[\mathsf{REAL}_{\mathsf{mPSI}, \mathcal{C}}(X, Y)] = Prob[Game_0].$$

$Game_1$: This game is same as $Game_0$ except that S_1 simulates π_1, instead of proving it. $\mathcal{Z}$'s views in $Game_0$ and $Game_1$ are indistinguishable because of zero-knowledge (simulatability) of the proof π_1. Therefore, there exists a negligible function $\epsilon_1(\kappa)$ such that

$$|Prob[Game_1] - Prob[Game_0]| \leq \epsilon_1(\kappa).$$

$Game_2$: $Game_1$ is same as $Game_2$ except that

(a) the simulator S_2 maintains a list χ_B and records all queries the adversary made to the random oracle $\overline{H}$.

(b) if the verification of the proof π_2 succeeds then the simulator S_2 runs the extractor algorithm for π_2 with $\mathcal{C}$ to extract the exponents r and $\{r_{y_1}, ..., r_{y_w}\}$. The simulator S_2 then extracts $\overline{H}(y_j) = \frac{d_{y_j}}{h^{r_{y_j}}}$ by extracting $d_{y_j} = \overline{H}(y_j)h^{r_{y_j}}$ from $\mathsf{dE}_{pk}(\overline{H}(y_j))$ in R_2, h from $pk = epk_A \cdot epk_B$ and using the exponent r_{y_j} for $1 \leq j \leq w$. The simulator S_2 then extracts y_j from $\overline{H}(y_j)$ utilizing the list χ_B for $j = 1, ..., w$. In this way S_2 extracts the private input set $Y = \{y_1, ..., y_w\}$ of B.

The simulation soundness of the proof π_2 makes $\mathcal{Z}$'s views in $Game_1$ and $Game_2$ indistinguishable. Consequently,

$$|Prob[Game_2] - Prob[Game_1]| \leq \epsilon_2(\kappa), \text{ where } \epsilon_2(\kappa) \text{ is a negligible function.}$$

$Game_3$: In this game the simulator S_3 has the knowledge of input set $X = \{x_1, ..., x_v\}$, secret key $esk_A = a_1$ of A and extracted set $Y = \{y_1, ..., y_w\}$ of B. Note that X is same as S_A in some order and S_3 has the knowledge of that. This game is same as $Game_2$ except that

(a) if the verification of the proof π_4 succeeds then S_3 outputs $X \cap Y$ as the final output of A making use of the extracted set Y,

(b) if the verification of the proof π_4 does not succeed or $\mathcal{C}$ aborts in mPSI protocol then the following cases arise:

⬦ if $\mathcal{C}$ sends $\langle \{s_{x_i}\}_{i=1}^v, \{s_{y_j}\}_{j=1}^w \rangle$ to S_3 in dispute resolution protocol then S_3 does the following:

    – for each $i = 1, ..., v$, computes $\frac{\bar{d}_{x_i} d_{\bar{g}} d_{\hat{g}}}{(C_{x_i})^{a_1} s_{x_i}} = \hat{x}_i$ using $esk_A = a_1$;

    – for each $j = 1, ..., w$, computes $\frac{\bar{d}_{y_j} d_{\bar{g}} d_{\hat{g}}}{(C_{y_j})^{a_1} s_{y_j}} = \hat{y}_j$ using $esk_A = a_1$;

    – outputs $\{x_i \in X | \hat{x}_i \in \{\hat{y}_1, ..., \hat{y}_w\}\}$ as the final output of A.

⬦ if $\mathcal{C}$ aborts in dispute resolution protocol then S_3 outputs $\perp$ as the final output of A.

By the simulation soundness property of the proof π_4, $\mathcal{Z}$'s views in $Game_2$ and $Game_3$ are indistinguishable. Therefore, there exists a negligible function $\epsilon_3(\kappa)$ such that

$$|Prob[Game_3] - Prob[Game_2]| \leq \epsilon_3(\kappa).$$

$Game_4$: $Game_4$ is same as $Game_3$ except that S_4 does the following after extracting $Y = \{y_1, ... y_w\}, r$:

(a) computes $X \cap Y$,

(b) constructs a set $\overline{X} = \{\bar{x}_1, ..., \bar{x}_v\}$ by including all the elements of $X \cap Y$ together with $v - |X \cap Y|$ many random elements chosen from $\mathbb{G}$.

(c) chooses $r', r_1, ..., r_w, \beta \leftarrow \mathbb{Z}_q$,

(d) computes $\bar{g} = g^\beta$, $\langle \{\mathsf{dE}_{pk}((\overline{H}(\bar{x}_i))^{rr'}) = (\bar{c}_{\bar{x}_i}, \bar{d}_{\bar{x}_i}), \mathsf{eE}_{epk_B}((C_{\bar{x}_i})^{a_1})\}_{i=1}^v$, $\{\mathsf{dE}_{pk}((\overline{H}(y_j))^{rr'}) = (\bar{c}_{y_j}, \bar{d}_{y_j})\}_{j=1}^w, \mathsf{dE}_{pk}((\bar{g})^{r'}) = (c_{\bar{g}}, d_{\bar{g}})\rangle$, where $C_{\bar{x}_i} = \bar{c}_{\bar{x}_i} c_{\bar{g}} c_{\hat{g}}$,

(e) computes $\langle\{\bar{u}_{y_j} = (C_{y_j})^{a_1} \cdot g^{r_j}\}_{j=1}^{w}, \{\mathsf{vE}_{vpk_{Ar}}(g^{r_j})\}_{j=1}^{w}\rangle$, where $C_{y_j} = \bar{c}_{y_j} c_{\bar{g}} c_{\hat{g}}$,

(f) sends $\langle\{\mathsf{dE}_{pk}((\overline{H}(\bar{x}_i))^{rr'}), \mathsf{eE}_{epk_B}((C_{\bar{x}_i})^{a_1})\}_{i=1}^{v}, \{\mathsf{dE}_{pk}((\overline{H}(y_j))^{rr'}), \mathsf{vE}_{vpk_{Ar}}(g^{r_j}), \bar{u}_{y_j}\}_{j=1}^{w}, \mathsf{dE}_{pk}((\bar{g})^{r'}), \bar{g}\rangle$ as $\langle\{\mathsf{dE}_{pk}((\overline{H}(x_i))^{rr'}), \mathsf{eE}_{epk_B}((C_{x_i})^{a_1})\}_{i=1}^{v}, \{\mathsf{dE}_{pk}((\overline{H}(y_j))^{rr'}), \mathsf{vE}_{vpk_{Ar}}(g^{r_j}), \bar{u}_{y_j}\}_{j=1}^{w}, \mathsf{dE}_{pk}((\bar{g})^{r'}), \bar{g}\rangle$ to $\mathcal{C}$ and simulates the proofs π_3.

As the associated encryption schemes $\mathcal{DEL}$, $\mathcal{EL}$ and $\mathcal{VE}$ are semantically secure, $\langle\{\mathsf{dE}_{pk}((\overline{H}(x_i))^{rr'}), \mathsf{eE}_{epk_B}((C_{x_i})^{a_1})\}_{i=1}^{v}, \{\mathsf{dE}_{pk}((\overline{H}(y_j))^{rr'}), \mathsf{vE}_{vpk_{Ar}}(g^{r_j}), \bar{u}_{y_j}\}_{j=1}^{w}, \mathsf{dE}_{pk}((\bar{g})^{r'}), \bar{g}\rangle$ is identically distributed in $Game_4$ and $Game_3$. Indistinguishability of the tuple $\langle\{\mathsf{dE}_{pk}((\overline{H}(x_i))^{rr'}), \mathsf{eE}_{epk_B}((C_{x_i})^{a_1})\}_{i=1}^{v}, \{\mathsf{dE}_{pk}((\overline{H}(y_j))^{rr'}), \mathsf{vE}_{vpk_{Ar}}(g^{r_j}), \bar{u}_{y_j}\}_{j=1}^{w}, \mathsf{dE}_{pk}((\bar{g})^{r'}), \bar{g}\rangle$ and the zero-knowledge (simulatability) of π_3 makes the views of $\mathcal{Z}$'s in $Game_3$ and $Game_4$ indistinguishable. Hence,

$$|Prob[Game_4] - Prob[Game_3]| \leq \epsilon_4(\kappa), \text{ where } \epsilon_4(\kappa) \text{ is a negligible function.}$$

$Game_5$: This game is same as $Game_4$ except that during the setup phase S_5 chooses $a_1 \hookleftarrow \mathbb{Z}_q$ and in *Step* 5 simulates π_5, instead of proving it. By the zero-knowledge (simulatability) of π_5 the views of $\mathcal{Z}$'s in $Game_4$ and $Game_5$ are indistinguishable. Consequently, there exists a negligible function $\epsilon_5(\kappa)$ such that

$$|Prob[Game_5] - Prob[Game_4]| \leq \epsilon_5(\kappa).$$

Let us construct the ideal world adversary SIM that uses $\mathcal{C}$ as subroutine, simulates the honest party A and controls $\bar{B}, \bar{A}r$ and incorporates all steps from $Game_5$.

(i) SIM first plays the role of trusted party by generating the global parameter $\overline{\mathsf{gpar}} = (\mathsf{ppar}, \overline{H})$. SIM then plays the role of honest party A by choosing $\bar{a}_1 \hookleftarrow \mathbb{Z}_q$ and publishing $g^{\bar{a}_1}$ as the public key $epk_A = y_A$. SIM also acts as certifying authority to obtain public keys epk_B, vpk_{Ar} of B, Ar. SIM then invokes $\mathcal{C}$.

(ii) SIM chooses $\breve{x}_1, ..., \breve{x}_v$ randomly from $\mathbb{G}$ and sends $\{\mathsf{dE}_{pk}(\overline{H}(\breve{x}_i))\}_{i=1}^{v}$ as $\{\mathsf{dE}_{pk}(\overline{H}(x_i))\}_{i=1}^{v}$ to $\mathcal{C}$ and simulates the proof π_1.

(iii) SIM maintains a list χ_B and records all queries the adversary made to the random oracle $\overline{H}$.

(iv) On receiving $R_2 = \langle\{\mathsf{dE}_{pk}(\overline{H}(y_j)), \mathsf{dE}_{pk}((\overline{H}(y_j))^r)\}_{j=1}^{w}, \{\mathsf{dE}_{pk}((\overline{H}(x_i))^r)\}_{i=1}^{v}, \mathsf{dE}_{pk}((\hat{g})^r), \hat{g}, \pi_2\rangle$ from $\mathcal{C}$, SIM verifies the proof π_2. If the verification does not succeed, then SIM instructs $\bar{B}$ to send $\perp$ to T, $\bar{A}r$ to send $b_A = \circ$ to T and terminates the execution. Otherwise, SIM runs the extractor algorithm for π_2 with $\mathcal{C}$ to extract the exponents r and $\{r_{y_1}, ..., r_{y_w}\}$. Utilizing $\{r_{y_1}, ..., r_{y_w}\}$ and the list χ_B, SIM extracts $Y = \{y_1, ..., y_w\}$ by extracting $\{d_{y_j} = \overline{H}(y_j)h^{r_{y_j}}\}_{j=1}^{w}$ from $\{\mathsf{dE}_{pk}(\overline{H}(y_j))\}_{j=1}^{w}$ in R_2, h from $pk = epk_A \cdot epk_B$. SIM then instructs $\bar{B}$ to send Y to T, $\bar{A}r$ to send $b_B = \circ$ to T and receives $S_A \cap Y = X \cap Y$ from T.

(v) $\mathcal{SIM}$ constructs a set $\overline{X} = \{\bar{x}_1, ..., \bar{x}_v\}$ by including all the elements of $X \cap Y$ together with $v - |X \cap Y|$ many random elements chosen from $\mathbb{G}$. $\mathcal{SIM}$ then does the following:

- chooses $r', r_1, ..., r_w, \beta \leftarrow \mathbb{Z}_q$;
- computes
$$\bar{g} = g^\beta, \langle \{ \mathsf{dE}_{pk}((\overline{H}(\bar{x}_i))^{rr'}) = (\bar{c}_{\bar{x}_i}, \bar{d}_{\bar{x}_i}) \}_{i=1}^v, \{ \mathsf{dE}_{pk}((\overline{H}(y_j))^{rr'}) = (\bar{c}_{y_j}, \bar{d}_{y_j}) \}_{j=1}^w, \mathsf{dE}_{pk}((\bar{g})^{r'}) = (c_{\bar{g}}, d_{\bar{g}}), \{ \mathsf{eE}_{epk_B}((C_{\bar{x}_i})^{a_1}) \}_{i=1}^v \rangle;$$
- computes $\langle \{ \bar{u}_{y_j} = (C_{y_j})^{a_1} \cdot g^{r_j} \}_{j=1}^w, \{ \mathsf{vE}_{vpk_{Ar}}(g^{r_j}) \}_{j=1}^w \rangle;$
- sends $\langle \{ \mathsf{dE}_{pk}((\overline{H}(\bar{x}_i))^{rr'}), \mathsf{eE}_{epk_B}((C_{\bar{x}_i})^{a_1}) \}_{i=1}^v, \{ \mathsf{dE}_{pk}((\overline{H}(y_j))^{rr'}), \mathsf{vE}_{vpk_{Ar}}(g^{r_j}), \bar{u}_{y_j} \}_{j=1}^w, \mathsf{dE}_{pk}((\bar{g})^{r'}), \bar{g} \rangle$ as $\langle \{ \mathsf{dE}_{pk}((\overline{H}(x_i))^{rr'}), \mathsf{eE}_{epk_B}((C_{x_i})^{a_1}) \}_{i=1}^v, \{ \mathsf{dE}_{pk}((\overline{H}(y_j))^{rr'}), \mathsf{vE}_{vpk_{Ar}}(g^{r_j}), \bar{u}_{y_j} \}_{j=1}^w, \mathsf{dE}_{pk}((\bar{g})^{r'}), \bar{g} \rangle$ to $\mathcal{C}$ and simulates the proofs π_3.

$\mathcal{SIM}$ executes following steps according to $\mathcal{C}$'s reply.

(vi) If $\mathcal{C}$ instructs both B and Ar to abort, then $\mathcal{SIM}$ instructs $\bar{A}r$ to send $b_A = \perp$ to T. Then outputs whatever $\mathcal{C}$ outputs and terminates.

(vii) If $\mathcal{C}$ instructs B to send $\langle \{s_{x_i}\}_{i=1}^v, \{s_{y_j}\}_{j=1}^w \rangle$, then $\mathcal{SIM}$ checks the validity of the proof π_4. If the verification succeeds then $\mathcal{SIM}$ instructs $\bar{A}r$ to send $b_A = \circ$ to T and sends $\{g^{r_j}\}_{j=1}^w$ to $\mathcal{C}$ and simulates the proof π_5. If verification fails or $\mathcal{C}$ instructs B to abort in mPSI protocol then the following cases arise:

$\diamond$ if $\mathcal{C}$ instructs Ar to send $\langle \{s_{x_i}\}_{i=1}^v, \{s_{y_j}\}_{j=1}^w \rangle$ in dispute resolution protocol then $\mathcal{SIM}$ does the following:
- for each $i = 1, ..., v$, computes $\frac{\bar{d}_{\bar{x}_i} d_{\bar{g}} d_{\hat{g}}}{(C_{\bar{x}_i})^{\bar{a}_1} s_{x_i}} = \tilde{x}_i$;
- for each $j = 1, ..., w$, computes $\frac{\bar{d}_{y_j} d_{\bar{g}} d_{\hat{g}}}{(C_{y_j})^{\bar{a}_1} s_{y_j}} = \tilde{y}_j$;
- instructs $\bar{A}r$ to send $b_A = \{\bar{x}_i \in \overline{X} | \tilde{x}_i \in \{\tilde{y}_1, ..., \tilde{y}_w\} \}$ to T. $\mathcal{SIM}$ then outputs whatever $\mathcal{C}$ outputs and terminates.

$\diamond$ if $\mathcal{C}$ instructs Ar to abort in dispute resolution protocol then $\mathcal{SIM}$ instructs $\bar{A}r$ to send $b_A = \perp$ to T. $\mathcal{SIM}$ then outputs whatever $\mathcal{C}$ outputs and terminates.

Therefore, the ideal world adversary $\mathcal{SIM}$ provides $\mathcal{C}$ the same simulation as the simulator S_5 as in $Game_5$. Hence $Prob[\mathsf{IDEAL}_{\mathcal{F}_{mPSI}, \mathcal{SIM}}(X, Y)] = Prob[Game_5]$ and

$$|Prob[\mathsf{IDEAL}_{\mathcal{F}_{mPSI}, \mathcal{SIM}}(X, Y)] - Prob[\mathsf{REAL}_{mPSI, \mathcal{C}}(X, Y)]|$$
$$= |Prob[Game_5] - Prob[Game_0]| \leq \Sigma_{i=1}^5 |Prob[Game_i] - Prob[Game_{i-1}]|$$
$$\leq \Sigma_{i=1}^5 \epsilon_i(\kappa) = \rho(\kappa), \text{ where } \rho(\kappa) \text{ is a negligible function.}$$

Thus we have $\mathsf{IDEAL}_{\mathcal{F}_{mPSI}, \mathcal{SIM}}(X, Y) \equiv^c \mathsf{REAL}_{mPSI, \mathcal{C}}(X, Y)$.

3. **A and B are corrupted.** This case is trivial as $\mathcal{C}$ has full knowledge of X and Y and the encryption scheme used by Ar is semantically secure. Therefore a simulator can always be constructed.

- **Case II (When the adversary $\mathcal{C}$ corrupts only one party)**
If only Ar is corrupted then Ar is not involved in the protocol as A and B are honest. Thus it is trivial to construct a simulator in this case. If only A or B is corrupted then the simulator can be constructed as steps (i)–(iv) of the case when A and Ar are corrupted or steps (i)–(iv) of the case when B and Ar are corrupted. The only change is that $\bar{A}r$ is honest and always sends $\circ$ to T in these cases.

Theorem 2. *If the encryption schemes $\mathcal{EL}$, $\mathcal{DEL}$ and $\mathcal{VE}$ are semantically secure, the associated proof protocols are zero knowledge proof and the associated permutations are random, then our* mPSI-*CA presented in Sect. 3.2 is a secure computation protocol for the functionality* $\mathcal{F}_{\mathsf{mPSI}-CA}$: $((X, |Y|), (Y, |X|))$ $\rightarrow$ $(|X \cap Y|, |X \cap Y|)$ *in the security model described in Sect. 2.1.*

Proof. We omit the proof of Theorem 2 as it is analogus to the proof of Theorem 1.

5   Efficiency

The computation overhead of our mPSI and mPSI-CA is measured by modular exponentiation (Exp), modular inversion (Inv) and hash function evaluation (H). On the other hand, the number of group elements (GE) transmitted publicly by the users in our mPSI and mPSI-CA incurs the communication cost. The complexities of our mPSI and mPSI-CA are exhibited in Table 2, where $\pi_1, \pi_2, \pi_3, \pi_4, \pi_5, \widehat{\pi}_2, \widehat{\pi}_3$ are associated zero-knowledge proofs. For instance, in *Step* 1 of mPSI protocol, party A encrypts each member $\overline{H}(x_i) \in S_A$ to

Table 2. Complexity of our mPSI and mPSI-CA

mPSI				
	Party A	Party B	Arbiter Ar	Total
Exp	$19v + 31w + 13$	$18v + 34w + 12$	$2v + 7w + 2$	$39v + 72w + 27$
GE	$8v + 11w + 10$	$12v + 18w + 16$	$v + 2w$	$21v + 31w + 26$
Inv	$v + w$	$2v + 2w$	w	$3v + 4w$
H	$w + v + 5$	$w + 6$	$w + 1$	$v + 3w + 12$
mPSI-CA				
	Party A	Party B	Arbiter Ar	Total
Exp	$25v + 42w + 35$	$29v + 40w + 34$	$2v + 7w + 2$	$56v + 89w + 71$
GE	$14v + 27w + 28$	$21v + 24w + 36$	$v + 2w + 1$	$36v + 53w + 65$
Inv	$v + w$	$2v + 2w$	w	$3v + 4w$
H	w		w	$2w$

GE = number of group elements, Exp = number of exponentiations, Inv = number of inversions, H = number of hash query, v, w are the sizes of input sets.

Table 3. Comparative summary of mutual PSI and mutual PSI-CA protocols

mPSI Protocol	Adv. model	Security assumption	Comm. cost	Comp. cost	Fairness	Optimistic	Group order	Arbiter
[34]	Mal	AHE	$O(w+v)$	$O(wv)$	no	no	composite	
[9]	Mal	Strong RSA	$O(w+v)$	$O(wv)$	yes	yes	composite	FT
[33]	SH	AHE	$O(w+v)$	$O(w+v)$	no	no	composite	
[19]	Mal	AHE,VE	$O(w+v)$	$O(wv)$	yes	yes	prime	SH
[18]	Mal	Dq-DHI, DCR, DDH	$O(w+v)$	$O(w+v)$	yes	yes	composite	SH
Our	Mal	DDH	$O(w+v)$	$O(w+v)$	yes	yes	prime	SH
mPSI Protocol	Adv. model	Security assumption	Comm. cost	Comp. cost	Fairness	Optimistic	Group order	Arbiter
[34]	Mal	AHE	$O(v)$	$O(v^2)$	no	no	composite	
[9]	Mal	Strong RSA	$O(w+v)$	$O(wv)$	yes	yes	composite	FT
Our	Mal	DDH	$O(w+v)$	$O(w+v)$	yes	yes	prime	SH

AHE = Additively Homomorphic Encryption, VE = Verifiable Encryption, SH = Semi-honest, FT = Fully Trusted Dq-DHI = Decisional q-Diffie-Hellman Inversion, DCR = Decisional Composite Residuosity, DDH = Decisional Diffie-Hellman, Mal = Malicious, v, w are the sizes of input sets.

Table 4. Comparison summary in terms of GE, Exp, fairness, optimistic and order of underlying group

Protocol	GE	Exp	Fairness	Optimistic	Group order	Arbiter
[19]	$7w + 53v + 2wv + 5$	$11w + 96v + 12wv$	yes	yes	prime	SH
[18]	$77v + 77w$	$156v + 156w$	yes	yes	composite	SH
our mPSI	$21v + 31w + 26$	$39v + 72w + 27$	yes	yes	prime	SH

v, w are the sizes of input sets.

get $\mathsf{dE}_{pk}(\overline{H}(x_i)) = (c_{x_i} = g^{r_{x_i}}, d_{x_i} = \overline{H}(x_i)h^{r_{x_i}})$ requiring $2v$ Exp. In this step, A sends $\{\mathsf{dE}_{pk}(\overline{H}(x_i)) = (c_{x_i}, d_{x_i})\}_{i=1}^v$ to B which contains $2v$ GE of $\mathbb{G}$. Apart from that, a zero-knowledge proof $\pi_1 = \mathsf{PoK}\{(r_{x_1}, ..., r_{x_v}) | \wedge_{i=1}^v (c_{x_i} = g^{r_{x_i}})\}$ is executed between A and B in this step. The complexity of π_1 is $m + 2\Sigma_{i=1}^m$(number of exponentiations to computeX_i) $= v + 2v = 3v$ Exp and $l + 1 = v + 1$ GE using Lemma 1 for non-interactive version in Sect. 2.4.

We briefly summarize the results on mPSI and mPSI-CA from prior work in Table 3. As far as we are aware of, till now the most efficient fair mPSI protocols are [18,19]. We compare our mPSI protocol with the construction of [18,19] in Table 4. Note that any modular operation over composite order group is more expensive than the operation over prime order group, where the composite number $(n = pq)$ is formed by the product of two such primes. Thus computing $156(v + w)$ exponentiations and transferring $77(v + w)$ group elements over composite order group are more expensive than computing $39v + 72w + 27$ exponentiations and transferring $21v + 31w + 26$ group elements over prime order group. In other words, our work is more efficient than the work of [18].

6   Conclusion

We have designed a fair mPSI protocol with *linear* complexity over *prime* order group in the ROM. The security of this protocol is achieved in presence of malicious parties under the DDH assumption. Our mPSI achieves fairness in the optimistic way i.e., by using an off-line semi trusted third party (arbiter). Particularly, our mPSI is more efficient than existing mPSI protocols in terms of both the communication and computation complexity. Further, we have proposed that utilizing two random permutations our mPSI can be extended to mPSI-CA, where the security properties remain invariant except that the security model is changed to standard model. To the best of our knowledge, our mPSI-CA is the *first* mPSI-CA achieving *linear complexity*.

References

1. Agrawal, R., Evfimievski, A., Srikant, R.: Information sharing across private databases. In: Proceedings of the 2003 ACM SIGMOD International Conference on Management of Data, pp. 86–97. ACM (2003)
2. Bellare, M., Goldreich, O.: On defining proofs of knowledge. In: Brickell, E.F. (ed.) CRYPTO 1992. LNCS, vol. 740, pp. 390–420. Springer, Heidelberg (1993). doi:10.1007/3-540-48071-4_28
3. Bellare, M., Rogaway, P.: Random oracles are practical: a paradigm for designing efficient protocols. In: Proceedings of the 1st ACM Conference on Computer and Communications Security, pp. 62–73. ACM (1993)
4. Boneh, D.: The decision diffie-hellman problem. In: Buhler, J.P. (ed.) ANTS 1998. LNCS, vol. 1423, pp. 48–63. Springer, Heidelberg (1998). doi:10.1007/BFb0054851
5. Brandt, F.: Efficient cryptographic protocol design based on distributed El Gamal encryption. In: Won, D.H., Kim, S. (eds.) ICISC 2005. LNCS, vol. 3935, pp. 32–47. Springer, Heidelberg (2006). doi:10.1007/11734727_5
6. Camenisch, J., Shoup, V.: Practical verifiable encryption and decryption of discrete logarithms. In: Boneh, D. (ed.) CRYPTO 2003. LNCS, vol. 2729, pp. 126–144. Springer, Heidelberg (2003). doi:10.1007/978-3-540-45146-4_8
7. Camenisch, J., Stadler, M.: Efficient group signature schemes for large groups. In: Kaliski, B.S. (ed.) CRYPTO 1997. LNCS, vol. 1294, pp. 410–424. Springer, Heidelberg (1997). doi:10.1007/BFb0052252
8. Camenisch, J., Stadler, M.: Proof systems for general statements about discrete logarithms. Technical report, Citeseer (1997)
9. Camenisch, J., Zaverucha, G.M.: Private intersection of certified sets. In: Dingledine, R., Golle, P. (eds.) FC 2009. LNCS, vol. 5628, pp. 108–127. Springer, Heidelberg (2009). doi:10.1007/978-3-642-03549-4_7
10. Cramer, R., Shoup, V.: A practical public key cryptosystem provably secure against adaptive chosen ciphertext attack. In: Krawczyk, H. (ed.) CRYPTO 1998. LNCS, vol. 1462, pp. 13–25. Springer, Heidelberg (1998). doi:10.1007/BFb0055717
11. Cristofaro, E., Kim, J., Tsudik, G.: Linear-complexity private set intersection protocols secure in malicious model. In: Abe, M. (ed.) ASIACRYPT 2010. LNCS, vol. 6477, pp. 213–231. Springer, Heidelberg (2010). doi:10.1007/978-3-642-17373-8_13

12. Cristofaro, E., Gasti, P., Tsudik, G.: Fast and private computation of cardinality of set intersection and union. In: Pieprzyk, J., Sadeghi, A.-R., Manulis, M. (eds.) CANS 2012. LNCS, vol. 7712, pp. 218–231. Springer, Heidelberg (2012). doi:10.1007/978-3-642-35404-5_17

13. Cristofaro, E., Tsudik, G.: Practical private set intersection protocols with linear complexity. In: Sion, R. (ed.) FC 2010. LNCS, vol. 6052, pp. 143–159. Springer, Heidelberg (2010). doi:10.1007/978-3-642-14577-3_13

14. De Cristofaro, E., Tsudik, G.: Experimenting with fast private set intersection. In: Katzenbeisser, S., Weippl, E., Camp, L.J., Volkamer, M., Reiter, M., Zhang, X. (eds.) Trust 2012. LNCS, vol. 7344, pp. 55–73. Springer, Heidelberg (2012). doi:10.1007/978-3-642-30921-2_4

15. Debnath, S.K., Dutta, R.: A fair and efficient mutual private set intersection protocol from a two-way oblivious pseudorandom function. In: Lee, J., Kim, J. (eds.) ICISC 2014. LNCS, vol. 8949, pp. 343–359. Springer, Heidelberg (2015). doi:10.1007/978-3-319-15943-0_21

16. Debnath, S.K., Dutta, R.: Efficient private set intersection cardinality in the presence of malicious adversaries. In: Au, M.-H., Miyaji, A. (eds.) ProvSec 2015. LNCS, vol. 9451, pp. 326–339. Springer, Heidelberg (2015). doi:10.1007/978-3-319-26059-4_18

17. Debnath, S.K., Dutta, R.: Secure and efficient private set intersection cardinality using bloom filter. In: Lopez, J., Mitchell, C.J. (eds.) ISC 2015. LNCS, vol. 9290, pp. 209–226. Springer, Heidelberg (2015). doi:10.1007/978-3-319-23318-5_12

18. Debnath, S.K., Dutta, R.: Towards fair mutual private set intersection with linear complexity. Secur. Commun. Netw. 9(11), 1589–1612 (2016). doi:10.1002/sec.1450

19. Dong, C., Chen, L., Camenisch, J., Russello, G.: Fair private set intersection with a semi-trusted arbiter. In: Wang, L., Shafiq, B. (eds.) DBSec 2013. LNCS, vol. 7964, pp. 128–144. Springer, Heidelberg (2013). doi:10.1007/978-3-642-39256-6_9

20. Dong, C., Chen, L., Wen, Z.: When private set intersection meets big data: an efficient and scalable protocol. In: Proceedings of the 2013 ACM SIGSAC Conference on Computer and Communications Security, pp. 789–800. ACM (2013)

21. ElGamal, T.: A public key cryptosystem and a signature scheme based on discrete logarithms. In: Blakley, G.R., Chaum, D. (eds.) CRYPTO 1984. LNCS, vol. 196, pp. 10–18. Springer, Heidelberg (1985). doi:10.1007/3-540-39568-7_2

22. Fiat, A., Shamir, A.: How to prove yourself: practical solutions to identification and signature problems. In: Odlyzko, A.M. (ed.) CRYPTO 1986. LNCS, vol. 263, pp. 186–194. Springer, Heidelberg (1987). doi:10.1007/3-540-47721-7_12

23. Freedman, M.J., Hazay, C., Nissim, K., Pinkas, B.: Efficient set intersection with simulation-based security. J. Cryptol. 29(1), 115–155 (2016)

24. Freedman, M.J., Nissim, K., Pinkas, B.: Efficient private matching and set intersection. In: Cachin, C., Camenisch, J.L. (eds.) EUROCRYPT 2004. LNCS, vol. 3027, pp. 1–19. Springer, Heidelberg (2004). doi:10.1007/978-3-540-24676-3_1

25. Furukawa, J.: Efficient and verifiable shuffling and shuffle-decryption. IEICE Trans. Fundam. Electron. Commun. Comput. Sci. 88(1), 172–188 (2005)

26. Hazay, C.: Oblivious polynomial evaluation and secure set-intersection from algebraic PRFs. In: Dodis, Y., Nielsen, J.B. (eds.) TCC 2015. LNCS, vol. 9015, pp. 90–120. Springer, Heidelberg (2015). doi:10.1007/978-3-662-46497-7_4

27. Hazay, C., Lindell, Y.: Efficient protocols for set intersection and pattern matching with security against malicious and covert adversaries. In: Canetti, R. (ed.) TCC 2008. LNCS, vol. 4948, pp. 155–175. Springer, Heidelberg (2008). doi:10.1007/978-3-540-78524-8_10

28. Hazay, C., Nissim, K.: Efficient set operations in the presence of malicious adversaries. In: Nguyen, P.Q., Pointcheval, D. (eds.) PKC 2010. LNCS, vol. 6056, pp. 312–331. Springer, Heidelberg (2010). doi:10.1007/978-3-642-13013-7_19

29. Hohenberger, S., Weis, S.A.: Honest-verifier private disjointness testing without random oracles. In: Danezis, G., Golle, P. (eds.) PET 2006. LNCS, vol. 4258, pp. 277–294. Springer, Heidelberg (2006). doi:10.1007/11957454_16

30. Huang, Y., Evans, D., Katz, J.: Private set intersection: are garbled circuits better than custom protocols? In: NDSS (2012)

31. Jarecki, S., Liu, X.: Efficient oblivious pseudorandom function with applications to adaptive OT and secure computation of set intersection. In: Reingold, O. (ed.) TCC 2009. LNCS, vol. 5444, pp. 577–594. Springer, Heidelberg (2009). doi:10.1007/978-3-642-00457-5_34

32. Jarecki, S., Liu, X.: Fast secure computation of set intersection. In: Garay, J.A., Prisco, R. (eds.) SCN 2010. LNCS, vol. 6280, pp. 418–435. Springer, Heidelberg (2010). doi:10.1007/978-3-642-15317-4_26

33. Kim, M., Lee, H.T., Cheon, J.H.: Mutual private set intersection with linear complexity. In: Jung, S., Yung, M. (eds.) WISA 2011. LNCS, vol. 7115, pp. 219–231. Springer, Heidelberg (2012). doi:10.1007/978-3-642-27890-7_18

34. Kissner, L., Song, D.: Privacy-preserving set operations. In: Shoup, V. (ed.) CRYPTO 2005. LNCS, vol. 3621, pp. 241–257. Springer, Heidelberg (2005). doi:10.1007/11535218_15

35. Pinkas, B., Schneider, T., Segev, G., Zohner, M.: Phasing: private set intersection using permutation-based hashing. In: 24th USENIX Security Symposium (USENIX Security 15), pp. 515–530 (2015)

36. Pinkas, B., Schneider, T., Zohner, M.: Faster private set intersection based on OT extension. In: 23rd USENIX Security Symposium (USENIX Security 2014), pp. 797–812 (2014)

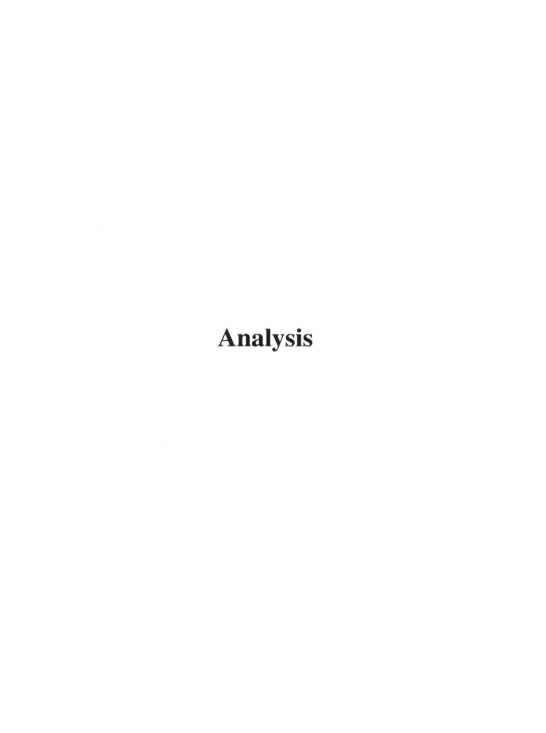

Analysis

Improved Results on Cryptanalysis of Prime Power RSA

Liqiang Peng[1,2], Lei Hu[1,2], and Yao Lu[3(✉)]

[1] State Key Laboratory of Information Security, Institute of Information
Engineering, Chinese Academy of Sciences, Beijing 100093, China
pengliqiang@iie.ac.cn
[2] Data Assurance and Communication Security Research Center,
Chinese Academy of Sciences, Beijing 100093, China
hu@is.ac.cn
[3] The University of Tokyo, Tokyo, Japan
lywhhit@gmail.com

Abstract. Recently, Zheng and Hu (SCIENCE CHINA Information Sciences 58(11):1–8, 2015) proposed a cryptanalysis of Prime Power RSA with two private exponents, namely, for a Prime Power RSA modulus $N = p^r q(r > 1)$, there are two pairs of public and private exponents. According to their work, when the two private exponents are small enough, this variant of RSA is insecure and one can factor $N = p^r q$ efficiently. Moreover, in C2SI 2015, Nitaj and Rachidi considered the implicit factorization problem. They showed that for two Prime Power RSA moduli $N_1 = p_1^r q_1$ and $N_2 = p_2^r q_2$, when p_1 and p_2 share a suitable amount of most significant bits, one can factor N_1 and N_2 in polynomial time. In this paper, we revisit these two works. More specifically, for Zheng-Hu's work, by solving two modular univariate linear equations and modifying the Zheng-Hu's selection of polynomials to construct lattice, we can further improve their result. For Nitaj-Rachidi's work, based on an observation that a desired solution of a modular equation is a factor of Prime Power RSA modulus, we can also improve Nitaj-Rachidi's bound. Our improved attacks are verified by experiments.

Keywords: Cryptanalysis · Prime Power RSA · Multiple private exponents · Implicit factorization problem · Coppersmith's method

1 Introduction

The famous RSA public key cryptosystem [19] has been widely used in practical applications for encrypting data. Thus, it is important to obtain higher efficiency in practical implementations, for now several variants of RSA have been proposed like CRT-RSA [25], Prime Power RSA [23] and so on.

On the other hand, in terms of efficiency of practical applications, one may choose small private exponents in RSA scheme and its variants to speed up the decryption process. However, this may lead to several successful attacks on

© Springer International Publishing AG 2017
S. Hong and J.H. Park (Eds.): ICISC 2016, LNCS 10157, pp. 287–303, 2017.
DOI: 10.1007/978-3-319-53177-9_15

Table 1. Overview of existing results on small private exponent attacks on Prime Power RSA (Numbers in the table indicate the largest exponent δ of $N = p^r q$ that once private exponent is smaller than N^δ, then modulus N can be factored in polynomial time. And the numbers in bold specify the best results for different r.)

r	[13]	[11]	[20]	[21]
2	0.222	0.222	**0.395**	**0.395**
3	0.250	0.375	0.410	**0.461**
4	0.360	0.480	0.437	**0.508**
5	0.444	**0.556**	0.464	0.545
6	0.510	**0.612**	0.489	0.574

RSA scheme and its variants if the private exponents are not properly chosen. Therefore, the research about the security of RSA and its variants has been given great attention.

1.1 Background

Small Private Exponent Attacks on RSA and Prime Power RSA. Coppersmith's method, which has been proposed in [3] to solve small roots of modular and integer equations by utilizing the lattice-based method, has a wide application in analyzing the security of RSA and its variants. For the original RSA scheme with modulus $N = pq$, Boneh and Durfee [1] successfully used Coppersmith's method to factor the modulus when $d \leq N^{0.292}$. Later, Herrmann and May [5] introduced unravelled linearization technique to simplify Boneh-Durfee's lattice construction and obtained the same result as [1]. For the Prime Power RSA with modulus $N = p^r q$, by utilizing Coppersmith's method, May [13] showed that one can factor the modulus in polynomial time provided that $d \leq N^{(\frac{r-1}{r+1})^2}$. Recently, Lu et al. [11] successfully improved this bound to $d \leq N^{\frac{r(r-1)}{(r+1)^2}}$ by choosing more helpful polynomials to construct lattice. On the other hand, Sarkar [20] used the algebraic property $p^r q = N$ to replace the monomial $p^r q$ by N appears in the polynomials which are selected to construct lattice and significantly improved the previous bound when $r \leq 5$. Recently, by optimizing the selection of polynomials, Sarkar [21] further improved result of [20]. Table 1 lists the existing small private exponent attacks on Prime Power RSA for different values of r.

Recently, from a new point of view, Zheng and Hu [26] considered the security of Prime Power RSA when two pairs of public and private exponents, (e_1, d_1) and (e_2, d_2) are used for a common modulus $N = p^r q$. More specifically, for (e_1, d_1) and (e_2, d_2), one can obtain following equations,

$$\begin{aligned} e_1 d_1 &= k_1 p^{r-1}(p-1)(q-1) + 1, \\ e_2 d_2 &= k_2 p^{r-1}(p-1)(q-1) + 1 \end{aligned} \tag{1}$$

where k_1 and k_2 are some integers. Therefore, the problem of factoring $N = p^r q$ can be reduced into finding the unknown (d_1, d_2) from the following modular equations,

$$f(x_1) = e_1 x_1 - 1 \pmod{p^{r-1}},$$
$$f(x_2) = e_2 x_2 - 1 \pmod{p^{r-1}} \tag{2}$$

By an application of Takayasu and Kunihiro's lattice construction method [24], Zheng and Hu combined the two modular Eq. (2) to construct lattice and obtained the following theorem:

Theorem 1 (Zheng-Hu, [26]). *Let (e_1, e_2) be two public exponents of Prime Power RSA with common modulus $N = p^r q$. Consider that d_1, d_2 are the corresponding private exponents. Then based on Coppersmith's method, one can factor N in polynomial time when*

$$\delta_1 \delta_2 < \left(\frac{r-1}{r+1}\right)^3,$$

where $d_1 < N^{\delta_1}$ and $d_2 < N^{\delta_2}$.

Moreover, Nitaj and Rachidi [16] also considered the similar attack scenario. Compared to the Zheng-Hu's small private exponent attack, Nitaj and Rachidi mainly focused on the difference between d_1 and d_2, namely, when the two private exponents d_1 and d_2 share some most significant bits, the value of $|d_1 - d_2|$ can be upper bounded. Then they transformed Eq. (1) into the following equation,

$$e_1 e_2 (d_1 - d_2) = e_2 - e_1 + (k_1 e_2 - k_2 e_1) k_1 p^{r-1}(p-1)(q-1) \equiv e_2 - e_1 \pmod{p^{r-1}(p-1)(q-1)}$$

Therefore, the problem of factoring $N = p^r q$ can be reduced into finding the unknown $d_1 - d_2$ from the following modular equation,

$$f(x) = e_1 e_2 x - e_2 + e_1 \pmod{p^{r-1}}$$

Then by utilizing the method of [11], Nitaj and Rachidi successfully obtained $d_1 - d_2$ when $|d_1 - d_2| < N^{\frac{r(r-1)}{(r+1)^2}}$.

Implicit Factorization Problem on RSA and Prime Power RSA. The implicit factorization problem on RSA is introduced by May and Ritzenhofen [14]. For the convenience of description of implicit factorization problem, we first describe the implicit hint of RSA as follows: Consider two n-bits RSA moduli $N_1 = p_1 q_1$ and $N_2 = p_2 q_2$, where q_1, q_2 are αn-bits ($\alpha \in (0, 1)$). And the implicit hint is that p_1 and p_2 share tn ($t \in (0, 1)$) least significant bits. May and Ritzenhofen proved that when $t \geq 2\alpha$, the vector (q_1, q_2) is a shortest vector in a two-dimensional lattice, then one can easily recover q_1 and q_2 by lattice basis reduction algorithm. Shortly afterwards, Sarkar and Maitra [22] transformed the implicit factorization problem into approximate greatest common divisor problem which can be solved by Coppersmith's method and obtained the same bound as May-Ritzenhofen's result. Since then there are many works about implicit factorization problem [4,9,10,18] and for now the best result is $t \geq 2\alpha - 2\alpha^2$.

Recently, Nitaj and Rachidi [16] considered the implicit factorization problem on Prime Power RSA and obtained the following result.

Theorem 2 (Nitaj-Rachidi, [16]). *Let* $N_1 = p_1^r q_1$ *and* $N_2 = p_2^r q_2$ *be two Prime Power RSA moduli. Then if*

$$|p_1 - p_2| < \frac{p_1}{2rq_1q_2},$$

one can factor N_1 *and* N_2 *in polynomial time.*

Note that, for the above theorem, we assume that q_1, q_2 have roughly the same bit-size as N^α and $(0 < \alpha < 1)$, p_1, p_2 have roughly the same bitlength as $N^{\frac{1}{r}(1-\alpha)}$, where N denotes an integer and has the same bit-size as N_1 and N_2. Then Nitaj-Rachidi's result can be rewritten as

$$|p_1 - p_2| < N^{\frac{1}{r}(1-\alpha)-2\alpha},$$

neglecting any small constant since N is relatively large.

1.2   Our Contributions

In this paper, we focus on the security of Prime Power RSA, in particular, we improve the Zheng-Hu's cryptanalysis of Prime Power RSA with two pairs of public and private exponents and Nitaj-Rachidi's cryptanalysis of implicit factorization problem on Prime Power RSA, respectively. And our improved attacks are both verified by experiments.

Improved Result on Zheng-Hu's Work. We firstly revisit the analysis of Prime Power RSA with two private exponents and utilize the technique of selecting polynomials [11] to improve the previous bound $\left(\frac{r-1}{r+1}\right)^3$ of Zheng and Hu's work [26] to $\frac{r(r-1)^2}{(r+1)^3}$. Comparing with the work of [26], we list some theoretical bounds in Table 2.

Furthermore, we extend the previous cryptanalysis to multiple private exponents and obtain the general bound. Specifically, for Prime Power RSA, assume that there are n pairs of public and private exponents (e_l, d_l), where $l = 1, \cdots, n$ with a common modulus $N = p^r q$. By using the method of [11], we show that the modulus can be factored when

$$\delta_1\delta_2\cdots\delta_n < \frac{r(r-1)^n}{(r+1)^{n+1}}$$

where $d_l \leq N^{\delta_l}$ for all $l = 1, \cdots, n$.

Note that, Peng et al. proposed an independent work [17] which similarly focused on the problem of multiple pairs of public and private keys with a common variant RSA modulus. The main work of [17] is to give the analysis of

Table 2. Comparison with the result of [26] on the theoretical bounds on two private exponents d_1 and d_2

r	$\|d_1 - d_2\| < N^{\frac{r(r-1)}{(r+1)^2}}$ ([16])	$d_1 d_2 < N^{\left(\frac{r-1}{r+1}\right)^3}$ ([26])	$d_1 d_2 < N^{\frac{r(r-1)^2}{(r+1)^3}}$ (Our result)
2	0.222	0.037	0.074
3	0.375	0.125	0.188
4	0.480	0.216	0.288
5	0.555	0.296	0.370
6	0.612	0.364	0.437
7	0.656	0.422	0.492
8	0.691	0.471	0.538

another variant RSA, CRT-RSA with multiple private exponents. For Prime Power RSA, Peng et al. simply used the conclusion of [24] to give the bound and ignored the detailed construction of lattice. Since Peng et al. used the same technique proposed in [24] as Zheng and Hu's work [26], when there are two private exponents, the bound in [17] is same as Zheng and Hu's bound in [26].

Improved Result on Nitaj-Rachidi's Work. We also reconsider the implicit factorization problem on Prime Power RSA and improve the bound $\frac{1}{r}(1-\alpha) - 2\alpha$ of Nitaj and Rachidi's work [16] to

$$\frac{1}{r}(1 - \alpha) - 2\alpha + 2\alpha^2$$

Specifically, let $\widetilde{p} = p_1^r - p_2^r$. Since p_1 and p_2 share some most significant bits, namely, the upper bound of $|p_1 - p_2|$ is determined, then the upper bound of $\widetilde{p}$ can also be determined. Then we represent N_2 as $N_2 = p_2^r q = (p_1^r - \widetilde{p})q_2$, the problem can be transformed into finding the common divisor of N_1 and $N_2 + \widetilde{p}q_2$, where $\widetilde{p}q_2$ is unknown. Inspired by the idea of [9], by utilizing Coppersmith's method, we can construct lattice and obtain $\widetilde{p}$ and q_2, moreover based on the observation that the one of desired solutions q_2 is a factor of the known modulus $N_2 = p_2^r q_2$, we introduce a new variable p_2^r to reduce the determinant of our constructed lattice. Finally Nitaj-Rachidi's bound can be improved. Comparing with the work of [16], we list some theoretical bounds in Table 3.

The rest of this paper is organized as follows. Section 2 is some preliminary knowledge on lattices. In Sect. 3, we analyze Prime Power RSA with multiple two private exponents. Section 4 presents an improved analysis of implicit factorization problem on Prime Power RSA. Finally, Sect. 5 is the conclusion.

2 Preliminaries on Lattice

Let $\mathcal{L}$ be a lattice which is spanned by k linearly independent vectors $w_1, w_2, \cdots, w_k \in \mathbb{Z}^n$. Namely, lattice $\mathcal{L}$ is composed by all integer linear combinations, $c_1 w_1 + \cdots + c_k w_k$, of $w_1, w_2, \cdots, w_k$, where $c_1, \cdots, c_k \in \mathbb{Z}$. Then the set

Table 3. Comparison with the result of [16] on the theoretical bounds on the value of $\log_N |p_1 - p_2|$

r	α, i.e., $\log_{N_i} q_i$	$\frac{1}{r}(1-\alpha) - 2\alpha$ ([16])	$\frac{1}{r}(1-\alpha) - 2\alpha + 2\alpha^2$ (Our result)
2	0.10	0.250	0.270
2	0.15	0.125	0.170
3	0.10	0.100	0.120

of vectors $w_1, \cdots, w_k$ is called a lattice basis of $\mathcal{L}$ and k is the lattice dimension of $\mathcal{L}$. Moreover, for any lattice $\mathcal{L}$ with dimension greater than 1, we can transform the lattice basis $w_1, w_2, \cdots, w_k$ to another lattice basis of $\mathcal{L}$ by a multiplication with some integral matrix with determinant ± 1. More details about the lattice can be referred to [15].

In [8], Lenstra et al. introduced the famous L^3 lattice basis reduction algorithm to find a lattice basis with good properties. More specifically, for any given lattice, one can use L^3 lattice basis reduction algorithm [8] to find out relatively short vectors with following lemma in polynomial time.

Lemma 1. (L^3, [8,12]) Let $\mathcal{L}$ be a lattice of dimension k. Applying the L^3 algorithm to $\mathcal{L}$, the outputted reduced basis vectors $v_1, \cdots, v_k$ satisfy that

$$\|v_i\| \leq 2^{\frac{k(k-i)}{4(k+1-i)}} \det(\mathcal{L})^{\frac{1}{k+1-i}}, \text{ for any } 1 \leq i \leq k.$$

Coppersmith's method: Coppersmith [3] successfully applied the L^3 lattice basis reduction algorithm to find small roots of univariate modular equations and bivariate integer equations, typically called Coppersmith's method. Later, Jochemsz and May [7] extended this technique and gave a general strategy to solve for small roots of multivariate equations. Since then, based on Coppersmith's method, many cryptanalyses [11,13,20,24,26] have been proposed to attack the RSA scheme.

Moreover, the following lemma due to Howgrave-Graham [6] gives a sufficient condition which can transform a modular equation into an integer equation. For the convenience of describing the lemma, we define the norm of a polynomial $g(x_1, \cdots, x_k) = \sum_{(i_1, \cdots, i_k)} a_{i_1, \cdots, i_k} x_1^{i_1} \cdots x_k^{i_k}$ as

$$\|g(x_1, \cdots, x_k)\| = \left(\sum_{(i_1, \cdots, i_k)} a_{i_1, \cdots, i_k}^2 \right)^{\frac{1}{2}}.$$

Lemma 2. (Howgrave-Graham, [6]) Let $g(x_1, \cdots, x_n) \in \mathbb{Z}[x_1, \cdots, x_n]$ be an integer polynomial with at most k monomials and m be a positive integer. Suppose that

$$g(y_1, \cdots, y_n) \equiv 0 \pmod{p^m} \text{ for } |y_1| \leq X_1, \cdots, |y_n| \leq X_n, \text{ and}$$

$$\|g(x_1 X_1, \cdots, x_n X_n)\| < \frac{p^m}{\sqrt{k}}.$$

Then $g(y_1, \cdots, y_n) = 0$ holds over the integers.

Then based on the above two lemmas, we give a brief sketch of Coppersmith's method. For a modular equation $f(x_1, \cdots, x_n)$ modulo p and the desired roots are $(y_1, \cdots, y_n)$, we firstly select polynomials $h_i(x_1, \cdots, x_n)$ have the same roots $(y_1, \cdots, y_n)$ modulo p^m. Then we construct a lattice whose row vectors correspond to the coefficients of the selected polynomials $h_i(x_1 X_1, \cdots, x_n X_n)$, where $|y_1| \leq X_1, \cdots, |y_n| \leq X_n$. In general, suppose that by applying L^3 algorithm to the lattice, we can obtain n polynomials corresponding to the first n reduced basis vectors with sufficiently small norm. Then due to Lemma 1, we have

$$||v_1(x_1 X_1, \ldots, x_n X_n)|| \leq \cdots \leq ||v_n(x_1 X_1, \ldots, x_n X_n)|| \leq 2^{\frac{k(k-1)}{4(k+1-n)}} \det(\mathcal{L})^{\frac{1}{k+1-n}}.$$

Moreover, since the obtained polynomials $v_1(x_1, \ldots, x_n), \ldots, v_n(x_1, \ldots, x_n)$ are some integer combinations of the polynomials $h_i(x_1, \cdots, x_n)$ which are used to construct lattice, $v_1(x_1, \ldots, x_n), \ldots, v_n(x_1, \ldots, x_n)$ have the same roots $(y_1, \cdots, y_n)$ modulo p^m. Then if the norm of $v_1(x_1, \ldots, x_n), \ldots, v_n(x_1, \ldots, x_n)$ satisfy the second condition of Lemma 2, namely if

$$2^{\frac{k(k-1)}{4(k+1-n)}} \det(\mathcal{L})^{\frac{1}{k+1-n}} < \frac{p^m}{\sqrt{k}},$$

we have that $v_1(y_1, \cdots, y_n) = 0, \ldots, v_n(y_1, \cdots, y_n) = 0$ hold over the integers.

Similarly as other lattice-based attacks, we ignore small terms that do not depend on p since p is relatively large, and only check whether $\det(\mathcal{L}) < p^{mk}$ does hold or not.

Then based on the following heuristic assumption, we can solve for the roots $y_1, \cdots, y_n$ from the polynomials $v_1(y_1, \cdots, y_n) = 0, \ldots, v_n(y_1, \cdots, y_n) = 0$.

Assumption 1. *Our lattice-based construction yields algebraically independent polynomials. The common roots of these polynomials can be efficiently computed by using techniques like calculation of the resultants or finding a Gröbner basis.*

3 Revisiting the Cryptanalysis of Prime Power RSA with Multiple Pairs of Public and Private Exponents

In this section, we first give an improved analysis on Zheng-Hu's work of Prime Power RSA with two pairs of public and private exponents, then we extend the cryptanalysis to multiple pairs of public and private exponents.

3.1 Two Public and Private Exponents Attack of Prime Power RSA

Firstly, we revisit Zheng and Hu's work [26]. By modifying the Zheng-Hu's selection of polynomials which are used to construct lattice, we obtain following result,

Theorem 3. *Let (e_1, e_2) be two public exponents of Prime Power RSA with common modulus $N = p^r q$. Consider that d_1, d_2 are the corresponding private exponents. Then under Assumption 1, one can factor N in polynomial time when*

$$\delta_1 \delta_2 < \frac{r(r-1)^2}{(r+1)^3}$$

Proof. For one modulus $N = p^r q$, there exist two pairs of public and private exponents (e_1, d_1) and (e_2, d_2), thus, we have that

$$e_1 d_1 = k_1 p^{r-1}(p-1)(q-1) + 1,$$
$$e_2 d_2 = k_2 p^{r-1}(p-1)(q-1) + 1$$

Hence, for the unknown (d_1, d_2) we have the following modular equations,

$$f_1'(x_1) = e_1 x_1 - 1 \pmod{p^{r-1}},$$
$$f_2'(x_2) = e_2 x_2 - 1 \pmod{p^{r-1}}$$

As it is shown, (d_1, d_2) is a root of simultaneous modular univariate linear equations modulo an unknown divisor, and the solutions can be roughly estimated by $d_1 \simeq X_1 (:= N^{\delta_1})$ and $d_2 \simeq X_2 (:= N^{\delta_2})$, neglecting any small constant since N is relatively large.

Let e_1', e_2' be the inverse of e_1, e_2 modulo N, respectively. Then we have

$$f_1(x_1) = x_1 - e_1' \pmod{p^{r-1}},$$
$$f_2(x_2) = x_2 - e_2' \pmod{p^{r-1}}$$

Using the technique of [11], for a positive integer t, we firstly select following polynomials,

$$f_{i_1, i_2}(x_1, x_2) = (x_1 - e_1')^{i_1}(x_2 - e_2')^{i_2} N^{\max\{\lceil \frac{t-(r-1)(i_1+i_2)}{r} \rceil, 0\}}$$

where $0 \leq \delta_1 i_1 + \delta_2 i_2 \leq \frac{t}{r+1}$. Note that, all polynomials $f_{i_1, i_2}(x_1, x_2)$ share the common root (d_1, d_2) modulo p^t.

Following Coppersmith's technique, we arrange the above polynomials with the order $(i_1, i_2) \prec (i_1', i_2')$ if

$$i_1 < i_1' \quad \text{or} \quad i_1 = i_1', i_2 < i_2'.$$

Then following this order, we can construct a triangular matrix whose row vectors are the coefficient vectors of $f_{i_1, i_2}(x_1 X_1, x_2 X_2)$ and lattice $\mathcal{L}$ which is spanned by the row vectors of this matrix. The diagonal entries of $\mathcal{L}$ are

$$X_1^{i_1} X_2^{i_2} N^{\max\{\lceil \frac{t-(r-1)(i_1+i_2)}{r} \rceil, 0\}}, \quad \text{for } 0 \leq \delta_1 i_1 + \delta_2 i_2 \leq \frac{t}{r+1}$$

Then the determinant of $\mathcal{L}$ can be determined as

$$\det(\mathcal{L}) = \prod_{0 \leq \delta_1 i_1 + \delta_2 i_2 \leq \frac{t}{r+1}} X_1^{i_1} X_2^{i_2} N^{\max\{\lceil \frac{t-(r-1)(i_1+i_2)}{r} \rceil, 0\}}$$
$$= X_1^{S_1} X_2^{S_2} N^{S_3},$$

where the exponents S_1, S_2, S_3 are calculated as follows:

$$S_1 = \sum_{0 \leq \delta_1 i_1 + \delta_2 i_2 \leq \frac{t}{r+1}} i_1 = \sum_{i_2=0}^{\frac{t}{\delta_2(r+1)}} \sum_{i_1=0}^{\frac{t}{\delta_1(r+1)} - \frac{\delta_2 i_2}{\delta_1}} i_1 = \frac{t^3}{6(r+1)^3 \delta_1^2 \delta_2} + \frac{\delta_1 + \delta_2}{4(r+1)^2 \delta_1^2 \delta_2} t^2 + \frac{3\delta_1 + \delta_2}{12(r+1)\delta_1^2} t,$$

$$S_2 = \sum_{0 \leq \delta_1 i_1 + \delta_2 i_2 \leq \frac{t}{r+1}} i_2 = \sum_{i_1=0}^{\frac{t}{\delta_1(r+1)}} \sum_{i_2=0}^{\frac{t}{\delta_2(r+1)} - \frac{\delta_1 i_1}{\delta_2}} i_2 = \frac{t^3}{6(r+1)^3 \delta_1 \delta_2^2} + \frac{\delta_1 + \delta_2}{4(r+1)^2 \delta_1 \delta_2^2} t^2 + \frac{\delta_1 + 3\delta_2}{12(r+1)\delta_2^2} t,$$

$$S_3 = \sum_{0 \leq (r-1)(i_1+i_2) \leq t} \lceil \frac{t - (r-1)(i_1+i_2)}{r} \rceil \approx \sum_{0 \leq (r-1)(i_1+i_2) \leq t} \frac{t - (r-1)(i_1+i_2)}{r}$$

$$= \sum_{i_1=0}^{\frac{t}{r-1}} \sum_{i_2=0}^{\frac{t}{r-1} - i_1} \frac{t - (r-1)(i_1+i_2)}{r} = \frac{t^3}{6r(r-1)^2} + \frac{t^2}{2r(r-1)} + \frac{t}{3r}$$

On the other hand, the dimension of $\mathcal{L}$ is

$$\dim(\mathcal{L}) = \sum_{0 \leq \delta_1 i_1 + \delta_2 i_2 \leq \frac{t}{r+1}} 1 = \sum_{i_1=0}^{\frac{t}{\delta_1(r+1)}} \sum_{i_2=0}^{\frac{t}{\delta_2(r+1)} - \frac{\delta_1 i_1}{\delta_2}} 1 = \frac{t^2}{2(r+1)^2 \delta_1 \delta_2} + \frac{2\delta_1 + \delta_2}{2(r+1)\delta_1 \delta_2} t + 1$$

Then due to the Lemmas 1 and 2, one can use the L^3 lattice basis reduction algorithm to $\mathcal{L}$ to obtain two integer equations which share the root (d_1, d_2) over the integers if

$$\det(\mathcal{L}) < p^{t \dim(\mathcal{L})}$$

namely,

$$X_1^{\frac{t^3}{6(r+1)^3 \delta_1^2 \delta_2} + o(t^3)} X_2^{\frac{t^3}{6(r+1)^3 \delta_1 \delta_2^2} + o(t^3)} N^{\frac{t^3}{6r(r-1)^2} + o(t^3)} < p^{\frac{t^3}{2(r+1)^2 \delta_1 \delta_2} + o(t^3)}$$

To obtain the asymptotic bound, we assume t goes to infinite and ignore all terms of $o(t^3)$. Putting the bounds X_1, X_2 into the above sufficient condition of obtaining integer equations, the inequality simplifies into

$$\frac{1}{6(r+1)^3 \delta_1^2 \delta_2} \delta_1 + \frac{1}{6(r+1)^3 \delta_1 \delta_2^2} \delta_2 + \frac{1}{6r(r-1)^2} < \frac{1}{2(r+1)^3 \delta_1 \delta_2}$$

which leads to

$$\delta_1 \delta_2 < \frac{r(r-1)^2}{(r+1)^3}$$

Under the heuristic Assumption 1, we can solve for the common roots (d_1, d_2) of these two integer equations. Then one can easily factor N, this concludes the proof of Theorem 3. □

Comparison with previous works: Note that, Nitaj-Rachidi's method [16] focused on the difference between d_1 and d_2, namely the size of $|d_1 - d_2|$. However, Zheng-Hu's method and our method mainly consider the product of d_1 and d_2, namely the size of $d_1 d_2$. Therefore, when the difference between d_1 and d_2 is small, Nitaj-Rachidi's method is more efficient, since the product of d_1 and d_2 may much larger than our method. On the other hand, when d_1 and d_2 are random number, which mean that $d_1 - d_2$ has the same bit-size as $\max\{d_1, d_2\}$, our method is more efficient.

Moreover, Sarkar [20,21] used the algebraic property $p^r q = N$ to replace every occurrence of monomial $p^r q$ by N appears in the polynomials which are selected to construct lattice and significantly improved the previous bound when $r \leq 5$. Due to Sarkar's work, for the case of $r = 2$, one can efficiently factor N when $d_1 < N^{0.395}$ or $d_2 < N^{0.395}$. However, due to our work, the condition is that $d_1 d_2 < N^{0.074}$, which leads to $d_1 \simeq d_2 \simeq N^{0.272}$. For the case of $r = 4$, Sarkar's result is that $d_1 < N^{0.508}$ or $d_2 < N^{0.508}$ and our result is that $d_1 \simeq d_2 \simeq N^{0.537}$. Therefore, when $d_1 \simeq d_2$, Sarkar's method is better than our result when $r = 2, 3$, and when $r \geq 4$, our method is better.

Experimental Results: To verify our attack, we implemented our analytical method in Magma 2.11 [2] on our PC with Intel(R) Core(TM) Duo CPU (2.53 GHz, 1.9 GB RAM Windows 7). We list some experimental results on the size of d_1 and d_2 that the Prime Power RSA moduli $N = p^r q$ can be factored for comparison between our method of Sect. 3.1 and Zheng-Hu's method of [26] in Table 4. Here we assume that $d_1 \simeq N^{\delta_1}$ and $d_2 \simeq N^{\delta_2}$ where $\delta_1 = \delta_2$.

Table 4. Experimental results on $\delta_1 \delta_2$ for various r in [26] and Sect. 3.1

r	N (bits)	The values of $\delta_1\delta_2$ [26]				The values of $\delta_1\delta_2$ (Sect. 3.1)			
		theo.	expt.	dim	time of L^3 (in sec.)	theo.	expt.	$(t, \dim)$	Time of L^3 (in sec.)
2	900	0.037	0.016	6	0.104	0.074	0.058	(2, 6)	0.016
3	1000	0.125	0.089	10	15.436	0.188	0.116	(9, 28)	4.040
4	2000	0.216	0.159	10	34.178	0.288	0.176	(13, 28)	7.894
5	1800	0.296	0.238	6	21.756	0.370	0.240	(8, 6)	0.016

We also list some experimental results with different bitlengths of N in Table 5.

Table 5. Experimental results on δ_1 and δ_2 for various r in Sect. 3.1

r	N (bits)	$(t, \dim)$	δ_1	δ_2	Time of L^3 (in sec.)
3	2400	(10, 31)	0.350	0.370	316.822
4	2500	(15, 28)	0.440	0.480	229.805
5	3000	(10, 10)	0.460	0.500	2.558

Note that, in the experiments when d_1 and d_2 satisfy the values in Table 4, we can always successfully obtained d_1 and d_2.

3.2 Multiple Public and Private Exponents Attack of Prime Power RSA

Moreover, we can generalize the result of Theorem 3 to multiple public and private exponents and obtain following result,

Theorem 4. *Let* $((e_1, d_1), (e_2, d_2), \cdots, (e_n, d_n))$ *be* n *pairs of public and private exponents of Prime Power RSA with a common modulus* $N = p^r q$. *Then under Assumption 1, one can factor* N *when*

$$\delta_1 \delta_2 \cdots \delta_n < \frac{r(r-1)^n}{(r+1)^{n+1}},$$

where $d_l \leq N^{\delta_l}$, *for* $l = 1, \cdots, n$.

Proof. For one modulus $N = p^r q$, there exist n pairs of public and private exponents (e_l, d_l), thus, we have that

$$e_1 d_1 = k_1 p^{r-1}(p-1)(q-1) + 1,$$
$$e_2 d_2 = k_2 p^{r-1}(p-1)(q-1) + 1,$$
$$\cdots$$
$$e_n d_n = k_n p^{r-1}(p-1)(q-1) + 1.$$

Hence, for the unknown $(d_1, \cdots, d_n)$ we have the following modular equations,

$$f_1'(x_1) = e_1 x_1 - 1 \pmod{p^{r-1}},$$
$$f_2'(x_2) = e_2 x_2 - 1 \pmod{p^{r-1}},$$
$$\cdots$$
$$f_n'(x_n) = e_n x_n - 1 \pmod{p^{r-1}}.$$

As it is shown, $(d_1, d_2, \cdots, d_n)$ is a root of simultaneous modular univariate linear equations modulo an unknown divisor, and the size is bounded as $d_l \simeq X_l (:= N^{\delta_l})$, for $l = 1, \cdots, n$, neglecting any small constant since N is relatively large.

Then, let $e_1', e_2', \cdots, e_n'$ be the inverse of $e_1, e_2, \cdots, e_n$ modulo N, respectively. Then we have

$$f_1(x_1) = x_1 - e_1' \pmod{p^{r-1}},$$
$$f_2(x_2) = x_2 - e_2' \pmod{p^{r-1}},$$
$$\cdots$$
$$f_n(x_n) = x_n - e_n' \pmod{p^{r-1}}.$$

Using the technique of [11], for integer t, we select polynomials as following,

$$f_{i_1, i_2, \cdots, i_n}(x_1, x_2, \cdots, x_n) = (x_1 - e_1')^{i_1}(x_2 - e_2')^{i_2} \cdots (x_n - e_n')^{i_n} N^{\max\{\lceil \frac{t - (r-1)(i_1 + i_2 + \cdots + i_n)}{r} \rceil, 0\}}$$

where $0 \leq \delta_1 i_1 + \delta_2 i_2 + \cdots + \delta_n i_n \leq \frac{t}{r+1}$.

According to a similar order, we can construct a triangular matrix which is spanned by the coefficient vectors of $f_{i_1, i_2, \cdots, i_n}(x_1 X_1, x_2 X_2, \cdots, x_n X_n)$. Then $\mathcal{L}_1$ is spanned by the row vectors of above triangular matrix and its diagonal entries are

$$X_1^{i_1} X_2^{i_2} \cdots X_n^{i_n} N^{\max\{\lceil \frac{t - (r-1)(i_1 + i_2 + \cdots + i_n)}{r} \rceil, 0\}}, \quad \text{for } 0 \leq \delta_1 i_1 + \delta_2 i_2 + \cdots + \delta_n i_n \leq \frac{t}{r+1}$$

Then the determinant of $\mathcal{L}_1$ can be determined as

$$\det(\mathcal{L}_1) = \prod_{0 \leq \delta_1 i_1 + \delta_2 i_2 + \cdots + \delta_n i_n \leq \frac{t}{r+1}} X_1^{i_1} X_2^{i_2} \cdots X_n^{i_n} N^{\max\{\lceil \frac{t-(r-1)(i_1+i_2+\cdots+i_n)}{r} \rceil, 0\}}$$

$$= X_1^{S_1} X_2^{S_2} \cdots X_n^{S_n} N^{S_{n+1}},$$

where the exponents $S_1, S_2, \cdots, S_{n+1}$ are calculated as follows:

$$S_1 = \sum_{0 \leq \delta_1 i_1 + \delta_2 i_2 + \cdots + \delta_n i_n \leq \frac{t}{r+1}} i_1 = \frac{t^{n+1}}{(n+1)!(r+1)^{n+1}\delta_1^2 \delta_2 \cdots \delta_n} + o(t^{n+1}),$$

$$S_2 = \sum_{0 \leq \delta_1 i_1 + \delta_2 i_2 + \cdots + \delta_n i_n \leq \frac{t}{r+1}} i_2 = \frac{t^{n+1}}{(n+1)!(r+1)^{n+1}\delta_1 \delta_2^2 \cdots \delta_n} + o(t^{n+1}),$$

$$\cdots\cdots$$

$$S_{n+1} = \sum_{0 \leq (r-1)(i_1+i_2+\cdots+i_n) \leq t} \lceil \frac{t-(r-1)(i_1+i_2)}{r} \rceil = \frac{t^{n+1}}{(n+1)!r(r-1)^n} + o(t^{n+1})$$

On the other hand, the dimension of $\mathcal{L}_1$ is

$$\dim(\mathcal{L}_1) = \sum_{0 \leq \delta_1 i_1 + \delta_2 i_2 + \cdots + \delta_n i_n \leq \frac{t}{r+1}} 1 = \frac{t^n}{n!(r+1)^n \delta_1 \delta_2 \cdots \delta_n} + o(t^n)$$

Then due to the Lemmas 1 and 2, one can use the L^3 lattice basis reduction algorithm to $\mathcal{L}_1$ to obtain n integer equations which share the root $(d_1, d_2, \cdots, d_n)$ over the integers if

$$\det(\mathcal{L}_1) < p^{t \dim(\mathcal{L}_1)},$$

namely,

$$X_1^{\frac{t^{n+1}}{(n+1)!(r+1)^{n+1}\delta_1^2\delta_2\cdots\delta_n}+o(t^{n+1})} \cdots X_n^{\frac{t^{n+1}}{(n+1)!(r+1)^{n+1}\delta_1\delta_2\cdots\delta_n^2}+o(t^{n+1})} N^{\frac{t^{n+1}}{(n+1)!r(r-1)^n}+o(t^{n+1})}$$

$$< p^{\frac{t^{n+1}}{n!(r+1)^n\delta_1\delta_2\cdots\delta_n}+o(t^{n+1})}$$

Assume that t goes to infinite and ignore all terms of $o(t^{n+1})$. Putting the bounds $X_1, X_2, \cdots, X_n$ into the above condition, then the sufficient condition of obtaining integer equations can be finally reduced into following,

$$\delta_1 \delta_2 \cdots \delta_n < \frac{r(r-1)^n}{(r+1)^{n+1}}$$

Under the heuristic Assumption 1, we can solve for the common roots $(d_1, d_2, \cdots, d_n)$ of these integer equations. Then one can easily factor N, this concludes the proof of Theorem 4. $\qquad \square$

4   Revisiting Implicit Factorization Problem on Prime Power RSA

In this section, we revisit the implicit factorization problem on Prime Power RSA which has been studied by Nitaj and Rachidi [16] and obtain the following improved result,

Theorem 5. *Let $N_1 = p_1^r q_1$ and $N_2 = p_2^r q_2$ be two different Prime Power RSA moduli. Assume that q_1 and q_2 have roughly the same bit-size as N^α ($0 < \alpha < 1$), p_1 and p_2 have roughly the same bit-size as $N^{\frac{1}{r}(1-\alpha)}$, where N denotes an integer and has the same bit-size as N_1 and N_2. Then under Assumption 1, one can factor N_1 and N_2 in polynomial time when*

$$|p_1 - p_2| < N^{\frac{1}{r}(1-\alpha) - 2\alpha + 2\alpha^2}$$

Proof. Let $|p_1 - p_2| < N^\delta$. Then we can estimate $|p_1^r - p_2^r|$ by

$$|p_1^r - p_2^r| = |p_1 - p_2| \sum_{i=0}^{r-1} p_1^{r-1-i} p_2^i < r|p_1 - p_2|p_1^{r-1} < N^{\delta + \frac{r-1}{r}(1-\alpha)}$$

Here we assume that r can be ignored, since N is relatively large.

Let $\widetilde{p} = p_1^r - p_2^r$. We have that $N_2 = p_2^r q_2 = (p_1^r - \widetilde{p})q_2$ and $N_1 = p_1^r q_1$, thus we obtain that $\gcd(N_1, N_2 + \widetilde{p}q_2) = p_1^r$. Hence, for the unknown $(q_2, \widetilde{p})$ we have the following modular equation,

$$f(x, y) = N_2 + xy \pmod{p_1^r}$$

The solutions can be roughly estimated by $q_2 \simeq X(:= N^\alpha)$ and $\widetilde{p} \simeq Y(:= N^{\delta + \frac{r-1}{r}(1-\alpha)})$. Note that the desired solution q_2 is a factor of the modulus $N_2 = p_2^r q_2$. Then we introduce a new variable z for the another factor p_2^r of N_2. Let $p_2^r \simeq Z(:= N^{1-\alpha})$ denote the upper bound of the variable z.

In order to solve for the desired solutions, for a positive integer m we firstly select following polynomials,

$$g_k(x, y, z) = z^s f^k(x, y) N_1^{\max\{t-k, 0\}}, \quad \text{for } k = 0, \cdots, m$$

where s and t are integers and will be optimized later. For all the selected polynomials, we replace every occurrence of the monomial xz by N_2 since $p_2^r q_2 = N_2$. Therefore, compared to the unchanged polynomials, every monomial $x^k y^k z^s$ and $k \geq s$ with coefficient a_k is transformed into a monomial $x^{k-s} y^k$ with coefficient $a_k N_2^s$. Similarly, when $k < s$, every monomial $x^k y^k z^s$ with coefficient a_k is transformed into a monomial $y^k z^{s-k}$ with coefficient $a_k N_2^k$.

Then we construct a triangular matrix which is composed by the coefficient vectors of $g_k(xX, yY, zZ)$. Then lattice $\mathcal{L}$ is spanned by the row vectors of above triangular matrix. Moreover, to keep the determinant of the lattice as small as possible, we eliminate the factor of N_2^s or N_2^k in the coefficients of the diagonal entries by multiplying the corresponding polynomial with the inverse of N_2^s or N_2^k modulo N_1. Then the diagonal entries of $\mathcal{L}$ are

$$\begin{cases} X^{k-s} Y^k N_1^{\max\{t-k,0\}}, & \text{for } s \leq k \leq m, \\ Y^k Z^{s-k} N_1^{\max\{t-k,0\}}, & \text{for } 0 \leq k \leq s-1 \end{cases}$$

Then the determinant of $\mathcal{L}$ can be determined as

$$\det(\mathcal{L}) = X^{S_x} Y^{S_y} Z^{S_z} N_1^{S_n}$$

where

$$S_x = \sum_{k=s}^{m}(k-s) = \frac{(m-s)(m-s+1)}{2},$$

$$S_y = \sum_{k=0}^{m} k = \frac{m(m+1)}{2},$$

$$S_z = \sum_{k=0}^{s-1}(s-k) = \frac{s(s+1)}{2},$$

$$S_n = \sum_{k=0}^{t}(t-k) = \frac{t(t+1)}{2}$$

On the other hand, the dimension of $\mathcal{L}$ is $\dim(\mathcal{L}) = m+1$. Then due to the Lemmas 1 and 2, one can use the L^3 lattice basis reduction algorithm to $\mathcal{L}$ to obtain integer equations which share the desired roots $(q_2, \widetilde{p}, p_2^r)$ over the integers if

$$\det(\mathcal{L}) < p_1^{rt \dim(\mathcal{L})}$$

namely,

$$X^{\frac{(m-s)(m-s+1)}{2}} Y^{\frac{m(m+1)}{2}} Z^{\frac{s(s+1)}{2}} N_1^{\frac{t(t+1)}{2}} < p_1^{rt(m+1)}$$

Let $t = \tau m$ and $s = \sigma m$. To obtain the asymptotic bound, we assume m goes to infinite and ignore all terms of $o(m^2)$. Putting the bounds X, Y and Z into the above sufficient condition of obtaining integer equations, the inequality can be reduced into

$$\frac{(1-\sigma)^2}{2}\alpha + \frac{1}{2}(\delta + \frac{r-1}{r}(1-\alpha)) + \frac{\sigma^2}{2}(1-\alpha) + \frac{\tau^2}{2} < \tau(1-\alpha)$$

The optimized values of τ and σ are $\tau = 1-\alpha$ and $\sigma = \alpha$, then we finally obtain the sufficient condition

$$\delta < 1 - 3\alpha + 2\alpha^2 - \frac{r-1}{r}(1-\alpha) = \frac{1}{r}(1-\alpha) - 2\alpha + 2\alpha^2$$

Under the heuristic Assumption 1, we can solve for the common roots $(q_2, \widetilde{p}, p_2^r)$ of these integer equations. Then one can easily factor N_1 and N_2, this concludes the proof of Theorem 5. $\qquad\square$

Experimental Results: To verify our attack, we implemented our analytical method in Magma 2.11 [2] on our PC with Intel(R) Core(TM) Duo CPU (2.53 GHz, 1.9 GB RAM Windows 7).

In [16], Nitaj and Rachidi presented an example to verify their method. For two moduli $N_1 = p_1^2 q_1$ and $N_2 = p_2^2 q_2$, where p_1, p_2 are 82-bit primes and q_1, q_2 are 26-bit primes, Nitaj and Rachidi successfully factored N_1 and N_2 when $|p_1 - p_2| < 2^{27}$. We similarly generate two moduli $N_1 = p_1^2 q_1$ and $N_2 = p_2^2 q_2$, where the bit-size of p_1, p_2, q_1 and q_2 are same as Nitaj and Rachidi's example. Based on our method, we construct a 21-dimensional lattice with parameters $m = 20, t = 17$ and $s = 2$, then we successfully factor N_1 and N_2 when $|p_1 - p_2| < 2^{34}$ and the running time of L^3 algorithm is 0.499 s and the running time of calculation of Gröbner basis is 21.060 s.

We also list some experimental results with different bit-sizes of p_i and q_i in Table 6.

Table 6. Theoretical and experimental bounds on the value of $\log_N |p_1 - p_2|$

r	Bitsize of (p_i, q_i), i.e., $((1-\alpha)\log_2 N_i, \alpha\log_2 N_i)$	The value of $\log_N |p_1 - p_2|$ (Sect. 4)			
		theo.	expt.	$(m, t, s, \dim(\mathcal{L}))$	Time of L^3(in sec.)
2	(400, 100)	0.247	0.231	(30, 26, 3, 31)	91.073
2	(400, 200)	0.080	0.060	(30, 24, 6, 31)	114.099
3	(400, 100)	0.166	0.131	(30, 27, 2, 31)	91.807

5   Conclusion

In this paper, we revisited the Zheng-Hu's work of two public and private exponents attack of Prime Power RSA and Nitaj-Rachidi's work of implicit factorization problem on Prime Power RSA respectively. By choosing more helpful polynomials to construct lattice, we firstly improved the Zheng-Hu's bound $(\frac{r-1}{r+1})^3$ to $\frac{r(r-1)^2}{(r+1)^3}$. In addition, we extended the analysis to multiple private exponents and gave a generalized bound. For Nitaj-Rachidi's work, we transformed the implicit factorization problem to finding a common divisor of a known number and a unknown number, where the value of unknown number is similar to a known modulus, then by utilizing Coppersmith's method, we also improved Nitaj-Rachidi's bound.

Acknowledgements. The authors would like to thank anonymous reviewers for their helpful comments and suggestions. The work of this paper was supported by the National Key Basic Research Program of China (Grants 2013CB834203 and 2011CB302400), the National Natural Science Foundation of China (Grants 61472417, 61402469, 61472416, 61502488 and 61272478), the Strate gic Priority Research Program of Chinese Academy of Sciences under Grant XDA06010702 and XDA06010703, and the State Key Laboratory of Information Security, Chinese Academy of Sciences. Y. Lu is supported by Project CREST, JST.

References

1. Boneh, D., Durfee, G.: Cryptanalysis of RSA with private key d less than N 0.292. IEEE Trans. Inf. Theor. **46**(4), 1339–1349 (2000)
2. Bosma, W., Cannon, J., Playoust, C.: The magma algebra system I: the user language. J. Symbolic Comput. **24**(3), 235–265 (1997)
3. Coppersmith, D.: Small solutions to polynomial equations, and low exponent RSA vulnerabilities. J. Cryptol. **10**(4), 233–260 (1997)
4. Faugère, J.-C., Marinier, R., Renault, G.: Implicit factoring with shared most significant and middle bits. In: Nguyen, P.Q., Pointcheval, D. (eds.) PKC 2010. LNCS, vol. 6056, pp. 70–87. Springer, Heidelberg (2010). doi:10.1007/978-3-642-13013-7_5
5. Herrmann, M., May, A.: Maximizing small root bounds by linearization and applications to small secret exponent RSA. In: Nguyen, P.Q., Pointcheval, D. (eds.) PKC 2010. LNCS, vol. 6056, pp. 53–69. Springer, Heidelberg (2010). doi:10.1007/978-3-642-13013-7_4
6. Howgrave-Graham, N.: Finding small roots of univariate modular equations revisited. In: Darnell, M. (ed.) Cryptography and Coding 1997. LNCS, vol. 1355, pp. 131–142. Springer, Heidelberg (1997). doi:10.1007/BFb0024458
7. Jochemsz, E., May, A.: A strategy for finding roots of multivariate polynomials with new applications in attacking RSA variants. In: Lai, X., Chen, K. (eds.) ASIACRYPT 2006. LNCS, vol. 4284, pp. 267–282. Springer, Heidelberg (2006). doi:10.1007/11935230_18
8. Lenstra, A.K., Lenstra, H.W., Lovász, L.: Factoring polynomials with rational coefficients. Math. Ann. **261**(4), 515–534 (1982)
9. Lu, Y., Peng, L., Zhang, R., Hu, L., Lin, D.: Towards optimal bounds for implicit factorization problem. In: Dunkelman, O., Keliher, L. (eds.) SAC 2015. LNCS, vol. 9566, pp. 462–476. Springer, Heidelberg (2016). doi:10.1007/978-3-319-31301-6_26
10. Lu, Y., Zhang, R., Lin, D.: Improved bounds for the implicit factorization problem. Adv. Math. Comm. **7**(3), 243–251 (2013)
11. Lu, Y., Zhang, R., Peng, L., Lin, D.: Solving linear equations modulo unknown divisors: revisited. In: Iwata, T., Cheon, J.H. (eds.) ASIACRYPT 2015. LNCS, vol. 9452, pp. 189–213. Springer, Heidelberg (2015). doi:10.1007/978-3-662-48797-6_9
12. May, A.: New RSA vulnerabilities using lattice reduction methods. Ph.D. thesis. University of Paderborn (2003)
13. May, A.: Secret exponent attacks on RSA-type schemes with moduli $N = p^r q$. In: Bao, F., et al. (eds.) International Workshop on Public KeyCryptography, PKC 2004, LNCS, vol. 2947, pp. 218–230. Springer, Heidelberg (2004)
14. May, A., Ritzenhofen, M.: Implicit factoring: on polynomial time factoring given only an implicit hint. In: Jarecki, S., Tsudik, G. (eds.) PKC 2009. LNCS, vol. 5443, pp. 1–14. Springer, Heidelberg (2009). doi:10.1007/978-3-642-00468-1_1
15. Nguyen, P.Q., Vallée, B.: The lll Algorithm. Information Security and Cryptography. Springer, Heidelberg (2010)
16. Nitaj, A., Rachidi, T.: New attacks on RSA with moduli $N = p^r q$. In: International Conference on Codes, Cryptology, and Information Security, pp. 352–360. Springer, Heidelberg (2015)
17. Peng, L., Hu, L., Lu, Y., Sarkar, S., Xu, J., Huang, Z.: Cryptanalysis of variants of RSA with multiple small secret exponents. In: Biryukov, A., Goyal, V. (eds.) INDOCRYPT 2015. LNCS, vol. 9462, pp. 105–123. Springer, Heidelberg (2015). doi:10.1007/978-3-319-26617-6_6

18. Peng, L., Hu, L., Xu, J., Huang, Z., Xie, Y.: Further improvement of factoring RSA moduli with implicit hint. In: Pointcheval, D., Vergnaud, D. (eds.) AFRICACRYPT 2014. LNCS, vol. 8469, pp. 165–177. Springer, Heidelberg (2014). doi:10.1007/978-3-319-06734-6_11
19. Rivest, R.L., Shamir, A., Adleman, L.: A method for obtaining digital signatures and public-key cryptosystems. Commun. ACM **26**(1), 96–99 (1983)
20. Sarkar, S.: Small secret exponent attack on RSA variant with modulus $N = p^r q$. Des. Codes Crypt. **73**(2), 383–392 (2014)
21. Sarkar, S.: Revisiting prime power RSA. Discrete Appl. Math. **203**, 127–133 (2016)
22. Sarkar, S., Maitra, S.: Approximate integer common divisor problem relates to implicit factorization. IEEE Trans. Inf. Theor. **57**(6), 4002–4013 (2011)
23. Takagi, T.: Fast RSA-type cryptosystem modulo $p^k q$. In: Krawczyk, H. (ed.) CRYPTO 1998. LNCS, vol. 1462, pp. 318–326. Springer, Heidelberg (1998). doi:10.1007/BFb0055738
24. Takayasu, A., Kunihiro, N.: Better lattice constructions for solving multivariate linear equations modulo unknown divisors. IEICE Trans. Fund. Electron. Commun. Comput. Sci. **97**(6), 1259–1272 (2014)
25. Wiener, M.J.: Cryptanalysis of short RSA secret exponents. IEEE Trans. Inf. Theor. **36**(3), 553–558 (1990)
26. Zheng, M., Hu, H.: Cryptanalysis of prime power RSA with two private exponents. Sci. China Inf. Sci. **58**(11), 1–8 (2015)

On Computing the Immunity of Boolean Power Functions Against Fast Algebraic Attacks

Yusong Du$^{1(\boxtimes)}$ and Baodian Wei^2

^{1} School of Information Management, Sun Yat-sen University,
Guangzhou 510006, China
duyusong@mail.sysu.edu.cn
^{2} School of Data and Computer Science, Sun Yat-sen University,
Guangzhou 510006, China

Abstract. The immunity of Boolean functions against fast algebraic attacks (FAA's) has been considered as an important cryptographic property for Boolean functions used in stream ciphers. An n-variable Boolean power function f can be represented as a monomial trace function over finite field $\mathbb{F}_{2^n}$, $f(x) = Tr_1^n(\lambda x^k)$, where $\lambda \in \mathbb{F}_{2^n}$ and k is the coset leader of cyclotomic coset C_k modulo $2^n - 1$. To determine the immunity of Boolean power functions, one may need the arithmetic in $\mathbb{F}_{2^n}$, which is not computationally efficient compared with the operations over $\mathbb{F}_2$. In this paper, we show that the linear (affine) invariance of the immunity of Boolean functions against FAA's can be exploited to observe the immunity of Boolean power functions against FAA's, i.e., the immunity of $f(x) = Tr_1^n(\lambda x^k)$ against FAA's is the same as that of $r(x) = Tr_1^n(x^k)$ if $f(x)$ can be obtained from $r(x)$ through a linear transformation. In particular, if $\gcd(k, 2^n - 1) = 1$ then the immunity against FAA's of $f(x)$ and that of $r(x)$ are always the same. The immunity of Boolean power functions that satisfy this condition can be computed more efficiently.

Keywords: Stream cipher · Boolean power function · Algebraic immunity · Fast algebraic attack

1 Introduction

Boolean functions used in stream ciphers, especially in the filter and combination generators of stream ciphers based on linear feedback shift registers, should have large algebraic immunity ($\mathcal{AI}$), in order to resist algebraic attacks [1]. They should also have the resistance against fast algebraic attacks (FAA's), because Boolean functions with large algebraic immunity (even the maximum $\mathcal{AI}$) may

This work is supported by National Natural Science Foundations of China (Grant No. 61309028, Grant No. 61472457, Grant No. 61502113), Science and Technology Planning Project of Guangdong Province, China (Grant No. 2014A010103017), and Natural Science Foundation of Guangdong Province, China (Grant No. 2016A030313298).

S. Hong and J.H. Park (Eds.): ICISC 2016, LNCS 10157, pp. 304–316, 2017.
DOI: 10.1007/978-3-319-53177-9_16

not resist FAA's [1,5]. Algebraic immunity as well as the immunity of Boolean functions against FAA's, has been considered as an important cryptographic property for Boolean functions used in stream ciphers resisting both algebraic and fast algebraic attacks [2,4,7,10,12–14].

Boolean power functions are a special class of Boolean functions and are widely studied because of their applications in cryptography, coding theory and sequence design. The immunity of Boolean power functions also received attention, but mainly on their (standard) algebraic immunity.

The upper bounds on the algebraic immunities of inverse functions, Kasami functions and Niho functions, which are typical Boolean power functions, were given respectively by Y. Nawaz et al. [11]. The lower bound on the algebraic immunity of inverse functions was also analyzed [3]. In 2013, on the basis of some experimental results D.K. Dalai conjectured that the algebraic immunity of inverse functions exactly arrives at the upper bound given by Y. Nawaz et al. [6]. Then X. Feng et al. proved that Dalai's conjecture on the bound of inverse functions is correct [8]. They also demonstrated some weak properties of inverse functions against FAA's.

Existing results can be applied to negative the immunity of Boolean power functions against FAA's because low algebraic immunity implies weak resistance against FAA's. But they may be *not* interesting to determine or to compute their exact immunity against FAA's. Consider the determination of the immunity of Boolean power functions against FAA's. For an n-variable Boolean power function $Tr_1^n(\lambda x^k)$ with $1 \neq \lambda \in \mathbb{F}_{2^n}$, in order to compute its immunity, by using the generic method of determining the immunity of Boolean functions against FAA's we may need the arithmetic in $\mathbb{F}_{2^n}$, which is available but not computationally efficient compared with the operations over $\mathbb{F}_2$.[1] Alternatively, we need to compute the algebraic normal form of the Boolean power function firstly, and then we can determine its immunity through the operations over $\mathbb{F}_2$, which is also inconvenient.

In this paper, we show that the linear (affine) invariance of the immunity of Boolean functions against FAA's can exploited to compute more efficiently the immunity of some Boolean power functions against FAA's. We give the fact that the immunity of Boolean power function $Tr_1^n(\lambda x^k)$ is the same as that of $Tr_1^n(x^k)$ if $\lambda = \beta^k$ and $\beta \in \mathbb{F}_{2^n}$. In particular, if $\gcd(k, 2^n - 1) = 1$ then the immunity against FAA's of $f(x)$ and that of $r(x)$ are always the same. We show that Niho functions satisfy the co-prime condition, and verify that a large number of odd variables Kasami functions also satisfy the co-prime condition. We give two classes of Boolean power functions with sub-almost optimal immunity, which are selected at an example from our experimental results. Furthermore, the sufficient condition can also be applied to the (standard) algebraic immunity

---

[1] For instance, basic matrix arithmetic operations over $\mathbb{F}_{2^n}$ are supported in Number Theory Library (NTL, a C++ library for doing number theory). One can verify on a personal computer that it takes about one minute to compute the determinant of a random square matrix of order 2000 over $\mathbb{F}_{2^{14}}$. But for a random square matrix of the same size over $\mathbb{F}_2$ it takes only 0.027 s.

of Boolean power functions because of the relation between the (standard) algebraic immunity and the immunity against FAA's.

2   Preliminaries

An n-variable Boolean function f can be viewed as a mapping from vector space $\mathbb{F}_2^n$ to binary field $\mathbb{F}_2$. We denote by $\mathbb{B}_n$ the set of all the n-variable Boolean functions. Let $\mathbb{F}_{2^n}$ be the finite field with 2^n elements. By identifying the finite field $\mathbb{F}_{2^n}$ with the vector space $\mathbb{F}_2^n$, an n-variable Boolean function is also a univariate polynomial over $\mathbb{F}_{2^n}$:

$$f(x) = \sum_{i=0}^{2^n-1} f_i x^i,$$

where $f_0, f_{2^n-1} \in \mathbb{F}_2$ and $f_{2i} = (f_i)^2 \in \mathbb{F}_{2^n}$ for $1 \leq i \leq 2^n - 2$. The *algebraic degree* of Boolean function f, denoted by $\deg(f)$, is given by the largest integer $d = wt_2(i)$ such that $f_i \neq 0$, where $wt_2(i)$ is the number of nonzero coefficients in the binary representation of i.

Let m be a divisor of n. A trace function $Tr : \mathbb{F}_{2^n} \mapsto \mathbb{F}_{2^m}$, is given by $Tr_m^n(x) = \sum_{i=0}^{n/m-1} x^{2^m \cdot i}$ where $x \in \mathbb{F}_{2^n}$. A cyclotomic coset C_k modulo $2^n - 1$ is defined as $C_k = \{k, k \cdot 2, \cdots, k \cdot 2^{n_k-1}\}$, where k is the coset leader of C_k and n_k is the smallest integer such that $k = k \cdot 2^{n_k}(\mathrm{mod}\, 2^n - 1)$, i.e., the size of the cyclotomic coset C_k.

We denote by $\Gamma(n)$ the set of all coset leaders modulo $2^n - 1$. An n-variable Boolean function f can also be written as a binary sum of trace functions:

$$f(x) = \sum_{k \in \Gamma(n)} Tr_1^{n_k}(f_k x^k) + f_{2^n-1} x^{2^n-1}, \quad f_k \in \mathbb{F}_{2^n}, f_{2^n-1} \in \mathbb{F}_2.$$

In particular, an n-variable *Boolean power function* is represented by a monomial or single trace function, i.e., $f(x) = Tr_1^{n_k}(f_k x^k)$ for some coset leader k. By convention, $f(x) = Tr_1^{n_k}(f_k x^k)$ is often written as $f(x) = Tr_1^n(f_k x^k)$ when $n_k = n$ or n/n_k is an odd integer.

A Boolean function $g \in \mathbb{B}_n$ is called an *annihilator* of $f \in \mathbb{B}_n$ if $fg = 0$. The lowest algebraic degree of all the nonzero annihilators of f and $1 + f$ is called *algebraic immunity* of f or $1 + f$, denoted by $\mathcal{AI}_n(f)$, and it has been proved that $\mathcal{AI}_n(f) \leq \lceil \frac{n}{2} \rceil$ for a given $f \in \mathbb{B}_n$ [1]. A Boolean function $f \in \mathbb{B}_n$ has the *maximum algebraic immunity* if $\mathcal{AI}_n(f) = \lceil \frac{n}{2} \rceil$.

Boolean functions with large algebraic immunity (even the maximum $\mathcal{AI}$) may not resist fast algebraic attacks (FAA's). The study shows that the attacker may launch a fast algebraic attack if for an n-variable Boolean function f there exists n-variable Boolean function g of low degree ($< n/2$) such that $fg \neq 0$ has not high degree with respect to n. The attack can be converted into solving an over-defined system with multivariate equations of degree not more than the degree of g and the complexity of establishing the over-defined system is mainly determined by the degree of fg [1,5]. Moreover, one can use the fast general attack by splitting the function into two $f = h + l$ with l being the linear part of f [5]. In this case, function g can be considered as the nonzero constant.

In order to resist FAA's, we hope that the degree of fg can be large for any nonzero n-variable Boolean function g of low degree ($< n/2$). In other words, the immunity of an n-variable Boolean function f against FAA's is determined by the minimum algebraic degree of $\deg(fg)$ where the minimum is taken over all nonzero n-variable Boolean function g of degree at most e and $1 \le e < n/2$.

However, an observation given by N. Courtois [5] reveals that there always exists a nonzero n-variable Boolean function g of degree at most e such that $\deg(fg) \le n - e$. It implies an upper bound on the maximum immunity against FAA's. The best case for us against FAA's is that $\deg(fg) \ge d$ holds for any nonzero n-variable Boolean function g of degree at most e, where $d = n - e$ and $1 \le e < n/2$. And $d = n - e - 1, n - e - 2$ can also be considered as good cases against FAA's. Therefore, if $\deg(fg) \ge n - e$ holds for any nonzero n-variable Boolean function g of degree at most e and any positive integer $e < n/2$, then we say that f has the *optimal immunity against FAA's*.

In [10] Boolean functions with the optimal immunity against FAA's are also said to be perfect algebraic immune functions. M. Liu et al. further proved that an n-variable Boolean function has the optimal immunity against FAA's only if $n = 2^s$ or $n = 2^s + 1$ with positive integer s [10]. They showed that $\deg(fg) \ge n - e$ may never hold for some n and e. In this case, we can determine whether $\deg(fg) \ge n - e - 1$ holds [9,12]. By convention, f is called a function with *almost optimal* immunity against FAA's if $\deg(fg) \ge n - e - 1$ holds for any nonzero n-variable Boolean function g of degree at most e and any positive integer $e < n/2$.

Similarly, in this paper, we say that f is a function with *sub-almost optimal* immunity against FAA's if $\deg(fg) \ge n - e - 2$ holds for any nonzero n-variable Boolean function g of degree at most e and any positive integer $e < n/2$.

Definition 1. *An n-variable Boolean function f has the optimal (resp. almost optimal, sub-almost optimal) immunity against FAA's if $\deg(fg) \ge n - e$ (resp. $\deg(fg) \ge n - e - 1$, $\deg(fg) \ge n - e - 2$) for any nonzero n-variable Boolean function g of degree at most e and for any positive integer $e < n/2$.*

3   Determining the Immunity of Boolean Functions

In this section, we recall the generic method of determining the immunity of Boolean functions against FAA's, which was used by M. Liu et al. in [10], and also discuss the relation between the (standard) algebraic immunity and the immunity of Boolean functions against FAA's.

Denote by $\mathcal{W}_e$ the integer set $\{x \mid 0 \le x \le 2^n - 1, \, wt_2(x) \le e\}$ and by $\overline{\mathcal{W}}_d$ the integer set $\{x \mid 0 \le x \le 2^n - 1, \, wt_2(x) \ge d + 1\}$ where $1 \le e < \lceil \frac{n}{2} \rceil$ and $d < n$. We also need to define the orderings of the integers in $\mathcal{W}_e$ and $\overline{\mathcal{W}}_d$ respectively. For example, the elements in $\mathcal{W}_e$ are lexicographically ordered, while those in $\overline{\mathcal{W}}_d$ are reverse-lexicographically ordered. But they do not essentially affect the results on the immunity of Boolean power functions in this paper.

Let f, g, h be n-variable Boolean functions and g be a Boolean function of algebraic degree at most e satisfying that $h = fg$ has algebraic degree at most d. Let $f(x) = \sum_{k=0}^{2^n-1} f_k x^k$ ($f_k \in \mathbb{F}_{2^n}$) and $h(x) = \sum_{y=0}^{2^n-1} h_y x^y$ ($h_y \in \mathbb{F}_{2^n}$) be the univariate polynomial representations of f and h respectively. Function g of degree at most e can be represented as

$$g(x) = \sum_{z \in \mathcal{W}_e} g_z x^z, \ g_z \in \mathbb{F}_{2^n}.$$

The algebraic degree of $h = fg$ is at most d. For $y \in \overline{\mathcal{W}}_d$ we have $h_y = 0$ and thus

$$0 = h_y = \sum_{\substack{k+z=y \\ z \in \mathcal{W}_e}} f_k g_z = \sum_{z \in \mathcal{W}_e} f_{y-z} g_z,$$

where operation '$-$' is regarded as the substraction modulo $2^n - 1$. These equations on g_z's are a homogeneous linear system with $\sum_{i=d+1}^{n} \binom{n}{i}$ equations and $\sum_{i=0}^{e} \binom{n}{i}$ unknowns. Denote by

$$U(f; e, d)$$

the coefficient matrix of these equations related to the Boolean funciton f, which is a $\sum_{i=d+1}^{n} \times \sum_{i=0}^{e} \binom{n}{i}$ matrix with ij-th element equal to $u_{yz} = f_{y-z}$, where y is the i-th element in $\overline{\mathcal{W}}_d$ and z is j-th element in $\mathcal{W}_e$.

It is not hard to see and was also shown in [7,10] that there exists no nonzero function g of degree at most e such that the product gh has degree at most d if and only if matrix $U(f; e, d)$ has full column rank. This means that $\deg(fg) \geq d + 1$ if and only if matrix $U(f; e, d)$ has full column rank. Therefore, one can determine optimal (almost optimal or sub-almost optimal) immunity by computing the rank of $U(f; e, n - e - 1)$, $U(f; e, n - e - 2)$ or $U(f; e, n - e - 3)$ for all possible integer e.

The method of determining the immunity against FAA's can also be used to describe the relation between the (standard) algebraic immunity and the immunity of Boolean functions against FAA's. With above notations, let f be n-variable Boolean functions and g be a Boolean function of algebraic degree at most e. If $fg = 0$ we have

$$h_y = \sum_{\substack{k+z=y \\ z \in \mathcal{W}_e}} f_k g_z = \sum_{z \in \mathcal{W}_e} f_{y-z} g_z = 0$$

for $0 \leq y \leq 2^n - 1$. This is a homogeneous linear system with 2^n equations and $\sum_{i=0}^{e} \binom{n}{i}$ unknowns. Denote by $V(f; e)$ the coefficient matrix, which is a $2^n \times \sum_{i=0}^{e} \binom{n}{i}$ matrix with ij-th element equal to $u_{yz} = f_{y-z}$ where y is the i-th element in $\{x \mid 0 \leq x \leq 2^n - 1\}$ and z is j-th element in $\mathcal{W}_e$. There exists no nonzero function g of degree at most e such that $fg = 0$ if and only if matrix $V(f; e)$ has full column rank.

Proposition 1. *Let f be an n-variable Boolean function such that $U(f; e, d)$ has full column rank, i.e., $\deg(fg) \geq d + 1$ for any nonzero n-variable Boolean function g of degree at most e, where $1 \leq e < \lceil \frac{n}{2} \rceil$ and $e \leq d < n$, then the algebraic immunity of f is at least $e + 1$.*

Proof. We use a proof by contradiction. Matrix $U(f; e, d)$ has full column rank. Suppose that the algebraic immunity of f is not more than e. If there exists an n-variable Boolean function g of degree at most e such that $fg = 0$, then we have $V(f; e)$ not having full column rank. Since $U(f; e, d)$ can be obtained from $V(f; e)$ by removing some rows it follows that $U(f; e, d)$ is not of full column rank, which is contradictory. If there exists an n-variable Boolean function h of degree at most e such that $(1 + f)h = 0$, i.e., $fh = h$. Since $d \geq e$ it follows that $U(f, e, d)$ does not have full column rank, which also leads to contradiction. □

We take $e = \lceil \frac{n}{2} \rceil - 2$ and $d = n - e - 3$. Then $n - e - 3 \geq e$. If $U(f; e, n - e - 3)$ has full column rank, by Proposition 1, the algebraic immunity of f is at least $\lceil \frac{n}{2} \rceil - 1$.

Corollary 1. *If f is an n-variable Boolean function with sub-almost optimal immunity against FAA's, then $\mathcal{AI}_n(f) \geq \lceil \frac{n}{2} \rceil - 1$.*

Similarly, we take $e = \lceil \frac{n}{2} \rceil - 1$ and $d = n - e - 1$. The inequality $n - e - 1 \geq e$ also holds. Then we have the following result, which has been well-known. It is considered here as a corollary of Proposition 1.

Corollary 2. *If f is an n-variable Boolean function with optimal immunity against FAA's, then $\mathcal{AI}_n(f) = \lceil \frac{n}{2} \rceil$.*

4   The Immunity of Boolean Power Functions

For n-variable Boolean power function $f(x) = Tr_1^{n_k}(f_k x^k)$ with $k \in \Gamma(n)$, the entries of matrix $U(f; e, d)$ are in $\mathbb{F}_{2^n}$ and to compute its column rank, $\mathrm{rank}(U(f; e, d))$, is not computationally efficient. In this section, we show that linear (affine) invariance of the immunity of Boolean functions against FAA's can exploited to determine the the the immunity of Boolean power functions against FAA's, i.e., the immunity of $f(x) = Tr_1^{n_k}(f_k x^k)$ against FAA's is the same as that of $r(x) = Tr_1^{n_k}(x^k)$ if there exists a linear relation between the two functions. Since $U(r; e, d)$ is a matrix over $\mathbb{F}_2$ its column rank can be determined more efficiently.

Consider n-variable Boolean functions with the univariate polynomial representation over $\mathbb{F}_{2^n}$. Let $\mathcal{L}(x) = \lambda x$ with $0 \neq \lambda \in \mathbb{F}_{2^n}$ be a non-singular linear transformation of variable x. Because of the linear (affine) invariance of the algebraic degree, we have $\deg(f(x)g(x)) = \deg(f(\mathcal{L}(x))g(\mathcal{L}(x)))$. If $\deg(f(x)g(x)) \geq d$ for any nonzero n-variable Boolean function g of degree at most e and $1 \leq e < n/2$, then $\deg(f(\mathcal{L}(x))g(\mathcal{L}(x))) \geq d$ for any nonzero n-variable Boolean function $g(\mathcal{L}(x)) = g(\lambda x)$ of degree at most e. Furthermore, for a given $\lambda \neq 0$,

$$\{g(x) \,|\, g(x) \in \mathbb{B}_n, \deg(g) \leq e\} = \{g(\lambda x) \,|\, g(x) \in \mathbb{B}_n, \deg(g) \leq e\}.$$

Therefore, in this case, $\deg(f(\mathcal{L}(x)g(x)) \geq d$ for any nonzero n-variable Boolean function g of degree at most e and $1 \leq e < n/2$.

Given an n-variable Boolean power function $f(x) = Tr_1^{n_k}(f_k x^k)$ with $f_k \in \mathbb{F}_{2^n}$ and $k \in \Gamma(n)$, if $f_k = \beta^k$ and $0 \neq \beta \in \mathbb{F}_{2^n}$, then $f(x)$ can be obtained from $r(x) = Tr_1^{n_k}(x^k)$ by a non-singular linear transformation $\mathcal{L}(x) = \beta x$, and their immunity against FAA's are the same.

Theorem 1. *Let $f(x) = Tr_1^{n_k}(f_k x^k)$ be an n-variable Boolean power function and $r(x) = Tr_1^{n_k}(x^k)$, where $f_k \in \mathbb{F}_{2^n}$ and n_k is the size of the cyclotomic coset C_k modulo $2^n - 1$. If $f_k = \beta^k$ and $0 \neq \beta \in \mathbb{F}_{2^n}$, then the immunity of $f(x)$ against FAA's is the same as that of $r(x)$.*

This fact can also be shown by using the generic method of determining the immunity of Boolean functions against FAA's described in Sect. 3. More precisely, for $f(x) = Tr_1^{n_k}(f_k x^k)$ and $r(x) = Tr_1^{n_k}(x^k)$, we show that $\mathrm{rank}(U(f; e, d))$ is equal to $\mathrm{rank}(U(r; e, d))$ if $f_k = \beta^k$ and $0 \neq \beta \in \mathbb{F}_{2^n}$.

Lemma 1. *For $m \geq n$, let $A = (a_{ij})_{m \times n}$ and $B = (b_{ij})_{m \times n}$ be $m \times n$ matrix with $a_{ij} = \beta_i \gamma_j b_{ij}$ and $\beta_i, \gamma_j \neq 0$ for $1 \leq i \leq m, 1 \leq j \leq n$. Then $\mathrm{rank}(A) = n$ if and only if $\mathrm{rank}(B) = n$.*

Proof. Denote by $\mathrm{diag}(x_1, x_2, \cdots, x_n)$ an $n \times n$ diagonal matrix with diagonal entries $x_1, x_2, \cdots, x_n$. Let

$$P = \mathrm{diag}(\beta_1, \beta_2, \cdots, \beta_m) \quad \text{and} \quad Q = \mathrm{diag}(\gamma_1, \gamma_2, \cdots, \gamma_n).$$

Then $\mathrm{rank}(A) = \mathrm{rank}(B)$ follows from $A = PBQ$. □

Theorem 2. *Let $f(x) = Tr_1^{n_k}(f_k x^k)$ be an n-variable Boolean power function and $r(x) = Tr_1^{n_k}(x^k)$, where $f_k \in \mathbb{F}_{2^n}$ and n_k is the size of the cyclotomic coset C_k modulo $2^n - 1$. If $f_k = \beta^k$ and $0 \neq \beta \in \mathbb{F}_{2^n}$, then $\mathrm{rank}(U(f; e, d)) = \mathrm{rank}(U(r; e, d))$.*

Proof. For $1 \leq i \leq \sum_{i=d+1}^{n} \binom{n}{i}$ and $1 \leq j \leq \sum_{i=0}^{e} \binom{n}{i}$, we denote by a_{ij} the ij-th element of $U(f; e, d)$ and by b_{ij} the ij-th element of $U(r; e, d)$. Only $f_k, f_{2k}, \cdots, f_{2^{n_k-1}k}$ are nonzero in the univariate polynomial representation of f. According to the definition of matrix $U(f; e, d)$ we have

$$a_{ij} = \begin{cases} f_{2^l k}, & \text{if } (y - z) = 2^l k \bmod (2^n - 1); \\ 0, & \text{otherwise.} \end{cases},$$

and

$$b_{ij} = \begin{cases} 1, & \text{if } (y - z) = 2^l k \bmod (2^n - 1); \\ 0, & \text{otherwise.} \end{cases},$$

where y is the i-th element in $\overline{\mathcal{W}}_d$, z is j-th element in $\mathcal{W}_e$ and $0 \leq l \leq n_k - 1$. Let $\beta_i = \beta^y$ and $\beta_j = \beta^{-z}$. If $(y - z) = 2^l k \bmod (2^n - 1)$ then

$$a_{ij} = f_{2^l k} = (f_k)^{2^l} = \beta^{2^l \cdot k} = \beta^{(y-z)} = \beta^y \cdot \beta^{-z} = \beta_i \gamma_j b_{ij},$$

otherwise $a_{ij} = \beta_i \gamma_j b_{ij} = 0$. It follows by Lemma 1 that $\mathrm{rank}(U(f; e, d)) = \mathrm{rank}(U(r; e, d))$. □

Note that $\lambda \in \mathbb{F}_{2^n}$ can be always written as the kth power of some element of $\mathbb{F}_{2^n}$, i.e., $\lambda = \beta^k$ and $\beta = \lambda^{k^{-1}(\bmod\ 2^n - 1)} \in \mathbb{F}_{2^n}$, if $\gcd(k, 2^n - 1) = 1$. Thus, we have the following corollary.

Corollary 3. *Let $f(x) = Tr_1^{n_k}(f_k x^k)$ be an n-variable Boolean power function and $r(x) = Tr_1^{n_k}(x^k)$, where $0 \neq f_k \in \mathbb{F}_{2^n}$ and n_k is the size of the cyclotomic coset C_k modulo $2^n - 1$. If $\gcd(k, 2^n - 1) = 1$ then the immunity of $f(x)$ against FAA's is the same as that of $r(x)$.*

Generally, let α be a primitive element of finite field $\mathbb{F}_{2^n}$. For $0 \leq i, j < 2^n - 1$ and coset leader $k \in \Gamma(n)$, if $(\alpha^i)^k = (\alpha^j)^k$ then $ik \equiv jk \bmod (2^n - 1)$. It follows that

$$i \equiv j \bmod \left(\frac{2^n - 1}{\gcd(k, 2^n - 1)} \right).$$

This implies

$$1, \alpha^k, (\alpha^2)^k, \cdots, (\alpha^{\frac{2^n - 1}{\gcd(k, 2^n - 1)} - 1})^k$$

are all nonzero elements that can be written as the kth power of some element in $\mathbb{F}_{2^n}$ with primitive element α.

Corollary 4. *Let $f(x) = Tr_1^{n_k}(f_k x^k)$ be an n-variable Boolean power function and $r(x) = Tr_1^{n_k}(x^k)$, where $0 \neq f_k \in \mathbb{F}_{2^n}$ and n_k is the size of the cyclotomic coset C_k modulo $2^n - 1$. If f_k is equal to one of element in*

$$\{(\alpha^i)^k \mid i = 0, 1, 2 \cdots, \frac{2^n - 1}{d} - 1\},$$

then the immunity against FAA's of $f(x)$ is the same as that of $r(x)$, where α is a primitive element of $\mathbb{F}_{2^n}$ and $d = \gcd(k, 2^n - 1)$.

Theorem 1 can be directly generalized to a small sub-class of Boolean functions with polynomial trace functions. The result may help us find a few of Boolean functions using the trace representation that have good resistance against FAA's.

Corollary 5. *Let Λ be a subset of $\Gamma(n)$,*

$$f(x) = \sum_{k \in \Lambda \subseteq \Gamma(n)} Tr_1^{n_k}(f_k x^k)$$

and $r(x) = \sum_{k \in \Lambda \subseteq \Gamma(n)} Tr_1^{n_k}(x^k)$ be two n-variable Boolean functions, where k is the coset leader and n_k is the size of the cyclotomic coset C_k modulo $2^n - 1$. If $f_k = \beta^k$ for each $k \in \Lambda$ and $0 \neq \beta \in \mathbb{F}_{2^n}$, then the immunity of $f(x)$ against FAA's is the same as that of $r(x)$.

Moreover, all the results mentioned above in this section can be applied to the (standard) algebraic immunity of n-variable Boolean power function $f(x) = Tr_1^{n_k}(f_k x^k)$ because of the linear (affine) invariance of the (standard) algebraic immunity of Boolean functions.

5   On Inverse Functions, Kasami Functions and Niho Functions

As the applications of Theorem 3, we consider three classes of Boolean power functions: inverse functions, Kasami functions and Niho functions. Let $\lambda \in \mathbb{F}_{2^n}$. An n-variable inverse function can be defined as $f(x) = Tr_1^n(\lambda x^{-1})$. An n-variable Kasami function can be written as $f(x) = Tr_1^n(\lambda x^{2^{2t}-2^t+1})$, where $1 \leq t \leq \lfloor n/2 \rfloor$ and $\gcd(t,n) = 1$. For odd integer $n = 2t + 1$, an n-variable Niho function can be defined as $Tr_1^n(\lambda x^{2^t+2^{\frac{t}{2}}-1})$ when t is even and $Tr_1^n(\lambda x^{2^t+2^{\frac{3t+1}{2}}-1})$ when t is odd.

For inverse functions, since $Tr_1^n(\lambda x^{-1}) = Tr_1^n(\lambda x^{2^n-2})$ and $\gcd(2^n - 2, 2^n - 1) = 1$, applying Corollary 3, one can directly see the fact that the (standard) algebraic immunity of $f(x) = Tr_1^n(\lambda x^{-1})$ is the same as that of $r(x) = Tr_1^n(x^{-1})$, which was also shown in [3]. Furthermore, the immunity of $f(x) = Tr_1^n(\lambda x^{-1})$ against FAA's is identical with that of $r(x) = Tr_1^n(x^{-1})$.

For Kasami functions, we did not find any Kasami function in odd n variables that does not satisfy the co-prime condition of Corollary 3 up to $n = 9999$. In fact, one can quickly check the (non-)coprimality by a computer.

On the contrary, unfortunately, all the Kasami functions in even variables can not satisfy the co-prime condition. This is because $2^{2t} - 2^t + 1 \equiv 2^n - 1 \equiv 0 \bmod 3$ if n is even and t is odd, i.e.,

$$\gcd(2^{2t} - 2^t + 1, 2^n - 1) = \gcd(2^{2t} - 2^t + 1, 2^{n-3t} + 1) \geq 3 \neq 1.$$

Hence, the result given by Corollary 4 can be applied to Kasami functions in even variables.

For Niho functions, we observe that an n-variable Niho function has always the same immunity as that of $Tr_1^n(x^{2^t+2^{\frac{t}{2}}-1})$ or $Tr_1^n(x^{2^t+2^{\frac{3t+1}{2}}-1})$ because of Propositions 2 and 3.

Proposition 2. *Let $n = 2t + 1$. If t is even then $\gcd(2^t + 2^{\frac{t}{2}} - 1, 2^n - 1) = 1$.*

Proof. It can be verified directly for $t \leq 8$. For even $t > 8$ applying the Euclidean algorithm, we have

$$\gcd(2^t + 2^{\frac{t}{2}} - 1, 2^n - 1) = \gcd(2^{\frac{t}{2}-1} - 9, 11).$$

Note that $\gcd(2^{\frac{t}{2}-1} - 9, 11) = 1$ if and only if $(2^{\frac{t}{2}-1}) \bmod 11 \neq 9$. But 2 to the power of any positive integer modulo 11 never results a number with factor 3. Therefore $(2^{\frac{t}{2}-1}) \bmod 11 \neq 9$ holds for any even $t > 8$.   □

Proposition 3. *Let $n = 2t + 1$. If t is odd then $\gcd(2^t + 2^{\frac{3t+1}{2}} - 1, 2^n - 1) = 1$.*

Proof. It can be verified directly for $t = 1$. For $t \geq 3$ applying the Euclidean algorithm, we have

$$\gcd(2^t + 2^{\frac{3t+1}{2}} - 1, 2^n - 1) = \gcd(2^t + 2^{\frac{t+1}{2}} - 2, 3 \cdot (2^{\frac{t+1}{2}} - 1)).$$

Since

$$\gcd(2^t + 2^{\frac{t+1}{2}} - 2, 2^{\frac{t+1}{2}} - 1) = \gcd(2^t - 1, 2^{\frac{t+1}{2}} - 1) = 2^{\gcd(t, \frac{t+1}{2})} - 1 = 1,$$

it follows that $\gcd(2^t + 2^{\frac{3t+1}{2}} - 1, 2^n - 1) = \gcd(2^t + 2^{\frac{t+1}{2}} - 2, 3)$. Note that $2^t \bmod 3 = 2$ and $2^{\frac{t+1}{2}} \bmod 3 = 1, 2$ for any odd t, which imply that $(2^t + 2^{\frac{t+1}{2}} - 2) \bmod 3 \neq 0$. Therefore, we have $\gcd(2^t + 2^{\frac{3t+1}{2}} - 1, 2^n - 1) = \gcd(2^t + 2^{\frac{t+1}{2}} - 2, 3) = 1$.   □

In 2013, with some new techniques of computing the (standard) algebraic immunity D.K. Dalai checked the (standard) algebraic immunities of n-variable Kasami function $Tr_1^n(x^{2^{2s} - 2^s + 1})$ and Niho function $Tr_1^n(x^{2^t + 2^{\frac{3t+1}{2}} - 1})$ for $n \leq 17$ and $n \leq 19$ respectively[2], where s is the largest integer such that $\gcd(s, n) = 1$ and $n = 2t + 1$ [6]. By Proposition 3, Dalai's experimental results is also applicable to odd n-variable Kasami function $Tr_1^n(\lambda x^{2^{2s} - 2^s + 1})$ and Niho function $Tr_1^n(\lambda x^{2^t + 2^{\frac{3t+1}{2}} - 1})$, where $1 \neq \lambda \in \mathbb{F}_{2^n}$.

6   Experimental Results

Note that the complexity of establishing matrix $U(r; e, d)$ directly is about $\mathcal{O}(\sum_{i=d+1}^n \binom{n}{i} \cdot \sum_{i=0}^e \binom{n}{i})$, which may still be large. Algorithm 1 can speed up the process of obtaining the matrix $U(r; e, d)$. The complexity decreases to

$$\mathcal{O}(n \cdot \sum_{i=d+1}^n \binom{n}{i}).$$

It is not hard to see the correctness of Algorithm 1. Only $r_k, r_{2k}, \cdots, r_{2^{n_k - 1}k}$ are nonzero in the univariate polynomial representation of r, where n_k is the size of the cyclotomic coset C_k modulo $2^n - 1$. According to the definition of matrix $U(r; e, d)$ we have

$$u_{ij} = u_{yz} = \begin{cases} 1, \text{ if } (y - z) = 2^c k \bmod (2^n - 1) \\ 0, \text{ otherwise} \end{cases},$$

where y is the i-th element in $\overline{\mathcal{W}}_d$, z is j-th element in $\mathcal{W}_e$ and $0 \leq c \leq n_k - 1$. If $(y - z) \bmod (2^n - 1) = k$, then $(y - k) \bmod (2^n - 1)$ must be in $\mathcal{RS}$ and step 05 of the algorithm will set u_{yz} to be 1. If $(y - z) \bmod (2^n - 1) = 2^c k$ with some positive integer c, then the while loop will set u_{yz} to be 1.

By the way, one should note a simple fact that Boolean functions with good immunity against FAA's should have large enough algebraic degree.

---

[2] In fact, he checked the *component algebraic immunities* of vectorial (multi-output) Kasami function $x^{2^{2s} - 2^s + 1}$ and Niho function $x^{2^t + 2^{\frac{3t+1}{2}} - 1}$, which are not more than the algebraic immunities of these functions as (single-output) Boolean functions.

Proposition 4. *Let* $f \in \mathbb{B}_n$. *If* $\deg(fg) \geq n - e - \delta$ *holds for any nonzero n-variable Boolean function g of degree at most e and every positive integer e less than* $n/2$, *where* $0 \leq \delta < n/2$, *then* $\deg(f) \geq n - \delta - 1$.

Proof. In particular, $\deg(fg) \geq n - e - \delta$ holds for $g = 1$. Then we have $\deg(f) = \deg(fg) \geq n - e - \delta$. This inequality still holds when $e = 1$, thus we get $\deg(f) \geq n - \delta - 1$. ☐

With the notations in Proposition 4, when $\delta = 2$, it is clear that if Boolean function f admits sub-almost optimal immunity against FAA's, then its algebraic degree must be not less than $n - 3$. This means that we only need to check the functions whose algebraic degrees are $n - 3$ at least if we want to search some Boolean functions with the sub-almost optimal immunity in practice.

Algorithm 1. [Establishing matrix $U(r; e, d)$ with $r(x) = Tr_1^{n_k}(x^k)$]

Initialize: $\overline{\mathcal{W}}_d$, $U(r; e, d) = \{0\}_{\sum_{i=d+1}^n \binom{n}{i} \times \sum_{i=0}^e \binom{n}{i}}$
01: $\mathcal{RS} \leftarrow (\overline{\mathcal{W}}_d - k) \bmod (2^n - 1)$
02: **for** i from 1 to $\sum_{i=d+1}^n \binom{n}{i}$ **do**
03:     $y \leftarrow$ the i-th element in $\overline{\mathcal{W}}_d$, $z \leftarrow$ the i-th element in $\mathcal{RS}$
04:     **if** $wt_2(z) > e$ **then** continue **else**
05:         $u_{yz} \leftarrow 1$
06:         $y_0 \leftarrow y$, $z_0 \leftarrow z$, $y \leftarrow 2 \cdot y_0 \bmod (2^n - 1)$, $z \leftarrow 2 \cdot z_0 \bmod (2^n - 1)$
07:         **while**($y \neq y_0$ or $z \neq z_0$)
08:             $u_{yz} \leftarrow 1$, $y \leftarrow 2 \cdot y \bmod (2^n - 1)$, $z \leftarrow 2 \cdot z \bmod (2^n - 1)$
09:         **end while**
10:     **end if**
11: **end for**

For all the functions $r(x) = Tr_1^{n_k}(x^k)$ with $k \in \Gamma(n)$ and $n \leq 15$ we compute rank($U(r; e, n - e - 2)$) and rank($U(r; e, n - e - 3)$) for each $e = 1, 2, \cdots, \lceil \frac{n}{2} \rceil - 1$ on a laptop computer (Intel Core i7-6820hq at 2.7Ghz, 8GB RAM, Ubuntu 16.04) by using NTL. For Boolean power functions that satisfy the condition in Theorem 1, our experimental results show that the majority of these functions except those of small variables are *not* almost optimal against FAA's, but some of them are sub-almost optimal against FAA's.

Although one may see the fact that some Boolean power functions such as inverse functions, Kasami functions and Niho functions are not the functions with good immunity against FAA's directly from their upper bound on (standard) algebraic immunity given in [11], our results provide more information on the immunity of some Boolean power functions.

For example, for Boolean power functions in 14 and 15 variables, we find in our experimental results that $Tr_1^{14}(x^{4091})$ and $Tr_1^{15}(x^{12279})$ are the functions with sub-almost optimal immunity against FAA's. Furthermore, since 4091 is co-prime to $2^{14} - 1$ and 12279 is co-prime to $2^{15} - 1$, by Corollary 3, all the

Boolean power functions $Tr_1^{14}(\lambda x^{4091})$ with $0 \neq \lambda \in \mathbb{F}_{2^{14}}$ and $Tr_1^{15}(\lambda x^{12279})$ with $0 \neq \lambda \in \mathbb{F}_{2^{15}}$ have sub-almost optimal immunity against FAA's. By Corollary 1, their algebraic immunity is at least 6 and 7 respectively.

The total time (in seconds used) of deciding the immunity of $Tr_1^{14}(x^{4091})$, including the time spent for establishing the matrices, is about 3.7 s, and that of $Tr_1^{15}(x^{12279})$ is about 33.3 s on our computer. In contrast, choosing a random element $0 \neq \lambda \in \mathbb{F}_{2^{14}}$, we tried to determine the immunity of $Tr_1^{14}(\lambda x^{4091})$ by computing the ranks of the matrices over $\mathbb{F}_{2^{14}}$. The process of establishing these matrices was also fast due to Algorithm 1 (an adapted version), but the computation was aborted by NTL after 528.112 s probably because there was insufficient memory available to complete the computation.

7   Conclusion

In this paper, we discuss the relation between the immunity of Boolean power function $f(x) = Tr_1^n(\lambda x^k)$ against FAA's and that of its reduced function $r(x) = Tr_1^n(x^k)$, where $0 \neq \lambda \in \mathbb{F}_{2^n}$. We show that the immunity of $f(x) = Tr_1^n(\lambda x^k)$ against FAA's is the same as that of $r(x) = Tr_1^n(x^k)$ if $f(x)$ can be derived from $r(x)$ through a linear transformation. This may help us compute the immunity against FAA's as well as the (standard) algebraic immunity of some Boolean power functions more efficiently. We also provide an algorithm that can speed up computing the immunity of the reduced function $r(x) = Tr_1^{n_k}(x^k)$.

References

1. Armknecht, F.: Improving fast algebraic attacks. In: Roy, B., Meier, W. (eds.) FSE 2004. LNCS, vol. 3017, pp. 65–82. Springer, Heidelberg (2004). doi:10.1007/978-3-540-25937-4_5
2. Armknecht, F., Carlet, C., Gaborit, P., Künzli, S., Meier, W., Ruatta, O.: Efficient computation of algebraic immunity for algebraic and fast algebraic attacks. In: Vaudenay, S. (ed.) EUROCRYPT 2006. LNCS, vol. 4004, pp. 147–164. Springer, Heidelberg (2006). doi:10.1007/11761679_10
3. Baev, V.V.: Some lower bounds on the algebraic immunity of functions given by their trace forms. Problemy Peredachi Informatsii **44**(3), 81–104 (2008)
4. Carlet, C., Feng, K.: An infinite class of balanced functions with optimal algebraic immunity, good immunity to fast algebraic attacks and good nonlinearity. In: Pieprzyk, J. (ed.) ASIACRYPT 2008. LNCS, vol. 5350, pp. 425–440. Springer, Heidelberg (2008). doi:10.1007/978-3-540-89255-7_26
5. Courtois, N.T.: Fast algebraic attacks on stream ciphers with linear feedback. In: Boneh, D. (ed.) CRYPTO 2003. LNCS, vol. 2729, pp. 176–194. Springer, Heidelberg (2003). doi:10.1007/978-3-540-45146-4_11
6. Dalai, D.K.: Computing the rank of incidence matrix and algebraic immunity of boolean functions. IACR Cryptology ePrint Archive 2013, 273 (2013)
7. Du, Y., Zhang, F., Liu, M.: On the resistance of boolean functions against fast algebraic attacks. In: Kim, H. (ed.) ICISC 2011. LNCS, vol. 7259, pp. 261–274. Springer, Heidelberg (2012). doi:10.1007/978-3-642-31912-9_18

8. Feng, X., Gong, G.: On algebraic immunity of trace inverse functions on finite fields of characteristic two. J. Syst. Sci. Complexity **29**(1), 272–288 (2016)
9. Liu, M., Lin, D.: Almost perfect algebraic immune functions with good nonlinearity. In: 2014 IEEE International Symposium on Information Theory, pp. 1837–1841. IEEE (2014)
10. Liu, M., Zhang, Y., Lin, D.: Perfect algebraic immune functions. In: Wang, X., Sako, K. (eds.) ASIACRYPT 2012. LNCS, vol. 7658, pp. 172–189. Springer, Heidelberg (2012). doi:10.1007/978-3-642-34961-4_12
11. Nawaz, Y., Gong, G., Gupta, K.C.: Upper bounds on algebraic immunity of boolean power functions. In: International Workshop on Fast Software Encryption, pp. 375–389. Springer, Heidelberg (2006)
12. Pasalic, E.: Almost fully optimized infinite classes of boolean functions resistant to (fast) algebraic cryptanalysis. In: Lee, P.J., Cheon, J.H. (eds.) ICISC 2008. LNCS, vol. 5461, pp. 399–414. Springer, Heidelberg (2009). doi:10.1007/978-3-642-00730-9_25
13. Rizomiliotis, P.: On the resistance of boolean functions against algebraic attacks using univariate polynomial representation. IEEE Trans. Inf. Theor. **56**(8), 4014–4024 (2010)
14. Wang, W., Liu, M., Zhang, Y.: Comments on a design of boolean functions resistant to (fast) algebraic cryptanalysis with efficient implementation. Crypt. Commun. **5**(1), 1–6 (2013)

Improved Fault Analysis on the Block Cipher SPECK by Injecting Faults in the Same Round

Jingyi Feng[1,2], Hua Chen[1(✉)], Si Gao[1,2], Limin Fan[1], and Dengguo Feng[1]

[1] Trusted Computing and Information Assurance Laboratory,
Institute of Software, Chinese Academy of Sciences, Beijing 100190, China
{fengjingyi,chenhua,gaosi,fanlimin,feng}@tca.iscas.ac.cn
[2] University of Chinese Academy of Sciences, Beijing 100049, China

Abstract. SPECK is a new family of lightweight block ciphers proposed by the U.S. National Security Agency in 2013. So far, there exist several fault analysis results on this family. In this paper, we propose an improved fault analysis on SPECK under the random byte fault model, which only needs to induce faults at one intermediate round to retrieve the whole master key. In this attack, the fault propagation properties of SPECK are fully utilized, not only to determine the locations and the values of the faults, but also to eliminate incorrect candidates of the key. Moreover, compared with the previous approaches, more characteristics of the nonlinear modular addition operation are exploited, and the relations between different pairs of ciphertexts are also taken into account, which greatly enhance the efficiency of the key recovery. Finally, the experimental results confirm the correctness and the effectiveness of our proposed attack.

Keywords: Fault analysis · SPECK · Fault propagation · Modular addition

1 Introduction

Fault Analysis (FA) is an important cryptographic implementation attack originally proposed by Boneh *et al.* [1] in 1996 to break the RSA cryptosystem. Shortly after, Biham and Shamir [2] extended this attack with differential analysis, and called it Differential Fault Analysis (DFA). DFA is implemented by injecting faults into a cryptographic device and analysing the correct and faulty ciphertexts of the same plaintext to reveal the secret key. So far, fault analyses on many other ciphers including 3DES [3], AES [4–6], CLEFIA [7], ECC [8] and RC4 [9] have been proposed.

SPECK [10] is a new family of lightweight block ciphers proposed by the U.S. National Security Agency in 2013, which is optimized for software implementations. The family consists of 10 instances specified as SPECK2n/mn, where $n = 16$, 24, 32, 48 or 64, and $m = 2$, 3 or 4. SPECK2n/mn employs a Feistel-type structure with 2n-bit block size, mn-bit key size and T-round iterations.

S. Hong and J.H. Park (Eds.): ICISC 2016, LNCS 10157, pp. 317–332, 2017.
DOI: 10.1007/978-3-319-53177-9_17

The round function is built only with basic arithmetic operations including modular addition, XOR, and bit rotation. Since the publication of SPECK, a number of cryptanalysis results have been presented, such as differential analysis [11–13], linear analysis [14,15] and so on. Besides, implementation attacks like fault analyses [16,17] have also been published.

In FDTC 2014, Tupsamudre *et al.* proposed the first fault attack against SPECK [16], in which a one-bit-flip fault is induced into the input of the last round. Based on the basic information leakage of the modular addition operation, the attack recovers the n-bit last round key with at least $n/3$ pairs of correct and faulty ciphertexts. In FDTC 2015, the attack is improved by Huo *et al.* in two ways [17], under the condition that all the ciphertexts are encrypted with the same plaintext. The first attack assumes that a random n-bit fault is induced into the input of the last round. By transforming addition modulo 2^n into a second-order algebraic system of equations, the attacker can recover the last round key with the Gröbner bases algorithm from about $5 \sim 8$ faulty ciphertexts. The second attack is based on the chosen-value fault model, which requires 4 specific faults to recover the round key. To the best of our knowledge, in order to recover the mn-bit master key of SPECK, all the existing attacks require to induce several faults into the last m rounds to reveal the corresponding round keys.

Our contributions. In this paper, we propose a new fault attack against SPECK under the practical random byte fault model. To retrieve the entire mn-bit master key of SPECK, the attacker only needs to induce faults at one intermediate round, such as the $(T - m)$-th round, as long as the full diffusion of the fault has not been reached until the last round. In this attack, the fault propagation and fault inheritance properties are fully utilized to deduce the location of the injection and the values of the faults. Compared with the previous works, more characteristics of the nonlinear modular addition operation are exploited in the key recovery, and the relations between different pairs of ciphertexts are also applied, which significantly reduce the number of the fault injections. Furthermore, based on the location of fault, an effective filtering rule is proposed to distinguish the non-conforming intermediates and exclude the corresponding candidates of the key. Finally, we conduct experiments to confirm the correctness and the effectiveness of the attack. In addition to posing a threat to SPECK, the proposed techniques can also contribute to the study of fault analysis on other cryptographic primitives using the modular addition operations for non-linear functions.

This paper is organized as follows. After describing the family of SPECK in Sect. 2, we present some useful properties of the algorithm applied in the attack in Sect. 3. In Sect. 4, we demonstrate the improved fault attack on SPECK, and provide the corresponding computation verification. Finally, we give our conclusion in Sect. 5.

2   Preliminaries

2.1   Notations

n, m, T: word size, key word size, and the number of rounds in SPECK
K^i: the i-th round key
(X^i, Y^i): the input state of the i-th round encryption
x_j: the j-th least significant bit of x
$\tilde{x}$: the faulty version of variable x
Δx: the bitwise difference $x \oplus x'$
$\oplus$, $\odot$: bitwise XOR operation, and bitwise AND operation
$\boxplus$, $\boxminus$: addition modulo 2^n, and substraction modulo 2^n
$\ggg$, $\lll$: circular right rotation operation, and circular left rotation operation
$||$: concatenation operation

2.2   Description of SPECK

SPECK is a family of lightweight block ciphers consisting of ten instances. The instance SPECK2n/mn employs a Feistel structure with 2n-bit block size and mn-bit key size, where n can be taken 16, 24, 32, 48 or 64, and m can be taken 2, 3 or 4. The instances are also different in the number of iteration rounds T and the rotation constants (α, β). Parameters for all versions of SPECK are specified in Table 1.

Table 1. SPECK parameters

SPECK2n/mn	Word size n	Key words m	Rounds T	α	β
32/64	16	4	22	7	2
48/72	24	3	22	8	3
48/96	24	4	23	8	3
64/96	32	3	26	8	3
64/128	32	4	27	8	3
96/96	48	2	28	8	3
96/144	48	3	29	8	3
128/128	64	2	32	8	3
128/192	64	3	33	8	3
128/256	64	4	34	8	3

The encryption procedure works as follows.

1. Let $P = X^0||Y^0$ denote the 2n-bit plaintext.
2. For $i = 0, \ldots, T-1$, $X^{i+1} = ((X^i \ggg \alpha) \boxplus Y^i) \oplus K^i$, $Y^{i+1} = X^{i+1} \oplus (Y^i \lll \beta)$.
3. Output $C = X^T||Y^T$ denotes the 2n-bit ciphertext.

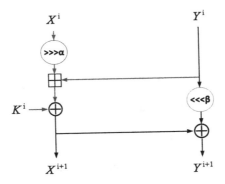

Fig. 1. The round function of SPECK

Fig. 1 illustrates the single round function of SPECK.

The key schedule of SPECK2n/mn employs the similar round function and generates the round key words $(K^0, \ldots, K^{T-1})$ as follows.

1. Let $K = (L^{m-2}, \ldots, L^0, K^0)$ denote the mn-bit master key.
2. For $i = 0, \ldots, T-2$, $L^{i+m-1} = (L^i \ggg \alpha) \boxplus K^i) \oplus i$, $K^{i+1} = L^{i+m-1} \oplus (K^i \lll \beta)$.

3 Characteristics of SPECK

This section demonstrates some characteristics of SPECK that are helpful in the following fault analysis. To simplify the description, the symbol $mod\,n$ in the subscript is omitted in the rest of the paper. For example, we refer to $X^i_{j\,mod\,n}$ as X^i_j.

3.1 Characteristics of the $\boxplus$ Operation

In this subsection, we focus on the input and output differences of the non-linear modular addition operation $\boxplus$ in order to retrieve the round key.

Take (X^i, Y^i) and (X^{i+1}, Y^{i+1}) as the i-th round input and output of SPECK. $K^i = (K^i_{n-1} \ldots K^i_0)$ is the round key, where the subscript 0 indicates the index of the least significant bit. Since $X^{i+1} = ((X^i \ggg \alpha) \boxplus Y^i) \oplus K^i$, the j-th $(0 \leq j \leq n-1)$ bit of K^i is computed as,

$$K^i_j = X^{i+1}_j \oplus X^i_{j+\alpha} \oplus Y^i_j \oplus c^i_j \tag{1}$$

where c^i_j is the carry bit in $\boxplus$ operation, and $c^i_0 = 0$,

$$c^i_{j+1} = (X^i_{j+\alpha} \odot Y^i_j) \oplus (X^i_{j+\alpha} \odot c^i_j) \oplus (Y^i_j \odot c^i_j), \tag{2}$$

Table 2 details the relationship among $X^i_{j+\alpha}$, Y^i_j, c^i_j, c^i_{j+1} and K^i_j.

Table 2. The relationship among $X^i_{j+\alpha}$, Y^i_j, c^i_j, c^i_{j+1} and K^i_j

$X^i_{j+\alpha}$	Y^i_j	c^i_j	c^i_{j+1}	K^i_j
0	0	0	0	X^{i+1}_j
0	0	1	0	$X^{i+1}_j \oplus 1$
0	1	0	0	$X^{i+1}_j \oplus 1$
0	1	1	1	X^{i+1}_j
1	0	0	0	$X^{i+1}_j \oplus 1$
1	0	1	1	X^{i+1}_j
1	1	0	1	X^{i+1}_j
1	1	1	1	$X^{i+1}_j \oplus 1$

Consider the case that a fault is induced into the round input, which turns (X^i, Y^i) into $(\tilde{X}^i, \tilde{Y}^i) = (X^i, Y^i) \oplus (\Delta X^i, \Delta Y^i)$ and leads to corresponding changes in carry bits and round output. Suppose (X^{i+1}, Y^{i+1}) and $(\tilde{X}^{i+1}, \tilde{Y}^{i+1})$, which denote the correct and faulty round outputs, respectively, are known to the adversary, then Y^i_j, $\tilde{Y}^i_j$ and ΔY^i_j could be directly worked out as,

$$Y^i_j = ((X^{i+1} \oplus Y^{i+1}) \ggg \beta)_j, \quad \tilde{Y}^i_j = ((\tilde{X}^{i+1} \oplus \tilde{Y}^{i+1}) \ggg \beta)_j \tag{3}$$

$$\Delta Y^i_j = Y^i_j \oplus \tilde{Y}^i_j \tag{4}$$

Moreover, if the value of $\Delta X^i_{j+\alpha}$ is known, Δc^i_j can be recovered as,

$$\Delta c^i_j = \Delta X^i_{j+\alpha} \oplus \Delta Y^i_j \oplus \Delta X^{i+1}_j, \quad \Delta c^i_0 = 0 \tag{5}$$

With the method above, the combination of $(\Delta X^i_{j+\alpha}, \Delta Y^i_j, \Delta c^i_j, \Delta c^i_{j+1})$ can be figured out bit by bit. We enumerate all 14 types of logical combinations in Table 3, and denote them as Type0, Type1, ..., TypeD. Besides, we summarize the equivalent expressions of c^i_j, c^i_{j+1} and K^i_j according to Table 2. For example, if $(\Delta X^i_{j+\alpha}, \Delta Y^i_j, \Delta c^i_j, \Delta c^i_{j+1}) = (0010)$, then the value of $((X^i_{j+\alpha}, Y^i_j, c^i_j, c^i_{j+1}),$ $(\tilde{X}^i_{j+\alpha}, \tilde{Y}^i_j, \tilde{c}^i_j, \tilde{c}^i_{j+1}))$ must be taken from $\{((0000), (0010)), ((0010), (0000)),$ $((1101), (1111)), ((1111), (1101))\}$. And it can be induced that $c^i_{j+1} = Y^i_j$ and $c^i_j \oplus K^i_j = X^{i+1}_j$.

So far, we are able to determine the secret information about carry bits and round key bits from the round outputs, and we sum it up in Property 1.

Property 1. Given a pair of correct and faulty round outputs denoted as (X^{i+1}, Y^{i+1}) and $(\tilde{X}^{i+1}, \tilde{Y}^{i+1})$. There are several ways to recover K^i_j $(0 \leq j < n-1)$.

(i) **Straightforward recovery of K^i_j [16]:** If the combination of $(\Delta X^i_{j+\alpha}, \Delta Y^i_j, \Delta c^i_j, \Delta c^i_{j+1})$ belongs to Type3/4/9/A, K^i_j can be directly retrieved with X^{i+1}_j and Y^i_j.

Table 3. $(\Delta X^i_{j+\alpha}, \Delta Y^i_j, \Delta c^i_j, \Delta c^i_{j+1})$ and corresponding expressions of c^i_j, c^i_{j+1} and K^i_j

$(\Delta X^i_{j+\alpha}, \Delta Y^i_j, \Delta c^i_j, \Delta c^i_{j+1})$	ΔX^{i+1}_j	c^i_j	c^i_{j+1}	K^i_j
Type0: (0000)	0	-	-	-
Type1: (0010)	1	-	Y^i_j	$X^{i+1}_j \oplus c^i_j$
Type2: (0011)	1	c^i_{j+1}	c^i_j	$X^{i+1}_j \oplus c^i_j \oplus 1$ or $X^{i+1}_j \oplus c^i_{j+1} \oplus 1$
Type3: (0100)	1	c^i_{j+1}	c^i_j	$X^{i+1}_j \oplus Y^i_j$
Type4: (0101)	1	-	Y^i_j	$X^{i+1}_j \oplus Y^i_j \oplus 1$
Type5: (0110)	0	$1 \oplus Y^i_j$	-	$X^{i+1}_j \oplus c^i_{j+1} \oplus 1$
Type6: (0111)	0	Y^i_j	Y^i_j	-
Type7: (1000)	1	Y^i_j	Y^i_j	-
Type8: (1001)	1	$1 \oplus Y^i_j$	-	$X^{i+1}_j \oplus c^i_{j+1} \oplus 1$
Type9: (1010)	0	-	Y^i_j	$X^{i+1}_j \oplus Y^i_j \oplus 1$
TypeA: (1011)	0	c^i_{j+1}	c^i_j	$X^{i+1}_j \oplus Y^i_j$
TypeB: (1100)	0	c^i_{j+1}	c^i_j	$X^{i+1}_j \oplus c^i_j \oplus 1$ or $X^{i+1}_j \oplus c^i_{j+1} \oplus 1$
TypeC: (1101)	0	-	Y^i_j	$X^{i+1}_j \oplus c^i_j$
TypeD: (1111)	1	-	-	-

Type0~2 denote the modular addition between uncorrupted $X^i_{j+\alpha}$ and uncorrupted Y^i_j.
Type3~6 denote the modular addition between uncorrupted $X^i_{j+\alpha}$ and corrupted Y^i_j.
Type7~A denote the modular addition between corrupted $X^i_{j+\alpha}$ and uncorrupted Y^i_j.
TypeB~D denote the modular addition between corrupted $X^i_{j+\alpha}$ and corrupted Y^i_j.

(ii) **Recovery of K^i_j based on carry bit c^i_j:** If the combination of $(\Delta X^i_{j+\alpha}, \Delta Y^i_j, \Delta c^i_j, \Delta c^i_{j+1})$ belongs to Type1/2/B/C, then K^i_j can be retrieved with X^{i+1}_j and c^i_j. The value of c^i_j can be pre-computed as follows.

- **Recovery of c^i_j based on the adjacent combination:** If the combination of $(\Delta X^i_{j+\alpha-1}, \Delta Y^i_{j-1}, \Delta c^i_{j-1}, \Delta c^i_j)$ belongs to Type1/4/6/7/9/C, then c^i_j is identical to Y^i_{j-1}.

- **Recovery of c^i_j based on another pair of outputs:** Suppose there exist another pair of correct and faulty round outputs, of which the round input difference and the carry bit difference are denoted as $(\dot{\Delta} X^i, \dot{\Delta} Y^i)$ and $\dot{\Delta} c^i$, respectively.

  –Consider the case that this pair of outputs are encrypted with both the same input and the same key as the given pair. If the combination of $(\dot{\Delta} X^i_{j+\alpha}, \dot{\Delta} Y^i_j, \dot{\Delta} c^i_j, \dot{\Delta} c^i_{j+1})$ belongs to Type5/6/7/8, then c^i_j can be figured out with Y^i_j.

  –Consider the case that this pair of outputs are encrypted with the same key as the given pair, but with a different round input. If K^i_{j-1} has been retrieved from $(\dot{\Delta} X^i_{j+\alpha-1}, \dot{\Delta} Y^i_{j-1}, \dot{\Delta} c^i_{j-1}, \dot{\Delta} c^i_j)$, and the combination of $(\Delta X_{j+\alpha-1}^{i}, \Delta Y_{j-1}^{i}, \Delta c_{j-1}^{i}, \Delta c_{j}^{i})$ belongs to Type2/5/8/B, then c_{j}^{i} can be figured out as $K_{j-1}^{i} \oplus X_{j-1}^{i+1} \oplus 1$.

(iii) **Recovery of K_{j}^{i} based on carry bit c_{j+1}^{i}:** If the combination of $(\Delta X_{j+\alpha}^{i}, \Delta Y_{j}^{i}, \Delta c_{j}^{i}, \Delta c_{j+1}^{i})$ belongs to Type2/5/8/B, then K_{j}^{i} is identical to $X_{j}^{i+1} \oplus c_{j+1}^{i} \oplus 1$. The value of c_{j+1}^{i} can be pre-computed as follows.

- **Recovery of c_{j+1}^{i} based on the adjacent combination:** If the combination of $(\Delta X_{j+\alpha+1}^{i}, \Delta Y_{j+1}^{i}, \Delta c_{j+1}^{i}, \Delta c_{j+2}^{i})$ belongs to Type5/6/7/8, then c_{j+1}^{i} can be figured out straightforward with Y_{j+1}^{i}.

- **Recovery of c_{j+1}^{i} based on another pair of outputs:** Suppose there exist another pair of correct and faulty round outputs, of which the round input difference and the carry bit difference are denoted as $(\dot{\Delta}X^{i}, \dot{\Delta}Y^{i})$ and $\dot{\Delta}c^{i}$, respectively.

  –Consider the case that this pair of outputs are encrypted with both the same input and the same key as the given pair. If the combination of $(\dot{\Delta}X_{j+\alpha}^{i}, \dot{\Delta}Y_{j}^{i}, \dot{\Delta}c_{j}^{i}, \dot{\Delta}c_{j+1}^{i})$ belongs to Type1/4/6/7/9/C, then c_{j+1}^{i} is identical to Y_{j}^{i}.

  –Consider the case that this pair of outputs are encrypted with the same key as the given pair, but with a different round input. If K_{j+1}^{i} has been retrieved from $(\dot{\Delta}X_{j+\alpha+1}^{i}, \dot{\Delta}Y_{j+1}^{i}, \dot{\Delta}c_{j+1}^{i}, \dot{\Delta}c_{j+2}^{i})$ and the combination of $(\Delta X_{j+\alpha+1}^{i}, \Delta Y_{j+1}^{i}, \Delta c_{j+1}^{i}, \Delta c_{j+2}^{i})$ belongs to Type1/2/B/C, then c_{j+1}^{i} can be figured out with K_{j+1}^{i} and X_{j+1}^{i+1}.

Based on the full understanding of the modular addition operation, Property 1 illustrates the key recovery methods not only from the point of straightforward way as previous works [16], but also taking advantage of the faults in adjacent bits as well as the faults induced in other encryptions to improve the efficiency of the recovery.

3.2   Fault Propagation Properties of SPECK

Let $X^{i} = (X_{n-1}^{i}...X_{0}^{i})$ and $Y^{i} = (Y_{n-1}^{i}...Y_{0}^{i})$ denote the i-th round input of the SPECK2n/mn. If a t-bit $(1 \leq t < n)$ fault is induced into the j-th bit location of Y^{i}, then $\Delta Y^{i} = Y^{i} \oplus \tilde{Y}^{i} = (...00\Delta Y_{j+t-1}^{i}\Delta Y_{j+t-2}^{i}...\Delta Y_{j}^{i}00...)$. As the encryption goes on, the fault propagates to the subsequent intermediates step by step in the way that Fig. 2 shows. In this figure, each intermediate is demonstrated as a bit string marked with the bit indexes and different colours. The fault infected bits are in grey, while the fault free ones are in white. To simplify the expression, when the bit index $a > b$, we abbreviate $s \in [a, n-1] \cup [0, b]$ to $s \in [a, b]$ and take a as the least significant index, on the other hand we take b as the least significant index for $s \in [b, a]$.

In the i-th round encryption, the modular addition operation $(\tilde{X}^{i} \ggg \alpha) \boxplus \tilde{Y}^{i}$ results in $(t + \delta_{1})$-bit fault in $\tilde{X}^{i+1}$, where δ_{1} denotes the number of drifting bits. Then the least significant index of bit string $(00...0)$ in ΔX^{i+1} can be represented as,

$$j + t + p_{1} = j + t + \delta_{1} \tag{6}$$

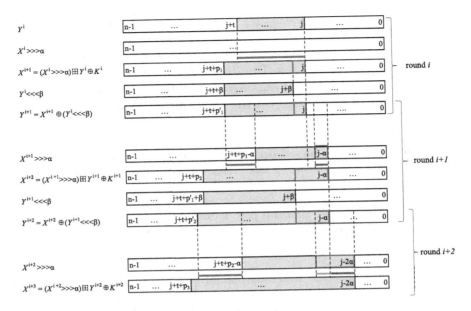

Fig. 2. The detailed fault propagation in the intermediates of SPECK (Intermediate are demonstrated as bit strings marked with the index of bits. The bits in grey are infected by faults, and the bits in white are fault free. The boxes of the same color indicates the faults in the boxes are equal. The purple horizontal lines denotes the modular addition between the infected bit of Y and the fault-free bit of X. The green horizontal lines denotes the modular addition between the fault-free bit of Y and the infected bit of X. The orange horizontal lines denotes the modular addition between the infected bit of Y and the infected bit of X.). (Color figure online)

According to Table 3, if the carry bit difference $\Delta c^i_{j+t} = 1$, then $(\Delta X^i_{j+t+\alpha}, \Delta Y^i_{j+t}, \Delta c^i_{j+t}, \Delta c^i_{j+t+1})$ must be taken from (0010) or (0011). Since $\Delta X^{i+1}_{j+t} = \Delta X^i_{j+t+\alpha} \oplus \Delta Y^i_{j+t} \oplus \Delta c^i_{j+t}$, then $\Delta X^{i+1}_{j+t} = 1$ and δ_1 is larger than 0. If $\Delta c^i_{j+t} = 0$, then $(\Delta X^i_{j+t+\alpha}, \Delta Y^i_{j+t}, \Delta c^i_{j+t}, \Delta c^i_{j+t+1}) = (0000)$ and δ_1 is no larger than 0. For example, when $(\Delta X^i_{j+t+\alpha-1}, \Delta Y^i_{j+t-1}, \Delta c^i_{j+t-1}, \Delta c^i_{j+t}) = (0110)$, ΔX^{i+1}_{t+j-1} is equal to 0 and δ_1 is smaller than 0. Referring to [16], it can be deduced that $|\delta_1| \leq 3$ with a probability of 0.968.

After the XOR operation $\tilde{X}^{i+1} \oplus (\tilde{Y}^i \lll \beta)$, $\tilde{Y}^{i+1}$ inherits the last β bits fault from $\tilde{X}^{i+1}$, which are outlined with red boxes. As for the bit string $(00\ldots0)$ in ΔY^{i+1}, the least significant index of it is set as $j + t + p'_1$, which satisfies the Eq. (7).

$$j + t + p'_1 = \begin{cases} j + t + max\{p_1, \beta\}, & p_1 \neq \beta \\ j + t + p_1 - \delta'_1, & p_1 = \beta \end{cases} \tag{7}$$

For the case $p_1 = \beta$, it can be induced that the number of fault bits wiped out by $\oplus$ satisfies $0 < \delta'_1 \leq 3$ with a probability of 0.875.

In the $(i + 1)$-th round encryption, the last β bits fault in $(\tilde{X}^{i+1} \ggg \alpha)$ are equal to that of $\tilde{Y}^{i+1}$, which are both outlined with red boxes. The least significant index of the bit string $(00...0)$ in ΔX^{i+2}, denoted as $j + t + p_2$, should be close to that in $(\tilde{X}^{i+1} \ggg \alpha)$ and $\tilde{Y}^{i+1}$, and the number of drifting bits satisfies $|\delta_2| \leq 3$ with a probability of 0.968.

$$j + t + p_2 = j + t + max\{p_1', p_1 - \alpha\} + \delta_2 \tag{8}$$

For $\tilde{Y}^{i+2}$, it inherits the last $\alpha + \beta$ bits fault from $\tilde{X}^{i+2}$, which are outlined with blue box. And the least significant index of the bit string $(00...0)$ in ΔY^{i+2} satisfies the equation below. And the number of fault bits wiped out by $\oplus$ satisfies $0 < \delta_2' \leq 3$ with a probability of 0.875.

$$j + t + p_2' = \begin{cases} j + t + max\{p_2, p_1' + \beta\} & , p_2 \neq p_1' + \beta \\ j + t + p_2 - \delta_2' & , p_2 = p_1' + \beta \end{cases} \tag{9}$$

In the following rounds of encryption, errors inherit and propagate similarly as the above. We generalize the relationships between the round output difference $(\Delta X^{i+r}, \Delta Y^{i+r})$ as below, where the symbol $*$ denotes the unknown bit. When $r = 1$,

$$\Delta X_s^{i+r} = \begin{cases} * & , s \in [j, \ j + t + p_1 - 1] \\ 0 & , s \in [j + t + p_1, \ j - 1] \end{cases} \tag{10}$$

$$\Delta Y_s^{i+r} = \begin{cases} \Delta X_s^{i+r} & , s \in [j, \ j + \beta - 1] \\ * & , s \in [j + \beta, \ j + t + p_1' - 1] \\ 0 & , s \in [j + t + p_1', \ j - 1] \end{cases} \tag{11}$$

When $r \geq 2$ and $t + p_r' + (r - 1)\alpha < n$,

$$\Delta X_s^{i+r} = \begin{cases} * & , s \in [j - (r - 1)\alpha, \ j + t + p_r - 1] \\ 0 & , s \in [j + t + p_r, \ j - (r - 1)\alpha - 1] \end{cases} \tag{12}$$

$$\Delta Y_s^{i+r} = \begin{cases} \Delta X_s^{i+r} & , s \in [j - (r - 1)\alpha, \ j - (r - 2)\alpha + \beta - 1] \\ * & , s \in [j - (r - 2)\alpha + \beta, \ j + t + p_r' - 1] \\ 0 & , s \in [j + t + p_r', \ j - (r - 1)\alpha - 1] \end{cases} \tag{13}$$

Apparently, before the fault has reached the full diffusion effect, some bits of the output difference remain 0s. Since the most significant index of bit string $(00...0)$ in ΔY_s^{i+r} is $j - (r-1)\alpha - 1$ and the least significant index of the induced fault in i-th round is j, it is easy to determine the location of the fault injection from the output difference.

In the remainder of this subsection, we will talk about how the fault propagation properties contribute to the key recovery. Suppose the output pair (X^{i+r+1}, Y^{i+r+1}) and $(\tilde{X}^{i+r+1}, \tilde{Y}^{i+r+1})$ have been retrieved by the attacker in the preceding analysis. According to Subsect. 3.1, Y^{i+r}, $\tilde{Y}^{i+r}$ and ΔY^{i+r} can be directly figured out, while only a few bits of K^{i+r}, X^{i+r}, $\tilde{X}^{i+r}$ and ΔX^{i+r} can be recovered with this pair of outputs, which means there still exists more than one candidate of K^{i+r} and ΔX^{i+r}. Then we can filter the candidate of K^{i+r} by examining whether the value of ΔX^{i+r} that recovered from it matches ΔY^{i+r} from the view of fault propagation. Moreover, if no candidate of K^{i+r} is left, it can be inferred that (X^{i+r+1}, Y^{i+r+1}) and $(\tilde{X}^{i+r+1}, \tilde{Y}^{i+r+1})$ are retrieved from a wrong candidate of K^{i+r+1}, which should also be eliminated. Property 2 illustrates the scope of the least significant index of $(00\ldots0)$ in ΔX^{i+r} and provides a way to distinguish the incorrect round keys.

Property 2. Based on the facts that $\delta_r \leq 3$ and $\delta'_r \leq 3$ with a high probability, $\beta \leq 3$, and $\alpha \geq 7$, it can be deduced from Eq. (6–9) that in most cases, $p'_r \geq p_r - \alpha$ and the least significant index of the bit string $(00\ldots0)$ in ΔX^{i+r} satisfies,

$$j + t + p_r \leq j + t + 3r \tag{14}$$

$$j + t + p_r \leq j + t + p_{r+1} + \alpha \tag{15}$$

For convenience, we define the variable $p_r^* = max\{p'_r, 3r\}$, which ensures that $(\Delta X^{i+r}_{j-(r-1)\alpha-1}\ \Delta X^{i+r}_{j-(r-1)\alpha-2}\ \cdots\ \Delta X^{i+r}_{j+t+p_r^*})$ is a all-zero bit string and leaks the secret information during the modular addition operation.

Property 3. Given the correct and faulty outputs, denoted as (X^{i+r+1}, Y^{i+r+1}) and $(\tilde{X}^{i+r+1}, \tilde{Y}^{i+r+1})$, though the complete value of ΔX^{i+r} can not be recovered without K^{i+r}, the sequential zero bits $(\Delta X^{i+r}_{j-(r-1)\alpha-1}\Delta X^{i+r}_{j-(r-1)\alpha-2}\cdots\Delta X^{i+r}_{j+t+p_r^*})$ can be determined in advance with the knowledge of fault position. Besides, partial faulty bits of ΔX^{i+r} can be deduced from ΔY^{i+r} according to the fault inheritance property.

Table 4 summarizes all the input difference of the $(i+r)$-th round modular addition operation that can be deduced from the output pair. When $(\Delta X^{i+r}_{s+\alpha}, \Delta Y^{i+r}_s)$ belongs to Case0/1/2/4, K^{i+r}_s could be worked out according to Property 1.

4   Fault Attack on the SPECK2n/mn

4.1   Fault Attack Under the Random Byte Fault Model

Based on the properties demonstrated in Sect. 3, we propose an efficient fault attack on SPECK2n/mn, in which the master key can be recovered by injecting t-bit faults into the i-th round intermediates. In this subsection, we will take the random byte fault model $(t = 8)$ and $i = T - m$ as example to demonstrate the procedure of the attack.

Step 1. Generate several pairs of correct and faulty ciphertexts.
   Randomly select a group of plaintexts and encrypt them with the same secret key. For each plaintext, repeat the encryption procedure and randomly induce a byte-oriented fault into the intermediate Y^{T-m} to obtain the corresponding faulty ciphertext. Neither the precise location nor the value of the induced fault is known.

Table 4. The input difference pair of the $(i+r)$-th round $\boxplus$ operation

$(\Delta X_{s+\alpha}^{i+r}, \Delta Y_s^{i+r})$		Range of s
$r=0$	Case0: $(0, \Delta Y_s^{i+r})$	$s \in [j,\ j+t-1]$
	Case1: $(0,0)$	$s \in [j+t,\ j-1]$
$r=1$	Case2: $(\Delta Y_{s+\alpha}^{i+r}, 0)$	$s \in [j-\alpha,\ j-\alpha+\beta-1]$
	Case3: $(*, \Delta Y_s^{i+r})$	$s \in [j-\alpha+\beta,\ j+t+p_1^*-\alpha-1]$
	Case0: $(0, \Delta Y_s^{i+r})$	$s \in [j+t+p_1^*-\alpha,\ j+t+p_1^*-1]$
	Case1: $(0,0)$	$s \in [j+t+p_1^*,\ j-\alpha-1]$
$r \geq 2$ and $t+p_r^*+(r-1)\alpha < n$	Case2: $(\Delta Y_{s+\alpha}^{i+r}, 0)$	$s \in [j-r\alpha,\ j-(r-1)\alpha-1]$
	Case4: $(\Delta Y_{s+\alpha}^{i+r}, \Delta Y_s^{i+r})$	$s \in [j-(r-1)\alpha,\ j-(r-2)\alpha+\beta-1]$
	Case3: $(*, \Delta Y_s^{i+r})$	$s \in [j-(r-2)\alpha+\beta,\ j+t+p_r^*-\alpha-1]$
	Case0: $(0, \Delta Y_s^{i+r})$	$s \in [j+t+p_r^*-\alpha,\ j+t+p_r^*-1]$
	Case1: $(0,0)$	$s \in [j+t+p_r^*,\ j-r\alpha-1]$

Step 2. Determine the location of the fault injection.
With the knowledge of the correct and faulty ciphertexts, (X^T, Y^T) and $(\tilde{X}^T, \tilde{Y}^T)$, we get the inputs of the last round encryption $Y^{T-1} = (X^T \oplus Y^T) \ggg \beta$, $\tilde{Y}^{T-1} = (\tilde{X}^T \oplus \tilde{Y}^T) \ggg \beta$ and $\Delta Y^{T-1} = Y^{T-1} \oplus \tilde{Y}^{T-1}$. Then, we can determine the location of the injection, denoted as j, from the most significant index of bit string $(00\ldots 0)$ in ΔY^{T-1}, denoted as j', with the equation $j = (j'+1+(m-2)\alpha) \bmod n$. If there exists no $(00\ldots 0)$ in ΔY^{T-1}, we will discard this pair of ciphertexts and execute Step 2 with another pair.

Step 3. Deduce candidate values of K^{T-1}.

Step 3.1. Compute the difference of variables that are related to $\boxplus$ operation in the $(T-1)$-th round. Based on the location of the fault injection and the inheritance property demonstrated in Table 4, we obtain a few bits of $(\Delta X^{T-1} \ggg \alpha)$ from ΔY^{T-1}. Since $\Delta c^{T-1} = (\Delta X^{T-1} \ggg \alpha) \oplus \Delta Y^{T-1} \oplus \Delta X^T$, the corresponding carry bit differences are also obtained. So far, several combinations of $(\Delta X_{s+\alpha}^{T-1}, \Delta Y_s^{T-1}, \Delta c_s^{T-1}, \Delta c_{s+1}^{T-1})$ are precisely recovered from a single pair of ciphertext.

Step 3.2. Recover n' bits of K^{T-1} with the least amount of ciphertexts.
Initialize an empty collection of the recovered key bits $\mathcal{K}^{T-1}$ and denote the number of recovered key bits as $\#\mathcal{K}^{T-1}$. If $\#\mathcal{K}^{T-1} < n'$, do as follows.
For each pair of ciphertexts, initialize the collection of the recovered carry bits $\mathcal{C}^{T-1}$ with $c_0^{T-1} = 0$, and denote the number of recovered carry bits as $\#\mathcal{C}^{T-1}$. Then, analyze on $(\Delta X_{s+\alpha}^{T-1}, \Delta Y_s^{T-1}, \Delta c_s^{T-1}, \Delta c_{s+1}^{T-1})$ bit by bit, and conduct the information retrieval according to Property 1 and Table 3 with the known values of key bits and carry bits. If the new information about K_s^{T-1}, c_s^{T-1} and c_{s+1}^{T-1} is obtained, add it into $\mathcal{K}^{T-1}$ and $\mathcal{C}^{T-1}$. Repeat the analysis on the current pair of ciphertexts until no more information can be get.

Algorithm 1. Recover n' bits of K^{T-1}

---

1 Set $\mathcal{K}^{T-1} = NULL$, $NumK_1 = \#\mathcal{K}^{T-1} = 0$, $L = l = 0$;

2 **while** $\#\mathcal{K}^{T-1} < n'$ **do**

3   **if** $NumK_1 = \#\mathcal{K}^{T-1}$ **then**

4       $\lfloor$ $l = l + 1$;

5   **else if** $NumK_1 < \#\mathcal{K}^{T-1}$ **and** $l > 1$ **then**

6       $\lfloor$ $l = 1$, $NumK_1 = \#\mathcal{K}^{T-1}$;

      /* If $\mathcal{K}^{T-1}$ is updated, re-analyse from the 1st pair of ciphertexts   */

      /* L denotes the number of ciphertexts used in key recovery   */

7   **if** $l > L$ **then**

8       $\lfloor$ $L = l$;

      /* Analyse on the l-th pair of ciphertexts   */

9   Set $\mathcal{C}^{T-1} = \{c_0^{T-1} = 0\}$, $NumC = \#\mathcal{C}^{T-1} = 1$, $NumK_2 = \#\mathcal{K}^{T-1}$;

10   Set ΔX^{T-1}, ΔY^{T-1}, Δc^{T-1} as the variables derived from the l-th pair of ciphertexts;

11   **do**

12       $NumC = \#\mathcal{C}^{T-1}$, $NumK_2 = \#\mathcal{K}^{T-1}$;

13   **for** $s = 0$ **to** $n - 1$ **do**

14   **if** $(\Delta X_{s+\alpha}^{T-1}, \Delta Y_s^{T-1}, \Delta c_s^{T-1}, \Delta c_{s+1}^{T-1})$ *are known* **then**

15   Execute information recovery with $\mathcal{K}^{T-1}$, $\mathcal{C}^{T-1}$ and Table 3;

16   **if** K_s^{T-1} *is recovered and* $K_s^{T-1} \notin \mathcal{K}^{T-1}$ **then**

17             $\lfloor$ Add K_s^{T-1} into $\mathcal{K}^{T-1}$, $\#\mathcal{K}^{T-1} = (\#\mathcal{K}^{T-1}) + 1$;

18   **if** c_s^{T-1} *is recovered and* $c_s^{T-1} \notin \mathcal{C}^{T-1}$ **then**

19             $\lfloor$ Add c_s^{T-1} into $\mathcal{C}^{T-1}$, $\#\mathcal{C}^{T-1} = (\#\mathcal{C}^{T-1}) + 1$;

20   **if** c_{s+1}^{T-1} *is recovered and* $c_{s+1}^{T-1} \notin \mathcal{C}^{T-1}$ **then**

21             $\lfloor$ Add c_{s+1}^{T-1} into $\mathcal{C}^{T-1}$, $\#\mathcal{C}^{T-1} = (\#\mathcal{C}^{T-1}) + 1$;

22         $s = s + 1$;

23   **while** $NumC < \#\mathcal{C}^{T-1}$ **or** $NumK_2 < \#\mathcal{K}^{T-1}$

      /* If $\mathcal{K}^{T-1}$ or $\mathcal{C}^{T-1}$ is updated, re-analyse on the current ciphertexts   */

24 **return** $\mathcal{K}^{T-1}$, L

Then introduce a new pair of ciphertexts and analyse. If $\mathcal{K}^{T-1}$ is updated, restart the information recovery from the first pair of ciphertexts with the latest retrieved key bits. The pseudo-code of this substep is demonstrated in Algorithm 1.

Step 3.3. Filter out the incorrect candidate values of K^{T-1}. Exhaustively search on the other $n - n'$ bits of K^{T-1} and enumerate the candidate values of the key. For each candidate, X^{T-1} and $\tilde{X}^{T-1}$ can be recovered as $X^{T-1} = ((X^T \oplus K^{T-1}) \boxminus Y^{T-1}) \lll \alpha$ and $\tilde{X}^{T-1} = ((\tilde{X}^T \oplus K^{T-1}) \boxminus \tilde{Y}^{T-1}) \lll \alpha$, respectively. If the least significant index of bit string $(...00...)$ in ΔX^{T-1} is out of the scope that illustrated in Property 2, the corresponding candidate of K^{T-1} should be filtered out.

Step 4. Reveal the master key.

With the knowledge of (X^{T-1}, Y^{T-1}) and $(\tilde{X}^{T-1}, \tilde{Y}^{T-1})$, we get $Y^{T-2} = (X^{T-1} \oplus Y^{T-1}) \ggg \beta$, $\tilde{Y}^{T-2} = (\tilde{X}^{T-1} \oplus \tilde{Y}^{T-1}) \ggg \beta$ and $\Delta Y^{T-2} = Y^{T-2} \oplus \tilde{Y}^{T-2}$. A similar procedure is executed as Step 3 to retrieve K^{T-2}. Also, K^{T-3} and K^{T-4} can be recovered in the same way when $m = 3$ or 4. Finally, derive the master key through the key schedule and the brute-force search.

4.2 Discussions of the Attack

According to the fault propagation properties, the bigger the word size n is, the more rounds are needed to achieve the full diffusion of the fault. It can be estimated from $p_R^* \approx 3R$ and the full diffusion condition $j - (R-1)\alpha + n = j + t + p_R^*$ that the distance between fault injection and full diffusion is about,

$$R = \lceil \frac{n - t + \alpha}{3 + \alpha} \rceil \tag{16}$$

Depending on various fault injection techniques, faults with different granularities can occur, such as single-bit fault, multi-bit fault, byte fault and word fault, among which the byte and word oriented fault can be obtained more easily due to the fact that the bit width of the register is a multiple of 8. Apparently, the length of fault also impacts on the feasibility of the attack. For the word-oriented fault ($t = n$), once the fault is induced, the full diffusion is achieved. So the attacker have to induce faults in every one of last m rounds as [17] does to retrieve the keys. However, things are different for the byte-oriented fault. For SPECK32/64, SPECK48/72, SPECK48/96 and SPECK64/128, if the fault is injected into the $(T-m)$-th round, there will exist no continuous zero bits in ΔX^{T-1} or ΔY^{T-1}, which lead to the result that the location of fault injection can not be recognized and no bit in ΔX^{T-1} can be determined. Hence, our attack does not work with the faults injected into only one intermediate round. While for the ciphers with 96-bit or 128-bit block size, injections in single round are enough. Besides, the fault can be injected earlier than the $(T-m)$-th round, as long as the complete diffusion effect of the fault has not been achieved until the last round. And if the attacker conducts an extra key recovery of K^{T-m}, the master key can be uniquely selected via the key schedule. Moreover, for the single-bit fault model, most of the instances in SPECK are vulnerable to the attack with single round injections, and it allows a more flexible choice of the injection round. Take both the precision and the flexibility of the fault injection into account, we suggest to apply our attack under the byte-oriented fault model.

Regardless of the brute-force search, the complexity of this attack mainly depends on the key size mn and the number of t-bit fault injections L, which is about $\mathcal{O}(mnL^2)$ according to Algorithm 1. And the implementation difficulty of the injections is also affected by the required number of faults. Therefore, we focus on the factors that have impacts on the number of injections and give some advice on parameters selection. According to Table 4, as the round distance r between the injection and the key recovery grows from 0 to $m-1$, the approximate maximum number of key bits that can be recovered from this injection grows from t, and stabilizes at $2\alpha+\beta$ when $r \geq 2$. Because $2\alpha+\beta > t$ in most cases without regard to the word-oriented fault, we suggest to induce at an earlier round in order to reduce the injections. Moreover, in this attack, at least n' bits of the intermediate are corrupted after randomly injecting L t-bit faults, it can be approximated as the occupancy problem [18] that n' out of n bins are corrupted after throwing tL balls, in which the growth of n' becomes slowly when it get close to n. So we suggest to trade-off between L and n' to ensure a proper number of injections and search spaces. However, as L grows, most bits of the intermediate are likely to be corrupted more than once. Thus, it has a quite small probability that the corrupted bit does not match any key recovery condition in Property 1, which ensures the number of required injections would not be too large.

4.3 Computation Verification

In this subsection, we implement simulations in C++ code on a PC to verify the feasibility of the attack under the byte fault model. The program generates several pairs of correct and faulty ciphertexts with random plaintexts and a fixed master key. The byte fault is randomly induced into the specific intermediate, and the attacker has no access to the value or the location of it.

The attack runs for 100 times and each takes a few seconds. Table 5 illustrates the comparison of the target intermediates and the average number of fault injections between our attacks and the previous ones under the random fault model, as well as the brute-force search space of master keys. As we can see, the existing attacks require faults induced at multiple rounds, while ours only needs to injected into 1 round. In our attack, the average numbers of injections can be close to those in [17], by altering the lower bound of key-bit size n',

Table 5. Comparision of the target intermediates, the average number of fault injections, and the brute-force search space of the master key

SPECK $2n/mn$	Random one-bit-flip [16]			Random n-bit-flip [17]			Random byte (This paper)		
	Target	Num	Search	Target	Num	Search	Target	Num	Search
64/96	$Y^{23}Y^{24}Y^{25}$	132	2^3	$Y^{23}Y^{24}Y^{25}$	18	2^3	Y^{23}	[a]9	2^9
96/96	$Y^{26}Y^{27}$	170	2^2	$Y^{26}Y^{27}$	14	2^2	Y^{26}	[b]18	2^7
96/144	$Y^{26}Y^{27}Y^{28}$	255	2^3	$Y^{26}Y^{27}Y^{28}$	21	2^3	Y^{26}	[c]20	2^4
128/128	$Y^{30}Y^{31}$	228	2^2	$Y^{30}Y^{31}$	16	2^2	Y^{28}	[d]19	2^8
128/192	$Y^{30}Y^{31}Y^{32}$	342	2^3	$Y^{30}Y^{31}Y^{32}$	24	2^3	Y^{29}	[e]28	2^8
128/256	$Y^{30}Y^{31}Y^{32}Y^{33}$	456	2^4	$Y^{30}Y^{31}Y^{32}Y^{33}$	32	2^4	Y^{30}	[f]32	2^{11}

[a] n' in the recovery of (K^{25}, K^{24}, K^{23}) are selected as $(31, 24, 24)$.
[b] n' in the recovery of (K^{27}, K^{26}) are selected as $(40, 41)$.
[c] n' in the recovery of (K^{28}, K^{27}, K^{26}) are selected as $(46, 42, 42)$.
[d] n' in the recovery of (K^{31}, K^{30}) are selected as $(58, 58)$.
[e] n' in the recovery of (K^{32}, K^{31}, K^{30}) are selected as $(62, 62, 57)$.
[f] n' in the recovery of $(K^{33}, K^{32}, K^{31}, K^{30})$ are selected as $(63, 63, 59, 58)$.

at the cost of brute-force search space. For example, in order to recover the master key of SPECK96/144, we induce 20 random byte faults at Y^{26} and obtain $46/42/42$ bits of $K^{28}/K^{27}/K^{26}$, respectively. Besides, with the help of the round key distinguisher, the complexity of the brute-force search is reduced from 2^{14} to 2^4.

Moreover, our attack shows similar results no matter the faulty ciphertexts are derived from the same plaintext or the different plaintexts.

5 Conclusion

In this paper, we propose an improved fault analysis on SPECK under the random byte fault model. In this attack, the faults can be injected into 1 intermediate round to retrieve the entire master key for most versions of SPECK. To determine the locations and the values of the faults, we demonstrate several helpful properties of the fault propagation under the condition that the full diffusion of faults has not been achieved until the last round encryption. Further, a filtering rule based on the location of fault is proposed to distinguish the incorrect intermediates and the corresponding key candidates. In the information recovery, compared with the previous results, our attack exploits more characteristics of the modular addition operation, and takes the advantage of the faults in adjacent bits as well as the faults induced in other encryptions to retrieve the current key bit, which is believed meaningful to the study of fault analysis on other cryptographic primitives using the modular addition operations for non-linear functions. In the end, the experimental results confirm the feasibility and the efficiency of our attack.

Acknowledgements. We would like to thank the anonymous reviewers for providing valuable comments. This work is supported by the National Basic Research Program of China (973 Program, No.2013CB338002).

References

1. Boneh, D., DeMillo, R.A., Lipton, R.J.: On the importance of checking cryptographic protocols for faults. In: Fumy, W. (ed.) EUROCRYPT 1997. LNCS, vol. 1233, pp. 37–51. Springer, Heidelberg (1997). doi:10.1007/3-540-69053-0_4
2. Biham, E., Shamir, A.: Differential fault analysis of secret key cryptosystems. In: Kaliski, B.S. (ed.) CRYPTO 1997. LNCS, vol. 1294, pp. 513–525. Springer, Heidelberg (1997). doi:10.1007/BFb0052259
3. Hemme, L.: A differential fault attack against early rounds of (triple-)DES. In: Joye, M., Quisquater, J.-J. (eds.) CHES 2004. LNCS, vol. 3156, pp. 254–267. Springer, Heidelberg (2004). doi:10.1007/978-3-540-28632-5_19
4. Piret, G., Quisquater, J.-J.: A differential fault attack technique against SPN structures, with application to the AES and KHAZAD. In: Walter, C.D., Koç, Ç.K., Paar, C. (eds.) CHES 2003. LNCS, vol. 2779, pp. 77–88. Springer, Heidelberg (2003). doi:10.1007/978-3-540-45238-6_7

5. Chen, C.-N., Yen, S.-M.: Differential fault analysis on AES key schedule and some countermeasures. In: Safavi-Naini, R., Seberry, J. (eds.) ACISP 2003. LNCS, vol. 2727, pp. 118–129. Springer, Heidelberg (2003). doi:10.1007/3-540-45067-X_11

6. Dusart, P., Letourneux, G., Vivolo, O.: Differential fault analysis on A.E.S. In: Zhou, J., Yung, M., Han, Y. (eds.) ACNS 2003. LNCS, vol. 2846, pp. 293–306. Springer, Heidelberg (2003). doi:10.1007/978-3-540-45203-4_23

7. Chen, H., Wu, W., Feng, D.: Differential fault analysis on CLEFIA. In: Qing, S., Imai, H., Wang, G. (eds.) ICICS 2007. LNCS, vol. 4861, pp. 284–295. Springer, Heidelberg (2007). doi:10.1007/978-3-540-77048-0_22

8. Biehl, I., Meyer, B., Müller, V.: Differential fault attacks on elliptic curve cryptosystems. In: Bellare, M. (ed.) CRYPTO 2000. LNCS, vol. 1880, pp. 131–146. Springer, Heidelberg (2000). doi:10.1007/3-540-44598-6_8

9. Biham, E., Granboulan, L., Nguyen, P.Q.: Impossible fault analysis of RC4 and differential fault analysis of RC4. In: Gilbert, H., Handschuh, H. (eds.) FSE 2005. LNCS, vol. 3557, pp. 359–367. Springer, Heidelberg (2005). doi:10.1007/11502760_24

10. Beaulieu, R., Shors, D., Smith, J., Treatman-Clark, S., Weeks, B., Wingers, L.: The SIMON and SPECK of lightweight block ciphers. Cryptology ePrint Archive, Report 2013/404 (2013). http://eprint.iacr.org

11. Abed, F., List, E., Lucks, S., Wenzel, J.: Differential cryptanalysis of round-reduced SIMON and SPECK. In: Cid, C., Rechberger, C. (eds.) FSE 2014. LNCS, vol. 8540, pp. 525–545. Springer, Heidelberg (2015). doi:10.1007/978-3-662-46706-0_27

12. Biryukov, A., Roy, A., Velichkov, V.: Differential analysis of block ciphers SIMON and SPECK. In: Cid, C., Rechberger, C. (eds.) FSE 2014. LNCS, vol. 8540, pp. 546–570. Springer, Heidelberg (2015). doi:10.1007/978-3-662-46706-0_28

13. Dinur, I.: Improved differential cryptanalysis of round-reduced speck. In: Joux, A., Youssef, A. (eds.) SAC 2014. LNCS, vol. 8781, pp. 147–164. Springer, Heidelberg (2014). doi:10.1007/978-3-319-13051-4_9

14. Ashur, T., Bodden, D.: Linear cryptanalysis of reduced-round SPECK. http://securewww.esat.kuleuven.be/cosic/publications/article-2666.pdf

15. Liu, Y., Fu, K., Wang, W., Sun, L., Wang, M.: Linear cryptanalysis of reduced-round SPECK. Inf. Process. Lett. **116**(3), 259–266 (2016)

16. Tupsamudre, H., Bisht, S., Mukhopadhyay, D.: Differential fault analysis on the families of SIMON and SPECK ciphers. In: Fault Diagnosis and Tolerance in Cryptography-FDTC 2014 Workshop on IEEE, pp. 40–48 (2014)

17. Huo, Y., Zhang, F., Feng, X., Wang, L.: Improved differential fault attack on the block cipher SPECK. In: Fault Diagnosis and Tolerance in Cryptography-FDTC 2015 Workshop on IEEE, pp. 28–34 (2015)

18. Feller, W.: An Introduction to Probability Theory and Its Applications, vol. 3, 3rd edn. Wiley, Hoboken (1968)

On the Effectiveness of Code-Reuse-Based Android Application Obfuscation

Xiaoxiao Tang[1]([✉]), Yu Liang[2], Xinjie Ma[3], Yan Lin[1], and Debin Gao[1]

[1] Singapore Management University, Singapore, Singapore
{xxtang.2013,yanlin.2016,dbgao}@smu.edu.sg
[2] Wuhan University, Wuhan, China
liangyu@whu.edu.cn
[3] Nankai University, Tianjin, China
mxjnkcs@nankai.edu.cn

Abstract. Attackers use reverse engineering techniques to gain detailed understanding of executable for malicious purposes, such as re-packaging an Android app to inject malicious code or advertising components. To make reverse engineering more difficult, researchers have proposed various code obfuscation techniques to conceal purposes or logic of code segments. One interesting idea of code obfuscation is to apply code-reuse techniques (e.g., Return-Oriented Programming) to (re-)distribute essential code segments before they are reconstructed at runtime. Such techniques are well understood on x86 platform, but relatively less explored on Android. In this paper, we present an evaluation on the extent to which code-reuse-based techniques can be applied to obfuscate Android apps. Moreover, we extend code-reuse-based obfuscation to the Android platform by proposing an obfuscation mechanism for both Java and native code. Results show that 835 gadgets are found in the C standard library (`libc.so`) which cover the entire Turing complete set. Furthermore, we implement a semi-automatic tool named AndroidCubo and show that it protects both Java and native code with comparable security to those obfuscated with Java reflection at a small runtime overhead.

Keywords: Obfuscation · Android application · Code reuse · Java Native Interface

1 Introduction

Android is now the most popular mobile operating system with more than 80% market share. The number of apps available on Google Play has climbed to more than 2 million. The popularity of Android operating system and applications also invites lots of pirated apps. In order to produce pirated apps, adversaries typically analyze benign apps with reverse engineering tools [1–3], modify the app to bypass verification algorithms, if any, and then re-package the apps with injected malicious code or advertising components.

© Springer International Publishing AG 2017
S. Hong and J.H. Park (Eds.): ICISC 2016, LNCS 10157, pp. 333–349, 2017.
DOI: 10.1007/978-3-319-53177-9_18

To make such attacks more difficult, app developers apply code obfuscation techniques. Google recommends developers to use Proguard [4] to obfuscate sensitive code in Android. However, this tool only obfuscates Java code and leaves native code as easy targets of attackers. Moreover, Proguard, like many traditional Java obfuscation techniques [5–7], only applies relatively simple obfuscation techniques, e.g., rename identifiers and remove debugging information. Although identifiers of classes and methods are no longer understandable after the obfuscation, names of the system APIs and the control flow of the program still enable reverse engineering to a great extent. For example, it is easy to figure out important functionality of an app by analyzing the system APIs invoked.

Return-Oriented Programming (ROP), which belongs to the bigger family of code-reuse-based techniques, was recently proposed as an attacking technique to exploit vulnerable programs [8–12]. It was subsequently used for code protection [13–15] and to provide program steganography, e.g., RopSteg [14]. The main idea of code-reuse-based obfuscation is to replace essential code with small code pieces distributed in the app and to reconstruct the essential code dynamically. These small code pieces, typically ending with return/return-like instructions, are called gadgets. Then, a payload, which contains addresses of the gadgets and parameters needed by them, is generated for code reusing. This payload is typically used to trigger some vulnerability (e.g., buffer overflow) and to invoke the hidden code by executing the selected gadgets one by one. With this technique, the semantics of the essential code in the original program are hidden in the payload. As part of the data in an app, payload is safer than the original code under the disclosure of reverse engineering tools. The hidden code can be further protected through dynamically downloading the payload from a trusted remote server. In addition to protecting benign code, this technique can also be used for hiding malicious behaviors by adversaries.

However, RopSteg and other code-reuse-based techniques cannot be directly applied to Android applications. First, Android apps are mainly developed in Java, while code-reuse-based techniques are based on native binaries typically compiled from C/C++. Second, Android devices are built on ARM architecture on which registers are used for parsing function parameters and saving return addresses [16], as opposed to x86 which is more dependent on the stack.

In this paper, we present the first evaluation on the extent to which code-reuse-based techniques can be applied on Android application obfuscation. Moreover, we propose an effective code-reuse-based obfuscation mechanism for Android apps. This mechanism helps developers to obfuscate small pieces of sensitive code, including both Java and native code. We evaluate gadgets found in binaries of Android apps and calculate the amount of gadgets in several common native libraries used by Android apps. Results show that 835 gadgets in the C standard library (`libc.so`) cover a Turing complete gadget set. We implement this idea in a tool called AndroidCubo (Android Code-reuse Based Obfuscation) and successfully apply it on real examples to protect both Java and native code with a small overhead. We show that the security of our obfuscated code is comparable to that obfuscated with Java reflection.

2   Overview

Android app obfuscation focuses on preventing reverse engineering by adversaries. We assume a threat model in which an adversary reveals essential code in Android apps with reverse engineering tools, such as Apktool and APKstudio. These tools help adversaries decompile Android APK and disassemble the resources to Java or assembly code. Then, adversaries can tamper the decompiled app and repackage it to perform malicious behaviors. Obviously, we assume that source code of the Android app is not available to the adversary.

An effective obfuscation technique has to achieve two goals when targeting Android applications. First, it should protect the compiled essential code from being reverse engineered to a human understandable format. Second, it should be generally applicable to any code segments to be hidden on any Android applications. In the context of code-reuse-based techniques, this means that a Turing complete gadget set that consists of frequently appeared gadgets is needed.

Figure 1 gives an overview of our code-reuse-based technique in obfuscating the essential code in an Android app. First, the essential code is replaced with a gadget sequence based on the Turing complete gadget set. The gadget sequence represents the semantics of the essential code and is also regarded as the code reuse program. Next, we prepare a payload according to the gadget sequence. After that, a segment of trigger code is embedded in the app to invoke the protected code at runtime. At last, when the protected app is running, the payload will be loaded into the memory of the app and passed to the trigger code for invoking the protected code.

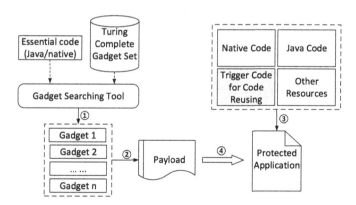

Fig. 1. An overview of our code-reuse-based obfuscation technique for Android apps.

The Turing complete gadget set is a fundamental requirement in this technique for providing enough gadgets to substitute the essential code. In the following sections, we first present our analysis of gadgets on ARM and then discuss the details of the code obfuscation mechanism.

3   Turing Complete Gadget Set

As we discuss in the earlier section, having a Turing complete gadget set is a necessary condition for a code-reuse-based obfuscation technique to be generally applicable to most Android applications. In this section, we present a Turing complete gadget set found available for code reuse obfuscation on ARM architecture. We also analyze the number of gadgets in each category. We focus our analysis on Android 4.4 on a Nexus 5 handset. In the following description, `Ra-Rd` and `Rx-Ry` denote different registers of ARM.

Previous studies [12,17] applied gadgets ending with `BLX Ra` in their code-reuse techniques. `BLX Ra` is an indirect jump instruction whose jump destination is specified by register `Ra`. Unlike return instructions, `BLX` cannot fetch gadget addresses from memory. Thus, a specific kind of gadget, called update-load-branch (ULB) gadget, is used to sequentially fetch gadget addresses to registers and chain the gadgets together. However, the ULB gadget is very hard to find in native libraries [12]. Besides that, this strategy doubles the length of the gadget sequence, which makes code-reuse-based obfuscation techniques more complicated and slows down the program. Hence, we explore the possibility in using another type of gadgets that ends with `POP {Rx-Ry, PC}`. This `POP` instruction loads an address from the stack to the program counter register `PC` directly. It always appears in the epilogue of a function and is more commonly found in native libraries than the `BLX` instruction.

Our gadget searching strategy is to look for basic blocks (instruction sequences that do not contain branches) ending with a `POP {Rx-Ry, PC}` instruction to minimize the effort needed to handle branches in instruction sequences and payload generation. We implement this strategy into a gadget searching tool in python. This tool searches for all available gadgets and their relative addresses in native libraries. It also categorizes the available gadgets to different classes according to their functionality.

We apply our gadget searching tool on several commonly used native libraries used by Android apps and compare the number of gadgets in our gadgets set with that in the gadget set proposed by Davi et al. [12], see Table 1. The results show that number of gadgets in our gadget set is much larger than that used by Davi et al. [12]. This is because `POP {Rx-Ry, PC}` is more frequently used than `BLX Ra` in the native libraries. With the larger number of gadgets, the probability of finding all gadgets needed in the Turing complete gadget set is higher. Besides that, the more gadgets we find, the more flexibility we have for essential code replacement.

Table 1. Number of gadgets found in different gadget sets.

Native libraries	libc	libruntime	libunity	libvideo	libcocos2d
# of Gadgets (Our gadget set)	835	2,244	21,483	317	12,913
# of Gadgets (Gadget set in [12])	77	1,326	10,734	148	6,126

Upon our analysis, we realized that gadgets that implement basic operations, such as memory operations, arithmetic, and logic operations, can be easily found through searching the corresponding instructions. Other functionality, including control-flow transfers and function calls, need to be constructed carefully. We carefully analyzed the gadget sets found and managed to form a Turing complete gadget set for converting sensitive code into gadget sequences, see Table 2.

Table 2. Number of different types of gadgets in our gadget set.

Gadget functionality	libc	libruntime	libunity	libvideo	libcocos2d
Load	127	151	2,484	60	1,607
Store	227	161	5,518	77	2,333
Add	20	3	878	23	204
Sub	30	1	78	3	35
Shift	12	8	20	2	689
And	6	8	137	3	60
Or	21	6	274	3	100
Xor	2	2	31	0	22
Unconditional branch	226	753	12,063	84	3,035
Conditional branch	28	15	1,107	29	29
Function call	8	187	865	5	458

The results show that libraries contain sufficient gadgets in each category of the Turing complete gadget set, with the exception of `libvideo` where there is no gadgets to perform `xor` operation. However, also note that `xor` could be indirectly implemented with other logical operators. This shows that many commonly used libraries are sufficient for providing gadgets for code-reuse obfuscation.

4 Code Obfuscation

With the Turing complete gadget set found in various native libraries covering different functionality, we now present details of the obfuscation mechanism for protecting a piece of essential code in an Android application. The code protection process, as shown in Fig. 1, consists of a few steps in (1) replacing the sensitive code with our gadget sequence; (2) generating code-reuse payload according to the gadget sequence; and (3) constructing trigger code to invoke the hidden code with payload in the app.

4.1 Essential Code Replacement

It is usually straightforward to replace the essential code to be obfuscated with gadget sequences. Most code-reuse techniques typically disassemble the essential code to instruction sequences first, and then substitute them with semantically equivalent gadgets. However, dealing with Android applications makes this process more complicated as we want to be able to obfuscate both the native and Java code. This makes our code-reuse-based obfuscation tool different from most existing ones.

For Android apps, native code is always compiled to native libraries (.so file) by the building module of Android Native Development Kit (NDK). Reverse engineering tools, such as IDAPro, Hopper, or the GNU Project debugger (GDB) can be used to disassemble the native libraries and to obtain the instruction sequences for the essential code to be obfuscated. We can then substitute instructions in the essential code with gadgets in the native binaries of the app. Since most of these native libraries contain Turing Complete gadget sets as shown in Table 2, we will always be able to perform this substitution successfully.

Dealing with Java code in Android apps is more challenging, since existing code-reuse techniques only support native code. Although a subset of the language-independent functionality (e.g., concatenation of strings can be implemented in Java as + operator and native code as `strcat()` method) can be implemented in native code as well, other functionality that uses classes or methods specifically provided by Java or Android cannot be directly implemented in native code (e.g., enable bluetooth can only be implemented in Java as `BluetoothAdapter.enable()`).

Fortunately, the Java Native Interface (JNI) provides a flexible connection for the communication between Java and native code [18]. JNI provides several native methods for accessing object's field from native code as well as methods for converting Java classes to native classes, including `GetObjectClass()`, `GetMethodID()` and `CallVoidMethod()`. These methods allow native code to use Java class objects and to call Java methods by providing corresponding class names and method names. In addition, JNI also provides methods to convert Java objects to native variables. For example, `GetStringUTFChars()` can be used to convert a Java string to native chars.

Figure 2 shows an example of the corresponding native code that can be used to replace a sensitive Java API `sendTextMessage()`. In this example, The JNI function `CallVoidMethod()` will call the sensitive API in native code after retrieving the class and method names.

In addition to the proposed method of implementing Java functionality in native code via JNI and then subsequently obfuscating the resulting native code, here we propose another method using shell command. We notice that many Java operations can be represented with shell commands in Android apps, e.g., reading SMS can be implemented through shell command `content query --uri content://sms`. Therefore, we propose to obfuscate Java code by first replacing it with a call to `system()` with the corresponding shell command, and then subsequently obfuscating the calling of `system()` with our code-reuse program. This method only needs two gadgets—the first one to move the address of the corresponding command to register R0, and the second to invoke the system call function. The actual shell command appears as parameters to the system call.

```
1   void * sendSMS(JNIEnv *env)
2   {
3       jclass smsclass = env->FindClass("android/telephony/SmsManager");
4       jmethodID get = env->GetStaticMethodID(smsclass, "getDefault", "()Landroid/telephony/
            SmsManager;");
5       jobject sms = env->NewObject(smsclass, get);
6       //Obtaining sendTextMessage()
7       jmethodID sendMethod = env->GetMethodID(smsclass, "sendTextMessage",
8       "(Ljava/lang/String;Ljava/lang/String;Ljava/lang/String;Landroid/app/PendingIntent;
            Landroid/app/PendingIntent;)V");
9       jstring destAddress = env->NewStringUTF("1234567890"); //Phone number
10      jstring text = env->NewStringUTF("native"); //SMS content
11
12      //Sending SMS with sendTextMessage() in native code
13      env->CallVoidMethod(sms, sendMethod, destAddress, NULL, text, NULL, NULL);
14  }
```

Fig. 2. The native code of calling sendTextMessage() with JNI.

Table 3 presents some common behaviors which can be represented by shell commands on Android. These commands are all feasible to be used on normal Android devices. The available shell commands can be found under the directory /system/bin in the corresponding Android devices. More complicated operations can be hidden in shell scripts written with available commands and be invoked through executing the scripts with system(). These shell commands include simple ones like file operations, process management, network configuration, as well as those provided by Android Debug Bridge (ADB) for activity management and package management.

Table 3. Examples of operations on Android and the corresponding shell commands.

Operations	Shell command
Open messenger	am start --user 0 -a android.intent.action.SENDTO -d sms:PHONE_NUMBER --es sms_body MESSAGE
Read SMS	content query --uri content://sms
Open dialer	am start --user 0 -a android.intent.action.DIAL -d tel:PHONE_NUMBER
Start browser	am start --user 0 -a android.intent.action.VIEW -d URL
Create directory	mkdir DIRECTORY_PATH

4.2 Payload Generation

The main advantage of code-reuse-based obfuscation tools over other obfuscation techniques is that the hidden code exists in the form of data rather than instructions. To achieve this, we need to prepare a payload according to the gadget sequence. Payload is a segment of memory content that contains semantics of the protected code and will be used for overwriting control data at runtime. A payload typically consists of three parts. The first part is the data that will be used to overwrite control data in memory to redirect control flow to the hidden code. The second part consists of the parameters and addresses for the gadget sequence which presents the semantics of the hidden program. The third part is a segment of buffer with data needed by the code reuse program and other padding data. Figure 3 is an example of the payload which has been loaded on the stack.

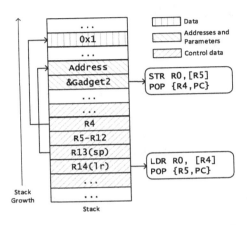

Fig. 3. Layout of the payload. The shadowed areas present different parts of the payload.

This payload is used for the gadget sequence that loads a number 0x1 from memory and stores it at another address. From bottom to top of the stack, the first part is the data that overwrites control data jmp_buf which is used to set register values of the execution environment. In the rewritten jmp_buf, R4 is set to the address of 0x1 and stack pointer is set to the beginning of the second part of the payload. The second part contains the parameter needed by the first gadget and the address of the second gadget. The last part of the payload contains other data—the number 0x1 to be loaded from memory and stored to the address specified by R5. To generate the payload, the most essential steps are store the address of the first gadget in lr and addresses of following gadgets on the stack. Thus, by changing sp, the gadgets will be executed in proper order.

4.3 Code Triggering

After preparing the payload, extra code needs to be added to the app as an entry point of the hidden code. This part of the code fetches the payload at runtime and uses it to trigger the code-reuse program. Code-reuse programs are commonly triggered through overwriting control data, including return addresses, function pointers, and jump buffer. The overwriting could be based on a set of vulnerable library functions that lack boundary checking, such as gets(), fread(), strcpy(), and sprintf(). As in some existing work [12], the control

```
1   typedef struct foo{
2       char buf[JP_BUFSIZE];
3       jmp_buf jbuf;
4   }FOO, *PFOO;
5   PFOO f;
6
7   void * overflow(char * filePath)
8   {
9       int i;
10      ... ...
11      i = setjmp(f->jbuf);
12      fread(f->buf, 1, BUFSIZE+256, sFile);
13      ... ...
14      longjmp(f->jbuf, 2);
15      ... ...
16  }
```

Fig. 4. Trigger code to be added to source code of the application.

data we choose to overwrite is the jmp_buf structure that is used to restore the execution environment in exception handling. The jmp_buf structure contains data that will be used to set values of registers which are used for storing parameters and the return address of a function call. Thus, it is convenient to redirect the control flow through overwriting jmp_buf structure on ARM.

Figure 4 shows an example of overwriting jmp_buf [12]. In this piece of code, function setjmp() and longjmp() are used to store and restore the execution context in variable jbuf. Reading data from sFile to buf will overwrite jbuf. Thus, longjmp() will direct the program execution to somewhere specified by the overwritten jbuf.

4.4 Payload Protection

Since the semantics of the essential code are hidden in the code-reuse payload, it is important that our obfuscation tool provides protection on the payload to resist and reverse engineering attempts. To protect the payload, we propose three possible solutions.

- Instead of storing payload as static resources of the Android app, the payload can be embedded in the resources using information hiding techniques. For example, the payload can be hidden in a segment of normal code, e.g., as an image, using steganography [19].
- The payload can exist in an encrypted form of data in the Android app, and be decrypted at runtime.
- To completely remove the payload from the APK file of the Android app, we can dynamically download it from a trusted remote server [15]. Dynamically, the app will request and receive payload from the server based on a reliable protocol.

In this work, we use the last, and the most secure, method.

5   Implementation and Case Studies

We manage to implement our idea of obfuscating Android application as a tool set, AndroidCubo. AndroidCubo takes as input the source code of an Android app and obfuscates selected native and Java code in it. We present some implementation details and applications of AndroidCubo on an app in this section. Experiments were performed on a Nexus 5 running Android 4.4.

5.1   Implementation Details

Code-reuse programming is complicated since it involves a lot of low level operations on memory and registers. We implement AndroidCubo as a tool set for helping Android app developers to obfuscate sensitive code with code-reuse technique. It contains a source code template to be inserted into the Android source code and a payload maintainer to execute on a trusted server.

The source code template contains a Java class named ObfuscateUtil and a C program named Hiding. The class ObfuscateUtil provides native interfaces for calling native methods in Hiding. It also implements network communication with the trusted server which maintains the payload for the code-reuse program. The Hiding program has a method named trigger() that uses the payload (received from communication with the trusted server) to trigger the obfuscated code.

This source code template can be directly added to the Android project for obfuscating a segment of sensitive code. The only additional code a developer has to add is for preparing parameters if they are obfuscating API calls. To use this template for obfuscating multiple segments of sensitive code, the user needs to add trigger methods in Hiding and the corresponding interfaces in ObfuscateUtil.

The payload maintainer on the server side has two parts. The first part is a payload generator that works in the following manner.

- **Native code obfuscation.** Our gadget searching tool lists available gadgets and their relative addresses for the developer to construct the gadget sequence. The developer can also use other existing tools, e.g. ROPgadget [20] or Q [21], to develop their code reuse program.
- **Java code obfuscation through shell commands.** The generator automatically generates the payload with a command provided by the user.
- **Java API obfuscation.** The developer specifies the addresses of the API and the corresponding parameters and our generator outputs the payload.

The second part is a program for sending payload to the app. This program is developed with PHP with which the server will handle the request of payload from the app, trigger the payload generator, and then send the payload over to the app.

5.2   Case Study: Obfuscating Native Code

To demonstrate AndroidCubo in obfuscating native code, we hide a simple comparison algorithm as shown Fig. 5(a), (b). This algorithm obtains and stores the larger one of the two input numbers. As described in Sect. 4, this simple algorithm needs to be converted to a sequence of gadgets first. AndroidCubo first executes the gadget searching tool and finds available gadgets and their relative addresses, and then generates a sequence of gadgets to substitute the original code as shown in Fig. 5(c). In this sequence, gadgets 1–3 are used to load the first operand to register R9. Gadgets 4–6 are used to load the second operand to register R3. The last conditional gadget is used to find and store the larger number.

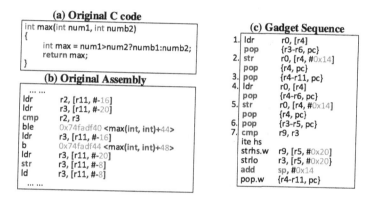

Fig. 5. Source code to be hidden and the corresponding gadget sequence. (a) Original C code; (b) Original assembly code; (c) Gadget sequence.

AndroidCubo then generates the payload based on the gadget sequence. In particular, the first part of the payload is the data used to overwrite the control data jmp_buf. jmp_buf directs the stack pointer to the beginning of the second part—the addresses and parameters of the gadgets. LR is then set to the address of the first gadget. The last part of the payload is a buffer containing junk data.

We recompile the Android app with outputs from AndroidCubo and execute the app with the corresponding payload. After executing the app and loading the payload to the stack, longjmp() successfully executes with the prepared jmp_buf, and the gadget pointed to by LR executes followed by other gadgets prepared in the payload.

5.3   Case Study: Obfuscating Java Code

We use another example to demonstrate using AndroidCubo to obfuscate Java code. In this example, we hide the Java code that kills a background process.

The operation of killing a background process is typically implemented by obtaining an `ActivityManager` object and killing the process by calling the method `killBackgroungProcess()` in Java. AndroidCubo hides this Java code through a shell command `am kill --user 0 PACKAGE_NAME` with two gadgets. The first gadget `MOV R0, R4; POP {R4, PC}` is used to prepare the shell command as a parameter for `system()`. The second gadget is a function call gadget `BLX R4; POP {R3-R5, PC}` to invoke the shell command. Figure 6 presents a view of the stack after our app loads the payload generated by AndroidCubo to overwrite a buffer.

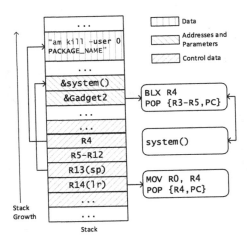

Fig. 6. Stack layout after loading the payload.

From bottom to top of the stack, the three shadowed areas present the corresponding parts of the payload. The first part is the overwriting of control data `jmp_buf`. In `jmp_buf`, register LR is set to the address of the first gadget. Function pointer SP is set to the beginning of the second part of the payload. Register R4 is set to the address of the command that will be assigned to R0 as the parameter of `system()`. The second part is the gadget addresses and parameters. The most essential data on this part is the address of `system()` and the address of the second gadget. The last part includes the padding data and the command string needed by `system()`.

5.4   Overhead

In our experiments in applying AndroidCubo to the Android apps, it introduces around 150 LOC to native part and around 250 LOC to Java part of the Android application.

6   Comparison with Other Obfuscation Techniques

There have been existing obfuscation techniques proposed, and in this section, we conduct a comparative test on sensitive API obfuscation among code-reuse-based method and other techniques, including control-flow obfuscation and Java-reflection-based obfuscation. Control-flow obfuscation techniques typically hides or protects the selected code by branching or looping garbage code. Java-reflection-based techniques typically hide sensitive API calls by using Java reflection to access the APIs through their names. We use these techniques to obfuscate an open source application named OverFlow. The sensitive API that we target to obfuscate is sendTextMessage().

6.1   The Experiment

We obfuscate the target app with all three techniques and then build the signed APK file. We use Apktool [1], dex2jar [3], and JD-GUI [22] to reverse engineer the APk files obtained to see how much information of the sensitive API can be reconstructed. Apktool is used to unpack the APK file and obtain the dex file. dex2jar converts the dex file to jar files which contain the byte code of the app. After obtaining the jar file, we extract the class files in the jar and use JD-GUI to reverse engineer class files to readable Java code. The above constitutes the most commonly used methods for reverse engineering Android apps.

6.2   Reverse Engineering Results

Figure 7 presents the reverse engineering output for the un-obfuscated app (Fig. 7(a)) and apps obfuscated by the three different techniques (Fig. 7(b)–(d)).

Although the control flow recovered in Fig. 7(b) seems opaque, it is easy to spot out the sensitive API call from the byte code at line 9. This shows that the control-flow obfuscation manages to introduce confusion in terms of how control transfers, but it fails to hide the existence of Java API call. From Fig. 7(c), we can also easily figure out the name of the API from the first parameter of getMethod().

Figure 7(d), on the other hand, substitutes the sensitive API call with a native function call whose functionality cannot be inferred from the name. That said, one could further analyze the native function CallVoidMethod() to see if it contains any hints of the API function to be called. We use IDAPro to reverse engineer the native function CallVoidMethod(), and find that the string sendTextMessage and (Ljava/lang/String;...)V can be recovered from the binaries.

6.3   Discussion

In our experiments of obfuscating the Android app with different obfuscation methods, AndroidCubo presents better security in hiding the sensitive API

```
1   private void sendMessage(String paramString1, String paramString2)
2   {
3       try
4       {
5           SmsManager.getDefault().sendTextMessage(paramString1, null, paramString2, null,
            null);
6           return;
7       }
8       catch (Exception paramString1)
9       {
10          paramString1.printStackTrace();
11      }
12  }
```

(a) Decompiled code of un-obfuscated sendTextMessage()

```
1   ... ...
2   // 131: goto -7 -> 124
3   // 134: aload 4
4   // 136: aload_1
5   // 137: aconst_null
6   // 138: aload_2
7   // 139: aconst_null
8   // 140: aconst_null
9   // 141: invokevirtual 105 android/telephony/SmsManager:sendTextMessage ...
10  // 144: return
11  // 145: astore_1
12  // 146: aload 5
13  // 148: astore_2
14  ... ...
```

(b) Decompiled code of function call obfuscated by control-flow obfuscation

```
1   private void sendMessage(String paramString1, String paramString2)
2   {
3       try
4       {
5           SmsManager localSmsManager = SmsManager.getDefault();
6           localSmsManager.getClass().getMethod("sendTextMessage", new Class[] { String.class,
            String.class, String.class, PendingIntent.class, PendingIntent.class }).invoke(
            localSmsManager, new Object[] { paramString1, null, paramString2, null, null });
7           return;
8       }
9       catch (Exception paramString1)
10      {
11          paramString1.printStackTrace();
12      }
13  }
```

(c) Decompiled code of function call obfuscated by Java Reflection

```
1   private void sendMessage(String paramString1, String paramString2)
2   {
3       try
4       {
5           nativeMethod(paramString1, null, paramString2, null, null);
6           return;
7       }
8       catch (Exception paramString1)
9       {
10          paramString1.printStackTrace();
11      }
12  }
```

(d) Decompiled code of function call obfuscated by AndroidCubo

Fig. 7. The decompiled code of calling sendTextMessage() and the decompiled code from obfuscated calling.

call from reverse engineering tools. At a high level, its idea is similar to Java-Reflection-based techniques in that both techniques replace the original Java call with another method call, and both techniques specify the underlying method to be called via a string. However, the replacement in Java-Reflection-based techniques is still a Java method call, which is relatively easy to analyze; on the other hand, AndroidCubo uses a replacement of native calls that are more difficult to analyze. Coupled with other string obfuscation techniques, we argue that AndroidCubo presents higher resilience in obfuscation compared to Java-Reflection-based techniques.

6.4 Limitations

Although applying the code-reuse-based obfuscation technique is feasible, there are a couple of limitations that are worth noting. First, AndroidCubo, in its current form, is a semi-automatic tool. Piecing together gadgets and writing long code-reuse programs are still a complicated process that requires the developer's attention and help. Second, applying code-reuse techniques for good, e.g., in obfuscating program logic, runs into the risk of being prohibited by code-reuse protection mechanisms. That side, current Android systems have no protection mechanisms to resist code-reuse programs, and advanced many techniques [23–26] are powerful enough to bypass most protection mechanisms.

7   Related Work

Traditionally, there have been three categories of obfuscation techniques proposed, including layout obfuscation [6], control-flow transformation [7,27], and data obfuscation. Layout obfuscation [6] removes relevant information from the code without changing its behavior. Control-flow transformation [7,27] alters the original flow of the application. Data obfuscation obfuscates data and data structures in the application. These techniques are certainly helpful in obfuscating Android apps; however, they are not specific to the Android platform and are especially weak in hiding code in Android apps.

There are also free or commercial obfuscation techniques specifically provided to Android developers. ProGuard [4] is a free and commonly used one that obfuscates the names of classes, fields, and methods. DexGuard [28] is a commercial optimizer and obfuscator. It provides advanced obfuscation techniques for Android development, including control-flow obfuscation, class encryption, and so on. DexProtector [29] is another commercial obfuscator that provides code obfuscation as well as resource obfuscation, such as the Android manifest file.

Code reuse techniques, including Return-into-lib(c) [30,31], Return-oriented programming [8,9] and Jump-oriented programming [10–12], are first proposed to exploit vulnerable apps by hijacking their control-flow transfers and constructing malicious code dynamically. Among these code-reuse techniques, only a few of them work on Android system or the ARM architecture. [12] proposes a systematic jump-oriented programming technique on ARM architecture. The gadget set proposed in this work consists of gadgets ending with **BLX** instructions. In this paper, we use a different type of gadgets that are more commonly found in native libraries.

Recently, several code-reuse-based obfuscation techniques [13–15] have been proposed. One of the code-reuse-based obfuscation techniques is RopSteg—a steganography technique on x86 [14]. RopSteg protects binary code on x86 architecture, while our code-reuse-based obfuscation on Android platform works for both Java and native code on Android platform. Another work [15] proposes a malware named Jekyll which hides malicious code and reconstructs it at runtime. Our obfuscation mechanism can be used for protection of either malicious or benign code.

8   Conclusion

In this paper, we present a code-reuse-based technique for protecting Android applications. This technique enhances the concealment of both Java and native code in Android apps through hiding essential code. Our evaluation shows that the limited binary resources in Android apps are sufficient for applying code-reuse-based obfuscations. We further implement AndroidCubo semi-automate the process of obfuscating essential code. Examples present that it is practical to protect applications with AndroidCubo.

References

1. Winsniewski, R.: Apktool: a tool for reverse engineering android APK files. http://ibotpeaches.github.io/Apktool/
2. Vaibhavpandeyvpz: Apk studio. http://www.vaibhavpandey.com/apkstudio/
3. Alll, B., Tumbleson, C.: Dex2jar: tools to work with android. dex and java. class files
4. Lafortune, E., et al.: Proguard. http://proguard.sourceforge.net
5. Collberg, C., Thomborson, C., Low, D.: A taxonomy of obfuscating transformations. Technical report, Department of Computer Science, The University of Auckland, New Zealand (1997)
6. Chan, J.T., Yang, W.: Advanced obfuscation techniques for Java bytecode. J. Syst. Softw. **71**(1), 1–10 (2004)
7. Collberg, C., Thomborson, C., Low, D.: Manufacturing cheap, resilient, and stealthy opaque constructs. In: Proceedings of the 25th ACM SIGPLAN-SIGACT Symposium on Principles of Programming Languages, pp. 184–196. ACM (1998)
8. Buchanan, E., Roemer, R., Shacham, H., Savage, S.: When good instructions go bad: generalizing return-oriented programming to risc. In: Proceedings of the ACM CCS (2008)
9. Shacham, H.: The geometry of innocent flesh on the bone: return-into-libc without function calls (on the x86). In: Proceedings of the ACM CCS (2007)
10. Bletsch, T., Jiang, X., Freeh, V.W., Liang, Z.: Jump-oriented programming: a new class of code-reuse attack. In: Proceedings of the ACM ASIACCS (2011)

11. Checkoway, S., Davi, L., Dmitrienko, A., Sadeghi, A.R., Shacham, H., Winandy, M.: Return-oriented programming without returns. In: Proceedings of the ACM CCS (2010)
12. Davi, L., Dmitrienko, A., Sadeghi, A.R., Winandy, M.: Return-oriented programming without returns on arm. System Security Lab-Ruhr University Bochum, Technical report (2010)
13. Ma, H., Lu, K., Ma, X., Zhang, H., Jia, C., Gao, D.: Software watermarking using return-oriented programming (2015)
14. Lu, K., Xiong, S., Gao, D.: Ropsteg: program steganography with return oriented programming. In: Proceedings of the ACM CODASPY (2014)
15. Wang, T., Lu, K., Lu, L., Chung, S., Lee, W.: Jekyll on ios: When benign apps become evil. In: Proceedings of the USENIX Security (2013)
16. Seal, D.: ARM Architecture Reference Manual. Pearson Education, Harlow (2001)
17. Davi, L., Dmitrienko, A., Sadeghi, A.-R., Winandy, M.: Privilege escalation attacks on android. In: Burmester, M., Tsudik, G., Magliveras, S., Ilić, I. (eds.) ISC 2010. LNCS, vol. 6531, pp. 346–360. Springer, Heidelberg (2011). doi:10.1007/978-3-642-18178-8_30
18. Google: Jni tips. http://developer.android.com/training/articles/perf-jni.html
19. Morkel, T., Eloff, J.H., Olivier, M.S.: An overview of image steganography. In: Proceedings of the ISSA (2005)
20. Salwan, J., Wirth, A.: Ropgadget (2012)
21. Schwartz, E.J., Avgerinos, T., Brumley, D.: Q: exploit hardening made easy. In: USENIX Security Symposium, pp. 25–41 (2011)
22. Dupuy, E.: JD-GUI: yet another fast java decompiler. http://java.decompiler.free.fr/?q=jdgui/. Accessed Mar 2012
23. Carlini, N., Wagner, D.: ROP is still dangerous: breaking modern defenses. In: USENIX Security Symposium (2014)
24. Davi, L., Lehmann, D., Sadeghi, A.R., Monrose, F.: Stitching the gadgets: on the ineffectiveness of coarse-grained control-flow integrity protection. In: USENIX Security Symposium (2014)
25. Göktaş, E., Athanasopoulos, E., Polychronakis, M., Bos, H., Portokalidis, G.: Size does matter: why using gadget-chain length to prevent code-reuse attacks is hard. In: 23rd USENIX Security Symposium, San Diego, CA, pp. 417–432 (2014)
26. Snow, K.Z., Monrose, F., Davi, L., Dmitrienko, A., Liebchen, C., Sadeghi, A.R.: Just-in-time code reuse: on the effectiveness of fine-grained address space layout randomization. In: Proceedings of the IEEE Symposium on Security and Privacy. IEEE (2013)
27. Wartell, R., Mohan, V., Hamlen, K.W., Lin, Z.: Binary stirring: self-randomizing instruction addresses of legacy x86 binary code. In: Proceedings of the ACM CCS (2012)
28. Dexguard. https://www.guardsquare.com/dexguard
29. DexProtector. https://dexprotector.com/
30. Wojtczuk, R.N.: The Advanced return-into-lib(c) Exploits: PaX Case Study. Phrack Magazine **0x0b**(0x3a). Phile #0x04 of 0x0e (2001)
31. Tran, M., Etheridge, M., Bletsch, T., Jiang, X., Freeh, V., Ning, P.: On the expressiveness of return-into-libc attacks. In: Sommer, R., Balzarotti, D., Maier, G. (eds.) RAID 2011. LNCS, vol. 6961, pp. 121–141. Springer, Heidelberg (2011). doi:10.1007/978-3-642-23644-0_7

Author Index

Printed in the United States
By Bookmasters